To [name]

Hope this inspires you to research your Civil War ancestors

All the best
Reid & Sari

Lincoln's Veteran Volunteers Win the War

Lincoln's Veteran Volunteers Win the War

*The Hudson Valley's Ross Brothers
and the Union's Fight for Emancipation*

D. REID ROSS

FOREWORD BY
DUANE A. SMITH

excelsior editions

Cover photo: battlefield sunrise © Kurt Holter / iStockphoto

Published by
State University of New York Press, Albany

© 2008 State University of New York

All rights reserved

Printed in the United States of America

No part of this book may be used or reproduced in any manner whatsoever without written permission. No part of this book may be stored in a retrieval system or transmitted in any form or by any means including electronic, electrostatic, magnetic tape, mechanical, photocopying, recording, or otherwise without the prior permission in writing of the publisher.

For information, contact State University of New York Press, Albany, NY
www.sunypress.edu

Production by Diane Ganeles
Marketing by Susan M. Petrie

Excelsior Editions is an imprint of State University of New York Press

Library of Congress Cataloging-in-Publication Data

Ross, D. Reid, 1922–
   Lincoln's veteran volunteers win the war : the Hudson Valley's Ross brothers and the Union's fight for emancipation / D. Reid Ross ; foreword by Duane A. Smith.
      p. cm.
   Includes bibliographical references and index.
   ISBN 978-0-7914-7641-3 (hardcover : alk. paper)
   1. Ross family. 2. Soldiers—New York (State)—Washington County—Biography. 3. Veterans—New York (State)—Washington County—Biography. 4. Brothers—New York (State)—Washington County—Biography. 5. Abolitionists—New York (State)—Washington County—Biography. 6. Washington County (N.Y.)—Biography. 7. Hudson River Valley (N.Y. and N.J.)—Biography. 8. Slavery—Emancipation—United States. 9. New York (State)—History—Civil War, 1861–1865—Social aspects. 10. United States—History—Civil War, 1861–1865—Social aspects. I. Title.

E607.R67 2009
973.7'47—dc22
                                          2007052571

10 9 8 7 6 5 4 3 2 1

This book is dedicated to my wife, Sari, and our three children—Kathy, Janet, and Peter—who had to exercise untold patience with my thirty years of dogged determination to write it. Their help also is immensely appreciated.

And to the descendants of the three Ross brothers who survived the war and had children, I also acknowledge their help in garnering family records that made this book possible.

Never doubt that a small group of thoughtful, committed citizens can change the world. Indeed it is the only thing that ever has.

—Margaret Mead

Contents

List of Illustrations	ix
Foreword by Duane A. Smith	xi
Preface	xiii
Acknowledgments	xix
Introduction	1
1. Why, How, and When They Fought	5
2. Stones River	39
3. Chancellorsville	59
4. After Chancellorsville	93
5. Gettysburg	107
6. Chickamauga	127
7. Missionary Ridge	153
8. After Missionary Ridge	189
9. Battle of the Wilderness	197
10. The Battle of Kolb's Farm	241
11. From Prisoner to Guard	263
12. Capture of Atlanta	287
13. March to the Sea and Beyond	301
14. Victory and the Grand Review	339
Epilogue: A Legacy of Sacrifice	351
Notes	369
Glossary	427
Bibliographic Essays	431
Index	441

Illustrations

Photographs

Melancton Johnson Ross	40
Daniel Reid Ross	60
Gen. Henry Slocum	68
Gen. Alpheus S. Williams	73
36th and 27th Illinois monuments on Missionary Ridge	176
William Henry Ross	198
Officers of the 93rd New York	200
Col. John S. Crocker with aides	204
Skeletons on Wilderness battlefield	239
Star of the South	285
John Doty Ross	302
Sherman's Veterans at the Grand Review	343
Daniel Reid Ross	366

Drawings

Gettysburg Artillery Battery in Action	118
Soldiers voting in camp	293
Sherman's troops destroying a rail line	310

Maps

Stones River	49
Chancellorsville	80
Gettysburg/Culps Hill	116
Chickamauga Battlefield & Vicinity	135
Chickamauga—Lytle Hill	139

Illustrations

Missionary Ridge	167
Wilderness	225
Kolb's Farm, action prior to Hood's assault	250
Kolb's Farm, Hood's assault	252
Slocum's route on Sherman's March to the Sea	303
General Williams's 20th Corps line, Siege of Savannah	314

Foreword

"You cannot qualify war in harsher terms than I will. War is cruelty, and you cannot refine it." Thus did William Tecumseh Sherman define war in a letter to the mayor of the recently captured Atlanta as this crucial Southern town lay in ruins. He is also credited with saying "war is hell." The War Between the States, the war for Southern independence, the Civil War—or whatever the participants elected to call it—certainly became that, in no uncertain terms.

Sherman was right on all counts, and either of his statements would do just fine in describing the Civil War experiences of the Ross brothers from New York and Illinois. They marched off to war more to the words of Julie Ward Howe's "Battle Hymn of the Republic":

Mine eyes have seen the glory of the coming of the Lord;
He is trampling out the vintage where the grapes of wrath are
    stored;
He hath loosed the fateful lightning of his terrible swift sword;
His truth is marching on.

They went to war with high religious idealism thanks to their Reformed Presbyterian heritage, reenlisted, and fought on as Veteran Volunteers. Their dedication and sacrifices illustrate the "better natures" of the human spirit. As President Abraham Lincoln noted at Gettysburg in November 1863, "The world will little know nor long remember what we say here, but it can never forget what they did here."

They found out, however, there was more truth in what Sherman wrote. Dan was captured and ended up in the hellhole called Andersonville. He survived and shortly after the war was one of the guards that took Jefferson Davis to Fort Monroe, Virginia. Will was killed at the

Battle of the Wilderness, and Lank was blinded by being hit in the eye with hot cinders. John fought with Sherman, was deafened at the siege of Savannah, continued fighting, and marched in the Grand Review in Washington at the war's end. In retrospect, while the 1861–65 conflict might seem glamorous and romantic, the Ross brothers' story testifies that it was anything but sentimental.

Before the Civil War ended, one or another of the four Rosses saw and participated in the greater part of the campaigning and combat in both the eastern and western war theaters. They fought in the eastern theater at Chancellorsville, Gettysburg, and Wilderness. They marched and fought with Sheridan and Sherman in the western theater at Stones River, Chickamauga, and Missionary Ridge, and from Atlanta through the Carolinas to the sea. Everywhere they went, they were involved in some of the bloodiest battles of the war.

They, like their comrades, experienced the excitement of the campaigns, the boredom of camp life, the privations and everyday life of the Union soldier, the horrors of battle, and the sorrow of losing friends and comrades. Through it all, they steadfastly stood true to their beliefs and their determination to carry the struggle through to a victorious conclusion.

Lincoln was their hero. They supported his Emancipation Proclamation and voted overwhelmingly for him in the 1864 election. In the end, like their surviving comrades, they returned home, but never forgot what they had seen, experienced, and felt during what was the high point of their lives.

The Ross brothers' story is that of their generation, who marched off to war in 1861 and returned home to a new and different United States in 1865. They had helped transform a people and a nation and been part of the birth of what we today call modern America.

Duane A. Smith

Preface

I became interested in American history, as well as in my family history and its cultural heritage, as a schoolboy in the 1930s. It was fostered by both my fifth-grade teacher and my father, who had a keen interest in history. In 1939, while still in high school, I read the entire four-volume first edition of Carl Sandburg's *Abraham Lincoln*, and was spellbound. My father could trace his family back 350 years to colonial days in New York, and my mother's to colonial Virginia for the same length of time.

Thirty years ago that curiosity began to consume me. Since childhood I had heard innumerable family legends but seen little documentation. My father and his sisters were aging. It was time to collect those records and record those who could still tell the legends. All I really learned from my family's oral history, however, was that many of my New York ancestors had participated as minor characters in a number of significant events in American history, including the colonial wars, the War for Independence, the War of 1812, and the Civil War.

I had to determine the validity of the family legends. For example, my father told this story of my grandfather's Civil War imprisonment: a guard would read off the names of those being paroled on a given day, handing each his pardon when he stepped forward. When the man standing next to him died, my grandfather took his identification papers, stepped forward when the man's name was called, and claimed that man's pardon.

There was at least a kernel of truth in the story, but finding that kernel was extremely difficult. It took years to find out the name of his regiment—the 123rd New York—as well as to learn that he had served in the cavalry and artillery, was an infantryman in Sherman's march on Atlanta, and was captured on the skirmish line thirty miles from that city. He was sent to Andersonville and four other prisons before being released from the prison in Selma, Alabama, after the city surrendered to Gen. James H. Wilson's cavalry raid.

Family Civil War records were scarce. All that existed was a seven-page memoir written by my grandfather, Daniel Ross, after the war and six wartime letters he and his brothers—Will, Lank, and John—wrote to each other, as well as one to their mother. Clearly, if I wanted to learn more about them, I would have to search beyond family records and my father's story of his father's capture near Kennesaw Mountain, Georgia. Actions would have to speak louder than words.

A moment of truth came when I learned that many opponents of slavery, including out-and-out abolitionists, were among the first to enlist. I knew that my grandfather and two of his brothers enlisted early, one within a week after Lincoln's call for volunteers, and two within five months. It took years of research before I finally was able to connect the dots.

When I began researching my family, I was not interested in merely building a family tree. I wanted to determine *why* my ancestors moved from the Old World to the New, *how* they adjusted to their new environment and *how* and *why* they contributed to their community. From the outset, I was interested in my grandfather, who enlisted in the Civil War for two three-year terms, the first on September 11, 1861, and was captured in June 1864.

I learned that his mother was descended from a line of Dutch and Walloon Calvinists, who arrived in New Amsterdam in 1624. His father's side were descendants of seventeenth-century Highland Scots Presbyterians who were followers of John Knox, the founder in Scotland of the Protestant Reformation. Both religions held stern convictions of righteousness and piety. Both families left the Old World for the New largely because of religious persecution. Their Puritan background gave them the moral courage to take strong stands even though they exercised little economic or political power.

I read Dutch and Scottish histories for further religious and economic explanations of why my first Dutch and Scottish ancestors left Europe for New Amsterdam. I examined the church records of two Dutch Reformed churches and two Reformed (Covenanting) Presbyterian churches to which five generations of my ancestors belonged prior to the Civil War. These churches held steadfastly to God's law and the Bible as their school textbook.

I found that their faith *and* their family history profoundly influenced my ancestors' beliefs and the decisions they made in the course of their lives. As Oliver Wendell Holmes, Sr., a Civil War veteran, put it, "We [veterans] are the trustees of the life of three generations . . . for the benefit of all that are yet to be." I also discovered that others who served in the three regiments in which the Ross brothers enlisted had similar family backgrounds.

Two revelations—the long-standing antislavery position of their church and the family's military history of fighting in the Revolution to create the Union and in the War of 1812 to defend it—opened up for me what had previously been a closed book. What Veteran Volunteers did and why were based partly on what their fathers and grandfathers did to achieve their aspirations. As the social historian Reid Mitchell noted, men's hopes supply armies as much as ammunition and food.

But my grandfather and his brothers wrote little about their views on such subjects. Therefore, I began searching for social historians who had read letters and diaries written by Civil War soldiers in which they described their motives for fighting and their determination to stay the course, at whatever cost to themselves. I thought they might have the answer to the question Sherman left unanswered. I read eighteen books, all written in the last fifteen years, by a dozen social historians. At least three had read soldiers' letters and diaries that revealed in their own words their moral imperatives and how and why they retained them throughout the conflict. They concluded that some soldiers who enlisted early in the war were motivated by their moral position to end slavery.

In order to ascertain their moral stance, I next read 649 letters and diaries—seven by the Ross brothers and the rest by their comrades, including officers. I also read 34 regimental histories written by the men who fought in them. Above all others, I found two recurrent themes: preservation of the Union and abolition of slavery.

Few Civil War soldiers had ever traveled very far from home, and been isolated from their families and friends. To describe to family and friends what they were seeing, doing, and feeling, they wrote millions of letters. These letters are not only the best descriptions of their wartime experience but, at least in the case of the regiments in which the Rosses fought, they also reflect the values expressed by their hometown newspapers, local religious leaders, and family backgrounds.

Since our nation's bicentennial celebration and the publication of Alex Haley's book *Roots,* countless more soldiers' letters and diaries have turned up in local history, genealogy, and manuscript collections of libraries across the country. Tens of thousands of people were inspired to search their attics for historical material and to donate it to libraries and historical societies. This previously untapped source has provided the clearest reflection of mid-nineteenth-century attitudes, values, and religious convictions.

By this time I was hooked. I wanted to learn not only why my grandfather and his brothers fought, but also in what battles and, if possible, what happened to them, their comrades, and their regiments. Two of the Ross brothers' regiments were Veteran Volunteers. The third was a three-year regiment organized in the fall of 1862 in response to Lincoln's July 2 call for 300,000 three-year men. More than 400,000 men responded to that call, knowing by then that war was not a glorious adventure that provided an opportunity to prove one's manhood.

I studied their regimental histories and numerous letters written by comrades to their families, friends, wives, and hometown newspapers describing battles and their contacts with ex-slaves, including some who had enlisted. I discovered others in their regiments were abolitionists to varying degrees. I also reviewed every "after-action" report in the *Official Records, War of the Rebellion* for every battle in which the brothers fought. Finally, I searched for corresponding Confederate accounts of those in regiments opposing them.

By the time I left retirement to enroll in a University of Wisconsin master's degree program, I had amassed numerous military records that described the battles in which the brothers participated. I needed help from my professors in identifying the religious, political, and social institutions forging the principles that led my abolitionist-leaning ancestors to be among the first to enlist and then to reenlist to war's end. Over two enriching and rewarding years, my professors led me to an understanding of the Reformed (Covenanting) Presbyterian Church's deep and abiding conviction that slavery was a sin in God's eyes and had to be abolished. The denomination was tiny, but its adherents' conviction was powerful.

My family had been members of such a church since before their arrival in the New World and for five generations after their arrival. I found members of each generation in church membership lists, and records of births, christenings, deaths, and/or marriages. Their enlistment records make it clear they were willing to see the war through, no matter what the cost. And cost it did!

In my thirty years of research, I have visited more than one hundred libraries, pored over hundreds of manuscript collections, and read more than 1,000 Civil War and other historical publications, personal memoirs, diaries, and letters. I read all six Washington County newspapers to uncover the community background that also helped to mold the four Ross brothers and others like them into the soldiers who made emancipation possible.

Through the soldiers' writings, I came to know about the food or lack of it available to them, the mud, rain, heat, cold, threadbare clothing, and even lice they had to endure, and how they tried their best to make light of it. I realized there were as many GI Joes in the Civil War as there were in World War II, but nobody like Bill Mauldin was around to make them into cartoon characters and quote their sardonic remarks.

So despite the paucity of documents written by the Ross brothers, I was able to weave family records together with primary source material with such public documents as deeds, wills, and administrations; tax, court, cemetery, and census records; and military, county, and oral histories. The result is a mosaic that reveals the pattern of the Ross brothers' family background and behavior as well as that of others like them. I did not set out to prove a point. Rather, I assembled the written records and let them speak for themselves. Having gained such insight, I decided to write this book.

Unlike other Civil War books, *Lincoln's Veteran Volunteers Win the War* attempts to describe *why* these committed Veteran Volunteers fought as well as *how* and *when*. As a result, it depicts those soldiers, their religious and community backgrounds, and the principles that motivated them to stay the course until the twin goals of preserving the Union and abolishing slavery were realized. In outlining the political and military strategies underlying why and when some of the bloodiest Civil War battles were fought, this book also provides the context for Veteran Volunteers' actions in those and other battles.

This book portrays the recruitment and service of these Veteran Volunteers and three-year men—who were essential to the North's victory—more completely than any other account I have read. Their moral imperatives and dogged determination have been, up to now, a sorely lacking element in scholarly accounts of the Civil War.

The endnotes for this book are guides to the primary sources used in writing it: letters, diaries, journals, memoirs, contemporary newspapers, regimental histories, the National Archives—including regimental and brigade order books, military, medical, and pension records of individual soldiers, after-action reports, and other reports in the *Official Records, War of the Rebellion*—and family, church, birth, death, land, and other public records in county courthouses, state archives, and numerous local and state historical societies.

The experiences of the Ross family reflect the commitments, dreams, and ambitions that mold a nation's history. Viewing history at this grassroots level, through families, small groups, and specific events and places, can fill in the detail not seen in the broad-brush view of traditional historians. A nation that does not know the history of its families does not know itself. By remembering the past and retelling its stories, we gain a crucial memory of our heritage as individuals and as a nation.

Acknowledgments

For decades, the American history faculty at the University of Wisconsin has included eminent Civil War scholars and produced dozens of academics who have taught in other universities and written numerous Civil War books. I chose the right university. My professors—Mac Coffman, Jurgen Herbst, Alan Bogue, and David Lovejoy, who taught courses on the Civil War—were intrigued with their sixty-five-year-old student who was older than they were, and knew exactly what he wanted to do as well as what help he needed. They were generous with their time, exceptionally patient, and helpful. Through their encouragement and guidance, I rediscovered the joys of scholarship. My professors also helped me to recognize the power of other motivations, especially Unionism or—on the Confederate side—states' rights and regional loyalties. Through this enriching experience I learned that the past is always present.

Detailed records of the Reformed Presbyterians in Washington County, New York, where the Rosses lived, were made available by the county historian, Doris McEachron, and the Presbyterian Historical Society. Rev. James MacNaughton, Jr., a retired Presbyterian preacher born in Washington County, whose ancestors arrived there at the same time mine did to settle on the Argyle Patent where my ancestors did before the Revolution, was also invaluable.

More recently, two valued friends were untiring and extremely thorough readers: Jack Pickering, whose career spanned decades of college textbook editing, and John Pocock, who recently retired as a history professor from Johns Hopkins University. My wife, Sari, and our three children—Kathy, Janet, and Peter—were careful and dedicated editorial critics.

Finally, I have to express my special gratitude to three outstanding Civil War scholars who have contributed enormously to the accuracy of details and interpretation of the battles and campaigns in which the Ross brothers fought: Professors James MacPherson and Duane Smith, as well as Ed Bearss, the retired chief historian of the National Park Service. And no author has had a more conscientious copy editor who also is as easy and pleasant to work with as Beth Green.

And last, but far from least, I am indebted for the knowledge shared with me by National Archives professionals and National Park Service battlefield historians including Don Pfanz, John Heiser, Jim Ogden, and Lloyd Morris, who sorted out fact from fiction. The service of interlibrary loan librarians and archivists in countless libraries will not be forgotten.

Introduction

> I think that all officers of experience will confirm my assertion that the men who voluntarily enlisted at the outbreak of the war were the best.
>
> —General William T. Sherman, *Memoirs*

In their exhaustive deliberations that led to the adoption of the U.S. Constitution and Bill of Rights, the founding fathers failed to resolve one issue that would haunt the nation for four score and seven years. To make certain that the thirteen colonies would each become part of the United States of America, they agreed to a tragic compromise on the issue of slavery.

Led by Thomas Jefferson and John Adams, they set in motion forces that ultimately destroyed slavery at the cost of 620,000 lives, but not before decades of political, social, and economic upheaval, endless debates, and sectional tensions almost sank the ship of state. With rare foresight, Adams predicted, "We must settle the question of slavery extension now, otherwise it will stamp our national character and lay a foundation for calamities, if not disunion."

The first real test of whether the compromise would work or simply postpone the crisis was the adoption of the Missouri Compromise in 1820. It extended the Mason-Dixon Line (36°30') westward into the Louisiana Purchase territory as a northern boundary for slavery, except for Missouri. Jefferson said of the Missouri Compromise "[T]his momentous question, like a fire bell in the night, awakened me and filled me with terror. I considered it at once as the knell of the Union."

In 1830, when there were only 5,000 slaves left in Northern states and 125,000 freed blacks, Senator John Calhoun, a South Carolinian, challenged the federal government over its power to regulate tariffs on imported goods. The hidden agenda in the debate was slavery, the South's "peculiar institution." He threatened in 1847 that if Congress rammed through the Wilmot Proviso, "the result would be political revolution, anarchy, and civil war." The proviso, which prohibited slavery in any territory acquired from Mexico, did not pass. In 1849, Henry Clay proposed another compromise—gradual emancipation, compensated by the sale of public lands—and it was soundly defeated.

By 1850, besides in the United States, slavery existed only in Brazil, Cuba, and Puerto Rico. Nevertheless, the 1850 debates that raged contentiously in the halls of Congress led to the adoption of the Fugitive Slave Act and other so-called compromises. Salmon P. Chase, who was to become Lincoln's secretary of the treasury, was convinced that while "the question of slavery in the territories has been avoided, it has not been settled." Indeed, it enraged the Northern abolitionists because it required U.S. marshals and their deputies to help slaveholders capture these runaways and imposed stiff penalties on those who hid or otherwise assisted fugitive slaves.

After another prolonged series of debates in 1854, Congress passed the Kansas-Nebraska Act, another compromise that virtually wrecked the Democratic Party by splitting it into Northern and Southern factions and laid the groundwork for the creation of the Republican Party. That year in the congressional elections, Republicans won forty-seven seats held by Democrats and overthrew their control of the House. Instead of banning slavery in Kansas, as well as all other states carved out of western territory, it permitted residents to vote on the slavery issue. Lincoln expressed his opposition to the legislation, saying that the North wanted to give Kansas pioneers "a clean bed with no snakes in it." Horace Greeley, editor of the *New York Tribune*, estimated that the Kansas-Nebraska Act made more abolitionists in two months than William Lloyd Garrison, a powerful abolitionist, did in twenty years.

By 1860, there were four million slaves and five million whites in the eleven states that would make up the Confederacy. Cotton constituted half of all U.S. exports. Southern planters were more prosperous and owned more slaves than ever before, and were more prepared to defend their peculiar institution. To do so, within five weeks after Lincoln's inauguration in 1861, they fired on Fort Sumter in South Carolina, and started the process of ripping apart the "national fabric," as Lincoln noted, that had been so carefully and uniquely woven by the founding fathers. The "irrepressible conflict" erupted, and fratricidal bloodletting began.

General William T. Sherman, who led a 1,500 mile march across Georgia and through the Carolinas to accept Gen. Joseph Johnston's surrender at the end of the war, considered the first men to volunteer for the Union army "the best." But he left unanswered the question that has intrigued many Civil War scholars and students: Why were they the best?

Sherman's "best soldiers" were powerfully motivated by convictions cemented in the 1850s, when they were coming of age. Many voted for their first time in 1860, for Lincoln, in the most important election ever held in this country. They were forged in the crucible of the hottest debates yet held in any election campaign. By the time those secessionist versus abolitionist debates climaxed in the Civil War, they were compelled to fight for their deep-seated beliefs. They would enlist so they could shoot as they voted.

Lincoln applied his belief that "all men are created equal" to both blacks and whites. In 1861, he said, "I have never had a feeling politically that did not spring from the sentiments embodied in the Declaration [of Independence]." On July 4, 1861, he told Congress that government's leading role was "to elevate the condition of man—to lift artificial weight from all shoulders—to clear the paths of laudable pursuit for all—to afford all . . . a fair chance in the race of life."

Through the course of the war, Lincoln issued multiple calls for volunteers to serve terms ranging from three months to three years. The 200,000 men who chose to become long-term volunteers—whether Veteran Volunteers or other early three-year men—would have the highest casualty rates out of the entire two-million-man Union army. They would fight in more battles, usually as the first ones in and the last ones out of these conflicts. Their regimental butcher's bill would be truly appalling.

The Ross brothers—Will, Dan, Lank, and John—would, like many of their comrades, fight until they were injured, captured, or killed. The dogged determination of such men would lead to their destruction in droves. By the war's end, two of the brothers' three regiments would be among those that suffered the greatest percentage killed and wounded—53 percent in one regiment and 41 percent in the other. Between them, the four Rosses would fight in eight of the largest and bloodiest battles of the war—including Gettysburg, Wilderness, Chickamauga, and Chancellorsville—and in two of its longest campaigns.

Social historians have concluded that many Union soldiers' motivation changed in the course of the Civil War. In the beginning, the goal of the vast majority was to preserve the Union. They knew the world was watching the United States, and the survival of its democratic government was at stake. The minority of Union soldiers who enlisted primarily to fight to end slavery believed that the Union could not be preserved without abolition. However, by the war's end many more had become convinced that emancipation was vital to restoring the Union. That commitment was key to their willingness to continue fighting despite high casualties.

Did the Ross brothers believe in immediate or gradual emancipation? Did they believe that all blacks should be given the vote? Their actions give an indication of their beliefs. In 1860 and 1864, Lincoln's support in their birthplace of Washington County, New York, was significantly stronger than in the nation as a whole. By then many Covenanting Presbyterians, including the Ross brothers' father, had joined the Republican Party. Lincoln's increasing strength there reflected the county's growing support for emancipation as the war dragged on.

The Ross brothers and their comrades-in-arms in the three regiments in which they served typify the 200,000 long-term volunteers with a strong moral commitment. The wellsprings of their loyalty and Unionism were the small Northern communities where they were raised. Their antislavery sentiments were nurtured by their churches. Many were recruited by their churches and communities, and their attachment endured to war's end.

A soldier in the brigade of one of the Ross brothers noted, "The soldier of '61 was full of life and patriotism... undampened by the stern discipline and Reverses of the War. The soldier of '65 was inured to hardship and adversity, and hoped less, but fought and accomplished more. The period of romance had changed to a period of system and endurance." The longer they fought, the better they fought. And Veteran Volunteers were the soldiers who fought the longest.

This is the story of the four Ross brothers and their comrades, and how they mirrored the 200,000 men in Veteran Volunteer and three-year regiments created by early 1862. In focusing on these dedicated volunteers and how their convictions were shaped, no disparagement is intended toward the vast majority of Union soldiers who sacrificed much, even though their service was shorter and their motivation may have differed.

1

Why, How, and When They Fought

> You know we are now in a business where we are very likely to be sent home crippled.
>
> —William Henry Ross, letter to his brother Dan, February 6, 1862

The four Ross brothers and their two sisters grew to adulthood in upstate New York's Washington County farming on both sides of the Hudson River. The verdant green hills belied the land's limited fertility. Frequent rains and bitterly cold winters only added to the challenges of growing crops. The Rosses took advantage of dense, virgin forests to supplement their farm income, cutting cordwood along the banks of the Hudson, then floating it downstream to Albany when the ice melted. Charles Wesley and Margaret Reid Ross moved their family three times as they prospered, seeking out larger acreage and woodlots and more fertile soil. One of their main crops was potatoes. Like lumber, this crop was floated downriver, on barges, to Albany.

William Henry was the oldest of the four Ross brothers, and the first to enlist. After his second enlistment, his mother pleaded with him to apply for a hardship discharge and return home to help operate the family farm, because she and her husband were crippled with rheumatism. On May 1, 1862, he expressed his concern for them in a letter, acknowledging that the "hard labor" of farm work was damaging his mother's health and leaving his father "feeble." He added that he owed his parents "a duty" that he could "never cancel."

Despite such concerns, Will and his brother Melancton (Lank) enlisted at the outset of the war. They also were among those 136,000 battle-hardened soldiers who reenlisted in regiments organized in response to Lincoln's first two calls for three-year volunteers. Dan enlisted soon afterward, serving in the cavalry, infantry, and artillery, something extremely few soldiers did.

Their sister Anna Marie was teaching in a girls' school in Mississippi, but once the war broke out, she returned home rather than remain in a Southern state. Their other sister, Charlotte, married a farmer and moved to a neighboring county, where she would spend the rest of her life. All four brothers wanted to help preserve a livelihood for their parents, as well as a home they could return to. They contributed part of their military pay to help with the farm mortgage payments.

Despite their sons' financial help, Margaret Ross's early concerns proved true. The spring and summer of 1864 were catastrophic for the family. One son was injured, another killed, and the third captured. At home, severe weather destroyed half their crops. Even with these tragic setbacks, eighteen-year-old John enlisted in Dan's regiment to replace his imprisoned brother—with his parents' approval. Soon after the war's end, with no help at home, Charles and Margaret Ross lost their farm to foreclosure.

What could have compelled all four brothers to risk not only their own personal safety, but the well-being of their parents and sister? Why would Will, Dan, and Lank reenlist when they not only had fulfilled their military duty, but also knew far too well what dangers they would face? What reasons could have driven John, who was under no obligation, to enlist and leave his home and family to fight in the war? Given the fates of his three brothers, he knew the risks were great.

The answers lie in their family's history and deep-seated faith. Their church had provided this family, as well as many others, with a moral compass, a definition of who they were. The Ross brothers' decisions stand as mute testimony to their pro-Union and antislavery sentiments. They felt no necessity to express those feelings to their parents or siblings in writing, because they already shared one another's convictions. Even their sister Anna Marie had acted on a commitment to those ideals when she went to Mississippi to teach in the 1850s. Immediately after the Reformed Presbyterian Church organized its Board of Missions for Freedmen in 1863, in response to Lincoln's Emancipation Proclamation, she went to Virginia to teach freedmen.

Most Northern families thought sending one son to fight the war was enough. *Everyone* in the Ross family sacrificed for the war. Between them, the four Rosses fought in virtually every major Civil War campaign and battle in both the East and the West, from Virginia and Pennsylvania to Tennessee, Georgia, and the Carolinas—an unusual distinction in itself. The family fully committed its personal skills and wealth, arguably the strongest position they could take.

As one historian wrote, only the church and the government could "legitimately ask Northern men to selflessly risk everything in pursuit of a common good.... Their Union was ... meant to be viewed by the rest of the world as God's model for the Millennium—the thousand years of ideal society in the Book of Revelation."

These Northerners were firmly convinced they were instruments of God, who required this great revolution in their country's social system to rid it of slavery.

Setting Their Moral Compass

Charles and Margaret Ross's forebears were Reformed (Covenanting) Presbyterians who had emigrated from the Scottish Highlands before the American Revolution. Their ancestors were products of the Protestant Reformation, the impact of which was greater in Scotland than any other European country. They brought with them their covenant with God, which decreed that when man's law—including the king's—conflicted with God's, they would obey God's law.

Covenanting was a basic tenet of Reformed Presbyterians' faith. To them the Bible was the supreme law of the land. They believed in God's direct rule on Earth, and in theocracy as a form of government. Armed resistance against sin was justified, because it was the individual's responsibility to implement God's law for the benefit of others. President Lincoln and other Calvinists shared this view. From the seventeenth century in their old country, "religious faiths had been battle flags, not just belief systems."

From the 1720s thousands of Ulster Scots began arriving in the American colonies, many settling on the frontier, west of New England, including in the Hudson River Valley. They came for both economic and religious reasons. Here they lived largely beyond the reach of government and law. Their Presbyterian Church was the only institution that followed them—indeed, it sometimes colonized them on land patents. Its ministers were not only among the best-educated people on the frontier, they were both religious and community leaders. So closely did the members of the congregation identify with and look to the church for guidance that it was often said they could not live without it. Their scriptural teachings included defining the duties of parents and children, and the importance of family worship.

Throughout the 1700s, there were probably never more than 10,000 Presbyterian Covenanters in America, and their membership grew slowly thereafter. The church and the church-sponsored school, with the Bible as its textbook, were the focal points of the Scotch-Irish community. The church had a stable, organized, governing structure that took care of the poor and the sick and provided discipline necessary for survival as they struggled in poverty. In 1773, as one Covenanter noted, "This is the best poor man's country in the world." The elders and the minister acted as a court in governing "sessions," in hearing and ruling on charges, in settling disputes over debts, land matters, and domestic conflicts, as well as in formulating and teaching church doctrine and moral discipline to the congregation.

Benedict Maryniak observed in *Faith in the Fight*, "The great formative events in the rise of England and then the United States were . . . wars—bitter fratricidal wars—accompanied by Puritan and abolitionist sermons and battle hymns." King George III regarded the Revolution as a Puritan and Presbyterian vendetta against the Anglican Church and the monarchy. A number of royal governors of the colonies as well as Anglican clergy vehemently voiced the same criticism.

Since the Covenanters saw slavery as a sin in God's eyes, they believed it had to be eradicated. Some even refused to recognize the U.S. Constitution, because it condoned slavery. There was no room in their religion for the whip, slave pen, or auction block. Their concept of freedom did not include the freedom to enslave others. They had fought in the old country for liberty from the oppression of the Crown. In the new, they called for liberty for the oppressed slaves. They believed that a nation built on the concept that all men are created equal could not also be the world's largest slaveholding nation.

Church members internalized, and were powerfully guided by, this set of moral principles. By the 1760s, Washington County had become a strong center for Highland Scots and Ulster Scots (Scotch Irish), many of whom were Presbyterian Covenanters. Members of those initial congregations were largely poor and uneducated, so Covenanter discipline was important in helping them form communities and survive in the wilderness.

Three generations of Rosses and at least one person from Margaret Reid's family belonged to the Old White Presbyterian Church of Cambridge, Washington County, whose part-time pastor, a Covenanter, became the first chaplain of Dan's regiment. Covenanters had organized this church in 1769, the second oldest covenanting church between Albany and the Canadian border. Its original congregation consisted of Scots, and its first ministers were Scots. Founded in 1785, the Reid family church to which Margaret's family initially belonged in Washington County also was a Covenanting Presbyterian Church. By the 1790s there were nine Covenanting congregations in Washington County.

Other ancestors of Margaret Reid Ross had a similar religious background. The Reids had intermarried with Dutch Calvinists named Krom, who were members of the Dutch Reformed Church, of Calvinist origin, the first of whom had arrived in 1624, escaping religious persecution.

The first recorded communion in the Rosses' church in Cambridge was held on November 9, 1794, when it had forty-three members. One member was William Ross, the grandfather of the four brothers, who joined on April 17, 1803, and was given an adult christening upon admission. Margaret Reid, the mother of the future soldiers, was admitted and baptized there on July 12, 1824. Shortly thereafter, she married Charles Wesley Ross, William Ross's son, who also was a member. William Henry Ross, the oldest of the four brothers, was baptized in the church on February 6, 1839. His sister also joined the church.

The Rosses' church was one of nine organized by Rev. Thomas Clark, MD, a Scotsman. He and congregation members who followed him from Scotland to Ireland were an ecclesiastical colony that had belonged to the Burgher Synod of Scotland. Dr. Clark, while still in Ireland, founded, in 1751, the Associate Presbytery of Down, Ireland's first Burgher presbytery. He and most of his congregations were Burghers who had seceded and would not "kiss the book," the legal form of oath-taking at that time in Ireland, nor would they take the sacrament from the King's Established (Anglican) Church. They were Covenanters who would hear no minister preach who had taken "the indulgence" after the National Covenant was signed in 1638. Ministers who took "the indulgence" surrendered the spiritual independence of the church to the tyranny of the king and his bishops.

Dr. Clark affiliated his nine churches, beginning in 1769, with the Associate Presbytery of Pennsylvania and, in 1776, with the Associate Presbytery of New York. By 1782, the Old White Church was affiliated with the Associate Reformed (Covenanting) Presbyterian Church. By 1858, it was one of seventeen churches that belonged to the United Presbyterian Synod of New York, nine of which were in Washington County. The 1850 U.S. Census recorded 35,660 church members in Washington County and eighty-one churches. Twenty-five were Presbyterian and accounted for 36 percent of total church membership in the county that year. In 1865, the two Presbyterian churches in Salem Township where the Rosses lived had a combined membership of 380, of whom 375 usually attended.

In 1858, the United Presbyterians declared that "slaveholding ... is a violation of the law of God ... that the law of God ... is supreme in its authority and obligations, and that where the commands of church or state ... conflict with the commands of this law, we choose to obey God rather than man." This synod resulted from a merger of the Associate Presbyterian Church and the Associate Reformed (Covenanting) Church. Both branches had repeatedly witnessed against slavery, keeping alive the tradition of the Scottish Covenanters. As early as 1787, the Synod of New York indicated its willingness "to procure eventually the final abolition of slavery." In 1800, the Covenanters agreed that "no slaveholder should be allowed the communion of the church." In 1811, the synod adopted an act declaring slavery a moral evil, directing members to free their slaves, and declaring that those who refused to comply were unfit for the fellowship of the church. In 1837, the delegate of the Presbytery of Troy, New York, to which the Ross family church belonged, introduced a motion to the Presbyterian General Assembly to get petitions on slavery read, but it was defeated.

By 1838, the church had split into Old School and New School factions. The New School faction then met in Auburn, New York, to organize. They were largely antislavery, and the events leading to the schism left little doubt that the Presbyterian was the first major church to split over the slavery issue. The Methodists formally split over the issue in 1844, and the Baptists in 1845. In 1840, correspondence was directed to Southern congregations asking them to agree to "moral emancipation," if they would not free their slaves. In 1850, the New School Synod declared the recently enacted Fugitive Slave Act null and void, and in 1854 called for the repeal of the Kansas-Nebraska Act because it would permit slavery in those states. In 1856, it inveighed against "American Slavery as a system which had its origin in violence, robbery, and blood ... [and] is a sin against God." In 1858, there were four synods in the Associate Reformed Church, and the Rosses' church belonged to one of them. There were only 367 congregations with 31,284 members in the entire North. Eleven of these congregations, with 2,037 members, were in Washington County.

Among the eighteen articles in the United Presbyterian Basis of Union, one dealt with slavery, declaring it "a foul blot on this fair land [and] a violation of the law of God and contrary both to the letter and spirit of Christianity." In 1860, the *Reformed Presbyterian* expressed its view that slavery should "be met with its own weapons.... [It] maintains itself by the sword. As it has chosen its mode of warfare ... those who are not disposed to submit to its demands should meet it ... with its own weapons." That same year, the *Presbytery Reporter* editorialized, "Even the fierce pro-slavery fervor of the South presents no cause for discouragement. It will either drive them madly on the rocks where their slave system will be wrecked, or there will be reaction. To stem the tide of human liberty which God is driving on in the world, is as insane an undertaking as to ... wade up the Mississippi River."

Covenanters often took the strongest position against slavery of any church of Puritan persuasion. How could they do anything less than send their sons—including the Ross brothers—to fight for putting an end to slavery?

Rev. Henry Gordon, a part-time pastor of the family church, would help to recruit the 123rd Regiment and serve as its first chaplain. Rev. Charles H. Taylor, another pastor of the church during the Civil War, allowed the church to be used as a recruiting station and made numerous trips to hold services for the troops in army camps. Likewise, in August 1862, Rev. James G. Forsyth, pastor of another Covenanting church in Washington County, preached to the 123rd New Yorkers while in camp in Washington, DC. In late April 1863, Gordon was temporarily succeeded as chaplain by Rev. A. B. Lambert, pastor of a neighboring Reformed Presbyterian church. Beginning one week after Lincoln's first call for volunteers, meeting after meeting was held in these two churches to gain public support for the war effort as well as to recruit volunteers for the two Washington County regiments, which three Ross brothers joined—the 93rd and the 123rd New York.

Shortly after he became chaplain of the 102nd Pennsylvania, in which capacity he served for four years, Rev. A. M. Stewart, a Covenanter, stated, "Slavery is now looked upon by all as a deadly bane on the body politic—a thing hated by God, accursed of men, and to be speedily and forever abolished." In 1862, the General Assembly of the New School Presbyterians sent Lincoln a message, declaring, "Since the day of your inauguration, the thousands of our membership have followed you with increasing prayer, besieging the throne of Heaven in your behalf." A year later, a committee of the Reformed Presbyterians told him, "By every consideration drawn from the Word of God [do not] be moved from the path of duty on which you have so auspiciously entered."

It was in this abolitionist environment that the Ross brothers grew to manhood and heard the twin issues of slavery and secessionism debated in the press and in the pulpit for years prior to the war. In perhaps their most impressionable years—the pre-Civil War decade—they heard, read, and felt the social, political, and economic issues that underlay the raging controversy. For them, their preacher was their "thought" leader.

From the 1830s, New York's abolitionist leaders were intensely active Reformed Presbyterians, Quakers, Methodists, Unitarians, Baptists, and Congregationalists. Had they not stimulated public debate on slavery, no one else would have. Dogged in their determination to abolish slavery, the Scots abolitionists helped stiffen the spines of their coreligionists in particular, and other abolitionists in general. Although there is no record that the Ross family were active or professed abolitionists—that they attended meetings, or circulated broadsides or pamphlets—they clearly were steeped in the beliefs of their church. Their actions as soldiers and the willingness of their parents to let all four brothers serve speak more loudly than any words they could have written or spoken.

Loyalty to church, family, and community was traditional among all the brothers' ancestors in New York, as it had been in Scotland and Holland. Community loyalty in the New World gradually extended to a wider patriotism, embracing all thirteen colonies that struggled to gain independence and then, as the United States, to keep it. They had tasted the fruits of self-government and never forgot its addictive flavor. A great-great-grandfather of the brothers served as a Hudson River shore guard in a New York militia regiment at the outbreak of the Revolution. Others served as sheriffs, school trustees, tax collectors, road masters, and—most importantly—as soldiers in the War of Independence and the War of 1812. Two great-great-uncles also served in the Revolution. Two of their grandfathers died in the War of 1812, and two great-uncles and another close relative served in it.

Margaret Reid Ross cherished a patchwork quilt she made from pieces of woolen uniforms worn by members of her family who had fought in colonial wars, as well as in the Revolutionary War and the War of 1812, to which she added scraps from her sons' Civil War uniforms. Her quiet pride in the fact that her ancestors, as well as her sons, would fight for their principles was woven into her quilt.

The Ross brothers' heritage stood firmly for both preserving the Union and removing its blemish of slavery. Apart from the armies of the Crusades, the American Civil War armies were probably the most religious that had ever fought. Northern Protestant clergy gave the war religious sanction. They were the single most important source of urgent patriotic appeals and earned more public respect than at any other time in the nation's history. It was during the Civil War that the phrase "In God We Trust" first was engraved on U.S. coins. Clearly, those soldiers who fought to end slavery acted on the deepest of religious convictions.

The Spread of Abolitionism

Covenanting Presbyterians were not the only faith community taking a strong stand against slavery in nineteenth-century America. Quakers and Mennonites in Pennsylvania had campaigned against slavery since 1688. By 1755 Quakers had banned slavery as a matter of principle. Nevertheless, during the 1830s, there were few abolitionists and most of them were scorned. Antislavery effort grew slowly but steadily through the 1840s, resulting in the emergence of new antislavery politics. By the 1850s, the simmering pot stirred by activists began to boil, and they gained both respectability and strength.

The Associate Synod, all Covenanters, was clearly at the vanguard of the abolitionist movement within the Presbyterian Church, and also led most denominations. In 1857, Albert Barnes, a leading antislavery New School Presbyterian spokesman, noted that "with the exception of the Quakers, there is no church . . . whose testimony has been more uniform . . . against slavery" than the Reformed Presbyterian.

As support for the abolition of slavery spread, it moved from churches into politics. In 1817, the state of New York had adopted an emancipation act. With the formation of the Anti-Slavery Society at a convention in Philadelphia in 1833, the movement became national. The convention was convened by William Lloyd Garrison of Massachusetts, editor of the *Liberator* and an admirer of the Covenanters. The publication's modus operandi was "to enlist the pulpit in the cause of the slave and to [purify churches] from all participation in the guilt of slavery." New York's Anti-Slavery Society became one of the strongest and had a chapter in Washington County as early as 1836. The *New York Evangelist*, a Presbyterian newspaper founded in 1830, became the leading abolitionist newspaper of the period. Abolitionist sentiment also was stirred by such African American writers and orators as Frederick Douglass, Sojourner Truth, and Harriet Tubman.

By 1857, the New School Presbyterians at their General Assembly condemned slavery and barred slaveholders from membership. Albert Barnes observed that "great reforms on moral subjects do not occur except under the influence of religious principle." By then he was an ardent Republican and strongly opposed admitting Kansas as a slave state. In 1861, Barnes's followers issued a call stating, "those . . . followers of the Prince of Peace who have no swords should sell their garments and buy them." He and other abolitionists argued that if slavery was not a sin, the Bible was the devil's book, not God's.

In May 1862, the Reformed Presbyterians urged both houses of Congress to remove the "foul blot upon the national escutcheon," arguing that the holding of slaves was a sin against God and that its continuance would invoke divine disapproval unless immediate emancipation was secured. The day before Lincoln announced the preliminary Emancipation Proclamation on September 22, 1862, a group from the Reformed Presbyterian Church in Washington urged Lincoln to free the slaves with the admonition that "God's wrath cannot be appeased." Shortly thereafter, the Scots Covenanters told the president that their church, "true to its high lineage and ancient spirit, does not hold within its pale a single secessionist," and congratulated him on the government's antislavery measures, foremost of which was the Emancipation Proclamation. Through this proclamation, in the eyes of the abolitionists, Lincoln had redirected the purpose of the war. Instead of a war merely to preserve the Union, the War Between the States became a war for freedom. The Covenanters enjoined him "not to be moved from the path of duty on which you have so auspiciously entered."

Since 1850, Lincoln and his wife had attended a Reformed Presbyterian church in Springfield, Illinois, and another in Washington while he served as president. Shortly after he issued the Emancipation Proclamation, however, Lincoln expressed concern that the majority of the public was not yet supportive. He wrote Vice President Hannibal Hamlin, "troops come forward more slowly than ever." Further, voters indicated their displeasure that fall by handing the Republicans a number of setbacks. In March 1863, Lincoln wrote to George W. Julian, "My proclamation was to stir the country; but it has done about as much harm as good." Fearing the proclamation would significantly weaken his support in the border states, he confided to another friend that "to arm the negro would put 50,000 bayonets that are for us against us."

During the decades immediately before the Civil War, the Liberty Party emerged on the national political scene. Its founders were upstate New York abolitionists, many of whom were preachers taking their first steps toward political action. In 1843, the party had resolved "that human brotherhood is a cardinal doctrine of true democracy, as well as of pure Christianity." The Bible was the party's creed. Some of its party conventions adopted resolutions based on biblical justifications for abolishing slavery.

The Liberty Party's mission was to make abolition a central issue in American politics. They ran James G. Birney as their presidential candidate on an antislavery ticket in both 1840 and 1844. A Kentuckian, Birney was nominated in Albany, New York, in 1840. His son, Maj. Gen. David B. Birney, also an abolitionist, was to become the division commander under whom Will Ross's regiment would serve. Another of Birney's sons would become a major general, recruit seven regiments of black soldiers, command a division of black troops, support equal pay for black soldiers, and systematically release slaves from Baltimore's city jails and slave pens. Because the Liberty Party was a one-idea party, it could only attract a small percentage of the popular vote.

Allied with the Liberty Party was the antislavery wing of the Democratic Party known as "Barnburners" because they would burn the barn to get rid of the "rats." One of the main planks in the 1848 New York Barnburner platform was restriction of slavery in the new western territories. Washington County was one of the five New York counties that in 1844 voted for Barnburner candidates by a majority of at least 60 percent. In 1848, at a convention in Buffalo, the Liberty Party merged with the Barnburners and others to form the Free Soil Party, with Martin Van Buren of New York as its nominee. Its campaign slogan was "Free Soil, Free Speech, Free Labor, and Free Men." They also were against the extension of slavery in territory where it did not presently exist. In 1850, the passage of the Fugitive Slave Act infuriated abolitionists who stood firmly behind the biblical passage in Deuteronomy, "Thou shall not deliver unto his master, the servant who is escaped from his master unto thee . . . thou shall not oppress him . . . "

This growing political momentum may have led Lincoln to state his position on slavery in 1852, namely, "opposition in principle, toleration of it in practice." Nevertheless, as antislavery sentiment increased in the North, pro-slavery attitudes hardened in the South. Northern and Southern radicals rejected further compromise.

By then, one churchman had concluded that trying to abolish slavery through the church was "like trying to pry up a stump with a bamboo crowbar." William Lloyd Garrison attacked the Constitution, describing it as "a covenant with death and an agreement with hell" and publicly burned a copy of it. More and more, abolitionists and slaveholders agreed that conflict was the only solution. The armed conflict in "Bloody Kansas" between free state and slave state settlers ("Border Ruffians") confirmed the belief that violence was inevitable.

Passage of the Kansas-Nebraska Act in 1854, sponsored by Sen. Stephen A. Douglas, was undoubtedly the most significant event in Lincoln's conversion to national antislavery activity and his resultant emergence as a national figure. It fired a political controversy that created unprecedented bitterness and led to vitriolic personal abuse, prompting some historians to argue that the Civil War started in Kansas. In 1854, the Republican Party was born, largely spawned by Northern indignation, if not fury, over passage of the Kansas-Nebraska Act. That year, the founding convention for the party in New York was held in Saratoga Springs, across the Hudson River from Washington County. By 1855, Abraham Lincoln had shifted his position on slavery, writing, "Experience has demonstrated, I think, that there is no peaceful extinction of slavery in prospect for us." That year he also wrote his friend Joshua Speed reminding him of a river trip they took together in 1841 when "ten or a dozen slaves [were] shackled together with irons" aboard the steamboat. "That sight was a continued torment to me [to this day]." In 1856, what remained of the short-lived Free Soil Party joined the newly formed Republican Party, which also included antislavery Whigs (Lincoln's party) and Democrats. In 1857, the Dred Scott decision handed down by the Supreme Court angered Lincoln, who called it, "a burlesque upon judicial decisions" and a "slander and profanation on the Founding fathers."

Lincoln threw himself wholeheartedly behind the party, as did many abolitionists. They ran John C. Fremont as their presidential candidate. On July 28, speaking on behalf of Fremont, Lincoln said, "We [the Republicans] would not strive to dissolve the Union; and if any attempt is made it must be by you.... We don't want to dissolve it, and if you attempt it, we won't let you." The campaign became a moral crusade against slavery and secession. Many Reformed Presbyterians joined, including Charles Ross. In the March 1858 local elections, entire slates of local Republican officials were elected in township after township in Washington County, and the Rosses became lifelong Republicans. Nationally, the Republican Party lost, but garnered 42 percent of the vote.

In 1858, Lincoln began his campaign against Stephen A. Douglas for the U.S. Senate seat from Illinois. In his opening speech on June 16, he summarized the depth of the controversy, saying, "I do not expect the Union to be dissolved ... but I do expect it will cease to be divided. It will become all one thing, or all the other." In his last debate he pleaded "let us re-adopt the Declaration of Independence, and with it, the practices, and policy, which harmonize with it ..." Lincoln lost to Douglas, but by that year, the Republican Party had gained majority support in Washington County.

In 1859, John Brown led a bloody, armed, and futile attempt to seize Harper's Ferry and start a slave rebellion. At least one newspaper in Washington County, the *People's Journal*, was sympathetic to him. By then, the Fugitive Slave Act had led to violence over returning runaway slaves to their masters. Many factors added fuel to the fire through the 1850s: the Kansas-Nebraska Act, expansion of the Underground Railroad, publication of Harriet Beecher Stowe's immensely popular *Uncle Tom's Cabin* (four hundred thousand copies were sold within a few years of its publication in 1851), the Dred Scott decision, the Lincoln-Douglas debates, John Brown's call at a Syracuse convention for arms to fight Kansas slaveholders, and the savage physical attack by Congressman Preston Brook of South Carolina on Senator Charles Sumner of Massachusetts on the Senate floor. The last straw was Lincoln's Cooper Union Speech in New York, which led to his nomination and election in 1860. He finished that speech by saying, "Let us have faith that right makes might, and in that faith, let us, to the end, dare to do our duty as we understand it."

Meanwhile, the Reid family's former church in Argyle, Washington County, New York, where Margaret's family initially settled, operated a station for runaway slaves along the "North Star Route" to Canada. Another station on this route, known as the Wheelhouse, was located near Cambridge (the site of the Ross family church) on the Turnpike Road to Vermont. Another three homes in Cambridge are thought to have been stations. Others in Washington County were located in a number of villages along the Battenkill, a major Underground Railroad route known as the Quaker Road that led from its mouth on the Hudson River eastward into Vermont. The Ross farm was on the Battenkill, and runaway slaves could have traversed it with or without the assistance of the family. Many other Covenanter settlements in the county were also on the Underground Railroad.

In 1854, Frederick Douglass gave seven lectures in Washington County. In 1858, the American Anti-Slavery Society held a meeting in Washington County at which Susan B. Anthony, a Quaker and New York agent for the society, spoke. Like the Rosses, as a child she had lived in that county along the Battenkill. During the 1850s she frequently lectured in company with a fugitive slave. A resolution was passed at that Washington County meeting condemning "all popular religions" except the "Old School" Covenanters as "eminently guilty of the sin of oppression." On another occasion, she observed, "[W]hile the cruel slave-driver lacerates the black man's . . . body, we, of the North, flay the spirit. . . . Let the North . . . prove to the South that she fully recognizes the humanity of the black man."

Gerrit Smith of New York, one of the wealthiest abolitionists of his day, gave farms to twenty-two black families in Washington County. Three were in Greenwich, two in Cambridge, and one each in Argyle, Salem, and Shushan. He also gave many more farms to black families elsewhere in New York.

In 1860, other leading radical abolitionists including Rev. Henry Ward Beecher, Horace Greeley, and Wendell Phillips spoke in the county. In April 1860, the Methodist Conference, to which Washington County churches belonged, adopted a resolution that read, "We are more than ever convinced of the great evil of slavery, and shall not cease to seek its extirpation by all wise and prudent means." The Congregational Church in Greenwich, founded on antislavery principles in 1837 by about a dozen Reformed Presbyterians, was the most active in the county in assisting runaway slaves. That church was only a few miles from where the Reid family first settled in 1765 on the Argyle Patent. Its founders agreed,

"It is our duty... to labor and pray for the speedy and entire abolition of slavery in the nation and throughout the world." Baptist and Quaker churches in Greenwich also took strong antislavery positions.

In June 1860, James B. McKean, the congressman representing Washington and Saratoga counties, said during a hearing on the state of the union, "Slavery and the Union cannot both exist; the one must destroy the other." He also noted that Southerners believed "the structure of white society must have a black foundation." Earlier in his career McKean had taught at the Jonesville Academy where Will, Dan, and Lank, as well as their sister Anna Marie, had gone to secondary school.

On both the political and religious fronts, New York had clearly emerged as a center of the politically active national abolitionist movement. Washington County was at the vortex of the movement in the Hudson River Valley. Lincoln's basic campaign argument was having its effect. Republicans, he argued, believed slavery was a moral, political, and social wrong, and the institution was an "unqualified evil to the negro, to the white man, to the soil, and to the State."

In 1860, enthusiastic "Wide Awake" Republican political clubs were organized in at least fourteen villages throughout Washington County. Members of the marching clubs wore black oilcloth caps and capes to identify themselves. Lincoln, leading the Republican ticket, had a total majority of 2,696 votes and carried every town in the county. He also swept into office Edwin Morgan, a Republican, as governor and carried the state's constitutional amendment for Negro suffrage by more than 1,000 votes in Washington County, even though it was defeated statewide. Governor Morgan won in Washington County by 6,108 votes to 3,504. Nationally, opposition to slavery had been the most important issue.

Southerners viewed Lincoln's election, only six years after the Republican Party was formed, as a Northern victory led by "Black Republican" fanatics who would use federal power to victimize them by denying their right to own slaves and to take them where they pleased. Lincoln's party did not carry a single Southern state. A point of no return had been reached.

Shushan, the village closest to where the Rosses lived, had the largest membership of all Wide Awake clubs. Members organized a rally of 800 people near the Ross farm for the "Rail Splitter," as Lincoln was known. The nearby Salem Club turned out 5,000 at its major rally. The windows were removed in the jam-packed Cambridge schoolhouse so the crowd outside could hear the speaker, District Attorney Archibald McDougall. Another rally in Hartford attracted 215 Wide Awakes, who heard James Rogers give an "excellent speech." Up to 1,000 uniformed Wide Awakes could be turned out almost anywhere. A number would be among the first to enlist. Rogers would become the lieutenant colonel of Dan and John's regiment, the 123rd New York, and later its colonel.

Four years later, after the sacrifice of inestimable blood and treasure, Washington County voted more than 63 percent for Lincoln, while statewide he received only 50.5 percent. Five Washington County newspapers were either strong supporters of abolition before the war or adopted that position during it. Only one opposed Lincoln and the Emancipation Proclamation.

The *Whitehall Chronicle* described slavery as a "noxious weed." The *People's Journal* noted that justice commanded "we lift the iron heel of oppression and prejudice from off the oppressed and restore them to their long lost right of citizenship."

The *Washington County Post* editorialized on November 15, 1861, "We earnestly hope that the first hand...lifted in Congress against the administration...for party purposes—be it emancipation, secession, or peace...may be palsied in its place." On March 28, 1862, the *Post* wrote, "Our confidence in the final and complete triumph of our government...over the curse of all curses—slavery...is in the God of our Armies...who will take care [of] wiping out the slave power in this our beloved land."

On July 11, 1862, the *Troy Daily Times*, published in an adjacent county but read in Washington County, stated that slaves should be armed so that "the Union cause may be strengthened...and in God's own time—perhaps sooner than most of us can now see—slavery itself may be abolished as the penalty of the madness of traitors."[1]

Acting on Their Faith

Shortly before the Civil War, Melancton (Lank) and William Henry moved from New York to join some of their Reid and Ross relatives, who, earlier, had moved to a farm near Somonauk, Illinois. A number of other Washington County families had moved there during the 1840s and 1850s, forming a Reformed (Covenanting) Church in 1842. The grandfather of one of its preachers had founded the Reid family church in Washington County in 1785.

The Somonauk church also operated an Underground Railroad station along the "Liberty Line" to help slaves reach Canada. Its preacher was a "conductor." A number of other Underground Railroad stations were established in nearby villages in Kendall, DeKalb, and adjacent Kane County, where there also was an Anti-Slavery Society beginning in the mid-1840s.

Will became a schoolteacher in Little Rock, Kendall County, six miles east of Somonauk, while Lank worked as a farmhand in Kane County, a few miles away.

When war broke out, the Regular Army numbered a mere 16,000 men in eighteen regiments. From the outset, Americans had disliked professional soldiers who killed for money. By the end of the war, only 67,000 had enlisted as Regulars, but there were never more than 26,000 at any point during the war. Early volunteers with a strong commitment to preserve the Union and/or abolish slavery became the backbone of the Union army.

Regular Army regiments were used intact, never to train volunteers or serve as a cadre in their regiments. Fewer than 90,000 men were drafted, and another 118,000 were hired to serve as substitutes for the conscripts. The overwhelming bulk of men in the Northern army—more than two million had served by war's end—enlisted as volunteers in 2,047 state regiments. Only 8 percent enlisted, like three of the Ross brothers, for a second hitch of three years as Veteran Volunteers.

Immediately following the April 13, 1861, surrender of Fort Sumter to Confederate forces, President Lincoln called for 75,000 volunteers to serve for three months.[2] Many Northerners viewed the attack on Fort Sumter as an attempt to destroy the first and only popular government ever created, a sentiment Will, Lank, and Dan may well have shared. Responding to a church elder's call for recruits, Will enlisted in the Somonauk company, one of the first organized in Illinois, on April 19, 1861. Charles Culver, a fellow Washington County transplant, also volunteered, as did other members of their church. The quota for Illinois was six regiments.

The Covenanting Somonauk Church was affiliated with a synod that had adopted a resolution in 1861 disavowing "all sympathy with traitors, styling themselves 'The Confederate States' [and pledging] that we will, as true patriots, defend this, our common country, against these and all like enemies." Somonauk Township would provide 311 men to the Union army, including 76 who enlisted with Will. In many Scots Reformed Presbyterian churches, all able-bodied men enlisted, forming companies of their own.

By midsummer, with the war escalating, initial enlistments like Will's expired. He was discharged from the 10th Ill. in late July 1861, after his regiment was disbanded. The men had been offered the opportunity to reenlist, but not enough of them chose to do so. Will returned to the family farm in time to assist his father and brothers Dan and John with late summer and fall chores.

Such short terms of service would not help win the war. So with congressional approval, Lincoln issued calls on July 23 and July 25 for

500,000 three-year men in 460 regiments. The Ross brothers were aware that the army's ranks had to be replenished quickly by three-year men. The devastating First Battle of Bull Run (Manassas) that ended on July 21 in a shameful, pell-mell, moblike retreat, led to a stark realization in the North: the magnitude and duration of the war would be greater than anticipated.

On July 29, the first organizational meeting of the 36th Ill. was held. Lank enlisted August 10, the third Ross brother in age, but first to sign up for a three-year stint. On August 20, 1861, he was mustered into Company E, the Somonauk company. The regiment was assigned by the state legislature to the First Brigade of Illinois Volunteeers.

The family of Lank's company commander, Lt. Lindsay H. Carr, were members of the Covenanting Somonauk Church. During the war, over half of the 36th would be killed, die of disease, or be wounded—more casualties than in any other Illinois regiment but one. Pvt. E. A. Crawford, assigned to Company C in the 36th Ill., wrote to his sister on December 7, 1861, that most of the men in his company were members of the United Presbyterian Church and were Covenanters.

Pvt. Walter V. Reeder of Company E, Lank's company, wrote home on July 29, 1862, that he witnessed slavery for the first time in Kentucky. "Several slaves...threshing wheat...I went down to the barn to see them work...three women, three men and a little boy...as I watched the poor things working away," he wrote. "I thought...I...would be willing to blot out this relict of barbarism, and if need be, to lay down my life for this end." He did at the Battle of Missionary Ridge after having been wounded at both Perryville and Stones River.

He was as strong a Union man as he was antislavery. He wrote, "Nothing short of the Union and the whole Union will we be satisfied with, though it may be cast in many trials and hardships and maybe our lives." In still another letter he wrote, "Badly as I want to go home I will fight them [Rebels] seven years, and, if need be sacrifice my life...the Union, one, and undivided, must, and shall be preserved."

Reeder did indeed sacrifice his life. He was wounded and captured at Stones River, returned to duty only to be wounded again at Missionary Ridge, and died shortly thereafter in the Chattanooga Military Hospital.

Included in Lincoln's two calls for three-year men was a quota of twenty-five regiments from New York. Washington County citizens would not accept the disgraceful Bull Run rout of their troops. Their commitment to putting down the rebellion led to the successful recruitment of three-year men in two new regiments, the 93rd N.Y. Volunteers and the 7th N.Y. (Black Horse) Cavalry. The War Department allowed prominent citizens to recruit these regiments independently, at their personal expense, under the supervision of, and in conformity with, the governors of their respective states. Almost 90,000 New Yorkers responded to Lincoln's July calls.

On September 11, 1861, after the harvest on the Ross farm, Dan enlisted for three years in the 7th N.Y. Black Horse Cavalry, the second brother to sign on for extended duty. He had graduated in June from a two-year course at the Jonesville Academy and intended to teach school like his brother Will and sister Anna Marie. Both had attended the academy earlier to become teachers. Lank also attended in 1860.

In a December 30, 1861, letter, Will advised Dan about what he should study if he wanted to teach "out West" and earn good pay, $25 to $30 a month plus board. "The best place for a young man of ambition and principles . . . is in a new village" like those in southern Illinois, he urged. Will earned $22 monthly, plus board and the use of a good horse, while teaching "twenty-two scholars" and having "a pleasant time." Summers, he worked on the farm where he lived, and finished husking corn before school started.

A fair number of easterners with secondary-school educations were moving to Illinois to meet the growing demand for qualified teachers after the state passed the Common School Law. By 1859, when Will moved to Illinois, private academies were being replaced by public schools so "the poor man's children [could] enter the school room on an exact equality . . . with the rich man's child."

A career in the classroom would have to wait, for both brothers. Dan and the fifty-four-man Salem company were not mustered in until November 6. When they left Salem to join the regiment in Troy, New York, local residents presented each member with a Bible and a blanket. Hundreds of friends and relatives gathered to bid them good-bye. The same day that Dan reported for duty with the Black Horse Cavalry, Will reenlisted, this time for three years in the 93rd N.Y. Infantry. Three brothers had now enlisted for three years.

During the first recruiting rallies in Washington County, when Dan enlisted, there was no mention of slavery. Rather, the focus was on preserving the Union. Rev. Henry Gordon, in his first recruiting speech to a packed audience at the Old White Presbyterian Church, told the crowd, "A great principle is at stake. Our free popular government is jeopardized." The silence on the subject of slavery was deafening—on Lincoln's part as well as that of the Ross family preacher and the committee that recruited Lank's regiment in Illinois.

Reflecting his combination of morality and expediency, Lincoln's sole rallying cry at war's beginning, as well as that of others, was saving the Union. This goal had overwhelming support in the North. In late April 1861, only a few weeks after Fort Sumter, Lincoln told John Hay, one of his assistants, "I consider the first necessity that is upon us is proving that popular government is not an absurdity.... If we fail, it will go far to prove the incapability of the people to govern themselves." Clearly it had the broadest, most urgent appeal.

For Dan, his preacher's appeal to help preserve the government was sufficient reason to postpone launching his teaching career and enlist. For others who had only political reasons, fighting for the Union was sufficient to justify enlisting. For those with deep moral/religious convictions, fighting to end slavery was another spoken or unspoken reason. In any event, relatively few Union volunteers mentioned slavery when they first enlisted.

Lincoln did not want to fight a long war. To avoid doing so, he had to keep the North united behind the war—Democrats and Republicans, radicals and conservatives. His war powers as commander in chief to put down an insurrection, the aim of which was to sever the Union, could not be constitutionally challenged. To save the Union, he also had to keep the border states neutral, if not supportive. Moreover, he wanted to maximize the possibility of a fraternal reunion at war's end.

The slavery issue, therefore, had to be tackled later, when he could justify emancipation as a military necessity. Even Lincoln's enemies recognized his concern about the border states. They ridiculed him by sneering that he "would like to have God on his side, but he must have Kentucky." He had participated in political events long enough to wait for the tide of events to move public opinion in support of his position, thereby gaining the consent of the governed.

Half of Will's regiment was recruited in Washington County, and the rest from neighboring counties. Will was off recruiting when he wrote to Dan on November 5, 1861, that Col. John S. Crocker had assured him of a commission as an officer if his recruiting efforts were successful. He also wrote that a patriotic Presbyterian preacher friend, Rev. Joseph Hulburt, "pledged himself unasked to help" and would be his "right hand companion and friend as well as adviser." Will was confident, assuring Dan his "prospects for an office [were] good." Until he was reimbursed for his expenses, he had to borrow money from his father. He wrote, "Father backs me up with true love not expecting to gain... I asked him to back me at the bank for sixty days which he has done readily." Apparently, though, he was not successful as a recruiter, particularly after Hulburt withdrew his help because of his mother's "poor health." In spite of that disappointment, Will enlisted as a private.

For two years prior to the war Col. Crocker served as an acting brigadier general in the First Brigade of the New York State Militia, and was active in recruiting for both the 93rd and, later, the 123rd. He was an abolitionist, whose grandfather had fought in the Revolution.

Crocker had been Will's father's attorney for ten years and later served as Lank's attorney in applying for his pension. He named the Ninety-third "Morgan's Rifles," after his close personal friend Gov. Edwin Morgan of New York, and raised it without offering bounties.

Crocker, age forty-one, mustered in the full regiment by November 15. The ladies of Washington County presented the regiment with a battle flag they had designed. Will's family church in Cambridge gave his company a prayerful, rousing, patriotic send-off the night before the men left by train. Crocker also helped to raise a company for the 22nd N.Y. He had spent $20,000 of his own money recruiting these regiments, for which he was never reimbursed. However, he had reimbursed Will for out-of-pocket expenses incurred in helping to recruit for the 93rd.

Crocker's cousin was editor and publisher of the *Washington County Post*, which came to support emancipation. Previously it had merely opposed the extension of slavery into Kansas and Nebraska and considered the matter a sectional, not a national, problem. Crocker had another relative, Rev. James N. Crocker, a Reformed Presbyterian who preached at the Charlton Freehold Reformed Presbyterian Church and was the principal founder of the academy there, a secondary school.

Meanwhile, Dan's regiment, commanded by Col. A. J. Morrison, arrived in Washington, DC, without mounts or arms. It was one of twenty-five Empire State regiments recruited in response to Lincoln's July calls. New York's quota was twenty-five thousand in twenty-five regiments. By the time Dan's regiment arrived November 25, there already were well over sixty regiments from various states guarding Washington. They were stationed at Camp Stoneman and assigned to help guard the capital. By March 1862, the War Department and General George McClellan determined that there were too few horses and too many cavalry regiments in Washington and discharged a number of them, including Dan's on March 31. His regiment was never mounted, even though its rank and file were described as intelligent sons of farmers and accomplished horsemen.

He returned home in April 1862 to work on the farm for his father, helping put in spring crops as well as harvest them. From correspondence between the two brothers that summer, it is clear that Dan was anxious to get back into the army. He wrote Will that he was plowing a field of corn stubble and felt a lack of something "prominent" to do. He also asked Will if he could assist in obtaining a position for him in his brother's regiment. On July 8, Will replied that it was "doubtful," adding, "[I] cannot give you any encouragement to leave . . . when father has so much business on hand. I am sure you can make yourself very useful" to him.

Lengthening casualty and sick lists made it clear that war was neither glamorous nor glorious. Four costly battles in the spring and summer of 1862—Shiloh, Seven Pines, Seven Days,' and 2nd Bull Run—had resulted in another 75,000 casualties in the Union army. Dan must have followed the demoralizing war news concerning the Seven Days' Battle in the local *Washington County People's Journal,* the *Salem Press,* and/or the *Washington County Post.* He surely attended the recruiting rally called by his township (Salem) war committee on July 22, 1862, held while the Army of the Potomac was still recovering from its disastrous defeat in the Seven Days' Battle that ended July 1.

After these heavy losses, Lincoln realized he should have recruited even more three-year volunteers. A few months earlier, in April, the Confederate Congress had extended for the duration of the war the enlistments of 400,000 Confederates who had volunteered in 1861. Meanwhile, Secretary of State William H. Seward met with various state governors, eighteen of whom petitioned the president to call on states for additional volunteers to "speedily crush the rebellion." Four of the governors were from the border states of Kentucky, Maryland, Missouri, and Tennessee. On July 22, 1862, three weeks after the last of the Seven Days' battles, Lincoln—ostensibly responding to this appeal—called for 300,000 more three-year volunteers.

New York State's quota was set at twenty-eight regiments, one of which was assigned to the state's senatorial district that included Washington County. Because enlistment fervor was on the wane, local recruiting committees went to work organizing rallies and war meetings in churches, schools, and halls, as well as parades. Governors called on men to join up, including Gov. Morgan. By war's end, New York had furnished a total of 250 regiments that served terms ranging from three months to three years, more than any other state.

With the crops in and heavy summer work over except for harvesting, Dan reenlisted at Shushan, the closest recruiting post to his home, on August 14, 1862. He and at least five other Black Horse cavalrymen were mustered in by Col. Crocker for three years in Company H of the 123rd N.Y., although he was not to be their commanding officer. Dan was the first of the Ross brothers to enlist for a second three-year hitch. It was five weeks before Lincoln released the preliminary Emancipation Proclamation on September 22.

Rev. Henry Gordon, who was known as a "rabid abolitionist" and the "fighting parson," served as their first chaplain. Born in Ireland, he was the son of Covenanter parents of Highland Scot extraction. Lt. Col. Rogers, the son of a New York congressman who served in the 123rd throughout the war, regarded Gordon as "the sunshine of the regiment."

The regiment's colonel was Archibald McDougall, a Lincoln Republican who joined the party in 1856 and was elected district attorney for Washington County in 1860 by almost a two-to-one margin. He had spoken at a number of Republican Wide Awake Club rallies during the presidential election campaign, and his family were members of the Reformed Presbyterian Church of Salem.

According to the *Troy Daily Times*, the caliber of many of these Washington County men was exceptionally high. They were not acting on romantic impulse, but from conscientious motives and with an understanding of what they would face. Dan and the others also could have been swayed by the new song that gained immense publicity, "We are coming Father Abraham 300,000 Strong." Written by an abolitionist newspaper editor, it was published first in the *New York Evening Post* on July 16, 1862, a week before Lincoln actually called for 300,000 more three-year men.

The 123rd enlistees consisted largely of sons of successful farmers. Reformed Presbyterian churches served ten of the seventeen Washington County villages from which most of these 1,089 three-year men were recruited. Not one was drafted. After completing their eight grades of public school education in a one-room schoolhouse, many also had attended private academies for secondary school education, like three of the Ross brothers. At least seven in Dan's regiment kept diaries, and thirty-seven others wrote vivid accounts, which have been preserved, of battles in which they participated and their moral commitment to fight. It was a highly literate regiment.[3]

Having already served almost five months, Dan was aware of the hardships and risks as well as the boredom of army life. Any dreams of glory, excitement, and adventure he may have had when he first enlisted had vanished. Military service was not his only option. The expanding wartime economy had created numerous city jobs, and farm boys like Dan were in the midst of a busy summer season. Hence, for many, a soldier's pay was not sufficient motivation to enlist, despite the fact that some had never seen a $10 bill.[4] They had to be compelled by a sense of purpose to sign up for three years, particularly knowing that the war could be prolonged.

Among them was Robert Cruikshank, a member of Dan's church who enlisted in the same company as Dan and later became its commander. Cruikshank's ancestors had been preachers, elders, and trustees of that church. They were among the original twenty-six to purchase a pew when the Old White Church in Salem was built in 1797. He had a wife and a fifteen-month-old daughter, and was a successful carpenter contractor. He wrote, "When President Lincoln called for three hundred thousand more men, I thought it my duty to go."

Sgt. Rice C. Bull enlisted for the same reason and noted that most men volunteered out of a sense of duty. He wrote, "We felt that if our country was to endure as a way of life planned by our fathers, it rested with us children to finish the work they had begun." Sgt. L. R.

Coy, an intensely religious man, and, like Cruikshank, a carpenter, also signed on.

On September 6, 1862, the *Troy Daily Times* described the newly formed 123rd as "composed of the very best material in the towns from which it has been recruited." It was the only regiment raised exclusively in Washington County. Men like Bull, Cruikshank, Coy, and the Ross brothers, who enlisted in the first year and a half of the war, remained the backbone of the army until war's end. They were in agreement with Lincoln when he said, "I expect to maintain this contest until successful, or till I die, or am conquered, or my term expires, or Congress or the country forsakes me."

There is no evidence that the Ross brothers were influenced by enlistment bonuses, nor is it known how many Union soldiers were. As "prebounty" men at the time of their first enlistments, Will, Lank, and Dan made their decisions "without price considerations." Not until Lank reenlisted for the second time did he receive a bounty. Will did not receive one until his third enlistment.

The War Department, aware of the difficulty in attracting three-year men in the summer of 1862, had authorized a $25 payment on the date of enlistment plus $75 more upon honorable discharge. Some states, cities, and counties offered additional bounties. New York's Washington County borrowed enough money to pay a $50 bounty to each recruit, and urged enlisting at a mass meeting so that it would not be compelled to resort to conscription. New York State also paid a $40 bounty, making Dan eligible for a total of $190 when he reenlisted.

In his message to Congress at the end of 1862, Lincoln said, "In giving freedom to the slaves, we assure freedom to the free [for which] the world will forever applaud, and God must forever bless.... We shall nobly save or meanly lose the last, best hope of earth." With this moral justification to enlist for three more years, Dan's bounty was useful to help pay the interest on his father's mortgage, but far from a principal incentive for reenlisting.[5]

The brothers did agree to share their military pay with their parents. In a later letter to Dan, Will said he was concerned about their father's financial affairs as well as his health. A mortgage payment on the farm was due shortly. He proposed to Dan that they and Lank together save $300 annually to pay the interest on the mortgage and let their father "and John look after a living for the family [and] keep the old house in order."

On May 3, 1863, Dan's regiment was on the front line in the Battle of Chancellorsville, the first battle they fought, and suffered 148 casualties, the greatest number it would experience in any battle. In response, the United Presbytery of Argyle, to which the Rosses' Old White Church belonged, sent the 123rd a resolution offering spiritual encouragement not to give up the struggle for the Union or abolition. They vowed "unfaltering and loyal attachment to the Government in its present struggles for maintaining the ordinance of God in its supremacy."

Chaplains were generally in favor of emancipation and had a significant impact on soldiers' attitudes. Rev. Henry Gordon, described as "one of the main props of the regiment," had assisted significantly in its recruitment, beginning with the initial rally on July 22, 1862, when he was nominated chaplain. On August 26, while they were in Camp Chase on Capitol Hill in Washington, Cpl. John C. Gourlie, of Company D, wrote to his sister that Rev. James G. Forsyth of Salem had preached a very good sermon on the parade ground. He also reported that he had gone to the Presbyterian Church three times one Sunday, and fifteen members of his company had attended a service. In November 1862, Gordon preached to the regiment every night and twice on Sundays. Shortly before the Battle of Chancellorsville, however, Gordon resigned as chaplain and returned to his church in Cambridge.

The price for their commitment would be profound in the Ross family. Charles Ross had lost needed help with his farm when two of his sons moved to Illinois and then enlisted. With only sporadic help from Will and Dan while they were between enlistments, he and John were increasingly unable to operate the family farm and wood business.

In April 1864, Lank was blinded while on his way to participate in Sherman's march on Atlanta. The following month, Will was mortally wounded in the Battle of the Wilderness and died May 6. In June, Dan was captured at the Battle of Kolb's Farm, during Sherman's march on Atlanta. He spent the next ten months in five Confederate prisons, initially in Andersonville, enduring cruelty, disease, starvation, thirst, and exposure that damaged his health for life.

In late July a severe hailstorm with walnut-sized hailstones struck, breaking countless windows in homes throughout Washington County, New York. Drought and violent winds followed in August and September, wiping out half the family's crops and vegetable gardens, and with them virtually all farm income. Nonetheless, on September 1, 1864, Charles Ross gave signed permission for John to enlist, taking Dan's place in his regiment and earning a $33.33 bounty. John was partially deafened three months after enlisting, when a shell burst near his head during the Siege of Savannah in the final days of Sherman's march to the sea. After a short hospitalization he returned to active duty, and remained until war's end.

Charles Ross had just lost about $2,000 from a bad investment. He was crippled by rheumatism in his hip, and his wife was disabled with the same illness. By the war's end, they had no choice but to default on their mortgage, surrender their farm, and move.

As the noted historian Arthur M. Schlesinger, Jr., has written: "At bottom the anti-slavery impulse was a moral impulse. No cause can command the deepest loyalties and the greatest sacrifice of men till it is presented under a moral aspect." Certainly sons of Northern farmers were not economically threatened by slavery. Religious convictions motivated many Union soldiers, while the ideals of Jefferson, Madison, and other founding fathers also provided inspiration.[6]

Veteran Volunteers

Men willing to fight for the North early in the war had choices other than the three-year terms chosen by the Ross brothers. Thirty-eight regiments were staffed with two-year men in 1861, and another ninety-two signed men for only nine months of service the following year.

By mid-1863, though, those men were due to be released—23,000 of them. In the first eight months of the following year, another 40,000 infantrymen in the Army of the Potomac alone would serve out their enlistments. By the end of 1864, with the war raging on, the North would lose 455 infantry regiments as their enlistments expired. Casualties also continued to take a dreadful toll on army ranks as well, 17,000 at the Battle of Chancellorsville in May 1863 and another 23,000 at Gettysburg in July, also in the Army of the Potomac.

Approximately 658,000 men had enlisted in response to Lincoln's first three calls for three-year men between May 1861 and January 1862; they were the only men eligible to become Veteran Volunteers. More than 89,000 were from New York, the most from any state. As the war dragged on, it became more and more obvious that it was vital to persuade the survivors among those experienced veterans to reenlist.

On June 25, 1863, the War Department offered a $400 bounty, payable in semiannual installments, to those who would reenlist for another three years or the duration of the war. In addition, they would receive a furlough of at least thirty days, exclusive of travel time, with paid travel expenses. At reenlistment, they also were to receive whatever bounty and back pay they were owed from their prior enlistment, plus the first $40 of the bounty, one month's advance pay, and a $2 premium. Hence, they were guaranteed money in their pockets when they arrived home on furlough. All installment payments of the $400 bounty, which became known as the Veteran Volunteer bounty, would be paid even if they did not serve out the full three-year term. For those killed in service, the unpaid balance would go to the man's legal heir. To be eligible, a soldier had to have initially enlisted for three years in 1861 or early 1862, and therefore already served at least two years. Most of these men had not seen home for that long. If three-fourths of a regiment reenlisted it would be designated a "Veteran Volunteer Regiment," given special chevrons of red and blue braid to be worn on the left sleeve, and furloughed in a body.

Regiments with high morale and popular officers were strongly motivated to preserve their regimental identity, despite the fact that many had seen the worst of war. An overwhelming majority of the 658,000 three-year men who had not died in service, been captured, or discharged for disability, though eligible to "veteranize," chose not to. They served out the remainder of their initial enlistment and were discharged. A total of 136,000 veterans reenlisted, almost three-fourths of the remainder, while their capable, experienced officers were retained in these hard-core regiments. Like the Ross brothers, they were prebounty veterans of 1861 and 1862 determined to stay on until the war was won. They were educated in what Sherman termed "the dearest school on earth." Another 51,000 three-year men, though eligible to veteranize, chose not to and were mustered out. Veteran Volunteers reenlisted with full day-to-day knowledge of what war was like—rain, mud, bitter cold, intense heat, bad food, near starvation, boredom, and the probability that they would be killed, maimed, captured, or infected by any number of incapacitating diseases.

Certainly the 36th Ill., Lank's regiment, knew what war was like. Almost 500 of their regiment were already casualties when they reenlisted. Six weeks earlier, they had been on starvation rations. When 227 of them "re-upped" on New Year's Day, 1864, in Strawberry Plains, Tennessee, the ink on the pen point was so cold that it froze. Hardship did not deter them.

Cpl. Day Elmore of Company H had first enlisted in August 1861. By November 1862 he had fought in three bloody battles—Pea Ridge, Perryville, and Stones River—and he wrote home, "If our Regt was Discharged tomorrow [and] . . . if this war was not at an End I would enlist again." After being shot in the lungs at Chickamauga, captured, imprisoned, paroled, and exchanged, he fought again at Missionary Ridge on November 25, 1863. On February 24, 1864, he reenlisted as a Veteran Volunteer and wrote his father, "I can not express myself so I will only say that my whole soul is wrapt up in this our countrys caus. I ought to be at school but I feel that I am only doeing my duty to myself and you, Pa."

Some may also have reasoned that they had a good chance to become casualties during the last months of their current enlistments. If not, they would probably reenlist anyway, so they concluded that by reenlisting now they would at least get a month's leave to visit home, family, wives, sweethearts, and friends. Without the furlough, a $1,000 bounty would not have been enough to induce most men to reenlist, since many had not seen home for two years. As one veteran put it, he was ready to endure "three more years of hell" in exchange for thirty days of heaven—home—perhaps including a Christmas vacation.

Another saw it differently but nonetheless reenlisted. He wrote, "they use a man here just the same as they do a turkey at a shooting match, fire at it all day and if they don't kill it raffle it off in the evening, so with us, if they can't kill you in three years they want you for three more—but I will stay." This inspired his comrade to say of him, "Well, if new men won't finish the job . . . as long as Uncle Sam wants a man, here is Ben Falls." Ben was killed two months later.

A Massachusetts soldier wrote his wife that not only would he get a furlough to visit her, but he would also receive a state bounty of $100 plus $20 monthly for six months after honorable discharge, as well as the $400 federal bounty. He concluded that would be enough "to buy a house and a few acres . . . and have a home for us when I return. I would want to buy it in your name." He also noted that he had nineteen more months to serve in his present enlistment, and the war probably would not last longer than that. Lank had nine months to serve out his initial three-year enlistment period, and Will had ten.

There were other reasons for veteranizing too. Victory seemed inevitable to many soldiers, and they could choose to participate in the triumph. Re-upping now would help demoralize the South, which was counting on them not to sign up; and thus re-upping possibly could help shorten the war. Many felt they had to finish what they had started. These men agreed with Elisha Hunt Rhodes, a Veteran Volunteer who fought from the first battle of the Army of the Potomac to its last. In camp during the 1863 Christmas holidays, he decided to reenlist as a Veteran Volunteer. "Tonight we have had a meeting of the officers to decide whether we are willing to remain in service . . . I decided without hesitation," he wrote. "I feel I owe a duty to my country . . . no one can tell when the end will come. But when it does come, I want to see it, and so I am going to stay." Hunt also wrote a few days after he was mustered out at the end of the war: "I thank God that I have had an opportunity of serving my country freeing the slaves and restoring the Union."

One "Lincolnite" in the 36th wrote in his diary, "The singleness of purpose to see the rebellion put down which characterizes these men, is such as completely surprises me; it is the men not the officers." Another Lincolnite who reenlisted in the 36th wrote his parents, "If this our boasted land of Freemen, the fairest land under the noblest government ever made by man, if this the famous Union *must* fall, I care not to survive it."

Peer pressure also was an important factor in encouraging reenlistment. With the onset of winter 1863, at the end of active campaigning, soldiers were told that if less than three-fourths of a regiment reenlisted, the remaining men would risk being consolidated with another depleted regiment. While the order was revoked by the secretary of war, the threat of lost regimental identity, comradeship, and cohesiveness—as well as the loss of officers in whom the men had confidence and trust—was a powerful motivation to reenlist as a unit. The sense of security they gave each other was a powerful binding force. They had developed strong loyalties to and dependence on their tent mates, messmates, companies, and regiments.

Many officers in the regiments that veteranized had been promoted from the ranks because of demonstrated ability. They were not inexperienced popinjay officers. Almost all of them had first enlisted in 1861 or early 1862. They had a wealth of experience, knew the men personally, understood their problems, and had their trust. They disregarded spit and polish, ceremony, and rank, thereby minimizing resentment toward them. It would have been impossible to replace these officers and men, and equally impossible to keep them against their will. By then, they had acquired an almost unerring ability to judge the military significance of a movement, for better or for worse.

The Ross brothers' regiments were typical of the long-term volunteers. By the spring of 1864, they had experienced two or more years of bloody battles, near starvation, and unspeakable fatigue and hardship. Regimental cohesiveness bound the men and their officers in Veteran Volunteer regiments into the most effective fighting machines in the Union army. By 1864 half of the captains and 90 percent of the lieutenants in Sherman's army had served as enlisted men. After three years of service, forty-seven enlisted men in the 36th, Lank's regiment, had been commissioned as officers. They had mastered many skills, including the logistics of supplying food, fodder, and ordnance, further increasing the combat effectiveness of their units.

The reappearance of these Veteran Volunteers at public receptions, fanfare, and speeches by local dignitaries while home on furlough stimulated recruiting activity. To replenish their ranks, the Veteran Volunteer regiments received many of the new recruits that responded to Lincoln's October 1863 call for another 300,000 volunteers.[7]

Two-thirds of the men whose time was expiring—26,767 in the Army of the Potomac—reenlisted, including 40 percent of Hancock's corps. These included William Henry Ross and the 93rd N.Y., the first regiment in the Army of the Potomac to reenlist. Will had acknowledged in his letter to Dan that he might end up crippled, yet he reenlisted.

Thirty thousand men in seventy-one regiments of the Army of the Cumberland, including Lank's 36th Ill., and thirty-seven other Illinois regiments, reenlisted—a larger number than in the Army of the Potomac.

Virtually every regiment in General McPherson's corps, also a part of Sherman's army, reenlisted as Veteran Volunteers, except a few from Iowa and Illinois. During their one-month furlough, their ranks were swelled by 8,000 new recruits, who were referred to as "squirrel shooters" and "hundred dollar men." Four of the nine regiments in Lank's brigade veteranized.

Dan's regiment, the 123rd N.Y., had enlisted for three years in September 1862, nine months before the War Department offered a $400 bounty to the Veteran Volunteers. With almost two years remaining in their term, men in the regiment were not eligible to reenlist in 1863. However, older regiments in the division to which the 123rd belonged that could veteranize, did so. By war's end, nearly 37 percent of the men in the 123rd were killed or wounded, or died of disease. Many of the veteranized regiments suffered equally severe casualty rates.

Will's and Lank's regiments were among the 300 Union regiments that experienced the greatest number of killed or mortally wounded by war's end. The 93rd N.Y. suffered a casualty rate of 41 percent. In Lank's 36th Ill., nearly 54 percent died or were wounded, a total of 709 soldiers. Because these regiments were the steadiest under fire, they were often the first to go into battle, and the last to leave. They also were frequently called on to skirmish with the enemy, the most dangerous and important role assigned to troops. Skirmishing required men who could act on the independent judgment they had gained through experience. They were the eyes and ears of the army, inspired by their officers' acts of bravery under fire and therefore unswervingly loyal to them. The more combat a regiment experienced, the more the bonds between men and officers were strengthened as they faced the same bullets. In Lank's regiments one man earned a Medal of Honor for conspicuous bravery, as did two each in Will's and Dan's regiments. While an officer's bravery was contagious, fear was equally so. That reality was demonstrated over and over by green troops led by green officers.

Veteran Volunteer regiments became tantamount to military families. The men were a band of brothers, and the officers were their father figures. The men even looked to officers for personal advice, because they made the men's problems their own, bridging the gap between the two-tiered caste system of officers and men. This bond of mutual support and trust resulted in even more esprit de corps. The steadiness, attention to duty, and discipline of these regiments under fire increased with every battle. There were no "coffee coolers," or stragglers. The faith the officers and men had in each other, plus their commitment to the Union cause, gave them the moral and physical courage to withstand the shock of battle after battle.

They were truly made of sterner stuff than short-term men, if not initially, then certainly through their shared experiences. No matter how brave soldiers may be, they rely on their comrades to advance as they advance and to respond to commands at the same time. They need to hear the voices and the shouts of those on either side and know that each has a firm moral grip on himself. Yet they all knew they could be injured or killed.

Those Veteran Volunteers who survived believed that abandoning the war would make a mockery of the sacrifices their comrades-in-arms had already made. Their military families not only included those still alive but those who had been killed, captured, or maimed, like Will, Dan, and Lank. So the survivors fought on to the bitter end. For some combination, if not all, of these reasons, many, upon returning from their Veteran Volunteer furlough, said they had had furlough enough and were glad to be back.[8]

The Growing Support for Emancipation

Paradoxically, while most secessionists feared abolition, most antisecessionists did not favor abolition. Many Southerners believed their economic and social welfare depended on slavery. Most Northerners, including President Lincoln, were willing to accept slavery—at least in the near future—in order to preserve the Union. Despite the fact that he had long regarded it as a moral evil, nearly a year and a half after the war started Lincoln wrote, "My paramount object in this struggle is to save the Union, and is not either to save or to destroy slavery."

By the end of the war's third year, emancipation was a much more widespread motivating factor in soldiers' decisions to reenlist than it had been at the war's beginning. By mid-1863, Union soldiers had reached the Deep South. They witnessed the arrogance and cruelty of slaveholders. As it began to anger them, they silently allowed runaways to pass through their lines or stay in order to perform menial labor. They refused attempts by masters to recapture runaways, especially when they would appear virtually naked, exposing backs horribly scarred from the lashes of whips. As this lesson ascended the chain of command, the Union army gradually became an army of liberation.

By late 1864, many Northerners had come to the conclusion that slavery caused the war, as, indeed, Lincoln recognized from its beginning. It had become clear that slavery was to the Confederacy what a keystone is to an arch. Remove the keystone and the arch collapses. As the war ground on, emancipation became more and more of a motivating force to the North. By war's end, the vast majority of soldiers in Sherman's army either believed in social and political equality for blacks or at worst held only a slight degree of prejudice against them. As Joseph T. Glatthaar noted, their opposition to slavery continued to grow as Sherman's troops marched through Georgia and then the Carolinas. By the time they reached Goldsboro and Raleigh, North Carolina, at war's end, campfire discussions focused increasingly on what peacetime rights freedmen should have. Some argued that blacks should have no political rights except freedom, that emancipation was a gift from Northern soldiers. Others supported emancipating and arming blacks without giving any thought to their postwar rights.

Support for preserving the Union was most clearly demonstrated by the border states, where slavery was permitted. The western part of Virginia actually became the Union state of West Virginia in 1863. It also became the first state to abolish slavery as a result of the war. According to some estimates, the border states of Maryland, Delaware, Kentucky, and Missouri had more men in blue than in gray, as did West Virginia. Certainly these border states provided many Union regiments, despite the fact that when Lincoln issued his first call for 75,000 volunteers in April 1861, Maryland, Kentucky, and Missouri refused to send a single soldier.

Yet Lincoln's emancipation policy did not drive these states into the Confederacy. Even well south of the border, the mountainous parts of eastern Tennessee and North Carolina, as well as northwest Georgia and western Virginia, resisted secession and sent 100,000 men to the Union army. As the war dragged on, the Appalachian South more and more came to believe that it was "a rich man's war and a poor man's fight." The *Nashville Union*, an influential Tennessee newspaper, advocated emancipation, editorializing, "We believe that slavery is an enormous curse, which will destroy our country." Tennessee was the next to last of the eleven Southern states to secede and the first readmitted to the Union after the war's end.[9]

Soldiers like William Henry, Lank, and Daniel Ross, as well as many, if not most, of their comrades who enlisted early in the war and re-upped as their initial terms of service expired, underwent a psychological and moral transformation from citizen to soldier as the war continued with no end in sight. Having fought the longest and hardest, these men were most altered by the war. They became hardened to death, violence, disease, discomfort, privation, even stealing and destruction. Their unaltered moral convictions, however, were that slavery had to be abolished and the Union had to be preserved. For many, emancipation became a means to achieve victory. For a few, it was an end in itself from the beginning.

The Synergistic Effect

The principles for which the Rosses and other Veteran Volunteers fought were underscored by a fatalistic religious conviction that they would die when God willed it. The comradeship of their fellow soldiers, many of whom were neighbors, relatives, friends, and schoolmates in civilian life, also helped to steel them at the battlefront. Above all, they had a strong sense of personal and public honor and wanted that honor to add to the reputation of their community. As citizens, they and their neighbors had helped to decide, through debate, ballot, and action, on the necessity of war. They had been recruited by their church and their community, and so they knew their cause was just. The ethos of many, if not most, of the early volunteers was rooted in the moral values of their communities and their churches and instilled by their families from childhood.

This moral resolve gave them a special kind of courage and a conviction that the cause warranted the risk. Community attachment endured to war's end, helping them bear the dehumanizing effects of military life. In that sense, they really never left home. Indeed, even in death, some of them did not leave home. By early 1862, cemeteries in Salem and Cambridge had set aside sections for soldiers' graves. The bodies of seventeen soldiers of the 123rd were brought back and buried with a single granite monument marking their graves in Salem, in addition to forty-five others buried in Cambridge. Fifty-one soldiers who served in the 93rd are also buried in Cambridge, along with sixty-one who served in other regiments. By taking up arms, they had not only fought for God and country but for their home, family, and community, rather than for glory or conquest. Death was feared less than dishonor.

Besides being strongly motivated, the Ross brothers, as sons of a farmer, had spent all their lives at hard labor. When they knew they had a job to do, they did it until it was finished. The hard work of their upbringing prepared them for the hardships of war. They were inured to adversity and the dull, grinding routine of farm life, and had the endurance, inner strength, and devotion to persevere. They could be soldiers as effectively as they could plow a field or swing an ax. Making war became their job, for as long as they were able to fight or until they were sent home either crippled or victorious.

Their Scottish Presbyterian faith had instilled in them a powerful predisposition against slavery. Their religion was based on the belief that perfectionism was the path to a personal union with God, so it followed that abolishing slavery was a way to form a more perfect Union. Hence, their sense of nationhood was fundamentally in harmony with their religion.

Among Unionists who were not antislavery, nationalism often had religious overtones, since many citizens believed the United States was guided by divine providence. Even the more secular-minded citizens often had faith in America's destined greatness and righteousness. Patriotism was especially strong among most foreign-born soldiers—chiefly from Germany or Ireland—who constituted a fifth to a quarter of the Union army. Of course, sectional patriotism, otherwise referred to as states' rights, imbued most Confederate troops, including the tenth who were foreign-born.

From the Scottish Presbyterian perspective, however, the South's case was morally and religiously weak. Since 1787, the South had done its best to perpetuate slavery. The framers of the Constitution gave the South overrepresentation in the House of Representatives and in the electoral college by counting every slave as three-fifths of a person without, of course, allowing any of them to vote. Further, the Missouri Compromise of 1820, the Fugitive Slave Act of 1850—which mandated the return of fugitive slaves from nonslave states—and the Kansas-Nebraska Act of 1854 all favored the protection and/or extension of slavery. This effort to protect as well as extend slavery remained consistent throughout the war. The *Richmond Whig*'s editorial page expressed it as late as December 9, 1864, by noting that abolition was "a repudiation of the opinion held by the whole South ... that servitude is a divinely appointed condition for the highest good of the slave."

When sentimental trappings were stripped away, the overriding war aim of the Confederate States of America was exploitation of one part of the human race by another. To the South, slaves were property subject to exploitation like any other property. Human equality applied to only part of humanity. Social stratification was necessary to control the masses, making slavery a fundamental social necessity. As Lincoln put it, the South wanted the "liberty of making slaves of other people."

In 1830, when Daniel Webster said in the Senate, "Liberty and Union, now and forever, one and inseparable," it fell on the deaf ears of plantation aristocrats. Perhaps the hollow center of the argument for slavery explains the complete and rather sudden collapse of the "Lost Cause."

Yet many Confederate veterans clung to the belief that they had fought to save a Jeffersonian, decentralized way of life. As pro-slavery apologists, in their view they were acting with the same zeal and moral righteousness as Northern abolitionists. As the slavery issue grew more and more heated by the 1850s, Lincoln asked a Kentuckian why this was so. The man replied from a slaveholder's perspective, "You might have any amount of land, money in your pocket, or bank stock [and] nobody would be wiser; but if you had a darkey trudging at your heels, everybody would see him, and know that you owned a slave ... it indicated the gentleman of leisure, who was above and scorned labor."

The bald truth was that the United States was two cultures sharing one nationality. The "irrepressible conflict" began at Fort Sumter, and the resulting bloody and costly clash of the opposing sides stirred the deepest emotions of any event in American history. The country was torn asunder physically, politically, emotionally, and morally for four fratricidal blood-letting years. Southern cities and the surrounding countryside were in utter ruin. By winning this war, the North overturned the world's most powerful slaveholding class, the Southern plantation owners. It freed more slaves than were held in bondage in the rest of the world.

2

Stones River

December 31, 1862–January 2, 1863

Though there is much suffering in a winter campaign, I think most of the men have come to the conclusion to do anything in their power to end this rebellion.

—Pvt. Walter Reeder, Company C, 36th Ill., October 1862

Melancton (Lank) Johnson Ross was the first of the Ross brothers to see combat, and he survived four of the bloodiest battles of the Civil War. The twenty-one-year-old farmhand was in Illinois in August 1861. He stood five feet ten inches tall and had brown hair, hazel eyes, and a fair complexion.

The war appeared to be far from over, yet the 75,000 men who had signed up to serve three months in the Union army—including his brother Will—were being discharged. Realizing this, President Lincoln issued a call for men willing to serve three years, and Lank responded. He enlisted on August 10 in the 36th Ill. volunteer regiment, which was recruited largely from Kane County. It was harvest season, and he and others like him easily could have found work at that time of year. Instead, ten days later he was mustered into the Bristol Light Infantry Company E, recruited by Capt. Charles D. Fish and 1st Lt. Albert M. Hobbs.

The 36th was one of seventeen Illinois regiments to be organized that summer; they were often described as "Lincolnites," in recognition of their coming from Lincoln's home state. Almost all seventy-eight original members of Company E were, like Lank, farmer's sons or farmhands from either Big Rock or the adjacent Little Rock Township, where Will had taught school. By war's end, about 4,000 Kane County men—13 percent of the population—would serve in the Union army.

Despite Lank's experiences in battle, before his first hitch was up in late 1863 he would reenlist for another three-year term. Fighting exclusively in the West, he saw more action before he was blinded in April 1864 than did Dan and Will together, even though both of them had enlisted shortly before he did.

The 36th Ill. was mustered in on September 23 at Camp Hammond, Aurora, Illinois, with 965 men. Lank and the rest of the lads in his company were issued 1841 Springfields, which were recently rifled muskets, plus bayonets, and cartridge boxes with belts to hold them. Known as the Fox River Regiment, the 36th distinguished itself in four major battles—Perryville, Stones River, Chickamauga, and Missionary Ridge—that prepared the way for Sherman's campaign to take Atlanta.[1] The regiment proved to be an outstanding example of how combat in typical Civil War close-order formation under fire created a comradeship that reinforced individual morale and bravery. Their regimental cohesion bound men into a brotherhood with a common objective; their collective will enabled them to function as a united whole. Serving under the four best fighting generals in the Union army—U. S. Grant, William T. Sherman, George H. Thomas, and Philip Sheridan—and led by company, regimental, and brigade commanders in whom Lank and his comrades had implicit confidence, further strengthened their belief that they could and would accomplish their goal.

The result of this cohesion was that Lank's regiment, like his brother Will's 93rd N.Y., stayed in the fight, putting them among the 300 Union regiments with the highest number of men killed or mortally wounded. The 36th Ill. would fight in all thirteen major battles and numerous minor engagements of the war in the West, losing 204 men, or nearly 15 percent, to immediate death or mortal injuries, the highest of

Melancton Johnson Ross

any Illinois regiment. Another 407 would be wounded or captured, and 128 would die of disease, for a total casualty rate of nearly 54 percent. Nearly two-thirds of the regiment's 739 casualties occurred in battles in which Lank fought.

In Lank's 130-man Company E alone, by war's end 29 were killed or died of disease. It would take a number of battle-tested regiments like the 36th to achieve the North's objectives in the West. Their goals were to (1) split the Confederacy by gaining full control of the Mississippi River; (2) liberate eastern Tennessee Unionists and keep Kentucky in the Union; and (3) sever the main railroad between Memphis and Richmond, then seize eastern and central Tennessee, depriving the South of their rich resources.

Between mid-July and early September 1862, the 36th had its first exposure to the Deep South while in camp near Rienzi, Mississippi. For part of that time, Lank served as a teamster. The weather was fearfully hot, and camp life was barren of incidents other than sporadic raids on the picket line, plus daily brigade and regimental drills during the cooler part of the day. Rations were plentiful, and sweet potatoes, vegetables, fruits, and berries were available nearby for foragers. All in all, idleness was the order of the day. Reading and writing letters were major occupations, as the men took shelter in the shade of venerable oaks. This time in camp gave Pvt. Walter Reeder, Company C, time to reflect on his and his family's deep religious convictions in letters to his parents, brother, and sisters.

On July 22, 1862, he wrote that a friend of the family who had recently seen his parents in Illinois was now visiting his regiment in Mississippi. "I asked him if Mother did not talk anti-slavery, and he said yes, strong." Reeder was very anxious that his father be named chaplain of the regiment, but an elder of his church, William Haigh, was selected three months later. On July 27 Reeder wrote, "I can not say any more about the prospect of Father getting the office [of chaplain] . . . I still hope for the best." Later in the letter he added, "I generally stand up for the negroes, and the boys try to make fun of me on that account, but they don't make much by it. Day before yesterday, the 7th Kansas Cavalry Regt passed here and they had 20 or more negroes in one squad. The negroes had arms as well as the Cavalry. I was glad to see it so." Charles R. Jennison, a leading, violent Kansas abolitionist, was colonel of the regiment.

On August 31, Reeder wrote, "I have no idea of wishing to back out of this business but want to go forward and see the end of this rebellion." On September 2, he told his mother, "I know that you want us to do our duty and try and help put down this rebellion. I tell you that I am proud of my Mother who so cheerfully gave up her sons to their Country."

In the fall of 1862, Lank Ross and the 36th Ill. were in Kentucky with the Army of the Ohio, initially under Maj. Gen. Don Carlos Buell and later under Maj. Gen. William S. Rosecrans. They were pursuing the Confederate Army of Tennessee, under Gen. Braxton Bragg, whose initial assignment had been to bring Kentucky into the Confederacy by occupying it with his army and arranging for the installation of a provisional governor. Bragg had failed to accomplish his mission. A chronically ill man of forty-five, he suffered from diarrhea, dyspepsia, migraine headaches, ulcers, and painful attacks of boils. Nevertheless, he was a hard taskmaster and a strict and skilled disciplinarian. He had won three brevets in the Mexican War, and his courage and character were beyond question.

Bragg's invasion of Kentucky came to an abrupt end in October 1862, when he retreated to Murfreesboro, Tennessee, on Stones River, after an inconclusive six-week campaign that ended with the Battle of Perryville, Kentucky. Lank and the 36th Ill. had fought at Perryville in a brigade that also included three inexperienced regiments. Their battle line was atop Peters Hill, where the Lincolnites fought under heavy artillery fire until they ran out of ammunition. They were flanked by enemy infantry and forced to fall back, "cursing and swearing." Much of the heavy fighting there was done by Gen. Philip Sheridan's division, which included the 36th Ill. Lank's regiment was positioned at the center for two hours; the men lay on the ground and discharged their muskets while their artillery fired overhead. Sheridan and the Illinoisans established their reputations as stubborn fighters in this battle. The butcher's bill for the 36th Ill. was the highest of the four regiments in its brigade: seventy-one casualties, more than half the total brigade.

Bragg planned to spend the winter in Murfreesboro guarding middle Tennessee's railroads and rich farmland. His withdrawal from Kentucky was a bitter disappointment to Confederate authorities. For different reasons, it must have been the same for Private Reeder. On October 24, he wrote his family, "I think we have passed through some of the prettiest country I ever saw. The land . . . produces almost everything a person would want . . . was it not for slavery, this state would be a desirable place of residence."

Bragg commanded neither respect nor admiration from his subordinates for his withdrawal and many other decisions, as well as for his tactlessness, moodiness, indecisiveness, and irascibility. Bragg also tended to use other officers as scapegoats for his failures. The South's defeat at

Antietam, followed by Bragg's retreat from Perryville, led the British government to decide against diplomatic recognition of the Confederacy.

After Perryville, Major General Buell—who had abandoned his campaign to control eastern Tennessee and Kentucky—chose not to attack Bragg's retreating army. Lincoln's impatience grew as Buell kept telegraphing excuses for his inaction. When he finally decided to return to his Nashville base instead of attacking Bragg, Lincoln replaced him with General Rosecrans who, on October 3 and 4, had just won a decisive victory at Corinth, Mississippi.

Rosecrans took command of the Army of the Ohio on October 30. A month later he bowed to pressure from President Lincoln and followed Bragg into Tennessee. He led the army into Nashville, starting November 7, to stave off Bragg's threatened capture of the city. The men helped build fortifications and settled in for the winter. "Old Rosy," who had graduated fifth in his West Point class, was six feet tall, brave, affable, a gifted strategist and hard worker, and immensely popular with his men. He had been an army engineer for a decade when he resigned to work for a railroad. He rode his horse with his back straight, sometimes standing in his stirrups, his head thrown back with a black campaign hat planted firmly over his forehead, an old blue overcoat enveloping him, and an unlit cigar stub clenched between his teeth. He had wavy hair, a bulbous red nose, and a fondness for whiskey. He had never lost a battle and knew how to plan and execute a campaign. However, under the stress of battle, he stammered and was impulsive, prideful, excitable (if not panicky), and impatient. He also resented interference from his superiors, and had a hair-trigger temper and brittle ego. Some of his division commanders censured him "because [they] could not turn their backs on [their] commands without his ordering portions of them away."

Tennessee had been the West's principal battleground since the war's beginning. By the end of 1862, neither army controlled it. Rosecrans's primary concern, therefore, was to assure the delivery of sufficient supplies by protecting the railroad between Louisville and Nashville from cavalry raids. His army arrived in Nashville hungry, cold, exhausted, and short of shoes, blankets, and tents. In late November, Lank and his brigade marched seven miles south of Nashville on the Chattanooga Pike and set up their new quarters in Camp Sheridan.

On the whole, they had marched through beautiful, fertile, and hilly country cultivated by numerous rich and productive farms. During their stay at Camp Sheridan, a contingent that included the 36th was ordered to penetrate the Rebel picket line. A slave volunteered to guide the troops to where they could ford a creek, since the bridge over it had just been burned. After accomplishing their mission, some of the lads invited the slave to return to their camp, which he did, making him the first "contraband" to be liberated by Lank's regiment.

On the day after Christmas, Rosecrans left Nashville, thirty-five miles from Murfreesboro, with 44,000 effectives to wrest control of the railroad from Bragg. It was slow going in the cold, torrential rains, sleet, mist, and fog. Wagons got stuck, and one trooper reported that with each step in the knee-deep muck, a man "lifted a square foot of mud three inches deep." The men had to sleep in wet uniforms under wet blankets, without camp fires to fight off the chill. As one wrote, "[W]e have plenty of mud for our beds." Visibility was sometimes near zero. Skirmishing was continuous for the four days it took to reach Stones River. On the night of December 29, having so far encountered little resistance, Lank and the others camped in a recently plowed cornfield, sleeping in ankle-deep, pasty mud. They collected cornstalks to make beds, over which they spread their wet blankets.

Lying there, within sight of enemy camp fires, they drifted off to sleep as regimental bands played patriotic songs to boost morale. With the first notes of "Yankee Doodle," a musical contest began as Rebel bands countered with "Dixie." The contest ended when the Northern bands played "Home Sweet Home" and the Southern bands chimed in while thousands of soldiers sang the words. It was a very poignant experience for men who were going to kill each other the next day. By the time the 36th reached Stones River, the regiment had been in service for fifteen months and traveled 2,800 miles—1,261 on foot, the rest by steamboat and railroad. They had fought in four battles by then, the most severe of which was Perryville.

Rosecrans's Army of the Ohio was made up of three corps, respectively commanded by Thomas L. Crittenden, George H. Thomas, and Alexander M. McCook, all West Pointers. Private Lank Ross and the 36th Ill. were in the 3rd Division of McCook's corps. Its division commander was Brig. Gen. Philip H. Sheridan, also a West Pointer.

At only five feet five and thirty-three years old, Sheridan's body was tapered like a wedge from his broad, muscular, square shoulders to his short, bandy legs. He had long arms, a handlebar mustache, uncommonly keen eyes, firm chin, high cheekbones, and close-cut red hair. He weighed less than 120 pounds with his spurs on and had a head as round as a cannonball. Lincoln described Sheridan as "a brown chunky little chap [with] a neck not long enough to hang him, and such long arms that if his ankles itch he can scratch them without stooping." He was a fire-eater in battle but quiet in camp, and inured to fatigue and hardship. He had falsified his birth certificate so he could enter West Point in 1848 at seventeen. The "bandy-legged buckeye" had a hot temper that had gotten him a year's suspension when, as a plebe, he became infuriated with a cadet officer and chased him with a bayonet. The incident ended in a fistfight, which he lost. He had the confidence of his superiors even though he could be brusque with them. He had earned the respect of officers and men in part because he treated them more democratically than most West Pointers. He was exacting on duty and hard on malingerers. From time to time he would walk through camp saying, "Smash 'em up, smash 'em up!" while thrusting his fist against his palm for emphasis. He never congratulated his troops after a battle or issued orders of encouragement beforehand. He assumed that they would do as well as they could, and they did.

At 4 A.M. on December 30, after a final alignment and a bugle blast, Sheridan's wet and shivering men, including Lank, began a slow, daylong advance in the fog and rain. Two companies were deployed as skirmishers to their right. Despite the miserable conditions, including no fires for cooking breakfast, the men of the 36th began the march with smiles and laughter. They could hear train whistles and the booming of artillery. At about 8 A.M. Sheridan's men met the enemy at Stones River, three miles from Murfreesboro, and with numb trigger fingers began driving back stubbornly resistant Rebel skirmishers. Bragg's line covered the approach to the Nashville and Chattanooga Railroad. Sheridan formed his line on a cedar-covered ridge at the edge of a corn and cotton field, on the right of the Nashville Pike but oblique to it. His men overlooked the field.

Brig. Gen. Joshua W. Sill, thirty-one years old, who had been in command of Sheridan's 1st Brigade—which included the 36th Ill.—for only eighteen days, occupied the center of his line. Sill graduated third in his class from West Point and had been Sheridan's roommate and personal friend. Sheridan and McCook both thought very highly of him. He was one of the youngest brigadier in the Union army and among the most promising young officers in the western army. Small of stature like Sheridan, he was a man of great energy and courage, and was gentle and modest, with a pleasant smile. Both were greatly admired for their coolness under fire. Sill, who had taught mathematics at West Point and Brooklyn College, combined his gentleness with strict discipline, and his men worshiped him.

By about 9 A.M., skirmishers from Sill's four-regiment brigade, accompanied by two of Sheridan's six-gun batteries—4th Ind. and 1st Mo. Light Artillery—had driven the enemy skirmishers into a cedar thicket on the opposite side of the cornfield within two miles of Murfreesboro. They lay in the cornfield until about 2 P.M. Lank's 36th Ill., with the rest of Sill's brigade, was then ordered to cross another plantation's fields of corn and cotton in front of the Rebel-held thicket. They crossed rapidly and in good order, but a storm of artillery shells and a hail of musket balls was unleashed at them from the cover of the woods. Many were killed and wounded in this advance. The 36th was in the front line, with the 88th Ill. on its left. The 24th Wis. was 200 paces behind Lank's regiment, while the 21st Mich. supported the 88th, all still on the right of the Nashville Pike. Union artillery fire forced the enemy to retreat five hundred yards across the field to the shelter of still another cedar thicket. There, Sill's batteries, after two hours of artillery dueling, silenced all eight of the enemy guns, including the feared Washington Battery of New Orleans, which had opened heavy fire on the 36th while they were advancing. The 36th then charged this battery with fixed bayonets and drove off its disabled fragments.

Next, they were ordered to support Bush's Indiana battery, which inflicted "terrible execution" on the enemy until dark, when it was withdrawn. Three men in Lank's regiment were killed and fifteen wounded; Lank was unscathed. By 4 P.M., the Union line of 43,000 men was continuous and faced 34,000 Confederates. McCook's corps—including the 36th Ill.—had reached the Wilkinson Pike and connected with Thomas's corps. They formed a compact double line fronting in places on rolling land and cultivated fields along a wooded ridge. A strong line of skirmishers was also "thrown out." In some places the opposing skirmish lines were less than 300 yards apart, separated by cornfields and cotton fields, which would become the contested ground the next morning.

The 36th Ill. remained on the battlefield through an intensely cold and windy night. A brilliant moon revealed their fallen comrades; the beards of the three dead men were white with frost. The fifteen who were wounded were held fast to the ground by their own frozen blood. Sill's brigade, exhausted after a five-day march, slept fitfully in line of battle, half in the woods and half in a cotton field. They had no tents, no fires, and only hard bread ("sheet-iron crackers" or "teeth dullers") and raw pork ("sow belly") to eat. The right of the brigade rested on the Wilkinson Pike, on a cedar-covered ridge, edged by open ground cut by chasms.[2]

Sill and Sheridan were both more concerned than McCook about Bragg's plan for the next day, since throughout the night they could hear his troops massing and wagons rumbling in the heavy cedar woods across an open valley. Sill never relaxed his vigilance. About midnight, he called for his horse and an orderly, visited his skirmishers to make certain they were alert, and listened and watched for enemy movements. Before daylight, he ordered that the wounded be carried to the rear.

Col. Nicholas Greusel, who was in charge of the 36th, sent his horse to the rear, preparing to share the dangers of the morrow with his men. Greusel was good-natured and much liked by his men. When vexed, however, he could swear and bellow dreadfully. Six feet one inch tall and forty-five years old, he was handsome and blue-eyed, and had an auburn beard. According to a soldier in the 24th Wis., "Old Nick" Greusel "like his men in the 36th Illinois . . . knows no fear, is generous [and] endures all the hardships and pleasures of camp." Sheridan and other generals also had high regard for Greusel's military skill, coolness, and bravery. Bavarian born, he had served as a captain in the Mexican War, where he had engaged in almost continuous battle with guerillas and Mexican soldiers. He served in the Civil War first as a major in the 7th Ill., then became the first colonel of the 36th, and had demonstrated his skills in two battles in 1862. He rigorously enforced a ban on alcohol, but encouraged sports, reading, and music. The regiment had an excellent band and glee club and would later acquire a library, using contributions from the men.

At 2 A.M., Sill and his aide rode to Sheridan's headquarters behind his reserve brigade, sheltered from the cold winter wind by a fallen tree trunk. They reported that they could hear the jingling of canteens, the clank of rifles, and other sounds indicating great enemy activity. Together the two walked into the tangled forest, where the 36th Ill. and the 24th Wis. were camped, to listen. Sheridan and Sill then mounted their horses and went to General McCook, their thirty-two-year-old corps commander. The West Pointer who had taught tactics at the academy now lay on a damp straw mat in an angle of a split-rail fence, having gone to sleep brimming with confidence. McCook shrugged off their information that artillery and infantry were being moved, saying that Rosecrans was aware the enemy was massing in his front, and then he went back to sleep. A fellow officer had once described McCook's grin as one that fostered the suspicion "that he is either still very green or deficient in the upper story."

Sill now held the far right of Sheridan's division. At his urging, Sheridan decided to send two reserve regiments to increase Sill's strength. They were placed a short distance from Sill's line behind the 36th. An hour before daylight, Sheridan deployed all twelve of his regiments and three batteries in battle formation and under arms. He awakened their commanders, conferred with them, and made certain his orders would be executed. He also made certain his cannoneers were at their posts and ready. Lank and the others hurriedly ate breakfast in the dark, chewing their hardtack while waiting for their coffee to boil. The men were cold, wet, puffy-eyed, and miserable. It was the last day of 1862. In a small tent, Rosecrans had just heard a mass delivered by Father

Tracy, the priest who always accompanied him. Both Sheridan and Sill had been up most of the night. Sill was convinced that the sounds he heard indicated the Rebels had moved far to the right of their division line and were probably massing for an attack. McCook leisurely shaved at the Gresham farmhouse as the men cooked breakfast.

Lank and the others in the 36th finished their breakfast at about 6 A.M., huddled around their fires, stamping their feet, and rubbing their hands in an effort to stay warm. An hour later they heard the distant rattle of musketry and the roar of a rifled Parrott gun. They were watching tensely as skirmishers fell back on their right when someone shouted "They're coming." At about 7:15 A.M., the Rebels charged out of the dense, fog-cloaked cedar forest "like a whirl-a-gust of woodpeckers in a hailstorm." Spread across the open field as far as the eye could see, they were followed by the roar of artillery salvos as they struck Sill's brigade. The men of the 24th Wis., a regiment of raw recruits, were the first to meet the attack. It was as if they were hit by a freight train. They fired a few rounds, but quickly suffered about 100 casualties. They retreated about 200 yards, leaving the 36th's right flank exposed. Lank's regiment was positioned on a cedar-covered hillock to the left of the 24th Wis., with an excellent field of fire.

Two reserve regiments moved up to replace the Badger Boys, as birds and dozens of jackrabbits, flushed from their holes, led the Confederate charge across the field. After the skirmishers had returned to the battle line, Colonel Greusel ordered the 36th to fix bayonets and fire from behind a low pile of rails. Cheered on by their officers, a heavy column of Alabamians advanced elbow-to-elbow across the field almost to the edge of the timber and within range of the Union muskets. At Greusel's command of "Get up," the Lincolnites rose and fired "a volley into their ranks causing them to stagger." Extending beyond both flanks of the 36th, the attacking column advanced into a wall of flame in a bayonet charge on the double quick, shrieking their bloodcurdling Rebel yell. The noise was so great that the Alabamians stuffed cotton in their ears. Sheridan's three artillery batteries positioned in front of Sill tore great gaps in their line. Firing from a kneeling position when the enemy was less than fifty yards away, Lank and the lads deliberately aimed their volleys into the faces of the Alabamians for half an hour, forcing a stumbling enemy retreat.

The Rebs and their commander, who was wounded, reeled back across the cotton field at great cost. The air was alive with whistling missiles and whizzing bullets. As the enemy returned fire from a prone position, Greusel shouted orders to Lank and the other Fox River lads for a bayonet charge. With the 88th behind them, the 36th rose up with

Stones River

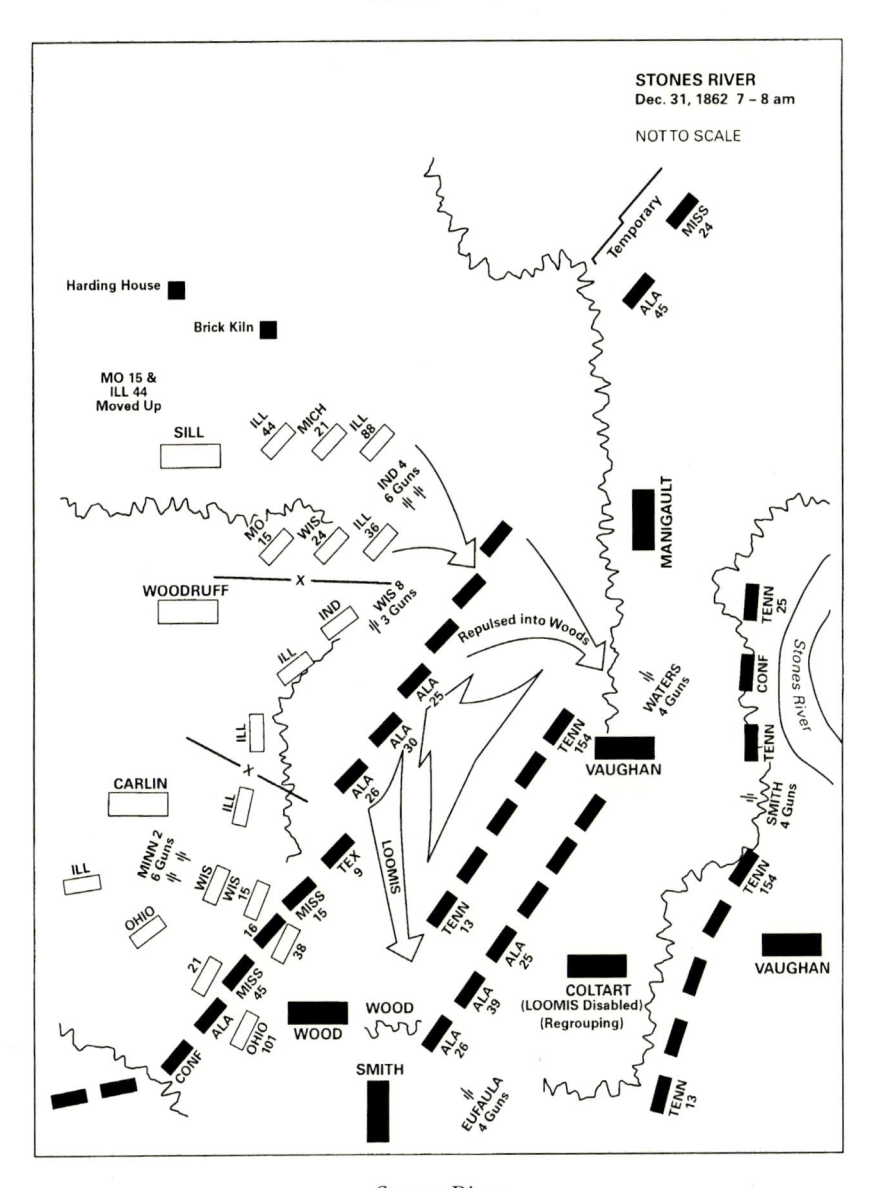

Stones River

a shout and a forest of bayonets. In confusion, the enemy fled across the cotton field and back into the woods, behind their entrenchments and out of range. By then the Lincolnites were almost out of ammunition and could not flush the Alabamians out of the woods. They had to fall back to their original line.

The two other divisions in McCook's corps, commanded by Johnson and Davis, had not anticipated the enemy advance, and so were not in the line of battle when the action began. Some were still eating a tardy breakfast with their rifles stacked, and artillerymen were still watering or harnessing horses in the rear. The Rebels captured several guns before they had fired three rounds.

Throughout the early morning hours, the air vibrated from the earthshaking, roaring thunder of both armies' artillery. Cut by shot and shell, trees splintered and crashed; broken limbs flew through the air as musket balls hissed and shells burst overhead. The barrage triggered a rush of Johnson's and Davis's panic-stricken, wild-eyed troops. Leaving their coffee pots and skillets simmering on their camp fires, some men even threw away their rifle muskets, shouting, "We are sold! Sold again!" as they retreated pell-mell out of the cornfield and across the open space toward Wilkinson Pike. In the forest of cedars and pines, both divisions were overtaken by the enemy. Meanwhile, terrified teamsters driving McCook's ordnance train of seventy-six wagons cut the mules and horses loose, then urged them on at top speed while riding them bareback, as many as three men per animal. The ground was strewn with pots, pans, kettles, camp stoves, tents, and boxes as wagons overturned. Scores of men, including officers, were hit by Rebel bullets. Some Federal cavalry also fled as Brig. Gen. Joseph Wheeler's 2,000 excellent horse soldiers—including Hardee's three brigades of Texas Rangers—pursued them.

In short order, six companies of the Federal 4th Regular Cavalry and the East Tennessee Volunteers arrived to protect McCook's ammunition wagon train. With the command "Draw sabres" followed by "Give them hell," a cavalry fight began. The wagon train was saved along with a number of teamsters who had been taken prisoner.

By 9:30 A.M., because of this front and flank attack, Sheridan's line bent and drew back through the dark cedar woods to escape utter destruction, but did not break. He patched his broken units together and conducted a fighting withdrawal behind his three well-positioned artillery batteries. The move of a mile and a half was necessary to avoid being fired on from the rear. They had to fight and retreat, then rally to fight again. His was the only division offering resistance, and Sill's was the last of Sheridan's brigades to withdraw. The brigade was in a meadow adjoining the Harding farm and behind the three batteries, with each man in an excellent position. The Texas Rangers twice charged the Chicago Board of Trade Battery, which was on a rise of ground and well supported by a pioneer brigade, but the attacks failed.

No reserves arrived to support Sheridan's division. While Sill's brigade, including Lank's regiment, was withdrawing to its new position behind some rails on commanding ground, Sill was shot off his horse and killed instantly. He had been leaning over his horse's head to tell a section chief to double-shot his gun, when he was hit under the left eye by a minié ball that buried itself in his brain. With his last breath, Sill ordered his brigade to charge, then fell dead between the guns. In the middle of the previous night, when Sill left Sheridan's tent after agreeing to strengthen his line, he had inadvertently picked up Sheridan's coat. He was still wearing it when he was killed. Colonel Greusel took command of the brigade and Maj. Silas Miller took over the 36th Regiment. Sill's body was carried off in a blanket and laid on the ground outside the Griscom House, which was being used as a hospital. Sheridan wept when he learned of Sill's death. Miller then turned to Capt. Hescock's Battery G, 1st Mo., and said, "Now give it to the scoundrels." He ordered Lank and the others to fire low and keep cool as they fought Vaughan's fresh Tennessee brigade, which was making a second charge, this time with bayonets. They faced the open cotton field from a slight rise in the dense cedar grove; some of the soldiers were protected by limestone outcroppings. Lank and the others fired with terrific effect until they were out of ammunition and the enemy, who outnumbered them, had flanked them on their exposed right, not fifty yards away. The batteries on each side were no more than 200 yards apart.

By command of Sheridan, Major Miller ordered a fighting retreat with tears in his eyes. He gave the order three times before the men obeyed. In the course of the retreat, Miller was wounded and taken prisoner, after which Capt. Porter C. Olson took regimental command in a hailstorm of minié balls. Impeded by rocky ground, cedar thickets, caverns, fallen trees, and heavy fire, the 36th continued the withdrawal with fixed bayonets. They formed a third line behind artillery batteries within 500 yards of the Wilkinson Pike. One Lincolnite reported, "No man could see the whole of his regiment." The heavy fire dropped men like wheat before the sickle. The Rebel artillery had thundered up to their rear and "at short range with grape and canister scattered death in our ranks," wrote Sgt. R. H. Watson.

Olson reported he was out of ammunition and down to 140 men, a staggering loss, but was ready to renew the fight as soon as his ammunition was replenished. The rest of Sheridan's men also had emptied their cartridge boxes and were fighting with bayonets and bare fists. Sheridan reported this to Thomas and told him they had to withdraw. His troops used roads cut through the cedars by pioneers to complete the withdrawal toward the Nashville Pike. McCook placed the 36th, including the rest of Sill's (now Greusel's) men behind Crittenden's corps when they arrived, sometime after 10 A.M.

The 10,000 fleeing Union troops from Johnson's and Davis's divisions abandoned some of their batteries and erupted in wild panic from the cedar thicket into an open space between the trees and the Nashville Turnpike. There Crittenden's corps, including two of his batteries, were massed awaiting the coming storm, their left protected by Stones River. They had been driven back nearly two miles. After a brief lull, long lines of Confederates shouting their demoniac yell emerged from the woods in their third attack. A Union soldier described the sight as he climbed a ridge in search of the ammunition train. "I saw the entire country...swarming with Confederates; the very earth seemed to be moving toward us. They came on in thousands, and so rapidly that we had barely time to turn tail and gallop down the hill and away, leaving them in possession of the train." A dazzling sheet of flame, followed by an iron blizzard, burst from Crittenden's guns and rifle-muskets as the Confederates surged forth in waves across the open field. For ten minutes, it was as if all the thunderclaps of heaven were sounding simultaneously. The advancing Rebels' front line was decimated before the choking gunsmoke enveloped both armies. Then the hand-to-hand fighting began as the batteries kept up an unceasing, deadly frontal and flanking fire, in a deafening roar one officer likened to the "continuous pounding of a thousand anvils."[3]

The Confederate penetration was being checked along the Nashville Pike, thanks to Crittenden's artillery and Sheridan's division, which was pinned against it. They had delayed by an hour the 10,000 troops led by Confederate Gen. William J. Hardee, giving General Thomas time to move his men to a position where they could retain possession of the pike and the railroad. Because of the delay, Hardee failed to break the spine of Rosecrans's army, as he struggled to organize his final offensive line along the Nashville Pike.

Of the three divisions in McCook's corps, only Sheridan's remained intact, with help from Thomas, as Rosecrans fortified his final line. Sheridan's decisive fighting retreat was probably never surpassed during the entire war. McCook had given no direction to the uncoordinated and hopelessly confused retreat of his corps. About 11 A.M. after the all-morning fight that had exhausted his ammunition, Sheridan finally was forced to retreat, dragging the remaining artillery with him, in a bloody running brawl across the Nashville Pike. But he did not fall back until the 36th Ill. and the 15th Mo. (the Swiss Regiment) had made two gallant bayonet charges against the Confederate Major General John M. Withers's attacking division. Withers reported that he had found Sheridan "fully prepared" and in a strong position. By then, Hardee's Louisiana brigade had lost a third of its men, and their colonel was wounded. He had faced Sheridan's men at Perryville with the same result, and his men now had no fight left in them. Private R. H. Watson of Company D, who was wounded and taken prisoner, later wrote his sister that before their retreat, he "could have walked over the dead bodies of our men from one end of the Reg't to the other without touching the ground."

Sill's (now Greusel's) brigade retreated across Nashville Pike with the rest of Sheridan's division and took refuge with their remaining pieces of artillery in a new defensive position behind the railroad track and embankment that paralleled it. It was a natural rifle pit, and the embankment provided some protection against enemy artillery. The 36th and the other regiments in the brigade needed to fill their cartridge boxes, emptied by five and a half hours of fighting over two miles of bloody ground, the last mile without ammunition. Only two of Sheridan's twelve regiments still had bullets. Fortunately, what remained of the ammunition wagon train had just arrived behind the railroad embankment. Sheridan, his angry face blackened with powder, swore like a teamster as he led back some of his survivors. Rosecrans, the stub of an unlit cigar clenched between his teeth, found him as he emerged from the cedars. "Here we are," Sheridan said, "all that are left of us. Our cartridge boxes contain nothing and our guns are empty." By then his men had repulsed four fierce attacks. Rosecrans told Sheridan to replenish his ammunition from the supply train one regiment at a time, relieve Wood's division, and get back into the fight. Captain Olson found Sheridan about noon and told him his men, including Lank, now had ammunition and were ready to return to the front. Sheridan told him to remain in his defensive position and await orders.

About 2 P.M., Sheridan re-formed his battle lines and ordered them back into the fight. They were to connect with Col. Bernard Laiboldt's brigade of Wood's division to the left of the railroad. The 36th led one more charge, driving the Rebels back a half mile, with more fearful slaughter from blasts of artillery fire on both sides. By dark, their last charge ended after they poured minié balls into those Rebels that were still standing. Sheridan moved a quarter of a mile to the rear for the night. The battle was essentially over. They had fought for a total of eleven hours. During the entire engagement, Sheridan calmly directed artillery fire and shifted his lines while smoking a cigar. Otherwise, with his "hat in one hand and sword in the other damning and swearing [he fought] as if he were the devil incarnate."

December 31, 1862, was a costly day for both sides. Although Sheridan, who was in the thickest of the fight, was unscathed, 1,633 of his 5,607 men were killed, wounded, or missing—30 percent of those who went into the battle. The casualty toll made Stones River one of the costliest battles of the Civil War. The 36th Ill. alone suffered 212 casualties, the most of any regiment in Sheridan's division and more than it suffered in any other battle in the entire war.

One of the wounded was Private Reeder, who was captured, paroled, and exchanged, and recuperated in hospitals in Murfreesboro and Louisville before returning to the regiment on May 22. On January 17, 1863, Pvt. J. H. Sacket of Company H wrote his father from Hospital No. 20 in Nashville that he was wounded in the hip but managed to get to the battlefield hospital in the manor house on the Harding Plantation. By the battle's end, the house held 100 severely wounded men, mostly from the 36th and 88th Ill. Another forty were on adjacent grounds, kept as warm as possible by huge fires and a few shelter tents. When the Rebels retreated, they took those prisoners that could walk to Murfreesboro. The remainder, including Sacket, were paroled and left with minimum rations at the Harding house until Union troops arrived on January 5 with forty ambulance wagons. Those who could be transported, including Sacket, were taken to Nashville, a long and excruciatingly painful ride.

Thirty-six casualties, including five who were killed, were in Lank's Company E, but Lank was unhurt. In addition to Major Miller, Captain Hobbs of Company E was captured. Hobbs was sent to Libby Prison, where he remained until he was paroled on June 3. Among the regiment's casualties were nine of its officers, including four wounded, two captured, one killed, one mortally wounded, and one missing. The regiment left sixty-five dead on the battlefield, the largest number killed in any battle it fought. The 88th Ill., positioned behind the 36th, lost 116 of the 420 men that went into battle. All three of Sheridan's brigade commanders, plus a replacement, were killed within three hours. He also lost sixty-nine other officers, and his own horse was killed under him. His leadership and lionhearted courage resulted in his promotion to major general, effective December 31, the hardest-fought day of the battle. Sheridan's star was detected in the firmament at Perryville, but it burned brilliantly at Stones River. In nine months he had risen from captain to major general.

In making their sacrifices, Sheridan's men, including the 36th, had breasted the Confederate tide long enough for Rosecrans to gallop around fearlessly in "many directions," impetuously making numerous new troop dispositions and encouraging his men by his presence. In the process, three of his mounted orderlies were shot dead. But by noon he cobbled together a second line that saved the 43,000-man Union army from the Confederate onslaught despite the fact that he countermanded numerous orders of officers under him. Thirty percent of Rosecrans's men were casualties. Bragg had not gained the railroad, or the Wilkinson or Nashville pikes that would have blocked a retreat by Rosecrans to Nashville. Rosecrans's supply line also was saved.

Sergeant O. Smith of Lank's Company E, one of four sergeants who were injured, was commended for bravery. Despite three wounds, Smith held his position, for which Greusel promoted him to 2nd lieutenant in front of the entire regiment. In turn, Rosecrans commended Greusel for "skill and courage." In his after-battle report, Sheridan also commended him for bravery, along with Maj. Silas Miller and Capt. Porter C. Olson. Only ten of the regiment's officers survived unscathed. Three brothers of Captain Olson served in the regiment; one, a lieutenant, was killed. Two orderlies, Private Pease and Private Knox of Company B, had horses shot out from under them. Private Day Elmore of the 36th wrote his parents after the New Year's Eve battle, "we drove [the enemy] from the ground until the two regiments on the right broke and run and still our regiment contested the ground . . . and drove them once [more] after our support had left us . . . until our brave colonel with tears in his eyes ordered us to retreat." The color-bearer Charles Ayres counted forty bullet holes in his uniform and blanket roll.[4]

Despite the steadfastness of Sheridan's division, as well as most of Thomas's corps, on New Year's Eve the Union line was bent into a horseshoe. This unfavorable positioning led Rosecrans to distribute the last of his scarce ammunition reserves and hold a council of war, during which they considered retreat. Thomas responded, "I know of no better place to die than right here . . . this army can't retreat." Sheridan added, "I request for my division the honor of leading the attack tomorrow!" Rosecrans's army stood fast, to Bragg's surprise.

Among the trees and limestone outcroppings, with snow in the air, Lank and the other survivors in Sheridan's division bedded down for the night on frozen ground. The battlefield was a scene "fit for ghouls." They slept on their arms and were not permitted to build fires. As the moon set and a frigid north wind gusted over the battlefield, Lincoln officially released the Emancipation Proclamation from the telegraph office at the War Department where he had gone to listen to news of the battle.

On New Year's Day, the 36th built breastworks on the Nashville Pike at Sheridan's headquarters and lay in readiness behind their log and stone redoubts, but did no fighting. Snow turned to heavy rain that fell for hours during the night, leaving Lank and the others knee-deep in mud. Tired and hungry, they were allowed to help themselves to rations. According to Pvt. Oscar Pecoy of Lank's Company E, the 36th quickly proved they were not too tired to eat. Sgt. Thomas J. Ford of the 24th Wisconsin reported that some men stole ears from a pile of forage corn near General Rosecrans's headquarters. Others ate meat from horses that had been killed. Between bites they wished each other a happy New Year. On that day, each army commander waited to see what the other would do.[5]

On the third day, January 2, Bragg attacked. Thanks to Union entrenchment, artillery placement on a ridge opposite Stones River, and a dreadful artillery duel, his assault was stymied by nightfall with a loss of 2,000 Rebels. The Union artillery had pulverized Bragg's men. Discouraged, Bragg retreated, protected from pursuit by the swollen Stones River, which was impassable for Rosecrans's artillery. Although both sides suffered heavy losses—the Union 13,000, the Confederate army 10,000—Bragg's retreat gave the North a needed victory. After the battle, Private C. A. Halsey of the 36th wrote his friend, "I shall never be sorry for what I have been through. I hope I shall live to see the end of this cursed rebellion and peace restored to our beloved country." Rosecrans was, he added, a "fighting son of a bitch" and the best general in the field. On January 5, on orders from Sheridan, a detachment from the 36th was sent to bury its sixty-five dead. They buried forty-one in a huge trench close to the battlefield, carved a headboard for each soldier, and erected a fence around the mass grave. They buried the remainder in single graves in other parts of the field. General Sill's body was taken by rail from the Murfreesboro courthouse to Cincinnati, escorted by ten companies of soldiers. The coffin was covered by a national emblem. The body lay in state until taken by train to his hometown for burial.

The men who fought at Stones River experienced the highest percentage of killed, wounded, or missing soldiers in any major Civil War battle. Of the 23,515 casualties, 13,249 were Union and 10,266 were Confederate. It was a high price, but made success possible in subsequent Union campaigns through the remainder of the war. With the capture of Murfreesboro, Rosecrans built the largest supply depot in the West and made it possible to supply the Union army at Chickamauga and Missionary Ridge as well as Sherman's march on Atlanta.

The Battle of Stones River ended the winter campaign for Rosecrans's Army of the Cumberland. His army encamped just south of Murfreesboro, where the troopers huddled for warmth in their poorly constructed winter quarters, and subsisted on a miserable diet. There they waited for the paymaster, whom they had not seen for six months. They had won the final battle to hold Kentucky in the Union and secured Nashville for the Union army. Bragg retreated farther south and made Tullahoma, fifty miles from Murfreesboro, his stronghold. Union supporters in Tennessee would now have easier going. On January 5, Lincoln telegraphed Rosecrans, "God bless you, and all with you! Please render to all, and accept for yourself, the Nation's gratitude for yours, and their skill, endurance, and dauntless courage."

President Jefferson Davis of the Confederacy noted, "our maximum strength has been mobilized while the enemy is just beginning to put forth his might." What he did not fully realize was that his western campaign had reached the turning point. His army had lost the initiative in its attempt to control the West.

Now Rosecrans's task was to reoutfit his entire army in preparation for capturing Chattanooga. To do so, he needed Sheridan, now a major general, and the Lincolnite lads of the 36th, who by now had developed a strong bond of affection with their division commander.[6]

Even obtuse Braxton Bragg realized he had only one last opportunity to hold part of the West for the Confederacy and redeem his reputation among his dispirited troops and officers after his failures at Perryville and Stones River. Corinth, Mississippi, had fallen on October 4, 1862, opening the way for a Union move on Vicksburg, the last Confederate stronghold on the Mississippi. Four days later, when Bragg retreated from Perryville, the Confederacy lost Kentucky and its potential for substantial recruits. "Little Phil" Sheridan's division, including the 36th Ill., had played a key role in halting the Confederate invasion of that border state. After the bloody Battle of Stones River ended on January 2, 1863, eastern Tennessee, including Nashville, was mostly Union territory. The next step for the Union was to open a corridor from Nashville through Chattanooga and Atlanta to the Georgia interior. To do this, Chattanooga had to be taken. This would be Bragg's last opportunity to prevent this.

On February 6 Colonel Greusel, who was worshipped by his men but in ill health and disgruntled, resigned because he had not been named to succeed General Sill as brigade commander. He wrote a long letter to his men thanking them for their courage and obedience. By April 11, Sgt. R. H. Watson was paroled from prison and returned to his regiment. On that day he wrote his sister that Capt. Porter C. Olson, "makes a good field officer and is cool and collected under fire and brave to a fault."

3

Chancellorsville
April 30–May 5, 1863

> I never shall regret taking part in the Battle of Chancellorsville...
> I would rather have lost a limb than not have taken part in the battle.
>
> —Lt. Robert Cruikshank of the 123rd New York,
> letter to his wife

After being the first of the Ross brothers to enlist, on April 19, 1861, Will served his three-month enlistment at Camp Defiance in Cairo, the largest city in southern Illinois. Grant, newly commissioned as a colonel, trained his first regiments at the camp, which had been established to curb secessionist activity in the region known as "Little Egypt." At the war's beginning, Cairo was the vital center of the West's military and political theater; it was strategically located at the confluence of the Ohio and Mississippi rivers. The mouths of the Cumberland and Tennessee rivers were less than forty miles to the east. All of these rivers were barriers as well as transportation routes for armies and their supplies. Control of the Mississippi had been a strategic goal since the war's beginning for both the North and the South. Will's company was one of the first to be raised in Illinois and included several volunteers who, like Will, had moved there from Washington County, New York.

By May 6, 1861, about 4,000 troops, including Will's company, were stationed in Cairo. The soldiers were so green that at bayonet drill one observer said they looked "like a line of beings made up about equally of the frog, the sandhill crane, the sentinel crab, and the grasshopper...jumping, thrusting, striking, jerking...and all gone

Daniel Reid Ross

stark mad." They drilled in homemade dark-blue denim uniforms and used a flag that had been made by local citizens. Nevertheless, as green as they were, they made reconnaissance expeditions to Columbus, Kentucky, and Benton, Missouri. Their real enemies at Cairo were ravenous mosquitoes, bugs, and the daytime heat. One soldier said the sun was hot enough to "cook eggs in 13 minutes." Malaria, resulting from mosquito bites, and typhoid were the prevalent diseases. By the end of Will's ninety-day enlistment in July 1861, the 10th Ill. boasted that it was "the crack regiment of the post."

Will returned home to New York after his ninety-day enlistment ended, helping his parents and brothers on the family farm. With the harvest completed, Dan enlisted, in September 1861, in the 7th N.Y. Black Horse Cavalry and reported for duty in November. At the same time, Will was recruiting for another New York regiment, the 93rd, hoping to secure a commission as an officer if he signed up enough men. He did not get his wish for a commission, but nonetheless reenlisted, this time for three years.

The day before he reenlisted, he wrote to Dan, "Mother feels very bad about my going into the Army . . . Father backs me up . . . with true love not expecting to gain . . . I asked him to back me at the bank for sixty days which he has done readily." The loan was to tide him over while he recruited soldiers for the 93rd N.Y. He also thanked Dan for a watch that "was really a godsend, and you may be assured it was gratefully received as a token of kind regard from a worthy brother of whom I am very proud."

Their parents' welfare weighed heavily on Will, who arranged for refinancing of their mortgage. Will was on a short leave in Albany, New York, on February 6, 1862, when he wrote to Dan, who was now in Washington, DC. He explained, "my business [at] home was to enquire into father's affairs," adding that their parents would need money by spring to pay off the "encumbrance" on his farm. Will complimented Dan on saving $50 from his wages and continued, "We owe a duty to our parents we can never cancel . . . Father is very feeble and I am afraid he will not long need a home." To help their father, Will had asked Dr. Gray, an ardent Lincoln Republican and the father of two of his comrades, to take over the mortgage. He suggested that the three brothers raise $300 a year from their soldiers' pay to repay the doctor. He further suggested that, if their father and youngest brother, John, were not burdened by the annual principal payments of $300 on the mortgage, they could at least "make a living for the family, pay the interest, and keep the old house in order." Dr. Gray agreed to his plan, Will wrote, adding that the doctor said he and his brothers "were doing nobly to look after the welfare of our parents." Will remarked, "Now I made [these] arrangements on the supposition that you and Lank would pitch right in. You know we are now in a business where we are very likely to be sent home crippled."

Will's company commander, Capt. Norman Gray, and one of his best friends in the 93rd, Quartermaster Sergeant Gray, were sons of Dr. Gray. The letter implies that Sergeant Gray encouraged his father to loan Will the money. Will and Dan could not have known that, despite the financial help they provided, their parents would lose their farm shortly after the war's end.

Dan Ross did not experience any direct confrontations with Confederate forces during his first three-year enlistment in the 7th N.Y. Black Horse Cavalry. The five-foot-nine aspiring teacher with brown hair and gray eyes had spent his time training and waiting until his regiment was deactivated in March 1862 for want of horses and proper equipment. He had served less than a year of his three-year term. It must have been frustrating to the twenty-year-old, who wanted to make a difference for the Union and strike a blow against slavery.

Will wrote to Dan a month after his return to the farm, asking, "How do you enjoy laboring after your long tour of suffering from want of something 'prominent' to do? I rather think by the time you have ploughed that field of corn stubble you will find you have permanent employment." He told Dan about the farm where he was bivouacked, which had been well cared for in the past but now was destroyed. The house, formerly Brig. Gen. Silas Casey's headquarters, was being used as the brigade hospital for 1,500 men and was known as Camp Misery. Located in a muddy, low-lying area, it accommodated those most seriously ill. He also noted that someone in his brigade had died in Camp Misery every day since his arrival.

Having Dan and their youngest son, John, at home on the farm still left the elder Rosses in dire straits. In a May 1, 1862, letter to his mother, Will responded to her request that he apply for a "hardship" discharge and come home to help run the farm. He wrote that he realized his parents needed his help, but he did not want to ask for a discharge even though he had been sick for two months. He acknowledged that hard farmwork was "injuring" his mother's health, and that he and his brothers were indebted to their parents. He hoped, though, that she could manage with Dan's and John's help. "You have borne your part of life's struggles," he conceded.

Will's regiment was chosen in May 1862 as headquarters guard for the Army of the Potomac under Maj. Gen. George B. McClellan. On May 19, his camp moved to White House Landing on the Pamunkey River, the major supply base for McClellan's army, which was only eleven miles from Richmond. The "White House" was Martha Washington's original home and was later owned by President John Tyler. Besides the hospital, 150 tents erected by the 93rd accommodated the sick, one for each regiment. Will, who also was sick, took care of the others in his tent and also was his company's left color sergeant. On the day he wrote to Dan, Will reported that he had attended ninety men in his brigade who were on the sick list and that malaria was the prevailing disease. Bad water, chronic diarrhea, wilting heat, fatigue, heavy rains, and high humidity in the Chickahominy swamp where they were camped added to their misery. Two daily rations of whiskey and quinine were issued to the troops. Dysentery and typhoid fever were major medical problems as well, and 3,600 wounded men from the Battle of Seven Pines, fought on May 31, also had to be treated at the landing before being loaded onto river transports for transfer to hospitals. Several hundred at a time were brought to White House Landing on the York River Railroad, their festering wounds infested with maggots. The hospital tents were filled with those who were sick, so as more and more wounded arrived, they were treated aboard hospital ships in the river.

As the provost guard at headquarters, the 93rd N.Y. operated a signal tower on top of a house. With the firing of a single gun as the signal, Lieutenant Swain ignited a holocaust on June 28, after McClellan's disastrous defeat at Gaines Mill. The house, camp, and supplies were torched, and the ammunition dump, locomotives, and bridges were blown up. That day the retreating troops began their movement by three river steamers, including the *North America*, to Harrison's Landing, twenty-five miles from Richmond and the ancestral home of two presidents. When all the troops arrived by July 2 at Harrison's Landing, they found conditions were worse than those at Camp Misery. They brought with them most of the 8,000 troops wounded in Malvern Hill and the Seven Days' battles. Almost one-fourth of the men who were not wounded became ill with malaria, typhoid, scurvy, or dysentery, and new cases were reported each day. Arriving in the rain, they were exhausted and hungry, but they were protected by Federal gunboats and gun emplacements around the landing, although Rebels occasionally lobbed artillery shells into camp.

The first night, each man bedded down in drenching rain in a recently harvested, stubble-filled wheat field. When ordered to change position, each man stuck his bayonet into a sheaf and carried it on his shoulders to his new campground to sleep on in the liquefied dirt. Will and the others awoke to find themselves virtually submerged in mud as the rain continued. The mud would not hold the tent pegs, and tents collapsed on their occupants. Two days later they moved to higher ground. Day and night, the heat and humidity were stifling, the water was bad, the sanitation was worse, and the swarms of insects were impossible. Shade provided small comfort. Disease spread rapidly, and death took a terrible toll. Many sought relief with whiskey, sometimes referred to as "busthead." An Indiana soldier described it as a mixture of bark juice, tar water, turpentine, brown sugar, lamp oil, and alcohol.

On July 8, still very concerned about their father, Will wrote Dan, "You should not think of leaving home just now when Father has so much business on hand. I am sure you can make yourself very useful and [I] see no way Father can spare you."

The following day, Lincoln and McClellan reviewed the troops on horseback, the last three hours in brilliant moonlight. The moon made thousands of bayonets sparkle. Troops cheered them, and cannons were fired throughout the review. Lincoln's black coat and silk stovepipe hat were coated with dust, which he repeatedly doffed as he smiled, revealing his anxiety and care for the men. It was clear that Will and the others loved him. Morale significantly improved. Because Will's regiment was assigned as headquarters guard for "Little Mac," he would have seen Lincoln up close. A Connecticut chaplain wrote that Lincoln's "arm with which he drew the rein, in its angles and position resembled the hind leg of a grasshopper—the hand before—the elbow away back over the horse's tail."

On August 1, the troops burned the house of Edmund Ruffin, the man who had fired the first Confederate cannon at Fort Sumter. On Sunday, August 17, Will wrote to Dan from Fort Monroe, where they had just arrived "in another grand skedaddle" aboard the river steamer *North America*. The New Yorkers were the last regiment to board the steamer. Will slept on deck, he reported, adding that he and his friend Gray had gone to town, had had a "tolerable dinner" at the hotel and "were going to church this p.m."

Before he could receive his brother's letter about the move to Fort Monroe, Dan reenlisted, again for three years, with the 123rd N.Y. Infantry. For reenlisting, he received $160 in state, county, and city bounty, plus another $100 in federal bounty to be paid at war's end. By the end of September, having drilled and done guard duty for about two weeks on Arlington Heights (an area that included what is now Arlington Cemetery), the men were issued Enfield rifles, and the regiment was given twenty mules to haul its wagons. The mules had never been harnessed and were as "green" as the men.

In mid-October, while Dan's regiment was camped near Harper's Ferry, Will's regiment marched through the area. Men in the two regiments, both recruited largely from Washington County, New York, had a joyous reunion for several days. The two brothers had not seen each other since a year before, when they were both home on the farm.

On October 17, 1862, Pvt. Will Ross was promoted to corporal by his regimental commander, Col. John S. Crocker, and assigned to Squad No. 1 of Company E. By then, the 93rd was in camp near Potomac Creek, Virginia. Will also was placed in charge of regimental ordnance. On January 9, 1863, he was promoted to regimental commissary sergeant. The commissary was an immense grocery warehouse filled with large quantities of food and supplies. With this promotion, his pay increased to $21 monthly.

Dan's regiment was attached to Brig. Gen. Alpheus S. Williams's division and remained with it to the end of the war. Dan's fall and winter duties involved guarding the Potomac River and occupying the north end of the Shenandoah Valley in what is now West Virginia to prevent Rebel cavalry raids on railroads, canals, and incursions into Maryland and Pennsylvania. His regiment also guarded the right flank of the Army of the Potomac. At night in late November, the men engaged in foraging, prompting Rev. Henry Gordon, the chaplain of the 123rd, to write, "It will be a month of Sundays . . . before the voice of a rooster or the chuckling of a gobbler is heard in [this] valley."

The next time Will and Dan might have seen each other was during Burnside's exhausting and futile two-day "mud march" that began on January 20, 1863. The march accomplished nothing except to demoralize the army and led to Burnside's resignation.

At the end of January 1863, the war's third year, President Lincoln chose Maj. Gen. Joseph Hooker as the third commander of the Army of the Potomac. Hooker, known as "Fighting Joe," aspired to a showdown victory against the Confederacy's Gen. Robert E. Lee. He felt confident that he would succeed where his two predecessors, George B. McClellan and Ambrose E. Burnside, had failed. Fighting Joe was a soldier's soldier, but he also was a heavy drinker, a "politico," and a braggart. Lincoln's assistant secretary of war once wrote a sarcastic letter in which he noted that an intensive search for Hooker was being conducted at Willard's

Hotel bar in Washington. Hooker wore well-tailored uniforms and had apple cheeks. Nevertheless, as a first-rate military administrator, he restored the Army's morale from rock bottom after its disastrous defeat at Fredericksburg, the miserable January 22–24 mud march, when soldiers in the 123rd marched one step forward and slipped back two, and Lincoln's Emancipation Proclamation. The proclamation infuriated a sizable number of soldiers, who argued that they had enlisted to preserve the Union, not to free slaves.

When Hooker took command of the Army of the Potomac, its squalid camps in the hills surrounding Falmouth were pestholes. One-third of the army was absent without leave, 15,000 soldiers were on the sick list, and desertions averaged 200 a day. The soldiers were dirty, cold, and miserable. Many drowned their sorrows in rotgut whiskey. Despotic "King Mud" ruled in camp until the weather finally improved in mid-April. Even Lincoln complained that "after deducting [for] the sick, the deserters, the stragglers, and the discharged, the numbers seriously diminish. . . . It's like trying to shovel fleas across a barnyard; You don't get 'em all there."

Within weeks, Hooker improved their health and morale and significantly reduced the length of the sick list. By also reducing corruption in the commissary department, he improved the army's supply system. He introduced basic rules of sanitation, moved many regiments, including the 123rd, to better campgrounds, vastly improved their diet, clothing, personal hygiene, and water supply, and policed their camps and hospitals. He also instituted a system of furloughs that reduced desertions by granting leave to two men and two officers per company at a time. Upon their return another four would be furloughed, and so on. However, if anyone deserted while on leave, the procedure ended for that company. He caught them up with their back pay, tightened security to discourage desertion, and kept them busy with drills, exercises, picket duty, and dress parades. Hooker also replaced incompetent corps commanders with those who were battle-tested or did not have personal ties with other high-ranking officers and therefore would be loyal to him. He also boosted unit pride by designing distinctive badges for each corps. Within a few weeks they cheered him as he rode through camp.

By early 1863, the Union's Regular Army artillery batteries were hopelessly short of both officers and enlisted men, and included only five regiments of "Old Army" artillery, each consisting of five batteries. No adequate measures were taken to obtain officers by promotion or to supply recruits. Brig. Gen. Henry J. Hunt, chief of artillery for the Army of the Potomac and a West Point contemporary of Hooker's, estimated that he was short almost 3,500 men in his field artillery to man twenty-eight pieces of regular artillery and fifty-six of reserve artillery. To meet this need, they recruited replacements from volunteer infantry regiments in the divisions attached to artillery batteries. Likewise, the only horses available for the batteries were those rejected by the ambulance corps and quartermasters for drawing wagon trains.

Four batteries were assigned to each division—at least one Regular Army battery, and the rest manned mostly by volunteers. The captain of the regular battery also commanded the volunteer batteries. Consequently, the experienced regulars in the artillery, who trained the volunteers, were usually outnumbered by inexperienced men.[1] The story of one raw recruit, Dan—at least raw with respect to artillery—demonstrates how quickly the newcomers learned, largely from on-the-job training.

In March 1863, Dan and a friend answered the call to transfer to the artillery. It was a timely decision. Union artillery would play a vital role in two decisive battles of 1863, Chancellorsville and Gettysburg. Lacking any experience with artillery, Dan and Sgt. Larned S. Amiden were reduced to the rank of private, by order of their regimental commander, Col. Archibald L. McDougall, while in camp near Stafford Court House, Virginia.

Although both Ross brothers were present for the battles of Chancellorsville and Gettysburg, their experiences were quite different. Now a corporal, William worked in the headquarters of the Union commanders, giving him more of an overview of the two battles than any of the soldiers directly involved in them could have. Dan experienced the battles as a cannoneer in the thick of the action, and saw little more than what was directly in front of him.

Pvt. Daniel Ross would be severely tested in the coming months. He was among the first of sixty-nine totally green volunteers recruited from his division. Thirty were assigned to Battery F, 4th U.S. Artillery, a Regular Army battery—including three others from Dan's regiment—to bring the battery up to its regulation strength of 120 privates. Many of these volunteers were beardless boys who were nineteen or less. Dan was nineteen.[2] Many volunteered for the artillery because of its glamour and dash, which were largely lacking in the infantry. Artillerymen's forage caps were a distinctive dark blue with insignia of crossed cannons, worn at a jaunty angle. Their brass-buttoned short jackets and blue trousers with reinforced seats were trimmed with scarlet piping, earning them the nickname "red legs." They carried sabers and sometimes pistols as sidearms, and wore boots instead of shoes. Dan paid $15.11 for his uniform and personal weapons out of his own pocket—about five weeks of his pay as a private.

While volunteer artillerymen may have been attracted by glamour, they were selected for self-reliance, intelligence, skill at handling horses and horse-drawn equipment, and mechanical aptitude. Dan was an excellent horseman and, having worked the family farm since boyhood, knew how to handle horse-drawn equipment. On the whole, these volunteers proved superior to Confederate artillerymen. Cannoneers probably never numbered more than 5 percent of the Union army.

When Dan reported to Battery F at Camp Williams near Stafford Court House, Virginia, in March 1863, he had never fired a weapon larger than an Enfield rifle-musket. Within the battery, there were two guns in each of three sections, each under the command of a lieutenant. Dan was pleased to find that his section chief, 1st Lt. Franklin B. Crosby, age twenty-one, also was a New Yorker who had enlisted in August 1861. Crosby was a volunteer, albeit a seasoned one, who enlisted after First Bull Run. The young lieutenant was the son of a prominent New York attorney, and was a rising young lawyer himself before being called to the colors.

The battery commander before Crosby had been Capt. Clermont L. Best, a West Pointer. Best had a sharp eye and a quick mind and was an excellent artilleryman. When the war began, Battery F was sent from Minnesota to the Washington, DC, arsenal, arriving April 18, 1861, three days after President Lincoln's first call for volunteers. Soon Best was promoted to 12th Corps chief of artillery, and Crosby replaced him as battery commander. Fighting with great skill and courage, Best had covered part of the Union retreat from Winchester to Harpers Ferry in the Shenandoah Valley. He earned extra laurels in September 1862, at the Battle of Antietam when he covered the 12th Corps during Stonewall Jackson's strong counterattack and blew the Rebels away like dust. Best was one of the more experienced artillery field officers Hooker placed in tactical control of artillery at the corps level.

The 12th Corps had been commanded by Maj. Gen. Henry W. Slocum since October 10, 1862. Small in stature and dapper, with black hair, beard, and eyes, he was a battle-scarred West Pointer who was severely wounded in the thigh at First Bull Run. Up to then, he had seen action in most of the battles fought by the Army of the Potomac. At age thirty-six, he was the second youngest Union officer to attain the rank of major general, which he did on July 4, 1862, only thirteen months after he had been appointed colonel of the 27th N.Y.

Slocum was well liked by his men. In 1852, as a cadet from Onondaga County, New York, he willingly expressed his abolitionist views in the face of strong pro-slavery sentiment at the academy. He was not only studious but also willing to help other cadets, including his roommate Philip Sheridan, and graduated seventh in his class. Slocum combined

Gen. Henry Slocum

prudence with courage and the ability to deal with the unexpected. He was careful, cautious, and competent, inspiring faith and confidence and would never fight until he had to. Once committed to battle, he was one of the hardest and toughest of fighters. He was a strict temperance man, and had a fierce temper, which he displayed when things went wrong. He and his outstanding division commander, Alpheus Williams, were friends who respected each other. Williams, who served as a colonel in command of a regiment in the war with Mexico, had reported for duty in the Civil War on October 5, 1861.

There were three sections in Battery F, each with two guns and under the command of a lieutenant. In the first five weeks after Dan was assigned to Battery F, Lieutenant Crosby, his section chief, trained him in specific drills known as the manual of the piece, the school of the section, and battery drill. Dan learned every position in the gun crew so that he could take the next man's job if necessary. They also had to learn the bugle calls. Drills were conducted daily, weather and mud permitting, in the barren hills and worn-out tobacco fields surrounding Stafford Court House, an antiquated, weather-beaten hamlet.

Each man at a cannon had a number and had a priority position with specific duties to perform at his designated station. All six horses hitched in pairs to the gun also knew their duties and stations. The pair closest to the gun was the "wheel team," the middle pair the "swing team," and the front pair was the "lead team," with a driver mounted on the "near" horse of each team. For safety reasons, the caisson holding ammunition was positioned a few feet behind its limber, a two-wheeled horse-drawn vehicle that also held ammunition. A second limber, in turn, was hitched to the cannon. A total of 1,218 rounds of ammunition were carried for a battery of six Napoleon twelve-pounders. The horses were unhitched and, if possible, hidden by the drivers a short distance to the rear before firing began. Each driver had to keep his two horses calm during battle and cut them out of their traces if they were killed or wounded.

Dan's gun was manned by a sergeant, or "chief of piece," two corporals, and thirteen privates, including seven cannoneers and six drivers. The sixteen-man platoon—or gun detachment—always served the same gun, and constituted the aristocracy of the artillery. Two platoons manned a two-gun section—a company in the artillery brigade. The sergeant sighted the gun. When not sighting, he was mounted so as to guide and otherwise superintend the piece. All sixteen platoon members were familiar with the manual, *Instruction for Field Artillery*, and the *Table of Fire*, which was glued to the inside cover of the limber chest. Artillery crews competed with one another in estimating ranges, cutting fuses to proper length, and mounting and dismounting guns. They also rolled cannonballs to one another for amusement.[3]

At the sound of a bugle, one man brought from the limber chest or the caisson a two-and-a-half-pound powder cartridge attached to a projectile consisting of solid shot, shell, spherical case, grape, or canister. These "fixed ammunition" were the standard military rounds. Another man shoved the cartridge-plus-projectile into the cannon muzzle. A third man rammed it down the barrel. When a shell (exploding projectile) was used, its fuse was cut to proper length before it was loaded. Following loading, the cartridge was pricked, the primer was inserted into the cannon's touchhole, the crew stepped back, and at the gunner's command of "Fire," the lanyard was attached and pulled. Lacking a mechanism to absorb the shock of explosion, a cannon leaped backward each time it was fired, and had to be resighted and manhandled back into position. Next, one man put his thumb, encased in a leather thumb stall, over the touchhole or vent at the breech to keep out air during the loading process. Another swabbed the barrel with a sponge on the end of a staff to extinguish any sparks. The process was repeated, as a fresh cartridge-plus-projectile was brought from the limber chest, inserted, and fired. A well-drilled crew fired their cannon twice a minute, four times when firing canister. Everybody moved in sequence like automatons, except that periodically the swab was dipped in a water bucket to help clean out the barrel.

Aiming and estimating the distance to a target consumed the most time. Men were instructed to achieve accuracy and not waste ammunition with poorly directed rapid firing. They took aim by sighting along the barrel. Next, the officer or gunner estimated distance to the target, fired the gun, and elevated or depressed it by turning a wheel screw located under the breech, depending on whether the previous projectile had fallen short or overshot the target. Hand signals directed the cannoneers to move the gun trail to the right or left to aim it.

If a cannoneer was killed or wounded, another stood ready to take his place. Those cannoneers not actually working the guns were provided with rifle-muskets and hand grenades and stationed nearby in case of assault. Cannoneers and their horses were prime targets for enemy infantry, sharpshooters, and artillerymen in their effort to put the dreaded batteries out of commission as quickly as possible. As a consequence, fifteen to twenty men were assigned to each gun to provide replacements. Cannoneers with pistols or sabers also repelled the enemy if they were overrun. During the spring of 1863, while he was training his red legs, Crosby wrote, "each one ... must do his duty [and with] a firm trust in God go forward on his path of duty."[4]

Dan's Battery F Napoleon guns were effective up to 1,500 yards, adequate range in the hilly, wooded countryside where many eastern Civil War battles were fought. When loaded with grapeshot or canister, they were vicious at a quarter mile, having the effect of a gigantic shotgun. A canister, otherwise known as "canned hell," was a tin can full of iron or lead slugs packed in sawdust, with a propellant at one end and a disk at the other. The can disintegrated when the gun discharged, spraying the slugs over the landscape in a fairly even pattern about twenty yards wide at a distance of 300 yards. A case shot was an exploding projectile that was filled with lead balls and activated with a timed or contact fuse. Canister was used at short range, case shot for long-range firing, with the burning time of the fuse set so that it would explode immediately in front of the enemy. In contrast to other artillery pieces, the Napoleon was a safe gun to fire. As late as July 1864, the Union chief of ordnance wrote there was no instance "of the 12-pounder bronze gun having worn out or ... [of it] bursting." All in all, the smoothbore Napoleon was the best gun for short-range fighting. It became the workhorse of Civil War artillery on both sides.

Dan's gunnery training was interrupted on April 6 by a visit from President Abraham Lincoln, his wife, and his son, Tad, together with

Secretary of War Stanton and General Halleck. They arrived in a blinding snowfall, accompanied by howling winds, for a four-day visit at the Aquia Creek landing on the Potomac River, the supply base for Hooker's Army. Lincoln's wife had urged him to make the trip to celebrate Tad's tenth birthday and escape from the dreadful daily pressures in Washington. A gaily decorated freight wagon greeted them on their arrival Easter Sunday and took the party five miles inland to Falmouth. There they were met by ambulances and a cavalry honor guard, which escorted them to their three large, floored tents, set up by Will and others from the 93rd N.Y. at Hooker's headquarters. After first visiting and talking to every wounded and sick soldier in the hospital tents at nearby Falmouth, Lincoln was to review the entire 160,000-man Army of the Potomac during the next two days. This was the largest and grandest review of the war to date. A reception was held in General Hooker's tent the next morning for about forty officers, including his staff and Captain D. E. Barnes of the 93rd, who was officer of the day. Despite looking careworn and thin, Lincoln shook each officer's hand as he was introduced.

The review, held about a mile away, began that afternoon with the cavalry and ended with Slocum's 12th Corps. Mrs. Lincoln rode to it in a four-horse carriage. Lincoln, Hooker, and other officers were in a reviewing stand on a gentle slope near an apple orchard. As each brigade passed in new uniforms and shoes, carrying new rifles with glinting barrels and bayonets, they dipped their colors, and the president returned the salute by bowing, taking off his stovepipe hat, and standing bareheaded as he was given lusty cheers that could be heard for miles. General Slocum's 12th Corps was reviewed on the second day, April 8, but the roads were so soft that the artillery came last in the review, the 200 guns making a loud, rumbling noise. Marching in formation, the 8,000 men in the corps, including the artillery, spanned two miles. The batteries were drawn by fine horses, and the officers and men appeared to be in excellent condition. They fired a deafening twenty-one-gun salute in Lincoln's honor. If Dan had a chance to see Lincoln, it would have been only at a distance. As part of Hooker's headquarters guard Will must have had a close-up look at the president, and may have helped guard him.

After the review that afternoon, Lincoln and Hooker rode through the camp, generating great enthusiasm among the men. Each time Lincoln halted his horse, men gathered around to salute or shout greetings, look into his sad-eyed but kindly, smiling face, and pat his horse. On strolls through camp, the president frequently stopped to talk with groups of soldiers.[5]

Seeing Lincoln, revered and beloved as he was, was a profoundly moving experience. His deep, personal appreciation of their military service cheered and encouraged the men. He was truly "Father Abraham" and so thoroughly enjoyed mingling with the men that he stayed an extra day. Yet on his small black horse, his high, battered silk hat bobbing as he rode by the troops, he presented a somewhat comical appearance. One soldier said his legs were so long they could be tied in a knot under the horse's belly. His pants crept above his boot tops, exposing his long white underdrawers. Hooker's enormous staff of at least 200 officers followed the president and his little son, who was mounted on an Indian pony.

At least one soldier in the 123rd wrote his mother, "Lincoln looks natural and quite like the pictures you have seen of him." Another soldier in Dan's brigade wrote that the "sight alone [of Lincoln] almost compensated us for our entire service in the army." Pvt. John Cutter, also of the 123rd, wrote his mother on April 17, "I feel as though I could go through any hardship. I know I am doing what is right and what I never shall feel ashamed of; I am not fighting for money, you know. I am fighting for my country, and Uncle Sam would get us, as willingly, if he did not pay a cent." Private Rich wrote that same day, "the boys are all well at present [and] are waiting for orders to march." Dan undoubtedly shared the feelings expressed by his fellow soldiers.

It was clear to all that in his way Lincoln suffered as much from the weight of responsibility for the war as did the soldiers who faced battles, disease, and physical discomfort. That realization and his manner of familiarity with them cemented a bond unlike that they felt with any other commander. When he left to return to Washington, thousands spontaneously cheered him. The trip had revived Lincoln mentally and physically. Curiously, the review was held about one and one-half miles from the Rappahannock River, across which was an enemy encampment with artillery batteries that could easily have shelled the Union forces, had they chosen to do so.

Preparations for the impending battle began April 12, in favorable weather—inspecting arms and ammunition, shoeing horses and mules, issuing provisions, emptying hospitals, and so forth. On April 15, the regiment received four months' back pay, $52 for Dan and every other private. The men were ordered to prepare to march at any hour. On April 21, Pvt. Henry Mosier wrote his uncle Asa that their "destination [was] not known to us and [we] don't care much where, if it will end the rebellion." That day, they turned in all except one change of clothing, an overcoat, and a blanket. General Williams told his daughter, "I never saw my troops in better condition, never more anxious to meet the enemy."

Chancellorsville was a vast plantation that bore the owner's name, located near the confluence of the Rappahannock and Rapidan rivers in northern Virginia. The area surrounding it, known as the Wilderness,

Gen. Alpheus S. Williams

was covered by virtually impenetrable stands of shrubs and small trees, mostly second growth, and cut by numerous streams and swampy ravines. The terrain and vegetation would play a key role in the battle, which would deal the Union Army a stunning defeat, despite its superior size and weaponry. With half the force of his opponent, Confederate Gen. Robert E. Lee would use the terrain and vegetation to his advantage. His audacity and Hooker's timid performance in combat would combine to result in a significant and embarrassing Union defeat.

On April 30, 1863, Best's 12th Corps artillery consisted of five batteries with twenty-eight guns manned by 14 officers and 507 enlisted men when they arrived at Chancellorsville in a drizzle late that afternoon. Three of these batteries, including Dan's Battery F, were assigned to Brig. Gen. Alpheus S. Williams' division, under Capt. Robert H. Fitzhugh, his division artillery chief. They were supplied with ammunition, equipment, food, and ambulances loaded with medical supplies, delivered by Potomac riverboat at the fortified Acquia Landing, a few miles from Stafford Court

House and fifty-five miles from Washington. The Richmond, Fredericksburg & Potomac Railroad had a railhead at the river landing at Acquia as well. By this time, Crosby had been promoted to chief of Battery F, and Lieutenant Floyd became Dan's section chief. The soldiers were finally on the move, relieved of the monotony of camp life.

The 123rd and Battery F's six guns, including Dan's, guarded the wagon train as it crossed the Rappahannock on two pontoon bridges at Kelly's Ford. Each man left camp with eight days' rations—hard bread, coffee, sugar, and salt—and sixty rounds of cartridges. Five days' rations of beef on the hoof followed the wagon train. Stafford Court House was eight miles from Falmouth, where Hooker's headquarters were then located, and twelve miles from Chancellorsville.

As the 12th Corps marched in high spirits through Falmouth past Hooker's headquarters on its way to the Chancellorsville battlefield on the Orange Plank Road, Dan and Will could have had a brief visit. The artillery had preceded the balance of the corps in order to guard the river crossing where the wagon train crossed. The corps then proceeded to a position near the Chancellor House where Hooker established his battlefield headquarters. The officers initially conferred with General Slocum, General Williams, and others for half an hour. Here, again, the brothers could have met. Dan's battery remained in reserve there until 6 A.M. the next day, when it moved to Fairview, where the 123rd had camped the night before and where they both would fight. That day, when Lee learned that Hooker had begun his offensive, he recalled Gen. James Longstreet from North Carolina, where Longstreet was foraging for badly needed food for Lee's men and animals. Longstreet got back too late to participate in the battle.

General Hooker's plan for his spring Virginia campaign was to maneuver General Lee into an open showdown. He divided his army into three parts. Maj. Gen. George Stoneman's cavalry corps was assigned to interrupt Lee's supply lines. Maj. Gen. John Sedgwick's reinforced infantry corps was assigned to feint a direct advance toward Fredericksburg and immobilize Lee there, while Hooker, with three corps, including the 12th, was to approach indirectly and turn Lee's left flank. To do so they took three and one-half days to follow a circuitous, sixty-five-mile route, whereas the direct route was only twelve miles. Hooker's strategy initially appeared to catch Lee in a trap from which he would have to flee or fight. If he chose to fight, it would be on Hooker's terms. Hooker kept his plans so secret that his corps commanders had only the fragments of information they needed to issue orders.[6]

When the audacious and aggressive Lee chose to fight, he took one of the great gambles of his career. In doing so, he displayed extreme self-confidence, whereas Hooker lost his nerve—and lost the fight.[7]

The armies met at Chancellorsville, where Hooker's larger numbers and superior artillery should have given him the advantage. Nevertheless, on May 1, he yielded the initiative, ordering his corps commanders to pull back and take defensive positions at Fairview near Chancellorsville, an order they protested but obeyed. Slocum shouted at the courier who delivered Hooker's order, "You are a damned liar. Nobody but a crazy man would give such an order when we have victory in our sights." He sent the courier back to explain the advantage of remaining to fight from his splendid position on a ridge facing open country. Hooker replied with an imperative to retire as ordered. The only action that afternoon was a contracted artillery duel until they retired about 6 P.M. at Fairview.

Lee sensed his psychological advantage and took the offensive. On the night of May 1–2, with the whistling whip-poor-wills "thicker than katydids up north," he sent Lt. Gen. Thomas J. "Stonewall" Jackson on a twelve-mile flanking movement around Hooker's right.

Dan and the other cannoneers spent most of the morning of May 2 behind the line in positions they had partially fortified on Fairview Heights near Hooker's Chancellor House headquarters. They dozed to catch up on sleep. In the morning, however, one two-gun section did return some enemy fire on a Confederate division, and in the afternoon three other sections, including Dan's, did likewise. They had not gotten to sleep on the ground until around midnight, and by then they had consumed most, if not all, of their eight-day supply of rations. That morning Capt. Hiram Wilson of the 93rd N.Y., Will's regiment that was guarding Hooker's headquarters, wrote his wife that by this battle "hangs the fate of the country. If we defeat the Rebel army they must give up and if we are beat . . . we can hang up the fiddle and the bow."

The infantry spent the day digging entrenchments and felling trees where they expected the enemy to attack. The only other noises were bugle calls, drumbeats, neighing horses, and braying mules. About noon, Hooker—handsome, dashing, and superbly mounted—was heartily cheered as he rode the lines, accompanied by his large staff. He was about to make a devastating misjudgment, though. When Jackson's flanking move was detected and reported to him, Hooker misinterpreted it to mean Lee's army was retreating. One of the lads in the 123rd, an ex-sailor, had climbed a tall pine tree and spotted Jackson's men marching away, as if in retreat. This was reported to General Williams' headquarters.

By 5:15 P.M. on May 2, Jackson attacked. By dusk, he had routed the one-armed Maj. Gen. O. O. Howard's 11th Corps. With darkness falling, Jackson's surge was stalled in large part by the 12th Corps. As enemy shrapnel and bullets whizzed over and through the 123rd, the bald-headed Colonel McDougall, whose arm was in a sling from having just been injured by a kicking mule, waved his sword and shouted,

"For God's sake boys, stand your ground. Don't let it be said the boys of Washington County ran." Captain Best also helped to check the Rebels by gathering all the guns he could at Fairview and firing them as rapidly as possible.

The red legs were instructed to cut their fuses short and aim their pieces so that the canisters would strike the ground at one hundred yards and ricochet. Then, at two hundred yards, the slugs would spread widely through the enemy ranks, penetrating bodies and trees. From then on, they were told to load and fire at will.

By about sundown, Best had massed forty guns, including Dan's two-gun section under Lieutenant Floyd, on Fairview. They fired on and off at the enemy in the woods 600 yards to a mile away until about midnight. The fire was directed with great delicacy over the heads of Williams's men 500 yards in front of the Fairview artillery line.

Jackson was seriously wounded about 9:15 P.M. when his own skirmishers from Lane's brigade mistakenly fired at him and his staff as they returned from a reconnaissance. They were in front of his skirmish line, so close to the junction of Berry's and Williams's line that they could hear the sound of axes as the Federals built fortifications. It was a brilliant, moonlit night. They were facing a potential onslaught by Stonewall Jackson's men, who formed in lines five and six deep in the woods.

When they were within about 200 yards, the Rebels fired a volley from their 5,000 muskets. The *New York Times* described the confrontation: "Among the most notable scenes . . . was the artillery fight of Capt. Best's guns . . . massed on the ridge . . . where the enemy was successfully checked Saturday night. . . . The reverberation the artillery rendered was very great, in consequence of the peculiar condition of the night air, and it seemed for one hour, as though the very heavens would fall."

Battery F had been extremely well positioned and was partially screened from enemy view after a rapid movement to shift the guns to cover the woods and the Plank Road. Horses heaved, strained, and snorted as they hauled the guns into the new position. From here, with each jerk of the lanyards, the flash of the Napoleons discharging canister, shot, and shell lit up the road or woods. The earth trembled and the noise was, indeed, deafening. Pvt. Albert Cook of the 123rd wrote his father, "the heavens and earth seemed coming together. It was the most sublime of all scenes."

Minutes after the shelling reopened about 9:30 P.M., the Confederate Maj. Gen. A. P. Hill, who had succeeded to Jackson's command, was painfully wounded by a minié ball that went through the calf of his left leg. Hill's disability created confusion and disorder, disheartening his troops. As 20,000 Confederates redeployed in the woods adjacent to the Plank Road, Best's cannoneers again raked the area and the road with a hail of fire. The tactic broke the charge and delayed a second Confederate attack until morning. Hill reported, "the enemy . . . concentrate a most terrible fire of artillery on . . . my division." They had filled the air with fire and thunderous fury for more than six hours.

According to Cpl. R. O. Fisher of the 123rd, the Rebels were driven back, yelling. Best's guns also wounded Col. Stapleton Crutchfield, Stonewall Jackson's chief of artillery. Battery F continued firing until about midnight, the full moon helping the gunners to sight accurately. As a result, they repeatedly silenced enemy guns. Captain Osborn recorded in his after-action report, "The practice of the artillery this evening was the most splendid I ever saw . . . we repeatedly tore the Rebel lines to fragments, and assisted our gallant infantry to drive them, shattered, to the rear. . . . Two batteries . . . commanded by Captain Best [namely, Crosby's and Winegar's batteries] did good service." Dan had a right to be proud of his performance in his first battle. Best's batteries also assisted the infantry in retaking artillery that General Howard's men lost late that afternoon.

The enemy advance was checked without injury to the Union soldiers. Their dead and dying lay in heaps as the survivors withdrew into the woods.

Aided by the 4,000-man engineer division, Best's exhausted redlegs—including Dan—worked until about two A.M., constructing small epaulments (earthworks) with shovels in front of each cannon to provide partial cover for the gunners. Some guns faced west, others south. The Union men heard Jackson's officers massing their disorganized men for a dawn attack. At the same time, the enemy could hear the axes of the Union engineers and infantrymen felling trees to make a fifty- to one-hundred-yard-wide clearing between their infantry and the enemy. The men in Company G of the 123rd had only two axes between them.

The felled trees were arranged with their three-foot stumps into an abatis and dirt-covered log breastworks in front of the infantry's first line. From the hill, the gunners again could fire over the heads of their infantry, entrenched behind three successive lines of log and earth breastworks four hundred to five hundred yards away. Capt. Henry C. Gray inspected the breastworks at 5 A.M. and said, "we had better build it a log higher." Forward of the breastworks was a boggy area filled with crisscrossed white oak saplings called "slashes." Rebels would be hard-pressed to make a coordinated attack through the trees, mud, and slash, while also facing artillery fire.

At about 2 A.M., Brig. Gen. Gershom Mott's 3rd Corps brigade had arrived and taken up a position to the left of the Plank Road, behind Williams's division and in front of the forty guns in Best's artillery. The night was cold, and the air was filled with sickening, stifling, sulphurous gun smoke and the screams of wounded men and horses roasting to death in the burning woods. One Stonewall brigade soldier wrote that they had encountered "the most terrible and destructive shelling that we were subjected to during the war." One Confederate officer wrote his wife, "heads [were] shot off or crushed, bodies and limbs torn and mangled, [all] the work of shells." There was much shooting, and the troops were nervous. Bodies of the Confederate dead and wounded were stripped of cartridges so that lines could be maintained and the firing could continue unabated. Soldiers from Brig. Gen. David B. Birney's 3rd Corps division made a chaotic midnight bayonet charge into the woods by moonlight to end the Confederate sharpshooting. Their charge created confusion among "Old Pap" Williams's division in the 12th Corps, but it also served, with the help of Best's batteries, to locate enemy lines and establish a more advanced position for the Federals. No lights of any kind were allowed, not even fires for coffee.

As the smoke finally cleared, the moon broke through to a chorus of katydids and whip-poor-wills. After about two hours of fitful sleep, Dan was awakened to eat a hasty breakfast of pork, hardtack, and coffee that had just been issued to them. He splashed cold creek water on his face to erase the sleep from his eyes and washed his gunpowder-blackened hands as daylight penciled its way through the sky. The 12th Corps Commander, Slocum, sleeping on the ground not far from Dan's battery, was awakened about daylight.[8]

As May 3 dawned, the Army of the Potomac braced for a resumption of fighting with General Hooker personally in command in the field. In Battery F, some of the ninety regulars and thirty volunteers were scattered around their guns, working on equipment and making ready for action. They filled sacks of grain and strapped them to ammunition chests, greased axles, and selected replacement horses for any that would be killed or injured. Other battery members were in the rear feeding and harnessing their 110 horses, marking the last time 13 of these splendid animals would receive such attention.

A perfect sun was just spilling over the trees. Heavy dew and slight fog covered the ground. "It was an ideal Sunday morning, warm and fair," noted Sgt. Rice C. Bull of the 123rd N.Y., one of the regiments manning Slocum's frontline entrenchments. "It seemed like a sacrilege that such a beautiful and sacred day should be used by men to kill and maim each other." The regiment had worked almost all night with the help of pioneers building new breastworks a short distance from their old position and at right angles to it, facing west. By then the enemy occupied their old works. The new ones proved effective against musket fire but not the devastating artillery barrage they would face. To build these breastworks they used tin plates, bayonets, and a "few axes that at other times would have been thought unfit for work."[9]

At 3:30 A.M., Lee ordered Maj. Gen. J. E. B. Stuart, the Confederate cavalry leader, to "dispossess" the enemy by turning his right (Berry's division of Sickles's corps), and at daylight to "drive him from Chancellorsville."[10] Stuart took over command of Jackson's corps after "Stonewall" and General Hill were wounded. At daybreak, skirmishers who were only fifty yards apart began to exchange fire. At about 5:45 A.M., Confederate Brig. Gen. Henry Heth's six-brigade division of about 11,800 men began to come into view through the fog, among the trees and dense undergrowth of endless vines atop a low ridge. With their wild whoops, the grayback sharpshooters drove the Union skirmishers back over the breastworks, and the "ball" (Civil War lingo for battle) opened, with the entire line engaged. As one New York skirmisher climbed the barricade he said to Sergeant Bull, "Get ready boys for they are coming and coming strong." Two North Carolina regiments in Colonel Lane's brigade headed straight for the New Yorkers and the 3rd Md. at the right end of Williams's line. There was no need for the order, "Fall in." The suspense of waiting for battle had been agonizing. Every man had already sprung into place, cocked gun in hand, and cartridge belt strapped on. Bullets whistled overhead.

The Rebels appeared as "one solid mass of living gray." The butternuts—another name for the Rebels—crossed the shallow, swampy Lewis Creek Valley—about one hundred yards wide and cut by ravines interspersed with slashes—and began to yell in high-pitched voices, "Remember Jackson!" It was a Rebel yell the Union soldiers would hear many times through the war.

Confederate Brig. Gen. James Archer's 1,400-man brigade (Heth's division), was the first to attack, on the Confederate right. They confronted Ruger's brigade at the left end of Williams's line in an attempt to flank it. Williams rallied the two regiments at that end and they fought valiantly, repulsing Archer's men twice. Many Rebels got mired down in the boggy ground or became entangled in endless vines, shrubs, and slashes.

General Williams, who by then had more battle experience than any other division commander in the Army of the Potomac and was the senior brigadier general in the entire army, was on the line about 500 yards in front of the artillery as the battle opened. "Old Pap" Williams had been commissioned as a brigadier general at age fifty-one with effective rank from May 17, 1861, giving him the same seniority as Grant and Sherman. This was the fourth battle in which he faced Stonewall Jackson's troops.[11]

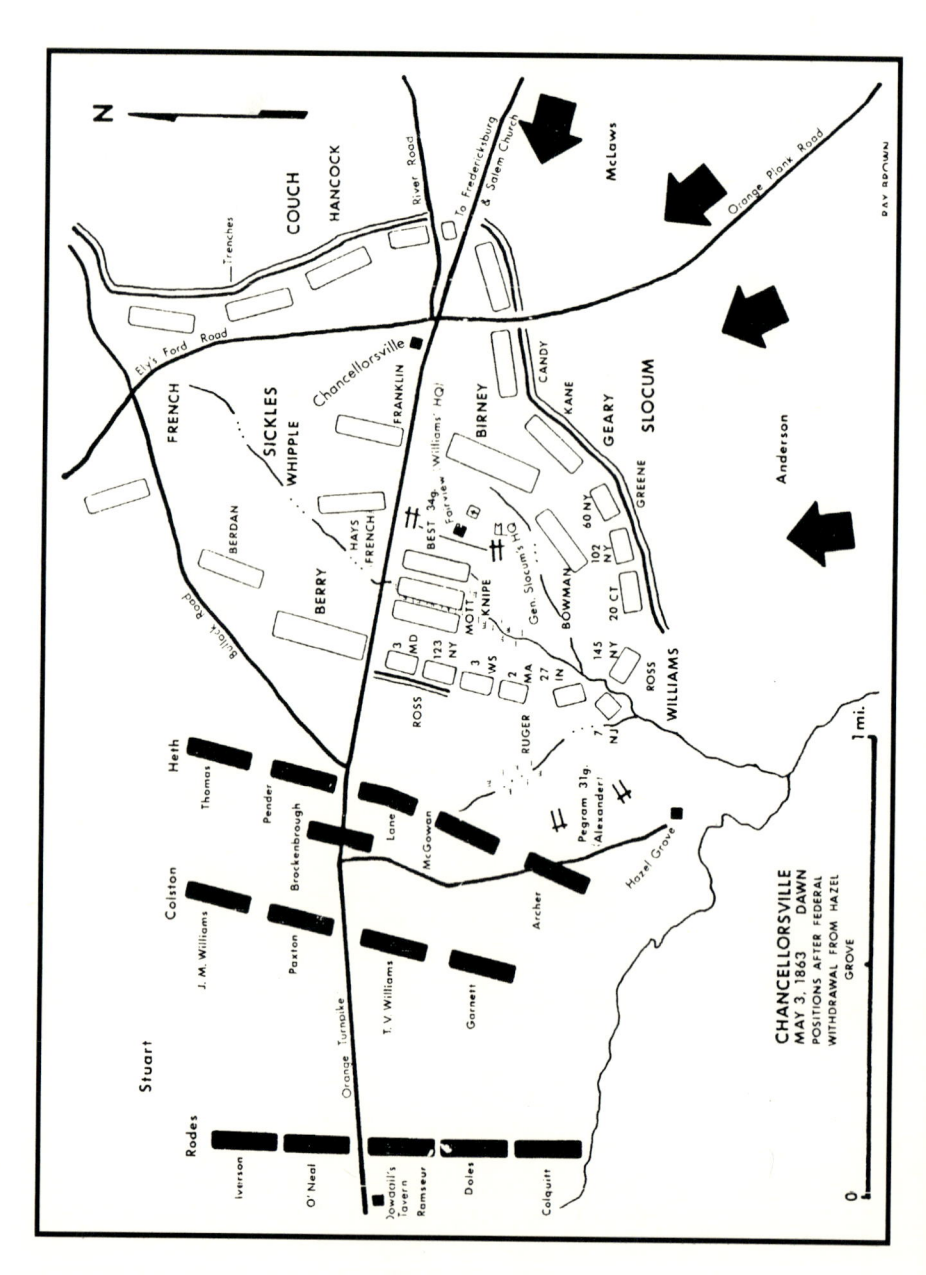

Chancellorsville

In an instant, the bugle call "Cannoneers to your post" rang out, followed by the next call, "In battery." Dan, his brown hair rumpled and gray eyes still bleary from lack of sleep, joined his crew as they leapt to their feet to take their stations. Adrenalin rushed through their veins and muscles tensed. The eagerly awaited command to fire was not given until the Rebel yell was heard. Until they emerged from the misty woods—driving in the skirmishers who had been slowing their advance—most of the attackers were screened from the view of Union artillerymen. At the commands "Load," "Ready," and "Fire," Best's batteries opened fire into the woods. The Sabbath sun dispelled the mist and turned into a bloodred ball of fire, foretelling what was to come.

Then appeared the whole of Stuart's mile-long first line of five brigades—7,000 men—in brigade formation with regiments massed in double columns hurling themselves at the Union line. When the first Battery F shells thundered forth, they were not more than twenty feet over the heads of New York's 123rd, who were positioned behind three-foot-high log works, completed only minutes before the action began.[12] "The noise of the cannonading was deafening, as shot and shell went howling and singing over our heads, the shells exploding only a short distance from our front," wrote Sergeant Bull. To some, the projectiles sounded "like a flock of blackbirds with blazing tails beating about in a gale."[13] The earth shook, and everything heaved and convulsed. Each gun fired a round about every ninety seconds. Dan found a moment to pray that he would not hit comrades from his own regiment who were hugging the ground. Shell fragments made a peculiar whizzing sound, an ear-piercing shriek, as they traveled in all directions. Others hissed like serpents as they flew through the air. Round shot crashed and thudded as it hit trees, buildings, the ground, and bodies. Screeching cannonballs tore into bodies, throwing them into the air. Corpses without legs and legs without torsos lay about. Grapeshot shattered skulls, splattering brains in every direction. Trees splintered, and gaping holes opened up in the ground. The night before, the Rebels had stayed in the woods. This time they charged out into the open.[14]

Initially, Best concentrated Union fire over the heads of Williams's men and onto the Orange Turnpike, which was crowded with Confederate ammunition trains, ambulances, troops, and artillery hurrying into position. To enter the battle from their position on the left of the Orange Turnpike, Rebels had to cross the road to face Williams's line. Three pieces from 1st Lt. Justin E. Dimick's battery were placed on the road behind earthworks in line with the infantry breastworks, to counter enemy efforts at breaking the Union line there. Confederate loss of life was frightful, as the road filled with dead and dying men and animals.

A cloud of fumes and dust enveloped the soldiers. They struggled to breathe, choking on the sulphurous gun smoke and fog rising from woods set ablaze by bursting artillery shells and smoldering wadding from rifle-muskets. The smoke stung combatants' eyes on both sides, further obscuring their movements from each other.

Gun smoke increased about 6:30 A.M., as thirty-one Confederate cannons began to return fire from Hazel Grove. One of its first victims was Col. Samuel Ross, in command of the brigade that consisted of the 123rd New York, 20th Conn., and 3rd Md. Wounded in the foot and leg by a bursting shell, he was carried from the field. Nevertheless, Best's artillery kept the enemy in check while the Union infantry rallied and advanced to regain position. Some of the enemy were so close that one battery fired with little or no trajectory, barely over the heads of their own soldiers. They drove the Rebels back up the hill in confusion as Union troops charged.[15]

By 8 A.M., the 12th Corps infantry had repulsed three Confederate assaults, the first two largely as a result of the terrible artillery fire. But now each attacking wave consisted of four or five brigades of fresh troops, in crowds rather than regular formation. According to Sergeant Bull, they were "mowed down like grass, by both our artillery and infantry." Led by General Paxton, the Stonewall brigade was in the second line of battle. Its 4th Virginia lost 160 of 355 men in ten minutes, and the 55th suffered severely. Paxton was shot through the heart and killed while he was on foot, attempting to re-form and reposition his brigade as it slowly advanced through a densely overgrown swale to within seventy yards of Williams's line. By the end of the battle, facing Williams's line, his brigade would suffer 493 casualties, 45 percent of his men. The dead lay in windrows in front of the breastworks.

Fifteen Confederate brigades, consisting of seventy-one regiments, were sent in one after the other over a four-hour period. As soon as Union troops repulsed each attacking wave with great loss, cheer after cheer went up among the men. They fired as fast as they could tear open a cartridge with their teeth and drive it home with a ramrod. On the first assault alone, the enemy lost eight stands of colors and about 1,000 men were captured. Some of these prisoners told their captors that the 123rd "was the devil to fight ... they never saw so hot a fire as we poured into them." Union Pvt. John L. Marshall of Co. E reported that his Captain, Henry C. Gray, fired both his seven-barrel revolver and a musket and "did a power of good shooting ... with cool and deliberate aim." He added that Lieutenant Hill "did not forget that a musket is a handy tool ... he must have done the Rebs a good deal of damage. These are the kind of officers to have."

Their faces were blackened with sweat-streaked powder, but their eyes were bright with anger and defiance. Nerves were strung tight, and the men were short of breath. They focused all attention on the job at hand, far too busy to concern themselves with the imminent danger they faced. They gave no thought to the past or the future, only to the present and the necessity to kill. The fear engendered by anticipation before the battle had disappeared. The first fire was the hardest. After that, all feelings and thoughts vanished, including concern for comrades who fell.

On the third assault, the 27th Ind., together with New York's 123rd, rose to unleash half an hour of murderous fire at the four regiments in McGowan's attacking brigade from seventy-five yards away. Simultaneously, two shells from Best's batteries behind them "burst in [the enemy's] midst which lay them in heaps. They ran back and a shout went up from the 123rd." Col. Silas Colgrove of the 27th Ind., who was wounded, wrote, "I can safely say that I never witnessed . . . so perfect a slaughter."

The two Union regiments then unslung their knapsacks and leaped over the breastworks to pursue the Rebels, picking their way over the dead and wounded enemies. Colonel McDougall of the 123rd shouted the order, "Go in boys—bully for the 123rd." He was beginning to earn his reputation as one of the most fearless and energetic officers in the 12th Corps. According to Pvt. S. Atwood, Sgt. Albert Cook, and Cpl. R. O. Fisher, the New Yorkers took 200 prisoners and two stands of colors with the help of the 13th New Jersey. Before Lieutenant Colonel Rogers ordered them back, they drove back the four regiments of McGowan's South Carolinian brigade seventy to eighty yards to their initial breastworks, firing with unusual accuracy. The order to fall back was given so that Best's redlegs could resume firing into the enemy ranks.[16] The attackers reported that exploding shells turned tree branches into deadly missiles. Lifeless human bodies hurtled through the air, and riderless horses galloped wildly in search of safety. Shortly thereafter, Georgia regiments from Dole's brigade (Rode's division)—the last line in the Confederate formation—overrode McGowan's entrenched line and flanked the Union line. But Dole's skirmishers could only get within 200 yards of Williams's line before grape and canister fire drove them back.

Sgt. Henry Morhous of the 123rd N.Y. described the action. "At virtually no trajectory, our batteries, at short range, hurled upon them grape and canister. The advancing column was cut and gashed as if pierced, seamed and plowed by lightning strokes. Companies and regiments melted away. . . . [The] batteries . . . left long lines of dead men piled where the grape and canister passed through, but [the lines were filled up] as fast as they were mowed down. The Rebels, half-crazed with whiskey, fought with the desperation of demons. [Their] cavalry drove the infantry on and allowed no man to skulk or retreat."[17]

Confederate Brig. Gen. Samuel McGowan and his successor were wounded while standing on the log works directing their brigade in the third attack, which became a retreat. He reported the Federals fired with fearful accuracy at his South Carolinians, who "stood in full relief upon the crest of the hill." The commander of the 13th S.C. in McGowan's brigade wrote that his regiment was "under a galling fire of shell, grape, canister and spherical case." One captain and seven lieutenants in the 14th S.C. were wounded. In vain, J. E. B. Stuart himself seized a brigade battle flag from the color bearer, waved it over his head, and rode forward shouting for the men to follow; he persevered even after his horse was killed under him.

On the Union side south of the Orange Plank Road, Ruger's brigade of Slocum's 12th Corps bore the brunt of McGowan's assault. By the end of the third Rebel attack, every one of Slocum's men had exhausted his sixty cartridges and even more that were taken from the dead and wounded. Slocum dispatched staffer after staffer to Hooker, pleading for resupply. Hooker replied, "I can't make men or ammunition for General Slocum." General Williams got the same answer. He was told he "must furnish [his] own ammunition, which, of course, was not possible through that volcano of flame and roar with a mule pack train."

Prior to the battle, Hooker had ordered forty guns and their horses sent to the rear. They had rumbled past the 12th Corps gunners at dawn "rocking and reeling, further and further away from the impending battle." Hooker had not arranged to bring up ammunition by mule train for the infantry or artillery, nor to use as replacements any of the more than 1,600 reserve artillerymen who were kept in the rear during the battle. He also kept three of his six infantry corps in reserve to cover his line of retreat. Hence, nearly half of his entire army was never engaged.[18]

At about 9 A.M., after a nearly exhausted supply of artillery ammunition and guns that were too hot to work forced a short lull in the battle, the enemy made its fourth advance, using a fresh brigade of Rodes's men. Rodes led them over the first breastworks in person, "in closed mass, backed and driven by their cavalry." By then, Williams's division had been on the battle line in the thick of it for more than three hours. His men had emptied their cartridge boxes, and were physically exhausted and weak from hunger, many not having eaten for twenty-four hours. To hold their position, they lay on the ground as the Rebels climbed over the breastworks ready to club the defiant Yanks. Only then did they jump up, fire a round, and use their bayonets. By this time, Slocum had moved corps headquarters back toward the Chancellor House.[19]

Shortly after this Confederate advance began, Lieutenant Crosby, Dan's battery commander, was killed along with another battery commander. Dan and the other cannoneers in Crosby's command pitted their Napoleons loaded with canister "against masses of infantry coming on with high, shrill Rebel yells—red, blue-crossed battle flags tossing here and there above them." Crosby was shot through the heart, probably by a sharpshooter from the right of the battery. The promising young lawyer lived five minutes, just long enough to whisper to Captain Best, "Tell father I die happy. Lord, forgive my sins." The *New York Times* reported, "The gallant young Crosby died at his guns." Williams regarded him as "a young officer of superior merit and fidelity." Crosby was carried to the rear by his own men. His body was later recovered under truce and sent home for burial.

Unable to bring up its ammunition and lacking reinforcements, Union infantry slowly and sullenly fell back, exposing the artillery to enemy attack on both flanks. Lt. George B. Winslow, commanding Battery D, 1st N.Y. Light Artillery on Crosby's immediate right, typified the plight of Union cannoneers. He ordered his men to load with canister and wait until the Union infantry fell back. When the enemy in their ragtag uniforms came down the hill in solid masses and out of the woods, Winslow said, "I gave the order to fire. In this way they were repeatedly driven back. They were, however rapidly closing around us . . . not more than 25 or 30 yards from my right gun, when I received . . . orders to limber up and retire." A small knot of Rebel riflemen, planting their colors by the side of the road one hundred yards away, fired ragged volleys and picked off Winslow's men and horses. Nevertheless, before he withdrew, he barked the order to load his six Napoleons with canister and fire. At that close range he blew the Rebels off the road. Confederate infantry then charged through the smoke again and took "several stands of colors."[20]

Between 9 and 11 A.M., Union infantry, partially resupplied with ammunition from a pile on the ground near the Chancellor House, continued to fall back, leaving the artillery increasingly exposed. Like the foot soldiers, the artillerymen were almost out of ammunition and could not be resupplied.[21] After Brig. Gen. Hiram Berry was killed, his division north of the Plank Road was the first to fall back. Sprinkled with inexperienced recruits, the 3rd Maryland on the immediate right of the New Yorkers also withdrew, leaving the latter's flank exposed and vulnerable to crossfire. The right wing of the 123rd then swung back, but not until they had driven back three attacks by Lane's North Carolinians. Lane's men then broke through and turned their rifle-muskets on Dimick's battery opposite them on the Plank Road, silencing it and mortally wounding Dimick. Williams's entire division south of the road then began to withdraw for a half mile through an open field, beginning with Ruger's brigade. In their fourth assault, at least three Confederate brigades penetrated Williams's line and reached Best's batteries. The enemy now controlled most of the Fairview Plateau. By then they also had advanced thirty pieces of artillery to within five hundred to six hundred yards of the Chancellor House. One of their shells had blown Slocum's headquarters to smithereens, and another had almost killed Williams's horse.

Lt. Robert Cruikshank of the 123rd N.Y. wrote his wife that as they pulled back, the enemy yelled like demons and fired at their backs. Dr. Connolly, the regimental surgeon, stayed on the field under a shade tree behind the center of the regiment, caring for the wounded until cross fire drove the regiment back through an open field, completely unsupported. It was the hottest time of the fight for the regiment. Cruikshank counted ten wounded, some mortally, that Connolly attended before the regiment retired. "Every piece of artillery behind us was worked as rapidly as possible and their shells seemed to graze our heads . . . as the enemy were but a few feet in front of us," Cruikshank wrote. "We fought the enemy until we got back to the creek then broke ranks and scattered as we went back up the hill [three-fourths of a mile] to the Chancellorsville House. While . . . going back the enemy opened on us with shell and solid shot. . . . The enemy [troops] came as far as the creek and as soon as we were out of the way our artillery opened on them with canister. . . . They did not make another charge."

According to Lt. Col. James Rogers, the enemy "got possession of one of our batteries stationed at a little distance to our left, and turned its fire on us." The 123rd lost nearly as many of their 135 dead and wounded while retreating as they had at the breastworks. After ordering his regiment to fall back, Colonel McDougall wrote, one solid shot from an enemy cannon "took a leg from one man, 2 legs from another, and a head from another man."

When Pvt. Albert W. Doane's leg was shot off, he shouted, "Boys the devils have hit me; but give them fits!" When last seen he was winding his gun strap around his leg stump and twisting it with his bayonet to stop the bleeding, to no avail. He died at Chancellorsville.

Pvt. James Sherman of Co. C received a slight wound. He felt his head and yelled, "Boys there goes a shingle off my roof." He kept on loading and firing until a second bullet grazed his skull. This time he yelled, "Hello, I'm d——ed if there ain't another shingle gone." Sgt. Henry Sartwell of the 123rd, severely wounded in the left arm, was sent a half mile to the rear, but returned to continue fighting until exhausted from the loss of blood. His bravery earned him the Medal of Honor.

The regiment temporarily lost its state flag, but fought some twenty minutes after the regiments on its flanks had withdrawn. The flag was later recovered by the 7th N.J. regiment.

As a result of the Confederate breakthrough, sharpshooting skirmishers on both sides of them cut down Union artillerymen and horses from one hundred yards or less. The cannoneers rammed charges down the barrels and fired canister and percussion rounds at them at point-blank range.[22] Lieutenant Cruikshank saw a shell strike a caisson, exploding it and killing several men. It stripped the clothes off another, blinded both his eyes, and severely burned him. The injured man cried pitifully for someone to kill him. As Corporal Fisher retreated, a shell "struck a little ahead of [him] and killed four men and wounded a number more. [He] could see men with arms, legs, and heads shot off." W. H. Armstrong, an officer on General Slocum's staff, wrote that two of his companions were struck by a shell, "cutting one of them in two and carrying away the head of the other." Another had his feet cut off just before his comrade reached him and "was struck again with a cannon ball" as his comrade was carrying him off the field. General Williams also recorded, "the getting away was worse than the staying. . . . Our line of retreat was over the ravine, up an exposed slope, and then for three-quarters of a mile over an open plain swept by artillery and infantry. . . . Many a poor fellow lost his life or limb in this fearful transit." Shot and shell plowed and replowed the ground while other shells burst overhead. Knapsacks and implements of war were scattered as if by a tornado. Nevertheless, the Rebel attack was driven back temporarily, accompanied by Federal cheers.[23]

Upon Lieutenant Crosby's death, Lt. John G. Floyd took command of a four-gun section of the battery. Lt. Edward D. Muhlenberg, with a three-gun section, was detached to support the six-foot-five-inch Brig. Gen. John W. Geary and his 12th Corps division. Dan and his Napoleon remained with Floyd. The brigade's gunners stood stoutly to their work, depressed their remaining guns, and continued to vomit canister at point-blank range, blowing back the enemy one hundred yards away.

They sponged and loaded with precision. The water in the swab bucket was black as night. Sweat-streaked burnt powder blackened every body. The heat was so intense that many gunners stripped to their waists, sweating like workmen at a furnace. Splinters flew from wheels and axles hit by musket balls, some thudding into horses' bodies. Terrified horses tore at their restraints, maddened by their wounds as their cursing drivers yelled to control them. Shot shrieked overhead and bullets whistled, hissed, and hummed past them, some ricocheting off wheel rims. The guns bellowed at short range until they were out of ammunition, leaving the ground littered with Rebel bodies mangled by canister, as the Confederates sullenly retreated into the nearby woods.[24]

Together with two Union infantry regiments, Best's artillery held off a fifth and final Confederate attack with grape and canister until Williams's division and the rest of Slocum's 12th Corps infantry emptied their cartridge boxes, then withdrew from their log barricade to avoid being flanked. Ramseur's brigade of four North Carolina regiments advanced for the final attack while General Stuart waved his plumed hat and offered "three cheers for Ramseur's brigades." The brigade suffered nearly 800 casualties—over half its strength—including more than 160 killed. Hunt ordered Best to retreat past the Chancellor House and over the hill to the brick hospital near U.S. Ford on the Rappahannock. Best's artillery had guarded the site while part of the army crossed there a week earlier on the way to the battle. Now the Orange Turnpike to U.S. Ford and the River Road were choked with troops, wagons, ambulances, cavalry, skulkers, and droves of cattle.[25] While retreating, Best's men were defended by whatever troops were immediately available, including some from the 123rd. He also was ordered to take charge of all batteries from every corps that massed there. The Twelfth Corps soldiers rallied and formed a new line out of range of Rebel artillery, got a cup of coffee, ate some hardtack, and refilled their cartridge boxes from ammunition carried by a deserted team of pack mules.[26]

Floyd's gunners, including Dan, then helped cover the withdrawal of the troops as well as the other batteries, whose ammunition chests were empty. Floyd positioned his guns halfway between Fairview and the Chancellor House. While limbering their four Napoleons and again dropping trail, Dan and the other gunners in Floyd's command were under direct fire from three enemy batteries at a one-mile range. Best's remaining twenty-four guns, soon reduced to eighteen, next took up a position across the road from the Chancellor House. With no earthworks for protection, they suffered severely. One battery, the 5th Maine (Leppien's), suffered 100 percent casualties in officers, men, and horses.

As the men jogged down the road to take position, they sang "I am going home to die no more." Upon arrival at the Chancellor House a 5th Maine gunner offered a prayer for his unit. The battery had to be withdrawn by infantrymen. The historian of Joseph Kershaw's Confederate brigade recorded, "A perfect sea of fire was in our faces from the many cannon parked around the Chancellor House and graping in all directions." Every inch of ground was contested as they got within fifty yards of the Union artillery.[27] Earlier, Hooker had been rendered temporarily senseless when an enemy shell struck a pillar of the Chancellor House porch as he leaned against it. Now his former headquarters was in flames.

By that time, Lieutenant Floyd had nine pieces from three batteries still operational under his command. He did not withdraw them until 11 A.M., when the enemy reached the Chancellor House. He had fired 1,380 rounds and had only three shells left. As a headquarters guard for Hooker at the Chancellor House, Will Ross was undoubtedly as preoccupied as his cannoneer brother, Dan. They were only a short distance apart but obviously too busy to attempt to find each other, even if they had known how close they were.[28] After cresting Fairview—the now Confederate-occupied hill from which Best's artillery had been driven—the enemy had to cross open fields commanded by Floyd's guns.

Dan and the others under Floyd fired into the advancing enemy with murderous results. They were still full of fight, displaying courage, grit, and skill. His voice hoarse, Lieutenant Floyd shouted rapid orders to the cannoneers, "Load—Canister—Double!" and ran from piece, to piece, cheering each crewman while demanding faster action. After a few thumps of the rammer head to drive home the load, the next order came, "Ready! By Piece!—At Will!—Fire!" Stripped to the waist, the men jumped back and forth for more than six hours. They fired, furiously muscled the cannon back into position, swabbed, rammed, primed, sighted, and braced themselves, awaiting the next signal to fire. Their only thought was to hurl as much death and destruction at the enemy as possible.[29] In the final retreat, some guns had to be removed by the infantry, but not a single gun was lost to the enemy. Before they heard the order "Limber to the rear," Dan and the other gunners had done much to cover the retreat of the infantry and other batteries. By noon it was complete. All of Muhlenberg's gunners had been killed or wounded, as were many of his horses. The infantry withdrew all three of his guns. Had Dan's gun stayed with Muhlenberg instead of Floyd, he would have been a casualty.[30]

By the time the 12th Corps artillery withdrew, there were only thirty-three guns in action, twenty-four under Best and nine under Floyd. Seven had been put out of action or had exhausted their ammunition supply. By 11 A.M., the enemy was in full possession of the field and only eighteen guns were left to withdraw. The *Cincinnati Daily Commercial* correspondent wrote that the engagement had lasted six hours and "our artillery literally slaughtered the enemy. Many of our batteries lost heavily but the guns were all saved."[31]

Sixteen men from Battery F—one-seventh of its complement—were killed, wounded, captured, or missing, along with nearly all of their horses. Two of the five missing cannoneers were reported as deserters. About noon the battery withdrew to their final position in the woods to protect U.S. Ford, rejoining the other remaining batteries of Best's artillery brigade. Here they replenished their ammunition. Dan survived without a scratch, after helping his battery fire 525 rounds.

The next day someone showed Sergeant Bull, who was among the 123rd N.Y.'s walking wounded and had been taken prisoner by the Rebels, where the artillery used canister with astonishing rapidity to cover the infantry retreat by holding back the final Confederate assault. Bull wrote, "the dead lay as they had fallen and so thickly upon the ground... that one could [step] from one body to another for the whole length of [the lead Confederate regiment]." By then the wounded had been removed. Some had burned to death elsewhere on the battlefield in fires ignited by bursting shells. Bull also went to the ridge atop Fairview Hill where the forty guns were initially engaged. Behind this position the bodies of the eighty horses killed in harness lay "scattered around the field... all were laying on their backs with feet in the air, their bodies swollen enormously."[32] By then, the skulkers, the bummers, and the stragglers that followed in the wake of every battle had arrived to rob the living and the dead. Soldiers' remains were scattered among cartridge boxes, knapsacks, rifle-muskets, and remnants of uniforms; their bodies had been stripped of clothing and valuables. Bull was later paroled and exchanged, as were all the other captured Union soldiers.

Captain Best, in his after-action report, cited the performance of Battery F. He also wrote that Lieutenant Muhlenberg "behaved with great discretion and gallantry... he well deserves the favorable consideration of the Government." He offered particularly high praise for Lieutenant Crosby. "My pen almost refuses to record his untimely death. Young, ambitious, highly educated, efficient as an artillery officer... [in him] the Service lost an officer of great value, and it seems yet a dream that his gallant heart is hushed forever.... [He] was a young man of fine promise, exceptional in his habits and moral character... and willing to stand by the government in all its measures."[33]

Muhlenberg, Floyd, and Field, two sergeants, and two corporals in the section in which Dan served were commended for bravery and soldierlike conduct. Best was promoted to major. Total casualties for Battery F in the three-day battle were seven killed, thirty wounded, and nine missing, presumably captured.[34]

Dan and his fellow cannoneers had shielded the 123rd N.Y. and a half dozen other frontline infantry regiments in Williams's division and well deserved their "favorable consideration." In the three-day Battle of Chancellorsville, the 123rd N.Y. Regiment suffered 148 casualties, 135 of them on May 3. The brigade logged 500 casualties; and its division logged 1,600, or one man in three. Slocum's 12th Corps incurred 2,800 casualties, one man in five. Williams's division lost almost half its field officers. In this one battle, Williams's division lost as many men as it would in General Sherman's entire four-month Atlanta campaign the following year.

The cannoneers and infantrymen, who had entered this battle with all the ardor and enthusiasm of youth, did not lose a piece of artillery. When it was over, consciously or unconsciously, they had crossed the line between boyhood and manhood. They were no longer rookies—they were now veterans. Sergeant Cook wrote, "Father I am proud to say that I have done something for my country. I never want to go into another battle but if I do with the help of God I shall fight harder than before." Certainly, Dan shared his view.

Captain Gray wrote, "The men did well. We are all proud of the 123rd. Col. McDougall did first rate; we all like him, if possible, better than ever. The men are in good spirits [and] ready to fight again." Corporal Fisher wrote, "We have got a great name, the Rebel prisoners said if the rest had fought like us that there would have been no chance for them to live.[35] Pvt. DeWitt Eldridge (Co. G, 123rd N.Y.), was more concerned about antiwar sentiment at home than the Chancellorsville military setback. He wrote his newspaper, "I earnestly hope there will be none of those copperhead demonstrations in our pretty little village."

Col. Charles F. Morse of the 2nd Mass., whose regiment was in Williams's front line along with the 123rd, wrote, "I don't believe any men ever fought better than our 12th Corps, especially the First Division [General Williams's] . . . they held their ground without any support against the repeated assaults of the enemy."

The enlisted men and their officers had not been beaten at Chancellorsville. Only Hooker had. Together with the losses Williams's division suffered and the impending discharge of his two-year and nine-month troops, Hooker's forces would dwindle to less than half of what they were before the battle. Although the Confederates won the battle, they suffered a heavy blow when Gen. Stonewall Jackson died of pneumonia on May 10, a complication after the gunshot wounds he suffered May 2 forced amputation of his left arm.

4

After Chancellorsville

> I doubt if the history of modern armies can exhibit a parallel instance of such palpable crippling of a great arm of the service in the very presence of a powerful enemy.
>
> —Gen. Henry Hunt, after-action report

Tactical errors led to Hooker's defeat at Chancellorsville. As a result, sixty-three men in the artillery of the 12th Corps were killed, wounded, or captured; ninety-seven horses were killed or wounded; six caissons were lost or blown up, and one was disabled. Infantrymen dragged several caissons off the field. Two of the eight battery commanders were killed. Another was shot in the spine and died a few days later. Yet another was captured. One had his horse shot out from under him and narrowly escaped death. Thirty-two horses were killed in one battery alone, five by a single shell. Confederate sharpshooters gave priority to shooting horses before gunners.

The morning of May 6 was cold, rainy, and foggy as Slocum's 12th Corps, including the artillery, crossed the Rappahannock on two pontoon bridges at U.S. Ford, six miles from where they had fought. They were followed by the rear guard of the retreating Army of the Potomac. The river—muddy, swollen, and angry—had risen nine feet in nine hours because of torrential rains that started the day before. Men placed cedar branches on the pontoon bridges to muffle the sound of their withdrawal. The unbearable stench of dead men and horses followed them as they crossed the river. Chilled to the bone, the dispirited men slipped and sloshed on the rain-slicked road, mud "sticking to each man like his brother." Hooker rode over the bridge looking sad and broken, and immediately retired to his tent.

Bone-tired, cursing redlegs hauled Dan's Battery F equipment by rope cables onto a bluff overlooking the river. Best was in charge of the artillery as it guarded the crossing against attack by firing at the enemy breastworks and artillery positions along the opposite riverbank. By 9 A.M. Hooker's entire army had crossed the river.[1]

Hailstones the size of hen's eggs pummeled the rain-drenched men as they slogged through the mud and waded through waist-deep creeks. After a fatiguing twenty-mile march that ended at sunset, the wet and wretched 12th Corps bivouacked for the night in its old camp at Stafford Court House, where they had begun the campaign. Many had left their knapsacks and tents behind and now had no shelter from the rain. The horrible stench in their campground was no better than that of the Chancellorsville battleground. The winter's accumulation of unburied offal from cattle slaughtered to feed the troops, plus the rotting carcasses of dead horses and mules made the air almost unbearable to breathe.

Despite the outstanding performance of the 12th Corps artillery brigade at Chancellorsville, Hooker's artillery chief, Gen. Henry Hunt, lamented the lack of experienced officers to command the batteries. Their "miserably insufficient staffs," in Hunt's opinion, "crippled the volunteer service." This was an obvious reference to Hooker's recent promotion or reassignment of a number of experienced artillery officers, leaving few to lead artillery corps brigades. When Hooker took command of the Army of the Potomac, he rejected advice to create a strong artillery arm under central control. Instead, he parceled out one battery to every brigade. If the brigade was in reserve, so was the battery. Without central control, it was difficult to mass batteries from different brigades and direct their fire.

When enemy action knocked batteries out of commission, Hunt lacked the authority to replace them with reserve units. The fault lay with Hooker's organizational change in the Army of the Potomac ten weeks before the battle. Hooker had effectively stripped General Hunt of the authority to command troops, post batteries in combat, or otherwise give orders to the artillery without prior approval. Hunt was reduced to a glorified orderly and sent back to manage the reserve artillery at Banks' Ford, far from the front lines where his tactical skills were desperately needed.

The army suffered severely—particularly Slocum's corps—from the absence of central control with a commander having overall authority. The result was confusion, lack of ammunition, and unused battery reserves. One artillerist noted that on the morning of May 3, "no one appeared to know anything and there was a good deal of confusion." Hunt, a West Pointer, had a genius for organization that even the Confederates admired, but Hooker had a deeply rooted dislike for him. Hunt had served in the war with Mexico, distinguishing himself in every battle he fought. He had further proven his abilities in the Civil War to the point that some considered him the best artilleryman in the Civil War, North or South.[2]

Two days after their retreat across the Rappahannock, Slocum reviewed Williams's division, a standard practice upon returning to camp after a battle or long march. He complimented the men for their performance in their first battle. Shortly thereafter, the 123rd was assigned to the 1st Brigade, commanded by Brig. Gen. Joseph F. Knipe, in Williams's division, and would remain in that brigade until the war's end. At the outset of the battle, it had been in Col. Samuel Ross's brigade, which was disbanded after his battlefield wound. Meanwhile, with spring in full bloom, the men were being introduced to a harvest of lice, ticks, chiggers, and fleas.

Hooker's performance at Chancellorsville drew the wrath of many who served under him. After the battle, General Williams wrote his daughter. "We have lost physically and numerically, but still more morally ... by a universal want of confidence in the commanding general ... I am greatly dispirited and almost disposed to resign ... this last [battle] has been the greatest of all bunglings in this war," he wrote. "I am not much of a military genius but if I could have commanded the Army of the Potomac at Chancellorsville I would have wagered my life on being in Richmond in ten days."

Meanwhile, Slocum wrote President Lincoln recommending Williams's promotion from brigadier to major general, describing him as constantly at his post during the campaign. This description fitted Williams in every battle he fought. By then he was the most experienced and one of the best division commanders in the army. Williams graduated in 1831 from Yale and spent the next five years studying law and traveling, spending most of his $75,000 inheritance. By the time of the Civil War, he had served as a judge, bank president, newspaper owner, and postmaster in Detroit and had played a prominent role in the militia activities of the city. He nursed contempt for the merits of a military education, did not sing his own praises, and refused to curry favor from reporters, a commonplace practice of generals. He was regarded as one of the least pretentious officers in the Union army.

Williams had been grumbling that he had been a brigadier longer than many less-experienced West Pointers who were promoted to major general over him. He also had more battle experience than any other division commander and had led his division longer than any other division commander had led one. It was as if he, a brigadier since May 1861, were the forgotten general of the Army of the Potomac.[3]

Slocum, whose temper was notorious when things went wrong, was highly critical of Hooker's timidity. He blamed Hooker's decision to go on the defensive and his failure to actively support the 12th Corps for their heavy losses at Chancellorsville. Slocum tendered his resignation, but Lincoln refused to accept it. When ordered west with his corps in September to reinforce Grant's army, Slocum refused to serve in it under Hooker, writing to Lincoln again with an offer to resign from the army. "The public service cannot be promoted by placing under [Hooker's] command an officer who has so little confidence in his ability as I have," he wrote. Lincoln again refused to accept his resignation, but compromised by transferring Slocum to General Rosecrans. Slocum joined his new command at Nashville and was given Williams's division to guard the Nashville and Chattanooga Railroad prior to the Battle of Missionary Ridge. Later Grant reassigned him to command the District of Vicksburg, and Hooker was transferred to Sherman's army.

Maj. Gen. Darius N. Couch, second in command to Hooker, not only refused to serve under him again, but also actively sought his removal from command. Outraged by Hooker's performance that led to the purposeless slaughter of his troops, Couch wrote, "I doubt if any orders were given by him to commanders... unless perhaps 'to retire when out of ammunition.' None were received by me." In response, Lincoln gave Couch a new command.

Maj. Gen. John Sedgwick, the commander of the 6th Corps, wrote his sister, "You have no doubt seen the disastrous termination of our late move... I will not attempt to say where the fault lay. It will someday be exposed." Maj. Gen. George G. Meade was disgusted with Hooker as well. A reporter for the *New York Tribune* observed privately that Hooker was "the mere wreck of what he was last fall... played out by wine and women."

Many men in the ranks shared the generals' disgust with Hooker. One soldier wrote after the battle, "Hooker's career is well exemplified by that of a rocket.... He went up like one and came down like a stick." First Lt. Haviland Gifford of the 93rd N.Y., Will Ross's regiment, served in Hooker's headquarters guard. He wrote his father, "I am today more and more confirmed in the opinion [that] had this Army been under the command of an officer who would not have been afraid of his own shadow the Army of the Potomac would have gained another victory over the Rebel Army." Col. Charles F. Morse, 2nd Mass., wrote, "I doubt if ever in the history of this war, another chance will be given with such odds in our favor as we had last Sunday [May 3], and that chance has been worse than lost to us." Lt. R. S. Robertson, another officer who served in Hooker's headquarters guard, wrote his father on May 6 "that 'Fighting Joe' has had his own way this time and failed... there is not a man but respects Hooker as a brave man. The difficulty is that they have no confidence in his leadership."[4]

When Lincoln got the news of Hooker's defeat, tears streamed down his cheeks. All he could say was, "My God! My God! What will the country say?" He refused to be comforted, later remarking, "If Hooker had been killed by the shot . . . that [only] stunned him, we should have been successful." The *Cincinnati Daily Enquirer* reported that Hooker "frankly informed the President that he will resign if this step is considered desirable to the Government."

Within an hour of hearing the bitter news on May 7, President Lincoln, General-in-Chief Henry W. "Old Brains" Halleck, and Secretary of War Edwin M. Stanton went to visit Hooker and his corps commanders. They traveled in a special train, consisting of a locomotive and a single car, from Aquia Creek landing. At a conference in Hooker's headquarters tent, the beleaguered general offered to resign, but Lincoln refused. Lincoln told one of Hooker's generals that he was "not disposed to throw away a gun because it missed fire once . . . [instead he] would pick the lock and try again." Lincoln resolved that he would not blame anyone, but his "countenance seemed to bear traces of sore disappointment," according to the *Cincinnati Daily Commercial*.[5] He appeared pleased with the troops' morale and fearful that army morale would suffer if he sacked Hooker.

Nevertheless, Lincoln indicated that the result was more disastrous to the country than any other battle had been. On this occasion, the president must have recalled his conversation with Hooker in early April, when he visited the Army of the Potomac before the Chancellorsville campaign began. He had told Hooker then, "[I]n your next battle, put in all your men." Despite this admonition, 35,000 fresh, mostly veteran troops were never used on May 3, almost one-third of his entire army. They included the entire 1st Corps (Reynolds's), Fifth Corps (Meade's), and part of the 11th Corps (Howard's), plus Averell's cavalry division of 3,500 horse soldiers. Three hours after that day's battle started, Hooker also had 246 unused pieces of artillery, most of them still in reserve at U.S. Ford. Yet no orders were issued to return to Slocum any of the guns ordered to the rear before the battle opened, much less to provide more ammunition. Lincoln was well aware of the severe criticism subordinate officers leveled at Hooker. On May 14, he wrote the beleaguered general, "some of your corps and division commanders are not giving you their entire confidence."

While the 12th Corps was back in its old camp at Stafford Court House, replacement men and horses had to be found for the artillery. Captain Best telegraphed General Hunt that forty horses were needed for Batteries E and F alone, to restore them to full strength of 110 horses each. The cavalry, medical, and quartermaster corps, however, had priority over the artillery for remounts. Hampton's battery was so depleted that it was disbanded, and its men, guns, and remaining horses reassigned to the division's three surviving batteries. Hampton himself had been killed, together with nine men and thirty-two horses. Two of the battery's ammunition chests also had exploded. Seeley's Battery K, 4th United States, lost 45 of their 120 gunners, and fifty-nine horses were killed or disabled.

A week after Chancellorsville, on May 12, Hooker consolidated the artillery that had been attached to divisions into separate, self-sufficient brigades, each attached to an infantry corps. He also restored Hunt to full field command of the artillery, and Hunt, in turn, selected the officers he wanted to command the brigades. These moves would significantly improve fighting efficiency, discipline, and training, beginning with the Battle of Gettysburg.[6]

Dan's artillery brigade drilled daily to train new horses and familiarize new replacement volunteers with their duties. Battery drilling was done largely with bugle calls, which the new men also had to learn. The drill was conducted in strict accordance with the manual Hunt wrote—a bible for artillerymen. Training, exercising, and teaching correct care of horses for the volunteer batteries was a major challenge.[7] As an excellent horseman, Dan was invaluable in tending to sick and wounded horses and training replacements. Proper care of artillery horses was essential. If weakened by disease, neglect, exhaustion, or lack of forage and water, they would not survive long, much less be capable of moving the guns. At every halt they had to be fed, with grain or grass cut from a farmer's field if necessary. The daily amount of forage and water consumed by the battery horses was enormous. Aside from those killed in battle, many others died of disease or exhaustion, as well as from exposure, thirst, and starvation. Demand for replacements was constant.[8]

Daily during training, the bugler sounded "stable call" at 6:15 A.M., right after reveille, and "water call" and "feed call" after breakfast. The men put leather buckets with food and water over the horses' heads, then harnessed up their horses when "Boots and Saddles" was sounded at 8 A.M. Noon was dinnertime for the men and feed time for the horses. Following afternoon drill, inspection of horses took place at 3:45 P.M., water call was at 4:00, and feed call at 4:15 P.M. When in camp and "stable call" was sounded, the horses were walked to cool them down, curried, and watered again, then tethered for the night to a long picket rope stretched between two trees. Then their canvas nosebags were taken to the grain pile, filled with oats or corn, and strapped on.

In the morning and after lunch when the bugle call sounded for drill, cannoneers leapt on their gun carriages. Batteries maneuvered at a gallop over rough, worn-out tobacco fields, with men and powerful horses straining every muscle, carriage wheels rumbling, drivers shouting, and bugles blaring commands. Cannoneers found it extremely difficult to stay in their seats as limber and caisson wheels struck every stone and stump in their path. Each maneuver was conducted in response to a different bugle call, some of which even the horses learned. If a horse fell, crippling itself, a cannoneer jumped down, cut the traces, and climbed aboard again while the gun was driven around or over the animal. If a gun carriage, limber, or caisson capsized, spilling the men who were riding on it, it was difficult to right it and keep the harnesses from entangling. If a wheel broke, they had to learn how to dismount the gun, sling it under the limber chest, and mount a spare wheel to replace the broken one. They also learned how to exchange a full limber chest for an empty one and memorized every piece of harness. Ironically, they seldom, if ever, practiced unlimbering a gun for target practice, or estimating distances for accurate firing. For repairs, a traveling forge and a wagon carrying spare parts accompanied each battery.

They also learned tactical safety considerations. To the extent permitted by the terrain, they were told to separate each gun in the battery, as well as the limbers, caissons, and horses to prevent the enemy from damaging or destroying more than one gun at a time. In seeking shelter, therefore, they were taught to take advantage of woodlots, shallow ravines, and reverse slopes, while always maintaining a clear field of fire. Finally, learning to position the battery so as to have access to an escape route was vital in case retreat became necessary. In actual battle, if they silenced an enemy gun and the occasion permitted, they would toss their caps in the air, shake hands, and shout.

Dan was probably assigned to a pair of horses as their driver. If so, he rode on the left horse while holding the rein of the off horse. A leg guard—an iron plate encased in leather—would be strapped to his right leg to prevent the limber pole from injuring him.

The weather was mostly dry and the dust stifling, which was preferable to heavy rain, during which gun carriages, limbers, and caissons could sink into mud above their axles. Then men would have to push the wheels while extra horses pulled on traces. Muhlenberg drilled Battery F until June 1, when General Hunt promoted him to 12th Corps artillery brigade commander. He was replaced by Lt. Sylvanus T. Rugg, who had served in the Regular Army since 1857 as an enlisted man until his promotion to lieutenant in 1862. Captain Best was promoted to Slocum's assistant inspector general on May 16.

The effectiveness of a battery depended on three things: (1) the skill and courage of the gunners; (2) the alertness, efficiency, and experience of the officers; and (3) the health and strength of the horses. Battery F was a far better battery after the Battle of Chancellorsville than it was the day that battle began.[9]

The outcome of the Battle of Chancellorsville had distinctly different impacts on the North and South. The morale of the Army of the Potomac, as measured by increased desertions and inability to recruit, suffered as severely as did Hooker's reputation. On May 21, The *Washington County People's Journal* published a letter by a soldier in the 123rd who called himself "Eyeglass." He wrote "[T]ruth compels me to say that the effects of the failure [Chancellorsville] has been depressing in the extreme." Meanwhile, the financial condition of the Confederacy was desperate. None of the border states had been won over by the South, denying it money, personnel, and other much-needed resources. The Confederacy needed a dramatic victory to gain support from Europe, particularly England and France. Lee faced a scarcity of food, clothing, transportation equipment, and supplies, including ammunition and forage for his horses. He now had to comb the area for rations, paying for them with Confederate dollars. His much smaller army had paid a hideous price at Chancellorsville, but morale, confidence, and discipline were high. Nonetheless, desertions were mounting as men went home for spring plowing.

Lee and his men were feeling invincible. Their victory at Chancellorsville had bred overconfidence and a special contempt for the enemy. The reality, however, was that his soldiers, many shoeless and vermin-ridden, had to comb the woods for sassafras buds and wild onions to prevent scurvy. Lee wrote to the Confederate secretary of war that his army was failing in health because of insufficient rations. Their daily ration consisted of eighteen ounces of flour and four ounces of poor bacon, occasionally supplemented by a few ounces of rice, molasses, or sugar. Horses died for lack of forage. They had cropped the grass and browsed the lower tree branches for miles around their winter camp. Good cavalry horses were in short supply. The Old Dominion's governments, schools, and churches no longer functioned. The Virginia countryside was devastated—houses had been deserted, fences and buildings leveled, and crops and cattle wiped out.[10]

Lee's army was meagerly fed, largely from the unravaged fields of Alabama and Georgia. He wrote later, "The question of food for [my] army gives me more trouble and uneasiness than everything else combined." His commissary general in Richmond said, "If General Lee wants rations, let him seek them in Pennsylvania." Pennsylvania had fields of ripening grain and fruit, fat cattle, and full granaries, all untouched by war. So did Maryland. And when Lee arrived on his march to Gettysburg, he ordered confiscated goods, including replacement horses that he sorely needed, to be paid for at market prices but with Confederate dollars. Soon sorely needed livestock and other food supplies were en route south in long wagon trains for his later use in Virginia. Lee's soldiers had paid as much attention to his order not to plunder as they would to a screech owl.

Lee was depressed for other reasons. He had lost Stonewall Jackson, his "great right arm." He had not gained any ground, nor had he driven the enemy out of Virginia. And his army had suffered a 22 percent loss, in contrast to 13 percent for Hooker. While Lee's Chancellorsville victory was a military masterpiece, it resulted in nothing more than a continuation of the war's stalemate in Virginia. In a candid moment, Lee told an aide of President Davis, "our loss was severe [and] we had not gained an inch of ground and the enemy could not be pursued." Both armies remained in defensive positions facing each other across the Rappahannock.

On economic grounds, Southern public opinion after both Fredericksburg and Chancellorsville demanded an invasion of the North. Taking Lee's army to the Keystone State would also give war-torn northern Virginia time to recuperate by removing both armies. Lee was convinced he had to free Virginia from the enemy's presence. Further, he mistakenly believed that invading the North might seriously hurt its morale and stimulate more resistance to the draft, thereby increasing Northern sentiment to accept a dictated peace that included Southern independence by strengthening the North's Peace Party. It also would divert troops away from Grant's siege of Vicksburg and elsewhere in order to defend Washington, Philadelphia, and Baltimore, thus enhancing prospects for British and French support of the Confederacy. Lee thought his army could crush the Yankees even in their own backyard. The South's poor intelligence, however, had significantly overrated the political strength of copperheads (peace Democrats, so called because of their poisonous views) within the North with respect to encouraging peace negotiations. The *New York Times* accurately predicted that Lee's invasion would, instead, "harmonize and consolidate the Northern people as nothing else could have done."

A large number of Union enlistments expired beginning in May. By the end of June, fifty-eight regiments would leave the Army of the

Potomac, reducing its strength to about 90,000 men. Lee hoped to discourage new recruits from replacing them. Additionally, drawing the Union Army away from Washington would open the way for its capture, particularly if a major Confederate victory in Pennsylvania forced evacuation of the capital. Washington was a huge training camp for recruits and a vital complex of supply depots. Lee's plan was to achieve this victory by forcing the Union army to attack him in a strong position of his choosing. A deep thrust into Pennsylvania also could sever telegraph, rail, and canal communications and interrupt transportation, while destroying heavy industry and coal mines. Further, if Lee could drive the Federals across the Susquehanna River he could control Maryland and possibly West Virginia. He even hoped this move would bring Maryland into the Confederacy. Finally, Lee also wanted to avoid being attacked again in the vicinity of Fredericksburg where, had he remained, the Union army could mobilize another sizeable force and initiate another campaign to capture Richmond, or at least to put it under siege and cut its supply lines. By moving into Pennsylvania, reinforced by General Longstreet's corps, Lee, in fact, diverted attention from Richmond to Washington and kept the main body of the Union Army close to the Union capital.[11]

Confederate President Jefferson Davis fully supported Lee's plan. On June 10, five weeks after the Chancellorsville battle, Lee began his great raid from Culpeper with 76,000 men, across the Blue Ridge, through the Shenandoah Valley toward Pennsylvania. That day he wrote Davis, "We should not . . . conceal from ourselves that our resources in men are constantly diminishing and the disproportion in this respect between us and our enemies . . . is steadily augmenting." He had unsuccessfully pleaded for substantial reinforcements from troops guarding Richmond and stationed elsewhere in the South.

Panic struck the North on the assumption that Lee was headed for the nation's capital. Pennsylvania and New York called out their state militias. Brig. Gen. Joseph Knipe, commander of the 1st Brigade to which the 123rd was assigned, was transferred to lead a Pennsylvania militia brigade and help bolster citizen morale in the Keystone State. Knipe had started out life as a Philadelphia shoemaker, fought in the Mexican War, been wounded in 1862, then been commissioned a brigadier general later that year. In December 1864, at the Battle of Nashville, he was credited with capturing 6,000 Rebels and eight regimental battle flags. Colonel McDougall took his place, commanding a brigade for his first and only time, until late July when Knipe returned.

Baltimore declared martial law. Lincoln issued a call for 100,000 emergency militia volunteers for six months from Pennsylvania, Maryland,

West Virginia, and Ohio. To checkmate Lee, Hooker reluctantly—only after Lincoln insisted—moved his 105,000-man Army of the Potomac northward to keep it between Lee's 76,000 men and Washington, DC, and asked the president to send him more troops. Hooker's army stretched more than forty-eight miles on this march. Brig. Gen. Marsena Patrick, in command of Hooker's Provost Guard, wrote, "He acts like a man without a plan, and is entirely at a loss what to do.... He knows that Lee is his master and is afraid to meet him in fair battle." When Brigadier General Haupt asked him what he planned to do on the march, Hooker replied that he did not know or care. He would simply do what he was told, and if disaster resulted, it would be someone else's fault, not his.

Williams's division began to move during the night of June 11, leaving Stafford Court House on the Dumfries Road after they destroyed their surplus stores. The 123rd was the lead regiment of its brigade and left camp at 5:30 A.M. the next morning, not knowing where they were going. They had been supplied with sixty rounds of ammunition and eight days' rations and, in case of attack, marched with loaded arms for the entire distance. Before they left, Dan and the other cannoneers in his artillery brigade strapped sacks of grain for the horses on the ammunition chests, greased the axles, and selected the best spare horses. Two days after June 11, the red legs followed the infantry, who had left at sunrise from Aquia Creek landing and set up camps around Leesburg on the Seventeenth.

On June 15, near Fairfax Court House, the troops were resting as General Slocum rode by. A line officer shouted for the men to clear the way. Slocum said, "Never mind boys, don't get up; my horse is not as tired as you are." It was one of the hottest days of the march, and the men were heavily laden with equipment. On June 17, after leaving Fairfax Court House at daybreak, the troops foraged extensively for fowl, milk, butter, eggs, onions, flour, meat, and honey. Rumors of the enemy's whereabouts were rife, and cavalry clashes were frequent. The men endured clouds of dust and sweltering heat, resulting in sunstroke for some and total exhaustion, fainting, and even death for others. The dust added grit to their rations and muddied the streams where they filled canteens. Some dropped out long enough to soak blistered, swollen, and aching feet in streams. Stragglers abandoned their knapsacks along the road. They were soaked in dusty perspiration. Their only relief from the heat and dust came in the form of four rainstorms, with sleet and hailstones as big as walnuts. The roads were narrow, deeply rutted, and full of chuckholes. One swollen stream they crossed after a rainstorm was so deep it almost covered the limber and caisson boxes as well as the artillery horses that pulled them.

On June 23, they reached Leesburg, which, according to Cpl. John Gourlie, was "a small village with decayed houses [in which] every inhabitant is Rebel to the heart." On June 25, it suddenly became clear to Hooker from signal stations, as well as from prisoners taken, that Lee was concentrating his army around Chambersburg, and probably headed for the Pennsylvania capital, Harrisburg, not Washington, DC.

On June 26, Muhlenberg was detached and ordered to Harrisburg to help build a system of fortifications around that panic-stricken city. The capitol building was denuded. Everything, from books in its library to portraits of governors, was readied for shipment in freight cars. Muhlenberg was ordered to correct shortages in ammunition and augment artillery emplacements in and near its Fort Washington, which protected Pennsylvania's capital. He also cleared trees and shrubs so the artillery would have a clear line of fire and extended trenches, since one of Lee's columns appeared to be approaching the capital. Prior to then, Muhlenberg's artillery brigade, including Daniel's battery, had crossed the Potomac at Edwards Ferry and encamped near Point of Rocks, Maryland. The 12th Corps had guarded the pontoon bridge crossing until Hooker's entire army was over. In contrast to Virginia, according to Lieutenant Robertson of the 93rd N.Y., the Maryland countryside was magnificent, and the farms were in splendid condition. The majority of residents were Unionists who were more than willing to provide food and drink to the troops.[12]

On June 27, while halted for lunch, the New Yorkers loudly cheered General Hooker as he rode by on his black charger. It was a rare demonstration of support after his Chancellorsville debacle. He had been refused permission to assign the 10,000-man Harpers Ferry garrison, temporarily reinforced by the 12th Corps, to attack Lee's rear. His intention was to cut Lee's supply line and sever his communications by destroying Potomac River bridges. That night from his Frederick, Maryland, headquarters, Hooker telegraphed Lincoln yet again, asking to be relieved of command. He disagreed with Lincoln, Stanton, and Halleck on the Army of the Potomac's mission, quibbled over orders, and questioned petty matters of procedure. Hooker and Halleck had a long-standing, instinctive dislike for each other. To compound matters, Hooker's own officers were undermining him. Lincoln, and undoubtedly others, feared that Hooker would be "outgeneraled" by Lee again as he had been at Chancellorsville.

Upon receiving Hooker's request, Lincoln and Secretary of War Stanton held an emergency meeting. They decided to replace him the next day with Maj. Gen. George G. Meade, a West Pointer who had served in the war with Mexico. Meade was one of Hooker's severest critics after Chancellorsville, although not publicly so. He was a Pennsylvanian, so Lincoln thought he would "fight well on his own dung hill."[13] At the time, he was in command of the army's 5th Corps. The change in command buoyed spirits in Williams's division. Meade was regarded as "a bear to his subordinates," but was their choice as commander. Other officers in the Army of the Potomac generally respected Meade for both his abilities as a soldier and his tendency to remain aloof from political maneuvering. He had shown great ability at Chancellorsville. His military specialty was engineering, which he used to help build Washington's defenses and would use superbly in laying out Gettysburg's defense. Even Confederate President Jefferson Davis thought Meade was "the most skillful general in the Federal army."

Meade was tall, thin, nearsighted, and utterly lacking in charisma, but courageous and cool under fire. He had been wounded twice and had a horse wounded under him. Hunt was pleased with Meade's appointment, as was Slocum, who outranked him. Slocum believed Meade was the logical choice to succeed Hooker. Meade had fought in every major eastern battle for the year prior to his appointment, and Slocum knew he was a skilled military engineer. Meade was quiet, practical, and businesslike, but he was an unknown quantity to the men in the Army of the Potomac except to those in his own corps. He was devoted to duty and hard work, and fully prepared to assume responsibility. Men received the news quietly and without demonstration. But they were ready to place more confidence in him than in Hooker. Williams's division had reached Frederick when the change of command took place.

General Lee often derisively referred to Hooker as "Mr. F. J. Hooker." In contrast, when Lee was told that Meade had succeeded Hooker, he told his staff, "General Meade will commit no blunder on my front, and if I make one he will make haste to take advantage of it." Lee, in fact, did commit a major blunder at Gettysburg, and, as he prophesied, Meade took full advantage of it.

As events dictated, Meade had only seventy-two hours to take up the slack in Hooker's reins and reflect on alternative strategies to find and confront Lee's army. He did not even know where all of his own units were, much less those of the Confederates. A reporter at the transfer of command ceremony noted that Meade stood "with bowed head and downcast eyes, his slouched hat drawn down, shading his features." Hooker praised Meade, shook his hand, and "with tears coursing down his cheeks, bade ... farewell." He told Meade he was glad to be rid of the responsibility. He said he had "had enough" and proceeded to brief him in his tent. Will, who was still serving in the headquarters guard, must have witnessed this scene.

On June 29, General Williams, Dan's division commander, recorded his thoughts on the change of command. "I had no confidence in Hooker after Chancellorsville.... I cannot conceive of greater imbecility and weakness than characterized that campaign from the moment Hooker reached Chancellorsville and took command," he wrote. "Still I don't despair. On the contrary [with Gen. Meade] in command I have renewed confidence.... But we run a fearful risk.... If we are badly defeated the Capital is gone and all our principal cities and our national honor.... I am full of faith and yet fearfully anxious. There must be a decisive battle, I think soon."[14]

Williams got his decisive battle, but not until his troops completed "a hard march.... it has been 20 days since we started it," as Pvt. Levi Eaton of the 123rd recounted in a letter to his wife shortly after the Battle of Gettysburg. During most of the march from Frederick, Maryland, to Pennsylvania, Dan and the other cannoneers in the artillery, and the wagon trains, took the roads, while the infantry marched through the fields on either side. As they moved into Littletown, Pennsylvania, civilians along the route sang and cheered, and fed them with pie, bread, and cakes. Fields of ripening wheat and corn and luxuriant meadows, orchards, and gardens lined their way. It was in stark contrast to the utter destruction and wasteland of Virginia. Their morale rose significantly. Fighting on their own soil increased their determination, as was the case with Rebel soldiers while fighting in Virginia.[15]

5

Gettysburg
July 1–3, 1863

> We had the advantage of excellent positions for artillery at good range ... the first half hour must have told them [it] was useless.
>
> —General Alpheus S. Williams

Unlike Hooker at Chancellorsville, Meade did not choose his battleground at Gettysburg. Nonetheless, when Brig. Gen. John Buford's cavalry division arrived there on June 30, he noted the defensible ridges and hills flanking the strategic crossroads. With his engineering skills, Meade used the terrain to full military advantage in order to fight defensively from this high ground. On the evening of June's last day, Dan and the other 12th Corps redlegs drew three days' rations at Littletown in preparation for battle. As they passed through, Littletown residents handed them food and water, and ladies waved handkerchiefs as they sang patriotic songs. Some were smiling, while others were in tears. The soldiers had marched thirty miles that day, starting at 5 A.M. with barely time enough for a cup of coffee. On orders from General Slocum, they camped that night about a mile outside of town.

Meanwhile, Lee's lead division arrived the next morning, July 1, and a two-hour fight ensued while couriers from both armies summoned reinforcements. By early that afternoon, a desperate battle was underway west and north of Gettysburg. Neither Lee nor Meade was present, nor had they intended to fight there. Lee arrived on the battlefield first and, despite his initial strategy to fight defensively from a strong position of his own choice, he approved the continuation of the Confederate attack. Waves of Confederates routed Union soldiers from their positions, sending them scampering through the streets, only to rally on Cemetery Hill south of the borough. Union artillery unlimbered on the hill, prompting the Confederate commanders to delay their attack. By dusk, the Union defense line was extended east to take in Culp's Hill, three-fourths of a mile from Gettysburg.

The 12th Corps infantry and artillery—including Daniel's Battery F and his old regiment, the 123rd N.Y.—arrived in the area at sundown on July 1. With Williams's division in the lead, they had marched since daylight, with an hour's break for lunch. General Williams was assigned temporary command of Slocum's 12th Corps. At about 5 P.M., Williams was told to take position on the Baltimore Pike—the highway to Washington, DC—near Culp's Hill. He was to defend the right flank of Meade's Army of the Potomac, the barb of Meade's fishhook-shaped line.[1] Williams had brought his division into position that afternoon on a five-hour march on a narrow, muddy road into dense woods. During the last two hours, the men moved at quick step without a halt, the sound of cannonading and musketry audible ahead. Sgt. L. R. Coy recalled the scene. "While we were on this step an aide-de-camp rode by saying, 'Boys, hurry up, you are all needed in front,' " he wrote. "All was wildest excitement [when] the welcome order came: 'Halt.' In a minute every man was flat on the ground resting while perspiration ran from our bodies in streams."

Williams's men were in line of battle within a mile of Gettysburg, when a Union battery to their front drove the enemy back. They then marched back and halted about 7 P.M. at Two Taverns, where Dan and the other redlegs in Battery F were positioned on high ground south of Rock Creek near the Baltimore Pike. Dan and the artillery brigade encamped there without supper. By then it was dark, and the night was warm and clear. Since he knew nothing of the topography, Williams put out pickets in all directions, then pitched his tent under a big oak tree. After determining where Geary's division was located, he rolled himself up in an India-rubber sheet and "slept most splendidly until daylight."[2] During the day, a Confederate prisoner brought into 12th Corps headquarters was asked, "What is Lee's objective?" He replied that it was the Army of the Potomac, adding, "He has whipped it many times and can do it now; then the way will be clear to Baltimore, Philadelphia, Washington, and on."[3]

On the battle's second day, July 2, following a breakfast of crackers and coffee at daybreak, the 12th Corps occupied the lower slope of Culp's Hill. They constructed substantial, chest-high log breastworks and entrenchments there, with the right end near Spangler's Spring on Rock Creek. The 4,000-foot line ran through a heavy growth of timber. Sgt.

Henry C. Morhous noted, "The boys, remembering Chancellorsville, were determined to have good works this time."[4] Several 12th Corps batteries, including Dan's, saw important action from Culp's Hill about 4:15 P.M. For an hour and a half, with enfilading fire, they engaged twenty-year-old Confederate Maj. J. W. Latimer's fourteen-gun battery atop Benner's Hill, about 800 yards away in a wheat field. By shortly after 5:30 P.M., they had silenced the Rebels. Benner's Hill was high, bare, and small, affording little shelter for horses, limbers, or caissons after the guns were crowded into the cramped open space. The well-directed fire of Williams's gunners and the 11th Corps artillery blew up three of Latimer's batteries and two caissons, caused severe casualties, and killed twenty-eight horses. With ammunition short and so many men injured, Latimer was forced to withdraw all but four guns. The "boy major" was mortally wounded as he remained with them.[5] Rebel shells had exploded near the Union artillery but nobody was hurt. Dan and the others in Rugg's battery were proud of their work on the second day. So was Hunt. That night Rugg's and Kinzie's batteries were moved to the artillery park on the Spangler farm, at the base of Powers Hill, and kept in reserve until needed.

When he arrived July 1, Lee had chosen the offensive, just as he had at Chancellorsville. But he did not get his troops into position until 4 P.M. on the second day, when some of the war's bloodiest fighting occurred. The Confederates temporarily penetrated the Union battle line in two places, but Meade's reinforcements arrived in time to plug the holes. Confederate artillery was unable to suppress Union artillery and could not advance to close positions in support of its infantry. Darkness ended the fighting on July 2. Unlike Confederate attacks at Chancellorsville, those at Gettysburg on the second day were disjointed, largely because of the late arrival of some of Lee's troops. Nor did Lee exercise the control he displayed at Chancellorsville. His orders resulted in poor coordination of his troops' movements.[6] In sharp contrast to Hooker's poor performance at Chancellorsville, Meade was quick and decisive at Gettysburg, moving troops to the right spot at the right time.

Culp's Hill was virtually abandoned between 6 and 7 P.M., when Meade's staff officers ordered all of the 12th Corps (except Brig. Gen. George S. Greene's brigade) to move left in support of the 3rd Corps. With Williams leading, Brig. Gen. Thomas Ruger's division marched four miles on the Baltimore Pike, all on the run with rifle-muskets at "right shoulder shift," according to Sergeant Coy. By the time they were ordered to halt at the bottom of Little Round Top, they fell to the ground exhausted. When they were ordered to the top, they discovered that the enemy had given way and they were not needed.[7] It was 10

P.M. when they returned to Culp's Hill under a full moon. They were within about 500 yards of it when they learned "the astounding intelligence" that their trenches at the base of the hill were now occupied by the enemy, who had driven a wedge up the slope almost to Abraham Spangler's farmhouse. The Confederates had halted within 200 yards of the Baltimore Pike, their shadowy figures visible as they moved about in the darkness. Ruger's division took up a position on the west side of the Baltimore Pike north of Powers Hill.

Meade ordered Williams to reoccupy Culp's Hill at dawn the next morning, at the urging of most of his top subordinates, including Slocum and Williams, who recommended that the rest of the army "stay and fight it out." Dan and the other artillerymen spent the night of July 2 replenishing ammunition chests, repairing damage, feeding horses, replacing wounded ones, and repositioning the batteries. Hunt himself was at the artillery reserve headquarters overseeing the issuance of projectiles to batteries whose supplies had run short, repairing damaged equipment, reorganizing decimated batteries, and replacing guns unfit for service.[8] Enemy-held trenches were in the woods only 500 to 800 yards away—"long-taw" range in cannoneer's lingo—so the work had to be done quietly. Nevertheless, the Confederates could hear Union soldiers moving about, chopping trees, and building breastworks; army wagons in motion on Baltimore Pike bringing up ammunition and supplies; and cannon rumbling as they were being positioned behind Union lines. Both the Confederate Maj. Gen. Edward "Allegheny" Johnson and Brig. Gen. George H. Steuart, however, mistakenly thought the summit of Culp's Hill was being evacuated and artillery moved elsewhere. They decided to use as many men as possible to attack at dawn. Few subordinates, especially those who had tried to take it earlier, thought it possible, even suicidal.

On the third day, as at Chancellorsville, 12th Corps infantry and artillery played a decisive role in the final stage of the battle.[9] By seniority, General Slocum held overall command of the Union right, while General Williams's 12th Corps was to make the assault on Culp's Hill. Meade regarded Slocum as "an officer of honor, dignity of character, and firmness of purpose," a trusted lieutenant. Slocum's men had only one day's supply of rations remaining. Both he and Meade knew the enemy would be hard to dislodge, because approaches were over open, marshy ground around Spangler's Spring, at the southern base of the hill. However, Slocum had five excellent, widely separated artillery positions at effective ranges to protect the advancing Union troops, including the 123rd N.Y., 495 strong. Williams's command had about 11,200 men in twenty-eight regiments from seven brigades in the Culp's Hill assault.

Meanwhile, Lee also decided on a dawn attack against Culp's Hill—vital to both armies—by about 10,500 men, also in seven brigades. This proved to be a grievous error on Lee's part. It was a cardinal rule that attacking forces needed to have at least double the number of troops against well-entrenched forces.[10]

Between midnight and dawn, Slocum's infantry regiments quietly moved into jump-off positions. Williams's 12th Corps was to be in the vanguard. Now the skirmish lines were so close together—not more than fifty yards apart—that during the night both Union and Confederate scouting parties were filling their canteens from the stream fed by Spangler's Spring.[11] After skirmishing for the division from 10 P.M. until after midnight under a brilliant moon, the 123rd—exhausted, hungry, and sleepy—spent the remainder of the night in a muddy cornfield over the crest of Culp's Hill.

Shortly after midnight, with only two hours of sleep, the 123rd heard the order "Fall in," as Rebel skirmishers opened fire on the entire regiment from the woods. In the confusion of the moment, Pvt. N. A. Taylor was killed by rifle fire from the 3rd Md. Regiment and/or the 145th N.Y. of his own division, as he helped return skirmish fire. But most men of the 12th Corps were bivouacked on protected ground in the open fields on both sides of the Baltimore Pike and slept on their arms until dawn, not far from the dead and dying of the previous day.[12]

The Confederates began their advance in the moonlight about 1:30 A.M. and moved into position at 4:00. If successful, Lee would draw Union forces away from Cemetery Hill and therefore be able to dominate it. He also would gain access to Meade's rear, including the parks for his supply and ammunition trains, artillery reserves, and his main line of communication along the Baltimore Pike. The pike was an easy musket shot beyond Culp's Hill, about 300 yards away.

According to Lee's plan, Meade's men also would be exposed to two-way artillery cross fire and a flanking movement while Longstreet mounted a simultaneous assault against Meade's left in the Wheatfield–Houck Ridge sector, the major battleground. When he received orders by courier from Lee to attack at dawn, the Rebel General, Ewell, vowed he would take the Baltimore Pike by moving up the heavily wooded, boulder-strewn slopes of Culp's Hill, or lose every man he had.[13]

General Williams knew he had both firepower and positions from which to deliver it that were far superior to what the Confederates had. Unlike as at Chancellorsville, he also had the authority to place his artillery. By 1 A.M., under orders from General Williams, Muhlenberg—just promoted to chief of the 12th Corps Artillery Brigade—positioned his ammunition train less than an hour away. He then boosted his firepower by moving up two of its four batteries, including Dan's F Battery under Rugg and Lt. David H. Kinzie's K Battery—ten guns in all. Both had been at the reserve artillery park on George Spangler's farm, south of Powers Hill, since the night before. In consultation with Hunt, Muhlenberg placed the two batteries on high ground above Williams's headquarters tent in a field near the Abraham Spangler farm buildings southwest of the Baltimore Pike. From this position, 100 yards behind the center of the battle line of the corps, Rugg and Kinzie could control enemy movements in the ravine or hollow between the Baltimore Pike and Spangler's meadow. They were immediately behind the infantry in Williams's division, now commanded by Ruger. The New Yorker, who had graduated third in his West Point class, was able, intelligent, and modest. A favorite of Williams, he had been wounded earlier in the war in heavy combat, and was commended for maintaining coolness and discipline among his troops while under fire.[14] Ruger's men were about 500 to 700 yards from the enemy entrenchments occupied by Steuart's Confederate brigade, which was supported initially by Walker's Stonewall brigade. With a clear field of fire, they could blast the enemy with canister should they advance up the meadow. The narrow, marshy Rock Creek swale was lined with woods and large boulders.

Since the previous evening, Muhlenberg had sixteen guns in position on nearby Powers Hill, about a half mile to the south and close to Slocum's headquarters. They were Capt. James H. Rigby's Battery A, 1st Md.; Lt. Charles E. Winegar's Battery M; and Lt. Charles Atwell's Battery E. One section of Winegar's battery was placed on McAllister's Hill. Rugg's and Kinzie's batteries brought the total to twenty-six guns. Rigby's Battery A also belonged to the artillery reserve and had been brought up earlier on Slocum's orders.

Rigby had six three-inch ordnance rifles, Winegar had four ten-pounder Parrotts, and Atwell had six. Rugg's and Kinzie's batteries manned ten smoothbore, twelve-pound bronze Napoleons, six in Dan's Battery F and four in K. No matter where the fire was directed, it could converge on the enemy. With such cross fire, they could bring to bear a heavy fire wherever the enemy chose to attack.

Battery F's regular strength at Gettysburg was 106—of whom 94 were present for duty—plus the same 31 men who had transferred to the artillery before Chancellorsville. Four of them, including Dan, were from the 123rd N.Y.[15] Lockwood's infantry brigade, together with the 150th N.Y., was positioned along the east side of the Baltimore Pike near Rugg's and Kinzie's two batteries. They were a reserve to be used as needed, to the right, left, or center, and to protect the two batteries in the interim.[16]

The Napoleon guns in these batteries originally had been designed for Emperor Louis Napoleon in the 1850s. The U.S. Army designated them the "Light 12-Pounder Gun, Model 1857," because the round, solid shot they fired weighed twelve pounds. By the beginning of the Civil War, the U.S. Army had acquired only a few dozen. By the time of the Battle of Gettysburg, the Napoleon was the most popular smoothbore cannon in both the Union and Confederate armies and remained so throughout the war. Almost half of the 320 guns in the Federal artillery at Gettysburg were Napoleons.[17] With a caliber of four and one-half inches, the Napoleon was much lighter and more mobile than other guns, and just as effective. Its maximum range was nearly a mile. Rifled cannon, such as the ten-pounder Parrott and the regulation wrought-iron three-inch gun, could fire farther and more accurately but were not so successful with canister. A Napoleon and its carriage weighed 3,800 pounds and required six powerful horses to drag it.[18]

The final positions of the five batteries were fixed by Williams and Muhlenberg in consultation with Geary, who was most concerned about retaking his entrenchments from the enemy.[19] The centralized control instituted upon General Hunt's urgent recommendation after Chancellorsville was a crucial change from that earlier battle. Williams and Muhlenberg had decisively demonstrated the defects in Hooker's command system there. At Gettysburg, instead of concentrating their guns as they had at Chancellorsville, they placed them on knolls in five different positions, concealed by the terrain or by woods where possible. They could thus maximize the possibilities of sweeping the woods and fields with enfilading, direct, and cross fire against attacking troops. This deployment also minimized the danger of having to withdraw all the guns at the same time in case of retreat, as had happened at Chancellorsville. At Gettysburg, moreover, the rocky, wooded, uneven terrain occupied by the 12th Corps afforded no single position for artillery close to the battle line. Consequently, the guns were largely out of accurate range for Confederate sharpshooters and artillery. Hunt had located the artillery reserve on the Taneytown Road, one and one-half miles south of Meade's headquarters, closer to the batteries and more able to supply them readily. At the reserve, he had consolidated broken batteries, replaced teams, and assembled a sixty-wagon ammunition supply train to send where needed.

At about 3:30 A.M., the Union right wing, including its artillery, was ready for its dawn attack. General Slocum's terse order was, "Hell, drive them out at daylight." Williams thought it was "an order that was more easily made than executed," but realized his biggest advantage was his artillery and the excellent positions they occupied. Standing next to the guns, Williams ordered Muhlenberg to open the attack on the enemy entrenchments at 4:30 A.M. with a fifteen-minute artillery barrage at a range of 600 to 800 yards. The general then enjoyed "a half hour or so of sleep on a flat rock sheltered by an apple tree."

When Dan heard the order "Cannoneers to your post," he had had no more sleep than General Williams. He and his comrades barely had time to boil coffee and munch hard bread. Under the watchful eye of General Hunt, Batteries F and K opened up, deep and heavy, and the other batteries joined them from their dispersed positions. Culp's Hill was ablaze with solid shot, shell, canister, and shrapnel being hurled furiously into wooded areas, the breastworks occupied by Steuart's brigade, and the Rock Creek swale. The Confederates had no artillery support and did their best to find cover, but the instant they stepped out from behind their captured works they were pounded by artillery. The earth literally trembled.[20]

Capt. Edward N. Whittier's 5th Maine Battery was stationed on Stevens Hill, 300 yards west of Culp's Hill. From his position he watched as "twenty guns converged and crossed their fire on the [enemy] entrenchments." In short order, the concussions were felt over a wide area. The 5th Regiment of Connecticut Volunteers was detached to support Winegar's Battery M at the outset of the barrage. The 150th and 107th N.Y. Volunteers supported the first two batteries from 4:30 A.M. until about 6 A.M.[21] Dan and his fellow redlegs, manning all ten guns of Batteries F and K, raked the woods and the Union-built breastworks now held by Steuart's Rebel brigade. As he had at Chancellorsville, Dan sometimes fired over the heads of the 123rd, his old infantry regiment. General Williams had created a gap between Ruger's and Geary's divisions of the 12th Corps, however, so that the artillery fire would go largely between them in a clear line of fire. Despite being noted for not exposing himself to fire in battle and for his flair at self-serving publicity, six-foot-six-inches tall, Geary had been wounded five times in the Mexican War and three in the Civil War. Williams did not admire his efforts to cultivate the press, while Geary thought Williams drank too much. Williams personally directed the battle from the center of the line near Geary's men. Slocum stationed himself at the right end of the 12th Corps line.[22]

At dawn all 12th Corps batteries were firing at short range from enfilading positions, as a prelude to the infantry attack, delayed just long enough to avoid being shelled by their own batteries. The air was filled with death. Lightning flashes leapt from the cannon mouths, followed by a murderous rush of hissing missiles hurtling through the air. The woods occupied by Steuart's men were filled with shells ricocheting and exploding among the boulders and trees. One Confederate officer reported, "The whole hillside seemed enveloped in a blaze. . . . The balls could be heard to strike the breastworks like hailstones on rooftops." The cannonading drowned out all other sounds, including musket fire, with the deafening blasts of artillery reverberating like thunder claps against the hillsides. At 4:45 A.M., "Cease fire" rang out to the artillery.

In a few minutes, Kane discharged his pistol and his brigade (Geary's division) began skirmishing on the left of the 12th Corps. Simultaneously, the right of the infantry line under Ruger, largely concealed in the woods, created a diversion. They cautiously probed the enemy with skirmishers, making noise to feint an attack, drawing attention away from Geary's men, and at the same time sending messages about enemy movements back to the artillery. This significantly increased the accuracy of the cannonading into the Union-built breastworks. At least two Confederate brigades now occupied these works, protected on their left flank by swampy ground at the confluence of Rock Creek and Spangler's Spring. Ruger's men were determining where to attack over marshy ground either to their front or on the enemy's right flank, should they abandon the breastworks. One gun fired by either Rugg's or Kinzie's battery fell short, killing one man in the 123rd and wounding another in the 20th Conn.

As daylight crept higher over the eastern hills and broke through the morning mist, troops could see to take aim. Heavy diversionary infantry fire commenced on the Union right, awakening any Rebel troops that had slept through the cannonading. In a few minutes, on the left of Williams's line, the rest of Kane's brigade moved out from behind their newly built log breastworks and overtook their skirmishers. The brief delay was sufficient to give "Allegheny" Johnson's Confederate division time at about 5 A.M. to move out in three lines from behind their entrenchments and advance, hugging the ground as they used stone walls, rock terraces, boulders, steep ravines, and dense clumps of trees for cover. They were accompanied by brigades in Rodes's and Early's divisions, all yelling in their distinctive style. Their orders were to seize Culp's Hill, and in a few hellish minutes a thousand rifles blazed away. The advancing Confederates had to fire at an angle of almost forty-five degrees to reach the Union breastworks on the crest of Culp's Hill. They also had two hundred yards of open ground and meadow to cross in their counterattack. Meanwhile, Longstreet's simultaneous early morning frontal attack never materialized.

Obviously, the Confederates' risk was calculated. They aimed straight for the Baltimore Pike and the Federal supply train and reserve artillery, as well as Meade's headquarters just beyond the meadow. Most of these Confederate troops also had faced Slocum's infantry and artillery at Chancellorsville, including Battery F. The Stonewall brigade had lost 45 percent of its men facing Williams's line in that battle. Now it was commanded by Brig. Gen. James A. Walker. This initial uncoordinated and uphill Confederate attack was checked and thrown back by

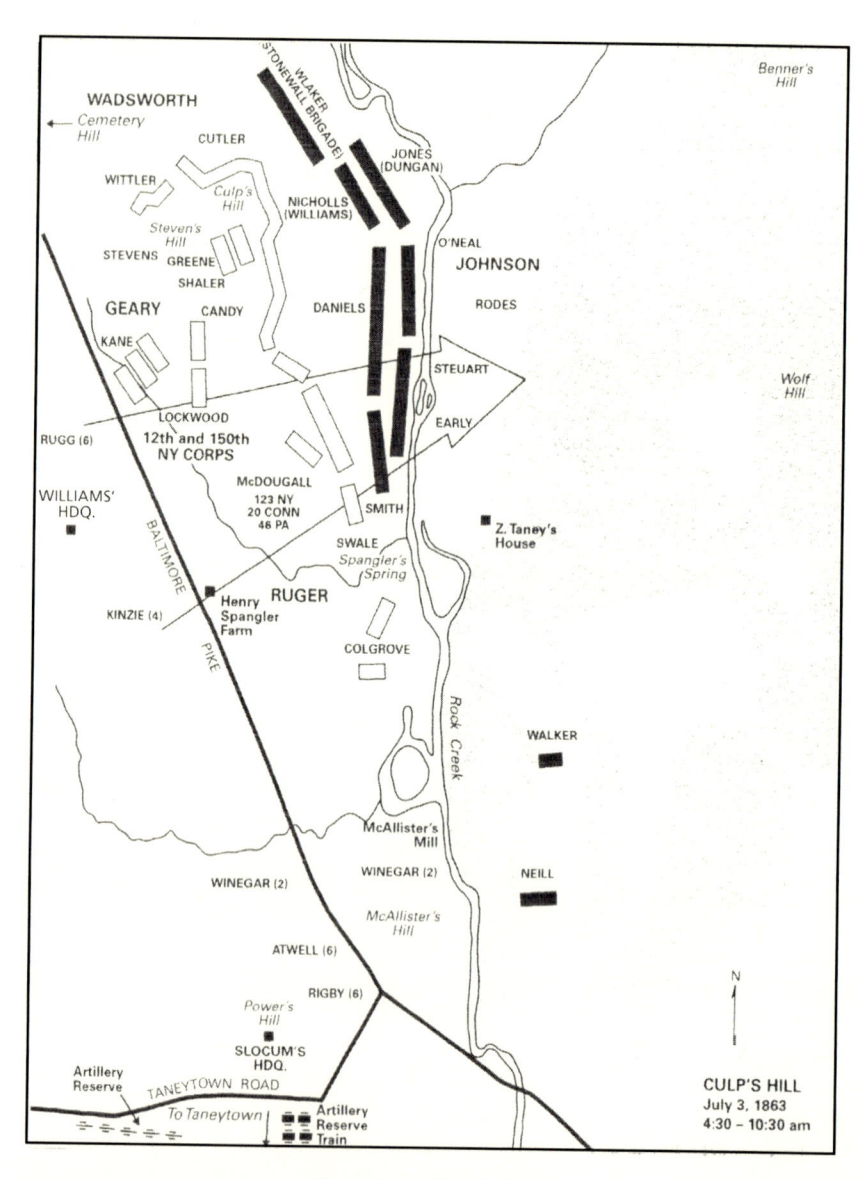

Gettysburg/Culp's Hill

Kane's counterattack. It was the first of four attacks that would be made. Confederate Lt. Col. W. G. Lewis reported that from about sunrise the regiment was "exposed to a most severe fire from a battery posted about 400 yards distant . . . of grape, shrapnel, and shell." This was from Dan's Battery F.[23]

Confederate Gen. Johnson quickly concluded that his troops would be pulverized by artillery if they stayed at the base of Culp's Hill. The question was whether they would be even more severely mauled if they advanced. He chose a seven-hour fight that raged up and down the boulder-strewn, tree-covered slope of Culp's Hill, the longest continuous fight in the three-day Battle of Gettysburg. Within minutes the battle spread like a prairie wildfire along Slocum's entire line. Kane's brigade advanced from behind trees and rocks, over numerous corpses, some of them dead from bayonet wounds suffered in the previous evening's battle. At 5:30 A.M., as the sun burned off the mist, the twenty-six guns under Muhlenberg again erupted like a volcano in support of the infantry, mercilessly raking the woods and the Rebel-held breastworks.

As the light grew stronger, swarms of men, horses, and artillery could be seen moving like ants on opposite hilltops. The Baltimore Pike was alive with curiosity seekers, stragglers, cavalry horses, prisoners, supply train teamsters, and—shortly after the battle opened—the wounded. As the fog and blue smoke of battle lifted like a stage curtain and was carried away by the morning breeze, signalers could be seen on the crests with their flags, communicating the battle's progress to Meade's headquarters.[24] Will Ross, on provost guard duty at that headquarters, must have seen this panorama of activity, possibly even his brother's battery blazing away.

July 3 was a sultry day, and the clouds hung low over the hills. On and off during the morning the batteries hammered away, sometimes firing just over the heads of the Union troops, as the enemy made three more dogged charges. Each charge was repelled with musket fire more terrific than the one before. Heavy cannonading accompanied the musket roar, pinning the Rebels down or forcing them to seek shelter. Edward O'Neal's Alabama brigade followed the Stonewall brigade over boulders slick with blood of the Virginians. In an appalling attempt to reach the crest, O'Neal reported they were "under a terrific fire of grape and small-arms," a double test of their resolve. Several of Geary's men in the 66th Ohio were felled from Powers Hill artillery fire shortly after 5:45 A.M. as they advanced too fast or too far in their effort to regain the Rebel-held breastworks. Atwell's Battery E and Kinzie's Battery K also fired at the enemy rear with devastating effectiveness to prevent

An artillery battery in action

Gettysburg Artillery Battery in Action

them from deploying in the woods and debouching suddenly in a surprise attack. Sgt. David Nichols of Battery E wrote his father that at one point a brigade of the enemy came out of the woods, in the second of Steuart's attacks, attempting to outflank the Union line, a move that the cannoneers prevented. "On seeing them our pieces was immediately opened in that direction when they fell back in confusion." In his diary, Nichols reported, "We poured shot and shell into them."

General Geary directed the fire of Atwell's battery from Powers Hill, sighting the pieces himself, "so as to command the enemy's position" in the woods and prevent a flanking movement by a battalion that was on open ground on top of Wolf Hill. Several times, the first around 9 A.M.,

Confederate troops, including the Stonewall Brigade, took cover at the base of Wolf Hill to rest on the Tawney farm, clean rifle-muskets, refill cartridge boxes, and eat what rations they had. Another time, two men brought them cartridges from Benner's Hill in a blanket slung over a fence rail.[25] About 10 A.M., three Confederate brigades—Steuart's, Daniel's, and Walker's—staged their last charge from their left flank, another frontal assault on Geary's well-entrenched position. They charged up the hillside, bellowing their ominous Rebel yell. Leading the charge, Steuart raised his sword and ordered his men forward over an open field with the command "Charge bayonets!" By this time he had about 900 men left in his brigade, half the number he had when the morning's battle began. Geary ordered his men to aim at their knees.

The effect was frightful. The Rebels barely reached their position, after leaving the shelter of the trees, when Federal guns (probably those on Powers Hill) opened "a murderous and enfilading fire." Geary's line began to waver convulsively from the attack but did not break. Winegar's Battery M also zeroed in on Steuart's brigade from McAllister's Hill. For forty-five minutes the Rebels were raked by musketry, grape, and canister as every battery belched its thunder. A North Carolina soldier wrote, "It was truly awful . . . how very fast did our poor boys fall. . . . You could see one with his head shot off, others cut in two, then one with his brains oozing out, one with his leg off, others shot through the heart." With their vision partially obscured, sight and sound guided Union gunners' aim. The Rebel yell redoubled, as did the artillery fire, until remnants of the devastated units, exhausted and defeated, were ordered back to the base of Benner's Hill for the fourth and last time. Their final assault had lasted no more than half an hour. During their retreat the Rebels were "exposed to an artillery fire exceeding in violence that of the early morning." As Steuart's men got back to the breastworks with decimated ranks and in hopeless confusion, the tearful general wrung his hands as he repeatedly uttered, "My poor boys! My poor boys!" At no time in the three-day battle was more artillery concentrated on such a small place, nor was more devastation wrought.

Compared to Chancellorsville, Gettysburg was a turkey shoot for Dan and the other Yankee cannoneers. The ground was too rough and steep for any Confederate batteries to be positioned close to Rock Creek for returning fire. In fact, Kirkpatrick's battery of Early's Confederate division, stationed behind a hill at the extreme left of his line, did not fire a single round. The Federal batteries, unlike those at Chancellorsville, were positioned on every little crest between Slocum's headquarters and Cemetery Hill, were well supplied with ammunition, and were out of small arms range, including that of sharpshooters. As a result, Rugg's

Kinzie's, Atwell's, and Winegar's batteries at Gettysburg fired 653 rounds, and Rigby's another 200, together using only twenty-six guns. In contrast, thirty-four guns had fired just 525 rounds at Chancellorsville.

The section of Winegar's Battery M on McAllister's Hill made a direct hit with its first shot at the Zebulon Taney house about 200 yards across Rock Creek. A squad of sharpshooters were firing from there on the 13th N.J. and 27th Ind. with fearful accuracy. The sharpshooting from the house terminated after about six shells exploded in it, but other sharpshooters filled the adjacent woods, firing from behind boulders.[26] Cannonading into the woods continued when it did not endanger advancing troops. The dazzling brass Napoleons leaped and bellowed, their shells shrieking through the treetops. Broken branches and twigs pelted the ground like a driving sleet storm. Other shells smashed boulders into countless flying stone splinters, forcing the Confederates to hug the ground or seek cover behind entrenchments, boulders, and trees as they advanced. Whizzing pieces of shrapnel flew in all directions, ripping bodies apart and flinging pieces of flesh over the stony landscape. Mangled bodies torn to pieces by exploding shells were everywhere, sometimes in heaps. Some soldiers, stunned by the concussion of bursting shells, were completely immobilized. After the guns went silent, more than 200 Rebels waved a white cloth signaling their surrender to the 27th Ind. One told his captors, "Lordy, you bastards had us between a shit and a sweat." When asked, "What did you quit for?" he replied, "the only thing we could do was wait for enough smoke to hide our asses and git!"[27]

By 10:30 A.M., Confederate regiments at Culp's Hill were forced to retreat to their former lines east of Rock Creek. For the third time in three days of fighting, the Confederates were compelled to give up ground they had taken. By this time, the smoke of the battle was so dense that soldiers on either side could not see each other unless engaged in hand-to-hand fighting. Otherwise they fired at each other's muzzle blasts. The noise was so overpowering that commands had to be shouted into soldier's ears. About 11 A.M., Colonel McDougall ordered the 123rd N.Y., which had been in reserve or supporting a battery until then, to lead a bayonet charge to relieve the 20th Conn. and 46th Pa. which, as skirmishers, had advanced the farthest over the dead and wounded. McDougall told them that the next time he saw them he hoped they would be masters of the works. The forty-six-year-old colonel, sporting a neatly trimmed beard, silver sideburns, and a bald pate, was acting brigade commander for the first time. The charge was preceded by shelling from the batteries on Powers Hill. The New Yorkers regained, "with a shout" and without loss of life, the breastworks they had built and then vacated the night before. According to Lieutenant Cruikshank, they immediately posted about two dozen pickets, the best marksmen in the regiment, including Pvt. Albert M. Cook. He took position behind a boulder and "blazed away" whenever a Rebel showed himself. By the time these New Yorkers reached the breastworks, the Rebels "were on a wild run through the woods beyond," according to Sergeant Coy.

By 12:20 P.M., the gap at Spangler's Spring was closed and the 12th Corps was in possession of its original line, from Culp's Hill to McAllister's Hill. The Union artillery chief Hunt was there to watch Union infantry regain the trenches.[28] As the Confederates withdrew to Rock Creek, the Union troops raised a tremendous cheer. Artillery fire continued for another hour. Musketry still flickered fitfully as skirmishers traded shots until the middle of the afternoon. By now, the July sun was intensely hot, and the air still, sultry, and choked with gun smoke. No breeze cooled the cannoneers or cleared the fouled air. Dan and the other red legs on the ridgetops had long since lost their forage caps, were stripped to the waist, sunbaked, coated with burnt gunpowder, and streaked with sweat, but otherwise unharmed.

In the afternoon Rugg's and Kinzie's batteries, as well as those on Powers Hill, took severe punishment from hidden enemy batteries whose projectiles passed over Cemetery Hill from Lee's right. This murderous bombardment, never equaled on American soil, heralded the major Confederate infantry attack, the Pickett-Pettigrew-Trimble charge, that began at 1 P.M. Muhlenberg reported that Dan and the other cannoneers "stood nobly under this . . . incessant hail, and displayed . . . the attributes of true soldiers." The 123rd N.Y. and the rest of its brigade remained in the entrenchments until nearly 5 P.M. Enemy sharpshooters also kept up an annoying fire. That afternoon one artilleryman in Dan's battery was wounded, in contrast to sixteen casualties at Chancellorsville. Battery F had taken the best cover their duties and ground afforded them. A total of 881 Union artillery horses were killed at Gettysburg, none from Battery F, which had lost 13 at Chancellorsville. At Gettysburg, only 8 men in the 12th Corps artillery brigade were wounded, a stunning contrast to the 1,215 casualties among the 8,295 infantry officers and men of the corps who fought in the three-day battle. Not all Union artillerymen were so fortunate. At Gettysburg one out of every ten artillerymen in both armies was either killed or wounded.[29]

Confederate Gen. Steuart had commanded the lead brigade in Johnson's fourth and last attack on Culp's Hill. His brigade initially was the most exposed and could not hold its position in line of battle. Instead, for an hour, the men had hidden behind rocks, a stone wall, and abandoned Union earthworks, where they suffered more from artillery and musketry fire than at any other time. "Mowed down with fearful rapidity . . . regiments were reduced to companies. . . . It came very near to being a rout. . . . " By 11 A.M. when they withdrew, Steuart had lost about 700 men.[30] The casualties started before their attack, as Steuart's men had been under fire for five hours. It was, as Ewell wrote later, "a task no troops could accomplish."

Chancellorsville and Gettysburg had savaged the ranks of the Stonewall (now Walker) brigade. Thirty years old and a West Pointer, General Walker had a fondness for whiskey, but he also had fight in his eyes. The 4th Va., one of his regiments, lost its battle flag and only sixty-five of its men survived the battle after advancing from boulder to boulder toward the Union breastworks. Combining losses in the two battles, this brigade suffered 823 casualties. It had taken five hours of musket and artillery fire in its front from Geary's men, and in its flank from Ruger's. Several wounded Rebels taken prisoner asked whether all the men who wore the red star of Williams's division were sharpshooters. They were, and they wanted to meet the Stonewall brigade again.[31]

By the early evening of July 3, Lee knew that he had lost the Battle of Gettysburg. Meade, in command of the Army of the Potomac for only a week, had outgeneraled him. Meade had captured and held the high ground and maintained a vastly superior intelligence network. Three Confederate divisions had failed to penetrate the Union center, and suffered enormous casualties in the effort. Both Ross brothers had participated in or witnessed Lee's defeat. Dan watched about 2,000 captured survivors as they were marched down the Baltimore Pike and across Rock Creek into a field, then placed under guard during the night of July 3–4. Will surely viewed Pickett's charge from Meade's headquarters, but could not have seen the action at Culp's Hill.

Late that afternoon, Williams's men discovered the havoc his artillery and infantry fire had inflicted. Twelve hundred to fifteen hundred enemy dead lay in mounds before the 12th Corps. Those who died in bayonet charges—Union and Rebel soldiers alike—were intermingled and lay "piled in heaps." Others had been dragged behind boulders, where they died lingering deaths, some clutching the earth in agonizing pain. More were scattered in every direction along the front, especially around Spangler's Spring.

Williams credited their strategic positions for their victory. "The woods in front and rear and above the breastworks held by the Rebels were filled with projectiles from our guns," he wrote. "It took two divisions two days of work burying the dead, and they could not finish before they had to leave. I have seldom seen the dead lie thicker on any battlefield than did the dead of Stonewall Jackson's [Walker's] famous old corps in front of Culp's Hill." He wondered why the Rebels had fought so long and concluded, "it requires no great stretch of fancy... that had the 12th Corps failed on the morning of July 3rd there would have been no victory." He had used about 9,000 12th Corps men on a front of about 1,200 yards who turned the battle into a disastrous tragic waste for Lee's army and laid the groundwork for its total defeat that afternoon.

Burial squads used rifles left on the field to mark the location of Union bodies by sticking their attached bayonets into the ground. Five thousand dead horses and mules were dragged into piles to be burned by farmers after the battle. One soldier reported that the dead lay as thick as pumpkins in a cornfield. The stench from decomposing bodies and horses was sickening. One officer wrote, "In some places you could not get a horse to go over the field on account of the horrid smell from the unburned corpses." It was like the breath of hell. Hundreds of wounded horses suffered in silence among the broken, scattered wagons.

Six thousand men and 3,000 horses and mules had died in the three-day battle. Separate, shallow trenches were dug in the hard, rocky ground for Union and Confederate bodies. Men from the 12th Corps buried 900 of the enemy dead by the next day. Many wounded Rebels remained on the battlefield. Others lay in Rock Creek, their glassy, vacant eyes staring from mangled, distorted bodies in the blazing midday sun. Only afternoon rain brought an end to their suffering, as floodwater engulfed them. Wounded 12th Corps soldiers were the most fortunate in the Union army. Their corps medical director disobeyed orders by bringing his medical supply wagons far enough forward that the soldiers could receive prompt medical attention.

Before the rain started, Union army ordnance wagons were loaded with discarded weapons and ammunition, while ambulances carried away the wounded. Eleven hundred Confederates were taken prisoner, and 5,000 small arms were picked up from the battlefield. Three stands of Confederate colors were captured, including the flag of one of the five regiments in the Stonewall brigade; it was later delivered to General Meade. In the three-day battle, the two armies suffered more than 50,000 casualties. Williams's 12th Corps alone killed 1,200 to 1,500 Rebels on July 3. Lee retreated in the drenching rain during the night of July 4, his two wagon trains carrying the 8,000 or more agonized wounded, together with his infantry, artillery, and supplies, headed for the Potomac. By the time they reached it, another 3,000 men had been killed or captured. Down mountainsides, through gorges, and over steep passes, the two wagon trains, totaling seventeen miles in length, took thirty-four hours to pass any given point. The roads were deeply rutted and crossed by countless raging streams. Merciless, hard-driven rain increased in fury by the minute, blinding horses, mules, and drivers as they traveled the forty-two-mile route.[32]

There were three main reasons for Lee's failure. First, On July 3, Longstreet had not executed Lee's plan for a coordinated frontal assault on Meade's left center. Second, Union cavalry had thwarted any effort by Confederate mounted troopers to strike the Union from the rear.[33] Finally, Slocum's forces—including the five batteries of 12th Corps artillery—repulsed Confederate efforts to exploit the toehold gained on Culp's Hill on the evening of July 2, and they drove the Rebels from this ground the next day. Ewell's vow to cut off the Union's escape route became a hollow echo as the Army of Northern Virginia prepared to retreat from Northern soil.

When the retreat began the next night in a torrential rain swept by powerful wind gusts, lightning cast eerie shadows on the dead still strewn over the battlefield. The blinding rain made it extremely difficult to keep torches lit in the black night. As the retreating army passed through Hagerstown, Maryland, citizens lined the streets shouting taunts such as "What's your hurry—[leave] anybody behind—eh??" and "Didn't get what you came for, did you?" Lee's wagon train, including commandeered farm wagons used as ambulances, plus infantry and artillery, was strung out helter-skelter as they headed for Williamsport to cross the Potomac. The wounded arrived at the river in waterlogged ambulances. Few of them had straw bedding, and none had wagon springs to lessen the excruciating pain from traveling the rutted, rock-strewn roads. Not one in a hundred had received adequate medical attention during the torturous journey. Tents and clothing were ripped apart to make bandages and tourniquets. Lee seized the two flatboats attached to wire ropes crossing the Potomac, and sent his wounded on to Richmond. By the time his entire army had crossed, Lee had suffered 27,125 dead, wounded or captured, including 19 generals and 171 regimental commanders. When Vicksburg was added, losses for July 1863 totaled 56,600, by far the largest Confederate loss for any month in the war and more than in all prior American wars put together. Two days before the crossing was complete, on July 14, Lt. Charles Brewster of the 10th Massachusetts, wrote home, expressing the widespread opinion of the troops. "What do people now think of the demoralized Army of the Potomac," he wrote. "If the growlers could have seen the desperate fighting . . . at Gettysburg I think they would shut up their potato traps."

As they ate a supper of "hardtack and gunpowder" on that postbattle night, after three days of nothing but light rations of hardtack, Williams, Muhlenberg, Rugg, and all the 12th Corps red legs, including Dan, must have pondered what they had learned from Chancellorsville. These lessons were manifest at Gettysburg, from the positioning of guns to their devastating fire and the light casualties among men and horses. Nevertheless, they slept on their arms that night without interruption except for the rain, not certain what the next day would bring. Five months earlier, Dan and sixty-eight other foot soldiers had been recruited by General Williams to serve as replacements in his artillery. Until then, the biggest weapon they had fired was a rifle-musket. Fighting as rookie redlegs at Chancellorsville, they lost their first battle, but in so doing they mastered their new assignment. They proved their mettle in their second battle by significantly helping to win it.

On the whole, Civil War artillery was not as effective as it had been at Gettysburg or even at Chancellorsville. Its value was more often psychological. The thunderous roar and smoke of the cannon and the whistle and hiss of the projectiles, grape, and canister were awesome and greatly feared by advancing troops. They knew that at close range grape and canister could cut a huge swath through their ranks. Consequently, when possible, the best marksmen with the newest rifle-muskets would be assigned to pick off the artillery officers, cannoneers, and horses one by one, putting the cannon out of action as quickly as possible.

At Gettysburg, however, unlike at Chancellorsville, the artillery positions picked by Williams were widely separated. Largely out of range of the Confederate marksmen and at least partially concealed, they were unopposed by enemy artillery. They could converge their fire and were well supplied with ammunition. Being so advantageously placed and supplied, Union batteries' cross fire confused the enemy, compelling them to seek shelter and re-form lines in the woods. Moreover, Union infantry regiments were assigned to protect cannoneers from any sudden enemy breakthrough. Williams had done a superb job. One of his staff officers later wrote, "General Williams was one of the finest military commanders in the eastern army . . . was thoroughly versed in all the arts of war and had a genius that inspired him where other men failed in a pressing emergency." Yet despite having more battle experience than any other division commander in the Army of the Potomac, he still was not promoted after Gettysburg.

Further, each artillery brigade was under the command of its corps rather than under a division commander. It took the debacle of Chancellorsville to force these basic changes at the Union command level. By centralizing control regarding where and when to locate batteries, how many to use, and what type of guns to employ—smoothbore or rifled—misuse and nonuse of artillery was minimized. An experienced artillery officer cited Hooker's handling of the artillery—or lack of it—at Chancellorsville as the major reason for his defeat. Unlike Hooker, Meade used artillery as a key element in his battle plans. He and Hunt worked as partners in the deployment of artillery to take full advantage of terrain, thus maximizing its effectiveness in supporting infantry.[34]

It is impossible to determine the age or experience level of the fifty-five detached volunteer infantrymen in Battery F, but Dan was not yet twenty-one. It can be assumed that most were just as young and inexperienced as he was. It is known that eighty-four of the eighty-nine detached volunteers who fought at Gettysburg with Battery B, the most famous in the Regular Army, were between eighteen and twenty-one, whereas the average age of a Union soldier was twenty-five. Thirty percent of the entire Union army was under twenty-one.[35]

6

Chickamauga

September 19–20, 1863

Sheridan's division, through no fault of his, went into the fight . . . with no more show than a broken-backed cat in hell without claws. . . . He held his position til he would have been a murderer to have asked his men to try to do so longer.

—Colonel Silas Miller, 36th Illinois

After the Confederate defeat at Stones River January 3, Maj. Gen. William Rosecrans spent nearly six months in Camp Schaeffer, near Murfreesboro. His goal was to convert that city into a gigantic warehouse for military stores and food, including one warehouse full of 40,000 boxes of hardtack. To do this, he had to repair and maintain his lifeline, the railroad link to Nashville. He requisitioned 18,450 horses and 41,680 mules, and built the largest earthwork of the entire war—three miles long and mounted by fifty artillery pieces.

On February 7, Pvt. George Cummins wrote his sweetheart, Maggie, from Camp Schaeffer, "The rantings of the hot-headed abolitionists and ravings of the secessionists in the north together with southern help makes me tremble for my country." He had undoubtedly concluded it was going to be a long, bloody war.

On April 9 at Camp Schaeffer, as acting brigadier, Col. F. T. Sherman detailed Lank Ross and fourteen others as provost guards for his headquarters. On April 11, Sgt. R. H. Watson was paroled from prison and returned to his regiment. He was reassured to see his company commander, Capt. Porter C. Olson, still in charge of the regiment. That day, he wrote his sister that Olson "makes a good field officer and is cool and collected under fire and brave to a fault." According to Private Cummins, on April 16 the regiment worked all day in the rain helping to build fortifications around the camp. While in camp, the men of the 36th voted to establish a regimental library and contributed $350 to get it started. Books were purchased as well as newspaper and magazine subscriptions, and religious tracts. A copy of *Webster's Unabridged Dictionary* was donated. On May 9, Pvt. Day Elmore wrote in his diary, "Report says that Bragg is advancing on us. I hope it is so for it will save us the trouble of going on to them . . . and we are ready." On May 17, General Lytle, now in command of Sill's brigade, sent his sick to the rear.

Lincoln believed that control of eastern Tennessee and Nashville would determine the war's outcome. The Nashville-Atlanta corridor was the Confederate lifeline. All spring the Union high command kept ordering Rosecrans to advance toward Chattanooga, a key railroad center and gateway to Atlanta, eighty miles from Murfreesboro. Railroads radiated from there to the Atlantic, the Gulf, and the Ohio and Mississippi rivers. Like a stubborn mule, Rosecrans resisted Lincoln's orders, arguing he had to resupply his army for a long campaign.

On May 22, after recovering from his Stones River wound, Private Reeder wrote his parents, "I don't believe the whole southern army could take this place as there are the strongest fortifications I ever saw. . . . Rosecrans could ask no better than to have the rebels attack him at this place." Rosecrans reviewed Sheridan's division in camp. As he passed the flag of the 36th, he said, "Well they say the old 36th will march further and do it easier than any regiment we have got."

They would not, however, confront Bragg at Camp Schaeffer. The same day Reeder wrote to his parents about the impressive fortifications, preparations got underway for a march on Bragg's army. Each man was issued forty rounds of cartridges, and another 2,000 rounds were loaded into each company wagon. Each man was ordered to roll up his blankets and pup tent and carry the roll around his neck. Each knapsack was to be packed with one shirt, one pair of drawers, and one pair of socks. Knapsacks were to be carried in the wagons. Mules were then ordered hitched to the wagons, which carried ammunition as well as rations for twenty-five days. All soldiers unable to march were sent to hospitals or convalescent centers. By then, a fair number were afflicted with the "Tennessee quickstep."

Shortly before the troop movement began, Colonel Miller was paroled from Libby Prison in Richmond and returned to his regiment, the 36th Ill. The entire regiment greeted him with huzzahs, wild cheers, and handshakes. It was as hearty a welcome as a regiment could give its commander. The band of the 24th Wis. played "Home Again." The celebration lasted several hours. Subsequently, Miller resumed his role as regimental commander.

Beginning on June 24, after deciding that the fall of Vicksburg was a certainty, Old Rosy moved his three corps—65,000 men—toward Chattanooga by three separate routes through gaps in the mountains. For Lank and all the others, the sheer novelty of finally marching was a welcome relief, despite the blinding rainstorm that back home they would have called a real "lamb killer." The rains lasted for seventeen days, making mountain trails virtually impassable and artillery almost impossible to move. One corporal described it as a "regular Baptist downpour." Water squirted from their shoes with every step. Men, animals, wagons, and artillery mired down in mud the consistency of thick, wet mortar. Horses and mule teams often had to be doubled and, at the steepest slopes, entire companies used ropes to help drag wagons and cannons uphill and then lower them, once over the crest. With cartridge boxes held high, men forded streams that were shoulder deep. They seldom had dry clothes, much less dry shoes. Rain soaked through their knapsacks, turning hardtack into paste, ruining their meat and coffee, and dissolving the sugar and salt. When the sun did come out, it baked them in their mud-caked clothes. On June 26, it took sixteen hours to march three miles. On Sunday night, June 27, they camped near a dam with a fifty-foot waterfall. Lank and the others took turns standing under it to gleefully wash off the mud.

McCook's corps, including the 36th Ill. and the rest of Sheridan's division, advanced toward Tullahoma in constant flanking maneuvers, with occasional skirmishes. They were the first to arrive, on July 2, with colors flying, drums beating, and the band playing "Down with the Traitor." After the Battle of Stones River, Bragg's army had spent the winter headquartered in Tullahoma, where he attempted unsuccessfully to block McCook's corps. Rosecrans's nine-day march on Tullahoma was brilliant and almost bloodless; nothing had been left to chance. It was one of the finest Civil War examples of feint and thrust, and kept Bragg completely on the defensive. They found the fort deserted, the siege guns spiked, and the tents and ammunition abandoned. A number of deserters also turned themselves in. Colonel Sherman of the 88th Illinois wrote his father, "All honor to Gen. Rosecrans, the greatest of American generals." The campaign resulted in only 560 casualties—fewer than 90 were killed—and cleared Bragg's army out of middle Tennessee, forcing him to retreat to Chattanooga, where he holed up.

The men of Sheridan's 1st Division celebrated the Fourth of July at Cowan, Tennessee, with band music played at noon in front of Brig. Gen. William H. Lytle's tent and at night in front of Sheridan's. Sheridan liked martial music. His band played almost continuously on the march as well as in camp. They also fired a National Salute at noon and at sunset. Lytle had recovered from his severe Perryville bullet wound, from which he bore a half-inch scar on the left side of his face. Since April 21, he had been in command of Sill's brigade, consisting of four regiments and an artillery unit. On July 8, they learned of the victory at Gettysburg and surrender of Vicksburg, and they fired a thirty-six-gun salute in honor of the victories. Excitement was intense. On July 22, Lytle wrote his sister that the weather at Cowan was "very fine" and they had "delicious spring water to drink."

On July 25, Stevenson, Alabama, was established as McCook's supply depot. The country around Stevenson swarmed with bushwhackers, who committed atrocious barbarities on loyal citizens as well as guerrilla warfare against the troops guarding the railroad. Rosecrans's advance through Stevenson toward Chattanooga was an exhausting summer campaign over rugged terrain on rain-soaked, muddy roads that had to be corduroyed for miles. Railroads and their bridges had to be repaired or rebuilt as well as guarded for the 212 miles between Nashville, his intermediate supply base, and Louisville, Rosecrans's closest secure supply base. The lads existed on half-rations, plus an abundance of blackberries picked en route. Huge quantities of forage were vital to the 43,000 horses and mules that Rosecrans's army needed to drive Bragg out of Chattanooga, which by then Rosecrans had decided to do. According to Col. F. T. Sherman, they passed through immense fields of corn and grain, but they would not be ripe until mid-August. Although much of it could be stockpiled in Stevenson, the junction point of two railroads, forage remained scarce throughout the campaign, and thousands of animals would eventually starve.

As soon as the railroad was rebuilt, Rosecrans ordered Sheridan's division to advance to Bridgeport from Stevenson to guard the supplies. After they arrived there August 1, Lank and the lads of the 36th built a chapel, superintended by Captain Smith of Lank's Company E and Captain Wakeman of Company H. Their library also arrived, and they organized a literary society and purchased subscriptions to the *New York Evening Post* and four magazines.

The twin victories at Gettysburg and Vicksburg in the summer of 1863 buoyed Union soldier's optimism. Pvt. George Cummins, in Lank's regiment, wrote a friend on August 25, "Notwithstanding the forked fangs of Copperheadism and the threats of arrant cowards, I think the dark clouds that have been hanging over the political horizon are beginning to rise ... proclaiming freedom to all classes and colors." On August 30, while still in Bridgeport, Cummins explained in a letter to his girlfriend,

Maggie, why he enlisted for three years. "I want the people to understand thoroughly what it means to become traitors [by attempting] to destroy our glorious Republic," he wrote. While there on August 9, the regiment he had recruited and initially commanded, the 10th Ohio, presented Lytle with a bejeweled gold Maltese cross.

With the Tennessee River swollen by unprecedented heavy summer rains, Sheridan's troops had to rebuild a 2,700-foot-long trestle bridge to carry railroad traffic at Bridgeport, under General Lytle's supervision. The retreating Rebels had recently burned all but the portion of this bridge still standing. Roads to the fords, boats, and a pontoon bridge also had to be built, and were completed by August 29. Day Elmore wrote in his diary on August 9, "The Rebs go in swimming on one side [of the river] and we on the other. We have great times talking with them and many a rich joke is passed."

On September 2, Lytle was ordered to break their comfortable camp and cross the trestle bridge. Each man was issued an extra pair of shoes. By September 4, the entire Army of the Cumberland (formerly known as the Army of the Ohio), including its wagons, artillery, and herds of cattle, had crossed the river unmolested by Bragg. That night Sheridan's division, including the 36th, camped in Hog Jaw Valley. Once across, they discovered ripened corn. Needless to say, the men and horses welcomed the change in diet. By September 6, Sheridan was within twelve miles of Winston's Gap at the foot of Lookout Mountain. On September 7, Bragg abandoned Chattanooga without a struggle to take a better position. The next day, Rosecrans outflanked him and a day later, Rosecrans ordered General Crittenden to occupy Chattanooga with a brigade.

Thinking that Bragg was retreating toward Atlanta, an overconfident Rosecrans followed him in a widely dispersed marching order through gaps in the mountains. In fact, though, Bragg was not heading to Atlanta. After five days of maneuvering by both sides, Rosecrans's three corps were finally within mutual supporting distance of one another, with Sheridan's division as the rear guard to the wagon trains. The Battle of Chickamauga, one of the biggest, bloodiest, and most confused ever fought on this continent, began on September 19. No one had the slightest suspicion what its magnitude would be, as measured in blood and flesh. The prize was Chattanooga, a huge natural amphitheater, twelve miles away, and the key to achieving all of Rosecrans's objectives.

Meanwhile, on August 28, two divisions from Joseph Johnston's army had arrived to reinforce Bragg. By September 10, Simon Bolivar Buckner's division also arrived, followed by two additional brigades from Johnston's army. By September 15, General Thomas's chief of scouts told him that these reinforcements had arrived, including prisoners paroled at

Vicksburg, who had not yet been exchanged. As fighting started, James Longstreet's corps of 12,000 in two divisions began to arrive from Virginia. Ironically, Longstreet and Rosecrans had been West Point roommates. Longstreet did the most to turn the battle into a tactical Confederate victory and to end Rosecrans's career. By then Bragg's army numbered 65,000, Rosecrans's 58,000. Despite repeated orders from Washington, Maj. Gen. Ambrose Burnside refused to send reinforcements to Rosecrans from Knoxville. Had he done so, the battle's outcome could have been significantly different.

Sheridan's division spent the nights of September 17 and 18 on grueling all-night marches. They marched at "route step" with "arms at will," ending at 3 A.M. on the 19th and resuming at 6:30 A.M. During the early hours of the 18th, a rich baritone voice had broken the silence of the march with a solo rendition of "John Brown's Body." A thousand voices joined the chorus, "Glory, Glory Hallelujah." A mighty volume sprang spontaneously from these throats as the men marched in perfect cadence to the song. By then, Lytle had caught a severe cold, and on the night of the 18th he wrapped himself in a buffalo robe and sat by the fire before he went to sleep. After midnight, Lytle's brigade, and the balance of Sheridan's division, serving as the rear guard of Rosecrans's army, saw their hardest marching—another night march guided by burning fences and huge bonfires, followed by only two hours sleep. Pvt. John Ely of the 88th Illinois wrote, "It was the longest hardest march that I ever endured."

Rosecrans's entire army now was positioned between Chattanooga and Bragg's army. A battle was inevitable. The day dawned bright and clear. The lads of the 36th made breakfast and coffee and by 10 A.M. resumed the march. Soon, however, a hundred small fires, kindled by soldiers to light their pipes and warm cups of coffee, spread through the dry leaves where the road traversed the woods. After an extended period of drenching rains and endless mud, it had not rained for weeks. The smoke, heat, and humidity were stifling as the men marched in quickstep through six inches of dust in humid, midday heat, listening to the distant muttering of cannon fire. Clouds of dust boiled up from thousands of feet, parching their throats and clogging their eyes and noses. Dust clung to them like flies to a honeypot. One soldier observed, "It was so dusty that when a grasshopper jumped, it stirred up enough dust to convince Rebels that the entire Federal army was on the march." Their first halt was at Crawfish Springs to allow men to get a drink of water, water their horses, fill canteens, and eat a few crackers. After a quick stop at about 2 P.M., they moved on to General McCook's 20th Corps headquarters to obtain extra boxes of ammunition for each company. An aide soon arrived and hastily exclaimed to McCook, "For God's sake General, send somebody down to hold Gordon's Mills... the enemy will be in our rear in fifteen minutes."

McCook turned to Sheridan, who dispatched Lytle's brigade. General Lytle, calmly smoking a cigar, received the order with stately courtesy. As he rode off he appeared the incarnation of courage and nobility. The brigade broke camp and then double-quicked another mile to Lee and Gordon's Mill, a number of men carrying the cartridge boxes on their shoulders. The dust was so thick that soldiers sometimes could not even see their file leaders. They were placed on the extreme right (southern end) of the twelve-mile-long Union line. While the battle raged north of them, Lytle positioned the 36th behind crude breastworks late that afternoon. They were about a quarter of a mile from the ford, the major crossing of Chickamauga Creek, when enemy skirmishers first made contact. The Chickamauga was deceptively deep—as much as ten feet—and safe to cross only at fords. The Lincolnites arrived in time to block the enemy attempt to cross the creek and seize the ford. Union and Confederate skirmishers were on opposite creek banks—a loud owl hoot apart.

Lank Ross had been serving as a provost guard at brigade headquarters since April 9. When Lytle arrived to take command on April 21, Lank had been retained at headquarters. Lytle drilled his brigade twice daily until they left Camp Schaeffer on June 24. On the eve of the battle, Lank was returned to his regiment.

Lytle was a hard-drinking, tobacco-chewing, widely recognized poet, brave as a lion; the general was possessed of keen military instincts, and kind to his men. He had served as a company commander in the war with Mexico, but saw no action. Courtly, small of stature, narrow-shouldered, and fair-skinned, and with masses of long, silken brown hair, he was from one of Cincinnati's leading families, and born to leadership. His father had been a major general in the Ohio militia and was now a congressman. His grandfather had commanded a company under Daniel Boone. His great-grandfather had fought the French in 1750 and the British during the Revolution. Lytle had been wounded twice and captured after being left for dead on the battlefield at Perryville. Effective March 17, 1863, upon his recovery, he was made a brigadier general. Lt. Henry Drake wrote his brother that Lytle was "a splendid officer and a fighting one too." Lytle had written, "I feel it my duty as long as I can to share with my generation its heavy burden and to stand along side of my brave comrades in arms to the last gasp."

Although fighting was heavy several miles to their north and across the creek, Lytle's brigade did not participate in the first day's main fight—the only brigade in Rosecrans's entire army that did not. After eating hardtack, Lytle's men built barricades; then, weary from their long forced march, they lay down on the cold, frosty ground with only their blankets for cover, keeping their arms at hand and cartridge belts on. A golden canoe of a moon and the stars shone down on them from a clear sky. No fires were allowed. In his farmhouse headquarters, Sheridan paced the floor, disturbed by the predicament he foresaw due to his exposed position at the extreme right of the army. He had suffered severely from similar exposure at Stones River.

During the night, Bragg prepared his main attack on the Union left, buoyed by reinforcements, including Longstreet's command. His plan was to seize the Rossville and Chattanooga Road and block Rosecrans's army from returning to Chattanooga.[1] However, the Union army had secure control of the Chattanooga-Lafayette Road as well as the Dry Creek Valley Road, which also led to Rossville. Fires were lit during the night to guide Thomas's troops into position along the latter road and warm the men when they halted. Sheridan and Charles A. Dana, President Lincoln's assistant secretary of war, attended a general's meeting with Rosecrans at about 11 P.M. at Widow Glenn's house, where they developed the next day's battle plans. The house was a three-room, weather-boarded log cabin on a small hill, fronting a large cornfield that provided an unobstructed view to the north and east. Widow Glenn's Confederate husband had been killed in action earlier in the war. After the meeting adjourned well past midnight, Rosecrans was too overwrought to sleep. He filled his pockets with hardtack and, with a canteen of cold tea, paced outside the cabin until dawn. Then he called for his personal priest to hear mass before the battle began.

At 2 A.M., Sunday, September 20, after a courier arrived from field headquarters, Lytle's men were awakened, drew rations and by 4:00 silently moved out, with a section of the division ammunition train and the ambulances. Lytle's cold had gotten worse during the night. He awoke feeling miserable, with hardly enough strength to move. His orderly begged him not to go into battle, but he was determined to do so. It was pitch-black and foggy, and the dust was as stifling as the day before. By daybreak they reached General Rosecrans's headquarters at Widow Glenn's house at the extreme right end of his line. McCook and Sheridan were also there. No better vantage point existed for his headquarters. Situated on a high hill overlooking a cornfield, it provided unobstructed views east and west. By the time Lank and the rest of Lytle's brigade had arrived, Rosecrans was filled with apprehension. He

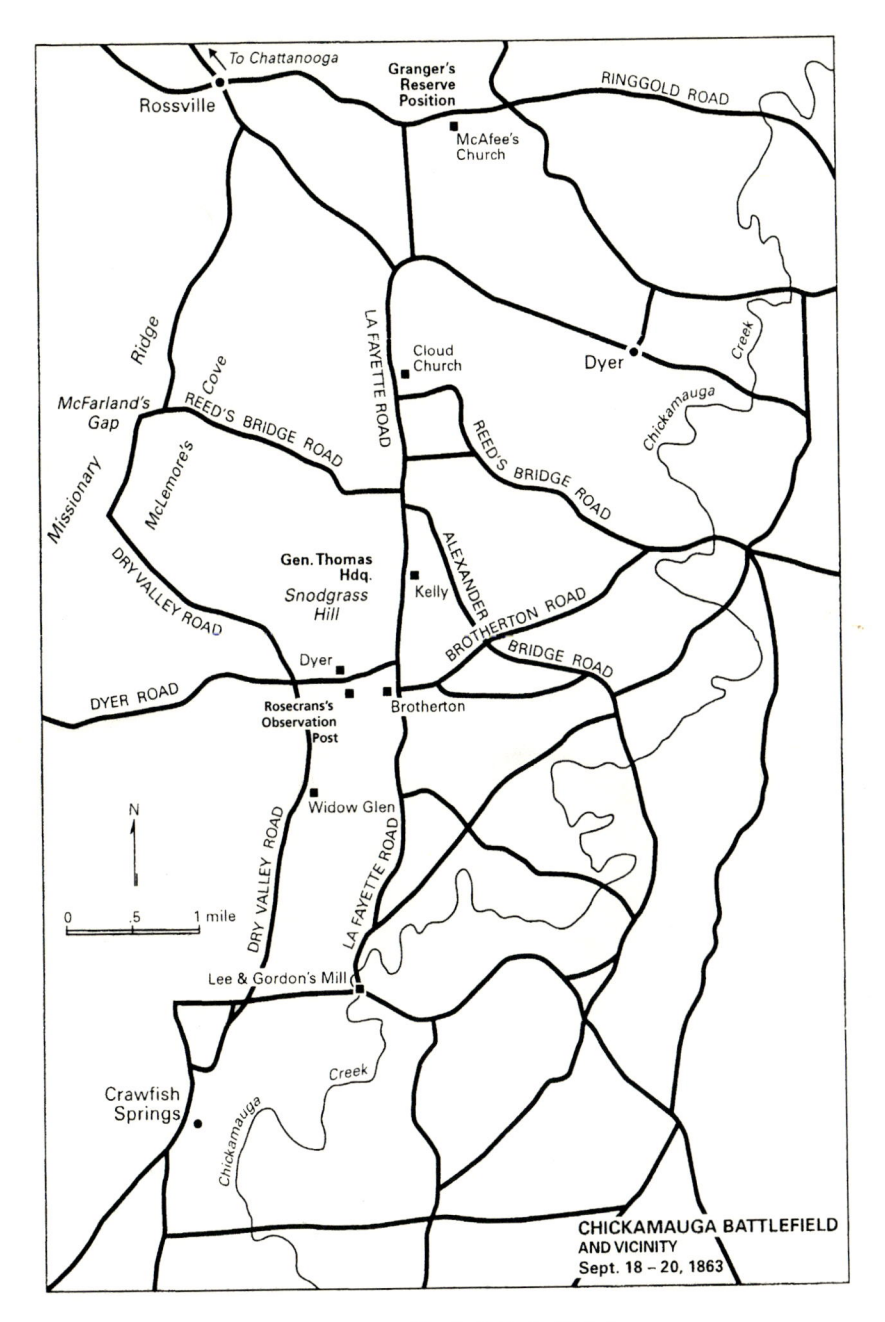

Chickamauga Battlefield & Vicinity

and staff officers had ridden three-fourths of a mile north to the highest hill on the Dyer farm, where he could observe his entire line as well as that of the enemy. Glaring problems were apparent. This eminence, near the intersection of the Dry Creek Valley and Brotherton roads, became his command post.

At the south end of the Union line, the morning air was cool, with an eerie mixture of smoke and fog so dense it isolated each man from sight and sound of his nearest comrades. Movements were almost impossible. The ground was white with hoarfrost. The fog, which had settled in the creek valley like a white veil of sorrow, did not lift until about 8 A.M., delaying action by both armies. While other troops moved out to take positions in the battle line, Lytle's and two other brigades of Sheridan's division (namely Laiboldt's and Bradley's) were ordered to stack arms and remain posted in reserve around Rosecrans's headquarters at Widow Glenn's, where they hastily ate breakfast. They also built breastworks from the rails and timbers taken from outbuildings and fences. The 88th Ill. shared their rations of bran pudding with Lank and the lads of the 36th, which they ate while shivering in the cold. Shortly thereafter, General Rosecrans rode up with his staff and escort. Having had little sleep or food for ten days, he was puffy-eyed, and his cheeks were flushed. He was operating on adrenalin, his nervous energy nearly depleted. He looked concerned, but his voice was cheerful, inspiring confidence in the men. He wore a plain blue coat, black pants stuffed into his boots, and a snow-white vest, and clenched his ever-present unlit cigar in his teeth. Rosecrans, a devout converted Catholic who swore but never blasphemed God, announced, "Boys, I never fight Sundays, but if they begin it, we will end it." He crossed himself before every battle, and carried a crucifix on his watch chain and a rosary in his pocket. His younger brother was an auxiliary bishop of the Catholic Church. Both were opponents of slavery. Lank Ross and the Fox River troopers waited anxiously, speculating as to what they faced. They were ready at an instant to take position as the fog slowly lifted to reveal a warm, beautiful day.

Calm and unmoved, Lytle sat on a bearskin rug spread under a tree by Joe Guthrie, his servant, while his aide fell asleep nearby on a blanket. Nevertheless, the general had a premonition of his own death. As he changed his uniform in his tent, he had told Guthrie he was completely exhausted. When Guthrie again had tried to persuade him not to go into battle, he had told his servant, "I never shrink from my duty but if I fall I want you to carry me off the field—and take care of my poor horse." Although the fog had lifted gradually, a thick cloud of smoke gave the sun a reddish hue, and hung like a funeral pall over the field and the adjacent forest. Brig. Gen. James A. Garfield, Rosecrans's chief of staff, predicted, "This will indeed be a day of blood." Rosecrans, McCook, and Sheridan were all in the saddle discussing the situation as the "ball" opened. They rode off silently on the Dry Valley Road both to check whether the line consisting of ten divisions was formed in accordance with Rosecrans's latest orders, and to locate high ground to which Rosencrans would move army headquarters. Rosecrans, Garfield, and the rest of his staff went off first. Lank and the other men completed the barricades for defense of the brigade. While waiting for new orders, Lytle calmly told his aide, Lt. Alfred Pirtle, that they were "going to fight two-to-one today." He had learned from Sheridan that Longstreet's troops had just arrived to join Bragg's forces. They would be fighting at a terrific disadvantage, he said, and made Pirtle promise to "stick to him to the last." While they snatched a quick breakfast, prisoners just captured from Longstreet's Corps were being marched by. A Rebel lieutenant announced, "You fellers will catch hell this morning."

For several hours, furious fighting could be heard to the north, where the battle opened first, with artillery fire. General Thomas's left flank—at the north end of the battle line—was turned, but the main line held. Fighting slowly spread south toward the center. After telling McCook and Crittenden on the battlefield to move troops into weak sections of the line, Rosecrans returned to Widow Glenn's house. There, a staff officer told him he'd been sent by Thomas to secure more support. With this new information, Rosecrans issued two written orders to McCook, the first at 10:10 A.M. directing him to reinforce Thomas as quickly as possible. That was followed five minutes later by orders to send two of Sheridan's brigades to Thomas immediately and to move the third brigade as soon as possible. These orders reached McCook at 10:55 A.M. By then, Rosecrans had issued a third order asking McCook to report to him in person, presumably so he could personally tell McCook where to position the brigades.

All together, Rosecrans had issued orders to nine corps and division commanders to reinforce Thomas and strengthen the weak mile-long stretch of line, leaving no reserves for the line's center. By then, they were all out of position to respond promptly and effectively. Unlike corps commanders, division commanders like Sheridan did not have the right to modify orders if circumstances dictated. Relying on inaccurate staff information and plagued by confusion and poor judgment, Rosecrans weakened the line even more where he wanted it strengthened, causing commands to get in each others' way, and thus lost control of his army. Rosecrans had been criticized at Stones River for issuing too many orders while his men were engaged. He did so again at Chickamauga.

By about 11 A.M., on Rosecrans's orders, McCook had moved out Laiboldt's brigade from an excellent defensive position at Widow Glenn's to cover the flank of Brig. Gen. Jeff C. Davis's two small brigades on the crest of a low ridge. Word was sent back to McCook that Laiboldt had arrived and taken the position. After a short lull, the battle recommenced, with hot work by Davis's and Laiboldt's men at the end of the battle line closest to Lytle.

Meanwhile, Sheridan returned on horseback to Widow Glenn's house, where he spoke to Lytle preparatory to inspecting his lines. Lytle then ordered his colonels to have their men ready to march. Immediately thereafter, Lt. Col. Gates P. Thruston, McCook's chief of staff, arrived with Rosecrans's written orders for Sheridan to move two brigades at once to support General Thomas. Sheridan expressed surprise, and the order was repeated. Sheridan then turned to Lytle and said, "You have heard the order general, put your brigade in motion at once." Both Sheridan and Lytle indicated their disappointment at being ordered to leave an excellent defensive position, just as the battle was approaching them. Nevertheless, with a voice like a trumpet, Lytle shouted, "Fall in! Forward—double-quick!" Every company commander repeated the order, and the men responded instantly. The order of march had the 88th Ill. in the lead, followed by the 36th Ill., 24th Wis., and 21st Mich. forming to the right of the 88th in that order. The artillery battery brought up the rear under Pirtle's command.

They marched about a half mile in column, four abreast, double-quick down the sandy, narrow, Glenn-Kelly Road. The pall of dust almost smothered the men. About a quarter of a mile from Widow Glenn's house, the 88th, as head of the column, suddenly turned off the road, crossed a dry streambed, and entered the woods at the base of a tolerably steep one-hundred-foot-high ridge. This movement was made on orders to Sheridan from McCook, who was in the road awaiting Sheridan's arrival. Rosecrans had just witnessed from his hilltop command the arrival of Davis's and Laiboldt's men at the battlefront, then ridden down the hill and found McCook. Somewhat relieved, he told McCook to hurry along Sheridan's other two brigades—Lytle's and Bradley's. These orders countermanded Rosecrans's previous ones for Sheridan to render assistance to Thomas. Sheridan's two brigades were now to assist Davis and Laiboldt, but lacked sufficient troops to replace those just withdrawn by Rosecrans.

Moments after the 88th started up the hill, Lytle turned in his saddle and, while his tall mount was prancing, gave the command to the 36th "On the right into line" and "Stand firm boys, stand like iron; never let the name of the brigade be disgraced." His next command was

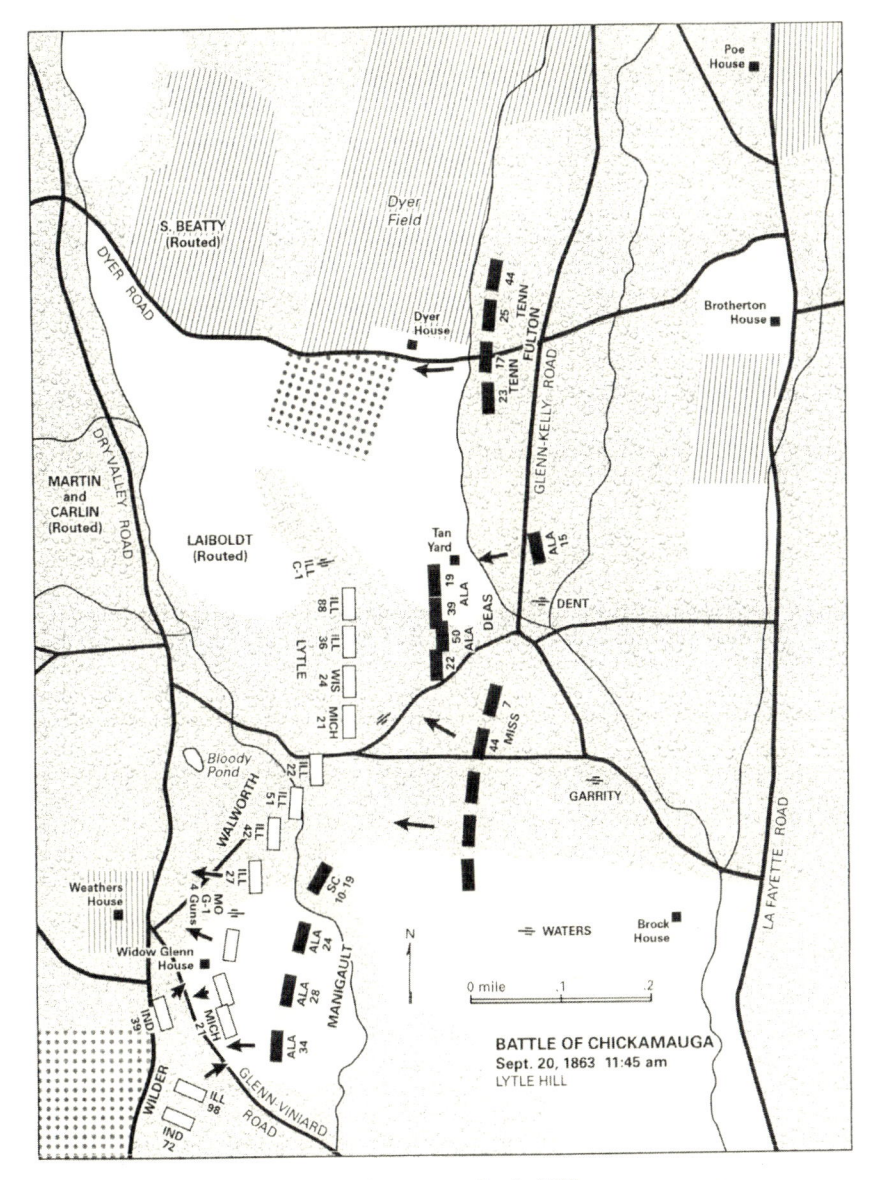

Chickamauga—Lytle Hill

"By company into line," which was executed under terrible fire. Lytle was determined to stall the attack on Davis's and Laiboldt's brigades as they withdrew in near panic. No sooner had Lytle's brigade entered the woods on Sheridan's orders and started toward the ridge about 11:20 A.M.

than men began to fall, cut down by enemy skirmishers firing from the ridgetop. The command "Forward double quick and into line" was given to the 88th by Lieutenant Pirtle who led them up the slope to connect with Laiboldt's brigade. When he reached the crest, he could barely make out Gen. Zachariah C. Deas's Rebel skirmishers in the woods. In a desperate charge led by Lytle with most of his staff, they rushed into line of battle with a cheer just as Laiboldt's and Davis's brigades collapsed and turned tail. They had charged up to the ridge at a hard run, taken the tree-covered crest, and, with a tremendous artillery and musketry fire, momentarily sent the enemy's first line scurrying back before they reached the summit and before the two regiments could jointly form a battle line. General Deas temporarily lost his grip on his four-regiment brigade as it came to a standstill. Meanwhile, the 36th formed its battle line below the ridge. Lytle wheeled his horse back down the hill, returned to the 36th, praised the men, raised his sword, and led them to the right of the 88th on the crest.

In another moment, the 36th was on the ridgetop, ready to join the 88th in the bloody conflict with Deas's Alabamians. They had fought this brigade at Stones River when it was commanded by General Loomis. Men in the 88th skirmish line were crouched behind a low rail fence at the edge of the woods, not seventy-five yards down the slope, with some of their skirmishers scurrying from tree to tree. Lytle dispatched his aide, Lt. J. M. Turnbull (formerly of the 36th), to the 88th skirmish line. He arrived on the crest just in time to witness Davis's fleeing troops and the Rebels pursuing them, leaving Laiboldt's skirmish line disconnected on its left. Turnbull reconnoitered through the underbrush about one hundred yards toward the front and could hear the enemy officers issuing orders in preparation for another attack. He ordered the 88th skirmishers to shift to the left and galloped back to Lytle with this information. Within minutes, a terrific volley of musketry opened on Lytle's men. Meanwhile, Lytle ordered Turnbull to bring up the 24th Wis. and the 21st Mich. and extend the battle line to the right of the 36th. In short order, Lytle formed a four-regiment battle line. He then rode along its front, cheering as he waved his hat and sword. Unable to be heard above the battle noise, Lytle gestured emphatically with his sabre to the cheering 21st Michiganders as they arrived, armed with Colt's repeating rifles. They moved forward on the double-quick, extending the battle line to the right. Their major was shouting, "Come on my brave boys. I won't ask you to go where I am afraid to lead." The 24th Wis. moved with more deliberation to assist the two Lincolnite regiments, which had suffered severely. Lytle then took a position thirty paces behind the 24th Wis., near their colors, where he could see his entire brigade as well as other units to the right and left, and the enemy. While he was behind them, the men heard him shout, "brave boys, brave 24th."

Lytle then exclaimed to his staff, "All right men, we can die but once. This is our time and place. Let us make a stand right here and die if necessary with our harness on." They stayed, knowing as he did how desperate the odds were. He then turned in his saddle and gave the command, "By company into line! Forward!" and moved to the crest of the hill within fifty feet of Deas's Alabamians.

Men dropped like flies from Rebel musketry, grape, and canister, but succeeded in keeping a good line, moving rapidly onto the crest of the ridge. Lytle also ordered two guns from Sutermeister's Missouri battery to be placed behind the 36th, as close as possible to the line of the 24th. The two pieces fired canister directly into the enemy with fatal effect, momentarily stopping their advance, but both the right and left of Lytle's line were hard-pressed. The Alabamians were within pistol range as Lytle told the 24th, "Boys, if we whip them today, we will all eat Christmas dinner at home."

The mid-morning reshuffling of half of his troops by Rosecrans had laid the groundwork for disaster to Sheridan's division. The army commander could not stop fine-tuning his battle line in the face of the enemy, which was obviously preparing to attack. By moving part of Wood's division to close an imagined gap near the center of his line, he opened a real gap near his right flank. At that very time, Longstreet launched his massive attack from a nearby forest, using eighteen brigades with 23,000 fresh and determined troops in deep columnar formation two brigades wide. At 11:20 A.M. two of these brigades—Deas's and Manigault's—had started driving 600 yards toward Lytle's brigade with bugles blowing and Rebels yelling. They were headed for the quarter-mile gap on the crest. Patton Anderson's brigade was 200 yards behind. Their orders were to take the ridge at any cost. It is unlikely that Longstreet even knew that Wood's withdrawal only ten minutes earlier had opened the gap. Instead, he probably thought his troops had created the opening by breaking the Federal line.

As soon as all four of Lytle's regiments were fully assembled behind hastily built rude log and rail breastworks on the ridgetop, his brigade unleashed a continuous hail of lead, slowing the Alabamians to a halt halfway up the slope. By this time, Davis's and Laibold's men, who had double-quicked in that order into the gap left by Wood, had already broken ranks, overwhelmed and disheartened by the superior numbers of Longstreet's men. A private in the 15th Mo., the last of Laibold's regiment to retreat, heard one of Deas's men yell, "Surrender you Yankee son-of-a-bitch." Sheridan climbed the ridge, where Pvt. John Ely, of the

88th, heard him speak cheerfully to the men, telling them—to no avail—to "keep cool" because they could "surely check" the enemy.

One soldier in the 36th later wrote that the sight was truly appalling. "The ground was covered with dry grass and old logs which the bursting shells had set on fire. A thick cloud of smoke had risen about as high as our heads and seemed hanging like a funeral pall in the air. Under this we could see, away down the slope of the hill . . . moving masses of men emerging from the woods and hurrying toward us," he wrote, referring to Mississippi regiments from Patton Anderson's brigade. "In our front not more than . . . seventy-five yards . . . the enemy's front line [Deas's Alabamians] lay secreted. We set forth with a will, while the ranks of the enemy belched forth a stream of fire, and a battery of artillery on the right flank tore the ground with grape and shell."

By then Lytle knew the situation was hopeless and that his men would pay for Rosecrans's blunder. They had to hold on. As he pulled on a pair of dark kid gloves, he was heard to say, "If I must die, I will die as a gentleman." McCook suddenly appeared to order Lieutenant Pirtle to place a two-gun section of Bush's 11th Ind. into a position down the wooded slope in front of the 21st Mich. Deas was stalled until Patton Anderson's reserve brigade of Mississippians came to his support. By this time the newly arrived battery was murderously enfilading the ranks of the 22nd Ala., the left regiment in Deas's front line. Meanwhile the 19th Ala., the other regiment in Deas's front line, was being mistakenly fired on from behind by the 15th Ala. In the smoke and confusion of the battle they had veered way out of line. Two of Anderson's Mississippi regiments charged the Union battery.

Manigault's men, now within rifle shot, fired on Sutermeister's battery. Captain Sutermeister ordered his Missouri battery to limber up, but too late to save the two sections of two guns each. A section commander, five cannoneers, and all the horses were killed or wounded. By superhuman effort, Sutermeister managed to withdraw his remaining equipment. However, pulled by frantic horses, one of his artillery wagons crashed into a tree, showering its branches onto the 36th. Anderson's support to the Alabamians gave them new courage, and they renewed their advance, but at a fearful cost. A section of Schueler's Battery G, 1st Mo. Light Artillery, also attached to Sheridan's division, pounded the Rebels with grape and shell while the Union musketry showered them with a cyclone of minié balls. Nevertheless, without the support of Bush's Indiana battery, Lytle's brigade suddenly found Confederates on three sides, less than 100 feet away. The 88th had been slowly driven back to the foot of the hill. Lank Ross's 36th began to break, its left flank exposed to a destructive cross fire as the 88th withdrew, but behind it, the 24th Wis. held. The 36th rallied about twenty yards behind their initial position. The 21st Mich. lay down to allow Sutermeister's Missouri cannoneers to pass over them in retreat. The Michiganders then rose and fired a withering volley, which checked the enemy advance. Then the 21st Mich. began to falter. The pressure on the 24th was now overwhelming.

Lytle was astride his horse behind the 24th, holding the reins in his left hand, his drawn saber in his right with the blade diagonal across his body, the point shoulder high. He wore high-topped boots, plain dark pants, a dark overcoat without insignia, and a gold cord on his cap, marking his rank as a general officer. His sorrel was decked out in finery. His face was lit with what was termed "battle-fire." His beard seemed electrified, his eyes sparkled, and his superb mustache was twisted and curled by his impatient fingers. He was close to the other guns of Sutermeister's battery, standing by their regimental colors, praising its men, and urging them to be calm and steady. In the dreadful noise, Lytle had drawn his sword, apparently to signal orders for a charge. He suddenly bent forward toward his aide and family friend, Lieutenant Pirtle, and calmly said to him, "Pirtle, I am hit." Pirtle asked, "Are you hit hard, General?" "In the spine. If I have to leave the field, you stay here, and see that all goes right," Lytle replied. He then began chewing his tobacco, as he always did when excited or suffering. This was his third wound in three battles.

The enemy's fire was now heavier, indicating that the Alabamians, reinforced with their Mississippi brigadiers, were approaching. Lytle's men were falling thick and fast. Pirtle asked the general whether he thought two more guns were needed. Lytle said no but that another regiment should be brought up. Pirtle saluted with his sword, galloped back down the ridge, and found the gallant officers of the 36th rallying the remnants of their regiment, including Lank. He conveyed Lytle's order to Colonel Miller, urging him to help his brigade commander. Pirtle dismounted and assisted in re-forming the regiment, as a flank fire from the left poured in on them, leaving no doubt they were outnumbered. Nevertheless, the 36th advanced toward the ridgetop for the second time. Shortly, when four shells exploded nearby, the 24th Wis. began to waver. The entire front line began to retreat behind the ridge, sullenly and slowly.

Then Lytle's riderless sorrel horse galloped down the hill. While apparently trying to give an order, Lytle had been hit again, this time in the face, filling his mouth with blood. As he slowly slid off his horse, Captain Green of the brigade staff eased him to the ground. Lytle implored Green to abandon him as the enemy closed in around his men, so that he would not be a burden. However, he handed his saber to a private in the 24th Wis. to be taken away. His beard and long hair soaked with blood, he died within a few minutes, after motioning to his troops to leave the scene. The last man in the 24th Wis. had withdrawn when Colonel Miller arrived. The 36th then became the only remnant of Lytle's brigade on the ridge. Miller now assumed command of the brigade, angry at the impossible circumstances his men faced.

The regimental command of the 36th shifted to Lt. Col. Porter Olson, another New Yorker who had moved to Illinois. He would be killed in the Battle of Franklin in November 1864. The conflict quickly grew more deadly and desperate. Miller, Olson, and Major Sherman were conspicuous everywhere, encouraging their men by example. Their troops sent well-directed volleys into the advancing enemy ranks, staggering and checking them. The Fox River regiment's colors were soon torn and the staff shattered. Cpl. Ezra Parker, one of the color guards, took a bullet through his head. After the battle, his replacement, Cpl. Charles Ayres, counted forty bullet holes in his uniform and blanket roll. Lank's company commander, Capt. A. M. Hobbs, was wounded, and Lt. Orison Smith, another officer in Lank's company, was killed. Both Hobbs and Smith had been wounded at Stones River. Two enlisted men were killed and ten were wounded, of whom five were captured, and at least one was sent to Andersonville. With every moment the ranks grew thinner. Within half an hour, the regiment had lost half of its 370 men. They were flanked on both sides and pressed in front by a horde flush with success.

It was as if they were a boulder in the midst of a stream with torrents of water pouring around both sides. They swung bayonets, and clubbed with muskets and rocks in hand-to-hand combat, but they were simply overpowered. Their line was broken, albeit at tremendous cost to the Alabamians. Col. Benjamin F. Sawyer of the 24th Ala. wrote afterward, "[O]ne-fourth of my regiment was cut down. Never before had I, nor since have I, seen such terrible execution in so short a time." The command to the Lincolnites to fall back behind the ridge was executed in good order, every step being contested. While withdrawing, they fought back from behind trees and boulders, slowing the enemy advance. By shortly after noon, when the enemy infantry and artillery using grape and canister reached the ridgetop, they had forced the 36th all the way down the reverse slope and back across the Dry Creek Valley about 300 yards into the smoke-filled woods. It was the last regiment to withdraw. Besides heavy infantry losses, Sheridan had lost eight guns in forty-five minutes. In the last attempt to rally the brigade at the foot of the hill, Rosecrans rode up to McCook and Sheridan and said, "charge them once more for Old Rosie." According to Corp. Arthur E. Stebbins, he then turned to what was left of the 88th and said, "Form a line! Don't fall back! Make a stand here! Hold the ridge for General Sheridan's sake!" To attempt a charge or to try to hold the ridge would have been murder. They chose not to. The battle was over in less than an hour.

The 23,000 men Longstreet used in his attack south of the Dyer Road outnumbered the force in Pickett's charge at Gettysburg. With a soldier's eye, Longstreet had spotted the gap Rosecrans had created. The meddlesome general had an unimpeded view of the activity from his hillside command post a few hundred yards southwest of the Dyer Road, all along the center of his line, including Longstreet's attack. In less than an hour Longstreet poured a rolling sea of his brigades through the gap with a front of 500 yards in three heavy lines. Six Union brigades—three of Sheridan's and three of Davis's in the Union right wing—had crumbled. Rosecrans watched the demoralized bluecoats run for their lives, and saw Lytle's bloodstained horse with an empty saddle come down the hill. He sent for Sheridan but waited only a few minutes for him.

Shortly after noon, he left a few staff officers to give Sheridan his instructions. Thinking his army had been destroyed, Rosecrans and two of his three corps commanders, McCook and Crittenden, and Assistant Secretary of War Dana fled to Chattanooga via the Dry Creek Valley Road and Rossville, where they would prepare for his army's next stand. He shouted to his aides, "If you care to live any longer, get away from here," and began forcing his way through a human wall of panic-stricken soldiers. When Rosencrans arrived at his Chattanooga headquarters, he was so emotionally shattered that he had to be helped off his horse. Until then, the forty-four-year-old Rosecrans probably possessed the most enviable reputation of any Northern general. Farther north, only Thomas stood firm, with his corps and remnants of the other two, unaware of the disaster that had just occurred south of him.

In the nick of time, Maj. Gen. Gordon Granger, hard as nails and a martinet, came to Thomas's rescue on his own initiative. Sometime after 11:30 A.M. he rushed back to his headquarters from McAfee Church with two of the three brigades in his Reserve Corps and 95,000 rounds of extra ammunition. Near the church he had climbed a haystack to see a cloud of dust on the horizon. At about 1:45 P.M. Granger took his two brigades up to Thomas's position on Snodgrass Hill, distributed ammunition, and rendered him the assistance that the brigades of Lytle and Bradley had initially been ordered to provide. Granger, a New Yorker, was a West Pointer. He had earned two brevets for bravery in the Mexican War. In the two hours that Granger's brigades, probably 3,900 men, were engaged, they suffered 44 percent in casualties but slowed and then broke the last Confederate advance. By 2:15, the thoroughly winded troops were rested and ordered into battle atop Horseshoe Ridge. Asked by Thomas if he thought his troops could clear the ridge, Granger reportedly replied,

"Yes my men are fresh.... They are raw troops, and they don't know any better than to charge up there." Granger was not there to lead his raw troops in triumph. He was busy at the Snodgrass house, doing what he liked best—positioning, aiming, and firing artillery.

As the 36th took refuge in the woods, the ambulances took up a position on the side of the road. The gunfire was still so terrible that survival seemed impossible. Streams of wounded men sought to reach the ambulances. About eighty wounded Fox River boys were loaded into ambulances. Once loaded, the ambulance drivers were urged to make all possible speed to Chattanooga, twelve miles away. More than 1,000 others from various regiments would be left behind. The rest retreated farther into the woods to the next ridge, where General Sheridan and Lieutenant Turnbull were attempting to form a new line with the demoralized men. Sheridan sent orders that as soon as they had rested sufficiently, each of his brigades should re-form where they were and report to him. Turnbull's horse had been shot under him and Lytle's riderless horse could be seen. Turnbull found another horse, mounted it, and organized about one hundred men into a new line with the help of other officers, including several of his staff. Sheridan shouted, "You are doing a good work ... fall back to the next ridge and gather up every straggler." After unsuccessfully attempting to re-form his men, he had concluded that further resistance on this part of the battle line was futile. Reaching the designated ridge, which was out of range of the murderous fire, his men could see Dry Creek Valley Road 300 yards below, jammed with wagons loaded with equipment, food, and munitions; ambulances; smashed gun carriages; caissons; horses; and men, wounded and unwounded, mounted and unmounted, streaming toward Chattanooga.

While falling back with the remnants of the 36th, Colonel Miller and Turnbull continued their attempt to help reorganize Lytle's brigade. Before long, Turnbull had mustered 200 to 300 men ready to follow Sheridan, who announced, "We are cut off from the main army and must reach General Thomas with the least possible delay." By 3 P.M. some 1,500 of Sheridan's men had recovered from their hysteria and rounded up a number of artillery pieces and caissons. In order to reach Thomas they retreated to the McFarland Farm near McFarland's Gap, on the Dry Creek Valley Road halfway to Rossville. By stationing regimental commanders at designated points along the way, members were assembled, including those from Davis's and other divisions. Colonel Miller also assembled the remnants of his brigade. Major Thruston, McCook's chief of staff, was dispatched at a gallop to Thomas to tell him that Sheridan (who was hopping mad) and Brig. Gen. Jefferson C. Davis had remnants of five brigades—several thousand troops—within supporting distance on the Dry Creek Valley Road.

Meanwhile General Negley had cleared McFarland's gap of enemy artillery on the road to within two miles of Rossville. He then put the 78th Pennsylvania to work there, collecting and organizing other scattered troops and stragglers on the nearby open ground. Shortly thereafter, he learned that Sheridan was approaching with about 1,500 men. Negley rode forward to meet Sheridan, asking him to join forces to assist Thomas. Sheridan stated that his first objective was Rossville. General Gordon Granger had been stationed near there with 4,500 fresh troops to keep the road open at all hazards by blocking any possible flanking movement around Thomas. Negley's reconnaissance discovered that the enemy cavalry had possession of the direct road to Snodgrass Hill, where Thomas was positioned. Furthermore, Confederate artillery were positioned so they could prevent a direct approach. After Negley reported this to Davis and Sheridan, the three finally agreed that it was advisable for all to proceed to Rossville and prevent the enemy from possessing the crossroads and thereby blocking Thomas's only retreat route. From Rossville, they agreed, Sheridan should move by the longer Lafayette Road route to support Thomas.

About 4 P.M., Thruston arrived back from Thomas with the message that he wanted them to try strengthening his right, since he thought the road leading to it was open. Thruston found Sheridan, Davis, and Negley farther down the road toward Rossville at the head of their columns. Lt. Col. Arthur Ducat, an aide to Rosecrans, was with them as they engaged in a heated discussion about what to do. Davis about-faced his troops, but Sheridan was convinced it would be dark before he could reach Thomas. With Thruston as his guide, Sheridan and what remained of his men reached the Cloud Church on the Lafayette Road three miles past Rossville before sundown. Colonel Miller's brigade, including Lank and the Fox River lads, took part in the advance. Night had drawn a curtain on the killing, and Sheridan's troops did not go into action, since the enemy had not pursued Thomas. The curtain, however, did not muffle the shrieks, cries, and groans at the Cloud Church, which was being used as a hospital for the wounded.

When Sheridan and Negley arrived at Rossville, they organized the troops, assembled abandoned artillery and caissons, and obtained ammunition from Chattanooga. Colonel Miller's brigade was still in the advance. In Rossville, Sheridan flew into a towering rage, swearing in the manner for which he was famous. He had lost faith in both Rosecrans and McCook. He told the other generals that his division had arrived exhausted from its forced march from Lee and Gordon's Mill to the battleground early that morning, had been shifted from one position to another without plan or purpose, and not once had had a fair show. He expressed particular bitterness about the sacrificial death of the brave, energetic, and chivalrous Lytle. While Sheridan was fiercely loyal to superiors he regarded as competent, he was even more concerned for officers and men under him.[2]

Sheridan's fury was largely justified. His men had had little sleep for three nights, the first two of which were spent in an intensely dark and fatiguing night march. The third night they were awakened at 2 A.M. to begin marching at four. When his troops had finally arrived at Widow Glenn's house that morning, they were assigned an extremely good defensive position. Then they were ordered to leave that position to aid General Thomas. While en route, they suddenly were ordered to take yet another position, which could not be defended against an overwhelming number of Longstreet's advancing troops. The result was slaughter and a hopelessly disorganized retreat for Sheridan's three brigades. One of his brigades, Bradley's, had already been badly mauled the day before. The fact that orders had been issued to Sheridan's troops without his knowledge only added fuel to the fire. Clearly, McCook had ordered Laiboldt's brigade up without informing Sheridan. Further, as Sheridan wrote in his *Memoirs*, "There did not seem to be any well-defined plan of action in the fighting, and this led to much independence of judgment in construing orders."

While Sheridan and others were being kept from going to support Thomas, he had held his ground around the base of Snodgrass Hill. There had been great slaughter as Thomas's corps repulsed Bragg's repeated attacks, which were reinforced with Longstreet's men. Here Thomas became known as the "Rock of Chickamauga." His presence was electrifying. About 5 P.M., Thomas had received telegraphed instructions from Rosecrans to fall back to Rossville and take a strong stand. He knew he could not hold out much longer. His men were almost out of ammunition, and it would be dark in two hours. Thomas told Sheridan it was futile to continue the attempt to hold Snodgrass Hill. Instead, he ordered Sheridan to cover the withdrawal of his exhausted men to Rossville. He was to block the Confederate cavalry, with whom Sheridan and the decimated 36th had been skirmishing, and prevent the capture of Thomas's wagon train. Thomas also had ordered Granger and what remained of his fresh troops to remain behind at Snodgrass Hill to prevent Rebel troops from pursuing him.

Thomas's men withdrew to Rossville over the debris of battle—overthrown and broken wagons, dismounted cannon, limbers, caissons, and such. Men rested or wandered about without purpose, either in groups or alone, but not panic-stricken. Some were put to work building breastworks. Colonel Miller reported that his men took position about dusk. The Fox River lads were within rifle shot of enemy camp fires during a very dark night. By "remaining remarkably quiet," they secured Thomas's wagon train and brought it back five miles to Rossville unharmed. Sheridan met Thomas on horseback at a crossroads near McFarland's Gap. At about 10:00 P.M. that evening they arrived at Rossville, the army's withdrawal complete. By then the moon was bright, and the night was clear and cold. Sheridan later wrote that Thomas's "firm purpose to save the army was the mainstay on which all relied after Rosecrans left the field."

They dismounted next to a split rail fence. Sheridan took a top rail from the fence and wedged it through lower rails to make a seat in an angle of the fence. Thomas was exhausted and depressed. After what Sheridan thought was an interminable silence, Thomas offered him a drink of brandy from his flask. Sheridan took a sip, thanked Thomas, and rode off to supervise the encampment of his troops.

Sometime after 9 P.M., the 36th—reduced to 168 men—bivouacked for the night near Rossville. They were tired and hungry, not having eaten since their early breakfast. Meanwhile, ambulances carried their 101 wounded comrades to Chattanooga hospitals. With the road from Rossville jam-packed for its entire twelve-mile length to Chattanooga, most did not arrive until about 9 P.M. Other men who were too severely wounded to be moved were left on the battlefield for as long as a week. One of the wounded was Pvt. Day Elmore, who had been shot in the lungs. Twenty others had been killed in action, and twenty were missing in action.

About 2 A.M., their move from Rossville to Chattanooga began, past the wounded, dead, and dying along the roadside. No lights, fires, or noisy movements were allowed. Sheridan sat patiently on his horse alongside the road waiting for the last of his men to arrive, before beginning the march. By 5 A.M., in a dense fog, his division reached the outskirts of Chattanooga, footsore, ravenous, and bone-tired. They halted for breakfast near the foot of Lookout Mountain and set to work digging rifle pits and felling trees to strengthen the half-finished defenses the Rebels had started in August when they occupied the city. That morning, the Fox River men took rations to their hospitalized comrades and dressed their wounds. A big tent was set up to accommodate them. About midnight, five hours before Sheridan's troopers arrived, Capt. Alfred Hough, one of his staff officers, had ridden six miles to find Rosecrans in Chattanooga and give him a report. He was physically and emotionally exhausted and crushed by his disaster. As Hough departed he looked back and saw the general down on his knees before his priest, praying and weeping.

At Chickamauga, Thomas had succeeded in keeping the Army of the Cumberland between Bragg's Army of Tennessee and Chattanooga, major supply base for whatever army held it. On September 21, two weeks after Bragg abandoned the city, the Stars and Stripes were hoisted over Chattanooga, the doorway to the Deep South and a natural fortress. The next day Lank and the other lads of the 36th entered the city, together with other remaining Union troops, including artillery, wagons, and ambulances. The Union now held a strategic railroad hub, the gateway to Atlanta, via the Western and Atlantic Railroad, and to Nashville, via the Nashville and Chattanooga Railroad. However, they had only ten days' full rations on hand.

That day, Bragg began to invest (surround) the city by posting batteries and signal stations and by moving his entire army onto the surrounding mountains in a semicircle from Chickamauga Creek to Lookout Mountain. In his retreat to Chattanooga, Rosecrans had abandoned these key positions outside the city as well as its supply routes. His men would again pay dearly. Some Rebels also appeared at the city's outskirts, and artillery fire began. Then Bragg sat down and waited, instead of pressing his advantage by either assaulting the city or at least severing its communication and supply lines. The Siege of Chattanooga had begun.

Bragg's men were to come as close to starvation as the Yankees they besieged. Cut off from their food supply, their plight endeared him even less to them. One of his privates wrote, "not a single soldier in the whole army ever loved or respected him." But they were convinced that the Union Army was not foolish enough to attack them.

With his heavily reinforced army, Bragg had failed to take full advantage of the blunders made by Rosecrans and other major Union mistakes, and he suffered crippling losses in the process. One-third of his men—18,500—were casualties, including 10 generals. Half of his artillery horses were killed. Bragg was despondent and pessimistic.

Rosecrans's casualties totaled 16,000, also one-third of his army. Almost 10,000 of his wounded were hospitalized in Chattanooga. His career as a field commander was over. In Lincoln's opinion, after Chickamauga Rosecrans was "confused and stunned like a duck hit on the head." As Lank's brigade commander put it, "The recent battles have taken the conceit out of the Army of the Cumberland." Less than a month later, on October 16, Thomas took command of the Army of the Cumberland, replacing Rosecrans. For his men, however, Rosie had a magnetic personality. As Pvt. John Ely of the 88th Ill. put it, "I think the worst calamity that has befallen us is the removal of Gen. Rosecrans . . . it seems to cause a depression of spirits throughout the army."

Assistant Secretary Dana telegraphed the war department: "Chickamauga is as fatal a name in our history as Bull Run." Sheridan's division suffered 1,517 casualties, of which 460 were in Lytle's brigade. The 36th Ill. had 141 casualties, including 18 in Lank's company, and, as at Stones River, the largest number in any regiment in the brigade. Again, Lank came through unharmed, but his company commander was wounded and captured, Lt. Orison Smith and a sergeant of his company were killed, and four men were captured. Elisha E. Lloyd, one of the four, was sent to four prisons, the last of which was Andersonville. He made one unsuccessful attempt to escape, for which he suffered severe punishment. He was near death when he was exchanged and paroled at Annapolis, where he recovered in the hospital. Counting the Battle of Perryville, Lank's good luck charm had gotten him through three of the bloodiest Civil War battles unscathed. Sheridan commended Colonel Miller, Lieutenant Colonel Olson, and Major Sherman.

According to legend, Chickamauga is an old Cherokee word meaning "river of death." After this battle, no one disputed the legend.[3]

7

Missionary Ridge
November 23–25, 1863

> If you write anything [about Missionary Ridge], don't forget Col. Miller of the 36th Illinois—one of the most gallant little fellows that ever drew a sword.
>
> —General Thomas J. Wood to a *Chicago Evening Journal* reporter

Missionary Ridge was the first battle in which Grant, Thomas, and Sheridan, all West Point graduates, combined their talents. It also was the first battle Lank fought under either Grant or Thomas, but the fourth in which he fought under Sheridan. Both Dan and Lank Ross would be involved in the effort to lift the Confederate siege of Chattanooga, but there is no record of their ever seeing each other there.

On the night of September 23, three days after the Battle of Chickamauga ended, Lincoln was summoned by Secretary of War Stanton. The president had been in the telegrapher's office at the Soldiers' Home reading war dispatches as soon as they arrived, but had gone to his cottage on the grounds and fallen asleep. Lincoln and his secretary, John Hay, galloped back in the moonlight to Washington. When Lincoln and the others were assembled, Stanton proposed that at least 20,000 of Meade's troops in the Army of the Potomac be sent by rail to assist Rosecrans, now under siege in Chattanooga. Lincoln had already written Rosecrans, "If we can hold Chattanooga . . . I think the rebellion must dwindle and die." Stanton argued that if 20,000 bales of cotton could be moved by rail, so could 20,000 men. Never, however, had such a transportation feat been attempted. Seven railroads, ferries, river steamers, and marches would have to be employed. Railroad gauges would have to be determined and altered where possible. Bridges had to be built, other trains sidetracked, and railroad managers and telegraphers alerted along the chosen route. The dubious president at last was persuaded, and by 2:30 A.M., orders were telegraphed to General Meade, to mobilize, and to Rosencrans to expect 14,000 to 15,000 men to arrive in Nashville in about seven days.

General Hooker was assigned to the command, which consisted of the 11th Corps and 12th Corps—17,615 men, ten artillery batteries, one of which was Dan's, and 3,000 horses. Railroad officials whose trains were commandeered were summoned to Washington to complete arrangements for the 1,200-mile journey. State governors, quartermaster officers, and War Department officials had to be involved. On September 25, the New Yorkers were ordered to assemble their baggage for shipment to Alexandria at 4 o'clock the next morning. Despite every effort to keep the movement secret, including pledges from newspapers to do so, the story was leaked on September 26 to the *New York Evening Post*. General Lee also obtained confirmation. According to an observer, "Stanton roared like a lion" and Lincoln "was exceedingly angry." Via the unseen but ever-present grapevine, rumors already were circulating that General Lee also was sending troops under General Longstreet to reinforce Bragg's Tennessee army.

Meanwhile, on September 28, nine days after the fight had started, one hundred ambulances were sent back to the Chickamauga battlefield to bring in the remaining wounded, who had been largely untreated and not fed for seven days. McCook was relieved of command, and his 20th Corps was consolidated with Crittenden's 21st Corps into a new 4th Corps. Lank's 36th Ill. was now part of the new corps, commanded by Maj. Gen. Gordon Granger, a New Yorker. Granger's support had been crucial to Thomas's stand at Chickamauga, and he was grateful for it.

Granger's troops admired his bravery and had complete confidence in him. He was rough in manner, particularly toward new recruits, but had a tender heart. His fearlessness in battle inspired acceptance of discipline as well, and he was a strict disciplinarian, sometimes whipping volunteers for neglect of duty. He was devoted to artillery and would sometimes take personal command of a battery. He had done so at the Battle of Chickamauga and would do so again at Missionary Ridge, until Grant reprimanded him. A West Pointer, Granger had served with distinction in the war with Mexico and had seen extensive frontier service. He never shirked responsibility and would rather act without authority—as he had at Chickamauga by supporting Thomas without orders to do so—than not act at all. His orders were brusque, his conversations to the point. To some he sounded harsh, if not arrogant.

The initial campsite of the 36th was at the bottom of a hillside, on the right of the army's line and resting on the Tennessee River. When it rained heavily the tents would flood, so Lank and the other Fox River lads were soon moved to a permanent site on ground that was higher, but still poorly drained. It was enveloped in thick fog through the night into early morning. The regiments in the brigade rotated picket duty, manned well-positioned, excellent trenches and rifle pits, and dug ditches to drain rain from the campsite. At night scouts would be pushed out and posted near the enemy lines. Beginning in early October, heavy rains flooded their campsite and found the holes in every tent. The men had to find a spot between leaks to sleep or sit, making it extremely difficult to keep things dry—clothing, diaries, books, everything. As the weather turned cold, the men shivered in their thin, worn-out clothing. Cadaverous mules and horses did their share of shivering in the cold rain as well, no longer strong enough to pull artillery. Hardly a blade of grass remained, and trees were all cut for fuel and fortifications. By the end of the siege, only fifty-one trees still stood in the city. Lank's camp was almost opposite Bragg's headquarters, which was in an old log hut atop Missionary Ridge. He could see the enemy's flag fluttering in the breeze. Nearby were the dilapidated Western and Atlantic railroad tracks that connected Chattanooga and Atlanta, Bragg's former supply line. On October 5, the Confederates bombarded Sheridan's men for seven hours, exploding 2,000 shells over their heads. Otherwise the shelling was sporadic and mostly at night, and injured no one.

During this period of anxious watching and waiting, heavy rains and gnawing hunger, the men counteracted stress and boredom with religious services, reading, and swapping stories and small belongings. The chaplain held two well-attended services on Sundays and prayer meetings every evening, weather permitting. The Lincolnite regiment must have been among the most literate in the army, measured by the quantity of reading material they purchased for their library—twelve copies of four monthly magazines, twenty copies each of several weekly newspapers, plus religious tracts, all avidly read, sometimes over and over like their mail. One newspaper correspondent who commented on picket conversations and exchanges dryly noted, "An examination of many a plug of the Indian weed [tobacco] in a picket's pocket would show the print of a Rebel's teeth at one end and a Yankee's at the other."

A sergeant was overheard to say, "Boys, I was eating a piece of hardtack this morning and bit on something soft. What do you think it was?" A private asked, "A worm?" The sergeant replied, "No by G——d, it was a ten-penny nail." By November, he might have longed for another "sheet-iron cracker" as the supply of bacon and hardtack was virtually exhausted. There were only four boxes of hard bread in stock in the Chattanooga warehouses. However difficult it was for the bluecoats, the Rebels and their animals surrounding the city were colder, wetter, and hungrier, and the morale lower. Bragg gave little thought to alleviating their suffering. One Confederate artilleryman reported that his "brigade has not drawn but one day's ration of beef in eight days." The weather was turning cold and windy, and uniforms and shoes were wearing thin, adding discomfort, if not frostbite. In both armies, many had no overcoats or blankets. The only hope the Rebels had was that they could block any attempted Union breakout.

Yanks quickly took to building brick fireplaces and mud chimneys in their tents so they could at least build fires for warmth. However, firewood was so scarce that they organized crews to go upriver to cut trees and float the logs downstream to where they could be carried on shoulders to campsites. Two tentmates posted a hand-lettered sign on their tent, "Dog Hole No. 1—Sons of bitches within." The siege necessitated issuing less than half rations to Lank, the other lads of the 36th, and 40,000 other troops. Rations consisted of moldy hard bread, also dubbed "Lincoln's Platforms," and dried beef, plus a quarter ration of sugar and coffee. The hardtack, if tenanted by weevils, could be eaten in the dark and not be distinguishable from untenanted crackers. Biting into them was like biting into a wooden shingle. Officers enjoyed the same rations as the men. Guards were posted to keep soldiers from stealing what little corn there was to feed the few remaining horses. Kernels that fell to the ground were salvaged, if possible, by nearby soldiers before the rats got them. They did not want to grant the rats "a monopoly of stealing," so they shot and ate the rodents as well. Some men grated what corn they could get by first punching holes through a tin plate with a nail. By rubbing the corn against the rough side, they made coarse corn meal, mixed it with water and salt, and baked it over hot coals in another tin plate. The grub was, according to some men, bad enough to convince a mule to desert and a hog to wish he'd never been born. Some men developed scurvy. Sutlers' prices for food were outrageously high. Many of the cold, wet, and hungry men were losing confidence in their leader. The same was happening among the Confederate officers and rank and file atop Missionary Ridge.[1]

On September 25, Maj. Gen. Henry W. Slocum, the 12th Corps commander, had again offered Lincoln his resignation, reiterating that his opinion of Hooker was so low that it would be degrading to accept a position under him. Lincoln refused the resignation and invited Slocum to the White House, promising to separate him from Hooker.

Slocum's 12th Corps, including Dan Ross and his artillery battery, had been on picket duty along the Rappahannock when orders for the move arrived. According to Lt. George I. Robinson of Company A, the New Yorkers had been camped at Kelley's Ford, Virginia. In a letter to his wife dated September 12, he wrote, "I shall be proud to think I done my share towards putting down the greatest rebellion the world ever saw. . . . I have done it . . . from a sense of duty that I and every man owes to his country and Government. Be as content as you can til I come home and will try to make up in love for the fusin I have caused you during the last years."

It took 600 passenger, livestock, and railroad boxcars in thirty trains to haul the 17,615 soldiers, artillery, horses, and baggage. Each train accommodated two regiments. The men huddled like cattle in the boxcars, on wooden benches along the sides and down the middle. The only ventilation was through holes the men punched in the ends of the cars with musket butts and axes. Officers occupied one passenger car in each train. Thirty-three flat cars were used for the ten batteries of artillery, including Dan's Battery F. Twenty-one livestock cars carried 3,000 kicking, snorting, and braying horses and mules, and 100 cars held ammunition, baggage, tents, and supplies. They carried 200 rounds of ammunition per gun as well as 570 wagons and 150 ambulances. Battery commanders rode in the horse cars or on top of them. Some of the men who were packed forty to a car chose to ride on the rooftops to escape the crowding as well as to enjoy the fresh air and scenery. A few fell off while asleep or drunk, despite an order to "close all drinking saloons at the principal stations." Needless to say, the men got little rest, much less sleep. Nonetheless, after two years of marching in Virginia, some troopers considered the train trip a holiday.

It was the largest troop movement by rail in the Civil War and included changing rail lines four times. On the afternoon of September 25, the first trainload of 11th Corps men left Brandy Station, Virginia, for Bridgeport, Alabama, about thirty miles west of Chattanooga. Dozens of others followed, including the one that took the New Yorkers. The 123rd left Brandy Station on one of the first 12th Corps trains at 3:30 A.M. on September 26. They traveled in delightful Indian summer weather with perfect moonlight to Bridgeport, almost 1,200 miles, in eight days. The artillery marched to Washington and entrained there. On September 28, the last of the Twelfth Corps men boarded trains at Bealton Station, Virginia. Some had waited two days to board. They had been given extra water before boarding the train, as well as extra salt, eight days' extra rations, and forty rounds of ammunition. The trains also carried five days' forage for the animals.

The first stop for the New Yorkers aboard the B&O was Martinsburg, West Virginia, at noon on September 27. The citizens served them coffee and food, waved handkerchiefs, towels, aprons, and flags, and cheered them on to victory. Ten years later, Dan would open his medical practice in Martinsburg. The next stop was at the Ohio River, where they detrained and marched across a pontoon bridge supported by coal barges and river scows. Cooks, waiters, cooking equipment, and food were stationed at intervals along the remainder of the route to feed the men fruits, freshly cooked food, bread, and coffee as the trains arrived. By ringing the courthouse bell, signaling the train's arrival, ample time would be given to farmers and others to bring, prepare, and serve the food. On September 29, they stopped for an oyster stew supper in Columbus. The Ohio gubernatorial election campaign was at its height. When citizens lining the tracks showed signs and shouted their support for Clement Vallandingham, the Copperhead candidate, the men reacted by pelting their tormentors with stones as they passed by.

Elsewhere in Ohio, they also were greeted by little girls with bouquets of flowers and young women who offered lavish refreshments and blew them kisses. One soldier wrote, "Our mouths were crammed with cakes, pies, cookies, meat, eggs and fruit, which the loyal Ohio people brought us without money or price." Soldiers wrote their names, addresses, and love notes on anything handy, including their paper collars, and tossed them to the girls. This experience may well have conditioned Dan to favor Ohio girls. In any event, he would move to Ohio and marry one five years later. Their marriage would last fifty-six years, until his death.

At Richmond, Indiana, Quakers fed breakfast to the hungry lads. Besides the food they received en route, ladies gave them handkerchiefs, towels, and soap to clean off the dust and grime from the journey. They stopped in Indianapolis long enough to have a good dinner at the Soldier's Home. At Jeffersonville, Indiana, the artillery was unloaded from the B&O and ferried across the Ohio to Louisville, where it was put aboard the L&N. Bands played patriotic airs and political speakers greeted them. Since they had received two months' back pay prior to departure, guards were stationed to prevent men who wanted to quench their thirst for whiskey from leaving the cars. As they passed through Murfreesboro on October 2, they saw their first colored regiment—recruited in Tennessee—lined up to salute the train as it passed. Pvt. Horace Mathews wrote in his diary that day, "they looked nice; I wish you could see them."

They arrived at Bridgeport, Alabama, at 3 A.M. October 3, then they slept until daylight. They selected a campsite by the Tennessee River, where they enjoyed their first bath in more than a week. The troops were to be assigned to protect the Union supply line to Chattanooga.

The two corps, including Dan's, were under "Fightin' " Joe Hooker's command, and immediately dubbed "Hooker's Potomacs" and "white-glove soldiers." Lincoln had authorized him to take possession of all railroads necessary for this operation and directed all railroad employees of these lines to obey Hooker's commands. A key role was assigned to Brig. Gen. Alpheus S. Williams's two-brigade division of 4,900 men, including the 123rd N.Y., 507 strong, and Dan's Battery F. They were to build and occupy fortifications along a ninety-mile stretch of the Nashville and Chattanooga Railroad between Murfreesboro and Bridgeport, the location of the Union supply depot and the terminus of the railroad from Louisville. They were an integral part of the lifeline to feed and supply the frontline troops defending Chattanooga. Complete stoppage could lead to their surrender. They had to prevent cavalry and armed guerrillas from blowing up bridges and tunnels, and destroying trackage.

By October 7, all the troops and animals had arrived. The lads of Battery F and the 123rd were more than glad to stretch their legs and pitch their tents for a good night's sleep after being cooped up for eight days and nights in boxcars with only rough-cut plank seats. General Williams's two horses also must have been grateful. His stallion was badly rubbed on both hips, and "Old Plug Ugly" had been bitten in the neck and his head and tail rubbed bare. On October 8, at Murfreesboro, the men unloaded the batteries. On that day, one soldier in the 123rd wrote his brother, "Boys [are in] good spirits. We gave up the notion long ago, of going home before our time was up, and so will stay contented for 3 years." He also reported that the Tennessee River at Bridgeport looked a lot like the Hudson River at Fort Miller, New York, near the Ross brothers' birthplace.

For the first two weeks in October it rained continuously, flooding their barracks with a foot and a half of water. The Bridgeport Road was so muddy that mules were mired down in it belly-deep. The railroad tracks they were guarding had been destroyed by Union troops previously, and the engines were old and in bad repair. Firewood for the engines was scarce. General Williams wrote from his Tullahoma headquarters, which he shared with Slocum, that it took a day to travel forty miles by train. To protect the trains, bridges, water tanks, culverts, tunnels, and telegraph lines, and to fend off Rebel cavalry, pro-Confederate guerrillas, partisan rangers, and bushwhackers, regiments were stationed at guard posts at intervals along the railway's ninety-mile route. The 123rd N.Y. was stationed initially at Bridgeport, as was Battery F, to guard a railroad bridge being rebuilt across the Tennessee River—a bridge the Confederates had destroyed when they had retreated. Ship's carpenters were brought in from the East to help rebuild the bridge. The 123rd also helped to run a sawmill and build steamboats, as well as to unload railroad cars. One hundred fifty New Yorkers, including every carpenter and mechanic in the regiment, were detailed at Bridgeport and paid extra to build flatboats and steamboats from late October until mid-March. Food was ample after the bridge was rebuilt and they could be supplied by rail. Later the regiment, including Dan's Battery F, was moved to Decherd, Wartrace, and various other way stations along the railroad as part of Brig. Gen. J. F. Knipe's brigade. Knipe's headquarters were in Decherd, a vital rail junction.

Dan and many of his fellow soldiers had their first up-close look at black troops in a regiment that was stationed between Decherd and Wartrace. One of Dan's officers wrote, "They seem anxious to fight." A soldier in the 27th Ind., another regiment in Dan's brigade, wrote, "The colored troops which we saw at this time impressed us with the exactness with which they executed orders." These Hoosiers felt that "if a Negro could stop a Rebel bullet, or better still stop the Rebel from shooting, let him come on." On October 12, Lt. George Robinson wrote his wife about the first black regiment he had seen. "They looked as clean and even cleaner than most of our white regts and the cleaner and best laid out camp I ever saw." He quoted one of the officers, "they are better than any white soldier he ever saw for they will obey orders and are more strict than whites. . . . There is no prejudice against them in this army for everybody knows they will fight. . . . No traitors. No desertions, and no shirking duty; and that is more than one can say for white soldiers."

They returned to Bridgeport on October 26 to guard the supply depot. While there Dan also could have seen the well-disciplined 1,000-man, 14th U.S. Colored Troops (USCT), who were doing picket duty, guarding wagon trains, and foraging in the vicinity. The soldiers were freed slaves recruited in Tennessee during the summer and early fall. Dan Ross had no idea that the supply line his battery had been guarding since October 3 was helping to keep his half-starved brother Lank alive, along with the rest of the Army of the Cumberland in Chattanooga.[2]

The 123rd had to guard a constant stream of at least 1,500 hungry, ragged, dirty, and miserable Confederate prisoners and deserters, mostly from Bragg's army, at Bridgeport. On October 18, Corp. Rice C. Bull, who was wounded at Chancellorsville, returned to the regiment and helped guard the prisoners. They also had to provide rations for large numbers of women and children. Lieutenant Cruikshank wrote his wife, "you [have] never seen poverty . . . their food is corn and pork. Their hogs run in the woods and fatten on nuts. The get about as fat as a northern fence rail." They also had to help build a large depot on the riverbank to store hardtack and other army rations for delivery by wagon fifty-five miles over a tortuous mountain road to Chattanooga. Despite the vital role that Slocum's men were playing in protecting Chattanooga's supply line, Hooker wanted him transferred to some other command. He wrote, "Unless [Slocum] gives more satisfaction in the discharge of his duties, he will soon find himself in deeper water than he has been wading in." Hooker also wanted to get rid of Williams, but Thomas vetoed that proposal.

On October 23, during a stormy night, Maj. Gen. Ulysses S. Grant arrived to assume command of all the troops at Chattanooga, accompanied by five big army wagons loaded with headquarters baggage. Dan and his fellow cannoneers received six months' back pay that day. One of Grant's first acts was to replace Rosecrans as head of the Army of the Cumberland with the six-foot, burly, grizzle-bearded Maj. Gen. George H. Thomas. Despite their half-starved condition, many soldiers were unhappy to see Rosecrans go. Maj. James A. Connolly wrote his wife, "General Rosecrans was my beau ideal of a leader. . . . This entire army was an army of crusaders under his leadership. He was the light and life of this army."

Thomas was a Virginia-born aristocrat and West Pointer who had freed his slaves and remained loyal to the Union. As a child, against his father's wishes, he taught the slave children at night what he had learned that day in school. Grant reputedly distrusted, if not disliked, Thomas because he was a Southern aristocrat. Thomas excelled at transforming volunteers into warriors. Thoroughly good-natured, he built a special bond with his soldiers, who came to call him "Old Pap." They knew he expected great things of them, and they did not let him down. His courage became their courage. He was as pugnacious as he was deliberate and careful. General Sherman respected Thomas for his excellent war record and his knowledge, but the two differed radically in their personal and tactical styles with one significant exception: both lacked the killer instinct. Interestingly, they had been West Point roommates. In November, Thomas was asked his opinion regarding enlisting blacks in the army. He replied, "I . . . think in the sudden transition from slavery to freedom it perhaps is far better for the Negro to become a soldier, and be generally taught to depend on himself for support, than to be thrown upon the cold charities of the world without sympathy or assistance."

By the time Grant arrived, supplies of hay and grain were so scarce that thousands of horses and mules died while hauling supplies on the hazardous wagon road over the 1,300-foot-high Walden's Ridge between Bridgeport and Chattanooga. The bodies of those that died in the city were heaped onto pyres that burned night and day. Raiding Rebel cavalrymen also set wagons on fire and shot the animals. The animals that survived were often so weak they had to be double-teamed in order to pull the wagons. Mules ate the bark off trees, wasting away until they were walking skeletons. Some fell dead while attached to their picket ropes. None were available to pull ambulances. Animals were so scarce that artillery horses were assigned to pull wagons. Torrential mountain rains made the road a deep-rutted, greasy, washed-out hell. To save the wagons stuck hub-deep in mud, weak, if not dead, horses or mules were cut out of their traces and their carcasses left to rot in roadside ditches. The combination of muck and carcasses was referred to as "mule soup." Tree trunks had to be laid across sinkholes and quicksand before wagons could cross, a tactic called corduroying. The besieged soldiers were on half rations of hard bread and "beef dried on the hoof." As a result, they were weak, listless, and low in morale. Their defeat at Chickamauga, as well as the removal of Rosecrans, made matters that much worse. On October 25, Lank's brigade commander, Col. Francis T. Sherman, wrote his father, the mayor of Chicago, "there is not a hog sty in all of Illinois that is not roomier and warmer than that which the enlisted man . . . has [here]."

After his Vicksburg campaign ended in victory on July 4, Grant had little to do for three months. He was suffering from boredom, and drank only when he was bored. His duty consisted almost exclusively of mopping up operations in western Louisiana and Mississippi, and building a new set of defenses around Vicksburg. During a trip to New Orleans in early September, he attended the Grand Review of twenty-thousand troops and a dinner in his honor where wine was served freely. Having overindulged, Grant borrowed a spirited, high-stepping charger, which got out of control when a hissing locomotive startled it. It bolted, ran into an oncoming carriage, and fell on top of Grant, rendering him unconscious for an hour. The left side of his body from armpit to knee was grotesquely swollen, and the pain was severe. Nursed by his wife, Julia, he partially recuperated from the injury in Vicksburg. Few officers were accompanied by their wives as often as Grant was. A strong and enduring bond existed between them. Not until September 25 was he even able to get out of bed and move with crutches. He was still weak, with purple bruises on his left hip and thigh. On October 21, when he arrived by rail in Stevenson to meet Rosecrans before his departure, he was on crutches, and still painfully bruised.

Battery F was in Stevenson when Grant arrived, and Dan may have seen him. In any event, Sergeant Bull recorded in his diary that he and others did see him. Grant took command from Rosecrans there, and the next day traveled by horseback in torrential rain over Walden's Ridge. His horse slipped, sending Grant head over heels to the ground. On arrival in Chattanooga, wet and muddy, with his crutches fastened to his saddle, he had to be lifted off his horse by two aides. He limped through the rain into Thomas's headquarters. After a quick inspection the next day, he returned to his headquarters and sat down to write a series of orders. A staff member of General Thomas observed that they outlined "vigourous and comprehensive steps in every direction throughout his new and extensive command." Grant also asked Capt. Horace Porter, one of Rosecrans's aides, about how much ammunition was on hand. Porter's reply was that they had only enough for a day's heavy fighting.

By the night of October 26, with Grant's sanction, a 1,350-foot-long pontoon bridge was completed over the Tennessee River. Thomas and his chief engineer, Gen. W. F. (Baldy) Smith, had recommended the bridge, but Rosecrans had never ordered it built. On October 28, Union forces took control of Brown's Ferry, between Bridgeport and Kelley's Ferry, from the Confederates, giving them complete control of that stretch of the river. That night, under Hooker's command, steamers, flatboats, and scows immediately began to carry rations from Bridgeport to Kelley's Ferry. On October 30, Lieutenant Robinson of the 123rd watched the first steamboat arrive from Chattanooga at noon to load rations and return there. Now wagons had to travel only eight miles from Kelley's Ferry instead of fifty-five, to reach Chattanooga with rations. Five days earlier Grant had traveled part of this miserable road on horseback in a torrential rainstorm and was familiar with it. On October 31, all the 36th had to eat was one hundred pounds of moldy and wormy hard bread. Two days later, with the bridge in place, 250,000 rations had arrived, including a small mountain of hardtack. Mail was also being delivered, and steamboats were bringing prisoners and wounded soldiers from Chattanooga hospitals. Pvt. Walter V. Reeder of the 36th wrote his parents on November 5, "Dinner today [consisted] of beef soup—'hardtack' and hominy. Provisions are much more plenty [sic] than when I came." Lank, who enjoyed the same meal, could not have known his brother Dan's regiment helped build the boats at Bridgeport that were delivering their food. Meanwhile, on November 7, Lt. Sylvannus T. Rugg and the other officers of Dan's Battery F treated Generals Slocum, Williams, and Knipe to a supper that included champagne and oysters. The generals had arrived on an inspection tour.[3]

The new "Cracker Line" was as great a surprise for the Union army at Chattanooga as it was for the enemy that surrounded the city. Bragg could no longer assume that by waiting he could starve Grant's army out of Chattanooga. Nevertheless, it would take some time to overcome the adverse impact of past severe food shortages on both men and animals. Morale was boosted November 14 when the 36th was paid off. The regimental chaplain, having been granted leave, agreed to take home $17,000 in back pay that men wanted to send to their families.

The money not sent home was used for gambling to relieve boredom. The men's hollow cheeks, sallow skin, physical weakness, and low morale began to dissipate after full rations were restored on November 15. Now Generals Grant, Sherman, and Thomas could turn their attention to recruiting Veteran Volunteers as much-needed replacements. Sherman visited Bridgeport that day to encourage reenlistment as veteran volunteers those eligible to do so.

With the danger of starvation removed inside the besieged city, Grant could now turn his attention to freeing Chattanooga from the noose around its neck and securing its railroad supply line. Thomas's weakened Army of the Cumberland was already reinforced by the two-corps army from the East, under Hooker. Now Grant ordered General Sherman to send two corps of his Army of the Tennessee from Vicksburg. Grant and Thomas planned a three-pronged breakout from Chattanooga. Hooker was to take Lookout Mountain at the south end of Missionary Ridge; Sherman was to attack Tunnel Hill at the north end; and Thomas was to hit the ridge's center. On November 19, while these plans were being laid, Lincoln delivered his Gettysburg address.

On November 20, Sherman's men, who were on their way to reinforce Grant, marched past the 123rd at Bridgeport. They mocked the "Potomac boys" as "tin soldiers." With feigned surprise, they elaborated, "Oh look at their little caps. Where are your paper collars? Oh how clean you look, do you have soap?"

Two days earlier, in a cold, clammy, disagreeable drizzle, Sheridan's division, including the Lincolnites, had been ordered to prepare rations for two days, carry eighty rounds of ammunition, and be ready to march at a moment's notice. Musicians were ordered to be ready with stretchers for the wounded. "This means something—our artillery have the same orders, but enough of this," wrote Lt. Richard H. Watson, of Lank's regiment, to his sister. On November 22, all day long the Fort Wood artillery heavily shelled Missionary Ridge, some five miles away. The fort was part of the semicircular fortifications between the city and Missionary Ridge.[4]

On the morning of November 23, the valley was filled with fog, but the veil slowly lifted, and it turned warm and windy, with a crystal blue sky. Thomas ordered Col. Francis T. Sherman's 1st (Sheridan's division), to which the 36th was attached, to be ready by 1 P.M. to move toward the front. Colonel Sherman had succeeded Lytle at Chickamauga. The maneuver was intended to explore the strength of the Confederate forces holding Orchard Knob, a 100-foot-high, steep, wooded eminence, only a mile and a half in front of the center of Missionary Ridge. It also would divert Bragg's attention from both ends of his line, where Hooker and

Sherman were positioning themselves for attack. In thus threatening the center of the line, Grant also could smoke out Bragg's intention to fight or retreat. Bragg had, in fact, notified Grant that he should move all noncombatants out of town, suggesting he was about to attack. The Confederate pickets from two Alabama regiments guarding Orchard Knob were within gunshot range, leaning lazily on their rifles or sitting on top of their little mounds like groundhogs in front of their burrows. They did not fire a shot.

The brigade was in two lines in front of its breastworks, with Col. Silas Miller of the 36th in command of the first line. Lt. Col. Porter Olson took command of the Fox River regiment. Born and raised near Niagara Falls, he would be killed a year later at the Battle of Franklin, Tennessee. About 2 P.M., as the clouds lifted and the drums beat the "long roll," the loud commands of hundreds of company officers could be heard amid countless bugles. Bands played martial tunes as the troops marched out in line of battle, their polished bayonets flashing like a flying shower of electric sparks. After eight days of full rations, they were at last marching on full stomachs. All four of Thomas's divisions, 23,000 men, participated in this maneuver in parade-ground order with their regimental flags, some bright and others tattered, waving in the afternoon breeze. Initially, the Confederates atop the ridge, including General Bragg, thought it was a grand review. They watched from the ridge as Grant, Thomas, Sherman, Hooker, Sheridan, and others galloped with their staffs along the line as if on inspection. The Rebels were awed by the size of the force facing them from below.

Colonel Miller, Lank's regimental commander, was an interesting man. He was twenty-three years old (a year older than Lank), short and dapper, a former schoolteacher and law student. Miller had completed his last two years of education in 1858 at the Fort Edward Collegiate Institute, a boarding school on the Hudson River in New York, near where both he and Lank had grown up. Miller had first enlisted for three months in the same Illinois regiment as Lank's brother Will. Since both were teachers from neighboring New York communities and first enlisted in the same Illinois regiment, they surely knew each other. Very early, Colonel Miller acquired a reputation as an expert in directing the skirmish line, having drilled the regiment in this tactic since early 1862. Undoubtedly because of his skill and courage, Miller became an intimate friend of Sheridan's. In less than a year, Will and Colonel Miller would meet the same fate on different skirmish lines.

Shortly before 3 P.M., in bright sunshine, with Sheridan's entire division dressed in their best uniforms, the bugles sounded "Charge." Each regiment was led by its color guard bearing both national and state flags.

On the double-quick, a thin line of skirmishers followed by two battle lines drove the enemy pickets positioned in the sparse woods back about 600 yards. The Confederates on the ridge thought they were watching just another "Potomac Review." Wood's division easily took possession of Orchard Knob, capturing the first line of Confederate rifle pits along with several hundred prisoners. Cheers rang out and bands played again. By 5 P.M. it was all over, and Grant's headquarters and a battery moved atop Orchard Knob. The enemy had retreated to another line of trenches and were digging in deeper. One of the Rebels who had watched the entire maneuver, called out, "Hello, Yanks, what's got the matter with you all over there?" A Yank replied, "We're out of wood." The Confederate's response was, "If you wanted wood why didn't you say so?"

By the time the shades of night gathered, Miller and the rest of the brigade had accomplished a great deal. They had taken their new position to the right of Orchard Knob, overrun the Rebel picket line, helped capture Orchard Knob, and deployed their skirmishers. They built rail and log breastworks three and a half feet high and banked with earth, brought up their artillery, and prepared to sleep on their arms during the clear and frosty night. Rebel musket flashes on the mountainside and ridgetop gave the appearance of twinkling stars. Three white greyhounds, mascots of the 36th who had led the advance, now dashed ahead of the skirmish line to chase a family of rabbits. Their yelps contrasted sharply with the musket fire. The new Union line gave the Army of the Cumberland a much larger, partially wooded area to occupy less than a mile from the new Rebel entrenchments. The Union skirmish line was very heavy; the men were stationed about four feet apart. No longer crowded, the troops also now had access to firewood. They could heat their bones that had been chilled for two months. An officer observed, "What a relief it was to get out of old works where we had stood, like cattle, for two months." They would stay in their new position for two days and two nights.

Grant and Thomas were astounded at the success. Grant wired Washington that "the troops moved under fire with all the precision of veterans on parade." Thomas's troops were still nursing their wounded pride about their losses at Stones River and Chickamauga, even though Sheridan's division had helped to avert disaster for the Union army in both battles. Already on the mend, Lank's morale and that of the 36th and other regiments in the Army of the Cumberland improved even more after Orchard Knob.

During the night, parallel rows of camp fires tended by the respective armies looked like "streams of burning lava, while in between, the flashes from the skirmishers' muskets glowed like giant fireflies." On November

Missionary Ridge

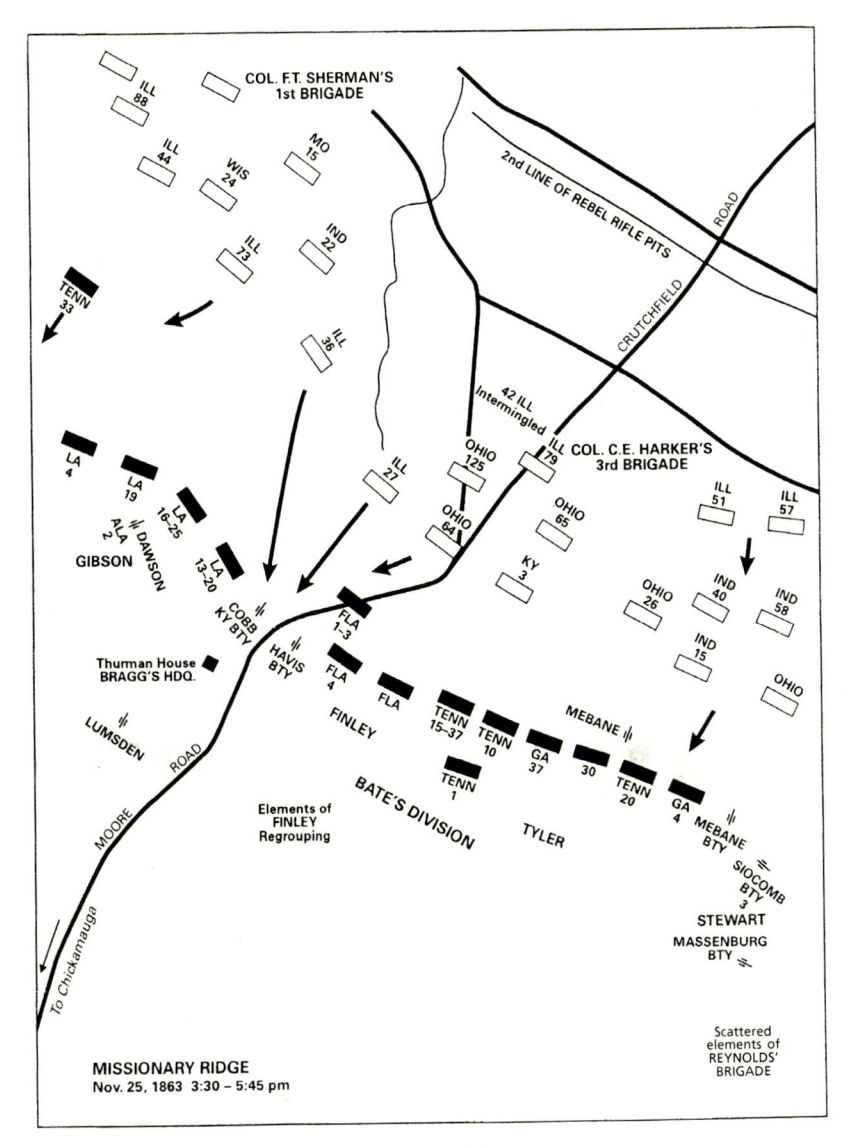

Missionary Ridge

24 at 4 A.M., four regiments of F. T. Sherman's first brigade—the 24th Wis., and the 44th, 36th, and 73rd Ill.—were placed to the right of Col. C. E. Harker's 3rd Brigade, behind hastily constructed, muddy, and cold rifle pits. This shift was necessitated because the battle line had lengthened. It was raining and cool.

One soldier wrote that while the boys were fortifying the lines, "I tried to get a little sleep by lying down close to a fire. [In doing so, I] burnt all the back out of my overcoat.... Afterwards... I often heard soldiers say... Golly didn't a shell come near getting that feller, look at the hole in his coat.'" The 73rd Ill. was known as the "Preacher Regiment." Its colonel, James F. Jacquess, as well as the lieutenant colonel, major, five out of ten captains, several lieutenants, the chaplain, and at least two enlisted men were Methodist preachers. Jacquess, a lawyer as well as a preacher and twice a college president, initially was commissioned as a chaplain and later recruited a regiment from church congregations. Many of the regiment's enlisted men were sons of prominent preachers and Methodist families, and a number were divinity students as well as educators. They held prayer meetings after morning and evening roll calls.

By dawn, it was bright and bone-chillingly cold in the river valley. A light fog on Missionary Ridge soon burned off, revealing a brilliant sun in a cloudless sky. The crest of Missionary Ridge stood in sharp relief against the bright sky. Men on the picket line were close enough to hear the Rebels coughing and to watch them wake up after sleeping under long, white blankets. One Lincolnite wrote in his diary, "They resembled the cranes on our [Illinois] prairies in the fall of the year."

About noon, while still in the position they were ordered to take at 4 A.M., Lank and his comrades watched General Hooker's men drive Confederates at a lively pace across open ground on the slopes of Lookout Mountain. A color bearer bravely waved on his comrades, then planted the Stars and Stripes atop the crest of the mountain. It was the first battle they had ever witnessed without being engaged. They cheered lustily in the drizzling rain, as the bands struck up "Hail to the Chief" and fifty cannon bellowed their praise for those who made the Rebels "git," as one soldier put it. Unfortunately, Hooker permitted some of Bragg's forces to move to Missionary Ridge. At the north end of the ridge, Sherman moved cautiously and slowly as both he and Hooker found themselves stalemated. That night, Grant gave Thomas the next day's orders "to carry the rifle-pits and ridge directly in front of them simultaneously" and "in cooperation with Sherman's advance along the ridge top from Tunnel Hill toward Bragg's center."

As Lank and the others turned in that night without tents, some slept fitfully, while others prayed and read the Bible, wrote home, or let a thousand thoughts and memories race through their minds. Fear, created more by the anxiety of waiting than anything else, manifested itself in dry throats, heightened perspiration, knotted stomachs, diarrhea, difficulty breathing, sinking or palpitating hearts, and nervous laughter.

On the morning of the 25th, Thomas ordered Sheridan to have his men drive in the Confederate pickets at his immediate front. They did so without firing a gun. By mid-afternoon, the Union center under Thomas was to bear the heaviest responsibility for lifting the siege of Chattanooga. Sheridan's division stayed at the base of Orchard Knob until noon that day, intently listening to and watching Sherman's battle for Tunnel Hill, at the north end of Missionary Ridge. By then Sheridan had armed and placed in line all his service troops, including quartermasters, cooks, and clerks.

This was the first time Sheridan would fight under Grant's command. About 2 P.M. that afternoon, "Little Phil" Sheridan rode in front of the two-mile line without a crook or a curve in it to make last-minute changes and closely examine the first line of the enemy rifle pits. They "seemed as though they would prove untenable after being carried," wrote Sheridan. As general field officer of the day, he had to receive verbal orders from Orchard Knob and relay them in the same manner—a process that inevitably led to some confusion. Since he had earlier driven in the Rebel pickets on his front and taken over their first row of rifle pits, he could now move his battle line forward some 300 yards to conform with the battle line of Wood's division on the left.

Harker's brigade held its extreme right with the 27th Ill. closest to the road. The left of Col. F. T. Sherman's brigade was also anchored on the Moore Road. His extreme left regiment, the 36th Ill., was directly below Thurman's log house on the crest, now Bragg's headquarters, and on the right side of the 27th Ill. Grant's headquarters was alive with couriers and aides on galloping horses arriving and departing in haste. Lank could see Bragg moving regiments to fill empty trenches on the ridge. Sheridan knew he would have to act quickly before the Rebels could significantly strengthen their positions. Although his 6,000 men were still concealed in the woods, their movement was observed by the Confederate cannoneers, who began shelling from the ridge. Of the nine regiments on the hill, five would be eligible to veteranize. Four of them would do so after this battle.

By about 10 A.M., a heavy line of skirmishers from companies A, B, and F, commanded by Maj. George Sherman, had been placed to the front and flank of the 1st. The balance of the 36th, including Lank's Company E, remained in the front rank of the brigade. At 1 P.M., the front rank was ordered to advance slowly to the picket posts from which the Rebels had been driven two days earlier. All these movements were done in plain view of the enemy, who then moved regiments, with blue battle flags flying, into vacant spaces in the rifle pits facing Sheridan. Sheridan's men then lay down on their arms in the timber to await further orders. By "grapevine dispatch," rumors soon began circulating that they were going to charge the rifle pits immediately in front of them. Nevertheless, some men in the line could be seen gambling, perhaps to distract themselves.

It was quiet as a graveyard. The blue line stretched to the left as far as the eye could see. By then, all were tense with nervous excitement and fear, many clenching their teeth behind compressed lips, and staring straight ahead. The waiting was dreadful as time moved on leaden wings. Men fidgeted, chewed tobacco, clenched their fists, or retied their shoelaces. Some had rubbery legs, broke out in cold sweats, or retched. Levity commingled with prayers, earnestness, and anxiety. Conversation was in monosyllables, usually only in response to questions. Otherwise they silently controlled their fears.

Somewhat later General Sherman signaled Grant from Tunnel Hill, saying that Bragg had transferred enough troops from Missionary Ridge to block his assault. It was therefore time for Thomas's Army of the Cumberland to move on Bragg's center. Grant then walked over to Maj. Gen. Thomas J. Wood, whose division was next to Sheridan's. He told Wood that Sherman "was having a hard time" and suggested an advance to the first line of rifle pits in order to help him by drawing troops back from Sherman's front. Wood responded that if ordered to do so, he would try it. Grant then turned to Thomas, who was observing Missionary Ridge through field glasses, and said, "Don't you think it's about time to advance against the rifle pits?" Thomas relayed the message to Granger. Ten minutes later Granger, standing on the parapet, gave the agreed-on sign to start the action, lifting and lowering his right arm in rapid succession as he shouted, "Number one, fire," and so on to "Number six, fire." It was about 3:40 P.M. Not much daylight was left. The rest of Thomas's army had been given similar orders. His entire line of 2,300 men covered a stretch of about two miles. About 9,000 Rebels occupied the first line of rifle pits. Pvt. John Ely of the 88th noted in his diary that they found it hard to believe they were to charge at least a half mile across an open field to take the first row of rifle pits.

When the first gun was fired, the bugles sounded, and the officers called their men to attention. The men were partially concealed from enemy view by leafless cottonwood trees and a thicket of bushes. Cheering and yelling, they sprang to their feet, rustling dead leaves and snapping twigs underfoot. An artillery battery arrived in front and unlimbered in the open. Field and staff officers also positioned themselves in front of the line, surgeons and stretcher bearers in the rear. Color bearers unfurled their flags. Fingers played with gunlocks and bands struck up as the men shouldered arms. Only about two hours of daylight remained.

In his *Memoirs*, Sheridan wrote that he discussed the feasibility of advancing no farther than the first line, but did not tell any of his three brigadiers to halt at these rifle pits, because they were too exposed to enemy artillery and rifle fire and the enemy's position was growing stronger by the minute. He could see Bragg's troops moving to fill unoccupied spaces in his line on the crest. Sheridan sent the only staff officer with him, Captain H. C. Ransom, at a mad gallop back to General Granger to ask if he was to carry the first line of rifle pits at the base or those on the ridge beyond. Ransom was still on this mission when the action started.

Meanwhile, Colonel Sherman relayed the order and signal to assault the first rifle pits to every officer and man in his nine-regiment command, including Olson and his Fox River regiment as well as to Major Sherman with the skirmishers. He did not, however, instruct them to remain in the rifle pits. The signal for the advance was to be the firing at two-second intervals of six Parrott guns in Bridge's Illinois battery on Orchard Knob. Lank Ross and his comrades saw Turnbull bring Sherman's order. Other officers were seen hurriedly mounting horses on Orchard Knob and riding toward the line of battle. Turnbull passed along the triple line from left to right, relaying the information. He said later, "I shall never forget [how] they received the order and nerved themselves for the conflict. [It] seemed to me ... that nothing but death would hinder them from carrying out the order." Turnbull reached the right end of the line as the signal guns fired.

When Granger shouted "Number six, fire" and the sixth gun was heard, another bugle call sounded. Major Sherman shouted "Forward boys" to the skirmishers, who had already started to move, and the ball opened, as the artillery in front of and behind them fired overhead from Orchard Knob. A perfectly aligned wall of blue moved forward in lockstep, as if on parade. One Rebel atop Missionary Ridge reported that his comrades thought the whole world was marching to battle them. Sheridan's three-brigade division poured out from the cottonwood trees bordering Citco Creek, a small stream, and swept without resistance into the broad, flat cotton field, flushing the Rebel skirmishers out of the underbrush.

The three ranks of Colonel Sherman's brigade, covering a front of more than a half mile, followed hard on the heels of the skirmishers like long tidal waves, as the artillery continued to fire overhead. One shell from Orchard Knob blasted Bragg's headquarters to smithereens. The Yanks advanced like impatient, restive mules unwilling to be restrained despite bits in their mouths. There was no dust. The air was clear and bathed in sparkling sunshine. Men began to fall in the face of intense fire from the rifle pits, but others filled the gaps they left.

In full dress uniform on his charger, Sheridan was in front of Harker's brigade, and therefore not too far from the 36th. He was accompanied by only one orderly so they would not attract enemy fire. Turning to look back, he told his brigadiers "to go for the ridge" and shouted over his shoulder, "Remember Chickamauga." They wanted revenge, and he knew it. He was always at the battlefront, cursing and swinging his sword, encouraging the brave and reproaching the laggards with alternate appeals and curses, setting an example to all. Lank's regiment held the left of its brigade front, closest to the Moore Road, as all three regiments maintained their advance in near-perfect alignment. No sooner had the valley floor come alive with the advancing Union troops than the entire ridge, enveloped in gun smoke, came ablaze with forty-two pieces of thunderous Confederate artillery issuing direct, plunging, and cross fire of shot and shell by the shovelful. The sound of shells leaving the cannon mouths was followed instantly by a halo of smoke surrounding a crimson flash. As each successive volley burst through the accumulating clouds of dull, gray smoke, a thousand mighty echoes deafened everyone, reverberating across the valley and growing fainter until drowned by the thunder of another volley. Most of this artillery fire proved harmless as it screamed over their heads, then burst above or behind them, or burrowed into the ground before exploding. Initial fear gave way to exhilaration as the men began to realize it was more sound and fury than danger. For veterans like Lank, their thoughts focused angrily on the enemy to their immediate front. No consideration was given to "showing the white feather." Further, the Confederates in the rifle pits on the ridge could not shoot at the advancing Union assault without endangering their own retreating skirmishers.

The experience of the Fox River boys was the same as that of Thomas's entire army. Not a musket was fired at them from the first line of rifle pits until they were within 300 yards, Civil War rifle-fire range. At that point, the 36th's bugle sounded twice, the signal for "Charge," and they ran into a hornets' nest of whizzing balls. Then a loud, spontaneous cheer went up from a thousand throats along the entire length of the line. They overtook their skirmishers, not halting to load and fire, but trusting to their bayonets. Advancing into this barrage of bullets, unable to return fire, was the greatest test of the bluebellies' moral courage. In a matter of minutes the Union front line captured their first line of rifle pits and a wet ditch connecting them before the surprised Confederates—one-fourth of Bragg's forces—realized the full extent of this movement. The skirmishers had already forced most of the Rebel pickets to retreat or surrender before the rest of the Fox River lads arrived.

Confusion reigned supreme as they collided with those who remained in the rifle pits. Some of the Rebels fell back toward the ridgetop, providing easy targets for Union artillerymen who encouraged their ascent by firing directly at them. The Southerners were obeying previous orders not to hold this line but to return fire when the bluecoats were within rifle range, and then retreat to the ridge. Others were told to hold their positions at all hazards. Nevertheless, large numbers of graybacks threw down their arms, surrendered, and were sent to the rear, taunted with such shouts as "You have been trying to get there long enough . . . now charge on Chattanooga." The exhausted bluecoats dropped into their enemy's pits for shelter and a breather, having run at least a half mile in the chilly fall afternoon, wrapped in woolen blankets on top of their overcoats.

In Sheridan's sector, the first rifle pits had been occupied by skirmishers from Gibson's Louisiana brigade, which had faced them at Stones River. Despite orders to hold their position at all hazards, these Rebels were simply overwhelmed. Meanwhile, Confederate rifle pits in the next line, as well as on the ridge, were still raining bullets, their red battle flags waving in defiance. Lank and the lads of the 36th had done what they were ordered to do, but a deluge of iron and lead forced them to either advance or retreat from what was becoming "a hideous slaughter pen." To the combat-wise, hunkering down in the rifle pits made no sense. Nevertheless, some worked frantically to "turn" the pits by moving the parapets to the opposite side, thereby affording some protection from minié balls and shells fired at them from the ridge.

The entire Army of the Cumberland was in the same position. According to the plan devised by Thomas and approved by Grant, the veterans of Chickamauga would take the rifle pits at the base of Missionary Ridge as soon as Sherman's army secured the north end of the ridge, thereby forcing Bragg to withdraw troops from his center. But Sherman had failed. Thomas's troops, therefore, realized that such a limited objective was now impossible. The aide to the commander of Sheridan's First Brigade, Lieutenant Turnbull, observed, "The officers of the field and line and the boys were the generals ordering the advance. . . . [I]t was a necessity understood . . . and acted on at once. . . . I believe our brigade was the first to start, and . . . the Ridge was now the objective point," even though they had one of the steepest and highest points to climb. The impetuosity of the combat veterans who first started forward was contagious. No one heard a bugle blow, a drumroll, or a shouted command. Pvt. John Ely of the 88th Ill. noted in his diary that they were carried away by their success, and a shout rang out along the line: "To the top, to the top." For the men it was a matter of both survival and pride. Staying where they were or retreating were not options. The 73rd had an additional motivation after Sheridan rode up behind them and shouted, "I know you; fix bayonets and go ahead." Looking down from atop Missionary Ridge, one Confederate likened the advance to "a huge serpent uncoil[ing] massive folds into shapely lines."

Having caught their breath, Colonel Sherman's 1st Brigade came out of the first line of Rebel pits and veered in disorder into a ravine to their left, thereby flanking the second or intermediate line of rifle pits, and forcing them to "skeedaddle" with a deadly cross fire. The advance was no longer shoulder-to-shoulder. The Lincolnites would stop, aim, fire, and then run behind a felled tree, or whatever cover they could find to reload. During this ten-minute race they were exposed to a maelstrom of grape, canister, and bursting shells, as well as musketry fire from rifle pits on their right, from which they suffered most of their casualties. As they raced uphill, they encouraged each other to advance far enough that the batteries would overshoot them.

Those Rebels not killed, wounded, or captured swarmed out of the second line of rifle pits, while Sherman's exhausted brigadiers swarmed in, panting and coughing. According to the *New York Times* correspondent, "A few [of the Rebels] turned and fired their pieces, but the greater number collected onto the many roads which cross obliquely up its steep face, and went onto the top." Some collapsed from exhaustion, gasping and retching, and were captured as they struggled in hopeless confusion to save themselves by zigzagging up the trails. Others made it to the top before collapsing. Still others crawled downhill on their hands and knees to surrender. Those that had been in the first picket line carried heavy knapsacks and three days' rations. Attempting to run uphill with this load was virtually impossible. The higher they climbed, the steeper the slope, in places as much as seventy-five degrees. Many were exhausted before they started, having spent most of the night digging their entrenchments.

Lieutenant Turnbull initially had stayed with the skirmishers rather than with the brigade staff, but soon reported to Colonel Sherman for further orders. At that time, the three companies of skirmishers were the only ones still advancing. Turnbull was sent back to the first line of rifle pits to urge forward those stragglers still there, a large number seeking the best protection they could find.

Captain Ransom and Col. S. B. Moe, Corps Commander Granger's chief engineer, arrived to tell Colonel Sherman his advance was contrary to orders. Turnbull told the couriers to deliver the message themselves to his brigade commander. He was busy urging the laggards forward. Shortly thereafter, Sheridan arrived to encourage their advance by cursing and swinging his sword, aided by Sergeant Realf, his aide-de-camp, who pricked "the skulkers with his sergeants sword." Sheridan's men were halfway to the second line of rifle pits, with the regimental flags of the brigade grouped together in advance of the line when Moe and Ransom arrived with the message from Granger to take only the line at the base and recall his troops if he thought it expedient. They had just reached the left of Colonel Sherman's line. It was too late. Sheridan jumped off his horse, threw his cape to his orderly, and shouted as he ran among the men, "Boys we are going to take this ridge. Forward and help your comrades." He then reached for his flask, took a gulp, and waved it at a group of officers he could see on the ridge with the salutation "Here's at you!" Two guns were immediately fired at Sheridan, showering him with dirt.[5]

One stretch in the Confederate line on the crest immediately below General Bragg's headquarters had minimal breastworks. Believing that Grant would not order a charge up that precipitous hill, the officer in charge of this section had not ordered entrenchments dug or artillery positioned until daybreak the day before, after the Union advance on Orchard Knob. In addition, the Rebels were short of entrenching tools, and the regiment that was to occupy this stretch was not moved into it until about 3:30 P.M., Bragg had ignored the fact that Grant had increased the size of his army and strengthened his position, and that his men were now well fed. He apparently was convinced that the half-starved Yankees could never make it up the ridge. Undoubtedly overconfident, he was much more concerned about his flanks. As a consequence, what breastworks they did build of logs, rails, and stones were inadequate.

The entire Confederate line across Missionary Ridge stretched for twelve miles, too long to be adequately defended at every point. Grant had captured a large number of the men on this line at Vicksburg, then paroled them because there was no room for them in Northern prisons. In violation of a previous agreement between the opposing armies, the Confederates unilaterally declared the prisoners exchanged, thus freeing them to fight Grant again at Missionary Ridge.

The first Illinois regiment to approach the top of Missionary Ridge (probably the 73rd, the "Preacher's Regiment") was initially driven back to where the men could find cover. Meanwhile, the 36th and 27th Ill. color-bearers ran from tree to tree, planted their colors, then sought cover in the deep ravine that led up to near where the Moore Road reached the crest. Cobb's four-gun battery, low on ammunition, was positioned to fire down or across the road. Smoke had settled into the ravine, offering further protection. For about twenty minutes, the worn-out Lincolnites of the 27th and 36th gathered one by one with their flag bearers in the ravine to recover from their exertion and prepare for their lunge to the top. Both regiments probably entered the narrow ravine under the lip of the ridge at about the same time. Having run uphill for nearly a mile, they were totally spent, puffing and perspiring profusely. They carried eighty rounds of ammunition plus all their equipment, but no knapsacks.

36th and 27th Illinois monuments on Missionary Ridge

Moving as fast as their courage and endurance permitted, they halted when they could take advantage of "dead ground" that sheltered them from Rebel fire. At the steepest parts, some men had to crawl on hands and knees, zigzagging up trails and over the dead and dying, now and then crouching for protection to recover their wind, reload, and fire. The once well-timbered, deeply furrowed hillside was now virtually devoid of trees. Lieutenant Turnbull noted that the timber immediately below the ridge had been felled to form an abatis.

They fixed bayonets in preparation for the final charge of fifty yards or so to the top. Hearing the enemy shout "Chickamauga" was like an electric shock that propelled them with even greater force. The front rank of the 36th, including Lank's Company E and the three companies of skirmishers on the extreme left of the brigade, gained the ridge interlocked with the 27th Ill. and captured Cobb's four-gun battery. Together, as the sun was nearing the horizon, they opened a gap through which others poured, possibly the first to plant their flags on this section of the ridge. Chaos reigned as others poured through the gap.

General Bragg's headquarters were immediately south of the Moore Road, behind the crest of the ridge. In front of the buildings, on the crest and adjacent to the south side of Moore Road, was Cobb's battery. To the left of the battery was a Louisiana regiment commanded by Maj. Francis Campbell. He had positioned the right of his regiment about one hundred yards to the left (or south) of the headquarters buildings, in a single line without reserves because of the distance they had to cover with few troops. Shortly after the formation moved into place about 3:30 p.m., it became actively engaged with a cloud of skirmishers, followed by the heavy first line of the 36th and 27th. To get a line of sight on advancing bluecoats below the crest, the Rebels had to stand up, thereby exposing themselves above inadequate entrenchments. If they lived to fire more than once, they were picked off by the Federals concealed in the folds and creases of the hillside as soon as they reappeared through the gun smoke, sharply silhouetted by the sun behind their backs.

After a half hour of sharp fire, the Rebels were driven back in confusion, but Campbell's regiment was nearly out of ammunition and had been instructed to save their cartridges and trust to the bayonet, if necessary. While Campbell sent for more ammunition, the Rebels hurled large stones down the ridge, repelling a vigorous attack by the Lincolnites' second line. A battalion of sharpshooters that had moved directly in front of the headquarters, astraddle the Moore Road, also fired on the bluecoats. Soon Campbell realized that gunners from Cobb's New Orleans four-gun battery on his left were running to the rear, abandoning their guns. Regiments on both sides had given way, and the Yanks were pouring over the top on both of his flanks. When the 73rd Ill. got within sixty yards of his left and the 36th and 27th were rapidly closing on his right, Campbell ordered his men to retreat down the reverse slope of the ridge. The move exposed them to fierce gunfire that led to heavy losses. Bragg himself barely escaped capture.

The two regiments were able to reach the crest at a point between the Moore Road and Major Campbell's Louisianans, capture the battery, and plant their flags. Lieutenant Hemenway and Sergeant Hall of Company E were the first to reach Cobb's battery. The gunners had vanished already, and their ammunition chests had been blown up. Many infantry had also retreated or precipitously thrown down their arms. Lank and his comrades arrived on the heels of their company commander and the sergeant as the sun disappeared over the ridge and a chill air settled in.

Sgt. Leverett Kelley discovered a Rebel captain hiding behind log breastworks, fixed his bayonet, and told the captain to surrender. The captain said, "Call an officer." The soldier's response was, "I'm officer enough . . . surrender or I will put the bayonet through you." A Union officer arrived and took the captain's sword, remarking that the soldier should have bayoneted him. The captain replied, "What do you mean? I have . . . never treated prisoners this way." The officer of the 36th said, "Then take off that overcoat you have stripped from [one of our] wounded comrades at Chickamauga." The officer took it off quickly, mumbling that they had been attacked so suddenly he forgot to take it off. Kelley would receive the Medal of Honor for his bravery in capturing the Confederate officer.

First Lt. Arthur MacArthur, Jr., adjutant of the 24th Wis. and father of Gen. Douglas MacArthur, also would receive the Medal of Honor for seizing the colors of his regiment at a critical moment and planting them on the crest. The Fox River-color bearer got so far ahead of the regiment that he lay down behind a log to catch his breath and wait for them to catch up. As he rose to continue his ascent, a sergeant saw a Confederate a short distance away aiming his musket. He whispered "Lie down" to the color-bearer. The sergeant then rested his musket on a log and took aim. "Now show him your knapsack." The color-bearer rose carefully on all fours to do so. The sergeant fired at the Confederate and missed. He reloaded and told the color-bearer, "Now do it again." The sergeant fired successfully and said, "Now we can go."

Colonel Miller permitted a young soldier who displayed cowardice at Chickamauga and was threatened with a court-martial to redeem himself in this battle. He was told that if he repeated his cowardice, he would suffer. He went in, stood his ground, and was wounded in the hand, proudly displaying his wound to Miller as proof he deserved redemption.

At the top, friend and foe became entangled in a surging mass. Sheridan had been behind his men, urging them on. His aide, Pvt. Benjamin T. Smith, heard Sheridan say, "Let them go, they will be over in five minutes." He had ridden up from the second line of rifle pits, where he signaled with a wave of his hat for Colonel Sherman's second line to move up. Captain Parsons of the 24th Wis., in the center of the second line, saw his cap-waving signal. Colonel Miller, in charge of the second line, a demibrigade of four regiments, was on horseback shouting "Excelsior" (Higher) to his men. Miller rode through the storm of iron and lead rallying and inspiring his men. When Sheridan arrived on the crest on horseback, Rebels turned their rifle butts toward him, symbolizing their surrender. He dismounted, since a few Confederate batteries elsewhere on the ridge were still firing. Meanwhile hundreds of other Confederates had already streamed downhill to surrender. Only forty-five minutes had passed since the six signal guns had opened the battle at 3:40 P.M.[6]

Col. Silas Miller of the 36th, had been slightly wounded at the base of the hill, but rode through the rifle and cannon fire to the summit ahead of his line nonetheless, inspiring his men by his courage and indifference to personal danger. When he reached the top, he called for volunteers to capture the two pieces in Stanford's Mississippi battery.

After Grant learned that Hooker's men had also topped the ridge and were heading north, he shouted, "Bring my horse! I'm going up there." Thomas wrote, "I fell among some of my old soldiers, who always took liberties with me—who commenced talking and giving their views of victory. When I attempted to compliment them for the gallant manner in which they made the assault, one man very coolly replied: 'Why, General, we know you have been training us for this race for the last three weeks.'" Grant, who had not ordered the assault on the crest, seemingly did not share fully in the elation, although he rode the lines, doffing his cap and thanking them, while the men greeted him with tumultuous shouts.

When Sheridan arrived on his black horse, having followed a winding dirt trail to the crest, he dismounted. Before he reached the ground, it appeared as if the men were going to lift both him and his horse on their shoulders. One soldier even clapped him on the shoulder. The lads of the 36th Ill. clustered around him, shaking his hand, cheering, patting his horse, and shouting, "How do you like this, General?" and, "Bully for Sheridan." Some shouted for food, others for whiskey. He raised his hat and said, "Boys in less than two hours time you will have all the hardtack, all the sow-belly and all the beef you want; as for the whiskey I can't say for sure." He then mounted one of the captured guns as if it were a horse, waved his hat like a cowboy on a bronco, and whooped it up.

When Granger arrived moments later, they exclaimed, "What do you think of this General?" He replied, "I think you disobeyed orders, you—rascals!" Exhaustion had given way to ecstasy as the men and officers yelled and cheered themselves hoarse while throwing their caps, blankets, canteens, and haversacks in the air, frantically drunk with enthusiasm. Others shouted, "Chickamauga, Chickamauga." It was truly a carnival scene, with Rebel flags scattered higgledy-piggledy on the ground. Laughing and sobbing, they slapped one another on the back, rejoicing in their victory. It was as if they had turned into an army of lunatics.

John Ely of the 88th Ill. recorded later that the graycoats had been driven off the ridge by the last volleys at about 6 P.M. in the moonlight. His regiment then re-formed its lines, stacked arms, and detached men to care for the wounded, gather them together, and build fires for their comfort. They exchanged their heavy rifle-muskets for lighter weight Confederate Enfield and Springfield rifles that had been abandoned by the 4th Fla., which went into the battle with 172 men and came out with 23. The gun Ely selected was smeared with Rebel blood. They also filled their boxes with English cartridges. Souvenir hunting then began as the Rebels had abandoned everything. The enemy dead were left where they fell. That night, Henry Fuller of the 88th wrote his father that his regiment had "lost about 40 killed and wounded." Another soldier in the 88th wrote his father that at 8 P.M. they were still bringing in the wounded and prisoners. Ely ate "a scanty supper" and afterward "took a walk by moonlight down the hill while waiting for the full rations Sheridan ordered from town for his men." The night was cold and frosty.

Lank's company commander, Lt. William H. Clark, was commended by the regimental commander, Olson, for his bravery and coolness. Only four men in Lank's Company E had been wounded, one of them hit six times. None was killed or captured. Pvt. Day Elmore was shot through the lungs, captured, hospitalized, and later paroled at Annapolis, Maryland. On November 26, he wrote his parents, "How long it will be before I am exchanged I know not but I long for that time. . . . I do not think [this] is the place for a soldier that is well. . . . I think I am quite able for duty." The regiment suffered surprisingly few casualties, with three killed and twenty-five wounded, one mortally. Colonel Sherman's brigade, however, suffered more than 20 percent casualties, the highest among the four brigades in Sheridan's division.

The Fox River lads bivouacked that night near the house Bragg had used for his headquarters. They were so exhausted they slept "forty miles an hour." During the night, ambulances arrived to take the wounded into town. Lincoln was in his sickbed with a mild form of smallpox when he received news of the victory. In one breath he told an old Illinois friend visiting him of Grant's success, and in another he said of his smallpox, at last, "I now have something I can give everybody."

The first time after the battle that Assistant Secretary of War Charles Dana saw Sheridan, he asked why he had led his troops up to the ridge. Sheridan replied, "When I saw the men were going up, I had no idea of stopping them... and after they had started I commanded them to go right on."

The next day was the national day of thanksgiving, the first ever proclaimed by a president. Union guns thundered a thirty-four-gun salute, while those killed in the attack were buried. Some of the survivors in the 36th met in a small tent, sang one psalm, read another, and held a prayer service for their fallen comrades.[7] Despite their losses, Missionary Ridge was sweet revenge for the lads of the 36th. They had been downcast for the drubbings they had taken at Stones River and Chickamauga. What faith they had lost in themselves was now restored. They were now heroes, and the tarnished reputation of Thomas's Army of the Cumberland was erased in the eyes of Grant, Sherman, and Hooker. Sheridan recommended Colonel Sherman be promoted to brigadier general and commended Colonel Miller, Lieutenant Colonel Olson, and Major Sherman for the inspiration they gave their men by personal example to perform "deeds of valor and heroism." On November 27, Sheridan commended his division. He wrote, "The storming of Missionary Ridge and the manner in which it was done, has not a parallel in this war nor in history... by your gallantry [it has become] a towering monument of your glory to future generations." His division captured 1,762 prisoners and 17 artillery pieces.

Today, two monuments about thirty yards apart in the battlefield park mark the positions where the 36th and 27th Ill. reached the crest of the hill. They flanked cannon, which is situated where the regiments captured Cobb's four-gun battery. Today's National Cemetery is located where the 36th was positioned before dawn on November 24, along with the 24th Wis., the 44th Ill., and the 73rd Ill.

After Missionary Ridge, the 36th returned to its old camp in Chattanooga for two days and participated in a jubilant victory celebration. On November 28, with rations for three days, they began a 110-mile march through the snow, rain, and mud in worn-out shoes. Together with Sheridan's division and the rest of Gordon Granger's 4th Army Corps, they were sent to relieve Maj. Gen. Ambrose Burnside's army in Knoxville by driving Longstreet's men out of East Tennessee. Lincoln wanted to aid Tennesseans loyal to the Union, who were suffering pitifully. Their wagon train carried ammunition only—no camp equipment. They arrived on December 6, shortly after Longstreet's siege had been lifted. He had assaulted the city's fortifications, but was easily repelled, and retreated. The Lincolnites were ill-clothed for a rapid winter march through the mountains of East Tennessee; they lacked sufficient shoes, hats, shirts, socks, pants, overcoats, India rubber ponchos, tents, and forage for their animals. Some made moccasins from their blankets. Their winter clothing and equipment were still in Murfreesboro. They subsisted on half rations since, at this time of year, there was nothing to forage and the Rebels had devastated the countryside.

On December 12, Lank's regiment left Knoxville to participate in other operations in east Tennessee. Then, on December 17, they bivouacked at Blain's Crossroads, Tennessee. It was in the buffer zone between east Tennessee, which was under control of the Union army, and the Confederate army in western Tennessee. Dressed in rags, by then they had marched 186 miles, over the worst roads they had yet encountered, in twelve days. Only on the twelfth day were they able to ride on top of railroad cars. It was the coldest winter the area had experienced for years. The snow-covered ground was frozen to a depth of six inches, yet the 36th had not one tent in the regiment.

On January 1, 1864, after returning from a foraging trip in rain and severe wind, Lank and more than three-fourths of his regiment—every able-bodied man—along with the 44th Ill. and nearly all of the eligible regiments in the 4th Corps, signed their Veteran Volunteer papers. Despite the privations they continued to suffer, Lank and twenty-seven others in Company E got the "Veteran fever" and "veteranized." An observer noted, "the smoke of the camp-fires was hurled in every direction, making it well-nigh intolerable to remain by a fire. . . . The ink with which the . . . papers were signed, froze on the pen . . . and had to be broken off . . . before another man could use it; the inkstand in the meantime [had to be] kept in contact with the fire. All honor to the noble men . . . who amid such severities . . . gave themselves afresh to their country's salvation." After signing, they were issued two ears of corn apiece for supper.

That night they built huge bonfires and stood so close to them they would roast on one side and freeze on the other while being nearly blinded by smoke. They still suffered from scant food, clothing, blankets, and shelter, and were infested with lice.

That same New Year's Day, Dan was still in Bridgeport, where Colonel McDougall of the 123rd N.Y. was provost marshal. Among his duties was helping to feed the civilian population, which was largely destitute. The stench of the hundreds of mules and horses that had died of starvation was unbearable. Cruikshank told his wife, "The curse of slavery shows itself in everything here."

By signing the new enlistment papers, Lank and the other Lincolnite lads had committed themselves to serve for three more years or the duration of the war. They did so after having spent the past year fighting three of the bloodiest battles in the West, enduring cold, rain, mud, and heat, without adequate clothing, shoes, or rations. By January 4, the requisite number of Fox River lads had signed on for three more years, despite the fact that nearly 500 had already become casualties. By war's end nearly 54 percent of Lank's company would become casualties, more than 700 men. The 36th was one of 133 regiments, including virtually all of Sheridan's old regiments, which reenlisted as Veteran Volunteers in the Army of the Cumberland. Like Grant, Sherman, Thomas, and Sheridan, they were prepared to hang on and slug it out.

In total, thirty-eight Illinois infantry and cavalry regiments reenlisted as Veteran Volunteers. They were used repeatedly as frontline troops and skirmishers for the remainder of the war. Having been shot in the lungs at Chickamauga and still recovering, Pvt. Day Elmore wrote his parents on December 6, 1863, "I can say that as long as I have served Uncle Sam I have done it well and am willing to finish my time and three years longer if need be." On January 9, after reenlisting, Private Reeder of the 36th wrote his parents, "I am willing to do, and suffer if need be, rather than see our glorious Union trampled underfoot by traitors and rebels.... If this the glorious Union must fall, I care not to survive it ... [while the pages of history call] to mind the suffering endured by men of the Revolution and later, to bestow on their posterity a land where men are free ... I hope that our men will never give over this contest." Soon after having signed on as a Veteran Volunteer, he died in the Chattanooga Military hospital from his Missionary Ridge wound, his third. His previous wounds were incurred at Perryville and Stones River. Another Lincolnite wrote, "The singleness of purpose to see this rebellion put down which characterizes these men, is such as completely surprises me; it is the men not the officers."

Lank and the other Veteran Volunteers then marched eighteen miles to Knoxville and boarded a train for Chattanooga. They arrived there on January 15. They were mustered in on January 18 and paid off January 27. While there, Lank may have witnessed the 14th USCT go through a drill, the same unit Dan may have seen months earlier. General Thomas had told its colonel that he "never saw a regiment go through the manual as well as this one."

Their trip home began on January 28. On February 5, they received their thirty-day furloughs in Chicago and a congratulatory telegram from the governor. Lank's Company E was welcomed with cannon fire and a banquet in Aurora, where they had been mustered in. Lank listed his residence as Little Rock, Kendall County, Illinois, where he had enlisted. To be eligible for the $400 bounty, War Department regulations required that the Veteran Volunteers reenlist in the district where they originally signed on. Lank received a $100 local bounty payment still due him, plus $60 toward the $400 federal bounty for reenlisting and one month's advance pay of $13. The Kane County, Illinois, board of supervisors also offered a $502 bounty to all veterans who reenlisted before January 5, 1864. Lank may have been eligible for this bonus as well, since he had lived in Kane County at the time of his enlistment. Although he enjoyed reunions with his friends in Illinois, he regretted that he was unable to visit his parents and friends in New York.

It is easy to eliminate two possible reasons for Lank's decision to reenlist. It was certainly not to seek adventure or glory. He had already seen nearly three years of carnage—thousands of blackened and bloated corpses, as well as thousands of horribly maimed men who would be disfigured, if not incapacitated, for life. He had lost 500 of his regimental comrades. In 1863 alone, the year just past, he had witnessed all the costs of combat and all the hardships of army life—starvation rations; bottomless mud, rain, heat, filth, monotony, freezing weather, and frozen ground to sleep on without adequate clothing, including shoes; and forced day and night marches without sleep or rest to the point of total exhaustion. Lank's motives for reenlistment could only have been commitment like Private Reeder's, comradeship, and/or bounty money, probably in that order.

Lank's regiment reassembled in Aurora, Illinois, and left for Chicago on March 19, to return to active duty from their Veteran Volunteer furlough. The Fox River Valley home folks had treated them to a series of banquets, parades, and balls. Thousands in Aurora saw them off. They were joined by 142 recruits, 20 of whom joined Lank's company. Some of the old-timers derisively observed that the government could have bought "mules much cheaper." Before they left, their chaplain, William M. Haigh, told the Veteran Volunteers and recruits, "Remember you are citizen-soldiers . . . who seek to implant in southern soil those sacred principles of freedom." Capt. A. M. Hobbs, Lank's company commander, had initiated the effort to recruit the chaplain in 1862. Within a year thereafter, Hobbs was wounded twice and captured once. He was a brave man, as well as devoutly religious.

The 36th was taken by train to Nashville. Pvt. George Cummins, a three-year man who did not veteranize, wrote home to his girlfriend, "The 'Vets' have returned and tell some big yarns I assure you. They have each got rid of from $250 to $500 apiece and now borrow from us." Lank had a lifelong reputation for spinning good yarns, some of which must have had to do with this furlough.

Other Veteran Volunteer regiments also were returning from their furloughs to rejoin their comrades. Two marched past the New Yorkers' headquarters to join their commands. On March 26, the Fox River men began to march in the rain from Nashville on a road that paralleled the 151-mile Nashville and Chattanooga Railroad route. They were told they had to march to their base at Cleveland, Tennessee, because Sherman needed all available rail transportation for hauling supplies to the front. Ammunition, food, fodder, and equipment were being stockpiled in Cleveland. Averaging about twelve miles daily, hard going for the fifty-nine recruits, they paused at the Stones River battleground, where the regiment had lost 200 men, to hold a service for their fallen comrades.

On March 31, on their way from Decherd to Cowan, Colonel Miller arranged for the regiment to ride atop a construction train. On April 4, they rode on top of the cars again, from Stevenson to Chattanooga, this time in the rain. Diaries of two soldiers in the 36th, plus the regimental history, confirm that the regiment marched most of the way from Nashville to Cleveland, except for two days when they were able to "ride the cars" by climbing on top of them. It was on one of those days that a hot cinder or spark from the engine's smokestack hit Lank Ross in his right eye, an excruciatingly painful injury. Lank stated in his pension application that his eye injury occurred in March when they were "guarding government property," presumably the construction equipment that train was carrying. It is extremely ironic that, having seen so much bloody conflict in four major battles, his only injury was received while off the battlefield. The Lincolnites arrived in Loudon on April 8. Rations were plentiful for the first time. They also held a Sunday service. Fruit trees were in bloom and fertile fields of wheat and oats were watered with bubbling springs and babbling brooks of pure water.

The regiment continued to their camp near Cleveland, arriving on April 21, and was assigned provost and guard duty. Cleveland was largely inhabited by Unionists who performed many kind deeds for the soldiers. Lank was admitted to the brigade hospital there on April 30, a month after his eye injury. Several men from the 36th and other regiments in the brigade were assigned as doctor's assistants or as hospital cooks, and undoubtedly tended to Lank, fed him, or at least visited him. Lank's pension and hospital records indicate that by the time he arrived at Cleveland he had inflammation in both eyes, because infection in the optic nerve had spread. He would never again see more than shadows.

The 36th remained in the Cleveland camp until May 4, when, without Lank, they started a march to Catoosa Springs to begin the Atlanta campaign. When it marched out of Cleveland, there were only 296 men left in the regiment. On May 9, Lank was sent from the brigade hospital in Cleveland to the Army General Hospital in Chattanooga and, on May 17, to Cumberland Army General Hospital. During September he was allowed to visit his parents in Washington County, New York. Then, on November 23, 1864, he was sent to Albany, New York, and subsequently furloughed March 3, 1865, for another visit with his parents. While Lank was home on furlough, Dr. Henry C. Gray, a family friend, examined him three times. Dr. Gray's medical report confirmed that Lank suffered from diseased eyes. He was discharged from the Ira Harris Army General Hospital in Albany on June 13, 1865, as totally disabled. On October 6, 1865, Lucien Hemenway, Lank's former company commander, certified that Lank had served in his company and "never missed a days duty until on or about April 28, when he lost his eyesight."

During December 1863, while in Bridgeport, Dan and his comrades had been "enjoying the richest blessings of a soldier's life, viz: good health, good quarters, good living" while guarding government stores. On November 30, Corp. R. O. Fisher wrote his father, "There is hardly a sick man in the Regt. We are the healthiest that we ever was." On January 1, Sgt. McLean wrote his father that they were well clothed but the troops still in Chattanooga were not. Since January 7, when they left Bridgeport, they had been foraging, fighting guerillas, and patrolling the river every two hours for some distance. They also guarded both ends of the railroad bridge on the Elk River near Decherd, Tennessee, midway between Nashville and Chattanooga, close to where Lank had been blinded a few weeks earlier.

On February 22, Pvt. Artemus Harrington, of the 123rd N.Y., wrote his parents that they also were "taking in all negros that wanted to come along" as well as rounding up robbers and bushwhackers who were "taken into custody." Dan and the boys from his home area were doing well, according to a letter written by one of his friends on February 27. Private Marshall wrote his parents that they had "excellent drinking water and the trains haul[ed] wood to each company," adding, "if you have any among you who still side with the Pro Slavery party I think a 3 months tour through the south will completely change their views."

The regiment they relieved had built wooden shanties with canvas roofs, brick fireplaces and chimneys, wooden floors, a double-decker bunk in each, and outdoor ovens. The swift, crystal-clear Elk River must have reminded Dan of the similar-sized Battenkill that bordered his family's New York farm. The lads explored a mile-deep cave the Rebels had dug nearby to mine saltpeter, an ingredient of gunpowder.

About April 1, Dan's Battery F turned over its six Napoleon twelve-pounders, which they had manned since Chancellorsville, to another battery in the 12th Corps, in addition to about a hundred splendid horses. Artillery horses had been given the lowest priority for food unless they were used to pull wagons, undoubtedly the reason Battery F and perhaps others were unofficially disbanded. Sherman estimated that 30,000 animal carcasses were rotting in the Tennessee Valley. Not even one cavalryman in ten had a horse. Dan then returned to the 123rd N.Y. as an infantryman. Six months later, by command of General Thomas, Battery F was officially disbanded at Atlanta on October 22, 1864.[8]

On April 4, Grant notified his adjutant general that Lincoln approved consolidating the 11th and 12th Corps under General Hooker. Slocum was to be relieved as 12th Corps commander so he would no longer have to serve under Hooker, and instructed to report to Sherman for assignment. Grant suggested to Sherman that he transfer Slocum to the Vicksburg District because there was "such a large proportion of colored troops ... and Slocum will take an active interest in this work." Lincoln concurred. Vicksburg was Grant's hardest-earned victory, and he wanted it kept under strict military control. Lincoln, Sherman, Grant, and Secretary of State Seward also wanted Slocum to crack down on rampant fraud. A solid commander and a man of high standards, he would command an army of 19,000 men occupying a huge territory. His job also would entail attacking corruption, including illicit traffic in contraband and goods, intercepting Rebel cavalry, and preventing Confederates from rebuilding their railroads or interrupting shipments of Union supplies. On April 20, Slocum was reassigned to command the post at Vicksburg.

On April 23, General Williams replaced Slocum as commander of the 12th Corps and reviewed the 123rd's brigade at Decherd. Dan participated in the review. Slocum had the confidence and respect of both General Sherman and General Thomas and would later return as a corps commander, replacing General Hooker, whom neither Sherman, Grant, nor Thomas liked. It would enrage Hooker.

The surrounding countryside, poor to begin with, had been ravaged by the Rebels, leaving the residents semi-starved, destitute, and ill-clothed, their houses in ruins. Hardly a blade of grass was available for their animals. The Union troops, including the 123rd, provided rations to them for the work they performed. Citizens were sorry to see them leave. One member of the regiment wrote home, "I am in hopes the day will soon come when this Civil War will end, and when the people once more, North and South, shall regard each others as brothers... why may it not be so?" In late April, the Ladies' Aid Society of Salem, New York, sent Dan and each of the other lads in Company H a gift. They were delivered by Lieutenant Cruikshank, who wrote a thank-you letter on behalf of his men.

Both Grant and Sherman were concerned about whether Sherman's Veteran Volunteers would return from their furloughs in time to participate in his next move. On April 25, Grant telegraphed Sherman, "Will your Veteran [Volunteers] be read[y] to enable you to start on the second of May?" Sherman replied that afternoon, "The Veteran Division cannot be up by May 2.... If you can, give me till May fifth." Grant wired back his approval.

On April 27 the New Yorkers, Dan included, were mustered for pay, then broke camp and started their fateful trek over the Cumberland Mountains, as part of Thomas's Army of the Cumberland, to join Sherman's march on Atlanta. The 20th Corps, which now included the 123rd N.Y., arrived in camp near Cleveland on May 3, awaiting orders from General Sherman to join his march on Atlanta. Although Lank was still in Cleveland in the brigade hospital, there is no record that Dan knew his brother was hospitalized nearby or could have gotten permission to visit him. Dan and his fellow New Yorkers did know, however, that they were in for a long, bloody campaign they hoped would end the war. The next night their camp, along with all the others, was ablaze with candlelight. Every soldier stuck his candle on his bayonet point or tent pole, and candles burned through the night while the men cheered.

On May 7, Hooker's corps began its march through the dangerous Nickajack Pass to join Sherman's march on Atlanta. A few days later they marched over the Chickamauga battlefield. According to Rufus Mead of the 5th Connecticut, some of the fallen had been buried where they fell in line of battles, while others were scattered across the field in graves so shallow that heads and feet were exposed. Whether Dan knew that day what a vital role Lank's regiment had played in the battle is unknown.[9]

8

After Missionary Ridge
The Turning of the Tide

> We now know that the only reliable hope for peace is in the vigor of our [military] resistance.
>
> —Jefferson Davis after the Battle of Missionary Ridge

Missionary Ridge was the last major battle of 1863. Grant had forced Bragg's Confederate army to retreat from Chattanooga, and made that city the strategic center and giant supply base for Sherman's march on Atlanta the following spring. He had gained a decisive victory for the Union and won a promotion for himself to three-star general in command of the entire Union army. The final blow that destroyed any hold the Confederacy had on the West came on November 29, four days after Missionary Ridge. Longstreet's corps attempted to take Knoxville that day and failed. His troops were massacred, and he retreated to Virginia. Gettysburg, Vicksburg, Stones River, Chickamauga, Missionary Ridge, Port Hudson, and Longstreet's repulse at Knoxville when Sheridan's men broke his siege—all these cost the South as much in loss of civilian and military morale as in loss of manpower, food, and equipment in the Confederate western armies.

In contrast, Grant's army had come to believe it was invincible. Military losses to the South in these battles totaled more than 92,000. For example, Grant's campaign to capture Vicksburg, the Confederate citadel, had cost the South 45,000 men, 60,000 muskets, and 172 cannon. In the course of this campaign, the capital of the state of Mississippi also was captured, and a large amount of war goods and manufacturing capacity was destroyed. In contrast, Grant lost 9,000 men.

As the Civil War historian Bruce Catton observed, "Cities, states, rivers, and armies had been lost and a larger burden would have to be borne by a diminished strength." Defeat was an unspoken word, but it was in the southern air that both citizens and soldiers breathed. In a conversation between Lee and Longstreet shortly after the Gettysburg disaster, they agreed the only hope left for the Confederacy was to win a great battle in the West. The reverse had happened, in spades. No two Southerners could have had better insight into the military capability of the North than Jefferson Davis, who had served as a U.S. senator and as a secretary of war, and Robert E. Lee, who had spent a lifetime in the U.S. Army.

Those Southerners who already had misgivings about slavery, if not feelings of guilt, had even less reason to fight for its continuation. The "20 nigger law" led to growing resentment against plantation owners by nonslaveholders and small farmers who were subject to conscription because they owned fewer than twenty slaves. The poor man felt he was fighting a rich man's war. He could not plant, much less harvest, his grain while he was fighting to protect the plantation owners' slaves, and lifestyle, a class conflict that further weakened support for the Confederate war effort. Clearly, the sun was setting on any possibility of Confederate victory.

Whatever optimism Robert E. Lee, or any other Confederate general, still had about winning the war should have been quashed by the end of 1863. All they had to do was follow the facts. Lee's own Army of Northern Virginia had been bled white at Gettysburg and was on the verge of collapse. He had played a high stakes game and lost. His hopes that Gettysburg would be a victorious battle of annihilation that would end the war had been shattered. Meade had maintained continuous pressure on Lee's army since Chancellorsville and Gettysburg, to the point that it could no longer assume the offensive. Lee's two attempts to invade the North—Antietam and Gettysburg—were costly failures. Lee himself was in the doldrums psychologically and in poor health. After Gettysburg, he candidly admitted to an aide of President Davis that his loss was severe, "[W]e had not gained an inch of ground and the enemy could not be pursued." The leadership of his army deteriorated. The best it could do was defend Richmond, where early that year desperate housewives staged bread riots because of severe shortages and inflated prices. Before Lee's army left for Gettysburg it had roamed the countryside searching for food and fodder. Sometimes farmers were paid with IOUs in Confederate dollars, but more often Lee's soldiers took what they needed, leaving crumbs for the civilian population. Then he had wrecked his army by sending it against the entrenched enemy at Gettysburg and virtually destroyed its logistical capability.

Bragg's western army also was in shambles. After these drastic military setbacks, the Confederacy was never the same. Those lost to death, disease, severe wounds, capture, and desertion could not be replaced. Tennessee, Louisiana, and Mississippi were Union-occupied. Foreign credit to the Confederate government vanished. The West and the four border states were lost, with Tennessee (including Chattanooga) and Vicksburg as its greatest losses. Grant had captured an entire army at Vicksburg, then gone on to defeat Bragg's army at Missionary Ridge. Lincoln said that as long as the South held Vicksburg, it meant "hog and hominy without limit." Now the hog and hominy were gone.

Control of the Mississippi River had been a strategic goal of Lincoln's from the war's beginning. Now the North held possession of the Confederate artery all the way to its mouth, cutting off Arkansas and Texas from the rest of the Confederacy. Rebel military operations west of the Mississippi were now unimportant. One hundred thousand ex-slaves, many from Mississippi River plantations, were serving in the Northern army, half of them bearing arms. Many more had fled their masters to follow the Union army. Lee's strategic concerns were focused on the war in Virginia. Unlike Grant and Lincoln, he and Jefferson Davis largely neglected the war in the West, with disastrous results. Lee was, at best, indifferent to the immense loss of western crops needed to feed his army, as well as its iron mines, and its munitions centers at Atlanta and Selma.

The South's foreign policy proved a bitter disappointment in 1863. Britain refused diplomatic recognition—a rejection that was worth "a second Vicksburg" to the North. Louis Napoleon's efforts to establish Maximilian as emperor of Mexico and to gain French diplomatic recognition of the Confederacy fizzled. The naval blockade of Southern seaports was strengthened as the Northern naval fleet dramatically increased. More than 1,000 vessels in the Southern fleet were immobilized, captured, or sunk, choking off the South's foreign trade. The British discontinued building ships for the Southern navy. War goods imported through Mexico were cut off, as were foodstuffs from west of the Mississippi. Sugar and molasses from the Mississippi Valley were no longer available to the Confederate army. Rebel soldiers referred to the only available meat, imported from Nassau, as "Nausea bacon."

Maryland, Missouri, and Mississippi were debating how to end slavery within their borders. The South's transportation system was a shambles. Most Southern roads were dirt tracks used by mule-drawn wagons, which were in short supply because they had been requisitioned by the army. Those that were available for civilian use were broken down, as were the animals available to pull them. Lee's army had to pasture horses across

Virginia and North Carolina to find forage no longer available locally. Yankee gunboats reduced river transportation to a minimum. There were only 9,000 miles of railroad tracks in the South as opposed to 22,000 miles in the North. What's more, Southern gauges varied from three to six feet, preventing cars from being transferred from line to line and adding to the time and cost of rail movements. At rail hubs, competing railroads did not connect, so freight often had to be hauled across town by wagon. The South's capacity to repair and rebuild its railroads was vanishing rapidly. Rolling stock was old and in disrepair, and spare parts were unavailable, making it extremely difficult to deliver food, equipment, and materiel to Lee's army. Under such conditions, he simply could not undertake a major offensive.

Such shortages, combined with the military defeats, were significantly damaging to morale as well as to the Confederate economy. Hunger and disease were civilian as well as military problems, particularly among North Carolina troops. Lee was too submissive to demand that his troops be equipped, clothed, and fed. His soldiers were described as "splendid scarecrows" and "magnificent ragamuffins." Medicines, as well as chloroform, clothing, and shoes were scarce. Five thousand soldiers had deserted after their Gettysburg and Missionary Ridge defeats. The South would not force its plantation owners to cut back on cotton and tobacco to produce much-needed food, because such a move surrendered agricultural land, once overtaken, to Northern armies. Nor were the plantation owners that did raise food crops willing to sell their produce at below-market prices. Instead, when possible, they sold to the North for greenbacks or gold.

Further, the Emancipation Proclamation encouraged an estimated 500,000 slaves to run away, seeking the sanctuary of Federal jurisdiction. Many of those who remained with their masters became "uppity" and "unfaithful." Since slaves constituted half of the workforce, the South's ability to produce crops was significantly diminished. Some plantation owners hired slaves out to bondsmen, who put them to work in war factories, further reducing agricultural activity. Another 150,000 slaves were taken to Texas so they could not be impressed into service by the Confederate Army. Still others were sold to plantation owners in the Deep South where Union armies had not yet penetrated. In the fall of 1863, the North was blessed with abundant harvests, while the gulf between the "haves" and "have-nots" in the South was widening. Plantation owners would not help neighboring dirt farmers. They had to cobble their own shoes out of canvas and wood, and to make clothing from old curtains and worn-out sheets, blankets from tattered carpets, and mattresses from whatever they could stuff in old grain sacks.

The Emancipation Proclamation also cemented radical support at home and coalesced liberal European opinion in Lincoln's favor as emancipation gained popular support among Northerners. The North had become a far bigger market than the South for British manufactured goods. Further, British cotton mills had found alternative sources of cotton in Asia and North Africa. Because Northern farmers were producing a surplus of grain, Britain became a steady market for it. The result was that Northern King Corn replaced Southern King Cotton.

The occupation of Chattanooga had cut off the supply of Tennessee coal, niter, and copper needed by factories in Virginia, Georgia, Alabama, and South Carolina. Inflation was rampant, as the government's gold and silver supply dwindled and individual states, as well as some cities, printed paper money. The South's banking system was chaotic. Inflation had eaten up the purchasing power of soldiers' pay and civilian income, having escalated nearly 70 percent in the four months after Gettysburg. At the beginning of 1863, it already took seven Confederate dollars to buy what cost one at the war's beginning. In contrast, the North's public credit was good, and its troops were paid more or less punctually.

In the Confederate congressional elections in the fall of 1863, of 106 congressional seats, 41 openly antiadministration candidates were elected. Sixteen of these were from North Carolina and Georgia, where anti-Davis sentiment was strongest. Their governors often refused to cooperate with President Jefferson Davis, because they were unwilling to allow him to create a strong central government. Many of his generals were angry with him. Twelve of twenty-six senators also were identified with opposition to the Davis administration. Even his vice-president opposed him throughout most of the war. The fragile Confederate coalition was coming apart, the honeymoon period of harmony and unity long over. Their concept of states' rights prevented the Confederacy from gelling.

By contrast, in 1863, Lincoln's Republicans won two bitterly contested gubernatorial elections against copperhead candidates in Ohio and Pennsylvania and carried two-thirds of the legislative districts in New York. In the Ohio election, 10,000 soldiers in the Army of the Cumberland voted in the field. Less than 300 voted for the copperhead candidate, Clement Vallandingham. The Republicans' margin of victory climbed 110,000 over the previous election. Despite popular resistance to the draft, the Republicans also made solid gains in Iowa, Illinois, Maryland, Minnesota, Pennsylvania, and Wisconsin. Copperheadism, which had peaked in the North after the Union's defeat at Chancellorsville, had been dampened after Gettysburg and Vicksburg.

The election was a watershed event, giving Lincoln a strong endorsement of his policies. Northern abolitionist strength was distinctly on the rise. Lincoln himself had set the tone in these elections. He could now get on with emancipation and restoring the Union by winning the war. Maryland and Missouri were debating how to end slavery within their borders. In contrast to Davis, Lincoln's personal popularity was growing, and he had learned a lot about how to deal with his generals. At the Republican Party convention in June 1864, William Lloyd Garrison reported that when someone proposed a constitutional amendment abolishing slavery as part of the party's platform, "The whole body of delegates sprang to their feet... in prolonged cheering." Clearly, Lincoln was a master politician, while Davis was a failure. Even his wife, Varina, doubted his leadership skills, writing, "He did not know the arts of the politician... and would not practice them if understood." He totally lacked charisma.

By the spring of 1864, the Confederate army was less than half the size of the Union's and had lost many irreplaceable officers. By then, the number of Confederate effectives numbered "generally less than half" of the total size of its army because of desertions, straggling, and other absences. Consequently, the privilege of paying someone to take one's place in the Southern army was abolished, age limits for the draft were expanded to include men between seventeen and fifty, and soldiers whose three-year enlistments were about to expire were required to remain in the army. Confederate desertions were escalating so rapidly that both President Davis and General Lee offered pardons to those deserters who would return within twenty days. It was clear that the South was suffering more casualties than it could afford.

By 1864, President Davis, unlike Lincoln, had proven himself inept at making military decisions. The Confederate congress was unwilling to enact legislation to force plantation owners to mobilize fully for the war effort. Davis himself personified the planter class in its aristocratic pride, feudal lifestyle, and total indifference to worldwide antislavery opinion. The Confederate supply system was riddled with corruption and inefficiency, and rations were short. Internal strife was tearing the Confederacy apart. Davis told his congress that traitors and spies riddled the government. Citizens of every state were more concerned about it than the Richmond government.

If Robert E. Lee had shown the leadership he displayed on the battlefield, he would have tried to convince President Davis—and what remained of his following—that the South could not win the war. Had Lee come to such a conclusion and made it unequivocally known, his opinion could not have been ignored, particularly if he had been asked or had chosen to resign because of it. In September 1863, on the eve of General Longstreet's departure to reinforce Bragg at Chickamauga,

Lee told him, "General, we must have a great victory out there. The success of our cause depends on it. We need only inflict one great disaster upon the Federal army to recover everything that has been lost." Instead, while Lee was checkmated in Virginia, the South suffered horrible losses at Chickamauga on September 19 and 20 and a disastrous defeat at Missionary Ridge on November 25, followed by Longstreet's retreat from Knoxville.

Lincoln's goal of disrupting the Nashville-Atlanta corridor, a Confederate lifeline, was finally realized after Chattanooga fell. A route was now opened for General Sherman to capture Atlanta, and with it, an all-weather supply line, the Western and Atlantic Railroad.

9

Battle of the Wilderness
May 5–7, 1864

> Comrade William Ross, in gathering sticks in the darkness, had brought along a thigh-bone of some skeleton, and when he noticed it by the fire, and picking it up and placing it alongside his thigh, said, "Well, that was a big Johnnie, and I don't know as I care to meet such a fellow." He was six feet himself and was a good soldier, never once flinching his duty, and poor Billy was killed.
>
> —Lt. C. T. Barnes, 93rd N.Y., Company C (Will's company) describing the early morning of May 5, 1864

Will Ross had served as regimental commissary sergeant since January 1863, drawing $21 a month in pay. During the summer of 1863, the post was abolished, and all Army of the Potomac regiments began drawing rations from brigade and division commissaries. As a result, Will was reduced in rank to private and assigned to Capt. Dennis E. Barnes's Company C on August 19, 1863. Despite being put on detached service guarding trains and prisoners, he did not complain, not even when his pay was reduced to $13 monthly.

In fact, with nearly a year remaining in his three-year enlistment, Will signed on for an additional three years in December 1863. It was his third enlistment, and although he had been close to battles as a headquarters guard, twenty-seven-year-old Will had served in the army for three years without participating in one. The Battle of the Wilderness would be his first, and his last.

It is impossible to gauge the part that antislavery convictions and commitment to restoring the Union played in Will's readiness to risk his life. In May 1864, he was in the prime of life, six feet tall and handsome, with light hair and blue eyes. There are several reasons to believe he was a staunch opponent of slavery, including his religious and family background and the sentiments of the upstate New York community in which he was born and raised. Arguably, few Union soldiers enlisted three times unless they were morally committed to preserving the Union and ending slavery.

At the outset, most Northerners, including President Abraham Lincoln, thought the Civil War would last three months. Three long, bloody years later, in the spring of 1864, Lincoln named Ulysses S. Grant commander of all Northern armies. The president told Grant, "There is no one but myself that can interfere with your orders; and you can rest assured that I will not do it." Grant responded, "The confidence you express for the future [of] my military administration is acknowledged with pride. It will be my earnest endeavor that you and the country shall not be disappointed." For the first time, Grant would go toe-to-toe with Lee.

William Henry Ross

Lee's first maxim of military strategy was to either outflank his enemy or split the enemy's army into segments at its weakest point, thereby reducing its effectiveness as a fighting unit. To do so at the Wilderness, he had to gain control of Brock Road, the key to the region. Lee was aggressive and audacious, willing to take desperate chances, as he had at Chancellorsville, where it paid off, and at Gettysburg, where it did not. Henry Heth, one of Lee's generals, said of him, "I have always thought [Lee] was the most belligerent man in his army." Yet he had never received one demerit in his four years at West Point. He had learned to carefully plan and delegate authority in the Mexican War. Like Grant, he lived plainly but for one luxury—a pet hen that regularly laid a single egg under his cot. Unlike Grant, Lee was an aristocrat, the scion of one of the first families of Virginia and married to a direct descendant of George Washington's wife.

Because of a host of soldiers like Will, the Army of the Potomac remained intact and held the crucial Brock Road by controlling its intersection with Orange Plank Road. From there, Grant's army went on to ultimate victory. The men of the 93rd N.Y. had spent two years guarding the headquarters of the Army of the Potomac and were referred to as its "pet lambs." They had served under generals McClellan, Burnside, Pope, Hooker, and Meade. They had been within sight and sound of the battles of Antietam, the Seven Days,' Fredericksburg, Chancellorsville, and Gettysburg. The regiment was a favorite at army headquarters because of its discipline and efficiency, but the men were eager to be reassigned to combat. Within ten days of their first battle, a man in the regiment earned the Medal of Honor.

The misfortunes that befell all four Ross brothers were directly related to General Grant's early 1864 decision to tie his operations against General Lee in northern Virginia to Maj. Gen. William T. Sherman's Atlanta campaign, thereby unifying military movements in the East and West. Up to then, Will, Dan, and Lank had survived three years of war without injury. Once Grant's strategy to destroy the two major Confederate armies—Lee's in Virginia and Joseph E. Johnston's in Georgia—was put in motion, ruthless determination took over. Although it led to a Union victory, the result was tragedy for the Ross family and many others.

May 1864 was the turning point of the war. Grant's objective was to crush Lee's army while it was defending Richmond, inflicting heavy casualties through constant attack. At the same time, Sherman would defeat Johnston's army as it protected Atlanta, the South's major transportation and manufacturing center. Sherman was to concentrate his troops at Chattanooga and move initially against Dalton, the "Georgian Gibraltar." He had under his command almost 100,000 men in three armies, who were to move down the Western and Atlantic Railroad to Atlanta. Grant had 118,000 men under his immediate command. The advance toward Richmond became a series of bloody, pitched battles and a siege. Unlike most Civil War campaigns, the struggle for Atlanta, called the "Battle from May to September," was continuous. Soldiers rarely escaped the sounds, if not the dangers, of combat.[1]

The Battle of the Wilderness, one of the bloodiest in the Civil War, began May 5, opening Grant's campaign to crush Lee's army and capture Richmond. Grant chose the direct approach on the theory that his superior numbers would make the difference, and he applied "horse sense" rather than military custom or doctrine in his decision-making. His objective was to capture the enemy's army. There would be no fancy maneuvers, no withholding of large bodies of reserve troops, no retreats to reorganize. He had a lifelong aversion to retracing his steps. "One of my superstitions [was] when I started to go anywhere not to turn back, or stop until the thing intended was accomplished," he wrote. He was determined "to hammer continuously against the armed forces of the enemy . . . [and] to

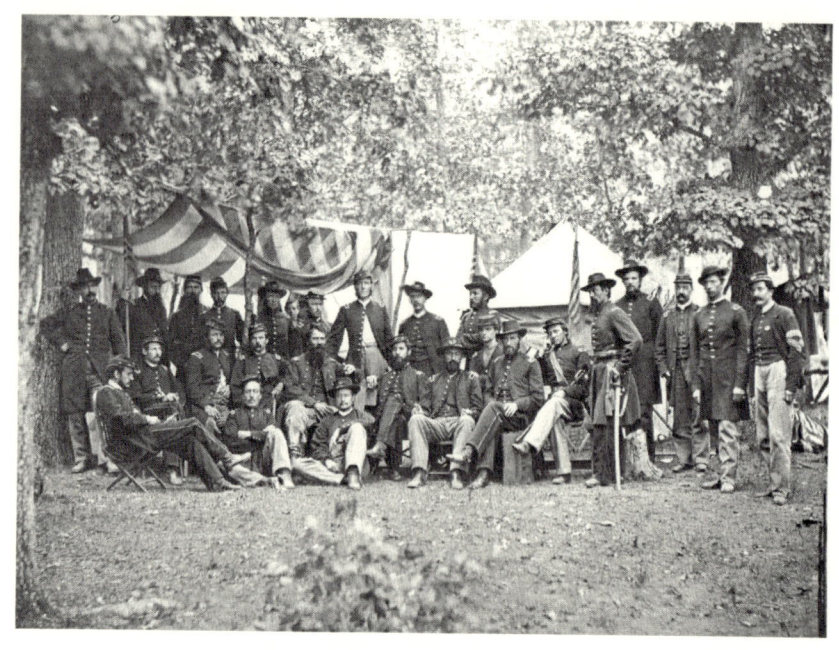

Officers of the 93rd New York, including Will Ross (far right)

fight it out on this line [to Richmond] if it takes all summer." He focused on what he could do to the enemy, not on what the enemy could do to him. Grant declared grim, ugly, destructive, total war.

Sherman's Atlanta campaign was set to start on May 7. Sherman's basic strategy was to avoid head-on confrontation with Johnston's troops while destroying the South's materiel—cities, railroads, munitions factories, arsenals, supply depots, cotton mills, standing crops, and cattle. "Of course I must fight when the time comes," he conceded, "but whenever a result can be accomplished without battle, I prefer it." The safety and support of his army were his paramount considerations. In the four-month march on Atlanta, Sherman's army suffered fewer casualties than Grant's army did during the first ten days of his march on Richmond.

Grant firmly believed it was better to suffer heavy losses in an effort to win than to suffer equally heavy losses in the stalemate the Army of the Potomac had been in during the first three years of the war. Grant, one of the finest horsemen the army ever produced, rode without affectation. As a boy he had developed an outstanding talent for handling horses, and he was fond of them. He liked farming and enrolled in West Point only because his domineering father got him an appointment. The only subject in which Grant distinguished himself was horsemanship. In fact, many of his classmates agreed that he was the finest horseman who ever attended the academy. As a cadet, he broke in all the new horses. He never punished an animal but slowly and skillfully let it know what he wanted it to do. He fought in the Mexican War, but hated it.

Grant knew he had to convince the Army of the Potomac that it no longer needed to be "afraid of Bobby Lee." He had only six weeks before the campaign began to instill self-confidence and aggressiveness in the army. Other than Gettysburg, it had few real victories to its credit in three years of fighting, and its veterans had painful memories of being defeated by Lee. Grant needed to convert the men into effective fighters before his army could become the steamroller he intended it to be. Grant was fearless. In every battle he fought he would ride, usually unaccompanied by his staff, to observe the action and the nature of the ground firsthand. He ignored danger, because he felt he could not rely on staff reports to make command decisions. He never flinched, blinked, or moved a muscle, much less swore. There was no show or pretense in his makeup.

Will spent July, August, and September of 1863 on detached provost duty in Washington, DC, initially guarding trains that were taking prisoners there and later guarding about 1,000 prisoners confined in the Old Capitol Prison. The prison was noted for its strict discipline, the spies incarcerated there, and its infestation of bedbugs. Had he not been on that assignment, Will might have seen his brother Dan again. In September, both their regiments were in line along the Rappahannock River near Bealton, Virginia, after pursuing Lee's army as it retreated from Gettysburg to Virginia through Manassas Gap. On September 26, Dan and his artillery battery left for Tennessee.

In early October 1863, 1st Lt. Haviland Gifford, of the 93rd N.Y., wrote his father that Northerners had a duty to help crush the "hydra headed monster that is eating at the very vitals of the Government ... laid down by our forefathers ... that we their offspring might enjoy the free institutions established by the works of their hands." On November 4, Robertson wrote his parents, "We [are] all jubilant tonight on the result of the New York election.... I had no fear, but that the Union ticket would be elected after the result of the Ohio and Pa. elections. Copperheads seem to be at a discount at present."

On November 9, 1863, the 93rd N.Y. arrived at Brandy Station, Virginia. Will was sick and was transferred to the Invalid Corps. His regiment received orders on December 3 to build a permanent winter camp for the headquarters of the Army of the Potomac. It took a great deal of work just to clear the ground for the camp. Winter quarters for Will and the other men consisted of log huts chinked with mud, eight feet square and four feet high, with a floor, and a shelter tent for a roof. Each hut accommodated three to five men and had an open fireplace with a chimney made of stone or wood. Every company built its huts in two rows facing one another along opposite sides of a narrow lane. Despite the bitterly cold Virginia winter, the huts were warm. To break the monotony, some would run down abundant wild hogs, rabbits, and squirrels in the surrounding woods, yielding great fun and good rations. Others, while on picket duty, would declare a truce for the day with enemy pickets on the opposite side of the river. In return for coffee supplied by the Yanks, on at least one occasion the Rebels sent tobacco across the river on a hand-carved, 14.5-inch boat propelled by sails made of Southern newspapers.

General Meade stayed in camp over Christmas to encourage his soldiers to reenlist. As an extra incentive, he extended their furlough to thirty-five days to allow for travel time. He anticipated that only half of the eligible men would reenlist, but his efforts were rewarded as nearly two-thirds did so. The 93rd was the first regiment in the Army of the Potomac to veteranize. By December 18, after a month of discussion, six companies had caught the "reenlistment fever," and a seventh joined up two weeks later. By Christmas, three-fourths of Will's company had followed suit. They received $110 of the $400 federal bounty payment—the balance to be paid in installments—$21.13 in clothing allowance, all back pay owed them, and paid transportation for their furlough home. The men received a service chevron to wear on their sleeves, identifying them as Veteran Volunteers. Will and others with these chevrons became known as "old sweats." Washington County borrowed $125,000 to pay a $200 bounty to each Veteran Volunteer. Those who re-upped with Will left camp on December 28 and arrived in Albany on New Year's Day 1864. There were 300 enlisted men and 22 officers, all with more money in their pockets than they had ever had before. One hundred sixty others recruited after the regiment took the field were not eligible for the furlough and remained in camp. In Albany, the men were greeted by Gov. Horatio Seymour and collected $75 each in bounty from the state. This would be the last time Will would visit his home, family, and friends. Lt. W. W. Braman, who was in Will's company, was the recruiting officer for the regiment. Braman wrote his cousin Emmie, "I tell you this Army is just a Bully Army" and added that most of the regiment wanted to be assigned to frontline duty. A fortnight after Will's reenlistment, his brother Lank reenlisted as a Veteran Volunteer in the 36th Ill.

When the 93rd N.Y. was reorganized in December 1863 under Lincoln's Veteran Volunteer proclamation, it was part of the provost guard at General Meade's headquarters. The regiment's duties included furnishing regular camp guards for officers' quarters, guarding railroads, improving roads, and protecting the army's huge wagon train. They also guarded Rebel and citizen prisoners, Union soldiers convicted of various offenses, and deserters held in the "bull pen" within the gutted Culpeper Court House slave pen. The provost guard issued visitor passes and processed paperwork for both officers and soldiers. They rounded up runaway shirkers and stragglers who were frequently on the sick list, and they patrolled the countryside for bounty jumpers. In battle, they were assigned to prevent straggling.

During the winter encampment, many families and friends visited officers of the Army of the Potomac. The men spent long winter evenings around fires gossiping, playing cards, and other games, writing letters, swapping yarns, singing, and dancing stag, sometimes to the accompaniment of a banjo, guitar, or harmonica. The camp also had churches, theaters, debate schools, and a football field. Every night, the regimental band's fifes sounded tattoo, accompanied by drums. Crows grew fat and sassy feeding on the entrails of animals butchered to feed the troops over the winter. Pickets fed their fires with wood from fences, barns, stables, and farm machinery. As Private Haley put it, during winter months, picket duty was significantly less than enjoyable. "If the army imposed a penny fine for every oath a picket uttered... some men would have sworn away their entire months wages in a single night."

On February 10, 1864, the 93rd returned to Brandy Station from reenlistment furlough, except for a recruiting party that stayed behind in Washington County until April 26 to further replenish the depleted regimental ranks. It took four days by train to complete the journey from Albany, New York. To fill their ranks, the men brought nearly a hundred recruits, referred to as "mud crushers," "bounty bought," and "hundred dollar men." On their way back to camp, they stayed overnight in Alexandria, Virginia. Col. John S. Crocker, commander of the 93rd N.Y., visited the slave pen and noted in his diary, "We can rejoice at the thought that this notorious slave pen, where so many men, women, and children have suffered the most cruel wrongs... from cruel masters, and more cruel dealers in human flesh, will hold no more slaves henceforth.... Let us rejoice." As early as August 1862, Crocker had called for freeing the slaves and "using them in all practical ways to crush the rebellion."

Col. John S. Crocker with aides

Many recruits were soon on the sick list. They lacked immunity to camp diseases the veterans had long ago acquired. Meade was still sick in Philadelphia and did not return to camp until February 16. Will's regiment at Brandy Station resumed its duty as headquarters guard for General Meade.

The previous December, Congressman Elihu B. Washburn had introduced a joint resolution to Congress to thank Grant and award him a gold medal. The two had known each other since their days in Galena, Illinois, and Washburn had sponsored every military promotion for Grant since being elected to Congress in 1854. Grant had responded with a letter to Washburn, acknowledging that he had already been honored by the government. He wrote, "I do not ask, or feel that I deserve, anything more in the shape of honors or promotion. A success over the enemy is what I crave above everything." Nonetheless, on February 1, 1864, Washburn introduced a bill reviving the rank of lieutenant general, expressly for Grant. The president signed the bill by the end of the month. Before then, only George Washington had held the rank; Gen. Winfield Scott had held it but only by brevet.

On March 5, Brig. Gen. Alexander Hays was assigned to command a new nine-regiment brigade in Maj. Gen. David B. Birney's new 3rd Division. Both were part of Maj. Gen. Winfield S. Hancock's new 2nd Corps. The 93rd N.Y. would soon join Hays's brigade. Hays established his headquarters in five large, canvas-roofed log cabins built in a semicircle in the front yard of a private home. Hancock's headquarters were located on Coles Hill at the edge of a peach orchard near Stevensburg. More soldier than scholar, the hard-drinking Hays had graduated from West Point in 1844 near the bottom of his class. Hancock was in the same class, and Grant was a year ahead of them. Hays had served on frontier duty, and was breveted once for gallantry in the Mexican War, three times in the Civil War. Grant and Hays had known each other at West Point, and the two had served together on their first assignment in Mexico in 1846. He also had been severely wounded in the Second Battle of Manassas, Bull Run. Between the Mexican and Civil wars, he had been a "forty-niner" and later a bridge builder.

Grant now commanded 533,000 men who were present and fit for duty out of a total of 800,000 in the entire Union army. During the fall and winter of 1863-64, every effort had been made to strengthen the North's military. With the telegraphic communications fully operational, it was possible for Grant to direct all his field commanders, even those who were as much as 1,000 miles away. At age forty-two, Grant was a veteran of twenty-seven battles, all of them victories. He had captured two Confederate armies and routed a third.[2]

On March 10, President Lincoln and General Grant traveled sixty miles from Washington, DC, to Brandy Station in a cold, driving rain to meet Meade. With Meade slightly indisposed, two of his staff met the train. From the train they had viewed nothing but devastation—burned homes, ramshackle outbuildings and fences, fallow fields, denuded forests, and the wreckage of railroads. The buildings still standing were being used for barracks, hospitals, stables, and command posts. By war's end, one-fifth of all battles had been fought in Virginia. On seeing Lincoln for the second time, Colonel Crocker recorded in his diary that the president appeared careworn but not despondent—his soul was committed to crushing the rebellion. At headquarters, Will's duties as guard enabled him to see Lincoln for the second time and Grant for the first. Meade greeted the two chieftains with a salute and a handshake. A regimental band played "Hail to the Chief," and the three men dined in Meade's tent. About the time of their arrival, paymasters left Washington, DC, with $8 million to pay the Army of the Potomac, and Hays ordered new shoes issued to his brigade. He also decreed, "straggling will not be permitted . . . when the Spring Campaign opens."

Lincoln and Grant returned to Washington the next day. Grant excused himself from a Grand Military Banquet at the White House, explaining to the president that he had devoted "enough time to this show business." He added, "A dinner to me means a million dollars... lost to the country." At least eleven other generals did attend the banquet, including Meade.

Silent and retiring, Grant made no effort to court popularity, and he hated politics. He had less than seven weeks to shuttle back and forth to Washington, meet with General Sherman, develop and transmit his plans, and marshal all his forces so he could launch the simultaneous movement of his armies. Meanwhile, Will and the other men in the 93rd were reading newspapers to learn what they could about Grant and endlessly discussing his battles. When Grant unassumingly walked through the camp, thrusting his left hand into his pocket and chewing an unlit cigar clamped between his lips, soldiers seldom saluted him. They watched him silently with a curious reverence. Most "old-timers" in the Army of the Potomac no longer idolized their top military leaders, who over the past three years had wasted the lives of their comrades. Instead, they were waiting, patiently and hopefully, to be led to victory rather than defeat. As Private Haley noted in his diary, "Somehow we all believed that a new day dawned with the advent of Gen. Grant." Lincoln told John Hay, his private secretary, that he hoped Grant could "do something with the unfortunate Army of the Potomac."

On March 23, Hancock returned from two and one-half months of recruiting for his 2nd Corps. He had not yet recovered from the extremely painful groin wound he had suffered at Gettysburg. For the remainder of the war, he traveled largely by ambulance until he was in the vicinity of the enemy. He would then mount his horse until the battle ended. Riding a horse further aggravated the festering wound, necessitating daily treatment by a surgeon. The considerable weight Hancock had gained while on his lengthy absence undoubtedly made riding even more painful. Hancock had written his wife that when on horseback, he suffered agony. Hancock's 2nd Corps, consisting of eighty-one regiments plus ten artillery, was the army's most formidable striking force, and Hancock was the army's most aggressive corps commander.[3] Meade welcomed Hancock warmly. He had written Meade, "I would sooner command a corps under you than have the supreme command." Grant regarded Hancock as a general who could make a great army function smoothly.

Grant arrived on March 24 and established his headquarters in a large tent on private property near Culpeper Court House. The snow was nearly a foot deep, and some regiments organized snowball fights while others built sleds and took sleigh rides. Grant's arrival triggered greater activity and stricter discipline. Trains and wagons arrived, loaded with provisions, all of which was due to the logistical skills and foresight of General Meade as head of the Army of the Potomac. The troops became increasingly confident about the plans Grant was developing to coordinate the simultaneous movements of all his armies, especially their army.

On March 26, Will's Company C, commanded by Capt. Dennis E. Barnes, the senior captain of the regiment, was assigned the extreme right flank position in the regimental line, even though at that point, they were still headquarters guard. It would prove to be a fateful assignment for Will. That same day General Hays wrote his wife that he had sent her $400, was not indulging in "spirituous liquors in any form," had "implicit confidence in [his] men, and believe it is returned with double interest." He also noted that two cows would bring up the rear of his brigade and that he had "a churn, and [had] turned dairyman." On March 30, Crocker was informed that since his was a Veteran Volunteer regiment and had a large complement, it would be brigaded. On April 11, by general order, Hays created two four-regiment battalions, leaving the 1st U.S. Sharpshooters separate and under his direct command for special duty. The 93rd New Yorkers received their pay for January and February on April 16. It totaled nearly $40,000, about half of which was sent home. The next day they were issued new Springfield rifles to replace their old Enfields.

Acting on confidential information from Grant, Meade ordered his commissary department on April 17 to load one million rations on suitable vessels and take them up the James and Pamunkey rivers by the end of April. He also ordered one hundred rounds of artillery ammunition per gun and one hundred rounds of rifle ammunition per man plus medical supplies for 12,000 wounded to be taken upriver when necessary. Siege guns and siege trains were also to be readied. Several thousand head of cattle for the campaign were herded together to feed the men.

On April 18, Will stood his last guard duty, posted in front of the guardhouse. The next day, General Meade relieved the 93rd from headquarters duty, and transferred them to Hays's newly created 2nd Brigade. That same day, after returning from one of his many trips to Washington, Grant wrote his wife that he was back in Culpeper by rail, his only difficulty having been that the engine jumped the track.

The 3rd Division commander, Birney, who had been slightly wounded at Gettysburg, was the senior of Hancock's four division commanders. He thought very highly of the 93rd N.Y. Born in Alabama and a Philadelphia lawyer, he was the son of James Birney, the abolitionist candidate for president in 1840 and 1844 on the Liberty Party ticket. Its primary goal, according to Birney, was "the grant of the Elective Franchise to the colored people." By the end of the war, General Birney's brother William recruited and commanded a division of black troops and was breveted a major general. In April 1864 he proposed a plan to raise fifteen black regiments in South Carolina, Florida, and Georgia. Each soldier's family was to be settled on forty acres with a house, family necessities furnished by the government at cost, and equal pay of $13 monthly, $11 of it to be sent to the family.

Eight of the ten regiments in Hays's brigade were either Veteran Volunteers or had enlisted for three-year stints in 1862. Like the 93rd, two of these regiments would suffer enormous casualties in the battle—namely, 192 casualties in the 17th Maine and 191 in the 63rd Pa.

Colonel Crocker of the 93rd was senior in rank to all other regimental commanders in the brigade and therefore next in command to Hays. Like the First U.S. Sharpshooters, Hays also kept the 93rd separate from the two battalions and therefore subject to his direct command for such activities as skirmishing. By virtue of Crocker's seniority, the 93rd became the brigade's lead regiment. Before the war he had organized, trained, and commanded a regiment of New York State militia. Crocker was a thorough and skillful disciplinarian and had the admiration and confidence of his men, because he always looked out for their welfare.

Hays's brigade was the largest in the 2nd Corps, and the 93rd was the largest regiment in his brigade, with 433 men and officers. On the opening day of the battle, Hays's brigade mustered 3,641 effectives out of 26,676 in the entire 2nd Corps. They were the best fed and clothed in the Army of the Potomac. At twenty-seven, Will was among the minority. Fewer than half of these men were twenty-five or older, and thousands would never reach that age. The 2nd Corps had a far greater percentage of Veteran Volunteers than the Union Army as a whole, and within that, the 93rd N.Y. had a particularly high number, 322. While only 6.5 percent of the Union Army was Veteran Volunteers, almost 40 percent of the corps—10,883 men—had veteranized. More than 10 percent of those in the 2nd Corps, 1,170, were from the Empire State, including 322 in the 93rd, over one-fourth of the total.

Lt. W. W. Braman, of Will's company, wrote home, "[W]e took our leave of Hdqrs with flying colors ... have left a good reputation, and hosts of friends.... The Brigade, Division, and Corps are all we could wish, their name (now ours) is above reproach as soldiers. And when the proper time comes the 93rd will do their share to sustain that name." Other New Yorkers shared pride in the regiment. One wrote the *Messenger*, "The regiment is the only one in the brigade to ... represent the Empire State [and] we shall do it with pride and honor to ... our state."

Ten days after the regiment was brigaded, Braman wrote his cousin, "We are having drills, reviews, and inspections, in succession, as sure as Tuesday follows Wash day." Six feet tall, erect, fearless, and an inspirational leader, Hays had a reputation that preceded him. He ordered cooks, waiters, and other noncombatants in the 93rd to shoulder arms. Meade, Hancock, Birney, Hays, and Crocker all admired and trusted one another. The officers and men in Crocker's regiment shared these sentiments. With that bond of confidence they would prove to be an extremely effective fighting machine. Further, Birney and Crocker felt strongly about emancipation, which surely bound men like Will and Captain Barnes, his company commander, even more tightly to their leaders. Captain Barnes's family were noted Washington County abolitionists. His grandfather served in the War of 1812, and his great-grandfather in the Revolution.

By early April, Maj. H. L. Abbott of the 20th Mass., another Veteran Volunteer regiment in Hancock's corps, wrote his friend George. "I suspect myself we shall have the biggest fight the world ever saw," he wrote. "Meade of course will be merely chief of staff to Grant, but as the former has shown himself quick-witted, skillful, a good combiner and maneuverer and is unquestionably a clever man intellectually, [while] the latter has got force, decision, etc., [and] the character which isn't afraid to take responsibility to the utmost, the union of the two may be the next [best] thing to having [one man] of real genius at the head."

It had rained heavily for thirty-six hours in early April, turning the Union camp into a sea of mud. The rains had washed out two railroads, cutting off supplies and daily mail deliveries. Warm, pleasant weather followed; the grass and trees turned a luxurious green, and flowers bloomed everywhere. Birds sang during the day and frogs and whip-poor-wills chorused at night. The surrounding forests had been wiped out for several miles, cut for firewood over the winter. Peach and pear trees blossomed on the plantations. Morale was high, the sick list was short, and those who needed extended treatment were sent to Washington on the Orange and Alexandria Railroad, a seven-hour trip.

As soon as the roads dried out, drill reviews, inspections, and daily target practice began. At 4 A.M. on April 22, Crocker was awakened on orders from General Hays to have his regiment ready for a grand review by General Grant. It was the first bright, sunny day in weeks. Generals Grant, Meade, and Hancock reviewed the 2nd Corps at noon; they had arrived in a handsome carriage drawn by four magnificent horses. An artillery salute signaled Grant's arrival at the parade ground. A bugle sounded the call to present arms, and the review began, as brigade bands played "Hail to the Chief." With Meade standing on one side and Hancock on the other, Grant tipped his hat, then saluted each regiment as it passed in review and dipped its colors. They paraded in close column with faultless uniforms, paper collars, white gloves, knapsacks, and haversacks, their greatcoats neatly rolled on top of the knapsacks. Meade said the 93rd was second to none in the review. Theodore Lyman, Meade's aide, wrote, "There seemed to be enough men to beat the whole world.... In each direction there was nothing but a wide, moving hedge of bright muskets ... Grant is very much pleased." Colonel Crocker's regiment was eager for its first frontline experience. One officer in Will's company wrote home, "We are at last to pay a maiden call upon the rebellious sons of our respected uncle."

A week of drilling followed the review. Drill sergeants became hoarse from issuing raucous marching orders. On April 23, Hays's entire brigade, with Crocker temporarily in command, practiced target shooting. Birney also issued a first-ever command, instructing them to remain on the firing line when engaged if they ran out of ammunition, and resort to the bayonet. They were also told to aim at the knees and fire only when a target was in their sights. That same day they learned of the Fort Pillow massacre of more than 200 black Union soldiers. A soldier of the 105th Pa. in Hays's brigade wrote his mother, "It makes my blood curdle. My opinion is that we should show no quarter whatever in time of action but massacre every bloody traitor as fast as opportunity present[s] itself."

The next day Hays inspected the brigade's arms, ammunition, uniforms, animals, wagons, ambulances, and pioneers' entrenching tools. Will and the other troops brushed and repaired their clothes, polished their brass, and shined their shoes. On April 25, Crocker wrote Birney that his regiment was short 7,420 rounds of ammunition, 6 rifles, 26 coats, and 218 pairs of shoes. On April 26 the regiment moved out of its filthy, marshy winter quarters into shelter tents, without fireplaces or chimneys, in preparation for the coming campaign. They torched their winter huts and sent all excess baggage and clothing, as well as the sick and disabled, to the rear of the procession. Officers were allowed to keep only what they could carry in an ordinary valise. Visitors and 280 sutlers left the camp, money was sent home, and all mail delivery to and from the army was suspended. No bands were allowed to strike up without permission from headquarters, and no drumrolls or bugle calls were to be sounded. That same day, Grant wrote Brig. Gen. John E. Smith, "[T]he Army of the Potomac is in a splendid condition and feels like whipping somebody. I feel much better with this command than I did before seeing it."

The new camp was located near Stevensburg, in a peach orchard in full bloom on good ground, with good water. They moved into log houses covered with split shingles that accommodated eight men each. As Private Haley wrote, they no longer had "to step in the fireplace or onto the table when they got out of bed... [or] to go out doors when we turned around."

On April 29, Crocker recorded in his diary that seven recruits had died and forty-four were on the sick list, but no veterans were in either group. In accordance with Meade's orders, long freight trains on the Orange and Alexandria Railroad had been busy delivering rations of hard bread and barrels of salt pork, uniforms, forage, weapons, munitions, blankets, and other supplies. Rations consisted of fresh beef and bread, potatoes, and other vegetables including onions, turnips, and cabbage. Because the diet included vegetables, scurvy was nonexistent. Furthermore, there was an ample supply of spring water. The men were well fed, dressed, and equipped.

In sharp contrast, General Lee had written the Confederate Secretary of War James A. Seddon in January 1864, "Short rations are having a bad effect upon the men, both morally and physically.... [As a consequence] desertions to the enemy are becoming more frequent.... Unless there is a change, I fear the army cannot be kept effective." There were as many veteran Confederates in Northern prisons as there were soldiers in Lee's army. Later, Lee wrote Confederate president Jefferson Davis, "[I do not see] how we can operate with our present supplies.... There is nothing to be had... for men or animals. We have rations for the troops to-day and to-morrow [only]." Scurvy was common among the men. Lee was seen eating a piece of corn bread and a dish of cold cabbage. When asked why he was dining like a pauper, he replied, "I deem it my duty to share the fortunes of my men."

Many of Lee's men were nearly barefoot, dressed in rags, and freezing in their miserable shanties. Some had returned to the battlefront from hospitals, not fully recovered from sickness or wounds. Other were conscripts or furloughed men returning to the ranks. An Alabama soldier in Lee's army wrote his wife that the weather "was as cold as the world's charity." He counted thirty-one shoeless men in his brigade. Every home, shop, church, tavern, and public building was being used as a barracks, stable, or hospital. Even the quality of the ammunition seemed to be on the decline. Nevertheless, the men still had faith in themselves and their leaders.

Since Gettysburg, Meade had streamlined his army's organization, appointed competent corps commanders, overhauled the army's staff, integrated new recruits into the ranks including Veteran Volunteer regiments, and improved morale. His popularity at all levels of the rank and file had grown through the fall and winter, well before Grant's arrival. Theodore Lyman, Meade's aide, wrote, "[A]s a rule I am much pleased with our... officers high and low. They... have a firm, quiet bearing.

You can often pick out those who have been through the thick of it by their subdued and steady look." With respect to fighting, the preservation of the Army of the Potomac was Meade's goal. The men knew he was prepared to use them but not squander them by risky assaults. He handed Grant an army that was steadfast, confident, and refreshed in mind and body, and that had a renewed sense of national purpose.

On April 29, Grant's men were ordered to keep three days' full rations and three days' short rations in their knapsacks, plus fifty rounds of ammunition. An additional ten days' rations per man were loaded in the supply wagons. Officers were allowed one wagon per brigade to carry their subsistence needs. One hospital wagon and one medical supply wagon were assigned to the brigade. Grant telegraphed General Halleck, "Send all the horses... here.... Horses [alone] are now worth more than men and horses." That night Grant wrote to his wife, "[I don't] know exactly the day when I will start or whether Lee will come here before I am ready to move."

Grant paid another visit to the White House on April 28, telling Lincoln, "I have an impression that the Army of the Potomac has never been fought to its capacity.... This time it will be." On April 30, Lincoln wrote Grant, "You are vigilant and self-reliant, and pleased with this, I wish not to obtrude any constraint or restraints upon you.... If there is anything wanting which is within my power to give, do not fail to let me know it." Lincoln was grateful that Grant did not shriek "for reinforcements all the time.... He takes what reinforcements we can safely give him... and does the best he can."

Meade, however, was less impressed with Grant, who was seven years his junior. Meade was also older than any of his corps commanders except Maj. Gen. John Sedgwick. After their first few weeks in camp together, Meade described Grant as "not a striking man.... I fancy his West Point education [is] all he ever had and since his graduation I don't believe he has read or studied any. At the same time he has natural qualities of a high order, and is a man whom the more you see and know, the better you like him." Grant had read Hardee's textbook, *Rifle and Infantry Tactics*, which most West Pointers virtually memorized, decided he knew better, and set it aside.

Sherman, who had fought under Grant for two years, had far more respect than Meade for Grant's leadership qualities. On April 5, 1864, Sherman wrote his brother, Senator John Sherman, "Grant is as good a leader as we can find. He has honesty, simplicity of character, singleness of purpose.... His character, more than his genius, will reconcile armies and attach people."

On Sunday, May 1, many Union regiments, including the 93rd, had their ambrotypes taken by a photographer who set up his equipment in a nearby field. Many of these photographs still exist, but not one of Will. A large number of the men also wrote letters to their families and friends. On the Confederate side, that same day Lee ordered that all baggage be sent to the rear. Two days later Grant ordered that three days' rations be cooked. On May 2, a torrential rainstorm and tornado-like winds blew tents around like paper kites and twisted large tree trunks like pipe stems. That same day Grant wrote his wife, "The train that takes this letter will be the last going to Washington. Before you receive this... the Army will be in motion. I know the greatest anxiety is now felt in the North." To reassure her, he added, "I believe it has never been my misfortune to be placed where I have lost my presence of mind, unless indeed it has been when I was thrown in strange company, particularly that of ladies." The train that took his letter left Brandy Station at 8 P.M. May 4.[4]

The night after Grant wrote Julia, he told his senior staff officers that his goal was Lee's army, not Richmond. He spent time that evening with his confidant, Congressman Washburn, discussing politics, war, and the prospects of success. On the afternoon of May 3, Grant's fast-riding couriers delivered sealed packets to Meade's corps commanders, including Hancock. About sunset, drummers from the 93rd beat an officers' call to summon them to Colonel Crocker's headquarters, where Crocker read the marching orders. Company commanders, including Captain Barnes from Will's company, ordered that bugle calls be sounded. They formed their men and examined arms, equipment, and clothing.

Barnes's fifty-nine-man Company C was composed of one second lieutenant, five sergeants, four corporals, and forty-nine privates, including Will. Only one reported sick, and two were in the guardhouse. Captain Barnes was a strict disciplinarian, and his men looked upon him as a father. The men cheered until hoarse the orders that signaled the end of the winter's inactivity. Thousands more were singing and laughing. They were resolute in the belief that their cause was just and they would succeed. Private Haley wrote, "We have no doubt but what Grant will give them as hot a fight as they will care to engage in."

In each company, lieutenants and sergeants attended to matters such as ammunition and rations, including raw beef, which was taken immediately to the company cooks' tents to be cooked over fires. Each company marched to its cookhouse to receive its rations. Officers and orderlies galloped through camp delivering orders. Boxes of hardtack arrived, and the crackers were "divvied up." Boxes of ammunition were opened and the contents distributed. Confusion and hubbub reigned, as men drank their last cups of coffee, struck their tents, and made other last-minute preparations. Within an hour the men completed their work, then turned in for a few hours of sleep, if indeed they could sleep.

At midnight the roll was called. Informal inspection was made of every man and his bedroll, arms, and equipment, and weapons were stacked along the company streets. Drums beat a quick assembly, and companies took their rifle-muskets and formed a line, the men shivering in the cool night air. Will carried his bedroll diagonally across his chest and over his left shoulder. He slung his rifle on his right shoulder and carried his haversack with rations on his back. He had a canteen and a full cartridge box containing fifty rounds on his belt, with another thirty rounds in his knapsack and pockets. Colonel Crocker took command as head of the brigade with his staff, and gave the order to march.

At 12:30 A.M. May 4, Will and his comrades moved out of camp in columns of four, their brigade leading the corps with Crocker temporarily in command and the 93rd having the advance. In an incredibly brief time, the entire Army of the Potomac was on the move. Their departure was so quiet that no one in Culpeper heard it. By this time, inefficiency and disorganization had been largely eradicated. Amateurs were no longer in charge and, after the reorganization of the army from five corps into three, the caliber of its generals was, by and large, first-rate. Shortly before departure, Hays had instructed his commissioned officers that if by act, word, or deed they indicated dissatisfaction with an order, they would be charged with mutiny. Further, they were expected to promptly execute all orders. They also were to submit names of their men who distinguished themselves in battle. Immediately behind Hancock's corps were the reserve artillery and the immense commissary and baggage trains.

The march began without bonfires, a drumbeat, or a bugle call, as staff officers and orderlies on horseback delivered marching orders. The night was clear, starlit, and breezy as the wind "tossed the leaflets on the trees, [which] seemed to moan and shudder." At 10 A.M., the brigade crossed the Rapidan at Ely's Ford on two swaying, 200-foot-wide wood and canvas pontoon bridges that shook for hours from the tread of soldiers' feet. Mounted officers forded the river. Brig. Gen. David Gregg's newly shod cavalry, in advance of Hancock's corps, had spent most of the night reconnoitering and repairing the road to Ely's Ford. The road was rough and crossed numerous ditches, ravines, and streams.

The New Yorkers marched with no halts, not even for coffee, except for a hurried breakfast at the ford. As dawn broke, the weather was clear, warm, and pleasant. The men were in good spirits, the road was dry and hard, and there was little straggling. The air was fragrant with the smells of honeysuckle, wild rose, and pine. Green buds tipped tree branches, dogwood trees bloomed, and wild flowers sprouted. In addition to eighty rounds of ammunition, each man carried rations in his haversack, plus a shelter tent, a blanket, a rubber ground cloth, and an overcoat. The sun shimmered on their bright bayonets, "resembling the glitter of frost in hedgerows in winter." They marched in step with regimental bands playing, banners waving, and men singing patriotic songs, including "John Brown's Body." By the time they completed the twenty-six-mile march under a blue sky, the road behind them was carpeted for miles with abandoned blankets, clothing, and other "unnecessaries." The regiment arrived at Chancellorsville fourteen hours later at 3 P.M.

Since Rebels could observe Union movements from lookouts, Grant had waited until after midnight to start the march. At first light, Lee's officers could trace Union movement by the cloud of dust that rose over the woods in a long, slow line parallel to the Rapidan River. Occasionally, the white canvas of the wagons was exposed. During the night, moving lights were visible, and troops could be seen marching past Federal camp fires. By 5 A.M. Lee was notified at his Orange Court House headquarters that Grant's army was moving to the southeast. From noon on, Grant watched in silence as the 5th Corps crossed the Germanna Ford, six miles from Ely's Ford. Smoking a cigar, Grant was seated with Washburn on the porch steps of an unpretentious and deserted old Dutch-gabled farmhouse on the river bluff. An aide recorded Grant's observation, "Lee must by this time know upon what roads we are advancing. . . . We shall probably soon get some indication as to what he intends to do." One-third of Lee's army was only twelve miles away.

Through the afternoon and evening of May 4, Hancock's hospitals were set up near Carpenter's House. Running water was nearby, and what was to become the battleground, about a mile and a half away, was accessible by two good ambulance roads. Four ambulances were assigned to each regiment. Two traveled with the regiment, and two with the division wagon train. There were only 619 ambulances for the entire army, manned by 2,300 drivers and stretcher bearers. In contrast, at Gettysburg there had been 1,000 ambulances to accommodate 20,000 fewer troops.

Some of the soldiers of Hancock's corps formed a battle line facing west, while the rest spread out along the Ely's Ford Road through meadow and forest for the night of May 4, waiting for the wagon trains to catch up. They were eight miles from Grant's headquarters. They stacked rifles like shocks of cornstalks, pitched rows of pup tents or simply spread blankets on the ground, and lit thousands of camp fires. Hancock's column extended from Chancellorsville back to the Rapidan at Ely's Ford. Birney's division camped just west of the Chancellorsville ruins.

For some of those who had fought at Chancellorsville a year earlier, camping on its battleground was not a good omen. The New Yorkers camped very close to Fairview Heights, where Dan Ross's artillery had been positioned in that battle. The delightful spring weather made the men momentarily carefree. Bands played music until sundown, while the troops cooked an evening meal of fried bacon and hardtack dipped in coffee. The coffee ration consisted of roasted whole beans, which men ground or pulverized with their rifle butts. They mixed the grounds with sugar in a small bag and would then spoon it out and boil it as needed for a meal.

Night came early as the fleecy white clouds turned crimson and then purple. Before "Taps," a band at Grant's headquarters played the "The Star Spangled Banner" and "Home Sweet Home." As they sat around camp fires, one brigade sang a hymn. Thousands of others, including Will, thought of home, parents, and the hardships and they were enduring, and they speculated what the next day would bring. Camp fires were extinguished at 9 P.M., and drums beat tattoo while horses neighed, officers shouted commands, and artillery unlimbered. Grant revealed his battle plan to the eight senior members of his staff, and smoked a cigar with Meade, offering him his flint and steel to light it. While smoking and talking, Grant received a telegram from General Sherman announcing that he had started his advance. Then he went to bed early. The lieutenant general's tent contained a narrow canvas bed stretched across a wooden frame with an inflated rubber mattress, a washbasin on an iron tripod, a crude, collapsible pine table for his maps and papers, two folding chairs, and a small trunk.

Never was an army in better spirits, despite the fact that many were lame and footsore from the long march. Will and the others bathed their feet in what water was available. The men slept near their arms, in battle order, as their supply train caught up with them. The 17th Maine was assigned picket duty for the brigade, going without sleep for a second night.

According to official reports, Grant had 118,000 men, 95,000 of whom were equipped for duty; 56,000 animals; and 6,000 creaking, lumbering wagons, including ambulances. In battle line two ranks deep, his army would have extended twenty-one miles. His wagons carried ammunition, ten days' rations, ten days' forage, and as little other baggage as possible. For wagons carrying hardtack, forty boxes constituted a full load. Three days' rations of fresh beef "on the hoof" accompanied the wagons. Grant stated in his *Memoirs* that his wagon train, if placed in a single line, would have reached from the Rapidan to Richmond, or sixty-five miles. The main wagon train, however, carried only half the ammunition. The other half was in wagons accompanying the infantry divisions.

The calculated risk Grant took was to get his wagons through the Wilderness, where he did not want to fight, before Lee could marshal effective opposition and destroy his supply line, capture his reserve artillery, and cut the railroad to Washington as well. To move the wagon train and the cattle, 20,000 men were required. Each wagon had the badge of its corps sewn onto each side of the white wagon cover. Its contents were also designated—ammunition, bread, forage, and so on. Grant wrote that between his supplies and what he could forage from the countryside, his army could last twenty-five days. The train was headed for Fredericksburg, which Grant had selected as his new supply base. It took two days to get the wagons, cattle, and artillery reserve across the Rapidan, behind Hancock's corps. The last wagons would not cross until the first day's fighting was almost over on May 5.

Lee chose not to contest Grant as he crossed the Rapidan, but instead to fight it out in the Wilderness. Lee had 62,000 men, about half of Grant's strength. Grant had 274 cannon to Lee's 224. Lee's cavalry had not scouted the size of Grant's forces, but knew they were larger than his own. Federal strength was estimated as 75,000 men. In the Wilderness, Grant's artillery and cavalry would be virtually useless, and the smaller Confederate army could be used to better tactical advantage. From his signal station atop 600-foot Clark's Mountain, Lee and his corps and division commanders had a commanding, panoramic view, which permitted them to watch Grant develop his plans, observe the terrain on which the battle would be fought, and signal Confederate corps commanders where to concentrate. However, Grant's signalmen atop Stony Mountain near Culpeper used a telescope to decipher one of Lee's messages to General Ewell at 9:30 A.M. and another in the early afternoon. They knew what Lee was being told. At daybreak on May 5, Grant's engineers were assigned to ride over the countryside between the two armies to examine the terrain.

This would be the first of many days to come that Grant and Lee would go toe to toe. General Grant awoke just after sunrise to breakfast in the big hospital tent he used as headquarters; it was pitched near the old gabled farmhouse on the high bank of the Rapidan some seventy feet above the river. Grant waited until most of his aides had eaten before he sat down. Breakfast consisted of cucumbers, "which he sliced and dipped into coffee, as he lingered, placid as ever. Then he . . . called for cigars, and his servant... brought him twenty. He put on a [silk] sash and [gold] sword and pulled on a pair of brown thread gloves. None of his staff had seen him bedecked in such fashion before." He was not one for spit and polish, perhaps because of the poverty he had experienced in civilian life. On being presented with a new dress coat after his appointment as lieutenant general, he observed unabashedly, "[T]here have been times in my life when the gift of an overcoat would have been an act of charity. No one gave it to me when I needed it."

Curiously, Grant had freed the only slave he ever owned when he could have sold him for as much as $1,000, money he sorely needed. He disdained pomp, ceremony, and fancy uniforms, and was usually dressed carelessly in a shabby uniform with mud-splattered trousers and scuffed boots. His new uniform had a tight collar and a gold-striped belt. The gloves were a recent gift to him from his wife. His black felt hat, corded with gold, also was new. He had short-clipped, thick and bushy chestnut-brown hair, a close-cropped, foxy-brown beard, a reddish-brown complexion, a firm mouth, and a stubborn chin. He seldom laughed and never joked. He always seemed preoccupied and immovably calm, hopeful, and civil. As one English military observer noted, "[Grant] struck me as a quiet and most unpretending thunderbolt of war." He buttoned his coat around his slim waist and had his black boots with gold spurs shined. He then lingered over his coffee. It would be his last wartime appearance in full dress.

Meanwhile, Meade had left at dawn to find a better location for army headquarters. He returned to suggest the Lacy farm, known as Ellwood, because a nearby knoll afforded the only view of part of the Wilderness region. Later that day Grant and Meade moved their headquarters to the Lacy farm, where Meade planted his headquarters flag on the knoll.[5]

According to one of his staff officers, Lee was buoyant on May 5, good-humored, and full of confidence. At his breakfast of coffee and biscuits, he said he was convinced that Grant "had put himself exactly in General Hooker's predicament" at Chancellorsville a year earlier. He knew, however, that Grant was canny and had a preference for all-out assaults. Lee wore a planter-type hat, light gray in color; a clean, tailored gray uniform; gauntlets; and high black boots. His only weapon was a Colt revolver. He had reduced his personal staff to three officers, a few clerks, a cook, and a servant.

On that same day, Will Ross awoke at 4 A.M. to the bugle call of reveille and the hum of a thousand nearby voices. He had slept fitfully in his dew-soaked uniform. He stirred slowly and sat up. Some of his comrades were still sleeping, some were filling their canteens, and others were cooking. His back and blistered feet ached, he was stiff, and his face was sunburned. His throat and mouth were still parched from the dust of the previous day's twenty-six-mile march. Pesky flies, hunger, thirst, aches, and thoughts of what today would bring brought him slowly to his feet. He splashed his face with water from his canteen, then refilled the canteen from a nearby spring. Frost was on the ground as dawn turned to daylight, and a bloodred sun soon dispersed a low-hanging fog, foretelling the day's activities. A more beautiful day never dawned, and it soon turned warm.

As birds caroled their songs, Will discovered that his regiment had camped among the shallow graves of both friend and foe who had been killed in the Battle of Chancellorsville. The campsite was also close to where his brother Dan had survived his baptism under fire one year earlier. The field was strewn with lead and iron fired from the thirty-four guns, one of which Dan had helped to fire. The skulls and bones of fallen soldiers and horses from that battle covered the ground, rooted from shallow graves by wild hogs. Others still lay unburied where they had fallen, with remnants of knapsacks, rusty canteens, moldy clothing and blankets, and equipment clinging to their skeletons. Some of those that could be identified as former comrades were buried.

Will ate a hastily prepared breakfast, including coffee and fresh beef, and awaited marching orders. Orderlies, staff officers, and an occasional general hurried by. He packed his knapsack, carefully examined his eighty cartridges, ran his ramrod down his musket barrel, and checked to see that all was in working order. According to orders received the night before, as daylight began to streak the eastern sky about 5 A.M., Hancock—riding in an ambulance—started the march of the 2nd Corps. They marched behind the cavalry at a moderate gait south from the Chancellorsville area, down the Furnace and Brock roads to the Catharpin Road, then toward Shady Grove Church. Colonel Crocker, who was still in command of Will's brigade, described it as a "bad road." He was to turn right near Corbin's Bridge onto a narrow, wooded lane to Parker's Store and cut off the Confederate advance by hitting it in its flank and getting around its rear. Thanks partly to the fine weather, spirits remained high. Thousands of men were shouting, singing, and laughing.

By 7 A.M., Meade learned that the enemy had been met on the Orange (Stone) Turnpike and were forming a battle line in front of General Griffin's 5th Corps division. The Rebels also were advancing on the Orange Plank Road. By 7:30 A.M., he telegraphed the information to Grant, adding that he had ordered Hancock to stop his advance at Todd's Tavern and await further instructions. Meade's order didn't reach Hancock until 9 A.M., delivered by a "galloper" on a foam-covered horse. A soldier in the 139th Pa. wrote that when this order arrived, there was "quite a flurry of excitement among the bunch of orderlies, aides, and officers [much like] the lively manner of hornets flitting around when their nest is disturbed."

At 7:50 A.M. Meade sent a message to Griffin instructing him to prepare his whole division to attack, but await instructions while reinforcements were forming. By 8 A.M., Meade also learned that the 5th N.Y. cavalry were being driven back by a heavy line of Confederate skirmishers to Parker's store on the Orange Plank Road, about eight miles from Grant's headquarters. The two divisions of the Confederate Gen. A. P. Hill's corps totaled 15,300 men, plus a reserve division.

Hancock's lead division (Gibbon's) was already a mile and a half or more beyond Todd's Tavern toward the Shady Grove Church, where he ordered it to halt. Strung out behind him on the Catharpin Road, the others, including his wagon train, had not even reached Todd's Tavern. Crocker then ordered his men to break ranks, stack arms, and rest. In the suffocating heat, they ate a lunch of hard crackers and hot coffee in a pine grove near Todd's Tavern. Unfortunately, Meade did not deem hasty action necessary as yet. An hour and a half earlier he had sent another dispatch to Grant saying, "I think the enemy is trying to delay our movements and will not give battle, but of this we shall soon see." Grant replied, "If any opportunity presents itself for pitching into a part of Lee's army, do so without giving time for disposition."[6]

By 10:30 A.M. Meade knew that if Hill continued to advance farther than he had first anticipated, Hancock would have to face the Confederates on the Orange Plank Road. He therefore dispatched another courier to Hancock, directing him to proceed from Todd's Tavern to the Brock Road intersection with the Orange Plank Road, report his arrival, and be prepared to move on it toward Parker's Store. For the second time that morning, the message was slow in reaching Hancock. Meanwhile, Meade also dispatched part of another 5th Corps division to reach Parker's Store. They never reached the store, falling short by about a half mile. By then it was too late to cut off the Confederates.

Hancock finally received the 10:30 A.M. dispatch from Meade at 11:40 A.M.—seventy minutes late—telling him that A. P. Hill's corps was moving in full force up the Orange Plank Road past Parker's Store. No explanation has ever been uncovered as to why the two couriers took so long getting through the woods to reach Hancock, but the delays were critical to what would happen that day. By this time, Hays had rejoined his brigade, resuming command, and Crocker had returned to the 93rd.

Lee rode ahead of the troops alongside Hill, who had graduated last in his West Point class and had a reputation for being impetuous and overaggressive, with an unquenchable thirst for battle. About midday, Hancock could hear cannonading and light musketry from the direction of Wilderness Tavern. At noon, this time by signal, he received his third message from Meade, elaborating on the order to countermarch along the narrow, forest-walled Brock Road to its junction with the Orange Plank Road, some four miles away. He was to report his arrival there, then prepare to move out the Orange Plank Road another two and one-half miles toward Parker's Store, and secure control of the intersection by preventing the enemy from reaching it.

Besides taking control of a vital intersection, Hancock's 2nd Corps was to connect with Warren's 5th Corps, two miles farther to the north. Hancock was also to support Brig. Gen. George W. Getty's three-brigade division, which would be at the scene before Hancock could get there. They had been held in reserve at the Wilderness Tavern, awaiting assignment. A scout for Getty reported that the Rebels were about to take control of the intersection. At 11 A.M., Meade had ordered Getty to the crossroads to drive the enemy back beyond Parker's Store. Spurring his horse, Getty led his staff and orderlies, with his headquarters flag flying, ahead of his troops and posted himself directly in the intersection about 11:30 A.M. He told his staff an organized force was arriving, and said, "[W]e must hold this ground at any cost. Our men will soon be up." They could see dead Confederate skirmishers less than thirty yards away and a few gray-clad figures up the road moving cautiously forward. The 5th N.Y. cavalrymen came "flying down the Plank Road . . . like a flock of wild geese . . . a few barely pausing to cry out that the Rebel infantry were coming down the road in force."

By this time Cooke's partially entrenched Confederate brigade straddled the Orange Plank Road near the intersection, with two regiments on each side of it and Stone's Confederate three-regiment brigade to its left. Most of these riflemen and sharpshooters were hidden in the thick, vine-tangled underbrush behind their skirmish line. Getty delayed the enemy advance a few minutes until the first of his regiments, the 93rd Pa. Veteran Volunteers, arrived on the double-quick, crossed the intersection, and fired a quick volley before skirmishing in the thick woods. They were attacked upon arrival, receiving a tremendous volley from just a few yards in front. They went in with a yell and, at a shouted command, formed a battle line as other Veteran Volunteer regiments of their brigade arrived and opened fire, fighting for over an hour until the enemy withdrew, leaving a few of their men as prisoners. By this time the rest of Getty's men were arriving and lost no time forming two lines across the Orange Plank Road. Having lost twenty-eight men, the Pennsylvania regiment was ordered to shift to the right and stack arms. At about 12:10 P.M. and again at 12:30, Getty received orders from General Meade to extend his battle line to the right toward Warren and "to hold this crossing at all hazards until the arrival of the 2nd [Hancock's]

Corps." Getty had already anticipated these orders. Hancock's job was to prevent flanking of Getty's line at either end. Getty's 6,000 effectives now faced Hill's two divisions of at least 15,300.

Leaving his ambulance behind at Todd's Tavern at about 1 P.M., Hancock and his staff found Getty anxious to attack as soon as the others were ready. Hancock then sent Lt. Col. Charles Morgan to inform Meade that he had joined Getty on the Brock Road. He needed Getty to give him "an idea where to put in the 2nd corps," and Getty needed time to complete shifting the position of his troops north, position his artillery battery, and make room for Hancock's troops. Despite not yet having orders to attack, Hancock realized the enemy was fighting aggressively. He sent staff officers back to hurry up his troops, since it was clear Getty needed support for his attack. Hancock's troops first had to dig entrenchments to fall back into if they were forced to retreat. The rest of the regiments in Getty's three-brigade division were still forming their skirmish and battle lines and entrenching the Brock Road.

For more than an hour after they had heard the order "Attention, right face, march," Hancock's men had been countermarching on the Brock Road to the sound of signal guns, sometimes "double-quicking," with the New Yorkers as the lead regiment and the 1st U.S. Sharpshooters as flankers. Bullets were flying across the road as the hot and thirsty men traversed it. Hancock's troops were delayed by six of their artillery batteries maneuvering into position on a clearing on high ground adjacent to the road. In addition, horsemen including generals and their staffs, newspapermen, and ammunition and supply wagons crowded the narrow, intermittently muddy road. It was no easy matter to move a six-mile column of 26,000 men in eighty-one regiments under these circumstances. It was evident that Meade did not realize how long it would take to complete the movement, although he knew Hancock moved troops as fast as any commander in the army. Grant was convinced that Hancock was the most capable corps commander in the Army of the Potomac. As Pvt. John Haley of the 17th Maine put it, "Braver officers than Hancock I have never seen." Hancock took fierce joy in fighting. This was his first time in the field in ten months, and he was itching for a fight. However, his recovery had been slow, and his groin wound required daily attention from the surgeon assigned to him.

In contrast to what was happening with Union troops, on the Rebel side, Hill was able to move his troops quickly on the wider Orange Plank Road. Two-inch-thick, sixteen-foot planks lay across the road, with occasional broken ones exposing the soft clay roadbed.

By this time, Getty, Hancock, and Meade clearly realized that if Lee flanked Warren's 6th Corps, the Army of the Potomac could be cut in half. By 1:30 P.M., when they could hear no gunfire from other divisions in Warren's direction, they realized he had not made contact with the enemy, nor had Crawford's 5th Corps division. Further, if this crossroads, the key to flanking movements for both armies, was not held, the Union Army could be trapped in the bend of the Rapidan, as it had been in the Battle of Chancellorsville a year earlier, and would risk destruction of its entire wagon train.

The crossroads were about to become the most important intersection in the country. The Brock Road was the route to Richmond that Grant had chosen to follow, and Getty's single division could not defend it. Nor had any other 5th or 6th Corps division been able to get into position to help. Hancock had to hold the intersection.

About 2 P.M., during a lull in the skirmishing by Getty's men, a cloud of dust could be seen rising above the treetops. The first of Hancock's dusty, sweat-begrimed troops, with Birney's division in the lead, had reached the intersection of the Brock and Orange Plank roads. Birney, pale and ascetic-looking, rode ahead of his men to receive orders. The 93rd N.Y. was the lead regiment, and Hancock and Birney were there when it arrived.

Finally, at 2:40 P.M., Hancock received orders from Meade to attack as far as one mile north of the Plank Road, through the virtually impenetrable forest, and connect with Warren's 6th Corps. Hancock's preference was to have all four of his divisions in position before he attacked. Nevertheless, at 3 P.M., he replied to Meade that he would use two of his divisions to support Getty on his left as soon as they could get into position, but added that "the ground was very bad—a perfect thicket."

Hancock had ordered his division commanders, beginning with Birney, to throw up log and earth breastworks three lines deep as soon as they began arriving. They did so on Getty's left, using tin drinking cups, casement knives, bayonets, and a few picks and shovels, assisted by a detachment of engineers and pioneers. By 3 P.M. or shortly thereafter, Birney's division had built their breastworks and Mott's division had arrived and was entrenching. On Hancock's orders, one section of Getty's artillery was positioned at the intersection, and the rest—Hancock's—was about a mile back toward Todd's Tavern, on a cleared place of high ground adjacent to the Brock Road, with a clear view in the enemy's direction. Positioning these six batteries and their caissons one at a time blocked the road, causing considerable delay and confusion in bringing the infantry forward to the crossroads from Todd's Tavern. Both Birney's division and Matt's brigade had fought alongside Dan's division at Chancellorsville.[7]

At 3:35, Meade's aide delivered a peremptory order, written twenty minutes earlier, directing Getty and Hancock, who was mounted, to attack at once in full force. Another of Meade's staff members instructed

Hancock to put a division on each side of Getty. Hancock expressed his regret to Getty that his entire corps was not yet formed, but said he would reinforce him at once on both flanks. He told the aide to inform Meade, "[I]t is very hard to bring up troops in this wood... but I will do as well as I can."

Confusion was hopeless at the intersection with the Orange Plank Road. Fifth Corps cavalry that had met the Rebels much earlier in the morning had been driven back from past Parker's Store to the intersection. Mott's 2nd division had begun to arrive, and Hays's 3,641 troops were trying to move north through it. According to Private Haley, Hays was flying around like a "parched pea" spewing an "opulence of oaths." As he tried to pass, a cavalryman struck him with a spur, prompting Hays to yell, "G——d D——n your old heels."

Birney's men had cheered loudly as they arrived and set to work building breastworks on Getty's left, assisted by an attachment of engineers and pioneers. Meade's aide thought there were "few officers who could command 10,000 men as well as [Birney].... I always felt safe when he had the division." They now faced Hill's two divisions, which were forming a line across the Plank Road on somewhat elevated ground about 300 paces from the Brock Road, in front of Getty's division. Hill's lead division was commanded by Maj. Gen. Henry Heth, who had been wounded at Gettysburg and was an old friend of Hancock. Its battle line stretched between two small branches of Wilderness Run, each flowing through thickly wooded, marshy ravines. Having skirmished to a stalemate with the enemy's sharpshooters since shortly before noon, Getty opened the battle full-scale, advancing 200 yards to his skirmish line in the woods. On the right end of Getty's line, which was on the north side of the Plank Road in the woods behind a partial cover of logs and rails, was Brig. Gen. Henry L. Eustis's brigade. By shortly after 2 P.M., it was extended farther to the north (right) by the 93rd. The battle lines were now only about fifty yards apart. From shortly before 1 P.M., two companies from the 10th Mass. and three companies of the 37th Mass. had skirmished fifty feet in front of Eustis's two-line brigade. When the signal was given, both skirmish and battle line advanced, driving back Rebel skirmishers to Chewning's Farm, despite reinforcements sent to aid them, according to Adjutant Jacob Seibert of the 93rd Pa.

According to accounts by Crocker and Sgt. A. J. Gibbs, by 2 P.M., as soon as they had arrived at the crossroads, Hancock personally ordered the 93rd N.Y. to enter the woods immediately. They were to form in line of battle and advance with all possible dispatch north of the Plank Road and engage the enemy with vigor. The regiment had only about ten minutes to rest and fill canteens with whatever water they could find. Crocker was promised support within twenty minutes, and told meanwhile

Battle of the Wilderness

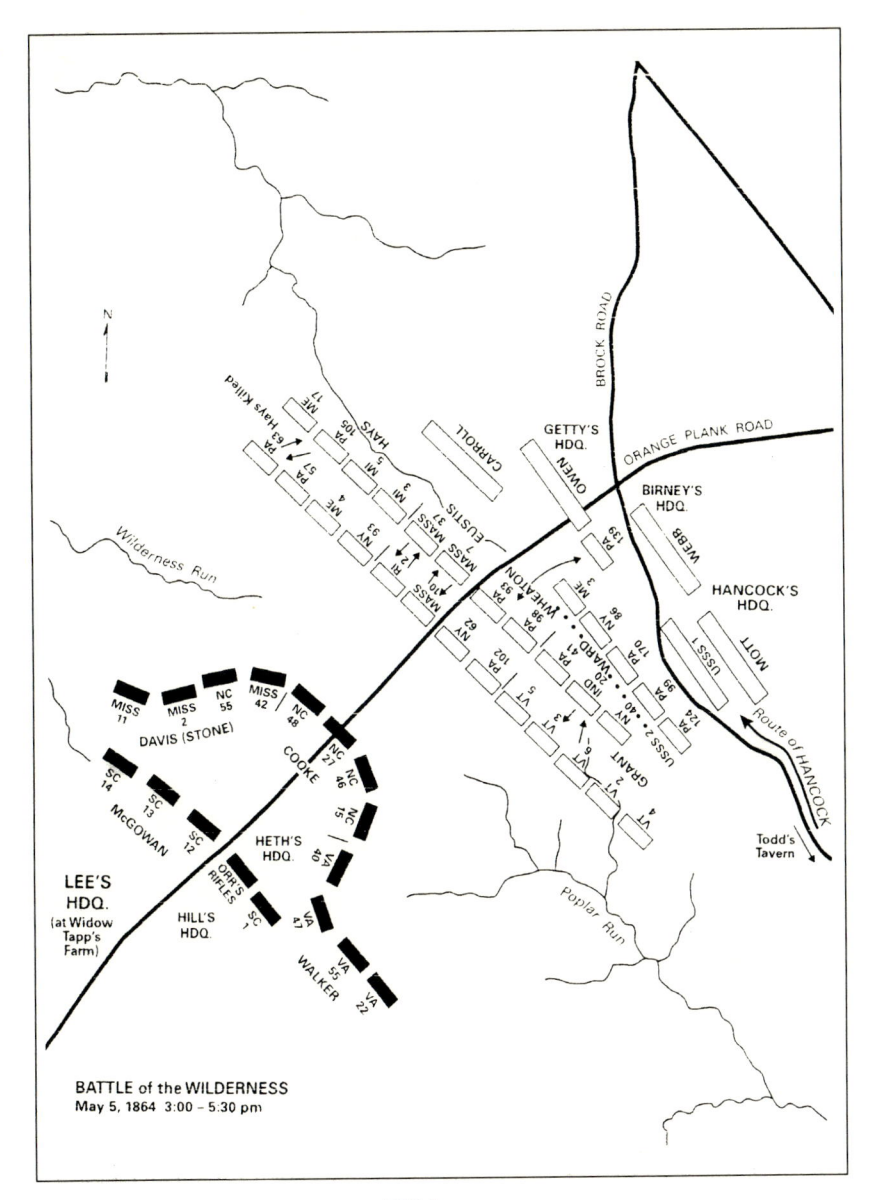

Wilderness

to gain possession of the ravine in front and to hold his position at all hazards until assistance arrived.

Will's Company C was on the regiment's extreme right flank, having been assigned that position by virtue of Captain Barnes's seniority in the regiment, and therefore went first to connect with Eustis's brigade. Flank companies were composed of men picked for their strength and courage. Since the tallest men in the company formed on the right, the six-foot Will was among the first to go in. A medical officer followed the regiment into action. The New Yorkers advanced as skirmishers. Despite their lack of battle experience, they were among the most disciplined troops after two years as headquarters guards. They reached the swampy ravine where dogwood and wild roses bloomed, along the easterly branch of Wilderness Run. They crossed several low ridges and hollows, noisily thrashing forward through matted and tangled underbrush and alder saplings, low-limbed, moss-shrouded pine trees, scrub oak, brambles, and prickly vines sometimes intertwined as closely as bars on a cage. Sunlight could barely penetrate the junglelike thicket, and the ground was littered with fallen trees and rotting logs overgrown with vines. Stumbling through the dense vegetation, they lost alignment. Few officers could use their horses. Companies were broken into small groups; briars tore the men's clothes and ripped their flesh as vines and logs snared their feet. As the New Yorkers advanced, the 93rd Pa. retreated precipitously through their ranks.

Despite the obstacles, it took the first men, including Will and Crocker's regiment, only five or ten minutes to move one-fourth mile and find the nearly invisible enemy. Stone's Mississippi-North Carolina Brigade unleashed continuous waves of heavy musketry fire from across the swampy, shallow ravine no more than a hundred yards wide. Joining with Getty's skirmishers, the New Yorkers opened fire, the first regiment in Hancock's Corps north of the Orange Plank Road to do so. The enemy line was within ninety yards, protected by the wooded crest of a slight elevation. The men bellied down behind the logs with their rifles at full cock, all eyes intent on the thicket in front. In the forest gloom, their gray uniforms made them all but invisible. Edward Steere, in his superb exposition, *The Wilderness Campaign*, wrote that Hays's regiments survived the first blast of Rebel fire "with splendid discipline."

About the same time he ordered the 93rd to advance, Hancock also ordered Hays to deploy the 1st U.S. Sharpshooters as skirmishers south of the Brock Road on the opposite end of Getty's line. They were to ascertain the position and strength of the enemy, who had been quiet there for an hour or more. Hays regarded the sharpshooters, known as "green breeches" for the color of their uniforms, as both the damnedest thieves and the damnedest fighters under his command. They had been in twenty-five engagements prior to this battle and were proficient, proud, and confident. They and the 2nd U.S. Sharpshooters would kill more Rebels than any other two regiments in the Union army. As skirmishers they had no equal.

Chaplain L. Barber of the 2nd U.S. Sharpshooters, known as the "Fighting Dominee" of the Army of the Potomac, "probably killed more Rebs than any man in this army." He also had helped recruit other sharpshooters for the regiment. A sergeant in the regiment described the fiery, zealous Methodist minister as "a fine man [who] doesn't hesitate to show his skills in shooting rebels." The sharpshooters had served as flankers for Hays's brigade since it started its march from Chancellorsville at 5 A.M. Now, on orders from Hays, they had less than a half hour's rest before they were pushed out on the double-quick to march through the dense brush out of sight of the road. They immediately came under enemy fire, and the 3rd Mich. moved up to support them.

Sometime after the 3rd Mich. moved up to support them, the sharpshooters withdrew, exhausted from all their flanking activity. Instead of the twenty minutes Hancock had promised Crocker, it took an hour and a half for support to arrive for the New Yorkers. About 3:30 P.M., Hays sent the 17th Maine to skirmish north of the 93rd, thereby taking the extreme right position of Hancock's 2nd Corps. They entered the woods about 500 yards north of the intersection and advanced obliquely to the right about a quarter of a mile. They skirmished sharply for more than an hour, drove the enemy skirmishers back, and took about thirty prisoners, but left their dead and wounded on the field. Private Haley of the 17th Maine recorded that "It was a continuous roar of musketry, rising and swelling like the sound of surf pounding on the shore." However, they became disconnected from the rest of their brigade's line to their left and were unable to find the 5th Corps on their right. In his after-action report, Lt. Col. Charles Merrill wrote, "Night coming on, and the supply of ammunition failing, no further advance was made, but the position was held till fresh troops arrived." Shortly after the 17th Maine went in, Hancock was ordered to employ his entire corps to attack in conjunction with Getty's command.

Will found himself in the midst of chaos. Regiments could not maintain continuous lines, and became separated from the flanks of their neighbors. Communication and coordination were impossible. The Union advance had no front and no direction. Neither army could exploit gaps in lines because nobody could see them. Only the flash of volleys forty or fifty yards away gave Will and the rest of his regiment any indication of the enemy's proximity. They saw flashes on the left, and realized they had to extend in that direction. Hugging the ground, they fired as rapidly as they could, pinned down by flank fire from unseen enemies. Will could hardly even see his fellow bluecoats in the sulphurous, choking gun smoke. Union and Confederate lines alike could only fire at enemy muzzle blasts, or fire by "earsight." It was largely a battle of invisibles against invisibles.

Guided by Hays on horseback, the New Yorkers extended to the left to help the played-out Rhode Islanders holding the extreme right end of Gerry's line. Will and his Company C were making the connection. Shortly thereafter they saw a gap on the right, which exposed that flank to Rebel fire. Company F, holding that end of the 93rd, shifted accordingly while the 37th Mass. moved up to replace the 2nd R.I. as it gave way in some confusion. Before the day was over, the 37th Mass. would suffer some 150 casualties, including 38 killed. Eight of 12 men who had prayed with the chaplain the night before were among the dead. Meanwhile, the 10th Mass., to the left of the Rhode Island men, had suffered 106 casualties and was out of ammunition. They were ordered to lie down while the 7th Mass. passed over them to take up the fire, and found the "Rebs thick as bees." The 10th then withdrew to replenish their ammunition. Such action typified the Battle of the Wilderness. By this time Will and the rest of the 93rd had been in action for more than an hour and had fired at least half of their rounds.

Confederate sharpshooters extended their line far beyond the 93rd's right flank, the position of Company F, exposing it for an hour to both front and oblique fire. By now Colonel Crocker realized that both flanks were suffering more than the center of the regiment. Crocker therefore advanced his line into the ravine about fifty yards closer to the enemy, where the rising ground afforded some protection. Company F remained partially sheltered in the shallow ravine, firing elbow-to-elbow from two ranks. The men of Company B were sharpshooters. They extended their line around the right of the enemy works to the rear of Stone's sharpshooters. The opposing lines were now less than one hundred feet apart, so close that the men used bayonets and clubbed muskets. With perhaps a third of the regiment killed or wounded and ammunition nearly exhausted, the men took cartridges from those who had fallen and continued the fight without yielding ground. In many places the dead and dying in both lines lay in heaps.

With their line decimated and no new support arriving, the regiment could not take those who waved white flags as prisoners. Crocker recorded in his diary that while in the ravine, his regiment fought one Rebel regiment on its front and two more on its right. Will was in the thick of it. The men of the 93rd first poured a murderous fire into the regiment in their front until it "broke and ran in great disorder. The New Yorkers then faced the two regiments on their right flank, charged and drove them off 100 yards in great disorder behind their several lines of log breastworks. In this two-hour fight, the 93rd expended 110 rounds each, killing an estimated 300 and wounding numerous others."

Initially, Colonel Crocker sought to maintain a linear battle line two men deep, one rank about two paces behind the other, with file closers several paces back. They were only fifty to a hundred paces from the enemy. The first volley was fired simultaneously by the front rank only; then the rear rank passed the muzzles of its guns over the shoulders of those in front who knelt and fired. After the first volley, each soldier reloaded and fired as fast as he could. When the front rank was exhausted, out of ammunition, or severely reduced by enemy fire, it was replaced by the second rank. While the front rank was engaged, the second rank often lay prone, hugging the ground. The New Yorkers, eager to prove their mettle under fire, formed their line as they had learned to do in drill after drill for almost two years. Elbow-to-elbow, they exchanged rifle fire with the enemy, not yielding an inch of ground.

For the first time in his nearly three years of service, Will had his chance to get in his licks with the enemy. Anticipating battle had surely strained his nerves almost to the breaking point as he waited for the ball to open. Yet, as soon as he was engaged in loading, aiming, and firing, fear and nervousness likely were replaced by what some called "battle rage," a mixture of fearlessness, excitement, total self-control, and concentration when the enemy is in sight. He wore a look of determination, his lips compressed, eyes fixed and bloodshot, and muscle and veins knotted. The dense, pungent smoke burned his eyes, nose, and throat. All thoughts beyond what to do at that moment were obliterated. Fighting blind was an intensely nerve-wracking experience. Rebels, lying silently behind their hastily erected barricades, had the advantage because they could at least hear the New Yorkers thrashing through the woods.

Sgt. A. J. Gibbs, file closer of Company F, described how they fought during the first ninety minutes. Each time men were hit, he and other sergeants, acting as file closers, would shout orders to dress (straighten) the remaining men to the right to close ranks and maintain alignment, one rank behind the other, all firing as rapidly as possible. Those killed usually fell backward, some flinging their rifle-muskets as they dropped. The wounded reeled in their tracks, clapped their hands over their wounds, and dropped to the ground. The rest kept on, teeth clenched, breathing heavily from exhaustion, fear, and the excitement of battle as spiteful bullets hissed around them. Pulses pounded as their faces, lips, tongues, and teeth were blackened by gunpowder and perspiration. Muskets became too hot to handle. Biting off the ends of cartridges left enough gunpowder in a soldier's mouth to create an intolerable thirst as well as cracked and bleeding lips. Some of the lads hurled expletives at the enemy; others would shout words of encouragement to their comrades like "Give it to 'em boys. . . . Stand by the flag, boys!"

About 4:15 P.M., Hays finally got his next three regiments through the jammed intersection. With a rallying cry, he ordered them to enter the fight behind and to the right of the 93rd's skirmish line. Hays went in with them to position the 4th Maine on the left, the 57th Pa. in the center, and the 63rd Pa. on the right, all regiments of the 1st Battalion. One by one, the regiments advanced, disjointedly, in battalion formation, into the leg-deep, swampy ravine and tangled undergrowth toward the Mississippi–North Carolina sharpshooters. By then Hays sent word back to Hancock that he needed reinforcements. A few minutes after this advance began, Hays was shot in the head with a minié ball and killed. With his staff and flag behind him, he was a perfect target for a marksman. It was typical for Hays to expose himself to danger. In previous battles, three of his horses had been shot a total of eleven times, and his leg had been shattered by a bullet at Second Bull Run.

It took half an hour for General Birney's aide to locate Colonel Crocker in the ravine and inform him that he was again in command of the 2nd Brigade. Crocker rode back over the brow of the rise about a third of a mile to the rear. By then six regiments of the brigade were completing the formation of two lines of battle near the Brock Road, and were partially engaged to the right of the 93rd. With Crocker in command, they then advanced into the woods on the double in an attempt to close the mile-wide gap between the 5th and 6th Corps. The entire brigade was now fully engaged and held its position until darkness.

The 93rd's regimental staff was splintered by lead and iron, and little of the tattered flag remained. Before the battle Crocker had been described as a fine disciplinarian and drillmaster. After the battle, 1st Lt. William L. Bramhall of the 93rd wrote that "Crocker was all fight and handled the brigade admirably." Sgt. S. E. Payn wrote, "Crocker is as brave a man as I ever saw." Both Crocker and Maj. Samuel McConihe had horses shot out from under them. McConihe, a lawyer from Troy, New York, who had succeeded Crocker as regimental commander, was slightly wounded.

Veteran Volunteers like Will had succeeded in stopping the Rebels from piercing the center of Meade's army despite the nearly impenetrable terrain. Their physical and moral courage allowed Hancock time to complete construction of entrenchments along Brock Road, feed more troops into the battle at both ends of Getty's line, hold the intersection, and protect the supply train. At 5:50 P.M., Meade was informed by dispatch from Lyman, "We barely hold our own; on the right the pressure is heavy. General Hancock thinks he can hold the Plank and Brock Roads, in front of which he is, but he can't advance." The road was blocked by the wounded and stragglers hobbling or walking to the vicinity of Grant's and Meade's headquarters or to one of Hancock's hospitals.

Will Ross was mortally wounded where fighting was heaviest, sometime between his regiment's initial charge at 2 P.M. and darkness. Most likely he was hit as his company led the regiment into the fight to connect with the 2nd R.I. As he felt and heard the thud of the bullet that hit him, the battle continued to rage around him. He must have been helpless as he fell, unable to shift position or seek shelter. The enthusiasm of battle was simultaneously replaced with fear as bullets flew over him and struck the ground beside him. He could not defend himself, nor could anyone else. No one could come to move him, give him a drink, or tend to his wound, because he was too close to the enemy line.

It would be a long, excruciating night for the twenty-seven-year-old teacher who had grown up on farms in the verdant hills of upstate New York and launched his teaching career in Illinois, only to interrupt it to support freedom and equality for all men. As his letters indicated, he understood his life could be altered, if not ended, on a battlefield. Now that was a reality. Perhaps he thought of his parents or of his brothers and sisters as blood flowed from his wound. After volunteering three times, he knew the risks he faced, but whatever sacrifices he might make would help preserve the Union his forefathers had fought to create and end the institution of slavery. It is doubtful that he regretted his decisions as his life slowly ebbed away on Virginia soil.

When the sad shadows of night ended the first day's fighting, the armies for the most part did not draw apart along the battle line. Many men stopped where they were, intermingled, facing every direction, not knowing where friend or foe might be. According to Sgt. George H. Blackman, they bivouacked for the night a short distance behind where they had fought. They then formed a picket line, ate a scanty meal, buried some of their dead comrades, brought off some of the wounded, and then, utterly exhausted, slept on their arms. A Confederate and a Union colonel were captured while drinking from the same stream. Enemy troops heard each other talking.

To link the Union picket lines after dark, Lt. Mason W. Tyler, Sergeant Graves (an experienced backwoodsman and surveyor) and four others of the 37th Mass., were dispatched from the right flank of Eustis's line past the 93rd and the rest of Crocker's brigade line to locate the position of Warren's 5th Corps. With the use of a compass, the connection was made in the dense woods, and the picket lines of the 5th Corps and 6th Corps were joined, about a half mile north of the Orange Plank Road and 900 yards west of the Brock Road. Private Haley, of the 17th Maine, recorded in his journal that "the last thing [the enemy] attempted, without success, was to wedge themselves in between our right and the troops of the 5th and 6th Corps." Alertness on the part of the Maine woodsmen, exhaustion on the part of the Confederates, and darkness thwarted their effort.

Nightfall had ended the battle's first day without a victory for either side. However, Lee's attempt to cut the Army of the Potomac in half at the very point where Will's regiment stood its ground had failed. The Orange Plank and Brock crossroads had not fallen into Rebel hands. Some of the Confederates facing the 93rd were compelled to fall back about a half mile. Units on both sides suffered similar setbacks. Grant's campaign of attrition had begun.[8]

After the firing ended about 8 P.M. on May 5, "at Grant's headquarters, the silence was awesome." It was broken when Meade said to Grant that the enemy had made a Kilkenny cat fight of the affair. Grant replied, "Yes, but our cat has the longest tail." By then Grant had smoked all twenty cigars his aide had handed him that morning. Grant did not eat supper that night until he issued orders to his commanders and medical officers to make every effort to find and help the wounded and bring them to brigade hospitals.

More than one-third of the forty-seven men in Will's company who went into the battle were killed or wounded that afternoon. A large number of wounded fell into enemy hands. He would not be among the wounded carried from the front on stretchers. Some managed to walk to brigade hospitals. Each corpsman made several trips, carrying the wounded to the hospital and returning to the front with boxes of cartridges in their stretchers to replenish the eighty rounds each man had brought into battle. Although the sky was completely obscured to the exhausted, nerve-racked troops in the dense woods, the night was clear and cloudless.

The misery of the Wilderness increased when the woods and dry underbrush, as well as the breastworks, caught fire from powder sparks and paper cartridge fragments, and burned through the night as a strong wind fanned the flames. It blew suffocating heat, hot ashes, and blinding smoke into men's faces. The agonized cries of the wounded, most likely including Will, could be heard all night. Live rounds in cartridge boxes attached to the belts of the wounded exploded, gouging ghastly holes in their flesh. One soldier, with both legs broken, cocked his rifle-musket and kept the ramrod in his hand, ready to kill himself should fire overtake him. Many, like Will, remained where they fell. Some tried to keep the fire from reaching them "by scratching the leaves away as far as they could reach." The only way to determine whether a corpse was that of a Rebel or a Yankee would be to turn it over to expose the unburned portion of its uniform.

During and after the battle, the influx of patients was so rapid and the numbers so great that it was not possible to record all of them. Corpsmen found wounded soldiers everywhere on the battleground. Some were moaning under the bodies of the dead. The hospital tents filled to overflowing. Amputated legs and arms piled up under the operating tables. Food and supplies at the hospital were insufficient. Many men begged for water, others for someone to shoot them. It was a scene from hell.

Capt. D. E. Barnes, Will's company commander, although wounded in the hand, went back in between the picket lines that night with three unarmed men to look for the missing in his company, including his brother, Lt. C. T. Barnes, and Will. Barnes and his trio captured three Rebels from one of four Georgia regiments that were within Union lines. The captured soldiers had arrived about sunset to relieve Stone's brigade, the 93rd's original opponents, indicating that the New Yorkers' position at nightfall remained unchanged and was crucial to the battle's outcome. Barnes found some of the mortally wounded who could not be moved. All they could do was make them as comfortable as possible and give them water to quench their thirst and wet their parched lips and throats made dry by the profuse loss of blood. Any movement attracted fire from the Rebel picket lines, which were very close.[9]

Already resupplied with ammunition, the regiment was awakened at 3:30 A.M. on May 6. They crept silently over the wounded to return to the position they had left the night before. As they advanced, at least one of Will's comrades must have seen him, still alive that morning, because his military service record says Will died on May 6. By then, there was probably nothing that could be done for him. The fighting resumed, and Captain Barnes who had been searching for his wounded brother, Lt. C. T. Barnes, was killed shortly afterward. The daybreak advance ended when they ran out of ammunition and had to fall back over the same ground. Perhaps the comrade who had seen Will at daybreak stopped to check on him as they fell back, or perhaps another noticed that he had died during the morning's fighting. Although his death is recorded, his body was never identified by the official burial party. Most likely, it was burned beyond recognition, like hundreds of others. Company commander Barnes's body, though, was found on the field, stripped of clothing, money, sword, and watch, then covered with boughs. Will's money, if he had any, likely was stolen as well, along with the watch his brother Dan had given him.

The casualty rate continued to mount on both sides, reaching 60 percent for the 93rd N.Y. by the second day when the battle ended. The regiment had gone into the battle with 433 men, and suffered 260 casualties, including 17 commissioned officers. At 60 percent, it was the highest rate among the brigade's nine regiments. Success had come at a very high price.

On the second day, Lee's sporadic attacks—Grant called them "confused"—were all thrown back. The last Rebel attack came in the late afternoon, and they suffered appalling casualties. Then, in Grant's words, "[d]uring the night all of Lee's army withdrew within their intrenchments." The Union commander in chief acknowledged that his army's losses in the Wilderness were "very severe," yet he claimed victory. As he later wrote in his *Personal Memoirs*, "Our victory consisted in having successfully crossed a formidable stream, almost in the face of an enemy, and in getting the army together as a unit."

Morris Schaff, a Civil War historian who served as an adjutant to General Meade during this battle, wrote, "There was no engagement during the war where the private soldiers of the army showed greater valor than up the Plank Road that afternoon. Bear in mind that they did all their fighting amid the umbrage and the terror of the woods, and not under the eye of a single general officer; not one in 20 could see his colors or his colonel. There was none of the inspiration of an open field with stirring scenes . . . their only companion [was a] sense of duty."

Use of artillery on a large scale had been impossible, but the violence of musketry fire surpassed any other two-day period in the history of the Army of the Potomac. In fact, the surgeons did not report one shell wound in Hancock's corps. Lieutenant Hunt reported that only an occasional shot was fired by artillery. The army had, in the words of a correspondent for the *Albany Evening Journal*, "never fought better."

Had Will survived the battle and been rescued, he would have faced further horrors. It took two weeks to collect all the wounded from the battlefield and move them by ambulance and wagon to Fredericksburg. Each division used its thirty-six hospital attendants and its drum corps of about 350 to collect and transport the wounded. Teamsters lashed their four- and six-mule teams while the wounded screamed, cursed, and sometimes fainted from excruciating pain as they jolted over the corduroy roads, from which Rebels had removed planks at intervals a year earlier to make them impassable. Many begged the drivers to shoot them. There was virtually no food or water, and they lay in their own filth in the wagons for twenty-four to forty-eight hours before they were even examined. Those who survived the trip had bone infections, secondary hemorrhages, gangrene, and broken adhesions. Flies swarmed around the wounded, and maggots infested many of their injuries. Amputees were loaded into ambulances or wagons according to which leg was amputated. All right leg amputees were placed together, since they would have to lie on their left sides, making it possible to pack more men into each vehicle. Thick beds of evergreen boughs lined the two-tiered, stiff-springed wagons, over which shelter tents and blankets were spread. The miles-long wagon trains had to cross broken bridges and be dragged through quagmires. The ambulatory wounded had to walk to Fredericksburg. Others were carried by horse or mule, two or three men per animal.

There were almost no tents or blankets available for the wounded until a May 7 search of the battlefield yielded more than 4,000 tents and blankets that were brought to Fredericksburg. Medical supplies warehoused at Alexandria did not arrive until May 10, and 300 additional tents arrived on May 20. Clothing for the wounded was practically nonexistent, and food was in short supply. The Fredericksburg "receiving hospital" was an old warehouse where some waited for days to be diagnosed, treated, or put aboard a train. There were only thirty or forty surgeons in Fredericksburg to care for the sick and wounded. Consequently, many had to stay in the wagons that brought them. As fast as possible, the wounded were moved from the wagons and given shelter in every warehouse or other available building in town. Those still alive inside the warehouse were lined up in rows on the floor, on muddy, blood-soaked blankets.

Wounded men from the 93rd occupied one room in an old rookery of a building. According to Lt. C. T. Barnes, the brother of Will's company commander, the room had a plank floor that "made a very hard bed." Sixteen days after he was wounded, the minié ball was removed from his abdomen, near his spine, without chloroform. The surgeon told him he had the worst wound created by a minié ball of anyone brought to that hospital. By the time the receiving hospital was closed on May 28, 26,000 wounded and sick soldiers from the Wilderness and several battles that followed it had been processed.[10]

According to the historian Bruce Catton, out of 118,000 Federal troops engaged in this battle, 2,246 were killed, 12,037 wounded, and 3,383 reported missing in action—a total of 17,666, or 15 percent of Grant's army. One-third of the casualties were in Hancock's corps. Some 62,000 Confederate troops were engaged and suffered about 13,000 casualties—21 percent of Lee's army.

Beginning May 8, trains of twelve cars each and several ships carried 8,000 of the Union's severely wounded back to Washington, DC, hospitals. Barnes was transferred by ship to an officer's hospital in Georgetown. The uniforms of the men were bloody, ragged, and dirty. Many had their pockets slit open and emptied of cash, watches, and other valuables. Many died en route, succumbing to the aggravation and infection of their undressed wounds while they were being loaded, unloaded, and transported, often without provisions. For three days and nights, an unceasing stream of ambulances carried the wounded from Washington's 6th Street wharf to the city's twenty-five hospitals.

The Battle of the Wilderness was the first direct confrontation between Grant and Lee, and one of the bloodiest battles of the Civil War. Grant said the battle "threw in the shade" anything he ever saw. He simply had not expected such resistance based on his experience fighting Confederates in the West.

The historian of the 11th N.C. reported that at one time, "[t]he regiment lay down behind a line of dead Federals so thick as to form a partial breastwork, showing how stubbornly they fought and how severely they suffered." One hundred fifty-seven dead Federal soldiers were counted in front of the 55th N.C. battle line, possibly including Will and many others of the 93rd, but the Rebels also suffered severely. One soldier in the 55th N.C., wrote his wife, that 2 P.M., "My company went in with 30 men and came out with 8 only and 2 taken prisoner. The rest all were killed and wounded." He reported that he shot his rifle sixty-one times. The 27th N.C. of Cooke's brigade straddled the road and took 60 percent in casualties. Pvt. Alexander Frank of the 48th N.C. wrote his father that his company "fought the best Navy troops that [they] ever fought."

On the Union side, Hays's brigade lost more than any other. Of the 3,641 effectives who went into battle, there were 1,390 casualties in the two days, almost 40 percent of his force. A total of 5,092 casualties were recorded in the twelve brigades of Hancock's corps—more than a quarter of them in Hays's brigade alone. Besides Hays, nineteen other officers in the brigade were killed, including four in the 93rd. Eighteen others in that regiment were wounded. All of Hays's staff but one were killed or wounded. Colonel Crocker, who replaced Hays as 2nd Brigade commander, and Maj. Samuel McConihe, who took Crocker's place as head of the 93rd, both had narrow escapes.

Crocker was injured two weeks later at the Battle of Spotsylvania and subsequently discharged for disability after examining surgeons pronounced him unfit for duty in November. His medical record indicated that he had inflammation in one leg and foot and was lame in both legs. During that battle his horse was shot and fell on him and a shell fragment seriously injured his foot. He had four horses shot out from under him between May 6 and May 20, the end of the Battle of Spotsylvania when he relinquished command of the regiment after returning to camp with 200 prisoners. He had been reduced to a skeleton, emaciated by chronic diarrhea and "bilious" fever (probably malaria).

A week after the battle ended, Grant wrote Washington, "[Meade and Sherman are] the fittest officers for large commands I have come in contact with." Meade was an ideal executive officer for Grant. His earnestness, bravery, and logistical and tactical skills were proven. He could comprehend and execute orders to the letter. Grant gave him general orders and left the details to him. He later wrote that Meade "proved . . . to be the right man in the right place."

Forty-three percent of the casualties that the 93rd suffered in its three and a half years of service occurred in this two-day battle. The New Yorkers continued to pursue Lee to Appomattox Court House, where they witnessed his surrender to General Grant eleven months later. They were skirmishing and taking prisoners until four hours prior to the surrender. Lee's Army of Northern Virginia never again carried the fight to Grant's army with such savage élan as it had at the Wilderness. To war's end, Grant kept Lee largely on the defensive, unable to maneuver or mount a general offensive, as he had consistently done throughout the first three years of the war.

A year after the battle, the regiment of Will's brother John, the 123rd N.Y., marched through the Wilderness battlefield and camped the night of May 14, 1865, on the Brock Road. They were on their way to the Grand Review in Washington, DC, before President Andrew Johnson and Generals Grant and Sherman. The New Yorkers found many dead, still unburied and lying where they had fallen a year before, beyond recognition now in moldy blue uniforms. Will's remains were surely among them, but unrecognizable to John or anyone else. The official burial party that arrived June 12, 1865, a month later, to inter these remains found only eight bodies that could be identified as soldiers of the 93rd, out of a total of sixty-seven who were identified from Hays's brigade. Of the 15,242 soldiers who were killed in the Battles of Fredericksburg, Chancellorsville, the Wilderness, and Spotsylvania and interred in the National Cemetery on Marye's Heights near Fredericksburg, only 2,472 are known; 12,770 are unidentified.

When Will's regiment was mustered out of the Army of the Potomac on June 29, 1865, at Bailey's Cross Roads, Virginia, only 85 of the original enlisted men and 2 of its original officers were among those discharged. Three hundred of its men had been killed or mortally wounded, died of disease, or been confined in Rebel prisons in its three and one-half years of existence. Nineteen died in prison, including 6 in Andersonville. Total casualties amounted to 559. Nine hundred and sixty-five men had enlisted initially in the regiment and 221 had been recruited or drafted, bringing the total to 1,186. Of the regiment's 47.1 percent casualty rate, almost half (260) were suffered in the two-day Battle of the Wilderness. The survivors, however, felt that their fallen comrades had not died in vain.

It is ironic that Will and a handful of others among those who were the first to enlist and then reenlist in the 93rd were killed on their very first day of combat. Lieutenant Robertson wrote his parents after the battle, "The 93rd has won a name that makes it famous in the whole army, but they have lost heavily. . . . Gen. Birney who commands the division says he can trust the 93rd to do anything." Both Birney and Hancock issued an order praising the regiment for its gallantry and efficiency. It was the only regiment in Hancock's entire corps that received such recognition.[11]

Skeletons on Wilderness battlefield

10

The Battle of Kolb's Farm
June 22, 1864

> Skirmishers can be distinguished by their peculiar fervor and patriotism . . . the hotter the fire, and the more dangerous the position, the more ardent and impulsive and eager are those tried veterans.
>
> —*Cincinnati Daily Gazette*, June 25, 1864

Following his return from the artillery, Dan Ross learned a new set of skills that would play a key role in Maj. Gen. William T. Sherman's conquest of Atlanta, a major turning point in the war. He would be in the lead, arguably facing greater danger as a skirmisher than any who followed him and his comrades into battle. After having escaped injury time and again as an artilleryman, his luck was about to change.

Seasoned volunteer infantry regiments that had learned the art of skirmishing mostly through trial and error were the most valuable of all. In fact, Sherman's 100-day Atlanta campaign was largely a skirmisher's war. As he said later, "The campaign was one immense skirmish with small battles interspersed," resulting in snail-like advances. Yet not until just before the beginning of his Atlanta campaign did Sherman issue orders for his regiments to conduct skirmish drills in camp—and he was one of the few Civil War generals serving North or South to do so. On May 8, 1861, three weeks after Lincoln's first call for volunteers, Sherman wrote the War Department offering his services "in the capacity for which [he] was trained." At that time he was president of the St. Louis Railroad Company. Previously, he had been president of a military academy that later became Louisiana State University. Three years later, when he launched his march on Atlanta, it was clear the War Department had fitted him into the right slot.

Skirmishing in Sherman's army became a post of honor. It took skill, stealth, endurance, steady nerves, dexterity, self-reliance, and ingenuity to effectively become the eyes and ears of the army. Yet skirmishers never earned the glory commensurate with the danger involved. Official reports merely recorded that "our skirmish line was advanced" or "our skirmishers were driven in." Skirmishers were almost always exposed to sharpshooter fire. The skirmish line was perfected in the Atlanta Campaign by those who needed adventure and challenge to offset the boredom of camp life and the drudgery of endless marches.

Dan, now twenty-one, was a member of one of Sherman's seasoned regiments, the 123rd from New York's Hudson Valley. The New Yorkers would be specially commended by their corps commander, Maj. Gen. Joseph Hooker, for "sublime conduct" in the little-known but crucial Battle of Kolb's Farm on June 22, 1864. Skirmishing was the job assigned to the 123rd N.Y. at Kolb's Farm and in many other engagements that became known collectively as the "Battle of May, June, July, and August." They were almost never out of the sound, if not range, of enemy gunfire. Skirmishing, neither described nor defined by most historians, was a skill these citizen-soldiers had mastered in little more than a year.

This opportunistic scouting and harassing action of soldiers fighting under loose command and not in tight formation epitomized the strategy of Sherman and his field commanders in splitting the Confederacy from West to East. He repeatedly used skirmishers like Dan to uncover the movements, feel the strength, harass the forces, and slow the advance of the enemy. Skirmishers were the fingers of the army, always feeling for the enemy.

The skirmishing at Kolb's Farm was a nearly perfect illustration of the specific tactical maneuvers involved in this strategy. Neither Sherman's Rebel opponent, Gen. Joseph E. Johnston, nor Johnston's field commander, Lt. Gen. John Bell Hood, relied as much on the tactic. Johnston relied more on fortified positions that he hoped would make Union advances too costly and thus feed political defeatism in the North. The rough, mountainous terrain of northern Georgia provided Johnston with excellent opportunities for delaying action from defensive positions. Hood's hope was that daring frontal assaults in compact formations would catch Sherman off guard and shock the North into suing for peace. Hood had to take regular doses of opium to dull constant pain from his amputated leg and bullet-shattered arm, which may have contributed to his aggressiveness. Both Confederate generals underestimated the skill of Sherman's skirmishers to detect and capitalize on weaknesses in either defenses or offenses confronting them. From time to time, Sherman himself would skirmish. He wrote, "I have many times crept forward to the skirmish line to avail myself of the cover of the pickets 'little fort' to observe more closely some expected result."

Like Johnston, Sherman enjoyed enormous admiration and affection from his men. They were both masters of their profession, and respected each other. Sherman sometimes slept among his men, preferably under a tree, and swam naked in the river, bathing with his troops. Somehow this behavior communicated to the men that his heart was with them. He was a perpetual motion machine, and was one of the lightest eaters and sleepers in the army. He was usually up by 4 A.M. which he called "the best time to hear any movement at a distance," and would pore over maps to plot his next move. He was untiring in his attention to detail. He also was "a steam engine in britches, furiously puffing blue cigar smoke but never finishing one before he lit another. On the battlefield, however, he puffs less on his cigar and talks less. Instead, he clenches his jaw, compresses his lips, squints so that he can see the action better, and assumes an expression of intense determination." Maj. Gen. J. D. Cox recalled that in the crisis of battle Sherman's mind was clear, his confidence strong, his temper calm and inspiring.

Unlike Sherman, Johnston was a trim, dapper, well-read aristocrat. He had served in the Seminole Wars in Florida as well as in the war with Mexico, was wounded six times, and had reason to be cautious. He wore silver spurs, a hat decorated with a star and feather, and a coat embellished with three stars. He also had spent the winter of 1863–64 turning Bragg's defeated, demoralized, hungry, and ill-clad army into a strong fighting force. Mistrust and desertions ended when he instituted a liberal system of granting furloughs and allowing families to visit soldiers in camp. He doubled rations, distributed tobacco and whiskey, and requisitioned new tents. Most of his army had faith in him. Unlike Sherman, who immensely admired President Lincoln, Johnston despised the Confederate president, Jefferson Davis—and that feeling was mutual.

Sherman observed in his *Memoirs*, "When a regiment is deployed as skirmishers, and crosses an open field or woods, under heavy fire, if each man runs forward from tree to tree, or stump to stump, and yet preserves a good general alignment, it gives great confidence to the men themselves for they always keep their eyes to the right and left, and watch their comrades." Some would camouflage themselves by placing foliage in their shirts.

Despite Union soldiers' skill in skirmishing, they did not underestimate the Rebels' skill in building entrenchments. One noted in his June 18, 1864, diary, "[T]he works we have just... taken from the Rebs are far superior to our own... they were built... of green logs and banks of earth... six or eight feet [thick] and far better too. [They] were enfiladed... and were as strong as man could make them." Sherman, who was exceedingly careful for the lives of his men, also believed in entrenching at night in preparation for fighting during the day. He used blacks who flocked to his camps to do the digging. His entrenchments were faced with a rail and log framework covered with the earth that was dug from the trench. If possible, they were topped with a heavy head log.[1]

Lt. Col. Franklin Norton was the only officer in the 123rd New York that had combat experience when the regiment did its first skirmishing at Chancellorsville on May 1, 1863, less than fourteen months prior to the Battle of Kolb's Farm. But by June 1864, in the northern hills of Georgia cut by rain-swollen, swift streams, most of the New Yorkers had experienced enough on-the-job training in the unsung art of skirmishing to have perfected their skills. Dan did not benefit from all that experience, however, because he had been temporarily assigned to the artillery corps. Skirmishing remained costly, though less so than fourteen months earlier. In the daylong battle at Kolb's Farm, the 123rd suffered forty-nine casualties on the skirmish line, in contrast to losing thirty men in two hours at Chancellorsville.

Prior to Chancellorsville, the regiment's range of military experience was limited to drill and picket duty. Because of his lack of military experience, Col. Archibald L. McDougall, the commanding officer, was capable of making sizeable blunders even while conducting a dress parade. One soldier wrote about the former lawyer, "He knows just nothing at all about military [matters] and most of his officers are as green as he is with the exception of Lt. Col. [Norton]." Because of their complete lack of training and experience in skirmishing, on the first day of the Battle of Chancellorsville, the regiment committed four basic errors that quickly cost them thirty men, including Norton.

First, they had halted and formed their skirmish line in full view of the enemy. Consequently, as soon as the skirmish line was established, the Confederate cavalry attacked, forcing a retreat. Second, they had delayed sending reinforcements to the skirmishers, so enemy troops were already advancing and firing before the 123rd formed its new battle line. Third, they had let the skirmishers get pinned down by enemy artillery, so they could not advance and were positioned in such a way that the balance of their regiment could not return fire without endangering the skirmishers. Finally, while one company of skirmishers had retreated into the woods and found shelter or got out of range, the other had retreated up the hill toward the regiment, exposing itself to both its own and enemy rifle fire through the entire distance.[2]

After the Battle of Gettysburg, the New York regiment had spent the rest of the summer of 1863 until September 23 pursuing Lee into Virginia, as did Dan's artillery battery. They were then transported by train from Virginia to Tennessee to support the Army of the Cumberland after its defeat at the Battle of Chickamauga. Hooker's 20th Corps was organized in the fall of 1863 and assigned to Grant's Western Army. A number of eastern regiments from the Army of the Potomac were transferred to the 20th Corps, including the 123rd N.Y. and Battery F. Soldiers from such western states as Ohio, Illinois, and Indiana at first referred derisively to the trim and natty appearance of "those paper collar galoots" from the Army of the Potomac. They were taunted with such shouts as "Hadn't you better stop and blacken your shoes?" and "Fall in for soft bread." In the beginning of the campaign the easterners would button a paper collar on their coats so that one end dangled, as if to suggest they did not know how to wear it.

Well before they reached Atlanta, however, the ridicule had ceased and the New Yorkers became known as Hooker's "Iron Clads." As a result of their new-found reputation, dozens of regiments and some brigade commanders requested transfer to Hooker's corps.

Despite his dismal performance at Chancellorsville, Hooker had earned his men's loyalty. He was exceedingly reckless of his own safety, which endeared him to his men because they could always see him during any fight. When he rode along his lines each day with only a single orderly, he would smile calmly at his men as a father might gaze on his children. He thoroughly understood how to build esprit de corps, and rousing cheers would greet him. From his initial nickname as "Fighting Joe," he soon became known as "Pugnacious Joe" and later as "P.J." No characteristic earned him more respect than his willingness to share the same dangers as his men. On June 18, Sergeant McLean wrote his parents, "Gen'l Hooker is around in the thickest of the fight, where bullets are flying. The boys are all for Joe and rather have him to command than any other man." Not only did Hooker earn such admiration, but so did Sherman, Williams, and Knipe.

Another Union regiment to earn its laurels by extremely effective skirmishing that day was the large 14th Ky. Veteran Volunteer Infantry. The unit's 700 men, recruited in the mountains of eastern Kentucky, had been on the skirmish line since May 24, engaging in actual "bullet intercourse" with the enemy for twenty-one out of twenty-nine days. Between February 15 and May 23, they had participated in six engagements, and since the regiment's formation had been in some thirty-two battles and skirmishes. In mid-April, they attacked 1,000 Rebels, killed or wounded twenty-five, and captured fifty men and a hundred horses. By then they were a seasoned regiment, in sharp contrast to the one Col. James A. Garfield, their brigade commander and a future president, had described in January 1862, a year and a half earlier. He wrote then, "The Fourteenth Kentucky is composed of excellent material [yet] . . . it can be considered but little better than a well-disposed, Union-loving mob, which, if its scattered fragments can be gathered up, may be converted into a very serviceable regiment." That year, the regiment's colonel, George Gallup, was described by one of his officers as having "more guts than brains."[3]

Some seventy-two participant and eyewitness accounts were written about the Battle of Kolb's Farm and the skirmishing that preceded it. Included among these are seven detailed diaries, six letters, and two regimental histories written by men in the 123rd, all of whom were on the skirmish or battle line. Five of the diaries were written by sergeants and one by Dan's company commander, who witnessed his capture. The *Official Records, War of the Rebellion* also includes fifteen detailed reports on this battle by officers of Maj. Gen. Joseph Hooker's 20th Corps, more than on any preceding battle in the first fifty days of Sherman's Atlanta campaign. Among those reports was one by Lt. Col. James C. Rogers, son of an ex-congressman, in command of the 123rd. Rogers had just succeeded Colonel McDougall, who had died in the Chattanooga Officers Hospital of a leg wound incurred a few days before this battle. Although McDougall had been a heavy drinker, his men sorely missed him. Sergeant McLean wrote his mother that the colonel was a brave and good soldier who never flinched. He always took his place in battle, never asking his men to go where he would not.

Clearly, the volume of written records on this brief battle suggests its importance to those who fought in it. Furthermore, Kolb's Farm is the only engagement in the first fifty days of the Atlanta campaign for which there are reports written by the opposing field commanders: Hooker and Brig. Gen. Alpheus S. Williams, Dan's extremely competent division commander, and their undistinguished opponent, Confederate Maj. Gen. Carter L. Stevenson. When these accounts are compared for consistency in detail, a vivid picture emerges of the immense value of two Union regiments as skirmishers: one from New York's Hudson Valley and one from the hills of eastern Kentucky. Stevenson, who had graduated near the bottom of his West Point class, and his entire division were among the 30,000 troops who surrendered to Grant at the fall of Vicksburg July 4, 1863. They were properly paroled on September 15, but not authorized to fight again until exchanged man for man with Union prisoners held in Confederate prisons. Without that exchange taking place, by the agreement the two armies had reached and honored since early in the war, they fought Grant again at Missionary Ridge ten weeks later. This time they would fight Sherman, still in violation of their parole.[4]

Besides his knack for using skirmishers, Sherman exercised great strategic skill as a flanker (to "gopher" the enemy, as his men said). He characterized himself as "scared as hell" of what the enemy would do out of his sight, and therefore relied heavily on skirmishers while flanking to keep track of every possible enemy movement. One of Sherman's soldiers said, "He's all hell at flanking.... He'd flank God almighty out of heaven, and the Devil into Hell." A revealing conversation between opposing pickets was initiated by the Rebel who asked, "I say Yank, who commands your army now?" "Billy Sherman. What makes you ask that question?" was the reply. "Cause," said the Rebel, "they said he was killed, but I know he wasn't for he has corkscrewed us out of some place every day." A Rebel prisoner described Sherman's tactics as follows, "Sherman gets on a hill, flaps his wings and crows; then yells out 'Attention creation! By kingdoms right wheel march!' And then we get it." Between June 17 and 30, scores of Hooker's skirmishers were killed or captured, while 507 were treated for gunshot wounds in the corps hospital, nearly a third of all those hospitalized from the corps in the entire month. Hooker, on occasion, would even deploy and lead his own escort as skirmishers. Nearly half of all the casualties in the entire Atlanta campaign were skirmishers.

The problem of loading made skirmishing particularly dangerous. The standard cartridge for a muzzle loader was a paper cylinder containing powder and a soft-lead bullet. The soldier bit open the cartridge, poured the powder down the barrel, then used his ramrod to push the bullet down the rifled barrel. If shooting a smoothbore, he had to insert a wad and perhaps some buckshot. For a rifle-musket, he used his ramrod to pack a tight-fitting patch of paper around the ball so it would take the spin imparted by the rifle's grooves. Then he had to place a percussion cap on the nipple to explode the charge. At best, it was extremely difficult for skirmishers who were also attempting to conceal themselves behind stumps, boulders, or logs, especially if they were in a prone position. It took the skill of a contortionist.

A few weeks prior to the Battle of Kolb's Farm, Johnston held Sherman in check at Big Shanty while the Confederate commander completed his formidable fortifications on Kennesaw Mountain. They were designed by engineers and built by slaves and soldiers. Recognizing this, the Union skirmishers built movable protection. They cut hoop poles, which were abundant in the vicinity, and wove them into hundreds of baskets about the size of flour barrels. They lined the baskets with grain sacks, then filled them with dirt and sand. A skirmisher could easily roll a basket across the field, safely concealed behind it. Protected by this movable breastwork and crawling as he pushed it, the skirmisher could get within easy rifle range of the enemy entrenchments. By the end of the second day of this skirmishing technique, the enemy had fallen back six miles to Kennesaw Mountain. Another group of skirmishers rolled a sixteen-foot log, with the men behind it, up a hill to within one hundred yards of the Rebel works. The log was then covered with brush and dirt from a ditch the men dug behind it so they could better conceal themselves. When advancing without such movable breastworks, one skirmisher would signal another to draw enemy fire so he could move more safely to the next tree, stump, hollow, or boulder.

The Battle of Kolb's Farm was a major step toward Sherman's outflanking of Johnston at Kennesaw Mountain a fortnight later. The mountain was the next to last natural barrier Sherman had to confront before his army could fight its way into Atlanta. The Union victory at Kolb's Farm demonstrated not only how Sherman got around Kennesaw Mountain but how he used skirmishers throughout the Atlanta campaign. Sherman had issued orders two weeks earlier prohibiting wounded skirmishers from being brought off the field by other combatants. Only musicians and ambulance corps noncombatants, wearing white armbands, could retrieve casualties as long as firing continued. The *Chicago Tribune* correspondent assigned to Sherman's headquarters noted that "skirmishing is the hardest and most dangerous work in the army ... it is every man for himself, as they rush to the nearest stump or tree for cover ... and the stratagems resorted to by our boys to uncover the Rebs are amusing. Occasionally a hat is cautiously raised on the end of a ramrod, and bang, bang, go half a dozen muskets at the unoffending [garment] which when lowered exhibits three or four ventilators."

On June 13, about the time the lads had perfected the science of skirmishing, Sgt. Rufus Mead, of the 5th Conn. in Johns's Brigade, wrote his parents of "the chering news of Uncle Abe's nomination ... by acclamation.... It did us a heap of good. I want to cast one more vote for him."

By then, for fifty days and nights there had been little time for rest, physically or mentally. They had marched almost continuously on the red clay of Georgia, which when wet, became as slippery as grease. They dug miles of trenches, attacked or repulsed attacks, withstood artillery fire day and night, stood picket duty, skirmished, buried the dead, suffered from lice, foraged to supplement their rations, and wallowed as well as slept in the trenches in knee-deep mud. The pant legs of some of the men were moldy. All the while they doggedly held on to the abiding conviction that the Union should survive, even if they did not.

Yet as Pvt. Noah Rich told his mother on June 21, "I am aboute ware out and the rest of the boys is to for it has been such a long campaign and I don't think it will be over for some time."

On the night of June 21, 1864, after a quiet day in the rain, the 123rd built works along their front and camped in a wheat field on the Atkinson plantation adjoining Peter Valentine Kolb's larger plantation. The move was made to gain Johnston's rear in preparation for a four-mile advance along the Powder Springs Road to Marietta, a Confederate railhead serving as a vast wagon yard for hauling supplies to the front.

The New Yorkers were told to be ready for an early start in the morning, and to have their cartridge boxes full and ten extra ones in their pockets. That night, Dan and his "bunkie" shared a shelter tent and a rubber blanket for protection against the wet weather. The tent consisted of two pieces of canvas, each three and a half feet wide and seven feet long, with eyelets and buttons on opposite borders so they could be joined. The two men cut a ridgepole and shorter end sticks from saplings to support it, and tied or staked down the edges. As substitutes for end sticks, they sometimes inverted their rifle-muskets, sticking the attached bayonets into the ground. At the ridgepole, the tent was only about three feet high, so the men had to crawl in and out of it. As usual, each company fortified its own ground as soon as officers had established the line. Troops were then issued a whiskey ration, perhaps because they had not been paid for six months.

June 22 was the first clear, bright, warm day after fifteen days of heat, rain, drizzle, mud, and storm. Weather had been the worst enemy for both armies, but now the morning air was perfumed with wild grape blossoms, hawthorn, and sweet grasses. By 6 A.M., Sherman's mood had turned as foul as the weather had been. Dan and the other men had eaten breakfast of salt pork, hardtack, and coffee, their steady diet for breakfast, lunch, and dinner for the last two months. The men were developing scurvy from lack of vegetables and fruit, because the overtaxed railroad supply line could not deliver adequate quantities of cabbage, the usual antidote. The Rebs had raided gardens and orchards before they retreated, leaving little for the Yanks to forage.

To gratefully acknowledge their first decent weather, as the sun rose brightly with little wind stirring and light fleecy clouds overhead, the Rebels raised "a loud and prolonged cheer... from the summit of Kennesaw which was taken up and carried along the entire line." Sometime before dawn, the Confederate general Hood had positioned his troops on a ridge that crossed the Powder Springs Road about a mile east of Kolb's Farm. Hood's purpose was to check Sherman's flanking movement and guard the railroad.

250   Lincoln's Veteran Volunteers Win the War

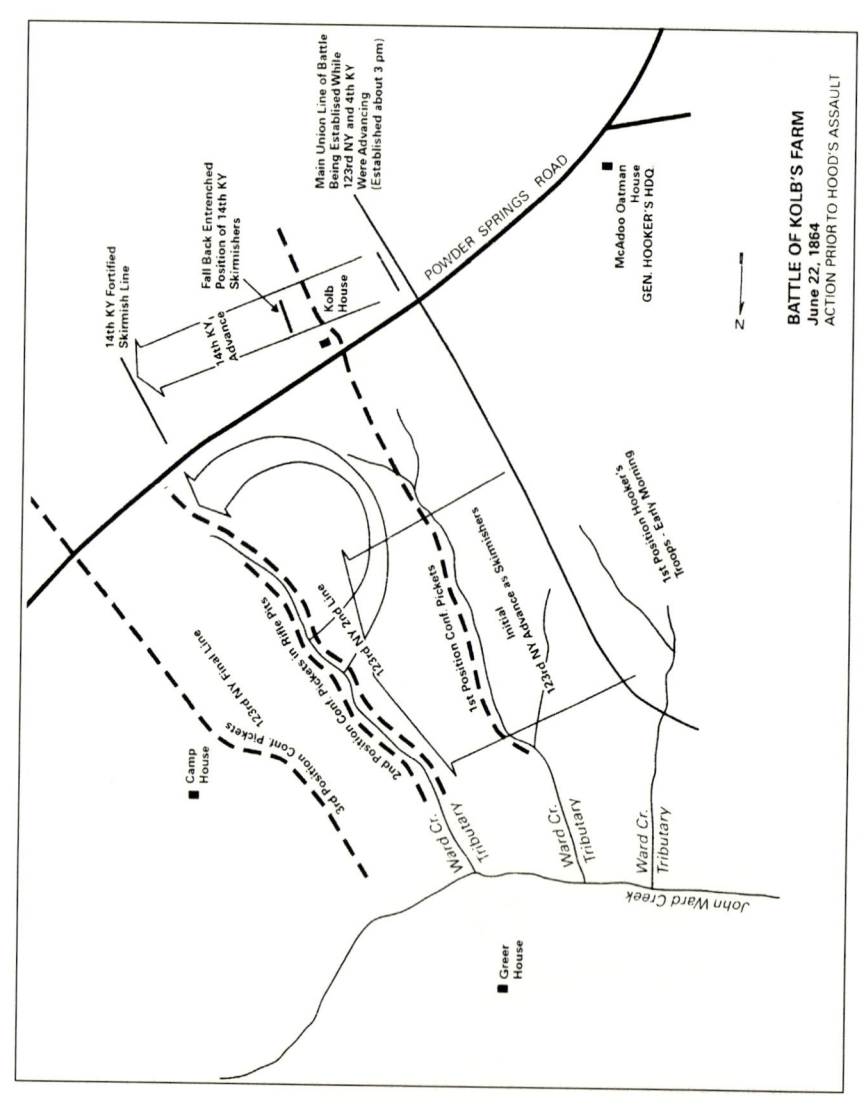

Kolb's Farm, skirmisher's action prior to Hood's assault

After breakfast the New Yorkers had packed, and, with their full boxes of ammunition plus ten extra rounds, were ready to be deployed. On the assumption that they might be gone overnight, packing up included putting their wool blanket and spare clothing lengthwise inside their gum-rubber sheet, rolling it lengthwise, then tying the ends together, thereby making a loop. Hospital tents were struck and an ordnance wagon and an ambulance train arrived. Staff officers and couriers scurried about as batteries awaited their horses, who were still feeding.

Shortly after nine, the regiment moved to the left of the Union line to deploy in front of Williams's entire division. Dan and the other skirmishers moved out in columns of four, with guns on the left shoulder and blanket rolls carried diagonally over their chests. They went along the north side of the Powder Springs Road in the direction of Marietta to determine the strength and position of the enemy. Each man was further weighed down with a full haversack, also known as a "bread bag," a cartridge box, a canteen, and a tin cup. The rest of their brigade, under Brig. Gen. Joseph Knipe, and the balance of Williams's division remained screened in the woods on Kolb's well-fenced farm, which was cut by ravines and drained by rain-swollen creeks with marshy banks. About 10:30 A.M., the skirmishers moved to the long crest of a wooded hill facing open ground, about 500 or 600 yards from Confederate rifle pits occupied by dismounted cavalry they had been forcing back. A section of artillery in Knipe's brigade (Winegar's Battery I) moved forward with the Union skirmishers to this ridge, which was to become the battle line, and shelled the enemy sharpshooters in their rifle pits. The battery's Napoleon smoothbore guns would fire a total of 669 rounds that day.

Another half hour's march through a ravine, during which firing began, brought Dan and his skirmisher comrades to heavy timber and thick underbrush on the summit of a longer ridge, where Federal pickets were firing briskly from their outer posts. They had advanced no more than half a mile from their division's line. As soon as the 123rd N.Y. reached this ridge, relieving the pickets along the way, several of the companies were deployed as skirmishers to the right and left, spread ten feet apart in a heavily wooded area. The rest acted as support to the skirmish line. At about eleven o'clock the bugle sounded "Forward" and the line advanced through the underbrush, unhurriedly. Within a half hour the New Yorkers were crowding the dismounted Rebel cavalry down the open cornfield in front of the ridge, across a ravine, and up the next densely wooded knoll, on the crest of which was a strong line of rifle pits. Although the Confederates were forced to give up these pits, they contested every foot of the way. They returned fire—sometimes at no more than fifty yards—as they ran through an old orchard, and then fell back to hold another hill, ravine, or shelter spot as long as they could.

By noon, under a broiling sun, Dan and the other lads had advanced about two miles, meeting most of their resistance along the Powder Springs Road. The advance had not been steady, or even, along the entire line as they forced the butternuts into an often hilly field cut by

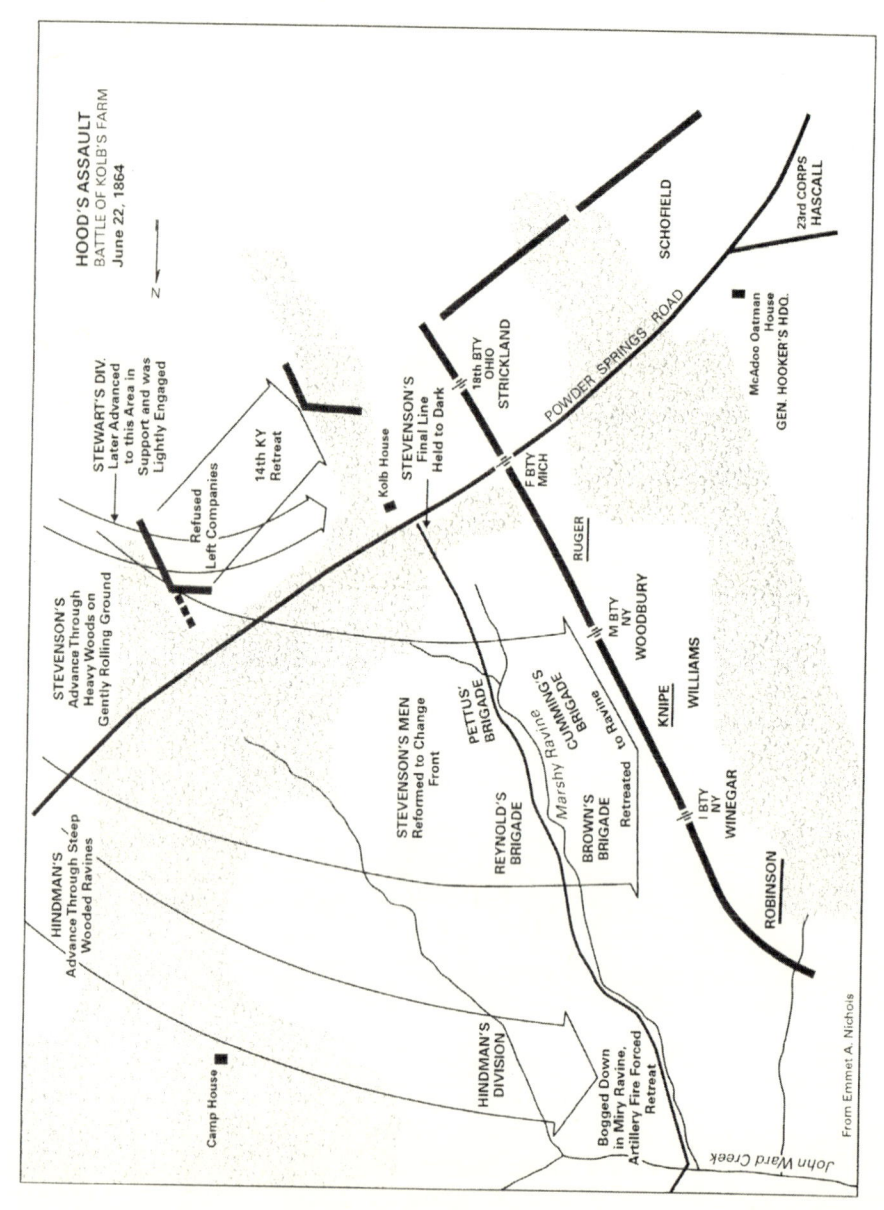

Kolb's Farm, Hood's assault

ravines. The Rebels doubled their skirmish lines and charged the Union line twice, driving it back at some points until the skirmishers rallied and advanced again, holding that position for about an hour, only to be driven back elsewhere before rallying once more. In the clash of the two skirmish lines, casualties on both sides were substantial. One man in Dan's Company H was killed and another mortally wounded. The latter died a week later in a Confederate hospital in Atlanta.

For nearly three hours beginning about 12:30 P.M., the lads of the 123rd N.Y. began skirmishing through a clearing, using every possible protection for cover, as did the retreating Rebels. The New Yorkers hid behind occasional trees and stumps, lay flat behind hummocks, and crawled into little ravines and gullies, as they slowly advanced and forced the enemy back into dense woods on the crest of still another knoll. The advance was man-by-man, gully-by-gully, stump-by-stump as they moved from one to the other "quicker than a heifer could switch her tail," continuing to load and fire. Sometimes they spread themselves on the ground—in the skirmishers' language, "as thin as butter on a slice of boarding house bread."

By 3 P.M., Dan and his comrades reached another line of well-protected enemy rifle pits (known as "gopher holes") in the woods on the edge of the clearing about 100 yards behind a long ravine. The Rebels dropped into these pits and gave the New Yorkers a defiant yell, as if to say, "Now get us if you can." In crossing the open ground the 123rd lost several more men.

After trying to advance again, the enemy charged in force, moving down the Powder Springs Road to where they had built field fortifications along the road. This advance pressed the 123rd back into the woods, outnumbered by twenty to one because of enemy reinforcements. With nothing for cover but scattered trees and stumps, three more of Dan's Company H comrades were wounded. The next order to the Union skirmishers was to advance and take the long ravine in front of the Rebel works. The skirmishers did so about four o'clock, checking the enemy by concealing themselves in the trees and underbrush at the bottom of the ravine, then exposed themselves as they crossed open ground, losing several men in so doing. Soon General Williams, via a mounted courier described by the troops as a "galloper," ordered Dan and the other skirmishers to advance again. The courier then dug in his spurs and rode off to deliver the same message to the 14th Ky. skirmishers. The enemy fired at him as he shouted and waved his "ventilated" hat, which had been pierced by a minié ball. The Rebels gave him a cheer in recognition of his courage and skill.

Sgt. Henry C. Morhous described how his comrades were transformed when the order was given to advance, charge, or fire at Kolb's Farm. It would apply equally to any battle. "With your first shot you become a new man. Personal safety is your least concern. Fear has no existence in your bosom. Hesitation gives way to an uncontrollable desire to rush into the thickest of the fight," he wrote. "The dead and dying around you, if they receive a passing thought, but serve to stimulate you to revenge. You become cool and deliberate, and watch the effect of bullets, the shower of bursting shells, the passage of cannonballs as they rake their murderous channels through your ranks, the agonies of the dying ... [your] feelings [become] so calloused by surrounding circumstances that your soul seems dead to every selfish thought. Such is the spirit which carries the soldier through the field of battle."

Meanwhile, General Knipe had followed the skirmishers into the woods to determine for himself where the enemy line was and to direct artillery fire accordingly. The brigade commander ordered a section of Woodbury's Battery M a to assume a position on a ridge and begin firing one gun at a designated treetop at five-minute intervals until he gave a signal. About 4 P.M., after the third shot, Knipe waved a white handkerchief from the woods and the battery fired about ten more rounds from each of two guns. A Rebel battery returned fire as Knipe ran back saying, "We have driven them back. They are trying to build breastworks.... I am going to fortify this ridge." His brigade then moved forward and stacked their rifles in order to bring forward thousands of fence rails at "right shoulder shift" to make breastworks.

Knipe, then forty-one, had served as an enlisted man in the Mexican War. He had been seriously wounded at Cedar Mountain, but returned to fight in the Maryland campaign and at Gettysburg, not yet fully recovered. Known as a heavy drinker, Knipe had served under Williams since the Battle of Antietam in September 1862, and they trusted each other. He was a brave and able commander, military in bearing, and a strict disciplinarian. He regarded the New Yorkers as "the best d——d regiment in my brigade." He used them either as skirmishers or on the front line in every battle his brigade fought in the Atlanta campaign. After the fall of Atlanta, Knipe was given command of a division in Maj. Gen. James H. Wilson's cavalry corps. In the Battle of Nashville in December 1864, he was credited with the capture of 6,000 Rebels.

By about 4:30 P.M. the courier delivered the order to Colonel Rogers to advance again. The right of the Union skirmish line was in the woods, the left in the ravine. The right had advanced considerably more than the left, thanks to better cover and lack of resistance in the woods. Lieutenant Quinn led an unsuccessful effort to straighten the line under terrific fire, and was shot in the face, after which the left moved up to a rail fence. Pvt. Willard Allen of Company C gained a position behind a large stump and did not fall back with the others. Having seen him, the Rebels began peppering the stump with minié balls, peeling off bark from each side and splintering the top. After he had shrunk himself into as small a target as possible they finally gave up, giving him the opportunity to make a few rapid leaps and rejoin his comrades unharmed. There they lay flat on the ground or hid behind large trees, no man speaking above a whisper. Their advance was so quiet that they got within 200 feet of the strong enemy rifle pits undetected. They could hear the enemy plainly, but the underbrush was so thick that the Rebels could not be seen. Their sounds indicated that they were massing their troops—men marching, orders given in low voices, horses tromping and neighing, bugles sounding in the distance. No Union skirmisher fired a shot.

Some of the skirmishers slid out of their knapsacks and noiselessly commenced fixing rails in front of them for breastworks. Lt. Robert Cruikshank, Dan's company commander, reported the enemy's proximity to the battalion commander, Major Tanner. Sgt. Rice C. Bull also crawled back to report this to his company commander, Capt. Alexander Anderson, who was at the regimental command post with Lieutenant Colonel Rogers. Rogers and Tanner went forward to the breastworks to do some listening for themselves, and immediately sent word back to General Knipe that the Rebels were massing in heavy force in front of the skirmishers.

At about 5 P.M., under orders from Tanner, Dan and the other skirmishers attempted another advance but had to fall back. Knipe reported this to the division commander, Williams, who relayed the information in person to Hooker. Hooker, impatient for an advance, ordered his main force to move up to within a half mile of the skirmishers, in line with the artillery, and to form a line of battle with Knipe's brigade. Knipe's men were in the center of Williams's line and had already advanced to align themselves with the artillery, giving the line a convex shape. Cheers rang out from other brigades as this movement was made. General Williams did not relay Hooker's order until he rode back and made certain his left and right flanks were protected. His men entrenched, using bayonets, tin cups, and bare hands, as the Confederates prepared to advance. Old Pap's troops also cut down some heavy underbrush in front of Knipe's brigade to give his men an unobstructed line of sight. While doing so, they also filled their tin cups with blackberries.

Knipe's two batteries of bronze Napoleon twelve-pounders and rifled guns, a total of twelve pieces, were already fortified with rails and logs on knolls at the battle line about a quarter of a mile apart, and had superb range on the Rebel skirmishers. Standing on a pile of rails, Williams ordered the guns loaded with double-shotted canister and case shot. He always positioned himself where the action was hottest. He was a hard fighter in battle but had a gentle soul. His men loved him because he took good care of them. Williams's stogie was spinning in his mouth like "a log in a peeler"—a direct reflection of the tension he was feeling. From this position he would watch the Confederates "rolled into a confused mass."

Meanwhile, Dan and the other New Yorkers, with guns cocked, listened to Stevenson's Confederate division preparing to attack from their position about a half mile west of the Mt. Zion Church. A volunteer from Dan's Company H was sent through the underbrush to verify this and barely escaped being shot. He reported to Cruikshank that the enemy were being formed into three battle lines at thirty-pace intervals. Massing the division for battle took about an hour. The Union skirmishers did not leave their places until shortly after 5 P.M. when they heard the bugle call and Stevenson's command of "Forward, double-quick, march."

General Williams wrote his daughter, "We had just begun to pile rails when [their] heavy skirmish line poured out of the woods and brush, screeching and yelling like so many wolves, in three long gray lines, about 100 yards apart, each in light marching order." They aligned on the left held by Cumming's Georgia brigade, which consisted mostly of inexperienced militia. It was as if they were on parade, Williams later wrote, "with colors and banners flying and officers dashing from line to line," waving their sabers in front of the men. Their bayonets glistened in the setting sun as they emerged from the woods. The Rebels fired a rapid volley of musketry at the New Yorkers as they boastfully floated their banners.[5]

The New York skirmishers on the Union right, facing Cumming's brigade, fired a parting salute at a distance of not more than 150 feet as they were called on to surrender. Then they beat a hasty retreat through the underbrush and woods toward the Kolb farm buildings, passing through the 14th Ky. skirmishers, who were positioned on the south side of the Powder Springs Road. They had been instructed to hold their position on the south side of the road until overcome, and did so until after the New Yorkers had passed and the Rebels were within ten yards of their position. Concealed behind their partially constructed barricades in the farmyard, the Kentuckians saved most of the New York skirmishers from capture. They had detained the Rebels for an hour and a half with their "yelping" seven-shot Spencer rifles. Some Rebel prisoners later asked where those guns came from, believing they were loaded on Sunday so they could be fired all week.

Facing Brown's Tennessee brigade—one of the best in the Confederate army—the New Yorkers fired a volley as a parting salute. They then ran a half mile with the Rebels on their heels, through open fields, every man for himself, loaded with full equipment. The right wing of the 123rd

N.Y. retreated into the wooded, rain-soaked Ward Creek ravine, where Hindman's Confederate brigades would get mired down soon afterward. Once in the ravine, the New Yorkers halted and fired another volley at Hindman's men. Slowed by the muddy ravines and repulsed by cannon fire, none of the Rebels got within rifle range of Williams's main line.

However, on orders from Major Tanner, two of the companies in the center—Cruikshank's Company H and Captain O. S. Hall's Company I on its right—had fallen back to make a stand at a pile of rails they had thrown together during their advance. No sooner had they taken this position than Tanner ordered every man to take care of himself. It was too late. Lieutenant Cruikshank noted in his diary that the enemy were within ten feet of him. They "gobbled" (captured) five of his men nearest to him, including Dan. The lieutenant avoided capture by running a half mile straight back to the main Union battle line, through the open field, across a ravine, and up the hill, hiding briefly behind a two-foot-wide stump to catch his breath. As he alternately ran and hid, bullets whizzed by him "like bees in swarming time." Facing Knipe's battle line he could see company officers pacing back and forth, ordering their men to hold their fire.

After resting, Cruikshank ran again and reached the Union line without a scratch, having watched the others run past him on both sides while he was concealed behind the stump. Dan and the other four lads from his company were probably captured by skirmishers of the 32nd Tenn. in Brown's experienced brigade, which got far out in front of the advancing line and spearheaded the heaviest assault made by the Confederates. Dan's company suffered more casualties than any other in the 123rd N.Y. or 14th Ky.—two killed, three wounded and carried off the field, and five captured. The day after the battle, the prisoners were interrogated by the 42nd Ga., a regiment held in reserve during the battle.

Rev. Edward Bartlett, chaplain of the 150th N.Y. Regiment, observed that "the skirmishers came running back as though the devil himself was after them." The route of the skirmishers' retreat saved many lives, since it dropped down into a ravine. Consequently, when the Rebels fired a volley at those in the ravine, including Cruikshank, and shouted for their surrender, the bullets mostly passed over their heads. Nevertheless, a total of sixteen men and one officer in the 123rd were captured, most in the muddy ravine. Thirteen of the seventeen captured were sent to Andersonville. Two were sent to other prisons and two died in Confederate hospitals. A total of six in the regiment were killed or mortally wounded, bringing the total casualties to forty-nine, compared with eighty-three for all other regiments in Knipe's brigade that remained on the battle line. No one would have dared to help the retreating skirmishers, twenty of whom were wounded, even if doing so had not been contrary to Sherman's orders. Those who got back—running full tilt a half mile while "their Blue blouses stuck strait out"—passed through the Federal line wherever they could and dropped to the ground completely exhausted, some in a dead faint. Then Lieutenant Cruikshank reported to his commanding officer that he thought all the men were in except those who had been captured.

After Hooker's skirmishers successfully retreated, the tide turned. When the Confederates, in good marching order and cheering defiantly, came within rifle-musket range of Knipe's brigade, metallic clicking rippled down the line as rifle hammers were cocked. The moment the balance of the skirmishers were all in, the men in blue responded to the order to fix bayonets, then leveled and aimed their rifles on command. The first of the three enemy lines was not more than fifty yards from Knipe's line. The next moment the bluebellies received the long-wished-for commands: "Ready, men," "Fire low," "Commence firing," and their guns exploded simultaneously. There was a prolonged cheer from the men as the crash and roar of artillery from five well-sited batteries and a storm of balls from 2,000 muskets roared from behind the breastworks on which the Stars and Stripes were unfurled. Like a plague of locusts, lead flew into the Rebels' faces. From then on, ramrods made a whirring noise as the men removed them, bit off paper cartridges, rammed minié balls home, and fitted percussion caps. Men fired at random, cursed, yelled, loaded, and fired again and again, as rapidly as they could. Meanwhile, the artillery vomited shell, grape, and double-shotted canister, or sometimes canister with a shell on top of it, tearing and smashing into the enemy columns, sweeping lanes through their ranks and sowing death at virtually point-blank range. Some of the artillery was positioned so that they could fire nearly lengthwise through enemy lines. Their front line wavered like wheat in a wind gust. One cannoneer wrote his parents, "We have considerable fun talking to the Rabbs [sic]. The boys will ask them how they like Joe Hooker's kids and if they want any more grape shot." Lt. Robert Gill of the 41st Mississippi described the confusion of the battle to his wife, "I think it was the heaviest fire I was ever under and I seemed to be every place but the right place."

Once again, Sherman's forces turned back a Rebel advance. By sundown the action was largely over. General Williams wrote his daughter that they "fled like scared sheep back into the woods," leaving their dead and wounded on the field like sheaves behind a reaper. Some of the Rebel wounded crawled up to the Union line. Williams's men, like the 123rd, who had been with him for two years, had long since learned his capabilities. Hooker, Thomas, and Sherman, however, were only beginning to realize his leadership qualities. In this battle, his one division had defeated two Confederate divisions.

At the Battle of Kolb's Farm, on June 22, 1864, Hooker's corps continued the momentum of the Union advance to Atlanta. More than a third of the Union losses in this battle occurred in the two regiments that spent the day skirmishing. The 14th Ky. suffered seventy-seven casualties, but were able to bring most of the wounded with them in their retreat. The 123rd suffered forty-nine casualties, ten of whom were in Dan's company, while Knipe's brigade suffered eighty-three casualties. Stevenson's and Hindman's divisions suffered more than 2,000 casualties. After the battle, under truce, the dead of both armies were buried on the field.[6]

―――

That evening, when the action was over, Sherman told a surgeon who called on him that he "counted the houses of Marietta" from an elevation near Pine Mountain. At midnight, Hooker wrote his battle report at his headquarters near the Kolb farmhouse. He told Sherman that both Knipe's and Maj. Gen. John M. Schofield's brigades had thrown forward skirmishers (the 123rd N.Y. and the 14th Ky.). He added, "Before advancing far they encountered the enemy in force and, in order to gain time to establish our lines and batteries, the advanced troops [skirmishers] were instructed to make a resolute defense, and only abandon their position when overcome by superior numbers. . . . The conduct of [all] the troops throughout the day was sublime." Schofield wrote Sherman, "[P]risoners say we are only a mile and a half from the railroad." Breaking the Confederate rail supply line from Atlanta was the main objective of the day's battle. In little over a year of fighting, the citizen-soldiers of the 123rd N.Y., like those of the 14th Ky., had learned dangerous lessons. Their skill in skirmishing continued to contribute greatly to the stunning successes of Sherman's Union armies in the western theater while Grant was stymied at Petersburg. In his June 22 diary entry, Sgt. Albert Cook of the 123rd wrote, "We received a good deal of praise from the Generals." The praise included that of General Knipe, who told Colonel Rogers after the battle was over that he had "the best d―――d regiment in my brigade."

How these hardened veterans felt about their high-ranking officers is revealed by what one soldier wrote in his diary. "Old Joe's boys and a part of the 4th [Thomas] and 23rd [Schofield] Corps repulsed the Johnnies, killing and wounding over two thousand of them. Our loss was small. The Rebs were trying to flank us upon the right but failed in every effort. Old Joe and Schofield were too wide awake for them." Colonel Robinson of Williams's division also praised Hooker, writing,

"I wish you could see him when a fight is underway. His enthusiasm is enough in itself to inspire any man." Lt. William Wheeler, commander of the 13th N.Y. battery in Geary's division, had written his mother two weeks earlier that Hooker immensely encouraged his men with cheerful words, coolness, and relaxed bearing. "He gets more fight out of his men than any officer I ever saw.... On the march he is continually among the troops." Wheeler, whose gunners were Veteran Volunteers, described himself as an "extreme emancipationist determined on seeing the end of the secession movement and of slavery." At the Battle of Kolb's Farm, a sharpshooter's bullet through his heart denied Wheeler his wish.

Union skirmishers at Kolb's Farm, including Dan, can be credited with at least eight accomplishments. They drove the Confederate cavalrymen, pickets, and skirmishers back to their main battle lines, thus preventing them from determining the strength and location of the Union forces or gaining any ground. They captured Confederate soldiers who provided major intelligence on Confederate troop movements and strength. They delayed the Confederates' attack for several hours by harassing them so effectively that they could not get their line of battle formed expeditiously, giving Hooker an hour or more to form his line. They helped direct artillery fire accurately. They became familiar with the terrain over which the Confederates had to attack so that they were able to delay the lead brigade and get the others out of alignment. They got close enough to enemy lines to overhear enemy orders and reported this information in ample time to allow for full-scale preparation. And they checked the advance of the lead Confederate brigade as it moved through heavy underbrush. The 14th Ky. skirmishers also separated Cumming's brigade as it retreated in confusion from the rest of the Rebel command, thereby preventing a coordinated attack.

Initially, skirmishers were principally used to locate and feel the enemy strength preparatory to a decisive blow by the main body of troops. By the end of the war, skirmishing was almost continuous, and skirmishers in Sherman's army were often used as assault troops, entrenching and even dragging cannon with them onto the skirmish line.

One newspaper account of the Battle of Kolb's Farm indicated that the skirmishers were so strongly entrenched as to be mistaken for a battle line, and that the skirmishers took artillery with them to this position. Instead of advancing in a tight, massed formation—fully exposed to murderous rifle and artillery fire from entrenched troops—skirmishers fought in extended order, taking advantage of all cover and spread out over a single line as much as a mile in length. This procedure became possible because of the veterans' confidence in themselves and one another. The Confederate general Hardee, author of *Infantry Tactics*, had learned in opposing Sherman that the skirmish line was as important as the battle line and that a heavy skirmish line could resist attacks by as many as three lines of battle.[7]

The Union general Jacob Cox, a corps commander under Sherman, described skirmishing tactics, noting that as an advance began, the skirmishers' flanks would be drawn in to about the "length of one brigade across the road." Skirmishers would trot "from a big tree to a larger stone" seeking cover while the main body was marching down the road four abreast behind them. When rapid rifle fire was heard ahead, the main column was halted and an officer dispatched to the skirmish line "to see what is up." If called for, a regiment was moved forward to "the nearest cover on each side of the road," together with artillery, to uncover the Rebels. After some artillery shelling, the regiment went "forward with a rush and a hurrah." If the vanguard regiment discovered temporary breastworks that required more than a regiment to overtake, more troops would be advanced. If they found "well constructed lines of defense," the troops were halted for "slower and heavier operations."[8]

Nonetheless, it was not until 1873, eight years after the Civil War ended, that skirmishing got scholarly recognition. Then Emory Upton published his revised *Infantry Tactics*, in which the heavy skirmish line became an ordinary tactical formation. According to Upton, the army's leading postwar analyst, skirmishers were deployed by the numbers, in groups of four, with the balance of the regiment immediately behind the skirmish line ready to feed it. His skirmish drill instructions were based largely on lessons learned from Sherman's Atlanta campaign. Upton himself had experienced a costly lack of skirmishing as a regimental commander at Chancellorsville. He specified that officers must impress on each soldier "the idea of his individuality and responsibility," including how to economize strength, how to fire only at targets, how to take advantage of any cover, and how to be self-reliant rather than wait for an order before taking action.[9]

The *Cincinnati Daily Gazette* wrote a dispatch three days after the battle at Kolb's Farm about the veterans in Hooker's corps. "In every engagement in which the 20th Corps has participated . . . the veterans can be distinguished by their peculiar fervor and patriotism. . . . [T]he hotter the fire, and the more dangerous the position, the more ardent and impulsive and eager are those tried veterans."[10] His description fits Dan Ross and the other three-year men of the 123rd N.Y. to a tee. Three of the seventeen who were captured—namely, the lieutenant and two enlisted men—later escaped from prison and returned to the regiment in deplorable condition. At least two of them were hidden by slaves to avoid recapture. The initial strength of Dan's regiment was 950 officers and men. While in the field throughout the war they added 165 recruits, and returned home with 525 men. They had suffered 53 percent casualties in seventeen battles and an unknown number of skirmishes.

By demonstrating their skirmishing and other skills, the lads of the 123rd N.Y. earned their laurels with the western troops. By the time they marched in the Grand Review before President Johnson and generals Grant and Sherman in Washington, DC, at the end of the war, they had become indistinguishable from the rest of the westerners known as "Sherman's Wolves." The New Yorkers had taken on the appearance and mannerisms of their comrades. "They [even] walked like Westerners." They were leaner; their uniforms were mud-spattered, dingy, and ragged; and they looked more battle-hardened, self-reliant, and determined. They wore large slouch hats rather than the tight caps of the Army of the Potomac, and looked taller, tanner, and more muscular. They also took swinging strides several inches longer than those of the easterners.[11]

11

From Prisoner to Guard
June 22, 1864–May 27, 1865

> I, with a dozen equally unfortunate comrades, overpowered and captured on the skirmish line... were marched in front of the [Andersonville] commandant's quarters and compelled to stand in the blazing sunlight until it seemed we could stand no longer, enduring the severest torture I ever experienced while his Highness ate his dinner.
>
> —Private Daniel Ross, memoir

In the ten months after he was captured on June 22, 1864, Dan was sent to five prisons, including Andersonville. Initially, he and the sixteen other New Yorkers were taken to a holding pen behind Confederate lines. Shortly thereafter, they were forced to march thirty miles to Atlanta, since Confederates were using the railroad to move a thousand or more of their wounded from Marietta to Atlanta hospitals. On June 25, three days after their capture, Lieutenant Martin wrote Lt. Col. Rogers, who commanded the 123rd, from the military prison in Atlanta that eleven of the captured men, including Dan, were in the city. Two others of the New Yorkers died of wounds in a Confederate prison hospital in Atlanta, and presumably are buried there.

After a short imprisonment in Atlanta, the majority of the seventeen surviving prisoners from Dan's regiment were loaded onto railway cars with captives from other battles, sixty men per car. The cars probably were part of a hospital train, which included other cars jammed with hideously wounded, sick, and dying soldiers, both Confederate and Yankee.

Dan and his comrades were held for a short time at Camp Oglethorpe in Macon, one hundred miles from Atlanta. One Union prisoner described the camp at Macon, which at that time held about 1,900 prisoners. "Each man was allowed a board sixteen feet long for the construction of a bunk. Sleeping quarters were fixed wherever between the ground and roof it suited an individual's fancy, so that he did not trespass on his comrades," he wrote. "The ground was nearly level, only at the rear end it declined rapidly to the ravine through which the stream passed ... as heaven's flood gates opened frequently the flat surface of the camp was often covered to the depth of several inches to the great discomfort of those who were without shelter, of whom there were always one or two hundred." A prisoner's daily food ration at Macon was a pint of unsifted cornmeal, two ounces of rancid bacon, a half teaspoon of salt, and an ounce of black-eyed peas or rice.[1]

From Macon, one of the New Yorkers was sent to Libby Prison in Richmond and paroled in December 1864. Twelve were sent to Andersonville, Georgia, where they arrived in early July. Work had just been completed July 1, expanding the sixteen-acre prison by ten acres.

In his Civil War memoir, Dan reported that he and his comrades arrived at Andersonville dejected, dispirited, exhausted, hungry, and thirsty, and were marched in front of the Confederate commandant's headquarters. They were compelled to stand in the blazing July sunlight to receive their prison assignment "while Capt. Henry Wirz, the commandant, ate." Dan then noted, "I asked a little darkey who was playing in the yard to bring me a drink of water from the spring that bubbled at our feet, but which we were not permitted to touch. The child filled a gourd with water and was in the act of handing it to me without any objection from the guard, when Capt. Wirz came out ... to call the roll and make the assignment. Seeing what the boy was doing he said to him with a fearful oath, 'Let the——Yankee——go to hell for water. If I catch you giving any prisoners water I shoots you.' The child's knees shaking, he dropped the gourd and fled."

Guards then stripped the men of their knapsacks, haversacks, knives, and other possessions, along with all but $20 of their money. Although he did not mention it in his memoir, Dan must have arrived shortly after July 11, the day Captain Wirz authorized the hanging of six brutal prisoners that had robbed, beaten, and terrorized the other inmates for months.

As he entered the prison through the huge doors of the north gate, Dan's first view was of walking skeletons, some naked and so covered with vermin and filth that they appeared to be painted black. The smell of excrement was suffocating. The prison was so crowded that each man had a space less than ten-by-four feet. They slept on the ground, which was infested with disgusting white worms so dense they resembled a blanket of snow. On foggy mornings, the whole camp was filled with white moths that flew into the men's mouths and noses, and disappeared only when the sun came out. The prisoners had unwillingly swallowed many. Dan and the other new arrivals were immediately surrounded by ragged inmates starved for any morsel of war information or prospect of parole or exchange. They were welcomed by prisoners, as were all other new arrivals, with the cry "Fresh fish." The first task Dan and his companions undertook was to build a "shebang," a makeshift tent of tattered blankets or clothing stretched over upright sticks.

Prisoners who were able to keep some money when they entered camp, including Dan, could supplement their starvation rations. Sutlers, as well as some of the prisoners, peddled their wares inside the prison stockade. Eggs cost $3 to $6 a dozen, a teacup of flour $1, salt $4 a pound, molasses $30 a gallon, and beans 50¢ a pint. Meal, dried peas, blackberries, potatoes, watermelons, and soda were also available for purchase. Guards or work gangs sold wood cut in nearby pine forests. In addition to staples, peddlers sold bunches of four or five green onions for $2 U.S.[2] Onions were a folk remedy for epidemic diseases—flu, measles, chicken pox, typhoid, and scarlet fever—as well as for lung congestion, colds, fever, and scurvy. Dan ate so many that he would never allow onions in his house after the war, because they brought back such painful memories of Andersonville. While there, Dan contracted typhoid fever and spent what little money he had buying onions in an attempt to cure it.[3] By eating onions, however, he at least warded off the scurvy that was directly or indirectly responsible for nine-tenths of the prison's fatalities.[4]

On July 15, about the time Dan arrived, several sergeants began circulating a petition with the approval of Captain Wirz, appealing to the Union government for an immediate prisoner exchange. General Grant opposed the idea because Confederates had refused to exchange blacks as equals to whites and because he considered Confederate prisoners the same as dead soldiers. To release them so they could return to the Rebel ranks would lengthen the war, in turn increasing Union casualty rates. On August 9, Wirz approved a committee of six prisoners to take the petition to Washington by train, but their effort was for naught. The petition did not change Union prisoner exchange policy.

In the summer and fall of 1864, the movements of Sherman's army through Georgia kept Confederate authorities searching for a secure place to hold prisoners. In anticipation of a raid on the grossly overcrowded prison, Gen. Joseph E. Johnston had sent President Jefferson Davis a telegram on July 11, urging him to transfer the prisoners immediately.

The evacuation of Wirz's prison did not start, however, until five days after Atlanta fell.[5]

Sherman did in fact authorize Gen. George Stoneman to conduct a raid on the Macon and Andersonville prisons. He also cut the sixty-mile railroad between Atlanta and Macon. His raiders, however, were stopped on July 30, two miles east of Macon, where Stoneman himself and 400 of his 5,000 cavalrymen were captured and taken to Andersonville. Apparently, Confederate officials were concerned that the next Union raid on Macon would succeed. A week after Stoneman's capture, they transferred 679 prisoners from Macon to Andersonville.[6] Efforts to transfer prisoners were accelerated after two days of drenching rain, on August 9 and 10, so severely damaged the Macon stockade that it took the entire guard force to save it.

The same two-day thunderstorm also drowned Andersonville, flushing a month of filth into its Stockade Creek. The deluge flooded tents and filled wells to overflowing. Stockade posts gave way to the floodwaters where the creek entered the prison, opening a one-hundred-foot gap. By this time, most prisoners were so weakened by the heat, scurvy, dysentery, and other diseases that attempting to escape was beyond consideration. Their condition contrasted sharply with that of hundreds of prisoners only a month earlier, when Dan had just arrived. At that time, they had made dozens of largely unsuccessful attempts to escape by tunneling under the stockade. Now many of them could barely walk to the "sinks" unaided, much less undertake a long flight to freedom. In fact, many of the weakest died from the effects of the punishing rain.

By the most fortuitous circumstance, the day after the last of the floodwaters had passed, a stream of clear water bubbled up from a deep, unpolluted aquifer just beyond the deadline. Men lined up with cups and buckets tied to poles, trying to reach the water. In an act of kindness, prison police diverted the stream so that it flowed into a reservoir dug by the prisoners. It became known as Providence Spring. By this time, a bakery was finally finished. It produced fly-infested bread that caused dysentery and other bowel problems. One prisoner reported that the bread was kneaded in a trough and shortened with flies, which were visible when they broke open the bread.

The prison population at Andersonville peaked at about 33,000 in August 1864, shortly before evacuation began. As the stockade became more crowded, the August sun hotter, and the rations per prisoner shorter, deaths by starvation, scurvy, dysentery, and gangrene increased. By then, the filthy, disease-ridden prison was the fifth-largest "city" in the Confederacy. When Dan and his comrades had arrived in July, the prison held 26,000 men on twenty-six and a half acres, almost 1,000 prisoners per acre. The arrival of 7,128 captives over the next month raised the number per acre to 1,200, leaving a space about the size of a grave per prisoner. At that time, 100 men died daily and 2,500 were hospitalized, while an untold number of others needed to be. In their death throes, they were often kicked to death by those semicrazed, desperation-driven fellow prisoners who wanted to rob them of their clothes and other possessions.

By August 14, a new prison site, Camp Lawton, was finally established five miles from Millen in east central Georgia. The Confederate general Braxton Bragg ordered another reopened at Cahaba, ten miles south of Selma, Alabama, both principally to house Andersonville prisoners.[7]

On September 2, Sherman's army occupied Atlanta. Dan's regiment, the 123rd N.Y., was among the first to enter the city. Shortly thereafter, Confederate orders were issued from Richmond to move 20,000 Andersonville prisoners by rail to Florence, Charleston, Savannah, and Salisbury, since Millen's Camp Lawton was not completed. Dan had been at Andersonville about two months when the transfer began at 7 A.M. on September 7. In order to discourage escape attempts during their two-day train ride, the captives were told there would be a general exchange of prisoners at Savannah. On September 13, the first exchange party returned. They had been taken to Rough and Ready, near Atlanta, instead of Savannah. There, General Sherman selected his own men for exchange—ingratiating himself to them—and sent the remaining Andersonville prisoners back. They were shipped in detachments of 270 and issued two days' rations. Those who were packed into cattle cars rode with manure still on the floors. It is not known when Dan left Andersonville, but it is certain that he was held there no more than two months. By September 15, about 11,000 prisoners remained at Andersonville, including 3,000 who were too sick to be removed. Ironically, those moved to other prisons in Georgia and South Carolina found themselves in Sherman's path as he advanced toward Savannah, and had to be moved again. By the end of October 1864, Andersonville held only 5,000 prisoners, all of them too sick or weak to be moved. By December 22, the day Sherman entered Savannah, all but 1,359 had died.[8]

Andersonville was a death trap in its fourteen months of existence. Twenty-nine percent of the 45,000 prisoners died, even though many of them, like Dan, had been confined there only a few months. If those who died after being transferred from Andersonville also are included, the prison's death rate approaches 35 percent. It is a stark contrast to the 15 percent death rate for all Union captives in Confederate prisons. Of all the Confederate prisoners in the twelve major Northern prisons, 13,000 died—the same as the toll at Andersonville alone.

Records for nine of the men from the 123rd N.Y. confined at Andersonville show that one died on August 24 from "improper treatment" only weeks after his arrival. After the war, the other eight, including Dan, would receive invalid pensions as a result of the diseases they contracted while in prison. Three suffered from heart disease complicated by rheumatism, lung, or chest problems. Other individuals had typhoid fever, eye disease, scurvy, lung trouble, chronic diarrhea, incapacitating rheumatism, or an unidentified disease. When they rejoined their regiment after being paroled or exchanged, one of the eight Andersonville survivors was described as "emaciated [and] entirely unfit for duty," and another as a "mere skeleton troubled with a lung difficulty." Still another described himself as "nearly starved to death." Dan contracted a rheumatic heart condition that would confine him to bed in his last years and eventually claim his life at age eighty-two. In a mere two months in Andersonville these prisoners had developed lifelong disabilities, and their ordeals were not yet over.

Those sent to Charleston or Savannah beginning September 7 thought they were being sent to an "oasis." Some men stumbled out of the boxcars and cattle cars at Savannah to a meager half pint of flour, nothing more. To stay warm in the new stockade near the Savannah jail, the prisoners burned a load of cordwood. But not all of the prisoners stayed in Savannah, which was threatened by Sherman. Without changing trains, Dan continued on the 236-mile Charleston-to-Savannah train trip, to newly completed Camp Lawton eighty miles northwest of the Georgia port city. Sherman arranged for articles of clothing, soap, and candles to be sent to Andersonville prisoners who were being transferred to Savannah and Millen. It is not known whether Dan received any of this largesse. Those men who lacked soap used sand to scrub their smoke-blackened faces and bodies. When Dan and about 1,000 other prisoners arrived at Millen on a foggy morning in early October, they doubled the population of Camp Lawton.

The prison camp was on the Georgia Central Railroad about five miles from the village itself and forty-five miles south of Augusta. The village was at a junction of railroads leading to Savannah, Augusta, Atlanta, and beyond to Richmond and the fertile agricultural districts of Georgia, Alabama, and Mississippi. It was an open stockade in a large clearing. A single line of unhewn vertical timbers enclosed forty-two acres, as compared with twenty-six at Andersonville. It was divided into thirty-two sections by sixteen-foot-wide streets. The location was better, but conditions were only slightly improved over those at Andersonville, except it was not as filthy or disease-ridden, because it was new. Camp Lawton was built on dry ground and had a stronger stream through the middle of the camp with ample clear water that was not bordered by a swamp. When Dan arrived, Rebel guards kept him and the other newcomers on one side of the brook until they could be counted and given mess assignments. The stream was about four feet deep in places and as much as twelve feet wide. A stretch of about thirty feet could be used for bathing. A privy was built over the stream at the low end of the stockade so that upstream water for drinking, washing, and cooking was not polluted.

There was minimal shelter, however, and bunks were provided for only 500 men. Timber felled in clearing the prison site was available to the prisoners for building shelters and for firewood until it ran out. Roots of tree stumps soon became the only available firewood. The weather was cold, windy, and rainy, and the saturated ground on which they slept was covered with a meager stand of hard, wiry grass. Heavy dew further added to their misery even for those who dug holes in the ground for shelter. Prisoners cooked their own meals. There was a row of bake ovens, each with two good-sized kettles for heating water. Food was somewhat better than at Andersonville, although Millen prisoners received little salt. The first night a cupful of good-quality cornmeal was issued to each prisoner. After that, daily rations consisted of two-thirds of a pint of cornmeal, three tablespoons of rice, four ounces of beef, and a teaspoon of salt. Sometimes bug-infested peas were substituted for rice. The beef ration was of better quality and double the amount that had sometimes been available at Andersonville.

Tents in one corner of the camp served as an inadequate hospital. Twenty to thirty-five prisoners a day died from exposure to cold, rain, snow, and less-than-subsistence rations. Scurvy, rheumatism, and diarrhea were major causes of death. After heavy rains, shanties and holes in the ground in which men lived had to be bailed out. During the first month Camp Lawton was in operation, 486 of the prisoners died. Another 926 died during October, almost all from Andersonville. The prison population peaked in late October when Millen held 10,229 men. In six weeks, one in ten had died. Those that survived were blue with cold, shivering constantly as they hugged their near-naked bodies with bony arms in a vain attempt to retain some body heat. A few froze to death. At night it was so cold that ice formed at the edge of the brook. Boxes of clothing sent to the prisoners by the U.S. Sanitary Commission were confiscated and used instead by the guards.

Surprisingly, the Millen prisoners were allowed to vote in the presidential election. Not surprisingly, they voted three-to-one for Lincoln over McClellan, 3,014 to 1,050. The Confederate government had allowed the prisoner vote to take place, believing that a McClellan victory would give Southern soldiers a boost in morale by reflecting weakened

Northern support for the war. This vote was taken after the prisoners knew that their chances of parole and exchange had vanished, and many were bitter at Lincoln because he had supported General Grant's August 27 order ending prisoner exchange.

Besides those at Millen, prisoners elsewhere took straw votes that supported Lincoln. One detachment of Andersonville prisoners conducted their own election. Out of 224 votes cast, 188 (84 percent) were for Lincoln, 36 for McClellan. In the Florence, South Carolina, camp, prisoners used two empty bags for ballot boxes. In single file, each voted with a black bean for Lincoln or a white one for "Little Mac." Lincoln won over McClellan by two and one-half to one. Officers in the Danville, Virginia, prison voted 274 for Lincoln, 91 for McClellan.

During the winter of 1863-64, the Confederates had refused to exchange prisoners in accordance with agreements reached in 1861. The North had captured about 40,000 prisoners as a result of victories at Vicksburg, Port Hudson, and other battles. There was no room in Northern prisoners for so many new captives, so the Confederate secretary of war met the prisoners in Mississippi and declared 20,000 to 25,000 of them properly exchanged and placed them in western armies, refusing to exchange them man for man. Confederate authorities also refused to exchange 5,000 black soldiers on any terms, but instead put them to work building fortifications or sold them back into slavery, while trying and punishing their white officers as criminals.

On November 15, as Sherman's army left Atlanta for Savannah, the Confederates gave the 9,000 prisoners remaining at Millen a ration of sweet potatoes and began moving them to other prison camps. These camps were at Savannah, Thomasville, and Blackshear in southern Georgia; Jacksonville, Florida; and Florence and Cahaba, Alabama. Dan was sent to the last of these. Many sick and wounded prisoners were paroled at this time, and a handful escaped, including one from the 123rd N.Y.[9]

While the prison commandant was preparing to evacuate Camp Lawton, General Kilpatrick and his Union cavalry were racing ahead of Sherman's army to liberate the Millen prisoners. They arrived on November 22, in time to watch from the river as the last of the 3,000 emaciated, sick, or wounded prisoners were herded into boxcars for shipment to other prisons. None of the prisoners knew of Sherman's advance. Large clouds of black smoke rose from bales of cotton and other stores that were burned to prevent them from falling into Yankee hands.

Orders for evacuation of Camp Lawton had been issued at 3 A.M. in a cold, driving rain. Dan and the others, most half-naked, were told to stand in ranks. Numb from the cold, and without fires or blankets, they waited in the rain until noon, when the open flatcars finally arrived.

By then, some had collapsed and died. Some of the survivors were taken to Florence. The others were first taken to Savannah, where a piercing wind replaced the driving rain. During the journey, they were given four ears of corn. Their teeth were so loose from severe scurvy that not one prisoner in a hundred could eat an ear, much less the hardtack they were given at Savannah.[10] More men died en route and, upon arrival at Savannah, were carried by a squad from each car and laid out in rows to be buried in shallow, sandy graves.

On December 3, Sherman's main force reached Millen, including the 123rd N.Y., in which young Pvt. John Ross had taken his captured brother's place. John could not have known that his brother had been imprisoned there. When the 20th Corps, to which John's regiment belonged, arrived at the prison, they found one fresh grave marked "650 BURRIED HERE." John likely agreed with the description Sgt. Rice C. Bull, of the 123rd, wrote in his diary. "There were many [of us] who visited the pen and I heard them say they would never be taken prisoner; they would prefer to be shot than put in such a place," he reflected. "I wondered what could have been their condition during wet weather. They must have been driven out [from their holes and caves dug into the earth] like rats from a sewer during a flood.

Five thousand to six thousand Andersonville prisoners who were taken by train to Savannah, including Dan, were consigned to the prison at Blackshear and given a few crackers before boarding. The rolling stock and rails of the Atlantic and Gulf Railroad at Savannah were in such deplorable condition that it was said to consist of no more than "two streaks of rust and a right-of-way." Grease was nonexistent, and the screeching of dry axles was agonizing to hear. It took four days to make the 150-mile trip from Savannah to Blackshear, not far from the Florida state line. Men who died en route were buried there.

Upon arrival at Blackshear, forty miles from the seacoast, the prisoners were offered parole, provided they promised not to bear arms against the Confederacy "until properly exchanged." They were in Blackshear only five days, but in that time were nearly eaten alive by a swarm of "galley nippers," insects much larger than mosquitoes. By this time, December 10, General Sherman's siege of Savannah had begun, so the prisoners were moved to Thomasville or Florence. A thousand were sent back to Andersonville.

Those who were returned to Andersonville were then sent by rail to Charleston and told they would be paroled and exchanged. They boarded the train to Savannah after signing parole forms and receiving two days' ration of cornmeal and fresh beef, convinced that at last they were on their way home. Instead, they were shipped from Savannah back to Charleston where, on December 13, weak from hunger, they received their first rations since they had left Charleston for Savannah. That day one of Dan's companions who had been captured with him was among those paroled and sent to the Union Army hospital in Annapolis, Maryland.

Meanwhile, after a few days in Charleston, the others, including Dan, boarded closed boxcars for a 120-mile trip to Florence, South Carolina, packed sixty to a car. En route to Florence, prisoners ripped off portions of the railroad car roofs to make cooking utensils. At Florence, the erstwhile parolees joined prisoners who had not signed parole forms. There were around 10,000 prisoners in Florence at that time, but the population of the fifteen-acre stockade soon reached 15,000. A visitor wrote he found the camp "full of what were once human beings . . . filthy, diseased, famished men, with no hope of relief except by death."[11]

Dan and a number of other prisoners continued by rail to Cahaba, near Selma, Alabama.[12] The prison was located fifteen miles southwest of Selma on the bank of the Alabama River, about a block from its confluence with the Cahaba River. It was a large building then known as Castle Morgan. The unfinished brick warehouse was an old cotton and corn shed with walls about fourteen feet high. About half of the building lacked a roof. Against the interior walls, five-tier-high "sleeping roosts" were built of rough planking with no bedding. They accommodated only 432 men. The rest slept on the ground. Confederate Army officers inspected the prison at least twice. In March 1864, when 660 prisoners were confined there, the inspectors reported that the building contained only one fireplace. About forty cooking fires were built inside the building; and without ventilation, the smoke became suffocating. The water supply entered the prison from a nearby artesian well through a 200-yard open street gutter carrying animal and human filth. One wheelbarrow was available to remove rubbish.[13] By July 1864, most of the prisoners at Cahaba had been captured in numerous engagements in and around New Orleans, Mobile, Vicksburg, Memphis, Nashville, and Chattanooga. They had served in various regiments attached to General Grant's Military Division of the Mississippi.[14]

In October, about a month before Dan arrived, a second prison inspection reported that a stockade fence, built of two-inch planks twelve feet high, had been completed around the brick structure so that outdoor cooking fires could be built. The fence enclosed a one-third acre site. The number of prisoners had more than tripled, totaling 2,151, despite the fact that the prison was built to accommodate 500. The choking smoke from 200 to 300 cooking fires was far worse than before. They had less than 17.5 square feet of space per prisoner, compared to 35.7 square feet at Andersonville when Dan arrived there. Prisoners exercised and cooked in a 35-by-120-foot area. Fall having arrived, the weather was colder, and prisoners needed clothing, food, blankets, wood, and water. By then the prison was infested with rats, lice, and swarming insects (muggers), making it almost impossible to sleep. Food consisted almost exclusively of bread and meat. No vinegar, vegetables, or sugar had been issued for months, although vinegar could have been easily supplied from Mobile, Alabama. There were numerous cases of scurvy, dysentery, diarrhea, and other diseases, as well as untreated war wounds. There was no hospital in the prison, although a small one was established in the Belle Tavern Hotel, two blocks away.

Nevertheless, the death rate was unusually low. The water supply came through pipes from a clear spring. Additionally, the prison had halfway decent toilet facilities and no serious shortage of medicines. Books loaned to prisoners by Mrs. Amanda Gardner, a lifelong resident of Selma, provided a mental escape for them. The prison commandant was humane and fair.

About the time of Dan's arrival, a hospital, known as the General Hospital, was established in a downtown Selma high school, several miles from the prison. Dr. Alexander Hart, a Confederate surgeon, was in charge of the 200-bed hospital, serving both Confederate soldiers and Union prisoners who were sick or wounded. Sixty-nine Union prisoners were hospitalized there, and another seventy-five needed to be. Dan volunteered to be an attendant to the hospitalized prisoners and undoubtedly ate the same food they did, a slightly better diet than the other prisoners were fed. Women of Selma also attended to the wounded, made bandages, and brought food. Before the assignment, Dan had given his word of honor that he would not attempt to escape. Shortly thereafter, excess prisoners not confined to the hospital were ordered transferred back to Millen, along with the prison's armament and equipment, but the order was never executed.[15]

By late November, when Millen was threatened by Sherman's march to the sea, more of its prisoners were sent to Cahaba. Castle Morgan became more overcrowded as the total number of prisoners rose to almost 3,000. Through the winter of 1864-65, horrible conditions existed at Cahaba, aggravated by flooding of the river and, in late January, very cold and snowy weather. By then, total space per prisoner averaged six square feet. Standard food rations consisted solely of raw meat and meal. The best meals they had were those they dreamed about night after night.

In January 1865, the Confederates finally agreed to exchange black soldiers, man for man, rather than treating them as slaves or traitors ineligible for exchange. Meanwhile, on January 20, 1865, while those in other prisons were being paroled and exchanged, the Cahaba prisoners mutinied and captured the guards. Soldiers from the post at Selma attacked the prison and put down the mutiny. On February 2, Grant relented, agreeing to exchange up to 300 prisoners weekly with the Confederates. He also supported efforts by Sherman and others to relieve suffering by Union prisoners. By March 1, the muddy floodwaters were several feet deep in the Cahaba prison stockade. The only benefit to the prisoners was that the flood drowned the rats and lice. By the time Maj. Gen. James H. Wilson's Union cavalry reached Selma after a nineteen-mile march on Sunday, April 2, 1865, only forty or fifty sick or wounded prisoners were in the hospital.[16]

After General Grant became commander in chief he made significant changes in strategy and personnel. He moved outstanding officers like Sheridan and Wilson into top positions and gave them independent commands—free reign to implement his orders. The cavalry raid that Wilson was assigned was the longest conducted by the North, using the greatest number of men. Further, Wilson is another example of how these men with independent commands—Slocum, Williams, Hooker, Lytle, Sherman, Hancock, Birney, and Hays—led their troops, exposing themselves to even more danger than their men.

When fully equipped for a march, the men of the 4th U.S. Cavalry under Capt. William O'Connell carried haversacks that held three days' rations in addition to their weapons. Each horse had a nosebag dangling from its neck. A bundle behind the saddle held as much as another 150 pounds of oats or other feed. The horse soldiers took excellent care of their mounts, resting and watering them as frequently as possible. Their reserve supplies were carried in wagons and on mules. It was the only cavalry regiment to remain mounted throughout the entire attack on Selma. As part of the Saber Brigade, the regiment was armed with sabers, Spencer seven-shot carbines, and revolvers. Just prior to the charge, some of Wilson's men watched a southbound Alabama and Mississippi trainload of Union prisoners waving their hats and cheering as they went by. Had Dan remained in the Cahaba prison instead of being transferred to the hospital, he undoubtedly would have been on that train and moved to still another prison.

On April 2 President Jefferson Davis abandoned Richmond as the Confederate capital while Gen. Robert E. Lee's army slipped out in retreat from behind the Petersburg lines. Lank had just suffered the injury that would ultimately cost him his sight in both eyes. Dan was still serving as a corpsman in the makeshift hospital at the Masonic high school, near the center of downtown Selma, when Wilson's horse troopers invaded the city. Dan watched the ensuing battle from the hospital roof, a vantage point few soldiers ever had. His memoir provides the only first-person account of a Civil War battle by any of the Ross brothers, made all the more significant because Dan, who had first enlisted in the cavalry, was watching cavalrymen capture the town.

Beginning in 1863, slaves built fortifications in a semicircle around the city. The barricade was four to five miles in length, meeting the Alabama River at each end. A space about two hundred yards wide between the two entrenchments was strewn with torpedoes and cross-wire baskets called "sheepracks." Every tree and stump for a half mile outside of the entrenchments had been removed. The river, its west bank fifty to one hundred feet below the city, formed the fourth side of the city's protective works. Each artillery battery was supplied with only twenty rounds of ammunition. Every effort was being made to get the military stores and prisoners out of the city, by rail or by river, filling the streets with wagons and drays.

Dan was awakened that bright Sunday morning by the distant boom of cannonading, the "long roll" of Confederate drums, and the clatter of countless horse hoofs. The spring air was fragrant with jasmine and dogwood blossoms.

Grant had picked one of his favorite generals to fight the battle, pitting him against the best cavalryman the South had ever produced. It was a force that even Sherman feared. At twenty-six, Wilson was the youngest major general in the Union Army, having graduated from West Point the year before the war started. A stoop-shouldered little man, in battle he would throw away the book and improvise on the spot how to fight it. Grant's first impression of him was that he looked more like a storekeeper than a general, but soon learned otherwise. Wilson described his men as "veterans of ripe experience." In fact, the majority of his twenty-seven regiments were Veteran Volunteers. Wilson had learned how to use cavalry as an independent strike force to attack entrenched infantry. Meticulous in selecting his mounts, he always kept these troopers of the 4th U.S. Cavalry at hand, mounted and ready to charge when the enemy broke.

Beginning at about 5 P.M., yelling and shooting as they ran, 1,500 dismounted troops in General Eli Long's Lightning Brigade penetrated the picket line, abatis, and outer works by advancing down the Summerfield Road through a hail of musketry and artillery fire. They were preceded by freed slaves who had followed Wilson's army. Armed with axes and ignoring enemy musket balls, these ex-slaves hacked openings in the stockade fence large enough for some of the dismounted troopers to crawl through. Others scaled the wall "as boys play leapfrog," the more active "boosting" their comrades over the stockade. Long led the charge himself and fell, wounded in the head. One-fifth of Long's men, more than 300, also became casualties, but others were able to leapfrog over the parapets and quickly open the stockade gate. Wilson's mounted 4th U.S. and 3rd Ohio followed.

The Confederate Gen. Nathan B. Forrest, the "Wizard of the Saddle," was in command of the militia manning the inner line. Forrest had grown up in southern frontier poverty. With only three months of schooling, he became one of the most successful slave traders in Memphis and had a temper that knew no bounds. Six feet two inches tall, he weighed 180 pounds, had gun-metal gray eyes, gaunt cheeks, and a grim countenance. He had twenty-nine horses shot out from under him, but was wounded only four times during the war and had killed thirty men in hand-to-hand combat.

Caught up in the frenzy of the attack, Wilson led his staff and the 4th U.S. as they charged 600 yards through the stockade gate into the city. Followed by the mounted 3rd Ohio Cavalry, the 4th U.S. then rode furiously to the very center of the Confederate inner line, which was manned by the militia, artillery batteries, Forrest himself, his guard, and Armstrong's brigade, the best in Forrest's corps. Wilson's artillery also breached the outer gate, then turned fire onto the forts and sharpshooter platforms of the inner line, as some of the mounted troops with drawn sabers rode straight through the inner gate into a hail of lead and grapeshot.

One cavalryman wrote, "[A]ll at once the whole top of the [interior] embankment was one sheet of fire, flame, and smoke and the bullets fairly piped and screamed through the air" as tornados of grape and canister ripped through their bodies. When close to the inner line of entrenchments, Wilson could hear an officer shouting, "[S]hoot that man on the white horse." On the signal of his Indian bugler, the mounted cavalry re-formed. Wilson held his horse in check, swung his sword toward the enemy, cheered his troops on as they charged a redoubt in the inner line at a single point and "went over the works with a shout."

Once inside the inner line, they wheeled to the left under a hail of musketry and artillery. Charging headlong on his spirited horse, "his jacket open in the heat, [Wilson and] the 4th U.S. galloped past the inner gate and down Summerfield Road into the city, waving drawn sabers.... The general himself was sent to the ground when a shot wounded his mount." Wilson, momentarily dazed, remounted his horse, which had regained its footing even though it had a bullet in its chest.

The regulars were badly scattered by enemy cannon volleys during the charge. Captain O'Connell also had his horse shot under him. Both

O'Connell and Wilson were bruised from their falls but unwounded. The 3rd Ohio Cavalry dismounted and deployed to both sides of the Summerfield Road. They reached a fort near the cotton gin and turned again to the left and carried the main works on the Plantersville (Range Line) Road. From there they entered the heart of the city.

Before the battle began Dan had watched as officers rode "hurriedly through the streets... assembling every combatant and non-combatant to man the breastworks and render what aid they could" in defending the city. He could see that "every man and boy that could shoulder a musket and many that seemed physically unable to do even that, were hurried forward to take their places crouched behind the earthwork fortifications."

The Rebels in the first line of works were soon driven into the second. Forrest's personal, hand-picked guard of Kentuckians and the second line of militia broke and fled through the streets and out the Burnsville Road. From then on, the battle became one of hundreds of individual combats. Dan saw the streets "strewn with dead and dying, some with their heads completely severed from their bodies, others with fearful gashes that told too well what a heavy and sharp saber can do.... The broad streets... were piled as far as the eye could reach with Union and Confederate cavalry, packed in so tight a mass that there was no escape except by cutting their way out, and this everyone seemed to be trying to do to the best of his ability." Wild-eyed horses were covered with the blood of their slaughtered riders.

Union batteries threw shrieking shells that crashed through houses, setting some on fire. The noise was deafening: men's wild curses and screams, officers' shouts, thundering hooves and snorting horses, frantic pistol and carbine shots, and clashing sabers. The battle raged from street to street, house to house, building to building. Clouds of dust made it difficult to distinguish friend from foe. From what Dan could see, "the fight could not have lasted more than thirty minutes" before the streets were emptied of fleeing survivors with the Union cavalrymen in close pursuit.

Some Confederates jumped their horses over the bluffs, fifty to sixty feet down to the deep, fast-flowing river in their attempt to escape. Mounted Union cavalrymen meanwhile charged down the Range Line Road, captured all the cannon, entered the center of the city, and pursued the Rebels to the river's brink, "cutting and slashing with their sabers."

Wilson carried his red battle flag into the city's public square, drawing the enemy's fire, while the 4th Cavalry's band was playing "Red, White and Blue." The major action was over by 6 P.M. By dark, Wilson had taken over Forrest's former headquarters at the Gee Hotel, six blocks from the hospital where Dan watched the action from the roof. He promptly appointed a provost guard to assist local citizens to establish order and extinguish fires.

Forrest barely escaped by riding his horse into the river without a moment's hesitation and swimming across it in the darkness. A squad of 3rd Ohio cavalrymen heard a slave shouting at the top of his voice, "Get him! Get him! Get him! That's General Forrest himself." He had just come out of the telegraph office where he had been dispatching orders, alerted by a boy who shouted to him, "The Yanks are a-comin." This was to be Forrest's first and only decisive defeat during the entire war. After it ended, he would go on to found the Ku Klux Klan.[17]

Sporadic house-to-house fighting continued into the night. Sgt. Thomas W. Giles of the 4th U.S. wrote, "We entered just at dark and such skedaddling I never saw." Those found hiding were taken prisoner. Others threw their guns away and surrendered in squads to the first Union soldier that appeared. Wilson used his hotel headquarters for the remainder of his stay in Selma to tend to casualties in both armies, refit his command, dispose of property with military value, enforce the protection of citizens, and prepare plans for the rest of the campaign.

Some 2,000 captured Rebels, including officers, were confined in a stockade once occupied by Union prisoners and Confederate deserters. Confederate officers were so indignant at their confinement that General Wilson threatened to put them in irons. Lt. Thomas H. Peabody of the 4th Mich. Cavalry (part of Col. Robert H. G. Minty's Saber Brigade) was put in charge of the Rebel prison and released the Union prisoners, including Dan.[18] It was the same cavalry unit that had guarded the flanks of the Union line when Dan was captured ten months earlier at Kolb's Farm.

Selma was the only remaining production center for Confederate cannon, bayonets, swords, and other munitions. It also sat astride the railroad that connected the southwestern states with Richmond. That connection was now broken. By April 1865, even foreign military supplies were cut off. Union troops promptly set about destroying every factory and all military supplies that had not already been destroyed by the Confederates to keep them from falling into Yankee hands. Arms and ammunition were found in almost every warehouse. Retreating Rebels had set fire to cotton warehouses containing 25,000 bales, and shot 500 surplus horses and mules, then thrown them in the river. What pillaging and plundering Union soldiers had not completed in the downtown business section before the fire, was finished the next day by Selma citizens. Ironically, Richmond, the Confederate capital, also caught fire that night, a few hours after Jefferson David fled that city. When it was over, not a thing was left in the stores. Many homes also burned, having caught fire from the shelling. Over the next three or four days, Dan witnessed that destruction, especially on the night after the city's capture when the countryside was lit by raging fires for at least twenty miles in every direction. Wilson's mission was to use his troopers to destroy this munitions complex and then to seize Montgomery, Alabama, the first capital of the Confederacy.[19]

On April 3, as soon as the sick and wounded under his care were provided for by Wilson's raiders, Dan was released from duty at the prison hospital. He reported to the general's provost marshal, Maj. C. L. Green, 7th Pa. Cavalry (Saber Brigade). Sixty-eight patients were left behind in the hospital with rations for forty days, plus medicines and supplies. A surgeon and an assistant were assigned to tend to them. A Union soldier wrote, "No men were ever treated better by the ladies of the town. They just flocked to the hospital to do what they can for them."

At his request, Dan spent the remaining two weeks of the war on assignment with the artillery, probably with Lt. George B. Rodney's Battery I, 4th U.S., armed with Napoleon twelve-pounders. This battery was attached to Edward F. Winslow's 1st Brigade of Emory Upton's 4th Division, a part of Wilson's command. Winslow had been placed in command of the city.

Three cavalry regiments of freed slaves, one for each of Wilson's divisions, were organized at Selma to accompany his army for the remainder of the war. The 137th USCT also was organized, on April 8. The officers of the black regiments, all white, had been noncommissioned officers who were recruited and promoted largely from regiments in the Saber Brigade. F. H. Bailey of the 4th Mich. was one of the white officers. On May 15, 1865, he wrote his parents, "[E]ven in the field I would as soon lead black soldiers as white ones for they will stand under as heavy fire and fight as well." According to Dan, the freedmen were "uniformed with white cotton duck shirts and pants, rawhide shoes, plantation hats and any kind of coats, mounted on mules and condemned horses and armed with whatever weapon they happened to pick up." They also did much of the heavy labor. Like the rest of Wilson's army, they subsisted on the countryside and frequently marched thirty-five or more miles daily.

In their last two weeks of fighting, after fording the dangerously swollen Alabama River, Wilson's cavalry captured Montgomery, Alabama, without firing a shot, then Columbus and Macon, Georgia. Dan helped to fire a Napoleon for his last time in the action to take Columbus, a well-fortified city. They were positioned at twilight under cover at commanding points behind the main forts on the elevated bank of the Chatahoochie River on the Alabama side, but within easy range of the city. The cannonading by Dan and the others in the three-gun battery preceded Winslow's cavalry attack; they fired enough shells to develop enemy gun positions as they exchanged shots. Not expecting an attack from the direction of the river, the 2,000 defenders offered feeble resistance, even failing to destroy the 1,000-foot bridge. Dan noted in his memoir that "a short acquaintance with our twelve pound Napoleon shells [convinced] the defenders that discretion was the better part of valor." The cavalry took Macon in short order, occupying it by 11 P.M. On April 20 they learned Lee had surrendered to Grant and Johnston had surrendered to Sherman.

At Macon, Wilson's cavalrymen and Dan received news of the assassination of President Lincoln. Many of the men in Winslow's brigade wanted to continue the war then and there. One noted that "there would be no mercy shown to any Rebs if we could only have a fight—we all pray that the truce of Sherman's and Johnston's may come to an end so we can go at it again."

Dan wrote that about thirteen miles outside of Macon, as they advanced in line of battle, he and the others in Wilson's army suddenly found themselves confronted by a Confederate "army whose arms were stacked and banners furled, welcoming us with the joyous news that the war was over." The Confederate Gen. Cherokee Robinson carried a flag of truce. While in Macon on May 7, a detachment of Wilson's men under Capt. Henry E. Noyes, aide-de-camp to Wilson, captured Captain Wirz, who was still paroling and transferring 3,000 sick prisoners per trainload from Andersonville to Florida via Macon and Thomasville, Georgia. They were paroled in Baldwin, near Jacksonville, Florida. A Georgia militia regiment marched the Andersonville prisoners they had been guarding out of the prison and abandoned them. On orders from Wilson, Captain Noyes brought Wirz to Macon for confinement while awaiting trial. Dan and forty or fifty other ex-Andersonville prisoners had to be kept from wreaking their vengeance on the Andersonville commandant when they discovered his closely guarded quarters. Dan wrote that "it required the unqualified pledge of [Captain Noyes] that punishment of Wirz would be swift and sure" before he and the other ex-prisoners decided not to render justice on the spot.

About May 20, Wirz was sent to Washington aboard a special train in the custody of Noyes and several troopers. On August 23, his trial began in the U.S. Capitol's basement. He was convicted and hung on November 10 for conspiring with Jefferson Davis and others "to impair and injure the health and destroy the lives . . . of large numbers of federal prisoners" and for "murder in violation of the laws and customs of war." General Hancock was in charge of the execution. Wirz was the only Confederate officer to be executed for war crimes. Undoubtedly, Dan would not have accepted Noyes's pledge had he known that at least two members of his regiment who had been captured with him were still at Andersonville. They were among the forty sick prisoners who were not paroled until April 28. The only prisoner held captive through Andersonville's entire existence died that day. Reduced to skeletons, most were too sick to be moved. Dan likely knew that one of his comrades already had died there. On May 4, Andersonville was effectively abandoned after the three last trains took 3,000 prisoners each to the Baldwin camp. At least two of those captured with Dan were released there.

Before leaving Macon, Wilson was instructed to give rations and provide transportation homeward to those Confederates who surrendered and were willing to take the oath of allegiance. Leaving behind only a small force to police Macon, Wilson's army marched to Atlanta, arriving about May 6. En route, on May 4, by order of General Wilson, Rodney's battery fired a 200-gun salute to mark the war's end. Dan certainly was one of the cannoneers who participated.[20]

As soon as communication was open to Augusta, Georgia, Dan requested and received permission from the Atlanta post commandant, Col. Berroth B. Eggleston, 1st Ohio Cavalry, to rejoin his New York regiment. The 123rd had pursued General Joseph E. Johnston's army to Goldsboro, North Carolina, where he surrendered on April 26. Since Dan's capture, the New Yorkers had marched more than a thousand miles. They had crossed Georgia from Atlanta to Savannah, marched through both South Carolina and North Carolina, and were well on their way to Richmond, Virginia, en route to Washington. Dan could not have known that John was in the regiment, much less exactly where the regiment was, beyond that it was in Virginia.

Dan boarded the first train he could catch to Augusta, a full day's journey from Atlanta, against advice that he should wait "till things settle down a little." It was dark when the train left, "unlighted and crowded with disbanded Confederates on their way home to their families." Fortunately, Dan had plenty of hardtack and other rations. "Before daybreak, by a generous distribution of the contents of my haversack . . . I had formed a bond of good fellowship with them that secured me from any annoyance from the few irreconcilables in the car [who] muttered threats to throw the d——d Yankee off the train. . . . The firm stand taken however by my new-made friends prevented any attempt to injure me."

Upon arrival in Augusta in the early evening, Dan reported to the colonel in command of the first regiment in Gen. Emory Upton's division to arrive there. He showed the colonel his pass to rejoin his regiment. To his surprise, the colonel turned to a nearby captain and said, "Equip this man and put him on duty." The regiment had come up the river from Savannah about May 3 to patrol the city and establish a military government. They had been sent there as soon as the news of Johnston's surrender was received. Dan spent about a week in Augusta on guard duty. The colonel told him, "I am here with a single regiment and there are ten thousand disbanded rebels in the city and more arriving every day. Many of them still retain their arms and were they so disposed, could easily over power us. I am disarming and sending them to their homes as rapidly as possible. I will put you on the first detail I send to Savannah." Dan found "pinetop" whiskey was plentiful, and vengeful leaders "were constantly inciting the [Confederate] soldiers ... to avenge their fancied wrongs."

Within a week, as soon as a brigade of reinforcements arrived on orders from General Sherman, the colonel fulfilled his promise. He offered to detail Dan to a small steam tug that was tied up on the riverbank below the city to take prisoners to Fortress Monroe. Dan gladly accepted the assignment. The tug had been sent upriver to remove torpedoes, and now the fifteen or twenty they had retrieved were lashed to the deck. The prisoners they were to take to Fortress Monroe turned out to be President Jefferson Davis, his family, and other Confederate officials.

According to U.S. Treasury records, when captured on May 10, Davis and his wife had $4,942.90 in gold and silver in their possession. The day before, General Wilson sent Secretary of War E. M. Stanton a telegram stating that Pritchard was taking every precaution to prevent Davis's escape. He wrote, "I don't think there are a hundred [Confederate] men who desire the release of Davis or would risk anything in trying to rescue him." In fact, on April 24, the *New York Herald* reported that former Confederates were hunting Davis, "induced by the reward of $2,000 offered by General Hancock."

At sunset on Sunday, May 14, the Confederate prisoners arrived from Macon at the Augusta railroad depot on a carelessly guarded special train. They were met by a half dozen carriages loaded with armed guards. Their wretched overnight train ride left Davis "haggard and ill." One of the guards described Davis's oldest daughter as "very pretty. The boys received some beautiful magnolia blossoms from her and will try to keep them for mementoes." The prisoners were driven down Telfair Street to the Lanier House, where Davis enjoyed a spacious room, had supper brought to him, and stayed the night. After supper, General

Wilson and Davis conversed. The next morning, Davis stood and tipped his hat while he and his family rode in a "jimber-jawed, wobble-sided barouche drawn by two raw-boned horses." At Augusta, while riding to the riverfront, they passed the home of nine-year-old Woodrow Wilson, who peeked through the blinds to witness the scene. They boarded the *Standish* four miles downstream, where it was tied up to avoid being detained by low water. The dirty harbor tug accommodated sixty men, but with no cabins and few furnishings. Davis sat on a suitcase, suffering from intense eye pain.

Dan was at the landing when Davis and his family got there. "Late in the evening a wagon load of trunks, boxes and bundles arrived at the landing followed by ambulances containing a dozen or more closely guarded prisoners," he later recalled. They included Davis, his wife, and their four children—Maggie, Jeff, Willie, and Varina, a baby. Many of the immense crowd of ex-Confederate soldiers lining the street to watch the procession shouted taunts and profane oaths at Davis: "Got any gold with you, Jeff?" "We want our pay!" "I haven't seen a dollar of my pay for two years." One Federal taunted a tattered Rebel, "Hey, Johnny, we've got your president." He yelled back, "And the Devil's got yours." There were enough guards armed with "seven-shooters" to keep the crowd under control.

At last, Dan was "homeward bound," or so he thought. He wrote, "No sooner were our distinguished prisoners safely on board than the lines were cast off and the boat headed downstream" for Savannah. He described Davis as "above medium height, of spare build with a face that expressed a high degree of intelligence yet showing in every outline the ravages of . . . terrific strain. . . . [I]t would have been an unforgiving nature indeed that felt not pity for the fallen but unrepentant man." Davis was dressed in a great coat and several mufflers, although the weather was warm. Another soldier described him as an "erect figure, with a somewhat martial bearing, brown hair turning gray, a keen strong face with a pallor in it . . . a look of sorrow about the lines of the firm-set mouth, a high pale forehead sharply defined above cold gray eyes that repelled sympathy." Still another soldier wrote that Mrs. Davis was as "haughty, scornful and insulting, as any woman I ever saw . . . but the children are pretty and innocent."

According to the official report of Lt. Col. Benjamin D. Pritchard of the 4th Mich., whose men captured Davis and the others on May 10, they boarded the *Standish* at 8 P.M. on May 14, and arrived near Port Royal in Savannah at 10 A.M. on May 16.

Prichard reported to Maj. Gen. Henry W. Birge, in command of the 1st Division of the Tenth Army Corps, which was occupying Savannah. The prisoners and the officers and soldiers guarding them, including

Dan, were immediately transferred to the river steamer *Emilie*. It departed for the major Union naval base at Hilton Head Island, South Carolina. Upon the *Emilie*'s arrival there, the prisoners and guards transferred to the oceangoing steamer *William P. Clyde*, a side-wheeler under the command of Capt. Enoch More. Colonel Pritchard allowed a *New York Tribune* correspondent aboard to write a story about Davis' capture. On May 16, about 3 P.M. the *Clyde* put to sea, escorted by the ten-gun sloop-of-war *Tuscarora*, captained by Commander James M. Frailey.

The *Clyde* arrived at Fortress Monroe at noon on May 19, after a stormy fifty-two-hour trip, during which almost all passengers were seasick. Captain More reported Davis was "terribly down," although he tried to keep up the morale of the prisoners and stayed on deck most of the time. En route, the captain served a bowl of punch in his cabin. While Dan stood guard outside the Davis cabin on one of the three ships, the Confederate president's oldest daughter, Maggie, age nine, stepped out. According to family legend, Dan attempted to pat her on the head, but she bit his thumb. Varina, Davis's infant daughter, had become a favorite with the guards. On the march to Augusta the soldiers had taken turns holding her for a while and then passing her along the line.

The *Clyde* and the *Tuscarora* anchored offshore at Old Point Comfort in Hampton Roads, surrounded by a cordon of warships, to await the arrival of Maj. Gen. H. W. Halleck the next day. Dan and the other guards remained aboard ship for three days, until May 22, dismissing all prisoners except Davis, Clement C. Clay, Jr.—who was suspected of involvement in Lincoln's assassination—and their families. The *Atlantic Monthly* wrote that there were men among the guards "who had been prisoners at Andersonville, but they spoke of [Davis] without malice; they only asked for justice as they recalled their fearful experience." Most likely, the correspondent spoke with Dan, who was one of the men he described.

About 3 P.M. on May 23, Davis and Clay were transferred by tugboat to casemates in Fortress Monroe, a six-sided stone structure surrounded by a moat, known as "the Gibraltar of the Chesapeake." Davis exhibited little emotion except when he said good-bye to his wife and children. The two Rebel leaders were turned over to Maj. Gen. Nelson Miles, who arrived from Baltimore aboard the steamer *Silas C. Pierce*. Once transferred to the *Pierce*, Davis was seated under a large American flag, his face "flushed but arrogant." He wore a thin, dark overcoat and a drab, slouched felt hat. Miles was elegantly dressed in his blue and gold uniform. At Fortress Monroe, Miles held Davis tightly by the right arm as he escorted him down the *Pierce*'s gangplank. Davis's wife and children were taken back to Savannah on the *Clyde*.

On the wharf at Fortress Monroe, Dan Ross and the other guards kept onlookers back a distance of 500 yards from Davis. Twenty-five 4th

Mich. cavalrymen armed with Sharp's repeating rifles guarded each side of the gangplank to prevent Davis from jumping overboard. Casemate number 2, a ten-by-fourteen-foot subterranean gun room, had been converted by stone masons into a prison cell for his incarceration behind the fort's thirty-foot thick granite walls. Forbidden to talk with him, six sentinels guarded Davis in silence. The cold, damp, rat-infested casemate contained only a table, chair, sofa, and iron cot with a straw pallet. The next day guards locked leg irons and chains to his ankles. No visitors were allowed unless issued a pass by the post commander. His accommodations improved somewhat over time, but Davis would remain in that cell for two years. Without ever being brought to trial for treason, he was released from prison on $100,000 bail in May 1867. By then his straw pallet was infested with lice and bedbugs. The case for treason was dismissed in February 1869.

On May 23, the *Tuscarora* sailed up the Potomac for Washington, DC, carrying Colonel Pritchard. He was under orders to deliver to Secretary of War Edwin M. Stanton some of the clothing Davis was wearing at the time of his capture—a lady's waterproof cloak and a shawl belonging to his wife. Pritchard's guard detail by then consisted of five officers and seventy men, including the officers and men from his own regiment and a detachment of Maine troops, which returned to Savannah aboard the *Clyde* to rejoin their regiment. The balance of the guard detail, including Dan, remained at Fortress Monroe under Gen. Nelson Miles, commandant.

Star of the South

Dan was released from guard duty and, on May 27, boarded the 650-ton steamer *Star of the South* at Fortress Monroe to complete his journey up the Potomac River to Washington, DC, and ultimately to rejoin his regiment. In November 1864, the *Star of the South* had been fitted with stalls to accommodate seventy-five cavalry and artillery horses. Before he could join his regiment, however, Dan was to assist in unloading a cargo of horses to be purchased in Maryland, upstream from the capital, and then shipped to Texas in June.[21]

According to family legend, somewhere near Little Georgetown, West Virginia, across the river from Maryland, while loading or unloading these horses, Dan was kicked by one. He remained behind a few days to recover, staying with a family named Ropp, whose farm bordered the Potomac River near the Johnston Ferry landing. Two years earlier Dan had formed an attachment to the area while serving there. Now, during his recuperation, Ropp urged him to return to the village and teach school after his military discharge.

He arrived in Washington, DC, on May 30, too late to join his regiment and his brother John in the May 24 Grand Review of Sherman's Army by President Johnson and Generals Grant and Sherman. On June 8, he was mustered out with his regiment and, on June 9, left Washington with the rest of the 123rd to return home with his brother.

Of the twelve men from the 123rd N.Y. sent to Andersonville, one died there and one escaped. Eight were paroled from there, and one from Charleston between November 1864 and April 28, 1865, two days after General Johnston surrendered to General Sherman at Bentonville, North Carolina. By April 28, only a handful of prisoners remained at Andersonville, including the last two New Yorkers, all of them walking skeletons.

Once the South finally agreed to exchange all prisoners in January 1865, several thousand a week were exchanged until the war's end. The Rebels, however, chose to exchange only those men who had been prisoners for at least six months and were therefore totally unfit for duty. They were exchanged at Rough and Ready, about twenty miles from Atlanta. Included among these were two of Dan's companions who had been captured with him at Kolb's Farm. At the time of their exchange, one was still at Andersonville, and the other was at Florence, South Carolina.[22]

The only compensation Dan received from the army for his imprisonment was for commutation of his rations, at the rate of 25¢ per day for the 286 days he spent in prison. This amounted to $72.50, and even that paltry amount was not paid to him until October 1868.

12

Capture of Atlanta
September–November 1864

> Whatever Old Billy does is right. He does the plotting and flanking; let us do the fighting and things will go on.
>
> —An old soldier in the 123rd N.Y.

While Pvt. Dan Ross was enduring inhuman treatment akin to Holocaust victims in Andersonville Prison, on September 1, 1864, his youngest brother took his place in the 123rd N.Y. Volunteer Infantry. President Lincoln had called for 500,000 more volunteers on July 4, assigning quotas to every city, town, and township in the country. The quota for Salem Township, Washington County, where John lived, was fifty-four. The call was filled promptly, and the only bounties John or any of the others received were $33.33 from the federal government and $50 from Washington County. On August 26, the *Washington County Post* published a letter from the 123rd stating, "All we want is a few able-bodied young men in Washington County to fill our regiment. . . . We will give them a hearty welcome and a good chance for honor and glory." That is all John needed to hear.

Elsewhere in the North, it took bounty payments as high as $1,000 to attract enlistees in response to Lincoln's call. Just over the minimum age of eighteen, John Doty Ross needed parental consent to enlist for one year in case he took liberty of the truth about his age. His father gave it, despite urgently needing his son's help on the family farm following a destructive hailstorm, a fearful wind, and then a drought that had destroyed half their crops. Charles and Margaret had faced the added burden of heartbreaking news received that summer about their three other sons: Will dead, Lank blinded and in the hospital, and Dan captured and sent to Andersonville, a hellhole of a prison. Pvt. John Ross, five feet seven and one-half inches tall, with light hair and complexion and brown eyes, was assigned to Dan's Company H, under Lt. Robert Cruikshank, who had been within ten feet of Dan when he was captured. John was the youngest of the fifty-four recruits, the majority of whom joined the 123rd.

After John and his fellow recruits left New York, they were sent first to Hart's Island in New York and then to the capital. Sprawling forts, camps, and earthworks were spread over thousands of acres around Washington, manned by tens of thousands of troops. Soldiers crowded into the streets, restaurants, and bars viewing the sights and otherwise doing the town. The city was crammed with hospitals accommodating 29,000 sick and wounded soldiers. Artillery, wagons, commissary warehouses, and horses were in overabundance. New regiments arrived constantly to replace those that already had received basic training and were leaving for the battlefront. John and the other newcomers also received rudimentary training while there.

The 123rd's last assignment, before entering Atlanta, had been to guard the railroad bridge across the Chattahoochie River. According to Sergeant McLean's letter of August 29 to his father, the bridge was on a trestle 180 feet above the river; Sherman's engineers had built the trestle as part of their supply line. Their pleasant and well-fortified camp was on the riverbank in a grove of large trees and guarded by artillery. The regiment had been there since August 25. After not having bathed for weeks they all went swimming. He wrote, "The river is full of Yanks all the time. Quite a novelty to see a thousand or two in the water at once."

The New Yorkers realized the political implications of capturing Atlanta, immediately following the surrender of Mobile Bay. Private Cutter noted, "Won't this help . . . elect Father Abraham . . . and end the war sooner. . . . We will attend to rebels in arms if the people at home will attend to the Copperheads." Sergeant McLean wrote, "The news of taking this place will not . . . help [McClellan] the Chicago [Democrat] nominee." Needless to say, Sherman also knew the vital importance of Atlanta to Lincoln's reelection. On August 25, he began his movement to isolate the city from the rest of the Confederacy. To do so, he left Slocum's entire 20th Corps well-entrenched at the railroad bridge and used the rest of his army to encircle Atlanta. Slocum's men, including the 123rd, were to guard the armies trains, the depot, reserve artillery, and the hospitals.

The main plank in the Democrats' platform was that Lincoln's war was a costly failure. Earlier that month, on August 6, sixty-three-year-old

Admiral Farragut directed his men to lash him to the mast of his flagship, twenty feet above the deck so he could see over the battle smoke. He ordered his eighteen ships to attack the defenses of Mobile Bay with his famous order "Damn the torpedoes! Full speed ahead." By August 23, all Confederate ships were sunk or captured and all forts surrounding the bay had been pounded into submission by continuous and heavy naval bombardment. The bay was now the North's.

At sunrise on September 2, the New Yorkers were ordered to be ready to march toward Atlanta in search of the enemy. At eleven o'clock, a 900-man battalion from at least a half dozen regiments in two other brigades of Slocum's corps, plus a cavalry detachment under Col. John Coburn, met the Atlanta mayor to accept his surrender of the city. General Slocum, who had been assigned by Sherman to replace Hooker as head of the 20th Corps on August 27, arrived around two o'clock, greeted by "hearty cheers as he rode along the line the first time." Rufus Mead, of the 5th Connecticut, wrote, "I am sorry Hooker has left us but he is not the only general we had confidence in; in fact we have all good ones here now." Slocum established his headquarters at the leading hotel, the Trout House, sent a courier to Sherman telling him Atlanta had fallen, and wired Washington, "General Sherman has taken Atlanta." The fact that Atlanta fell two days after McClellan's nomination was a body blow to his presidential campaign against Lincoln. The New Yorkers were the first complete regiment to enter the city, arriving about three o'clock. The first thing they did was help themselves to a three-month supply of cigars and tobacco. According to Sergeant Bull, they cheered as they entered the city singing, "We will hang Jeff Davis on a sour apple tree," "Hail Columbia," and "The Red, White and Blue," accompanied by loud huzzahs for Uncle Billy.

About 9 P.M., with bands playing, General Williams led Knipe's and one other of his brigades into the city. Williams reported that he heard a window open and a woman's voice cry, "Welcome." Other women waved white handkerchiefs or brought buckets of water for his troops, who had quick-marched into the city and were sweating profusely. Blacks lined the streets hailing the soldiers as their deliverers sent by God. Sherman and his staff did not arrive until the morning of September 7, without fanfare. Nevertheless, Sherman was in what he called his "high feather" mood, having accomplished his mission.

According to Pvt. John Cutter, the New Yorkers arrived in Atlanta with only their guns. Their haversacks and other gear "were brought up last night [September 3] by wagons. Meantime we have been living on rebel corn, blackberries, a few apples, and almost anything we could get. Johnnies had stripped the countryside. The citizens feed a great many of the boys gratis... we slept in some shanties built by the rebel soldiers." On September 3, Sergeant MacLean wrote, "Talk about Nero fiddling while Rome burned, we beat that here. I saw a Yankee sitting on top of a large pile of smoking timbers... playing away on a harp he had picked up.... He cut quite a grotesque figure, outNeroing Nero, completely." Cruikshank wrote his wife, "[T]he campaign is over [and] we all feel pretty well used up." While the city was under siege, out-of-control Rebel soldiers had raided shops and homes and terrified the citizens. Residents did their share of looting as well. Sherman's troops carried off what they wanted of whatever was left in the deserted stores, but made little effort to disturb the citizenry. Private Eaton wrote his wife that many of the "Secosh [sic] [had left] the [city] and those that are here seem to be very fine people and treat us very well." Guards were soon posted and all the pilfering stopped. Some soldiers initially camped in the yards of good Union families and made friends with the children. In at least one case soldiers befriended a good Union dog who slept in one corner of their tent.

The captures of Atlanta and Mobile Bay, one of the last major port blockades, and Sheridan's month-long raid throughout the Shenandoah Valley had broken a military and political logjam. Sheridan had destroyed the last vestige of forage for confederate man and beast in the Shenandoah Valley, after which the press labeled him "peace commissioner." At the same time, from the military standpoint, war goods that were produced in the west of the Confederacy could no longer feed major military action in the east, from Savannah to Richmond. They assured Lincoln's reelection, pumped up the North's will to win, and shattered much of the South's remaining will to fight. Lee had sent Gen. Jubal Early into the valley to threaten Washington, with the hope that Grant would withdraw some of his troops from Petersburg to defend Washington. It didn't work. Next, Grant ordered General Sherman to pursue General Early "and follow him to the death." The political scale tilted from one side to the other, accelerated by Fremont's withdrawal on September 19 from the presidential race, thereby preventing the Republican vote from splitting and further reducing McClellan's chance of defeating Lincoln. Sergeant Mead wrote his folks, "Such news as this won't help McClellan stock any." The next day General Williams celebrated his fifty-fourth birthday by reviewing his division. Afterward the troops marched in review past Sherman's and Thomas's headquarters. In the rain, while everybody got "pretty well soaked," Sherman came out to the street and declared that Williams's soldiers could never be beaten. Each general received "three as hearty cheers as were ever heard." Later, Williams ordered that the troops be issued a ration of whiskey, presumably to help celebrate his birthday.

After Slocum's entire 20th Corps, including the 123rd, entered the city, Slocum was put in charge of garrisoning it and resupplying the entire army in preparation for its "grand march," as Sherman put it. He had just completed a similar assignment at Vicksburg after its capture.

Atlanta was the wall that had protected the Cotton State. Its fall electrified the North and its voters. Northerners celebrated as if it were the end of the war. Crowds marched, cheered, and sang. Orators had a field day. Firecrackers exploded. Vicious newspaper and political attacks on Lincoln ceased. Church bells rang in every city. Lincoln ordered a one-hundred-gun salute in Washington and in every navy yard and arsenal. Lincoln also urged that thanks be offered to God the following Sunday "in all places of worship." Grant celebrated by ordering every gun "bearing upon the enemy" to fire a salute toward Petersburg, which he had under siege.

In contrast, the Confederate generals Lee, Bragg, and others called for clemency, amnesty, or pardons for deserters, and reduction of the number of civilian occupations exempted from conscription, including millers, blacksmiths, shoemakers, even justices of the peace. James Seddon, the Confederate secretary of war, estimated that 50 percent of eligible men were absent from the army, while President Davis estimated that two-thirds were absentees. Grant urged Sherman to rest his troops in Atlanta, but to begin another campaign as soon as possible in order to press the enemy continually. He sent Horace Porter, his staffer, to determine Sherman's plans, explaining, "My object now in sending a staff officer is not so much to suggest operations for you as to get your views and have plans matured by the time everything can be got ready." When Porter arrived by freight train, Sherman was seated on the front porch of his headquarters, a comfortable brick house near the Courthouse Square. He was reading a newspaper, his feet in slippers, his coat unbuttoned, and his black felt hat pulled down onto his forehead.

In the four months it took Sherman's army to reach Atlanta, the 20th Corps had done more hard fighting, suffered more casualties (over one-third of its initial strength), and put more Rebels out of action than any of the other six corps in Sherman's army. The men needed a rest. Yet it was vital they help Sherman convert Atlanta into a fortified military depot, a Gibraltar that could be held by a small garrison. This conversion, completed by October 1, required the evacuation of some 1,600 hostile civilians, in order to avoid the burden of governing and feeding them. Sherman had seen whole divisions of troops used to feed and protect civilians after Memphis, Vicksburg, New Orleans, and Natchez were captured. He would not allow that to happen again in Atlanta, where there was no food to feed the local population. Garrisoning required shortening and retracting defensive works toward the center of the city, which meant destroying some of its finest homes, because they were left outside the defense line. Citizens and freed slaves helped with this work, according to Sergeant Cook. One hundred of the New Yorkers were assigned daily to this task, demolishing unneeded buildings and using the remaining buildings for stockpiling massive military supplies for the coming campaign. Work continued night and day until completed. Evenings were now getting cooler, and the mosquitoes were, fortunately, dying off. To encourage the men to perform this arduous labor, their rations were doubled and a half gill of whiskey was issued daily.

On September 4, their first Sunday in Atlanta, almost all the New Yorkers attended church. Cruikshank wrote his wife that this was the first time in a year that he had been inside a church. He also assured her, "I make it a practice to read two chapters in the Bible every day and more if I have time." On September 11, the entire brigade was moved to the northeast quarter of the city on a commanding ridge that gave them a strong defensive position in case the city was attacked. It was a pleasant place with good water. They built "excellent quarters" that were paragons of "neatness and regularity," using lumber, doors, and windows salvaged from the demolished buildings. Sherman also barred sutlers and traders from entering the city. Many men considered sutlers "the vultures of the army."

On September 22 they heard the glorious news of Sheridan's victory in the Shenandoah Valley. Rufus Mead, of the 5th Conn., wrote, "How encouraging everything progresses lately."

On September 29, Lieutenant Martin, who had been captured on the skirmish line at Kolb's Farm the same day as Dan, arrived in Atlanta to rejoin his regiment. What a surprise, and what a sorrowful sight! He had escaped from the Charleston prison twice. To escape, he bribed a Confederate officer, hid in a swamp overnight, and was bitten by a snake but recovered. After he was recaptured, he was returned to the Charleston prison, fed two spoonfuls of rice and one of lard daily until September 25, then escaped again. He smuggled himself aboard a railroad car and went as far as Macon, Georgia. From there, with another escapee, he traveled by foot to Atlanta, eluding bloodhounds. He reported that "the rest of our boys [including Dan] are at Andersonville and [are] starving." He was granted twenty days leave. However, upon learning that the army was likely to leave Atlanta before his leave expired, he refused to take it. Martin had been an out-and-out McClellan man before his capture. But Rebel guards told him during his captivity that if Little Mac were elected president, he would save the Confederacy, which was enough to make him a strong Lincoln supporter. Likewise, Pvt. John Gourlie of

Soldiers voting in camp

the 123rd, switched his allegiance from McClellan. He wrote that he had become "a Lincoln man to the backbone."[1]

On October 3, Sherman took the rest of his troops, some 55,000 men, out of Atlanta to repair and guard his Western and Atlantic Railroad supply line and pursue General Hood's battered army to keep it from breaking his communications, food, and supply lines. Knowing that Hood was nowhere nearby, Slocum began to forage liberally in the countryside in order to feed his troops and 4,000 almost starved horses and mules. Meat was scarce. However, 8,000 head of cattle were safe from Rebel raids at Atlanta but the rail line was not repaired until October 14.

Meanwhile, they repaired the railroad all the way back to Chattanooga so that supplies could be delivered. At one point, the Rebels ruptured the line for eight miles. To repair it, 10,000 men worked for a week replacing 35,000 ties and six miles of iron. This and other incidents convinced Sherman that he could not protect the railroad from Atlanta all the way back to Chattanooga. He wrote Grant, "By attempting to hold [these] roads, we will lose a thousand men each month, and gain no result. [Instead] I can make this march to Savannah and make Georgia howl. We have on hand over 8,000 head of cattle, and 3,000,000 rations of bread, but no corn. We can find plenty of forage in the interior."

On October 18, election commissioners came from New York and several other states to gather the soldiers' vote in the presidential election. Private Mathews recorded in his diary that he voted that day and sent the ballot to his father, as did Sergeant McLean. The New Yorkers voted 336 for Lincoln, 30 for McClellan, a 91 percent majority for Uncle Abe. Company A voted unanimously for Lincoln, according to Cook. John's Company H voted 22 for Lincoln, 5 for McClellan. Ninety other members of the 123rd were too young to cast ballots, and John had not yet arrived. By then the men had probably heard the news that on October 13, Maryland voters had adopted a new state constitution abolishing slavery. A soldier in the 147th Pa., another regiment in William's division, recorded, "The expression in the army is nearly universal for Lincoln . . . at least in our Div. . . . The Copperheads will receive a terrible rebuke from the army on election day." Clearly, by election day Sherman's army was solidly behind Lincoln. Sergeant Mead of the 5th Conn. had predicted in a September 19 letter to his folks, "We will all vote for him, almost to a man."

On October 18, General Williams wrote his daughter, "[I]f I was at home I would vote for A. Linkum." Williams had had only one personal contact with Lincoln. In early October 1862, when Lincoln visited the Antietam battlefield, Lincoln and Williams sat on a log for a long talk. Williams described Lincoln as "the most unaffected . . . honest and frank man I ever met." On October 19, Sherman wrote General Halleck that "his March to the Sea was not purely military or strategic. . . . They don't know what war means; but when the rich planters of the Oconee and Savannah [rivers] see their fences and corn, and hogs and sheep vanish . . . they will have something more than a mean opinion of the 'Yanks.' Even now our poor mules laugh at the fine corn-fields, and our soldiers riot on chestnuts, sweet potatoes, pigs, and chickens." On October 21, Cruikshank wrote his wife about the election. "I feel confident that Mr. Lincoln will be reelected," he wrote. "I have done all I could for him . . . I would rather stay in the service another year than have it settled as the Copperheads would have it."

On October 21, at daylight, 7,000 men, including the 123rd, took part in a four-day foraging trip beyond Stone Mountain for both the men and the poor animals. Scurvy had become a problem because of lack of fresh vegetables, and fresh meat was in short supply because of lack of forage. While foraging they were enraged to find the still-warm bodies of Union soldiers who had been hanged, some with their throats cut. The area had abounded in corn, fodder, sweet potatoes, honey, poultry, farm animals, and nuts, but foraging activity had been so intense within a radius of twenty miles that the landscape was devastated. They returned October 24 with 928 wagons—128 more than they started with—loaded with corn and fodder. Sergeant McLean wrote in his diary, "Our [wagon] train presents a comical appearance. Vehicles of all kinds drawn by all sorts of animals."

On September 23, Lieutenant Cruikshank wrote his wife that if the men were not paid before they were to vote on October 18 in the presidential election, "it will make many votes for McClellan." If Lincoln actually did lose votes to "Little Mac" because payday was eighteen days after they voted, it was a mere handful, since only thirty votes altogether were cast for him.

By October 31, the 20th Corps had been told to "pack up" and get ready to move, but did not know where or when they were going. Sherman had told Grant he was ready to move as soon as the election was over. By telegram Grant convinced Lincoln that "Sherman's proposition is the best that can be adopted." Within three hours after receipt of this telegram, Secretary of War Stanton telegraphed Sherman his complete approval. The trio of Lincoln, Grant, and Sherman was now harnessed. All was bustle and confusion in Atlanta with preparations for the march, which Sherman wanted to coincide with the fall harvest season. On November 2, each man was issued an extra pair of shoes, and all surplus baggage was sent to the rear. Each officer in a company had to consolidate his baggage into a single valise. On November 6, the paymaster arrived and gave veterans eight of their ten months' back pay, then completed arrangements to send it home. Chaplain White left for his home in Salem, close to where the Rosses lived, taking with him many of the lads' back pay to deliver to their families.

Not until the next day did Grant give Sherman final, unqualified approval for his march to the sea. Both men knew that if Sherman should fail to capture Savannah, a seaport and a new Confederate supply base, he would destroy both his army and his reputation.[2] Protecting Sherman's rear was an army of 31,000 under Maj. Gen. George H. Thomas. Thomas faced Hood's Army of Tennessee, 40,000 strong, as well as Forrest's 7,000 roving cavalrymen. Sherman wrote Grant, "On the supposition always that Thomas can hold the line of the Tennessee... I propose to act against the material resources of the South." Sherman was both confident and respectful of Thomas. They had been West Point roommates and served for ten years in the same regiments. When Lincoln offered Sherman a brigadiership at the beginning of the war, he refused it. He suggested instead that the president nominate Thomas, asserting "Old Tom... as a soldier... is superior to all on your list."

In contrast to Thomas's odds, Sherman had to contend with only about 15,000 untrained, untested, and poorly led Georgia militia able to take the field at any one time. Some 3,400 Confederate cavalry under General Wheeler were available to support the militia and harass Sherman's foragers, but they were no match for Sherman's horse soldiers.

Prior to launching his march to the sea, Sherman made an offer to Gov. Joseph E. Brown of Georgia. In exchange for withdrawal of his state militia from Confederate service, the Union army would cross the state with minimum impact, paying for all the corn and fodder they used. If not, Sherman vowed to inflict destruction across its length and breadth. Brown declined on the pretext that they were needed to harvest the crops, so Sherman destroyed the rail and telegraph lines to Chattanooga as they left Atlanta, including eleven bridges that he had rebuilt, and anything remaining in Atlanta that could be used against him. By November 12, all rail and telegraph communications with the North were severed. Sherman's reputation as the grim reaper was established. He told his newest aide, Maj. Henry Hitchcock, "[W]e have been fighting Atlanta all the time ... have been capturing guns, wagons, etc. etc.... and now since they have been doing so much to destroy us ... we have to destroy them, at least to prevent any more of that." This included "unbuilding" the Southern railroads. Instantly struck by Sherman's self-confidence and character, Hitchcock noted in his diary that Sherman's intelligence was "the sort of power which a flash of lightning suggests"—clear, intense, and rapid.

It took John and his thirty-two fellow 123rd recruits two and a half months to reach their regiment in Atlanta on November 11, four days before Sherman's march to the sea began. They would have reported to Lieutenant Cruikshank. The recently appointed provost marshal for the brigade, Cruikshank likely told John details about his brother Dan's capture at Kolb's Farm, since he had actually witnessed it.

Together with ten other new recruits who had arrived in Atlanta September 23, the newcomers plus convalescents who had returned to the regiment, swelled the ranks of the 123rd N.Y. to 465 men and officers. They had started the Atlanta campaign at Chattanooga with 523 effectives. Forty-two men and three officers were now in John's Company H, including two of his fellow Washington County recruits. The regiment had lost 11 officers and 141 men, including Dan, during its four-month march with Sherman from Chattanooga to Atlanta between April 27 and September 2, virtually the same number of casualties it incurred in the two-day Battle of Chancellorsville. Many of these casualties, like Dan and the sixteen others captured with him on June 22, occurred on various skirmish lines before reaching Atlanta.

John and the other new volunteers were about to learn the art and science of skirmishing from the veterans in the regiment. Lt. Col. James

C. Rogers reported the newcomers were "a good class of men but . . . there was little opportunity to properly instruct them in drill."

When Sherman began his march to the sea on November 15, 1864, his army had 62,000 men in 218 regiments. Of those, there were 55,000 tough and robust infantrymen in 173 veteran regiments. Two of the four regiments in John's brigade were Veteran Volunteers and the other two were three-year men. More than 78 percent of these men had enlisted first in 1861 or early 1862. Nearly all had fought in the West, where campaigns and marches were long and food and supplies short. Nearly half of Sherman's men had reenlisted as Veteran Volunteers, compared to one in sixteen in the army as a whole. All of the eligible regiments in General Williams's division, to which the 123rd N.Y. belonged, had reenlisted as Veteran Volunteers. Many of these veteran regiments had begun the war with 1,000 men, but now were reduced to an average of 320. The 123rd had 408 enlisted men present for duty before the 43 recruits, including John, arrived in September and November. Most of the veterans had survived two years of war, heat, cold, mud, dust, fatigue, disease, starvation rations, and wounds. Yet they were restless in their pleasant camp that had good water and desirable accommodations.

Sherman stated he was committed "to demonstrate the vulnerability of the South . . . and to make its inhabitants feel that war and individual ruin are synonymous terms." Unlike other Northern generals, he was convinced that the war had to be waged against the entire South, not just its armies. In particular, he wanted the plantation class, which had precipitated the war, to pay for their folly personally. Sherman's mission was to consume and destroy, not to fight, so he and his soldiers vastly preferred attacking affluent plantation owners' property to battling Southern soldiers. Significantly, poor farmers, on the whole, gave his army little trouble, even with respect to emancipation of slaves. With Sherman's encouragement, they set out to ruin the plantation class, and did so.

The realization that the war in Georgia could weaken the Confederate effort in Virginia was a significant strategic factor to Grant, to Sherman, to the Army Chief of Staff Henry Halleck, and to Lincoln. Grant had urged Sherman to commit total war in Georgia, writing, "[M]ove against Johnston's army, to break it up and to get into the interior of the enemy's country as far as you can, inflicting all the damage you can upon their war resources." Halleck wrote, "I am fully of the opinion . . . that the conduct of the enemy . . . will justify you in gathering up all the forage and provisions which your army will require, both for a siege of Atlanta and for your supply in your march further into the enemy's country. . . . I would destroy every mill and factory within reach which I did not want for my own use."

Despite their relative inexperience, John and most of his fellow recruits would prove they could measure up to the vigorous battle-hardened veterans. Medical inspectors had purged his army of men who were sick, wounded, old, infirm, or otherwise unfit for a long march. Some, with soon-to-expire terms who thought the march was too risky, elected to go home. The rest were sent back to Chattanooga or Nashville. Sherman regarded them all as "trash." A few men who arrived in Atlanta so lame they were incapable of marching were sent by Dr. Kennedy to a convalescent hospital in Chattanooga, against their will. A few of the New Yorkers had arrived lame in Atlanta. Sergeant Cook's ankles and feet were so swollen he could not march, probably because of scurvy. He had not told his parents about his condition until after he arrived in Chattanooga.

Those that remained in Atlanta were experienced, well armed, newly clothed, physically strong, well equipped, immune to camp diseases, and unencumbered by excess baggage. Their sickness rate while on the march was about half that of the rest of the Northern army during the same period. They also were very young. Many regimental colonels were under thirty, and most men were in their late teens or early twenties. Sherman wrote General Halleck, "We have good corporals and sergeants, and some good lieutenants, and those are more important than generals." As a result of two or more years of campaigning, company-level noncoms and officers had learned to perform tasks independent of higher supervision. Sherman's incredible understanding of these officers proved invaluable when he needed to select some for special assignments. By then, he had rid his command of incompetent political appointees and regular army officers. Lieutenant Cruikshank was an example of the men he wanted. He had enlisted as a private, earned a commission, and become Dan's company commander before he was captured in June 1864. By the time John arrived in Atlanta, 1st Lieutenant Cruikshank had been promoted to acting provost marshal of his brigade.

The remaining men gained a sense that they were an elite corps. Motivated by supreme confidence in themselves and their officers, especially Sherman, they had boundless esprit de corps. Simply put, they idolized him, and called him "Uncle Billy" out of admiration, devotion, and obedience. Sherman was mindful of the value of that devotion: "Men march to certain death without a murmur if I call on them, because they know I value their lives as much as my own." He was bold, daring, and self-confident, and inspired the same attributes in his men. General Slocum was convinced that Sherman's self-confidence was nothing less than remarkable. Sergeant Mead wrote his parents, "You ought to see [Sherman] as he rides along... he reminds you of a circuit preacher. So sober and thoughtful... he is the least pretending of any of our generals."

Sherman had fought more battles, marched farther, served in more theaters, and faced more Southern generals than any other Northern general. Yet to him "the glory of combat... is all moonshine; even success, the most brilliant, is over dead and mangled bodies." Sherman praised Williams in his role as 20th Corps commander and for his fighting abilities, and recommended him for promotion to major general. In turn, Williams considered Sherman "daring and sagacious in his plans but never rash.... He moved the large subdivisions of his great army with the precision and harmony of the field-day maneuvers of a well-drilled division."[3]

In preparation for leaving Atlanta, trains headed north with the sick and the wounded, along with surplus artillery. They returned with food and ammunition, recruits, and veterans returning from furlough. Soldiers sent surplus baggage to Chattanooga and received winter clothing in return. Sherman was using only forty wagons for every 1,000 men instead of fifty-two, the standard number, carefully overhauling and loading every one of them for a wagon train that would stretch twenty-five miles. It included 600 ambulance wagons for those who would become ill or be wounded during the march. Most wagons were needed to haul ammunition, provisions, forage, and cooking utensils. From the start his army was exceptionally free of disease and remained so throughout the march, aside from some mild scurvy. Sherman's only personal health problem was asthma. Little canvas was carried, because Sherman believed that tents were a luxury to be used in camp but not in the field. He allowed tents only for the sick and wounded, and used only a tent fly and pine boughs for his own shelter and bed.

On this count, Sherman was in sharp contrast to General Thomas, whose men referred to his campsites as "Thomasville." Sherman wrote his wife, "[I]f one tent is carried, any quantity of trash will down the wagon. I will set the example myself." The artillery mounted sixty-five guns, about one for every 1,000 men; each gun was drawn by an eight-horse team. A fifth of the wagons hauled ammunition, enough to provide 200 rounds per man. Rations loaded into the wagons at Atlanta consisted of twenty days' hard bread, forty days' sugar and coffee, and eighty days' salt. A herd of 10,000 cattle—forty days' beef on the hoof—accompanied the wagon train. Officers subsisted on the same rations as the men. The average load on a six-mule wagon weighed 2,500 pounds.[4]

At the start, the mules were in very poor condition, most not having recovered from near starvation at Chattanooga. One soldier wrote,

"You never saw a dead mule and rarely a dead horse. Here roads are McAdamized with them—creeks, springs, rivers, houses, barns, everywhere there are living dead about, the whole county is putrid with them." As many as ten a day belonging to John's brigade died in Atlanta for lack of forage. To feed them, they were driven out of the city every day, under guard, to graze. Many more died or were killed during the march, but were replaced by healthy animals acquired on foraging expeditions. By the end of the campaign, the mule teams were in splendid condition. Fresh food for the men and forage for horses and mules became abundant by the third day of the march. As Sherman anticipated, plantation crops had already been harvested and stored in barns and granaries. This abundance and easy access to it were fortunate for his 25,000 animals, since Sherman had started the march with only four days' rations of oats and corn for them. Meanwhile the men foraged ample fresh sweet potatoes, corn, wheat, rice, poultry, pork, lamb, and beef.

When a group of foragers confiscated one flock of sheep, the farmer appealed to Sherman, who replied that Confederate soldiers had broken his railroad supply line. Because his army was "a strong, hungry crowd [and] Uncle Sam was deeply interested in our continued health ... we deeply preferred Illinois beef but mutton would have to answer." Foragers were more often referred to as "bummers," "smokehouse rangers," "corn crib commandos," or "professors of foraging." Bummers also served as "feelers." By keeping in advance and on the flanks of the main column they could spy out the land and the enemy. John undoubtedly did his share of foraging.

Sherman's saddlebags contained cigars, a change of underwear, and a flask of whiskey. Sherman's army was now ready to fulfill Grant's prophecy: "Sherman's army is somewhat in the condition of a groundmole when he disappears under a lawn. You can here and there trace his track but you are not quite certain where he will come out, till you see his head."

13

March to the Sea and Beyond
November 1864–April 1865

> I do believe that the whole United States, North and South, would rejoice to have the army turned loose on South Carolina [and] it would have a direct and immediate bearing on your campaign in Virginia.
>
> —Gen. William T. Sherman, Letter to Lt. Gen. Ulysses S. Grant, December 13, 1864

At 4 A.M. on November 15, the regimental drum corps beat the morning call and clear-toned bugles sounded reveille. The only other sound that could be heard was the neighing of horses. Once again, the 123rd New Yorkers would be in the lead brigade of the 20th Corps as it marched eastward out of Atlanta at 7 A.M., four days after John arrived. This would be his first daylong march with a full pack. He and the other recruits must have spent most of their four days in Atlanta sweating mightily while loading mountains of supplies into Sherman's 2,500 wagons. By the time the march began, the men had cooked and eaten breakfast, packed their haversacks with two days' rations of bacon and hard bread, five of sugar, and ten of coffee and suet. They surely must have thought about their future accommodations as they dismantled the comfortable little cottages with floors and windows. Flankers and skirmishers went out first to send any would-be Rebel attackers "kiting."

At the command "Right shoulder shift," the troops shouldered their well-used rifles and strapped on knapsacks. Next came "Forward march" and they began their long, swinging strides eastward along Decatur Road, singing "John Brown's Body" and "The Battle Hymn of the Republic," favorites of the abolitionists. Major Hitchcock, Sherman's aide, wrote that "never before or since have I heard the chorus of Glory, Glory, Hallelujah done with more spirit, or in better harmony of time and place." As John Ross looked back over his shoulder, he could see the appalling smoke and flames of the burning city. It was a raging inferno, huge waves of fire roiling into the sky. Prior to the army's departure, individual fire-setting was strongly discouraged. In fact, General Slocum offered a $500 reward for the arrest of any of his soldiers caught setting a fire.

John Doty Ross

Nevertheless, the night before departure, campfires were lit and the happy-go-lucky ones fed them with the furniture they had built or accumulated. The last message sent before the telegraph wires were cut was to General Thomas: "All is well." Atlanta could no longer produce 25,000 small-arms cartridges a day or any other war materiel, much less ship it.

John was participating in his first campaign with the Army of Georgia under Maj. Gen. Henry W. Slocum, with General Williams commanding the 20th Corps. His brother Dan had fought under Slocum and Williams at Chancellorsville and Gettysburg. It was also under Slocum that Dan had guarded the railroad supply line to Chattanooga that fed their brother Lank and his comrades. A small man with a large mustache, Slocum combined the qualities of a hard-bitten, hot-tempered, brusque soldier with a soft heart. He wrote his wife a week before they left Atlanta, "I wish for humanity's sake that this sad war could be brought to a close. While laboring to make it successful, I shall do all in my power to mitigate its horrors." Sherman described Slocum as "one of the best soldiers and best men that ever lived." He would not tolerate a word against him.

The march began on a fine day, cloudy and cool; the road was hard and dry, and no enemy was in their path. The 123rd marched fourteen

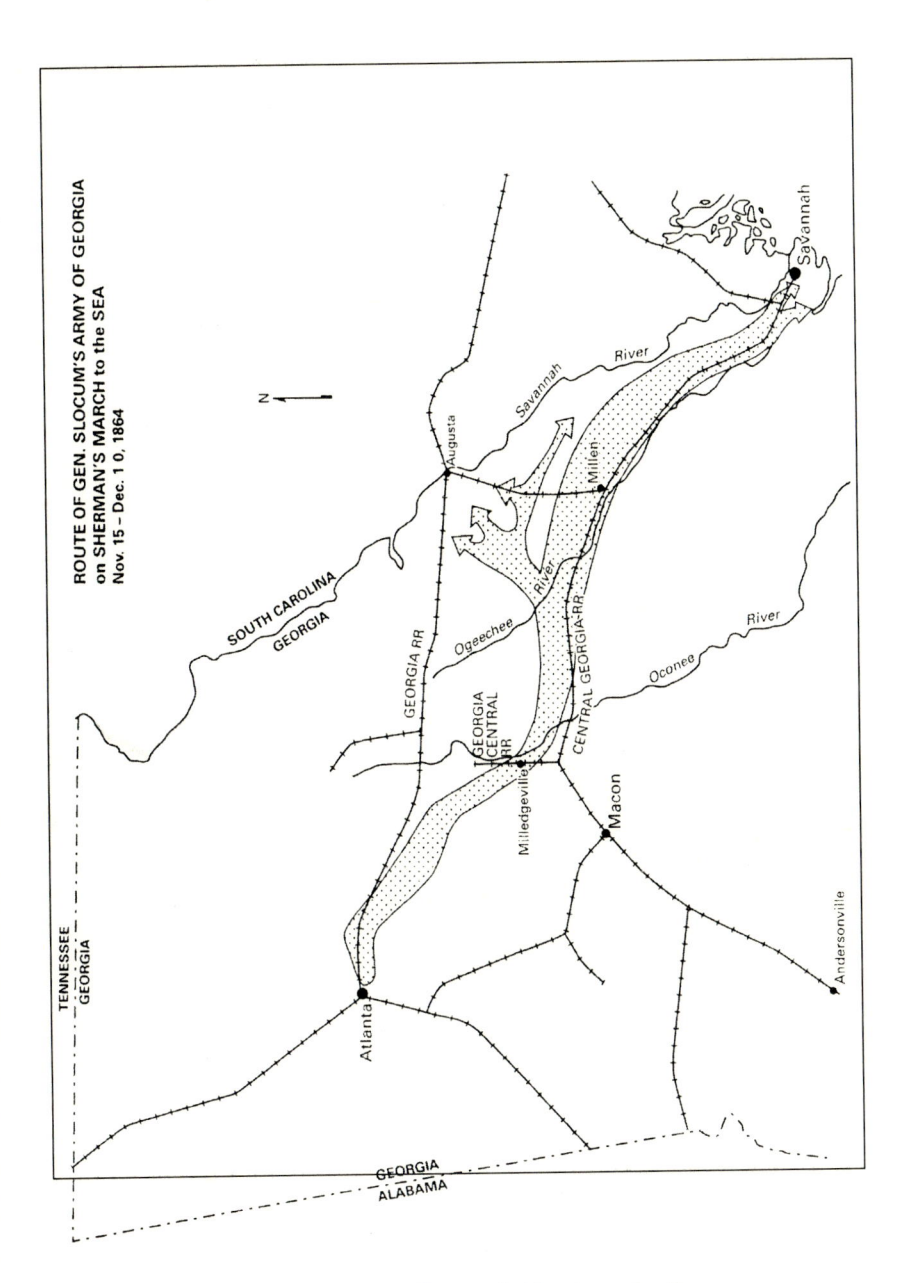

Slocum's route on Sherman's March to the Sea

miles and camped on Veales Plantation near Stone Mountain, close to the Georgia Central Railroad. They were tired and hungry but happy to be on the move.

John marched with his rifle and 40 rounds of ammunition in his cartridge box and 160 more in his pockets and haversack, his India-rubber poncho, a blanket, and his extra pair of shoes. Also on his hips and shoulders hung his "commissary department"—a canteen, tin cup, knife, fork, spoon, and his haversack, which would soon become his odorous lunchbox. Sometimes he carried his frying pan by sticking its handle in the end of his rifle barrel. Like all other soldiers, he also took along a pencil and writing paper. He and two others, undoubtedly veterans, constituted a mess, who slept under one tent fly. In the morning, they took turns cooking, filling canteens, and packing up. The night before they left Atlanta, they decided which coffeepots, hatchets, and stew pans to take in the supply wagon assigned to the regiment. Private Theodore Upson wrote, "[A]ll the boys are ready for a meal or a fight, and don't seem to care which it is."[1]

The 1st Brigade of the 1st Division, 20th Army Corps, to which the 123rd was attached, had one ammunition wagon, one ambulance, and one supply wagon assigned to each of its four regiments. Each of these wagons had a toolbox in front, a feed trough behind, a wooden water bucket on the side, and an iron grease bucket suspended from the rear axle. The supply wagon for the 123rd was kept full by those assigned as foragers. However, it was never allowed to stop while the foragers loaded it. They would return in some conveyance they had confiscated, riding majestically atop the load dressed in outlandish clothing to jests and cheers from their comrades. By November 18, when they reached Social Circle, three men had been wounded while foraging. General Slocum, however, was so concerned about his foragers wasting ammunition to shoot poultry and livestock that he levied a 50¢ fine for each unnecessary cartridge used.[2]

At Social Circle the first emancipated slaves began to follow the army. The regiment averaged twelve miles daily, with only one day's rest in the twenty-six-day march to Savannah. The rest of the wagons in the corps not assigned to individual regiments would travel in a train six miles long. Since the wagon trains had the right-of-way, the men often had to march on the roadside. By the time the trains had passed, the rutted red clay roads would be virtually impassable and have to be corduroyed by the pioneers using nearby fence rails, pine saplings, or split logs. They often had to cover the logs with brush to protect the animals from catching their hooves and possibly breaking their legs. One company of pioneers, consisting of able-bodied freed slaves, was assigned to each division, largely to repair and improve the roads. Otherwise, they were assigned to lead and care for the pack mules. Drinking water was usually ample and clean, minimizing diarrhea and dysentery. At many cool, clear stream crossings, soldiers stripped and bathed naked, leaving their clothes and guns on the bank. The weather was unusually fair for all but five rainy days when the roads turned to thick mud. On one occasion the 1st Division held the rear of the 20th Corps as it marched through a swamp in the rain. On that day roads were so cut up because of the wagons, artillery, mules, and soldiers ahead of them that it took five hours of hard work to march two miles. Howling winds also made marching difficult.

In the course of the march, a typical day for John would begin before daybreak with the sound of the foragers' horses as they left for their day's work. The glow of countless campfires would slowly fade as daylight crept over the horizon, gradually revealing the sleeping soldiers under their blankets. The dying pine-knot fires would still fog the air. Soon the other horses would be greedily devouring their fodder while the mules brayed fearfully. The bugles would finally break the soldiers' silence with reveille, followed by drumrolls. For John and the rest of his brigade, reveille would sound between 4 and 6 A.M., depending on whether the brigade was to be first or last in order of march that day. If they were the lead brigade, they would assign flankers to prevent surprise attacks. Unwillingly, the bluecoats would dress, and roll call would sound. They would begin the search for water and firewood, stir ashes, and rekindle the previous night's fires, then start cooking breakfast and brewing coffee. They frequently suspended a pan over the fire on the end of a ramrod to cook their food. After cooking with a frying pan, they would use a few leaves to wipe it out, but leave a coat of grease for the next meal.

When the brigade moved, it would march for fifty minutes and rest for ten. There was no halting for a noon meal, so men ate on the march unless they had to stop for a roadblock. By 6 P.M., the end of the day's march, the sun would be down and John and the others would make camp. Officers who rode ahead selected campsites, giving preference to well-drained, sloped sites that were close to water and close to trees or fence rails for firewood. As soon as they heard they were approaching camp, each man would appropriate a roadside fence rail. Since Georgia nights were cool in November, John would build a fire close to his tent and feed it with fence rails during the night. He and the other New Yorkers would sit around the fire cooking, eating, listening to the regimental band when it played, talking, singing, and sometimes dancing until tattoo sounded. For supper they would cook whatever meat they had foraged—beef, pork, chicken, or sometimes turkey—in a well-larded frying pan or on the end of a stick. With roasted sweet potatoes, corn, or hoecakes, they were indeed well fed. They would top this meal with coffee beans boiled in water.

Some of the boys had confiscated a large accordion that accompanied the singing and dancing after supper. By eight o'clock, John would be ready to sleep, having carried more than fifty pounds of equipment all day long. Like the others, he lay down on the ground under his blanket, usually in his clothes in case of emergency, and fell asleep to the sounds of cattle lowing, mules braying, and sentries shouting "Halt! Who goes there?" If fortunate, he found and cut brush for a bed, but by morning he would be chilled to the bone. With his teeth chattering, he would get up, get the fire started again, and cook breakfast with his messmates.

Cockfighting would become a significant pastime on the march after camp was set up in the evening. Roosters captured by foragers would be tested for valor and skill, with the losers relegated to the stew pan. Winners were named "Billy Sherman," "Pap Williams," and the like. Crowing triumphantly, they would ride proudly on artillery caissons or mules' packsaddles, or be carried under the arms of infantrymen. Each regiment, brigade, division, and corps headquarters had its own champion.[3]

Sherman's army, including John and the other New Yorkers, unquestionably engaged in wanton destruction as they passed through hundreds of large cotton plantations; they particularly targeted cotton gins, sawmills, and gristmills. However, it is equally true that as much, if not more, plundering and scavenging were perpetrated by hoards of deserters, looters, and stragglers from both armies. Local people and probably fugitive slaves who were seeking revenge on disliked neighbors or ex-masters also participated. Moreover, President Jefferson Davis urged his cavalry and the Georgia State Militia to "destroy all roads in Sherman's front, flank, and rear [and] burn what you cannot carry" so that his army would starve after his path was stripped of "Negroes, horses, cattle, and provisions." They also wrecked bridges and planted mines in roads. Commenting on the utility of Georgia militia regiments, one Confederate general caustically noted that they consisted of "3 field officers, 4 staff officers, 10 captains, 30 lieutenants, and 1 private with a misery in his bowels."

In the course of the march, Sherman would be "the most restless man in the army at night." In the middle of the night he would be seen poking around the campfire in his slippers, red flannel underwear, wool shirt, an old dressing gown, and a blue cloak. He would often awaken around three, be the first in the saddle, and remain awake, taking only short naps during the day. He could sleep anywhere. He wore a dingy, old, black slouch hat pulled down so far over his head that he was hardly recognizable. While riding on "Old Sam," a very fast walking horse, he would avoid the road as much as possible so as not to break into a regiment or brigade. Instead, he would ride through fields and thickets or plunge through swamps. Old Sam was as indifferent to shot and shell as was Sherman. The general's face was a nest of wrinkles, which twisted with each animated expression as he talked. When waving his arm to make a point, Sherman used his cigar stub like a baton. However, like Grant, who also was careless in his dress and lacked a military bearing, he was steady as a rock and single-minded in battle. They both needed an intimate and, as blood brothers, they served that purpose for each other. Without their mutual trust and support, Grant might not have assigned Sherman to lead the march to the sea.[4]

Slocum led the left wing of Sherman's army, and the one-armed Maj. Gen. Oliver Otis Howard, led the right. Howard was an outspoken abolitionist and a devout Presbyterian who did not want to fight on Sundays. Sherman kept in touch with his wing and corps commanders such as Williams by a telegraphic system that was in constant need of repair. Popular and solid, Williams led the 20th Corps as it marched across a six- to seven-mile front on the left side of the Atlanta and Augusta Railroad. The 14th Corps marched on its right until November 19, when they reached Madison. At night the two corps communicated by rocket. The brigade band played the "Battle Hymn of the Republic" and other lively tunes as they marched through the village. A number of wealthy families lived there, and their slave families, including children, abandoned their shanties to join the army.

During November 22–24, they entered Milledgeville, the Georgia state capital, in parade formation and camped on the bank of the Oconee River, close to the village. The main street was lined with black faces. The 20th Corps destroyed large quantities of arms, ammunition, accoutrements, salt, 2,000 cotton bales, immense piles of sawed timber, bridges, and other public property, including the penitentiary, and five miles of railroad by "burning and bending the rails." The state legislature, wealthy citizens, and Governor Brown, who had opposed Jefferson Davis throughout the war on the grounds of states' rights, already had fled the city, and the Union flag flew over the capitol. When he left by rail, Brown took a cow, a supply of cabbage, and some of his furniture, leaving government records behind. Upon arrival, Sherman moved into the governor's residence, sleeping on the floor because it had been stripped of furniture, curtains, carpets, and even food. He located the residence of Howell Cobb, whom he regarded as one of the "head devils" of the Confederacy, on one of his plantations. Having observed the miserable condition of Cobb's slaves, Sherman invited them to help themselves to the plantation's food. They hesitated, prompting Sherman to tell them, "Come on! We're your friends. You needn't be afraid of us. All this is for you—corn, wheat, molasses."

Slocum established his headquarters at the Milledgeville Hotel, and was ordered to tear up the Georgia Central Railroad and the telegraph line to the Ogeechee River. It took his men three days. While sitting around campfires one evening a few skeletal figures slowly appeared out of the darkness. They were Andersonville prisoners who had escaped and traveled a hundred miles, evading bloodhounds and Rebel patrols to reach Milledgeville. Their condition "sickened and infuriated" the troopers.

On November 26, they had their first skirmish with Wheeler's Confederate cavalry, supported by artillery. Wheeler commanded almost all of the Confederate troops they encountered. After a two-day running fight intended to delay the Union advance, in which bluecoat troops suffered fifteen casualties (but none in the 123rd), Wheeler withdrew. It was Wheeler's cavalry that had wrought havoc almost a year earlier on General Grant's Cracker Line that supplied Lank and the others in Chattanooga. Wheeler's horse soldiers also were looting and destroying property, possibly even more than Sherman's bummers. In contrast to the near-starvation diet Lank endured in Tennessee because of Wheeler's horsemen, John was enjoying an abundance of vegetables of all kinds, plus sorghum, fresh flour, corn, beef, and fowl. In fact, the cattle train was so long it was difficult to drive. At night the cattle were herded into immense fields of unharvested corn.

On November 28 and 29, the New Yorkers participated with others in the continued destruction of the Georgia Central Railroad tracks. On November 30, they moved up the Ogeechee River to near Louisville and skirmished again with Wheeler's cavalry. The Ogeechee was the last of three rivers they had to cross before they could begin an easy, unbroken descent to the sea at Savannah, 125 miles east. They crossed the river without even a skirmish, much less a battle, and halted for dinner on a large rice plantation. They destroyed five large government warehouses, railroad tracks and stations, a sawmill, and bridge and railroad timber.

On December 1, the 20th Corps began its march along the Louisville and Savannah Road, from Louisville down the peninsula through magnificent pitch pine country between the Ogeechee and Savannah rivers. From there they would cross dark, sluggish tidal streams winding through moss-hung, swampy forests. At night, John and the others used pitch pine torches to light their way in camp until the night fog spread like a blanket over the campground, so dense that the torches were of little use. The road was built on a thin crust of sand, four inches to a foot deep, and the enemy had destroyed all the bridges and placed many roadblocks in the way. When the road was wet, wheels on heavy-laden wagons cut through to deep quicksand, forcing construction of miles of corduroy. That day John's brigade guarded the 12th Corps wagon train, managing to cover only five miles.

The 123rd N.Y. started its march before daylight on December 3, and halted for lunch about three miles from Millen, near Camp Lawton, the prison camp where Dan had been confined until recently. The camp, completed only a month earlier, held 10,230 prisoners until Confederate officials realized that Sherman's army would release them as soon as it reached the village. By the time John and the lads of the 123rd arrived, the forty-two-acre prison pen was empty, but evidence of the horrors of prison life were abundant. Although John could not have known his brother had been imprisoned there almost since its completion, he now knew what his brother was enduring. The pen was located in a clearing surrounded by a dense pine forest and enclosed by a stockade fence, with no shelter for the inmates. A small stream ran through it. The seven-foot palisade surrounding the prison pen was built of logs fastened by iron bands. The deadline inside it was a single, rail fence. Well-used stocks for seven prisoners were near the entrance. Sentry boxes stood on platforms above the fence at fifty-yard intervals. Eleven cannons were mounted on high ground surrounding the prison to prevent escape. The hospital, which accommodated 300 patients, was a quarter of a mile from the prison. Over a recently dug mass burial trench outside the hospital hung a crude board sign, reading "650 buried here." Headboards for groups of fifty marked other trench graves. The soldiers buried three bodies they found in the huts. All the Millen prisoners had been transferred in three days ending on November 22, eleven days before the 123rd N.Y. arrived and shortly before Brig. Gen. Judson Kilpatrick's cavalry made a belated attempt to free them.

John and the other New Yorkers were enraged and sickened when they entered the prison. A few huts and burrows that were little more than kennels, not fit for hogs, were the only shelter some prisoners had from heavy dew, biting frosts, and cold, pelting rains. The rest lived in filthy "gopher holes" dug by hand in the barren soil. Sergeant Bull of the 123rd noted that some of the holes were "quite large where several men were together." Another man described the prison as "the barest spot I ever saw. The trees and stumps to the smallest fiber had been dug out for fuel; not a rag or a button or even a chip could be found." Every soldier who visited the prison "came away with a hardness toward the Southern Confederacy he had never felt before." In retaliation, Sherman gave the troops permission to burn the town's railroad station and warehouses. They had already destroyed all the tracks between Louisville and Millen, and now burned the prison to the ground and shot a pack of bloodhounds.

By December 8, John's regiment arrived at Eden's Crossroads, after more than a week of crossing flat and swampy lowland countryside, mostly forested with huge, widely spaced pines, eighty to ninety feet tall. John had cut more than his share of pine trees along the Hudson River, and surely thought this was a lumberman's paradise. Large ponds dotted the landscape every mile or so, and the creeks and bayous spread out into miry branches. As they approached Savannah, the tidal streams and ponds grew deeper. The road's sandy surface was only slightly above the level of the inky swamp water, inhabited by much-feared alligators and snakes. The road was soon cut through, and black pioneers had to resurface it with miles of corduroy. At swamp crossings, the enemy had cut trees to obstruct the road. Foraged supplies, however, were abundant, and the weather was fine. The entire route of the march reeked with the smell of rotting cattle, hog, mule, and horse carcasses. One man wrote, "Earth and air were filled with innumerable turkey buzzards feasting upon their thickly strewn death feasts." In addition, hundreds of runaway slaves who followed the army also died of disease, starvation, or exposure along the way. According to Cruikshank's diary entry, it was the most disagreeable day's march of the campaign.

After almost a month of marching, the men had become true ragamuffins. The two pair of shoes issued to each infantryman in Atlanta were either worn out or full of holes, to the point that many men tied

Sherman's troops destroying a rail line

gunnysacks on their feet. Their clothes were rags. Since they had no soap, their bodies were coated with resin, soot, and smoke from pine knot bonfires, plus accumulated dirt and grease. Yet one soldier wrote, "I wouldn't have missed [the march] for fifty dollars."

Slocum had his own method of destroying railroad tracks. The night before the work was to begin, he detailed a group of men, the number dependent on the amount of track to be destroyed. Others were ordered to guard against a surprise attack. Knowing his men worked best on full stomachs, he insisted they have "roast turkeys, chickens, fresh eggs, and coffee" for breakfast. After stacking arms, their officers divided them into three groups. The first was positioned alongside a rail, at opposite ends of a tie. Each man stuck his bayoneted rifle into the ground within easy reach. On the signal "Yo heave," the men on one side would lift the ties and overturn them. The second squad loosened the ties using sledgehammers or handspikes, stacked the ties into a pile, laid the rails on top, and then set them afire. The heated rails would bend of their own weight. Wielding giant wrenches, men in the last group would then further bend and twist each rail around a tree to make a "Sherman necktie," "Jeff Davis necktie," "hairpin," or "doughnut." The latter also was referred to as a "Lincoln gimlet." Other more artistic soldiers bent the rails to form the letters "U" and "S" and placed them where the locals would see them. One Irish soldier engaged in this activity remarked, "[W]hen the war is over General Sherman will buy a coal mine in Pennsylvania, and occupy his spare time with smoking cigars and destroying and rebuilding railroads."[5] By the time Sherman's army left Eden, it had destroyed 250 miles of railroad lines and all the facilities needed to operate a railroad.

On December 9 at 7 A.M., John's 1st Brigade led the 20th Corps advance from Eden to Savannah, twenty miles away. Theirs was the lead regiment of their division as it marched east toward the impenetrable Monteith Swamp, thirteen miles from Savannah. As usual, John and the others were laughing, joking, and singing, unmindful of any potential Rebel threat. They were approaching a small, open hilltop in the woods when a shell exploded directly overhead, followed by several more. A half mile away on another rise in an open field, John and his comrades could see smoke rising from a gun. Ahead of them, the enemy had felled trees and left piles of slash to block the road through the wide swamp.

Advancing farther, the Union vanguard also could see two redoubts in an open field on the edge of the swamp, manned by guns and cannoneers. One piece of artillery protected by fallen trees commanded the road. General Williams arrived and ordered the 1st Brigade, including John, to form a battle line close to the slash, send out skirmishers, and have pioneers clear the way. The other two brigades in Jackson's division occupied the flanks, one on each side of the road. Slash crossed the road into the swamp on both sides, forcing the New Yorkers to wade through two feet of water. As soon as the pioneers began to clear the timber, the enemy—estimated at 400 to about 1,000—opened artillery and musket fire, preventing the pioneers from removing the slash. Col. James L. Selfridge, John's brigade commander, then ordered the entire brigade to advance through the slash, the dense junglelike foliage, and the swamp on the left of the road in the best order possible, assuring them he would lead the charge. The 5th Conn. Veteran Volunteers took the skirmish line, cheering as they waded through the black muck and knee-deep water into heavy minié ball fire, and replied to it as best they could. The Rebel artillery fire was accurate and wounded several men. However, the Confederates were vulnerable to being flanked by the other two brigades in Jackson's division, which advanced over a mile through the swamp until they reached solid ground. After firing one more volley, the Rebels limbered up their guns and caissons and, within an hour, beat a hasty retreat, many men dropping their rifle-muskets. The 40th N.C. abandoned four guns and two caissons in the retreat, as well as small arms, clothing, other accoutrements, and a few prisoners. This was the last Rebel attempt of any consequence to disrupt Slocum's advance on Savannah, but they would encounter substantial resistance when they reached Savannah and beyond.

The 123rd reported one man wounded. According to his medical record, Pvt. John Ross suffered partial loss of hearing from a shell bursting overhead. Undoubtedly it happened during this confrontation on the Monteith Road. Seven men in John's division were wounded there, including one in his regiment, undoubtedly John. Twelve days later, John was hospitalized in Savannah for partial deafness as well as chronic diarrhea, which had begun at Hart's Island in New York while he awaited transportation to Atlanta. Until Savannah was evacuated by the Confederates on the night of December 20, however, John remained on active duty.

That night John's brigade camped on a Monteith plantation owned by Confederate Brig. Gen. George Paul Harrison. They had moved about a mile and a half in line of battle after their encounter with the enemy. The next day, as they marched southward, they destroyed two miles of railroad. About four miles from Savannah, on the Augusta Road, they encountered felled trees that were larger than the obstructions encountered the previous day. A flooded rice field three feet deep on both sides of the road also impeded their advance. While John's brigade attempted to penetrate the slash, Confederate artillery fired thirty-two-pound shells at them from a strongly fortified position about a half mile away. Although

Union sharpshooters silenced the artillery, skirmishers could not force the Rebels to retreat, and had to fall back, although seven deserters did surrender to the New Yorkers.

Conditions were about to change in more ways than the physical environment they were traversing. Up to now, the men had eaten well, thanks to an abundance of vegetables and livestock along their route. But now rations and forage were getting scarce. Most of the rations brought from Atlanta were not issued until the siege of Savannah began.

The siege of Savannah had begun. According to Sherman's men, by that time "[a] crow could not fly from Atlanta to Savannah without a haversack." With communications cut off along Sherman's route, officials in Washington, DC, had not known where his army was until they arrived at Savannah. About 10 P.M. on December 10, the 123rd N.Y. camped between the Augusta Road and the Savannah River. They had marched only six miles that day, guarding the wagon train through torrential rains that mired them down mercilessly. At their camp, they built light breastworks in the thick woods facing a flooded rice field and canal. Foragers had come in empty-handed, so supper consisted of a half ration of hardtack and tough, stringy, freshly slaughtered beef. Exhausted, they covered the damp ground with fragrant pine boughs and needles they called "soldier's feathers," augmented with long veils of hanging moss taken from oak and cypress trees, then bedded down in line of battle. In their twenty-six-day march over 300 miles, through forty of the richest counties in Georgia, they had met scant opposition. The regiment had lost only one man, a forager who was captured.

Sherman occupied all three roads and the two railroad lines between the Ogeechee and Savannah rivers, all of which were built on causeways leading into the city. The causeways, however, were commanded by heavy ordnance, which, although it was too strong for Sherman's light field artillery, did no damage. Now within four miles of Savannah, the 123rd was near where Pipe Makers Creek enters the Savannah River. A Rebel skirmish line consisting of rifle pits protected by rows of sharpened logs lay about three hundred yards from them.

Sherman's advance troops had driven the besieged Confederates back into their entrenchments, where 13,000 Confederates with eighty-one artillery pieces held the line, commanded by Gen. William J. Hardee. Sherman had 62,000 men outside the city. The 20th Corps faced 2,000 of the Confederates with twenty guns along a two-and-one-half-mile segment of the Rebel line.

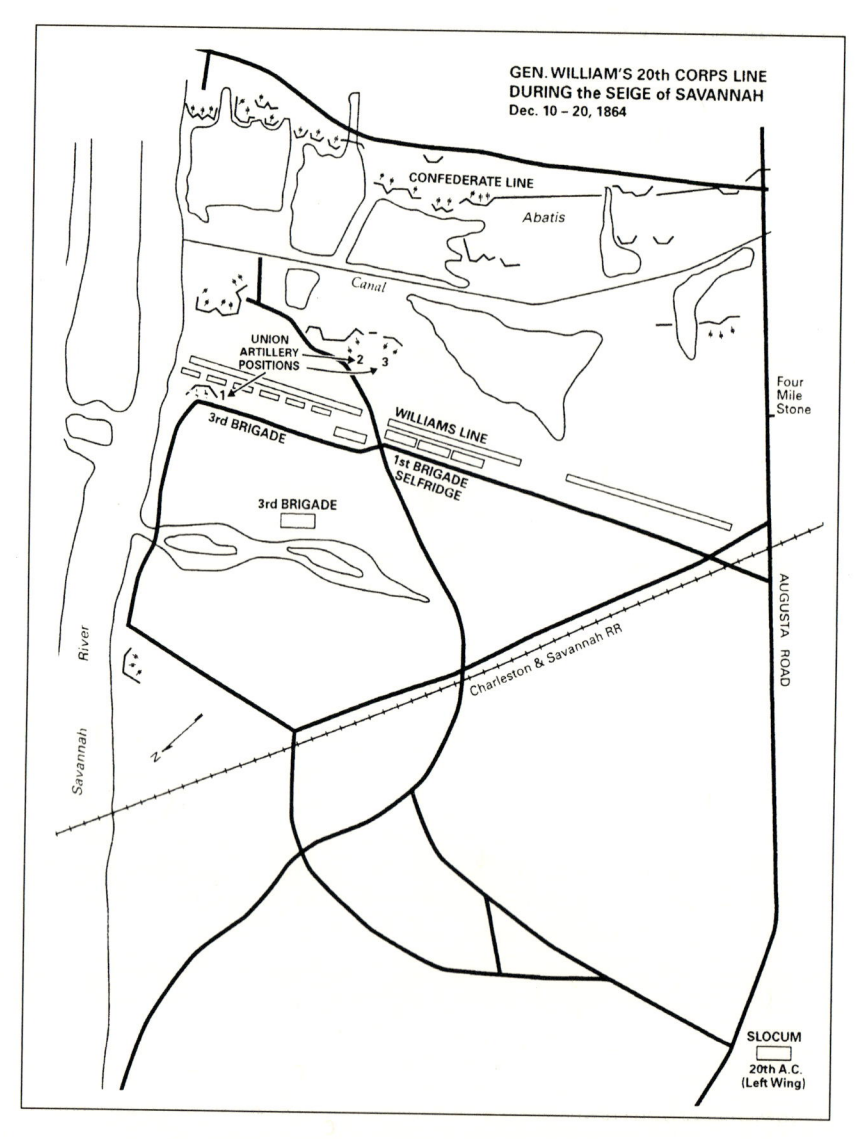

General Williams' 20th Corps line, Siege of Savannah

The only way to advance toward the city was on the roads, since the Confederates controlled the gates and dams between the river and the irrigation canals. By opening the appropriate gates or destroying dams (swamp dikes), they could flood any rice field, making artificial ponds several acres in size and as much as six feet deep. To counter the obstacle that flooding presented, the New Yorkers ingeniously bundled canebrakes and rice straw to support a floating bridge between dikes. Continuous shelling from the twenty guns commanding the three roads did little damage. During the ten-day period between December 10 and 20, the shells mostly whistled harmlessly through the treetops. During this time, the 123rd was engaged in skirmishing to determine the enemy's strength, reconnoitering their lines, and making preparations for an attack. In John's entire brigade, only one man was wounded by a piece of shell.

The city was clearly visible from the riverbank. Within a few days, the pickets from both sides were on friendly terms, talking and trading with each other. At night, John and his comrades could hear church bells and wagons rattling down streets. For amusement, the boys would sail "all over the river in small boats."

Not until December 19, the ninth day of the siege, did Sherman's army draw rations of crackers and sugar, when ships from the Federal fleet came upriver. The ships also delivered weeks of mail for some of the men. Newspapers printed Lincoln's annual message to Congress, delivered on December 6, in which he reported that the North's resources were larger than ever, and inexhaustible. He also noted that the U.S. Navy was the largest in the world, with 671 warships, adding the Union had "more men now than . . . when the war began . . . and [could] maintain the contest indefinitely." He called for bipartisan passage of the Thirteenth Amendment to the Constitution abolishing slavery. If any of the men needed a boost to their morale, Lincoln's speech did it. The weather was now warm, and abundant butterflies flitted from plant to plant in the sunshine. But such delights meant little to Savannah citizens, who were on the verge of starvation until shiploads of donated food arrived from the North.

Like Pvt. John Cutter of the 123rd, the men were not all that concerned about the shelling they were receiving. He wrote his father, "We have been here about a week now and the rebels have shelled us almost continuously night and day, but have not hurt any in our regiment. . . . Our pickets are so close that they call to each other, and when they send a shell the rebels will say 'How do you like that, Yanks?' . . . [In reply] the first thing you know over goes a shower of bullets from our boys."

Sherman also was nonchalant about the shelling. On one occasion, he was within about 800 yards of a Rebel battery on the Georgia Central Railroad tracks leading into the city. Sometimes enemy guns were mounted on platform cars that were run up close to Sherman's line. A few volleys would be fired rapidly, and the car would be run back. This time he was personally reconnoitering enemy lines, when he saw a puff of white smoke and caught sight of a thirty-two-pound round shot coming straight at him. He cautioned his staff to scatter and stepped aside himself. The ball struck the ground and ricocheted, hitting a nearby fugitive slave under his jaw, killing him. Sherman described the incident to his wife, but told her the slave only lost his arm.

During the siege, Union troops were far more concerned about their rations than the daily shelling. Pvt. Cutter wrote that they had drawn only "fifteen crackers apiece in the last thirty-five days . . . we have gone sometimes on very empty stomachs but we don't mind it, as it is all for the Union." Hardtack had been withheld while foraging provided ample food for the men. Now a scant supply of poor beef picked up on the march was soon devoured. Many roasted their portion on a stick held over the fire. After that it was rice for breakfast, rice for dinner, and rice for supper, for the officers as well as the men. Abundant fields of ripened rice were nearby, some already harvested and the grain piled high on the plantations. Occasionally, John and the other lads were able to forage some sorghum. Horses, mules, and cattle were living on rice straw. Some of the men roasted rice to make coffee. They hulled the rice in their mess pans with their rifle or bayonet butts, then placed it on a blanket and tossed it in the air to separate the chaff. Meanwhile, the flour supply from an old rice mill up the river on Argyle Island was diminishing daily.

On December 16, under a flag of truce, Sherman sent his final surrender demand to Confederate General Hardee, who asked for twenty-four hours to deliberate, then refused on the next day. In response, Sherman ordered Slocum to position six thirty-pound Parrott siege guns to shell the heart of Savannah and prepare to assault it as soon as he was ready. The guns commanded every position held by the enemy. Hardee's forces had dwindled by half, from nearly 18,000 when the siege began to 9,000 when, on December 20, Rebel batteries returned fire with heavy cannonading. They kept it up all day with unusual briskness. By afternoon, Confederate gunboats joined in, shelling the 20th Corps until dark and intermittently through the night, preventing the troops from sleeping and building fires. About forty men were wounded and nine killed. Maj. Henry Hitchcock, one of Sherman's staff officers, wrote his wife prior to this heavy bombardment, "Now and then a gun booms from somewhere along the lines, louder or duller or nearer or further off—probably Rebel shots for they have done a great deal of spiteful and useless firing since we came."

At 3:30 A.M. on December 21, General Williams, 20th Corps commander, received word that Savannah had been abandoned. Williams ordered General Geary, commander of the 1st Division, to see whether the other Rebel works around the city were unmanned. After his skirmishers confirmed the report, he ordered his men forward. At four o'clock, Savannah's mayor, R. D. Arnold, and a delegation of aldermen unconditionally surrendered the city to Geary. He unfurled the national and division flags over the U.S. Custom House and the City Hall, and General Slocum thereupon sent a report to Sherman, "We are in possession of the enemy's exterior line of works. . . . We are pushing forward toward the city." The Rebels had built ingenious pontoon bridges of rice flats and shallow barges, all lashed together, on which to retreat across the river into South Carolina, leaving behind their heavy artillery and a great deal of field artillery. The night had been so windy the gusts deadened the sound of troop and wagon movements, and fog obscured the view.

John Ross's 1st Brigade broke camp without breakfast, as they had nothing to cook. At six o'clock, they moved out of their works, passed their picket line, and occupied all the enemy's entrenchments within a mile of the city. They found the cannon spiked and the enemy gone. They entered the city by daylight, shouting and hurrahing from the bottom of their lungs, and captured an immense quantity of stores and a number of cannon. A civilian mob that was already breaking into stores and houses had to be dispersed with bayonets by a provost guard that Geary quickly established. Before the Rebels retreated, Wheeler's cavalrymen also had rifled through the stores. What they did not want was strewn in the streets. That night, after burning Rebel boats, John's brigade camped upriver just outside the city, with their headquarters established in a plantation mansion known as Marble Hall. Two days later they heard from Rebel sources that Lincoln had been reelected and that General Geary was appointed commandant of the city. Four days afterward they spent Christmas in Savannah. By then, though, John was hospitalized for his deafness and diarrhea.

Twelve men from the 20th Corps were killed in December and another 88 wounded. Although no one from John's brigade was killed, 6 of his mates were wounded and twenty-two captured. In addition, enemy cavalry had captured 165 of the brigade's stragglers and foragers. During the entire march the corps had captured 1,430 horses and mules and destroyed, lost, or abandoned 926. It also captured 324 prisoners. It left Atlanta with 429 cattle, captured 2,204, slaughtered 889 en route, and arrived at Savannah with 1,744, which were in poor condition. Since leaving Atlanta, John's brigade had destroyed twenty miles of railroad, five cotton gins, and seventy-three bales of cotton, and had not lost a single wagon. About 100 fugitive slaves attached themselves to the brigade. Except for John and a handful of others, his regiment and the balance of Sherman's army arrived in excellent health and in higher spirits than when they left Atlanta. For many of his soldiers, Sherman's march had been a lengthy, federally funded holiday.

John and the others, however, came to understand the short life expectancy of slaves who worked the rice fields around Savannah, wading through ponds to plant, weed, and harvest rice. The proprietors were wealthy enough to live in big cities, even in Europe. The overseers they left in charge treated slaves as brutally as if they were mules. Their poor diet and the prevalence of malaria were of no concern, because profits were so immense that it made little difference whether a slave lived or died. This realization strongly reinforced antislavery leanings for John as well as most, if not all, of his fellow bluecoats.[6]

By the time Sherman entered Savannah and was being resupplied, General Thomas had virtually destroyed Hood's army in Tennessee. Grant had Lee neutralized in the trenches of Petersburg and Richmond, and Atlanta was in shambles, under Union control, and useless to the Confederates. Sherman was ready to turn Savannah into a "grand depot" from which he could launch his next movement.

In Savannah, an ebullient Sherman enjoyed his Christmas dinner at his headquarters in the residence of Charles Green, a wealthy British cotton merchant. He soon noticed that a number of British flags flew over Savannah buildings, marking where cotton for sale to England had been stored. No sooner had he ordered its seizure than a pompous Englishman burst into Sherman's office vehemently insisting that his cotton was protected by the British flag. "Stop, Sir," Sherman said. "This is not your cotton, Sir, but my cotton; my cotton in the name of the United States government, Sir." "Well, Sir," replied the Englishman, "I shall report your conduct to my government, Sir." "Oh! Indeed." Sherman responded, "I hope you will report me to your government. You will please say to your government, for me, that I have been fighting the English government all the way from the Ohio River to Vicksburg, and thence to this point. At every step I have encountered British arms, British goods of every description, Sir." Sherman's position was that "all cotton in Savannah was prize of war. . . . [It] had been one of the chief causes of this war; it should help pay its expenses . . . all cotton became tainted with treason."

General Williams reported that he had a delightful winter residence with an abundant supply of old vintage wine, and the weather was superb. While in Savannah, Williams was finally breveted a major general after having served as a division and corps commander longer than almost all other brigadiers, a delay he attributed to his unwillingness to "pander to the paid puffers of the press." Undoubtedly he was referring to General Geary, whom Williams considered a consummate self-promoter. For his part, Geary was convinced Williams drank too much.

By midday almost every day, it was hot in the sun but cool in the shade. As the brigade provost marshal, Lieutenant Cruikshank was assigned a clerk and a servant to take care of his clothes and his horse. Headquartered in a private house, he slept on a featherbed in a nicely furnished room in the boardinghouse run by a family from an eastern state. When the regiment was paid in Savannah he received back pay of $1,050 and promptly sent $800 of it home to his wife. He wrote her that he had to keep his uniform clean and his shoes blackened—services that his servant provided for him. Sergeant McLean recorded in his diary that he "had a good dinner and a warm argument" with a "secesh" family on his second night in Savannah. He had a hospital tent for an office, furnished with sofa chairs, and was very comfortable. He and his bunkmates even put a floor in their tent.

McLean reported there was no looting in the city, likely because Sherman forbade foraging and destruction of property. To make certain he would be obeyed, he ordered that any soldier caught committing "unsoldier like deeds" would be "shot on the spot." To the delight of citizens, he also kept the streets clean, organized a fire department, and established a guard to provide security. Sherman also distributed supplies to Savannah civilians, in sharp contrast to his treatment of Atlanta civilians. McLean noted that most of the boys went to church on Christmas. That day, in the rain, Sherman also reviewed the troops and then dismissed them so they could cook their Christmas dinners. On Christmas Day, to rid his army of dead weight, Slocum called for dismissal of all "officers who, by intemperance, inefficiency, or ignorance of their duties, have shown themselves unqualified for the positions they hold." Further, he limited furloughs for officers and men to only those with a surgeon's excuse.

Sergeant Morhous recorded that upon arrival in Savannah two boys from the regiment set out to find something to eat. Knocking on the first door they came to, they made their wants known and discovered they were at the mayor's home. In short order, the mayor arrived at the door with a pan of bread and cakes. With many thanks, the two lads placed the food in their haversacks and departed. Three days after the army entered Savannah, it began publishing its newspaper, The *Loyal Georgian*, with the motto "Redeemed, regenerated and disenthralled—the Union must and shall be preserved."

A few days after Christmas, John was out of the hospital and joined his comrades in moving the regimental camp a half mile, tugging their shanties through the mud. Starting the day after they arrived in Savannah, they had laid out streets and built quarters in their first camp. Now they had to shift to a campground on the riverbank. It was well shaded by large India oak trees, green as summer, but the ground was swampy and mosquito-ridden. Although a few men contracted malaria, most of the regiment was in good health. Other troops built wooden shacks, or shebangs, for quarters in the town squares. The men had not been issued new clothing, so their uniforms were ragged, dirty, and permeated with the smell of the smoky pitch fires they had built on the march. General Sherman staged a review on December 30 to display his army to Savannah citizens, at which bands played, to the delight of thousands of local blacks. The well-to-do stayed home with their shutters tightly closed, but there were a number of Union sympathizers who watched the parade. The bands struck up "The Star-Spangled Banner," "Yankee Doodle," and "Dixie." On the whole, Sherman was convinced that "[n]o city was ever occupied with less disorder. Women and children . . . walk its streets with as much security as they do in Philadelphia."[7]

Yet camp restrictions were bothersome to the soldiers in Savannah. They were men of action who wanted to move on and finish whipping the enemy so they could go home. The only enemy they had to fight while in camp was lice, otherwise known as graybacks, which "sticketh closer than a brother." There was no sure way to kill them, not even by boiling clothes. The best, but not always effective, method was developed before they reached Savannah. By holding their clothes and blankets over campfires, especially ones burning pine logs, the soot and smoke clinging to the clothes would rid them of lice, at least for a while. Some men also found a little diversion when they discovered an immense oyster bed that was exposed at low tide in the river near Fort Pulaski. They could collect a bushel or so, row back to camp, and feast on raw oysters.

New Year's Day passed quietly. By January 5, John and the other lads began to receive new clothing, shoes—for which they were especially grateful—blankets, and equipment in preparation for their departure from Savannah. They also drew part of their back pay, and were reviewed by Sherman again. Sergeant McLean wrote his mother that the 20th Corps made "the best appearance" and that General Williams, the corps commander, said "our regiment was the best in the corps." January 9, Sgt. Benjamin Smith, who had been captured along with Dan, returned to the regiment after six months in prison. While being moved from Andersonville to another prison, he had escaped with about fifty other prisoners by jumping off the train into a swamp between Savannah and Thomasville. Most of the escapees were captured with the help of bloodhounds, but a half-breed Indian helped hide and feed Smith and four others in the swamp for several weeks, then brought them, half-starved, to Atlanta's picket line. A week later Sergeant McLean requested a twenty-day furlough for Sergeant Smith. When Secretary of War Stanton arrived on January 12, instead of giving a speech he proposed three cheers for "Old Abe." The men responded with enthusiasm.

General Geary wrote his wife about an occasion when Sherman asked permission to preach in a Savannah church. After some "hemming and hawing," the Episcopal rector told Sherman that the diocese of Georgia required him to pray for certain persons and asked Sherman if that was objectionable. Sherman conceded that he should certainly pray for both Jeff Davis and the devil, because "I don't know any two that require prayers more than they."[8]

Northerners now knew they could win the war. Sherman's march on Atlanta and his march to the sea had disemboweled the Confederacy. Food, forage, munitions, cotton, animals, bridge-building timber, factories, warehouses, and other supplies needed by General Lee and General Hood had been utterly destroyed. Thomas had dealt Hood's army a disastrous defeat at Nashville, leaving the Confederate forces in need of food, supplies, and time to recover. By year's end, 53 percent of Hood's army was absent. The "Garden Spot of the Confederacy," the area Sherman marched through after leaving Atlanta, was in ruins. Some 320 miles of railroad and the facilities to operate them were rendered useless for supplying Lee's army in Virginia. As a result, Lee's army was starving and cold, their uniforms and shoes in tatters. The men had no overcoats or blankets. Atlanta munitions factories and warehouses were destroyed. Savannah and its port were rendered useless to the South. Lee was also cut off from food and munitions from Macon and Columbus, Georgia. About 25,000 runaway slaves had followed Sherman's army, robbing the Confederacy of their forced labor to produce food and cotton. Sherman had liberated more slaves than any other Union general. Knowing that every plantation owner used hounds to run down escaped slaves and Union prisoners, Sherman's army had shot every dog in their path. Nonetheless, less than 7,000 of these freedmen reached the coast. Most were unable to keep up with the march.

Confederate civilian morale plummeted while army desertions soared. Sherman, in his grim and unrelenting style, was largely conducting economic warfare against plantation owners, striking a powerful psychological blow. For the 7,000 ex-slaves who reached Savannah with him, for others who lived there, and for the 110th Regiment of USCT that had been sent to him, Sherman issued his Field Order No. 15. It divided all abandoned, rich plantation land within thirty miles of the coast from Charleston to Jacksonville, Florida, into forty-acre, tillable plots for each family, and provided them with seed, farm equipment, and clothing. He also gave them surplus army mules, an action that became the derivation of the term "forty acres and a mule."

Sherman wrote his wife, "I want [the Negro] treated as free and not hunted and badgered to [be] made a soldier... when his family is left back on the plantation." In contrast, as Lieutenant Cruikshank wrote his wife two days before they left Savannah, "[T]he slave owner talks about his good stock of negroes as much as a northern man does of his cattle or sheep and talks about improving it the same."

By June 1865, some 40,000 ex-slaves had colonized the region. To assist blacks in preparing for freedom, the American Tract Society opened schools for their children. A total of 500 enrolled, and ten black teachers were hired to teach them. Savannah's black population contributed $81,000 to assist their fellow blacks in preparing for freedom.

Sherman knew his 60,000 soldiers were prepared to persevere, based on what he saw in them by the time they occupied Savannah. He wrote, "[T]hey seem so full of confidence in themselves that I doubt if they want a compliment from me, [but whatever called on to do]... they have done it, with alacrity and a degree of cheerfulness unsurpassed." He did acknowledge, though, some had been "a little loose in foraging, they did some things they ought not to have done!" On the march north from Savannah, he would call on them to destroy food supplies, railroads, arsenals, and other war resources in South Carolina and North Carolina. The Carolinas constituted the only remaining region from which the South, particularly Lee's army, could draw food and supplies in any quantity.

Sherman knew that he could not be resupplied until his forward units reached Fayetteville on the Cape Fear River, twenty miles upriver from the Port of Wilmington. Fortunately, Fort Fisher and the other Rebel forts guarding that port fell to Maj. Gen. Alfred H. Terry's forces on January 15, two days before John's regiment marched out of Savannah. Confederate blockade runners no longer had a safe haven on the entire Atlantic coast and could not help feed Lee's already hungry army. Sherman believed his march north from Savannah would be ten times more difficult than the one from Atlanta and ten times more important to ending the war. Until he reached Fayetteville, foraging would be an absolute necessity to feed his 60,000 men.

When Lincoln fully realized Sherman's plan, he said, "Grant has the bear by the tail while Sherman takes off its hide." South Carolina civilians awaited the arrival of Sherman's army with fear and trepidation, and as they also feared General Hardee's troops, who had left Savannah to defend South Carolina. One observer wrote, "The officers are worse than the men. The men desert at every opportunity and run without any cause and without shame." South Carolina was virtually defenseless against Sherman's onslaught. Pillaging and burning in both South Carolina and North Carolina made Lee's soldiers from these states desert from his Richmond trenches in droves to save what they could of their farms and homes and feed their families.

Rain of nearly biblical proportions, swollen rivers, and overflowing swamps delayed Sherman's departure. The evening of January 16, 1865, John Ross's company received orders from Provost Marshall Cruikshank to be ready to march at 7:00 A.M. John and the others packed their knapsacks, discarding items unnecessary for a long march. Now all veterans, they had learned the hard way not to load themselves down. They were ready and willing to leave the charms of Savannah and start the march through the Carolinas. General Geary was relieved as commandant of the city, replaced by Maj. Gen. John G. Foster, whose command included a number of black troops.

When the bugle sounded "Forward" the next morning, Sherman's army marched six miles out of camp and across the same pontoon bridge and dikes that General Hardee's Confederates had used to evacuate Savannah on December 20. Despite not having their wagon train, which was blocked by extraordinary floodwaters, the 123rd and all the other regiments gave three cheers as they crossed into South Carolina. The regiment's roll call counted 416 present, 5 of whom were sick. They camped that night near Hardeesville, South Carolina, on the Charleston Road.

General Hardee's instructions were to stop Sherman at South Carolina's wide Coosawatchie River, but he made no attempt to do so. It was the wettest winter in two decades, and after several weeks of rain, the lowlands and causeways were flooded. From January 21 to January 28 they could not move. As the river rose, many pontoon bridges and causeways were washed away and had to be rebuilt. As soon as the wagons could move, the troops waded through swamps and marched through knee-deep mud and water, often in cold, if not freezing, rain, advancing only a few miles daily. The Rebels had felled trees in the roads to impede the artillery and wagon trains. A thin coat of ice frequently formed overnight, and sopping wet clothes and shoes were covered with mud. For weeks at a time the men's feet were always wet. One New Yorker wrote his father that because he had no stockings, his feet got "all cut with gravel which gets in my shoes." Enraged soldiers cursed as they dragged Sherman's 2,500 wagons, 600 ambulances, and seventy cannon through the axle-deep mud and treacherous quicksand. Sometimes the roads had to be corduroyed for miles before the equipment could be moved.

Often General Williams helped with the corduroying. He had a rugged constitution and boundless energy. His men regarded him as firm but fair, and appreciated that he worked them no harder than he worked himself. The men slept in shallow, cold water while pickets patrolled campsites in boats. On at least one cold evening a ration of whiskey was issued that resulted in "songs and shouts of laughter," according to Sergeant McLean. On one occasion, the *New York Herald* correspondent found General Williams nestled in the bend of a tree with a blanket wrapped around him, smoking a cigar. His staff was in the same tree, seated on higher branches. Sherman also slept in a tree one night during a flood.

Rations were cooked in fires that sputtered in the rain, the pine smoke bringing tears to men's eyes. They soaked hardtack overnight in cold water, then salted it, and browned it in pork fat for breakfast. The biscuits were six inches square and slightly less than one inch thick. Made in Boston, the hardtack was stamped "B.C.," which the men said stood for "Before Christ," thus explaining why it was so hard. To make a stew, they would put one cracker into a cup, pound it into crumbs with a rifle butt, and mix it with coffee. Lieutenant Cruikshank called them "Ironclads." Others called them "skillygalee." The new uniforms and shoes the men had received in Savannah were in hopeless condition. As food supplies dwindled and troops were given only quarter rations, foragers went out every day. All in all, it was an "irksome and laborious campaign," according to General Williams. Skirmishing with the Rebels was an almost daily occurrence for the regimental foragers until about March 1, but there was almost no other contact between the enemy and the New Yorkers.

In 1832 and again in 1851, South Carolina planters had made unsuccessful attempts at secession. Nevertheless, Sherman's army met no substantial resistance there. The governor, Andrew J. McGrath, wrote President Davis, "It is not an unwillingness to oppose the enemy, but a chilling apprehension of the futility of doing so, which affects the people." Their concern was justifiable. Before entering the state, Sherman had telegraphed President Lincoln, "The whole army is burning with an insatiable desire to wreak vengeance on South Carolina." Retaliation for the death and destruction resulting from four years of Civil War was severe. General Williams wrote, "The soldiers quietly took the matter in their own hands." A blackened swath seventy miles wide marked the army's path through the heart of the state. Magnificent magnolia and cypress trees were cut by the thousands to corduroy roads and build bridges through the swamps and bayous. One Union soldier wrote, "If we don't purify South Carolina, it will be because we don't have a light." Everything that would burn, including houses and barns, was torched, with the exception of most Negro huts, which were left untouched. Sherman told Slocum, "Don't forget that when you [cross] the Savannah River you will be in South Carolina. You need not be so careful there about private property.... The more of it you destroy the better it will be." Slocum opposed the widespread destruction wrought in South Carolina, but admitted, "It would have been a sin to have had the war brought to a close without bringing upon the original aggressor some of its pains."

Sherman also wanted to destroy every other vestige of the South's war power that was in his path. Just before reaching Columbia, the capital of South Carolina, Sherman spent one cold night trying to sleep on the floor of an abandoned plantation house. He awoke cold and renewed the fire by burning a bedstead and a wooden mantel clock, "the only act of vandalism done by myself... during the war."

John and the rest of the 123rd and the 5th Conn. spent day and night from January 31 to February 4 at Sisters Ferry on the Savannah River, fifty miles north of Savannah. They corduroyed roads, rebuilt a bridge, built a dock at the ferry landing, and unloaded supplies, including a half-million rations and ammunition from four steamboats that came upriver from Savannah. A gunboat was there to protect them. Lt. Alonzo T. Mason of the 123rd wrote his wife, "The weather here is terrible. Rains—floods—mud—winds—roads near the river all submerged as deep as 8 feet in some places... [we] shall move the troops as soon as a man can keep his feet on the bottom and his head above water." Often they tied their shoes, socks, and pants to their rifles before wading in. At least, however, they now could draw full rations and read their mail.

On February 7, Lieutenant Beadle, who had been captured at Gettysburg and spent twenty months in Confederate prisons, returned to the regiment, just before it left Sisters Ferry. A week earlier, he had escaped from a train in South Carolina while being transferred to yet another prison and then had come across Sherman's army.

At least twelve bands played as the army marched into Columbia on February 17. John's regiment never entered the city, but camped and marched close enough to see the sky lit up as it burned. After fire completely destroyed Columbia, Sherman said, "Though I never ordered it and never wished it, I have never shed any tears over the event." General

Williams recorded in his journal that Confederate Gen. Joseph Wheeler left a letter offering to stop burning cotton if Sherman would stop destroying private property. Williams forwarded the letter to Sherman, who characteristically replied that he would thank Wheeler to continue burning cotton and save him the trouble, and that he had given no order to destroy private property except in cases of outrageous conduct. There is no evidence that the 123rd New Yorkers did anything more than forage for provisions, destroy railroad tracks and cotton, steal horses and fodder, and rejoice that others were forcing South Carolina to pay its debt to the Union. Nevertheless, according to Sergeant McLean, "the boys [in the 123rd] were determined to raise the devil in S. Carolina." Williams wrote that his bummers were doing just that—putting "the flames to everything."

Meanwhile, Sherman arranged for the 21st regiment of USCT to be the first to enter Charleston and accept its surrender. Many in its ranks were ex-slaves from the city. Sherman forced the evacuation of Charleston by severing three railroads that served it, thus cutting off its food supply. Rumors that he would enter the city also prompted citizens to flee. He did not lose a man in capturing the city.

Had John known of the bloody confrontations his three brothers already had experienced with South Carolina troops he would have felt more than somewhat vengeful upon setting foot in the state. At Chancellorsville on May 3, 1863, McGowan's brigade of South Carolinians had fought head-to-head with the 123rd N.Y. and Dan's Battery F, 4th U.S. Artillery. A year later, the same South Carolina brigade also fought Will's brigade to a standstill by nightfall May 5, 1864, in the Battle of the Wilderness, where he was mortally wounded. Still another South Carolina brigade (Manigault's) poured murderous fire into Lank's brigade at Stones River on December 31, 1862, Chickamauga on September 20, 1863, and the Battle of Missionary Ridge on November 25, 1863. It also had participated in the Battle of Kolb's Farm where Dan was captured on June 22, 1864.

On March 2, reveille was sounded early, and by 6 A.M. the 1st Brigade was again on the march through rolling country, at the head of the corps. The 123rd was the third regiment in line, acting in support with the 141st N.Y. and the 5th Conn. ahead and the 46th Pa. in the rear. Shortly after the march began, the brigade heard skirmishers' shots from a 300-man Rebel cavalry unit a half mile ahead. Colonel Selfridge, the brigade commander, ordered the first two regiments to deploy as skirmishers, with the 123rd and the 46th Pa. as their support. A battery moved to the front and fired a few shells; then the advance began. Rebel artillery replied, but the skirmishers and their supporters quickly drove them through the village of Chesterfield and across the two fortified Thompson's Creek bridges, to which they set fire as they retreated. Two Johnnies were killed and several wounded. The skirmishers saved the bridges from total destruction, and the brigade crossed and spent the night in a swamp protecting one. The Rebels "skedaddled" during the night after throwing a few harmless shells at the Yanks. Sherman was with the 20th Corps as the Johnnies "skedaddled," and later wrote in his *Memoirs* that a slave told him they fled so fast "you could have played cards on der coat-tails." It was their last contact with the enemy in South Carolina. Now they were on their way to Fayetteville, North Carolina.

On March 3, Congress established the Freedmen's Bureau. On March 4, inauguration day for Lincoln's second term, troops fired captured ammunition in celebration. Slocum's corps also began its departure from South Carolina after John's brigade repaired the bridge. That day, Capt. Dexter Horton of Slocum's staff wrote, "Reached N.C. line about 3 o'clock. Goodby land of Secesh. Your country is now desolate." South Carolina, which had been feeding Lee's army, would now have to be fed by others.

On March 7, during the night, John's brigade crossed a pontoon bridge over the Pee Dee River and made their first cup of coffee in North Carolina at 4 A.M. For at least half the way across South Carolina, the army had been compelled to corduroy roads in order to move the wagon trains through the swamps. They had waded, swum, and marched through countless downpours, and bridged more rivers in South Carolina than they cared to count. Now, however, the weather was warmer, the roads were drying out, and the men began to call the swamps "frog heaven." Forage was abundant and the train of refugees was growing longer.

Sherman admonished his men to deal fairly with the citizens of North Carolina—and they did. There was little plundering compared to what had happened in South Carolina. They reverted to their old ways in Georgia, foraging for food and fodder, and destroying public property, but not homes or lives. Each company in the regiment assigned three mounted men as foragers. The countryside through which they marched was poor. The principal products were tar, pitch, and turpentine made from mammoth pines.

March 11 dawned sunny after three days of rain. On fairly decent roads, they marched twenty miles, then camped within two miles of Fayetteville about 9:30 P.M. This far into North Carolina, not a single house had been burned. The city was newly occupied by other Union troops, after a little skirmish and cavalry fight had driven out the Rebels. That night, one of John's comrades commented, "If I had the contents of my mother's swill pail tonight, you can bet that I would rob the pigs of their supper." The next night, however, foragers brought both quantity and quality of ingredients that more than made up for the previous night. The dead body of one New York forager was found on the roadside. On the 13th they marched into Fayetteville and, after scraping the mud and grime off their rags, were reviewed by Sherman at noon. He called them his "ragamuffins." They then marched the rest of the way through town, crossed the Cape Fear River on a pontoon bridge, and camped about five miles beyond the town. By this time, General Johnston, who had opposed Sherman on his march to Atlanta, arrived to take charge of the forces now gathering to stop the bluecoats from continuing north.

Fayetteville was an inland port on the Cape Fear River, upriver from the Port of Wilmington. Sherman was intent on destroying the large former U.S. arsenal in the city, which had been seized a week after Fort Sumter fell in April 1861. The Confederates had installed gun-making machinery, taken from Harpers Ferry early in the war, and now manufactured cannon, their carriages, and fixed ammunition there, as well as storing thousands of rifles in the facility. Union forces also targeted for destruction government buildings, a large textile mill, warehouses, and the printing plant of the *Fayetteville Observer*, a staunch Confederate newspaper. Slocum sat on a hotel verandah "watching the progress of the flames." The next day the army tug *Davidson* and a navy gunboat arrived and delivered some mail, newspapers, and supplies—including some sorely needed clothing—to a cheering throng of soldiers. Some of the New Yorkers had only one sleeve left in their shirts, others no sleeves, and still others no shirts at all. Sherman had the steamboat skipper remain until nightfall so his men could have time to write letters home, giving every soldier his first opportunity since leaving Savannah to send as well as receive letters. They were issued rations that had been brought upriver by transport. The boats then returned to Wilmington with sick and wounded soldiers and refugees, black and white, who had joined Sherman's army. Lieutenant Beadle also departed on a leave of absence. A much larger crowd of refugees who could walk or at least ride in whatever wagons were available or on broken-down horses and mules traveled to Wilmington in column, escorted by 200 soldiers. After crossing the Cape Fear River, shortly after leaving Fayetteville, "Uncle Joe" Young of Company D, age forty-three, the oldest man in the regiment, single-handedly captured two fully armed Rebels on the picket line. When asked how he did it, he replied with a straight face, "[W]hy I surrounded them."

On March 16, Slocum's forces left Fayetteville and marched about four miles in a pelting rain beside the muddy Cape Fear River Road. Before reaching Averysboro, they heard distant cannonading ahead. Kilpatrick's dismounted cavalry was sent forward as skirmishers, with infantry support. Until now, rain had been their only enemy. Now they also faced Rebels entrenched behind earthworks with artillery support on a hilltop that was skirted by a creek-filled ravine. The 123rd took up a position behind crude breastworks as the Rebels fired on the cavalry, driving them back over the 123rd's skirmish line. In their "mud armor," the New Yorkers and other regiments in the line then opened with deadly volleys, exchanging both rifle and artillery fire for about three hours. At the order to advance, they waded through thick vegetation, mud, swamp water, sometimes two or three feet deep.

It rained all day as they drove the enemy back about a mile, then came to a second, much stronger and more heavily manned line of entrenchments blocking the road to Raleigh. The entrenchments stretched from the Cape Fear River to the Black Creek and were flanked by swamp. The New Yorkers dug in, exchanging artillery and rifle-musket fire with General Hardee's rear guard in the pine forest through the rest of the day and into the night. Wind and rain continued to plague them through the night as they slept fitfully on their arms in the swamp. By dawn on the 17th they realized the enemy had retreated toward Averysboro, leaving behind pickets and others who surrendered by waving handkerchiefs. Five of the New Yorkers were wounded in the battle. Altogether, Williams's division took 217 prisoners and three guns, and buried 108 Rebel soldiers. Sixty-eight of the prisoners were wounded. As far as the New Yorkers were concerned, this skirmish should have been called the Battle of Averysboro. When they left the battlefield, the roads were so bad that it took three hours to march a mile and a half. In the worst places, they unhitched the mules so the men could pull the wagons.

On March 18, on their way to Goldsboro, John and the lads waded waist-deep through Black Creek, a flooded, almost shoreless, stream flowing through endless swamps and lowlands. They had to hold their cartridge belts over their heads. When they finally reached the opposite shore they halted long enough to wring out their clothing. Wagons were mired in the mud until noon. At 11 P.M. they finally reached brigade camp, exhausted, having made only eight miles in sixteen hours. The camp was in a pine forest set on fire by those who tapped it for turpentine. The black smoke of the pitch added one more layer of tar to their bodies. They slept with their shoes on for fear the leather would shrink so badly it would be painful, if not impossible, to put them on again.

On Sunday, March 19, the foragers provided them with the best meal they had eaten in a week. During a pleasant morning, the 123rd had marched about seven miles on the Smithfield road toward Goldsboro when they heard cannonading. They pushed forward about two miles on the double-quick for nearly an hour to protect the wagon train. In a large, open field skirted by thick woods, they faced the enemy. The Battle of Bentonville had begun. Filing through a gap in a rail fence, the boys each grabbed a rail as they advanced to a thicket and quickly threw up breastworks, then were ordered forward to support a battery in the rear of the battle line. They remained there until dark, when they were sent forward to relieve another regiment in the front line. They lay on their arms for the night and discovered in the morning that the enemy had retreated toward Smithfield during the night, leaving behind their pickets and their dead. Several of the New Yorkers brought in Rebel wounded and spent most of the day burying some of the dead. This was the last major Civil War battle in North Carolina.

On March 23, seven miles from Goldsboro, the New Yorkers brought up the rear of the corps and therefore did not leave camp until about 10 A.M. By 1 P.M. they crossed the Neuse River at Cox's Bridge. Waiting at the bridge to welcome them was a brigade of General Alfred H. Terry's 10th Corps, recently recruited black troops in spotless new, well-fitted uniforms, shiny new shoes, and brand new guns of the latest model. They could not have presented a greater contrast to the New Yorkers in their filthy, ragged uniforms, with faces as black as pure soot as the soldiers who welcomed them. Sergeant McLean wrote in his diary that day, "[S]aw a division of colored troops and was agreeably surprised to find them making such good appearing soldiers." On April 8, 1865, Pvt. John Marshall, who also had seen General Terry's black troops, wrote his parents about what may have been his first view of black soldiers. "If I was not an abolitionist before I came South I am one now and if I was one then I am doubly so now for I learn from what I have seen that slavery is a curse to the South," he wrote. "I hope and pray that the Amendment to the Constitution for the freeing of our Country from this National Shame may soon be adopted.... [W]e ... took a look at their camp and equipment ... and the universal opinion ... was that they were a Good Institution instead of the Peculiar Institution we hear so much about."

On March 24, they finally reached Goldsboro, the junction of two railroads. As they marched into town, many shoeless and shirtless in muddy, pitch-coated clothes, their lean bodies hard as iron, generals Slocum, Schofield, and Terry reviewed the brigade. They then marched three more miles, and encamped in a pine forest near the Weldon railroad. On the torturous Goldsboro Road through the pine barrens that were blocked by the enemy, they had fought two battles, and a number of skirmishes. Their 500-mile march took sixty-six days; on twenty-one of them it rained. They had destroyed miles of railroad and telegraph lines and many buildings. They had crossed nine swollen rivers and scores of tributaries, and waded through endless swamps. The roads were so bad that in several places the mules and horses could not touch bottom. The animals had to be unhitched from their wagons and artillery so the men could pull them through the mud.

A large part of the time, Williams's 20th Corps had the lead. Seventy-seven of the men in the corps were killed and 477 wounded in five battles and various skirmishes. In the 123rd, several had been taken prisoner, one was killed, two died of disease—one a recruit that arrived in Atlanta with John—and a half dozen had been wounded, none seriously. Several contracted smallpox. Some of the lads were barefoot, and others had bound their feet in rags. Yet many marched with pet squirrels on their knapsacks or raccoons tied to strings. On their heads they wore an untold variety of commandeered hats, if they wore any hat at all. On some days they had marched from daylight to 11 P.M., according to Private Law. Both men and animals needed a rest. Nevertheless, they were in good health and spirits, despite having to live off the land because rations had been available only sporadically.

In Goldsboro, General Schofield's 23rd Corps were entertained royally by Sherman's "corn crib [and] fodder-stock . . . commandos," who wore silk stovepipe hats, long-tailed butternut overcoats, and every imaginable kind of clothing. They were mounted on any kind of animal, while vehicles of every description—carts, buggies, hacks, wheelbarrows—carried the forage and food, including chickens, turkeys, bacon, corn, meal, and oats. En route to Goldsboro, John's brigade had captured forty-six prisoners and buried sixty of the enemy killed in front of the brigade. At Goldsboro, they were assigned a good campground on which they built log huts and had a good supply of water and wood. Their first cry was for soap, which they had not seen for sixty-six days. Sherman described his army as "dirty, ragged, and saucy." Supplies and newspapers, including the *Albany Journal* and the *New York Times*, began arriving the day after the troops did. Having just suffered from three virtually sleepless nights, they were battle-worn and hungry. According to Slocum, however, both men and animals were in better condition than when they left Savannah. Some had even gained weight. They were in excellent health.[9]

In Goldsboro, John and the lads of the 123rd drew full rations for the first time in weeks, took regular doses of quinine, received a whopping three months of mail, and got their first pay since leaving Savannah. Sherman himself was so broke that he could not buy a new pair of boots that he sorely needed. His wife also was so short of money that he borrowed $200 from the quartermaster to send her. They were issued replacements for their tattered, greasy, malodorous uniforms, which they burned or buried. They also received new shoes to replace whatever remnants of shoes, if any, they had tied to their sockless feet. They took baths with soap, boiled their clothes and blankets or destroyed them to rid themselves of lice "tenants that had lodgings within their flannels," and rested their weary bones while luxuriating in the spring weather.

In contrast, strict orders were issued for foragers to dismount and return to their regiments, and for all extra animals to be handed over to quartermasters at headquarters. However, the countryside between Fayetteville and Goldsboro had already been stripped of food and forage for twenty miles around. Harvey Reid, an aide to Maj. Gen. William T. Ward, who commanded the 2nd brigade, described the behavior of the 20th Corps. "Our soldiers could take from the poorest almost the last morsel of food," he wrote. "General officers allow[ed] the men to pillage helpless women and children [and] burn their houses without a word of prohibition or punishment... If anyone thinks that the people of South Carolina can ever be 'loyal' [to our] government he must have a very strong faith in the meekness of human nature."

Goldsboro became the army's supply base for the rest of the campaign. The army was one immense camp for five miles along the river. John and the rest of Sherman's army had a seventeen-day rest there. The New Yorkers had an excellent camp on a pine-forested hillside, complete with a chapel they built. On the whole, the weather was warm and pleasant. Flowers and fruit trees were in bloom, and grass was turning green.

Sherman now commanded 95,000 troops in six corps. When news reached them that Richmond had just fallen to Grant, the lads went berserk with delight. Some smashed their rifles against tree trunks. One soldier wrote that the army had never "had such a day of rejoicing.... Such cheering, shouting, gunfiring [and] band playing... I never heard before." Bands played "John Brown's Body" and "Marching through Georgia." Some celebrated with John Barleycorn. Church services were held in the open air, and nearly the entire regiment attended. The entire Northern population celebrated just as joyously.

While in Goldsboro, on April 4, Sherman replaced popular "Old Pap" Williams with Maj. Gen. Joseph A. Mower, a combative regular army officer but not a West Pointer, as head of the 20th Corps. Sherman regarded Mower as "one of the boldest and best fighting generals in the entire army," indifferent to personal danger and always confident in battle. He had been with Sherman during all of his Mississippi campaigns. Many officers and men in the 20th Corps were upset and strongly resented losing Williams to the aggressive Mower, whom they considered a little too careless with their lives. In part, the popularity of "Old Pap" rested on his willingness to do such things as carry rails with his men to corduroy roads. He was almost universally regarded as one of the best officers in Sherman's army, with no blunders or failures in his record. Nevertheless, Sherman was adamant, justifying his position on the grounds that in case of a final battle, Mower would be more aggressive. Williams cheerfully returned to command his old division, describing Mower as "a very pleasant, gentlemanly man." Williams's ego proved to be nowhere near as brittle as Hooker's when he was serving as 20th Corps commander the previous July and resigned when Sherman promoted General Howard over him.[10]

Shortly after his arrival in Goldsboro, Sherman placed Schofield in charge and left for City Point, Virginia, to meet with Lincoln and Grant on March 27 and plan final operations. When Lincoln arrived on the paddle wheeler *River Queen* for the meeting, he was greeted by his son Robert, who was serving as Grant's aide. They met in Grant's roomy log cabin to hammer out peace terms. When Sherman left, Lincoln said to him, "Sherman, do you know why I took a shine to you and Grant?" Sherman replied, "I don't know Mr. Lincoln." Lincoln explained, "Well you never found fault with me." While there, Grant suggested to Lincoln that they visit the colored troops of the 18th Corps nearby. On horseback, they rode to their camp. The enthusiasm of the black troops knew no bounds. Horace Porter, Grant's aide, wrote, "They cheered, laughed, cried, sang hymns of praise.... They crowded him, fondled his horse; some of them kissed his hand.... The President rode with bared head; the tears had started to his eyes, and his voice was so broken by emotion that he could scarcely articulate the words of thanks." While Lincoln was at the 18th Corps camp, General Lee made his last assault on Grant's line and was soundly defeated. A few hours later, Lincoln viewed that battlefield.

On Sunday, April 2, Chaplain Myron White held services in a chapel with log seats, attended by nearly the entire 123rd N.Y. Meanwhile, President Jefferson Davis and his cabinet were evacuating Richmond and General Lee abandoned Petersburg. That same day, Dan Ross was released from prison in Selma, Alabama.

When reveille was sounded at 4 A.M. on April 10, John Ross and his two messmates took down their tent fly, packed their knapsacks, and ate breakfast. They had completely recuperated from their 500-mile march and were resupplied for another thirty-day campaign. The regiment fell in shortly after five o'clock as drums rolled, bugles sounded, and the orders "Shoulder arms. Right face. Forward march!" were heard. They moved out in high spirits, the New Yorkers leading the 20th Corps, on their way to Raleigh. When this movement was reported to General Johnston, he immediately moved his troops toward the same city. The 20th Corps marched through Goldsboro; they were headed west with the intention of establishing communication with Grant's Army of the Potomac in Virginia. The road had to be corduroyed, and progress was slow.

After marching six or seven miles, they bore right on the Smithfield Road and heard firing ahead. The advance escort soon galloped back to inform them of a large cavalry body east of Moccasin Swamp, which was under the command of Gen. Wade Hampton, one of the richest planters in South Carolina. The mounted escort had fired a few shots at the Union skirmishers, then withdrawn for help. Supported by the rest of its brigade, the 123rd in the lead did all the skirmishing on the right of Smithfield Road. They were ordered forward to confront 300 or 400 of Hampton's cavalry about half a mile away in a cleared field. Two companies initially deployed as skirmishers advanced at once and were fired on. The balance of the regiment, including John and the other lads of Company H, then moved forward to support the skirmishers. The Johnnies fired while falling back, keeping out of gunshot range but contesting every inch of the way so as to prevent artillery from gaining a better position. The New Yorkers drove them back about two miles and halted to re-form their regimental skirmish line with the 141st N.Y. as their support. When the whole line moved forward with artillery, the firing became heavy as the enemy retired in haste.

By noon, John and his comrades had advanced so fast and so far that they were soaked with perspiration and an April shower. They had been running and floundering through field, forest, and swamps full of tangled roots and vines, and climbing fence rails while carrying all their equipment. By 1 P.M. they forced the enemy into the detestable black muck of Moccasin Swamp, which was full of thick underbrush and bordered Moccasin Creek. The enemy had broken a dam a mile above the crossing, flooding the creek and adjacent swamp there. After crossing them, the Rebels had removed the bridge planking that traversed two channels through the swamp. They then entrenched behind breastworks made from the planking, as the New Yorkers waded into the swamp unaware of how deep the channels were. One hundred yards into the swamp, the men of the 123rd were waist-deep and had not crossed the first channel, which was about twenty feet deep. While standing in the water, the New Yorkers kept up a steady fire for an hour. Many had to hold up their cartridge boxes to keep their powder dry. Shorter men placed cartridge boxes on their shoulders. While under fire, one man was killed and four were wounded, but not one man retreated.

Colonel Rogers ordered his men back to find planks and rebuild the first bridge. They crossed it single file under heavy fire from several hundred Rebels, reentered the swamp, and advanced again while returning fire, until they came to the unanticipated second channel. The enemy continued firing, but the dense foliage obscured the New Yorkers from view, so most of the balls whizzed harmlessly over their heads. When one of the Union batteries began shelling the Johnnies, they abandoned their earthworks. John and his comrades soon repaired the second bridge, crossed to dry ground, and deployed again in a skirmish line. While the rest of the brigade crossed the two bridges, John and the other lads of the 123rd, dripping wet, charged the retreating enemy, who were in full sight. The Rebels continued firing their muskets, but failed to aim true and were too far away to inflict any harm.

After about a mile, the wet and exhausted New Yorkers halted on a knoll at dusk with the rest of the brigade, by order of General Williams. They bivouacked in line of battle about four o'clock in a pine grove on the Atkinson Plantation, and built large fires from fence rails to dry themselves out and make coffee. They had marched, waded, and fought for eighteen miles and were exhausted, but had caused the enemy to "dust out." While advancing, they had seen two dead and eight wounded Johnnies, all North Carolinian cavalrymen; a few of the wounded were captured. This was the last skirmish Pvt. John Ross and his comrades fought. Lieutenant Cruikshank wrote his wife that they "did splendidly and got a great deal of praise from all officers in the Corps."

Pvt. William H. Toohey had survived every other battle and skirmish in the regiment's history unscathed, only to be killed in this final skirmish. He was, in fact, the last man to be killed in Sherman's army. Four others in the regiment were wounded. About 9 A.M. on April 12, near the town of Smithfield, Colonel Rogers ordered the regiment into line and read them a short order from General Sherman announcing Lee's surrender to Grant at Appomattox.

John and the others went wild. Cheers billowed through their line of march as men broke ranks shouting, shaking hands, hugging, parading, singing, and dancing, until exhausted. Some turned somersaults or stood on their hands. They shot off guns and rockets and filled the air with hats, cracker boxes, and anything else that could be thrown. Bonfires were lit. Some men even smashed their rifles. Some shot off mines, others celebrated with barleycorn and still others with "milk juice." Jubilation knew no bounds. Every band, drum, and fife added to the deafening noise in the Smithfield town square. When Sherman told General Williams of Lee's surrender, the army commander shook John's division commander's hand for minutes, shouting "Isn't it glorious?"[11]

The celebration gave way to sheer exhaustion, but resumed the next morning with the regiment's departure on the march toward Raleigh, North Carolina, which Wheeler's cavalry had raided the night before.

That day John and the lads of the 123rd marched eighteen miles on a dusty, sandy road under a hot sun. They were the first to reach it early the next day in a pouring rain. The men sang, shouted, and fired their muskets as they marched, the downpour doing little to dampen their spirits. The bands played national airs that evening as the Stars and Stripes waved from the dome of the Capitol. The men got little sleep, talking of home late into the night around their campfires. They arrived 415 strong, including 5 men who were sick. John was among them, having suffered a flare-up of his diarrhea in Goldsboro.

Orders were issued to cease foraging and not molest Rebel soldiers or civilians. A guard was stationed at every house, and receipts were to be issued for everything taken from civilians. Sherman's men behaved as well as they did in Savannah, and mingled freely with paroled Confederate soldiers. Private Cutter wrote his father, "I have talked to many of them, they come through here by hundreds on their way home, and they are the most tickled lot of fellows you ever saw. One told me a few days ago, while he was on his way home, that if their cause had been *just* they would not have been whipped."

Sherman's army, plus Schofield's and Terry's, were held in readiness in Raleigh, awaiting Gen. Joseph E. Johnston's formal surrender of his 30,000 men, plus 14,000 from Hood's defeated Army of the Tennessee, which had recently arrived by rail to assist Johnston. These reinforcements included Gen. Carter Stevenson's division that the 123rd had skirmished with at Kolb's Farm. While waiting, John and the others grew feverishly anxious to begin the homeward march.

While Sherman was preparing to board a train April 17 to meet Johnston and begin surrender negotiations, a telegrapher rushed up to Sherman with a telegram reporting President Lincoln's assassination. Sherman handed Johnston the message and watched for his reaction. Johnston broke out in a sweat, and declared, "It's a disgrace to the age. The greatest possible calamity to the South. I hope you don't charge this to the Confederate government." Sherman indicated that while he suspected President Jefferson Davis might be responsible, he agreed the Confederate military did not perpetrate the outrage.

None of the men in either army was aware of the assassination until Sherman returned from his meeting with Johnston and announced it to his army that night. "In an instant," wrote Maj. Henry Gray of the 123rd, "those who were happy at the idea of peace [were] made desolate [and] desperate." Some stood around in knots talking in subdued and bitter tones. Others wept silently, hoping and wishing that General Sherman would not accept General Johnston's surrender. Still others were stunned into silence. The feeling was universal that the war should last as long as a Rebel remained unpunished. Private Haley of the 17th Maine wrote that a soldier who said he approved of Lincoln's death was dragged to a frog pond and held under water until he nearly drowned. A wave of gloom washed away the joy of victory. Then anger supplanted the gloom. Sherman posted trustworthy guards for several days to surround camps and prevent soldiers from wreaking vengeance on people and property. He also ordered the troops to drill twice daily and answer roll call four times per day.

Both Sherman and Johnston had feared the Union soldiers would explode in uncontrollable rage if they learned of the president's death before the surrender was final. When they were informed of the murder of "Father Abraham," Sherman told them that truce talks had begun. It was days before they recovered from their anger and grief. The shock of personal bereavement had affected every soldier. One officer wrote, "Everywhere men were seen to weep who had never flinched in the white heat of battle." Despite this, the Yanks and the Rebs gathered around campfires, swapping stories, tobacco, coffee, whiskey, and meat. One New Yorker wrote that he had talked to hundreds of Rebels and "all they want is peace. They are whipped and they all own it and are pleased to get off so easy."

On April 19, the New Yorkers marched more than fifteen miles with wagons to collect fodder for their animals, passing a number of paroled Confederate soldiers on their way home. At the same time, Grant was at the White House viewing President Lincoln's body lying in state. He wept profusely that day while Confederate armies were still surrendering to Sherman.

Sherman's troops were ordered to act magnanimously, and they did. Raleigh civilians were impressed, and even astonished, by their good conduct. On April 22, Sherman held an imposing review of the 20th Corps on its campground near the city. It was one of a series he held for each corps in his army. The 123rd had the lead of the corps. Bands played familiar tunes and officers saluted with their sabers. One of the best-drilled units in the corps was a division composed entirely of black troops. The next day Pvt. Philo Smith was buried. He was the last man in the regiment to die—ironically, it was of measles.

Sherman had had four goals when he started his march on Atlanta. Ten months later, he had fulfilled them all. He had denied Lee's army food and military supplies by capturing Atlanta and Savannah, destroying railroads that delivered to them, and obliterating croplands in the Carolinas and Georgia, especially the "Garden Spot of the Confederacy." He had utterly destroyed the slaveholding, aristocratic plantation society in these three states. He had minimized the possibility of Lee's army being reinforced, and he had significantly reduced Confederate military and civilian morale. The Veteran Volunteers and three-year regiments, like the 123rd New Yorkers, acted on Sherman's goals. In the process, they were able to realize their own goals of restoring the Union and abolishing slavery.

14

Victory and the Grand Review
April–June 1865

THE ONLY NATIONAL DEBT WE CAN NEVER PAY IS THE DEBT WE OWE TO THE VICTORIOUS UNION SOLDIERS.

—Sign hanging on the Treasury Building during Grand Review, May 23–24, 1865

After the final terms of a surrender agreement of all Confederate troops east of the Mississippi were reached on April 26, Sherman offered ten days' rations to Johnston's 30,000 paroled Confederates to take with them on their homeward journeys. He actually furnished 250,000 rations and wagons necessary to haul them, in the hope that giving the defeated enemy enough food to get most of them home would minimize the possibility that they would organize guerilla bands to forage en route. However, more than 8,000 of Johnston's men already had deserted and were not present to receive rations. Many took a horse or a mule with them as well as their personal property. Their officers had made little or no effort to stop them. As they started their journey home, they raided and pillaged the property of local citizens along the way.

Hood's men surrendered at Greensboro and other points in the military district. He also encouraged his generals "to relieve [their soldiers'] present wants and to encourage [local] inhabitants to renew their peaceful pursuits and to restore the relation of friendship among our fellow citizens and countrymen." Against orders from Jefferson Davis, Johnston gave each of his soldiers $1.15 for transportation home, all the money in his possession. It was paid from the gold and silver in the Confederate treasury and Richmond banks. On April 28, two days after the surrender agreement, Pvt. Matthew Moneghan arrived in camp. He had been taken prisoner with Dan and sent to Andersonville. After being paroled in Savannah, he managed to return to the regiment.

April 29, Easter Sunday, Rev. Henry Ward Beecher eulogized Lincoln to a packed New York City congregation. He said, "Four years ago, oh Illinois, we took from your midst an untried man, and from among the people. We return him to you a mighty conqueror. Not thine anymore, but the nation's; not ours but the world's . . . a sacred treasure to myriads who shall pilgrim to that shrine to kindle anew their zeal and patriotism." While this eulogy was presented, the New York lads and their officers spent the entire day "skirmishing with graybacks," which they did not want to march with on their last days in the army.

The next day, in delightful weather, Sherman's men began their 300-mile homeward march with Williams's division in the lead. The birds that awakened them could not have sung more sweetly or flown more happily. With the sick sent to Washington by ship, the rest of the New Yorkers started their march at 5 A.M., having lightened their load by turning in all ammunition except twenty-five rounds. Citizens along the route expressed good feelings about peace and "seemed to have lost their hostile feelings." Some offered pails of drinking water to the troops. That night they were mustered for two months' pay, still leaving them short eight months'. They took only eleven days to reach Richmond, crossing eleven rivers on pontoon bridges to do so, many nearly dropped from fatigue. They passed numerous ex-Confederates who were already home, plowing, hoeing, and planting their fields. They also saw large, handsome plantations where blacks were still working. On May 11, they marched through Richmond, past the Capitol and the infamous Libby Prison where Colonel Crocker of the 93rd N.Y., Will's regiment, had been imprisoned in 1862. As they marched past George Washington's statue, they carried their rifles in salute—with bands playing and flags flying—then camped about four miles north of the city. Private Cutter wrote his sister that they were reviewed in Richmond by Secretary of War Stanton.[1]

No sooner had they arrived in camp and set up their tents, than the heavens opened with a horrendous downpour, accompanied by violent bolts of lightning and deafening thunderclaps. The wind collapsed almost every tent. From then on, the march to Washington would be over wretched, war-torn roads made even more impassable by continued, drenching downpours and mud. Making matters worse, the weather grew hot and humid.

On May 15, four days after leaving Richmond, the 123rd reached the Chancellorsville and Wilderness battlefields, crossing the Orange Plank Road on which Will Ross and his regiment had marched the night before he was mortally wounded. According to Sergeant Cook, scarcely a tree stood where General Hancock's men, including Will, had fought a year earlier, on May 5, 1864. They halted for three hours, giving John ample time to see the earthworks on the low hill where his brother Dan's battery had been positioned on Sunday, May 3, two years earlier. He also saw the fence rails and felled trees marking the Chancellorsville battle line where the 123rd stood its ground until exhausting its ammunition in their first and bloodiest battle. John and his regiment buried the exposed, bleached skeletons of fallen comrades, sad sentinels of the battleground, in shallow graves. John surely must have wondered whether he would ever see Dan again and marveled that he had survived that battle. He was told of the cross fire of musketry and shot and shell to which Dan's battery was subjected as the enemy overran the Union line and forced his battery back to the Chancellorsville house. Now birdsongs replaced the sounds of battle.

General Williams halted the men on the line his division had held in that battle and went over the ground with Generals Sherman and Slocum. Lieutenant Cruikshank, Sergeant McLean, and other lads who had participated also silently walked over the ground on which they had fought. John must have then walked the short distance to the Wilderness battlefield, perhaps down the Brock Road where Will's regiment entered that battle, wondering whether his brother's rain-washed skeleton was among the unburied who still littered that battlefield a year later. When the official burial party arrived a month later, however, it found only eight bodies that could be identified as soldiers in Will's regiment, 93rd N.Y.[2]

On May 19, four days after visiting Chancellorsville and four months after they left Savannah, the New Yorkers marched through Alexandria to Arlington Heights, Virginia, footsore and exhausted. They camped near Ft. Runyon, not far from Arlington House, General Lee's home, which had been used as Union army headquarters since the war's beginning. By then, many Union soldiers had been buried there, in what would become Arlington Cemetery, and a Freedmen's Village had been built on the premises. They joined a thousand other camps on both sides of the Potomac, their regimental bands playing daily and smoking campfires twinkling nightly. They knew their marching days with knapsack and rifle were finally over, and a new life was about to begin. John had marched 1,100 miles in the six months since he had left Atlanta.

John and his comrades remained in Arlington Heights until May 23, preparing for the Grand Review before President Andrew Johnson, Generals Grant and Sherman, and other dignitaries. President Johnson had ordered the Grand Review at least in part to boost the morale of those still grieving over the loss of their kith and kin, and over Lincoln's assassination. The military trial of John Wilkes Booth's coconspirators for assassinating President Lincoln, which had already attracted a number of onlookers into the city, was adjourned during the review. John was the only one of the four Ross brothers to participate in the parade. Will was dead; Dan was on guard duty taking Jefferson Davis to Fortress Monroe; and Lank was in the Albany, New York, military hospital being treated for blindness. John and his comrades were told to break camp at midnight. They had brushed, mended, and cleaned their tattered uniforms by washing them in the Potomac, received some new clothing, polished their buttons, blackened what was left of their shoes, polished their cartridge boxes, and cleaned their muskets and bayonets until they glistened. As Sergeant Bull remembered, "Our guns which were our pride and joy could not have looked better."

Upon his arrival, Sherman wrote Grant, who had informed him to prepare his troops for the Grand Review, "I will be all ready by Wednesday [May 24] though in the rough. Troops have not been paid . . . and clothing maybe be bad but a better set of arms and legs cannot be displayed on the continent." Capt. George I. Robinson of the 123rd wrote his wife on May 19 that he was embarrassed by their appearance. "I think it is a shame that the government does not pay off Sherman's army so that the officers can appear [decent for the] review." Nevertheless, according to Private Mathews, their officers mustered as much style as they could, holding themselves stiff "like a dog shitting on a briar." On May 20, 21, and 23, visitors arrived from Washington County to greet their sons and witness the parade. Since they were not returning to Arlington after the review, the New Yorkers packed everything they had in their knapsacks.

Nobody in Sherman's 178 regiments slept the night before the parade began. At midnight they ate breakfast of hardtack and coffee, since they were still on short rations. They were told to break camp, then called into marching order at 2 A.M. The 123rd N.Y. led its brigade, which in turn led the 20th Corps and Slocum's Army of Georgia. Undoubtedly, the 20th Corps was selected for this honor because of its well-earned reputation for being the crack corps and for having the highest percentage of casualties in Sherman's army. It had fought gallantly in every battle, and had never lost a piece of artillery or a stand of colors. Each man marched with his blanket roll over his right shoulder and two day's cooked rations in his haversack at his left hip. By 5 A.M. sergeants were barking roll calls, and about 6 A.M. they halted at Long Bridge, spanning the Potomac River, about three miles from their Arlington camp. By daybreak, the entire corps was in place, and the weather was very pleasant. Sergeants barked out orders to start the march by company across Long Bridge, and along the east side of the C and O Canal. They assembled in the rutted streets around the capital, the dust settled by two days of cooling rain. In the fall of 1862, when the untested 123rd had crossed that bridge in the opposite direction, the regiment had numbered 1,000. Now a scant 400 passed in review.

Both the soldiers and the country needed a celebration, after four years of war, with more than 600,000 fatalities and untold grief, a presidential assassination, the manhunt to find the assassin, and a new presidential administration. Boats from Alexandria, roads from Maryland, and trains from all parts of the North brought people by the tens of thousands, including parents with their children to witness the historic event. For a week prior to the parade, hotels and boardinghouses had been jammed to their rafters, and many spectators had slept outdoors or

Sherman's Veterans at the Grand Review

stayed up all night. Private homeowners rented bed space in parlors and attics. The 100,000 visitors plus 150,000 residents added considerably to the monumental logistical problems created by the one hundred fifty thousand soldiers and 25,000 horses participating in the two-day review. Providing food, accommodations, water, forage, and sanitary facilities, including manure disposal, strained the capacity of all concerned. Cavalry patrols were posted along the parade route to keep the crowds clear of Pennsylvania Avenue.

Grog shops were closed for three days to minimize rowdiness and possible brawling, which upset a number of men. Nevertheless, speakeasies on the outskirts of the city were in business. Police spent their time arresting pickpockets, horse thieves, prostitutes, and those passing counterfeit money. By daybreak, the crowd began to line the avenue. All traffic on the parade route had been suspended for hours before it began and the streets were patched, swept clean, and watered by the street and fire departments. The buildings along the parade route were bedecked with American flags, bunting, floral displays, and black crepe ribbons to reflect mourning for President Lincoln. For the first time since his assassination, flags were raised to full mast. Welcome signs and banners were suspended from buildings and across street intersections. Over the entrance of the Treasury Building hung the torn flag of the Treasury Guard Regiment. Arches of flowers and evergreen boughs bridged Pennsylvania Avenue. Another banner stretched over the street read, "ALL HAIL OUR WESTERN HEROES."

People gathered at windows, rooftops, and porches—vantage points that were rented to them at "fabulous prices." Government clerks sat on the roof of the Treasury Building. Schools were dismissed, and boys climbed trees and lampposts to view the parade. Sobbing mothers lifted their babies above the crowd to see the soldiers. Others waved handkerchiefs and flags. Some people were issued special "curb tickets" so they could get to the front of the crowd to view the spectacle. By the time the parade started, the crowd was eight or more deep on each side of the street, waving miniature flags and shouting, "Sherman! Sherman!" By then, President Davis had spent his first night as a prisoner in shackles at Fortress Monroe.

At 9 A.M., while church clocks chimed, an artillery piece was fired. The 70,000-man parade of 178 regiments and 14 artillery batteries began uncoiling like a gigantic fifteen-mile-long python up Pennsylvania Avenue. At the front of each company were its tallest men. Sherman led the parade, accompanied by General Howard, one of his corps commanders and now head of the Freedmen's Bureau. With his empty right sleeve pinned to his jacket, Howard had to guide his horse with his left hand. Looking straight ahead and taut with pride, Sherman rode slowly like a Roman emperor on Lexington, his favorite horse, both of them bedecked with flowers.

As Sherman passed Lafayette Square on his dark bay, followed by his staff and escort, he recognized and saluted Secretary of State Seward, who stood at the window of a brick house on the corner of the square. Sherman guided his horse with his left hand so he could salute with his right. Seward, still feeble and bandaged from the severe wound he received the night of Lincoln's assassination, returned the salute. The cavalry rode stirrup-to-stirrup, as precisely as the infantry, while staring straight ahead and ignoring the garlands onlookers tossed at them. Apprehension finally overcame Sherman as he passed the Treasury Building. He glanced once over his shoulder to see how well his men were aligned, noting how the "glittering muskets [with fixed bayonets] looked like a solid mass of steel moving with the regularity of a pendulum." His eyes were wet. The sight was the most satisfying moment of his life. They were his war-worn warriors.

Each regiment of stagestruck country boys marched twenty abreast, from curbstone to curbstone, accompanied by its drummers, the ranks as straight as tightened twine. Each brigade marched to its own band; some of the men looked like "moving flower gardens," bedecked as they were with flowers and bouquets that had been tossed to them.

The troops marched under blue skies with light white clouds, moderate temperature, and a cool breeze. As they entered Maryland Avenue, they drank from barrels of ice water placed there by citizens. A roofed presidential stand was on the White House lawn, decorated with bunting, flags, and banners with names of battles won by the western armies—Stones River, Chickamauga, Missionary Ridge, Atlanta, Savannah, all battles in which the 123rd had fought. Two regimental pet oxen, "Chattanooga" and "Chickamauga," were led along with scarlet ribbons tied to their horns.

Grant, President Johnson, his cabinet members, and the diplomatic corps occupied the stand. Grant's wife Julia and son Jesse were at his side. Sherman's wife, Ellen, and his son, Tom, also were in the stand. Another stand for congressmen, public officials, lesser notables, and the press stood across the avenue in Lafayette Square. Two other reviewing stands were erected by private citizens, including a Boston financier, for use by wounded and sick soldiers.

Sherman saluted the president with his sword while the band played the popular new song "Marching through Georgia." Everyone in the presidential stand acknowledged his salute by taking off their hats, rising to their feet, and cheering. The men were astonished to see "Uncle

Billy" in a new uniform, an unfamiliar stiff-brimmed hat, and a trimmed beard. His appearance prompted more than a few snickers, wisecracks, and whistles from some of his men. Sherman merely smiled.

After passing the presidential stand, he dismounted and entered the stand to review his own troops. As each corps passed the stand, its commander and division commanders took a seat with the president, including General Williams. A deafening roar rose from the crowds lining the street—cheering, shouting, clapping. Sherman acknowledged the cheering by nodding his head, first to the right and then to the left. They sang along when familiar war songs were played. They also wept and laughed, waved flags, and threw flowers until they blanketed the avenue. Some soldiers even heard people praying. The enthusiasm was boundless, and Sherman raised it to fever heights. The troops were awed as well as delighted. These farm boys were not exactly accustomed to throngs of admirers. As it passed the reviewing stand, each regiment halted momentarily and dipped its flag. Many flags were stained, bullet-ripped, and ragged, but the color sergeants carried them as if they were "Roman Army eagles." One was barely big enough to "wad a gun." The loudest cheers were prompted by the most bullet-torn and tattered colors. All were festooned with flowers and black streamers of mourning, for both Lincoln and their fallen comrades.

The day before, Sherman watched Meade's Army of the Potomac in their flawless uniforms and white gloves. Seated next to Meade in the reviewing stand, he remarked, "I'm afraid my poor tatterdemalion corps will make a poor appearance tomorrow when contrasted with yours." He also cringed as he saw that some of the men were out of step and turned their eyes "like country gawks to look at the big people in the stand."

Sherman and his senior officers decided to include in their parade what Meade had not. He actually wanted the crowd to see his army as the Confederates had seen it, including "bummers, freedmen, and pioneers." To do so, he had the pioneers—runaway slaves in their ragged plantation clothes—march proudly in front of each division carrying picks, shovels, spades, and axes on their right shoulders, keeping perfect alignment. In the rear of each division were its artillery and six mule-drawn, worn-out ambulance wagons, three abreast, with bloodstained stretchers strapped to their sides. Two pontoon boats followed, one covered with canvas and the other a skeleton to reveal how it was constructed. Roses blossomed from the muzzles of the cannons. Behind each brigade were black men using rope bridles to lead gaunt mules and jackasses loaded with packs from which hung pans, kettles, baskets, gridirons, coffeepots, sides of bacon, hams, and such. On top of the packs rode the soldiers' pets—dogs, roosters, raccoons, and the like. Cows, sheep, pigs, and goats accompanied the pack beasts. One mule reputedly had been taken from Jefferson Davis's Mississippi plantation. Entire black families rode in farm wagons or carts. Others, leading or riding animals laden with forage, walked along with their children. The "Bummer Brigade," which had spent the night raiding barnyards and henhouses foraging for these animals, nearly stole the show.

The troops marched in perfect cadence as each guided left. Only a single footfall was heard. Some men were barefoot and bareheaded; others wore floppy caps of straw or wool that looked like empty flour sacks. Still others wore black slouch hats, like Sherman usually wore. The tread of Sherman's 60,000 soldiers was akin to a moral earthquake, destroying the blot of slavery that had sullied the Declaration of Independence for four score and seven years.

The uniform interval between companies was maintained with precision as they marched past the reviewing stand with long, swinging strides, their polished guns at right shoulder shift. One private remembered, "We couldn't look at the reviewing stand. If Lincoln had been there, I'm afraid our line would have broken up."

Lean, rough-looking, hard as iron, and sunburnt, they were all muscle, gristle, and bone, and looked like frontier soldiers. They were taller, leaner, and younger than eastern men, who dubbed them "Sherman's Mules." They wore tattered, loose, dirty blouses instead of trim jackets, and ragged pants tied around their legs. Many had dirty locks hanging to their shoulders and shaggy beards. Beautiful they were not, but impressive they were. Every soldier held his head high and eyes front with a confident, brash, look of glory on his face. Some surely must have popped their buttons, if they still had any, as they swelled with pride. By midmorning it was intensely hot and the men perspired profusely. The crowds cheered and wept for the entire six and one-half hours it took Sherman's army to complete the review. Sherman stood the entire time. A ghost marched with every two soldiers in the review; one soldier in every three that had served in the Union army was killed in action, mortally wounded, or died of disease.

It was noon before John and the Army of Georgia began their march under General Slocum, who received a tremendous welcome from the crowd. Onlookers festooned Slocum's horse with wreaths and flowers. The New Yorkers cheered the president as they passed his reviewing stand. Although he had been replaced as their commander, "Pap" Williams rode at the head of the 20th Corps. His troops, known as the Red Star Division because of their distinctive badge, "carried off the palm for best appearance in all the two days show." The Prussian ambassador who saw the 20th Corps during the parade commented, "An army like that could whip the world." The ex-senator Tom Corwin of Ohio concluded, "They marched like the lords of the world," and a New York Times reporter described "Sherman's Wolves" as the "best material on earth for armies." New Yorkers at hotels along the avenue or on the sidewalks, including relatives and friends of those in the 123rd from Washington County, shouted themselves hoarse. Slocum's staff followed in a single line that stretched from curb to curb. Following it was Slocum's escort, led by Lt. Walter F. Martin, of the 123rd, who had been captured at Kolb's Farm, escaped twice with the assistance of slaves, returned to the regiment at Atlanta, and refused the offer of a leave so that he could join Sherman's march to the sea.

By three thirty, the review was finally over. A friend of Sergeant McLean who had watched the review told him he "would not have taken the $500 for the sight." Some were so exhausted they fell out of ranks and flopped to the ground. Women and children handed them glasses of water and milk. After recuperating, the men marched off to new camps northwest of the city, at last resuming the long, easy route step they had used on so many marches. Spectators lingered after it was over. Sherman, with his wife and son, did not leave until four thirty, after the last of the pack mules and their riders were out of sight. Then the street and fire department took on the task of cleaning up after the thousands of horses that had imbued the city with the aroma of a gigantic stable. Sherman bid his troops farewell by expressing his belief that "as in war you have been good soldiers, so in peace you will make good citizens." The 123rd marched through Washington four miles to the north and camped, exhausted, near the Bladensburg Pike and the Baltimore Railroad, having marched thirty miles that day. Their campsite was in an open pine woodland near Fort Lincoln, along the Anacostia River. Wagons brought their knapsacks. The baggage they had sent to the rear before they left Atlanta also arrived. Visitors who remained overnight discovered the White House doors were open to the public for the first time since Lincoln's assassination.

Dan had arrived in Washington on May 30, a week too late for the Grand Review. He reported to the provost marshal general, then to the brigade provost marshal, Lieutenant Cruikshank, whom he hadn't seen since the day he was captured almost a year ago. He then rejoined his regiment, where he and his brother John had a joyful reunion after a three-year separation.

On June 1, they observed President Andrew Johnson's proclamation to set aside the day for fasting and prayer, and Colonel Rogers was breveted as brigadier general. They remained in camp a week, until June 8, when they were mustered out. During that period John and the others did all the sightseeing and shopping in the capital they could, including visiting the White House, the Smithsonian, the Navy Yard, and an ironclad ship of the *Monitor* class. The streets, restaurants, and bars were crowded with soldiers "doing the town."

On June 9, they boarded the homebound train and left for New York City, arriving June 10.[3] That night they boarded the river steamer *John Taylor* and sailed up the Hudson to Albany, arriving the next day at 6 A.M. They marched to the barracks two miles outside the city on the Troy Road, and on June 14, they were given their discharge papers in Albany. When the two brothers were discharged at Albany, thirty-five members of Company H were present. They were the survivors of the original seventy-eight volunteers plus nine subsequent enlistees in the company. Twenty-one had died and at least eighteen had been wounded. John and Dan arrived home that afternoon for a tearful reunion with their parents and their sisters Anna Marie and Charlotte.

They may have learned when they arrived in Albany that their brother Lank was still in the Albany General Hospital, where he had been since April 27. He would remain there until June 30. If not reunited at the hospital, the three certainly reconnected when Lank came home on furlough from the hospital. The 1865 New York State Census records all three brothers at their parents' home on June 23, when the census taker arrived to enumerate New York veterans. Anna Marie was also at home and reported her occupation as schoolteacher. Charlotte was married and living on a nearby farm. The three veterans reported to the census taker that their oldest brother, William Henry, had been mortally wounded at the Battle of the Wilderness and died on the battlefield the next day, May 6, 1864.[4]

General Slocum resigned his commission in 1865 and returned to Syracuse, New York. From there he moved to Brooklyn and was elected to Congress for three terms beginning in 1868. General Williams returned to civilian life in Michigan and was elected twice to Congress in 1874 and 1876. Colonel Crocker moved to Washington, DC, to resume his legal practice and settled numerous pension claims for veterans of the Civil War, including Lank's. Later he served three two-year terms on the District's Board of Aldermen, and was warden of the U.S. jail in Washington until his death. Colonel McConihe, who succeeded Crocker as commander of the 93rd N.Y., joined the Regular Army and served until 1876.[5]

Epilogue

A Legacy of Sacrifice

> War is horrible but it is in this case waged for a good and holy cause. We shall win, and if I do not live to enjoy the benefits of our government as a single unit, my children will. The fathers of the Revolution died that we might reap the harvest that they prepared for us.
>
> —Colonel Francis T. Sherman
> (Lank Ross's brigade commander),
> letter to his mother, June 7, 1863

Will, Dan, Lank, and John Ross set aside their family responsibilities and personal interests—working the family farm, teaching careers, education, and other possible ambitions—to fight for two larger moral imperatives. They knew, as they enlisted, what the risks might be, but none could have predicted the magnitude of impact their military service would have on them and their family. Nor could they have known what long-term impact their dedication to those goals would have on their fellow soldiers and the outcome of the war, as well as their country.

If courage is basically the willpower to not quit but keep on fighting, soldiers like the Ross brothers and their regimental comrades were the most courageous, morally and physically. From the beginning, they were among the one out of ten soldiers who fought for preserving the Union *and* abolition. Their unflinching determination to fight to the last set the example for, and maintained the morale of, the one-year men, new recruits, bounty men, and draftees.

Union Veteran Volunteers were the counterparts of the soldiers in the Continental Army who enlisted after mid-1776 for either three years or the duration of the war. By the end of that crucial year, it had become clear to George Washington that one-year militiamen, let alone six-month volunteers in state militia units, could not win the war. As a volunteer in the struggle against tyranny, the Continental soldier believed he would be immortalized for his steadfastness. Whether he lived or died, posterity would be grateful for his courage and commitment. A song recorded in the orderly book of the Second New York Continental Regiment, which was largely recruited in the Hudson Valley, included a verse that proclaimed, "The rising world shall sing of us a thousand years to come /And tell our children the wonders we have done."[1]

Like the Revolutionary War Continentals, Veteran Volunteers in the Civil War saw their military service as the fulfillment of a contract between the living, the dead, and the unborn. Many Civil War soldiers were, like Will, Dan, Lank, and John, grandsons or great-grandsons of Revolutionary War and War of 1812 patriots. Knowing that their nation was founded with their ancestors' blood, they would save it with theirs. They were determined to prove themselves capable of defending that legacy. Like many abolitionists, they tended to interpret the Declaration of Independence as a theological, as well as a political, document. On their shoulders, they believed, rested the very survival of the legacy of 1776, as embodied in that document—namely, that "all men have certain unalienable rights, including the right... to institute new Government."

Perhaps Pvt. Walter V. Reeder, a Lincolnite in the 36th Ill., still recovering from his second wound, best summed up this commitment when he wrote his parents on June 9, 1863, "If this, our boasted land of Freemen, the fairest land, under the noblest Government ever made by man... must fall, I care not to survive.... While they have such examples before them as those of Washington, Jefferson, and Jackson... calling to mind the suffering endured by men of the Revolution and later.... I hope that our men will *never* give over this contest until success shall crown our efforts."

Lincoln would reinforce his men's commitment when he spoke to the 148th Ohio during the 1864 election campaign, "Whenever I appear before a body of soldiers, I feel tempted to talk to them of the nature of the struggle in which we are engaged. I look upon it as an attempt to... maintain the government and institutions of our fathers... and transmit them to our children and our children's children forever."

Beginning in 1864, Grant's and Sherman's armies fought almost continuously. Only moral commitment, iron resolve, physical endurance, and courage kept the veterans going, while bounty men, conscripts, short-timers, and substitutes straggled or deserted in increasing numbers. By then, many of the veterans were convinced that they were fighting for the world's citadel of freedom, a temple of liberty. Many Europeans also believed that no combination of circumstances had ever existed that were more conducive to a republican form of government than in the United States. If it failed, that would be the end of freedom. If secession resulted in a *dis*-United States, tyrants and aristocrats everywhere would argue the breakup proved that men do not have the capacity for self-government, that government of, by, and for the people *will* perish from this Earth.

Lincoln and the Republican Party had won the 1860 election in a three-way race. Lacking a majority vote as president, he was in a position of having to dispense civilian and military patronage to Democrats whenever possible. He had to appoint volunteer officers as well as West Point graduates to high-ranking positions. Most of the appointees, like Gen. George McClellan, were not opposed to slavery. Lincoln possessed an uncanny ability to hold together, on a knife edge, a coalition of abolitionists, border-state Unionists, war Democrats, and Republicans, which gained strength as the war dragged on. He walked that fine line between what was morally right and what the public would support. Congressman George S. Boutwell astutely described Lincoln as having an "almost divine faculty of interpreting the will of the people without any expression from them." It was, he said, as if Lincoln had an "inner political tuning fork that reverberated with the rhythm of the common man."

He also earned the undying affection and support of his troops. Lincoln visited more wounded and sick soldiers than any other president, before or since. The ordinary soldier's morale was almost always on his mind. In reviews he not only doffed his hat to each regiment but often bowed as they passed him. Small wonder soldiers called him "Father Abraham."

Alexis de Tocqueville observed that participant generations know far better than later generations "the movement of opinion [and] the popular inclination of the times." Lincoln and Unionists like the Ross brothers and their comrades concluded that the time was *now* to recognize slavery as the supreme issue that divided the South from the North. They perceived that the nation could not be economically, politically, or socially united until slavery was abolished. It was a simple choice: the nation *or* slavery would survive, not both.

If committed men had not enlisted and reenlisted throughout the war to support the North's twin principles of preserving the Union and abolishing slavery, it is entirely possible that neither goal would have been realized. The Union citizen soldiers—along with Lincoln's leadership—played a crucial role in ending the illegal slave trade, abolishing slavery in Washington, DC, and the territories, advancing the Emancipation

Proclamation, enrolling freed slaves in the army and navy, and finally gaining public and congressional support for the 13th Amendment, which abolished slavery.

Veterans like the Ross brothers wanted a president who assured them that their sacrifices to restore the Union and abolish slavery would not be in vain. Their folks at home shared this commitment. "I was taught by you to abhor slavery but never did I hate it as I do now," Private Reeder wrote his parents. "There are but few soldiers but what are abolitionized to a greater or lesser extent. They look upon the 'institution' as a doomed thing and seem to be glad to get rid of the curse of slavery.... I trust that slavery will be *now* and *forever* [banished] from this our boasted land of free men." On May 8, 1863, five days after Chancellorsville, the *Whitehall Chronicle* concluded, "As the blood of martyrs is the seed of the church, so the blood of the patriot soldier is the food upon which the tree of Liberty thrives and lives."

Some men among the early volunteers quickly became converts to emancipation, at least in part because of the example set by more committed soldiers like the Rosses, and in response to what they saw of slavery's detestable effects. An officer of the 22nd N.Y.—which had been recruited early in the war, partly from Washington County—exemplified that transformation. "I am anything but an abolitionist," he wrote a family member on October 25, 1861, "... but having once seen the land where the 'peculiar institution' has flourished ... I must ... say that the experience and acquaintance does not justify the opinion ... that Negro servitude is the palladium of civilization, but on the contrary all history goes to prove it at best the handmaid of an effete, emasculated nationality." Another soldier from the same regiment wrote on November 2, 1861, "I have often heard it expressed by soldiers who had sympathized with slavery [that they] come here and see its effects and say they will never vote again with pro slavery men." In January 1862, a sergeant in the 27th Ind.—which fought alongside the 123rd N.Y. at Chancellorsville, Gettysburg, and Kolb's Farm, on the march to the sea, and to the war's end—wrote, "The more we see of slavery the more detestable it appears."

The majority of Union soldiers, however, were somewhat slower to embrace the abolition of slavery. During the first year or two of the Civil War, Union officers and soldiers usually, although not always, returned runaway slaves to their masters. Often they resented being slave catchers, but they were ordered to do so by Generals McClellan and Halleck in accordance with the provisions of the Fugitive Slave Act. In fact, during the first year of the war, Lincoln appointed his friend Ward Hill Lamon as marshall of the District of Columbia to uphold the Fugitive Slave Law.

Lt. Charles Brewster resisted upholding the law from the outset. "I never will be instrumental in returning a slave to his master in any way, shape or manner, I'll die first," he vowed in a letter to his mother in March 1862. Two years later, Brewster fought in the 10th Mass. alongside the 93rd N.Y. at the Battle of the Wilderness.

Meanwhile, by October 28, 1861, Senator Charles Jennison of Kansas, a staunch abolitionist, organized the 7th Kansas Cavalry, the first regiment that included both black and white soldiers. Another all-black regiment was commissioned by the Massachusetts governor by the end of 1862, but disbanded. The *Troy (NY) Daily Times* editorialized on July 28, 1862, "Why not... give a chance to all the colored people of the North to join the army?" Moderates among elected officials were coming to the same view. On August 14, Senator John Sherman wrote his brother, General Sherman, "I am prepared for one to meet the broad issue of universal emancipation."

Lincoln, a master of timing, had learned to wait for the tide of events to move public opinion to support his position, thus gaining the consent of the governed. Until late 1862, Lincoln had feared that advocating emancipation would divide his soldiers rather than unite them. When issuing his Preliminary Emancipation Proclamation on September 24 that year, he observed, "I hoped for greater gain than loss; but of this I was not entirely confident." Morale was low, and the responses of most Union soldiers ranged from temperate to indifferent. It probably stimulated desertion in the ranks and officer resignations. Only a few prayed for it. Four days later he explained, "[W]hat I did, I did after full deliberation, and under a very heavy and solemn sense of responsibility... I can only trust in God I have made no mistake." Morale suffered initially, exacerbated by McClellan's second dismissal by Lincoln in November 1862, Burnside's bloody defeat in December at Marye's Heights, and his miserably demoralizing Mud March in late January 1863. The decline in morale, however, was short-lived.

On December 1, in his annual message to Congress, Lincoln laid the groundwork for acceptance of his Emancipation Proclamation. In his concluding statement, he noted, "We shall nobly serve or meanly lose the last best hope of earth." Lincoln's leadership stood the test, as the idealists and the pragmatists slowly reached agreement and morale improved. Letters and diaries reveal that idealists' resolve grew even stronger as their searing battle experiences hardened their commitment. What had been a gradual shift in attitude toward abolition was, on balance, actually accelerated.

On January 1, as he affixed his signature to the Emancipation Proclamation, Lincoln said, "I never in my life felt more certain that I was doing right than I do in signing this paper." The following day, the *Troy Daily Times* in New York editorialized that it was the best document written since the Declaration of Independence, adding, "Slavery is to go down or the Union is to perish." Troy was a major stop on the Underground Railroad north into Canada. On January 8, the *Washington County People's Journal* wrote, "We regard it as the heaviest blow that has been aimed at the Slaveholders Rebellion yet." News of the proclamation was communicated through the slave grapevine with astonishing speed. A correspondent for the *Cincinnati Gazette* reported that slaves in Corinth, Mississippi, were all familiar with it. The trickle of runaway slaves became a torrent, washing away the plantation labor force in a flood tide.

Those who were most committed to emancipation for religious reasons had been quickest to support Lincoln. Robert D. Owen, chairman of the American Freedmen's Commission, wrote, "God who made the liberation of the Negro, the condition under which alone we could succeed in this war, has now, in his Providence, brought about a position of things under which it would seem that a full recognition that [the] Negro's rights as citizens becomes indispensable to stability of government in peace."

Ironically, even after the Emancipation Proclamation became effective, General Hooker, in command of the Army of the Potomac until late June 1863, was still granting passes to plantation owners to enter his camps, search for runaway slaves, and put any they found in chains and under the lash. Opinions were changing among the soldiers and other officers, though. Col. Oliver Edwards of the 37th Mass., which fought next to the 93rd N.Y. at the Battle of the Wilderness, wrote his mother on January 13, "[T]he term abolitionist is the proudest name one can bear." Sgt. Samuel E. Nichols, also of the 37th Mass., expressed his changing views in a February 26 letter to his cousin Phebe. "I am an abolitionist, but not a Negro worshipper. I am uncertain whether Negro fighting will amount to much. But if it does not, his freedom is due him at our purchase," Nichols wrote. "The wrong done him by keeping him enslaved for generations is great enough, and now we must cause him to make greater sacrifices and push him to greater dangers. His being caught fighting by the Rebels is certain death. It looks sometimes dishonorable to put him into active service with such certain conditions."

Not everyone agreed. Another soldier in the regiment who had enlisted for three years in August 1862, Pvt. Joseph Taylor, was strongly supportive of preserving the Union. He wrote his father on November 22, "If I live to return to my friends, I shall be proud . . . of having done my duty, and if I fall, you will never have to say you were ashamed of me. The long[er] I remain in the service the more enthusiastic am I, and the more determined I am to see the end of this struggle, or die with a knapsack on." But neither this nor his later letters reveal any interest in the Emancipation Proclamation or the plight of slaves.

The slavery issue among Union soldiers was still extremely divisive as late as the summer of 1863. A significant number of Union officers, particularly in the Army of the Potomac, including McClellan—"Little Mac"—for whom the 93rd had served as the headquarters guard—expressed their pro-slavery views. They did so publicly and privately, disparaging both Lincoln and Stanton, his secretary of war. Undoubtedly, at least some of the rank and file of the 93rd believed McClellan was the greatest general under whom they had served and continued to resent his November 1862 dismissal. William B. Peck, who signed his letter "W.B.P., Co. D, 93rd Reg't N.Y." wrote his local newspaper that when Lincoln, supported by those "troubled with Negrophobia, relieved 'Little Mac' from his command, and our worthy president issued his famous Emancipation Proclamation, [these] two ill-advised measures prolonged the war at least a year."

The political dissension was troubling to soldiers. On February 17, 1863, Samuel Timmons, of the 1st Ohio, which had fought at Stones River along with the 36th Ill., wrote his father, "It is shameful the manner in which the [Ohio] people are becoming divided in political affairs at home.... We have boys in our company whose Fathers have of late become anti-war ... while the one [the son] is trying to put down treason honorable, the other [the father] is against him and in favor of selling his birthright for a mess of pottage.... We ask our friends to stand by us. Are they to desert us in this late hour?" William H. Dobbin (123rd N.Y., Company A), had been captured at Chancellorsville and paroled. A Democrat before Chancellorsville, he wrote the *People's Journal* on August 13, 1863, "Now I am not blood thirsty, but if I am called by my country to kill traitors, let me have a crack at home of those double-dyed treason steeped villains who have not courage to come out and fight for the cause they pretend to espouse." In March 1863, Colonel Crocker, Will's regimental commander, indignantly denied that the Emancipation Proclamation had demoralized the army. He also stated that no Northern men hated copperheads more than soldiers in the Army of the Potomac.

While the Emancipation Proclamation changed some soldiers' views on abolition, it was the growing role of black soldiers in the Union army that had the greatest impact on them. Charles D. Wills, an Illinois soldier in Sherman's army, exemplifies the transformation in countless Union soldiers. He enlisted on April 26, 1861, as a twenty-one-year-old private in response to Lincoln's call for 75,000 ninety-day men. He rose to major and served throughout the war. Wills volunteered solely for the purpose of restoring the Union. His initial views on emancipation were unsympathetic. By the fall of 1862, however, he was prepared to confiscate slaves as contraband rather than return them to their masters. By January 1863, Wills readily accepted emancipation, and by June he strongly supported arming blacks.

Soon after the Emancipation Proclamation, Grant assigned his adjutant general, the West Pointer Lorenzo Thomas, to create regiments of freed black soldiers, initially in the Mississippi Valley. On April 17, 1863, Generals Grant and Thomas inspected the artillery brigades at Milliken's Bend. Afterward, Grant told them of his new policy regarding arming "contrabands." The men cheered. Thomas was an ardent abolitionist and undertook the assignment with enthusiasm, recruiting 20,000 former slaves in his first six weeks on the job. Grant selected Maj. Embry Osband, commander of his personal mounted escort, to command one of these regiments—the 3rd U.S. Colored Cavalry. By the end of 1863, more than thirty-two black regiments had been recruited. The unanswered questions were how they would fight and whether they would be accepted by whites. On June 7, 1863, the African Brigade organized by Gen. Nathaniel Banks using untried black soldiers, participated in vicious fighting against a Confederate attack by 1,500 to 2,000 Rebels on the Milliken's Bend supply depot. In July, black troops bravely fought two more battles—Port Hudson and Fort Wagner. By August 23, 1863, Grant wrote Lincoln, "I have given the subject of arming the Negro my hearty support." After one battle a Union general wrote, "It is impossible for men to show greater gallantry than the Negro troops in this fight." A Confederate officer noted that his charge "was resisted by the negro portion of the enemy's forces with considerable obstinancy, while the white or true Yankee portion ran like whipped curs." Because of the success Generals Grant and Banks had in raising and using black troops, Lincoln told Stanton to reinvigorate their efforts to recruit black soldiers along the Mississippi River. On August 30, Grant also wrote Congressman Washburn, a friend from Galena, Illinois, "[s]lavery is already dead and cannot be resurrected." By then many white soldiers, reluctantly or otherwise, had decided blacks made good soldiers and potential fellow citizens.

In fighting for the North, blacks faced even greater dangers than their white counterparts. On July 30, 1863, Lincoln made it abundantly clear to the South that he was fully prepared to retaliate for the atrocities committed against black Union soldiers. That day he issued an executive order stating, "[F]or every soldier of the United States killed in violation of the laws of war a rebel soldier shall be executed." This order was never carried out for fear there would be no end to its implementation.

Private Reeder wrote to his parents—ardent supporters of the war—between the battles at Stones River and Missionary Ridge, on May 30, 1863. "Speaking of slavery makes me think to tell you that there are but few soldiers [that are not] 'abolitionized' to a greater or less extent," he wrote. "They look upon the 'institution' as a doomed thing, and seem to be glad to get rid of the curse of slavery." In August 1863, after Reeder returned to his regiment from his furlough home with his brother, who served with him in the 36th Ill., his mother wrote, "I have never been the least afraid that my boys would desert. If they should I would be ashamed to own them, then I could no longer call them my brave boys." A soldier in the 93rd N.Y. wrote his hometown newspaper on June 8, "The new movement of arming the blacks will give us a half million additional troops who have shown at Port Hudson that they will fight, and to the last man."

Many of the white soldiers, particularly those who marched through plantation country, came to the same view as Congressman Thaddeus Stevens: "Slavery and Aristocrats go hand in hand.... Corrupt and rotten aristocracy had brought on the war and must be eradicated." John Ross, who participated in the march to the sea and through the Carolinas, surely must have had his abolitionist leanings reinforced by what he saw of slaves' living conditions, as well as what kind of soldiers they became. He also was aware that slaves had helped two men and an officer from his regiment to escape from prison and return to the regiment. A fourth, Lieutenant Beadle, had also escaped after his capture at Gettysburg, undoubtedly with the help of slaves, and returned to the regiment.

In the fall and winter of 1863, Dan saw his first black regiment perform among the best that were assigned to guard the railroad in Tennessee along with his 123rd N.Y. One soldier in his regiment wrote, "I have ... talked with some ... non-commissioned officers [in that regiment] and uniformly found them bright, energetic, and vain. They seem anxious to fight." At the close of the war, Dan also witnessed the creation of several black regiments at Selma and remarked favorably on them, noting that they gave "on every occasion good evidence of courage and loyalty." Seven months after Lank was blinded and still in the hospital, his regiment participated in the Battle of Nashville under Gen. George H. Thomas, as did four regiments of black soldiers—the 14th, 17th, 18th, and 44th USCT. On December 15, 1864, those black soldiers fought side by side with a brigade of white troops. Partly because of their combined efforts, Thomas was victorious in his charge. But it was a brutal day for the black soldiers, who suffered more than 300 casualties. The next day, the 2nd Colored Brigade participated in another charge, and were initially repulsed by Hood's troops. They made a second charge and the enemy gave way, retreating precipitously.

Afterwards, General Thomas rode over the battlefield and saw the commingled bodies of black and white soldiers. He turned to his staff and said, "Gentlemen the question is settled; Negroes will fight." One of these regiments had previously received high praise from Thomas for capturing a Rebel battery. The 36th witnessed this action, since they participated nearby in another part of the battle as one of the seventy-one Veteran Volunteer regiments in Thomas's Army of the Cumberland.

The growing role of black soldiers in fighting the war swung the tide of opinion. In 1862, blacks had been employed as laborers, teamsters, and trench diggers by the Union Army. Hostility and ill will were so predominant that the North would not enlist blacks to fight alongside whites. By July 1, 1863, there were only nineteen regiments of black soldiers. Two years later, by July 15, 1865, there were 139 black regiments in the army, totaling 123,156 troops. Altogether by war's end, 186,000 black soldiers had served in 178 Union regiments, while many thousands more worked for the army; 4,125 of these men were recruited in New York, while 68,000 were recruited in three Southern states: Louisiana, Tennessee, and Kentucky. There were more black men in the Union army than white men in Lee's Army of Northern Virginia. One-third of the black troops became casualties, most the result of disease; a total of 40,000 lost their lives, but only 2,900 were killed or died from their wounds. They had fought in 39 major battles and 410 minor engagements, armed with inferior weapons, earning lower pay, and receiving poorer food and medical care. Seventeen black soldiers had won the Medal of Honor. Since four-fifths of these men were ex-slaves, they confirmed the prophetic wisdom of the abolitionists that as freedmen they could and would fight.

Toward the end of the war, the synergistic effect of witnessing the inhumanity of slavery, having personal contact with slaves, and recognizing the contributions of black soldiers in the war shifted opinion. A growing number came to view slavery as a curse and vowed to abolish it. This was particularly true among those who had been taught that hard work was the way to achieve independence. They saw that rather than improving his circumstances by working hard, a slave only improved his master's lot in life. Although many of these men had not gone to war to free slaves, they came to agree that they were willing to free the slaves as a military necessity in order to win the war and save the Union. Every emancipated slave weakened the South's war effort and thereby strengthened the North.

From a pragmatic standpoint, unpaid slave labor in the South had impacted Northerners by holding down wages, a menace to the North's free labor economy. Those who opposed the draft supported the enlistment of blacks as a way to minimize the need for conscription. The instinct for self-preservation led still other soldiers to accept blacks who could stop a bullet as well as they could. As the historian Earl J. Hess noted, a fusion of such pragmatic reasoning and moral principle—or, at least, altruism—strengthened the resolve of ever-increasing numbers of soldiers to abolish slavery. They came to realize that blacks were their allies. Many befriended blacks as the war continued. Acts of kindness and assistance became more frequent, including teaching runaways how to read and write. It had finally dawned on Northern civilians that it was totally illogical to return or guard slaves, who were considered Rebel property, while the owner was fighting to destroy the Union.

One author, Joseph T. Glatthaar, who has studied Sherman's army extensively, has noted that by war's end, the vast majority of Sherman's army was composed of men who believed in social and political equality of blacks, or at worst held a slight prejudice against them. Sherman's army also had the highest percentage of Veteran Volunteers and three-year men. According to Lieutenant Cruikshank, Sherman's soldiers reduced to ashes those towns and plantations where they found slave pens, auction blocks, whipping posts, stocks, or bloodhounds used to track and maim runaway slaves.

Union soldiers' growing commitment to ending slavery not only sustained them through the war, but also played a key role in Lincoln's reelection. By 1864, 71 percent of Northern soldiers favored freeing slaves and enlisting them in the army. They recognized that by fighting, black soldiers were not only establishing their own worth, but that of their white champions as well. Some argued that black soldiers would thereby learn self-reliance and responsibility, which would better prepare them for freedom. Fighting for the Union, as well as their own freedom, was proof that blacks not only deserved but had earned emancipation. Having enlisted, they staked their claim to full citizenship.

On June 25, 1864, after Lincoln had been renominated in Baltimore, and three days after Dan was captured at the Battle of Kolb's Farm, a soldier in his regiment wrote the *People's Journal*. "You have renominated Lincoln. Thank God for that!" he exulted. "As the soldiers friend and the honest frank friend of our country, he receives our confidence as well as he will our support [in the coming election]. Nine out of ten of the Army of the Cumberland endorse the resolutions and nominations of the Baltimore [Union Party] convention." In September 1864, the *Washington County People's Journal* printed the letter of an officer (probably in the 123rd N.Y.) that said, "I have yet to find that officer or soldier who is not in favor of Abraham Lincoln." And a private in Sherman's artillery commented shortly before the election, "In the evening a general discussion took place on the 'nigger' question, politics, etc." His battery ended up voting 75–0 for Lincoln. He added, "I can cheerfully bear all the discomforts of a soldier's life for the overthrow of this monster evil."

By October 1864 support for Lincoln among Veteran Volunteers and three-year men had been forged by the heat of innumerable battles. These soldiers wanted desperately to vote to express "their deep devotion to their country," and to punish the party that "would have deprived us of that right." Since election laws were written and enforced by states, those controlled by Republicans made it easier to vote in the field, while those controlled by Democrats made it more difficult. Grant wrote Secretary of War Stanton that soldiers "have as much right to demand that their votes be counted as those citizens who remain at home; Nay more, for they have sacrificed more for their country."

Only twelve states—not including Illinois—permitted soldiers to vote in the field and have their ballots tabulated separately. Officials from those twelve states delivered voting tickets to soldiers but were not allowed to electioneer, although some of them apparently did. Illinois soldiers had to vote in person at home. Seven other states allowed soldiers to vote but did not keep a separate tally. For example, New York allowed proxy voting only, which meant that 70,000 ballots were sent home from the field to be counted. These ballots had to be delivered by local voters to appropriate polling booths on election day, together with affidavits authorizing the votes to be cast. The affidavit was, in fact, a soldier's power of attorney, signed and witnessed wherever the soldier was stationed. The *Washington County Post* published an editorial urging relatives and friends of Washington County soldiers to "fight with the ballot." It stated, "We . . . earnestly advise every man who has a relation or friend in the service to procure [voting] tickets at once and forward them to the soldier." The record is clear that the 123rd fought with the ballot as well as with the bullet.

Eighty-nine percent of the votes in Dan and John's regiment, the 123rd N.Y., went to Lincoln—336, compared to 30 for McClellan. Their Company H voted 22 for Lincoln, 5 for "Little Mac." Pvt. John Gourlie of the 123rd wrote his brother about a comrade, a staunch McClellan man, who had sworn he would see "Old Abe d———d before I would vote for him." However, during his capture and imprisonment, he heard his guards say that if McClellan were elected, he would save the Confederacy. That converted the prisoner into a "Lincoln man to the backbone." According to Lieutenant Cruikshank, this overwhelming regimental vote for Lincoln was cast despite the fact that the men had not been paid for ten months and had fought all summer. Colonel Rogers, the regimental commander, reported that his men conducted the election with less partisan heat and influence than elections at home.

Had Lank and Will's regiments been able to vote, there is little doubt they also would have cast a ten-to-one vote for Lincoln. On November 8, 1864, Pvt. Day Elmore of the 36th Ill. wrote his parents, "If George B. McClellan [is] elected . . . then will we soldiers take the rains [sic] of this government in our own hands and 'go on with the war' until the dear old flag [floats] from every housetop . . . in the so-called 'corn-fed' states." Unlike the 123rd, which was in camp, the 93rd N.Y. was in the front line at Petersburg and could not take the time to vote.

It is inconceivable that Veteran Volunteers would have fought two or three years for the Union and then have voted against it. Their vote for Lincoln was the heaviest. One soldier from Washington County informed the *Salem Press*, "Of one thing, you may feel assured, that in the regiment I belong to [probably the 93rd N.Y.] there are not ten men that would sooner see death staring them in the face, than to have any but the present incumbent in the chair." Sgt. Rice C. Bull of the 123rd declared, "The prevailing feeling among the men was a desire to finish the job." Pvt. John Cutter of the 123rd told his father, "I did not get a chance to vote for we were on the march from Adairsville to Atlanta. It is as well, if I had a thousand votes Lincoln would have them. I have seen a number of village papers [from Washington County] and would like to drop one in the rebel lines, just to make them huffy."

One scholar who examined numerous letters from Illinois soldiers, as well as other compelling evidence, concluded that as early as June 1862, many favored emancipation and that by 1864, most would have voted for Lincoln. One Illinois soldier summed it up when he wrote, "The sentiment of the army is 'God Bless Abraham.' . . . On this question [namely, emancipation] the army has been far in advance of the people." Gen. George McClellan had been the most popular commander the Army of the Potomac ever had. Many of his soldiers had virtually worshiped him. But McClellan had guaranteed his ignominious defeat with respect to the soldier vote by the repeated use of his campaign slogan, "The Constitution as it is, the Union as it was."

All during the summer and into the fall, stump speakers and pamphlets stirred heated political debates over "Little Mac" vs. Lincoln in army camp rallies and meetings. During the campaign, a soldier in the 83rd Ohio wrote home, "I did at one time think that the 'Little Napoleon' would have commanded a large vote . . . but . . . there has been a great falling off of the 'Faithful' [copperheads] since those vile traitors proclaim this war a failure."

The army was "Lincolnized," especially after McClellan referred to him as "nothing more than a well-meaning baboon." Of the total 154,300 soldiers who voted, more than three-quarters—120,000—cast their votes for Lincoln, compared to 34,300 for McClellan. Ohio's wounded and sick soldiers in Washington's hospitals and camps voted ten to one for Lincoln. Among Sherman's 173 Veteran Volunteer regiments, only one gave McClellan a majority vote. Altogether, approximately 12 percent of the 1,307,000 soldiers eligible to vote actually voted.

After the election in November 1864, 1st Lt. Haviland Gifford, adjutant of the 93rd N.Y., wrote his father, "Glorious news has reached here from the election in New York. . . . [T]he People [of New York have] solemnly avowed to support the administration of our worthy President . . . and we [the 93rd N.Y.] pledge ourselves, our lives and our sacred honor to carry on this war . . . until the shackles fall from off the toes of the last slave."

On November 12, when the election news reached the front, Pvt. John Haley of the 17th Maine wrote that Lincoln, "that friend of humanity and champion of human rights[,] is again at the helm of the ship of state. A better or truer man was never entrusted with power." Other soldiers lit bonfires and tar barrels and wildly celebrated. They did it again at his second inauguration and were particularly moved when he said in his inaugural address that the nation needed to care "for him who shall have borne the battle, and for his widow and his orphan."

Clearly, a soldier's vote for Lincoln was his vote for continuing the war and a mandate for emancipation. Grant recognized this when the election returns reached him. He telegraphed Lincoln that his "[v]ictory was worth more to the country than a battle won." Grant was also deeply impressed with the orderly way in which the election was conducted, as, indeed, were many Europeans. There were no riots and few fraudulent returns. Those that were detected were handled in an exemplary manner.

In contrast to the 78 percent of soldiers who voted for Lincoln, only 55 percent of the civilian population supported him in 1864—up, however, from 40 percent in 1860. He had received 350,000 more votes in 1864 than he did in 1860. He carried all but three states—Delaware, Kentucky, and New Jersey—and the Republican Party won 75 percent of the congressional seats. The Union candidate for Kentucky governor, a border state, also won in this election, indicating growing antislavery conviction there. The race-baiting, hysterical invective and unprincipled dirty tricks used to smear Lincoln and the Republican Party backfired and became the straw that broke the camel's back, assuring the death of slavery in the country.

The soldiers' change in attitude aided in turning around public opinion. By year's end, black freedom was widely viewed as a vital war measure, among soldiers as well as civilians. In his 1864 year-end message to Congress—after Maryland, Missouri, and Louisiana had emancipated their slaves—the recently reelected president urged quick adoption of the 13th Amendment to the Constitution, abolishing slavery. "May we not agree that the sooner the better?" Lincoln said. "The abolition of slavery by constitutional provision settles the fate for all coming time, not only of millions now in bondage, but of unborn millions to come." On January 31, 1865, by a two-thirds majority, the House of Representatives passed the constitutional amendment. It had already passed the Senate. On February 9, the *Washington County People's Journal* proclaimed January 31 nearly as important as the 4th of July. The *Washington County Chronicle* editorialized on January 13, "The late election will make millions more in bondage into freemen . . . the pretensions, the claims, the merits, and the influences of slavery have been weighed and found wanting."

By the end of the war in 1865, few Northern soldiers accepted the Southern view that servitude was a "divinely appointed condition for the highest good of the slave." One New Yorker wrote his parents on April 8, 1865, "If I am spared to come home I shall bring a black boy home with me. I know of some very good boys who would make good help and would be glad of such a chance and they are as much entitled to our care and our assistance as many who have a whiter skin but blacker hearts."

By war's end, a deeply rooted *national* consciousness had emerged. Until the Civil War, most thought of themselves as citizens of a community and state. People's loyalties were local rather than national. Small towns were crucibles of the concept of duty to one's community. There were few strong forces that tied them together nationally. Federal services to most citizens had been largely confined to mail delivery. With the war came a federal income tax, national currency and banking systems, a military draft, an expanded federal court system, the first homestead act, and a national railroad system that the federal government had helped fund. The war itself, however, played the most important role in linking Americans to their nation. Lincoln's and the army's ability to attract the devotion of citizens and soldiers to the national effort for reuniting the nation was crucial to creating this national consciousness.[2]

The three surviving Ross brothers all returned to upstate New York, to learn that their parents would soon lose the family farm. John would remain in New York, working as a slater, carpenter, and farmhand. He married the daughter of a neighboring family that owned a wool mill that was down the road from the family's farm and had made horse blankets for the Union cavalry. They had a son who died in infancy and four daughters. John eventually received a pension for his hearing loss suffered on Sherman's march. He died of typhoid fever in 1893 at the age of forty-eight.

Charles and Margaret Ross moved in with John initially, then bought a tiny farm where they lived for a few years with Anna Marie.

Daniel Reid Ross

Like John, their daughter Charlotte remained in the Hudson River Valley, raising chickens and turkeys, and growing corn, fruit, and potatoes with her husband and children on their farm.

The rest of the Rosses all left New York at some point after the war.

Spurred by memories of his winter stay near there in 1862, Dan moved to Berkeley County, West Virginia, two months after his discharge. While there during the war, Dan likely had been aware that President Lincoln signed a bill admitting that state to the Union, provided it emancipated its slaves. Now, like so many of his former comrades in arms, Dan wanted to forget the war and build the future. Whatever bitterness or hatred he had felt during the war was erased as soon as it ended. Instead, the war triggered his moral impulse to spend the rest of his life serving those in need, Union or Confederate.

Dan became the first public school teacher in Little Georgetown, Berkeley County, fulfilling the goal for which he had trained before the war. He also became the first depositor in the Old National Bank of Martinsburg, the county seat. Fifty years later, the bank—which was established to help finance the rebuilding of the county—published a half-page ad in the local newspaper thanking him for being their first depositor.

Epilogue

In 1868, Dan left his adopted state to study medicine in Ohio, where he met and married Samantha Mathews (Mantie), the daughter of an innkeeper. Family legend holds that this inn, The Ohio House, had been a station on the Underground Railroad. Three years later, in 1871, his parents and Anna Marie joined them in Ohio.

Lank received a pension soon after his discharge. He sold insurance to local citizens until he joined his parents and siblings in Ohio around 1872. In 1875, he married Mantie's sister, Ada.

Meanwhile, Dan went into medical practice with one of his teachers after finishing his schooling in Columbus, Ohio. With his training completed, he was ready to return to West Virginia, taking his wife and mother, in 1874. His father, Charles, had died in Ohio, and Anna Marie remained in that state until moving west to San Luis, Colorado, in 1878, and resumed her work teaching in Presbyterian mission schools. Dan would eventually have his father's remains moved from Ohio and reinterred in West Virginia, where they rest with those of his mother, who died in 1892. He also had the remains of his firstborn child, who had died in infancy, moved from Ohio and reinterred in West Virginia. On the four-sided tombstone he erected, he also memorialized Will's death at the Battle of the Wilderness.

Lank and his family followed the others to West Virginia some time after marrying Ada, but eventually moved his family back to Ohio. His wife gave music lessons and he became a blind tailor, but mostly they subsisted on his pension. He died in Painesville, Ohio, in 1914, of Bright's disease. Following her husband's death, Ada returned to West Virginia to live with Dan and Mantie until her death.

Dan spent his last fifty years as a country doctor and leading citizen of his adopted county, tending to countless residents who had been sympathetic to the Confederacy, as well as Unionists. He seldom billed any of his patients and often accepted payment in kind from farmers, grocers, and merchants. He also served as a section surgeon for the North Mountain Division of the Baltimore & Ohio Railroad, in exchange for lifetime passes for his family.

He was one of the few doctors in his county who would treat black patients. Dan also initiated the effort to open a public school for black children and raised funds to build the first high school in his district. He served on the school board for twenty years, reflecting his Reformed Presbyterian heritage. Three of his six children became teachers, imbued as strongly with the importance of education as with the concept of human equality.

Dan finally, in 1893, received a Civil War invalid pension for the heart problems and rheumatism he developed while in Andersonville and other Confederate prisons. It amounted to $8 a month. He died in 1924, at the age of eighty-two, having been bedridden the last two years of his life. By that time his pension had reached $12 a month.

On the day he heard of the death of Jefferson Davis, December 6, 1889, Dan sat down to write his only Civil War memoir at his home in Hedgesville, West Virginia, near Little Georgetown. He reflected on his experiences as a prisoner of war.

> I never saw any actual cruelty deliberately planned and practiced except at Andersonville ... [T]he site of that prison was chosen for the very purpose of killing as many prisoners as possible. . . . [W]hy were the guards, numbering not less than three thousand, camped on the stream that afforded us our water supply and we were compelled to drink their drainage? . . . In happy contrast to this was the conduct of a great majority of the men that fought the battles of the Southern cause. . . . [Except for the guards at Andersonville] I never, during the time I was a prisoner in their hands nor during the many years since that I have lived among them, have heard an unkind word or seen an unkind act done by those that formed the "rank and file" of the Rebel army to their Yankee neighbors.[3]

The Ross brothers and their comrades, like many committed emancipators, could well have been proud of the part they played by word and deed in laying the groundwork for the acceptance of the black man as a soldier, and ultimately as a citizen. Thanks to the dedication of such men, the end of the war became a true, albeit slow, beginning in making effective the crucial phrase in the Declaration of Independence, "We hold these Truths to be self-evident, that all Men are created equal."

Without the initial impetus of those one-in-ten soldiers like the Rosses, their comrades, and 200,000 others who became Veteran Volunteers and three-year men, the outcome of the war could have been very different—at worst, a negotiated peace that did not end slavery or, at best, an even more prolonged, tragic, and costly war. Even now this nation has not yet reached the goal set by Abraham Lincoln and the Civil War. When we do, only then will the price of 600,000 Union and Confederate lives lost, and an unknown but significantly larger number of others that were forever altered, prove to be worth it.

Notes

Document Key

AHG-HP: Alfred H. Guernsey, *Harper's Pictorial History of the Civil War* (New York, 1866)

AMC-L: Sgt Albert M. Cook (123rd N.Y.) letters

AMC-D: Pvt./Sgt. Albert M. Cook (123rd N.Y.) diary

BL: *Battles & Leaders of the Civil War*

CJ-WC: Crisfield Johnson, *History of Washington County New York 1737–1878* (Interlaken New York, 1991)

CS-AL: Carl Sandburg, *Abraham Lincoln* (New York, 1954)

CWTI: *Civil War Times (Illustrated)*

DE-L: Pvt. Day Elmore (36th Ill.) letters

DE-D: Pvt. Day Elmore (36th Ill.) diary

DHK-H93: David H. King, *History of the Ninty-Third Regt New York Volunteer Infantry 1861–1865* (Milwaukee WI, 1895)

EJH-BB: Earl J. Hess, *Banners to the Breeze* (Lincoln NE, 2000)

EJH-LV: Earl J. Hess, *Liberty, Virtue, and Progress* (New York, 1988)

EJH-US: Earl J. Hess, *The Union Soldier in Battle* (Lawrence, KS, 1997)

EL-GH: Edward E. Longacre, *A Biography of General Henry Jackson Hunt* (New York, 1977)

EL-GC: Edward E. Longacre, *Grant's Cavalrymen* (Mechanicsburg, PA., 1996)

ERB-IN27: Edward R. Brown, *Twenty-Seventh Indiana Volunteer Infantry* (Gaithersburg MD, 1899)

F4US: *Record of Events of Battery F Fourth Artillery* undated pamphlet (copy in author's possession)

FAL-TF: Francis A. Lord, *They Fought for the Union* (New York, 1960)

GP-LW: Geoffrey Perret, *Lincoln's War* (New York, 2004)

HCM-R123: Henry C. Morhous, *Reminiscences of the 123rd Regt. N.Y.S.V.* (New York, 1879)

HP-CG: Horace Porter, *Campaigning with Grant* (New York, 1991)

HSC-BG1: Henry Steel Commager, *Blue and Gray*, vol. 1 (Indianapolis, IN, 1973)

HSC-BG2: Henry Steele Commager, *Blue and Gray*, vol. 2 (Indianapolis, IN, 1973)

HSC-CWA: Henry Steele Commager, *Civil War Archive* (New York, 2000)

JB-CaC: John Bowers, *Chickamauga and Chattanooga* (New York, 1994)

JB-CoC: John Bigelow, *Campaign of Chancellorsville* (New Haven, CT, 1910)

JGC-NH: Jeffrey Gordon Charnley, "Neglected Honor, The Life of General A. S. Williams," (PhD dissertation, Michigan State University, 1983)

JGN-AL6: John G. Nicolay and John Hay, *Abraham Lincoln, A History*, vol. 6 (New York, 1890)

JGN-AL7: John G. Nicolay and John Hay, *Abraham Lincoln, A History*, vol. 7 (New York, 1890)

JGN-AL8: John G. Nicolay and John Hay, *Abraham Lincoln, A History*, vol. 8 (New York, 1890)

JGN-AL9: John G. Nicolay and John Hay, *Abraham Lincoln, A History*, vol. 9 (New York, 1890)

JGN-CW: John G. Nicolay and John Hay, *Complete Works of Abraham Lincoln* (New York, 1905)

JES-RN: Joseph E. Stevens, *1863: The Rebirth of a Nation* (New York, 1999)

JMM-A: James M. McPherson, *Crossroads of Freedom: Antietam 1862* (New York, 2002)

JMM-BC: James M. McPherson, *Battle Cry of Freedom* (New York, 1988)

JMM-CC: James M. McPherson, *For Cause and Comrades* (New York, 1997)

JMM-DS: James M. McPherson, *Drawn by the Sword* (New York, 1996)

JMM-OF: James M. McPherson, *Ordeal by Fire* (New York, 1982)

JMM-SE: James M. McPherson, *The Struggle for Equality* (Princeton, NJ, 1964)

JSC-D: Col. John S. Crocker (93rd N.Y.) diary

JTG-MS: Joseph T. Glatthaar, *The March to the Sea and Beyond* (New York, 1985)

JYS-PG10: John Y. Simon, *The Papers of Ulysses S. Grant*, vol. 10 (Carbondale, IL, 1982)

JYS-PG11: John Y. Simon, *The Papers of Ulysses S. Grant*, vol. 11 (Carbondale, IL, 1984)

JYS-PG12: John Y. Simon, *The Papers of Ulysses S. Grant*, vol. 12 (Carbondale, IL, 1984)

KJB-S: K. Jack Bauer, ed., *Soldiering, The Civil War Diary of Rice C. Bull* (Novato, CA, 1977)

LGB-H36: L. G. Bennett & William H. Haigh, *History of the Thirty-Sixth Regiment Illinois Volunteers* (Marengo, IL, 1999)

LJD-DG: Larry J. Daniel, *Days of Glory* (Baton Rouge, LA, 2004)

LJD-CG: Larry J. Daniel, *Cannoneers in Gray* (University, AL, 1984)

LT-GG: Larry Tagg, *The Generals of Gettysburg* (Mason City, IA, 1998)

LVLN-GC: L. Van Loan Naisawald, *Grape and Canister* (New York, 1960)

MOLLUS: Military Order of the Loyal Legion of the United States

MQ-CM: Milo M. Quaife, ed., *From the Cannon's Mouth: The Civil War Letters of General Alpheus S. Williams* (Detroit, 1959)

OR: *Official Records War of the Rebellion*

PC-BL: Peter Cozzens, ed., *Battles and Leaders of the Civil War*, vol. 5 (Chicago, 2002)

PC-NA: Peter Cozzens, *The New Annals of the Civil War* (Mechanicsburg, PA, 2004)

PC-TS: Peter Cozzens, *This Terrible Sound* (Chicago, IL, 1992)

PC-SH: Peter Cozzens, *Shipwreck of their Hopes* (1994)

PHS-M: Philip H. Sheridan, *Memoirs of P. T. Sheridan*, vol. 1 (New York, 1891)

PSP-PAL: Philip S. Paludan, *The Presidency of Abraham Lincoln* (Lawrence, MA., 1994)

PVS-SL: Philip V. Stern, *Soldier Life* (New York, 1961)

RCB-S

RC-D: Robert Cruikshank (123rd NY) diaries (typescript copy at Bancroft Public Library, Salem NY)

RC-L: Robert Cruikshank (123rd NY) letters

RED-CW: Robert E. Denney, *The Civil War Years* (New York, 1992)

RHS-HD: Richard H. Sewell, *A House Divided* (Baltimore, MD, 1988)

RL-ND: Robert Leckie, *None Died in Vain* (New York, 1990)

RM-S: Roy Morris Jr., *The Life and Wars of General Philip Sheridan* (New York, 1992)

RO-SI: Richard O'Connor, *Sheridan the Inevitable* (Indianapolis, IN, 1953)

SPH-WT: Stanley P. Hirshson, *The White Tecumseh* (New York, 1997)

WCM-L: Sgt. William C. (Clark) McLean (123rd NY) letters

WCM-D: Sgt. William C. (Clark) McLean (123rd NY) diary (copy in author's possession)

WKK-AL: William K. Klingaman, *Abraham Lincoln* (New York, 2001)

WML-EG : William M. Lamers, *The Edge of Glory* (New York, 1961)

WTS-M: William T. Sherman, *Memoirs of General William T. Sherman* (New York, 1875)

WVR-L: Pvt. Walter V. Reeder (36th Ill.) letters (University of Wisconsin MS Collections)

WWB-L: Capt. W. W. Braman (93rd NY) letters

WW-L: William Wheeler, *Letters of William Wheeler* (Cambridge, MA, 1876)

Source Key

AMHI: US Army Military History Institute

FCHS: Filson Club Historical Society, Louisville

LC: Library of Congress

NYHS: New York Historical Society

NYSL: New York State Library

NA: National Archives

Chapter 1. Why, How, and When They Fought

1. Ross family records and correspondence (copies in author's possession); military and pension records of the Ross brothers, Record Group 94, National Archives; Oscar and Lillian Handlin, *Liberty and Power* vol. 1 (New York, 1986),

pp. 11–12; James Hay Beveridge, *The Church of Pioneers* (Somanauk, IL, 1911), pp. 15–17; *Journal of the Illinois State Historical Society*, vol. 18, no. 3 (October 1925), p. 702; *Elgin Daily Courier*, April 20, 1861, and March 7, 1862; D. S. Fares, "The Covenanter Church in the Civil War," *The Christian Nation*, October 4, 1911, vol. 55, p. 6; Arthur M. Schlesinger, Jr., *The Age of Jackson* (Boston, 1946), p. 432; Carleton Mabee, *Black Freedom* (New York, 1970), p. 218; EJH-US, p. 75; *Washington County People's Journal*, March 6, 1858, and vol. 11, no. 29, July 21, 1864; *Washington County Post*, November 15, 1861, and March 28, 1862; *National Anti-Slavery Standard*, vol. 18, no. 42, March 6, 1858, p. 2; Hon. Jas. R. McKean of New York, speech entitled "Democracy Alias Slavery," delivered in the U.S. House of Representatives, June 6, 1860 (copy in author's possession); Ira Berlin, "To Canvass the Nation: The War for Union Becomes a War for Freedom," *Journal of the National Archives*, Winter 1988, pp. 237, 238, 242; Berlin, ibid., p. 165; Gerald Sorin, *The New York Abolitionists* (Westport, CT, 1971), pp. 5, 119, 127; Andrew E. Murray, *Presbyterians and the Negro* (Philadelphia, PA, 1966), p. 116; *Washington County Post*, vol. 73, no. 495, September 7, 1860, p. 2; ibid., vol. 73, no. 475, April 20, 1860, p. 2; ibid., vol. 74, no. 556, November 15, 1861, p. 2; E. A. Crawford (36th IL), letter to his sister dated December 7, 1861 (copy in author's possession); James W. Geary, *We Need Men* (DeKalb, IL, 1991), p. 40; Herbert Aptheker, *AntiRacism in U.S. History* (Westport, CT, 1993) p. 156; Kevin Phillips, *The Cousin's War* (New York, 1999), pp. 398, 400; V. Jacque Volgeli, *Free but Not Equal* (Chicago, IL, 1970), p. 83; Roger Butterfield, *The American Past* (New York, 1947), p. 149; Dave Thornton, "The Civil War Editor: Rufus King Crocker" (unpublished typescript, n.d.), pp. 10, 23, 27, 45, 47; Charles K. Whipple, "Relation of AntiSlavery to Religion," AntiSlavery Tract no. 19 (n.d.) Massachusetts Historical Society; Robert Hastings Nichols, *Presbyterianism in New York State* (Philadelphia, PA, 1963), p. 8; *Troy Daily Times*, July 11, 1862; Albert Barnes, *The Church and Slavery*, pp. 133, 202; Randall M. Miller, *Religion and the American Civil War* (New York, 1988), p. 78; Rev. E. W. Hicks, *History of Kendall County, Illinois* (Aurora, IL, 1877), pp. 215–16; Morton L. Dillon, *The Abolitionists* (DeKalb, IL, 1974), pp. 159, 190, 202, 223; Samuel Eliot Morison, *The Oxford History of the American People* (New York, 1965), pp. 592, 595, 653; CS-AL, pp. 131, 165, 235; Victor B. Howard, "Presbyterians, The Kansas-Nebraska Act, and the Election of 1856," *Journal of Presbyterian History*, vol. 49, no. 21 (1971), p. 143; Tom Calarco, *The Underground Railroad Conductor* (Schenectady, NY, 2003), pp. 14, 57, 59; Noah Brooks, *Abraham Lincoln* (New York, 1895), pp. 107–11; Richard H. Sewell, *Ballots for Freedom* (New York, 1976), p. 292; Briece Chadwick, *The American Presidents*, (Secaucus, NJ, 1999), p. 270; Robert W. Johannsen, *Lincoln, the South, and Slavery* (Baton Rouge, LA, 1991), pp. 20, 21, 23, 57, 63; Tom Calarco, *The Underground Railroad in the Adirondack Region* (Jefferson, NC, 2004), p. 155; Randall C. Jimmersen, *The Private Civil War* (Baton Rouge, LA, 1988), pp. 2, 3, 12, 13; Doris K. Goodwin, *Team of Rivals* (New York, 2005), p. 112; J. F. Cleveland, Compiler, *The Tribune Almanac* (1861), pp. 41, 46; J. F. Cleveland, Compiler, *The Tribune Almanac* (1865), pp. 48, 52; *CJ-WC*, pp. 278–79; NYHS, private correspondence from its manuscript department, dated March 13, 1991; O. R. Ser. 3, vol. 1, correspondence, pp. 386, 452, 675; *Troy Daily Times*, July 11,

1862; RC-D, March 1, 1863; James Oakes, *The Radical and the Republicans* (New York, 2007), pp. 52, 74; JMM-BC, p. 711; Deuteronomy, Chapter 23, Verse 11, Ward H. Lamon, The Life of Abraham Lincoln (Boston, 1872), p. 347. Elisha P. Thurston, *History of the Town of Greenwich* (Salem, NY), p. 59. H. Jack Lane, *The Wit and Wisdom of Abraham Lincoln* (Cleveland, 1942), p. 43; James M. McPherson, *Abraham Lincoln and the Second American Revolution* (New York, 1990), p. 54.

2. FAL-TF, pp. 1, 4, 7, 8; JMM-CC, pp. 58–59, 165–68; Clement Eaton, *A History of the Southern Confederacy* (New York, 1954), p. 93; RED-CW, p. 41; JTG-MS, p. 187; Phillip Shaw Pauludan *"A People's Contest"* (New York, 1998), p. 214; Gabor S. Borrit, *Why the Confederacy Lost* (New York, 1992), p. 115; Charles Royster, *A Revolutionary People at War* (New York, 1979), p. 46; William C. Davis, *Lincoln's Men* (New York, 1999), pp. 157–58; John S. Crocker, (93rd N.Y.), affidavit dated January 1, 1864, John S. Crocker Papers, NYHS; Robert W. Johannsen, *Lincoln, the South, and Slavery* (Baton Rouge, LA, 1991), p. 7.

3. Ross family records and correspondence; *Washington County People's Journal*, vol. 11, no. 13, March 31, 1864; *Washington County Post*, vol. 72, no. 450, November 15, 1859, p. 2; New York State Census of 1865; FAL-TF, p. 3; Dave Thornton, "The Civil War Editor: Rufus King Crocker" (unpublished typescript, n.d.), pp. 30, 32; *Troy Daily Times*, September 16, 1862; DHK-H93, pp. 494, 496, 625; *History Today*, July 2000, p. 24; WKK-AL, p. 138; John S. Crocker, affidavit dated January 21, 1864, John S. Crocker (93rd N.Y.) Papers, NYHS; JMM-CC, p. 19; Charles W. Wills, *Army Life of an Illinois Soldier* (Carbondale, IL, 1996), p. 22; Lynn Calvin, Saratoga County Historian, private correspondence to author dated 10/10/03; James MacNaughton, Jr., *The Argyle Patent and Its Early Settlers* (Hopkinsville, KY, 1999), pp. 298–99; EJH-LV, p. 25; LGB-H36, p. 12; *Report of the Provost Marshall General, Executive Documents of the House of Representatives*, 39th Congress, 1st session, 1865–66, table 2 (Washington, DC, 1866), p. 160; Ross family records; Mark H. Dunkelman, *Brothers One and All* (Baton Rouge LA, 2004), p. 17; Daniel E Sutherland, "Abraham Lincoln, John Pope, the Origins of Total War," *Journal of Military History*, (October 1992), p. 574; Kenneth Williams, *Lincoln Finds a General*, vol. 1 (Bloomington, IN, 1949), pp. 118, 399n30; RED-CW., pp. 60–61; O. R., ser. 3, vol. 4—Correspondence, p. 1264; PSP-PAL, p. 26.

4. JTN-BC, pp. 251–52, 409–10, 491–93; Fred Albert Shannon, *The Organization and Administration of the Union Army*, vol. 1 (Gloucester, MA, 1965), p. 259; *North and South*, vol. 2, no. 2, (January 1999), p. 8; RC-D, foreword (typescript copy in author's possession); KJB-S, p. ix; FAL-TF, p. 5; *Troy Daily Times*, July 2, 1862; Joseph Allen Frank, *With Ballot and Bayonet* (Athens, GA, 1998), p. 57; David W. Blight, ed., *Union and Emancipation* (Kent, OH, 1997), p. 118; GP-LW, pp. 291, 292; private correspondence from Mom and Dad Johnston, dated February 4, 1972 concerning Pvt. L. R. Coy, (123rd N.Y.) (copy in author's possession).

5. FAL-TF, p. 4; Ross family records; JES-RN, p. 14; *Troy Daily Times*, September 6, 1862; Joseph Allen Frank, *With Ballot and Bayonet* (Athens, GA, 1998), p. 52; WKK-AL, p. 138; *Centennial Celebration of the Salem Old White Church* (New York, 1898), pp. 46–47; GP-LW, p. 293.

6. Ross family records and correspondence; military and pension records of the Ross brothers, NA; Oscar and Lillian Handlin, *Liberty and Power* vol. 1

(New York, 1986), pp. 11–12; *Journal of the Illinois State Historical Society*, vol. 18, no. 3 (October 1925), p. 702; *Elgin Daily Courier*, April 20, 1861, and March 7, 1862; D. S. Fares, "The Covenanter Church in the Civil War," *The Christian Nation*, vol. 55 (October 4, 1911), p. 6; Arthur M. Schlesinger, Jr., *The Age of Jackson* (Boston, 1946), p. 432; Carleton Mabee, *Black Freedom* (New York, 1970), p. 218; EJH-US, p. 75; *Washington County People's Journal* vol. 11, no. 29, July 21 and August 1, 1864; Royden W. Vosburgh, ed., *Records of the First United Presbyterian Congregation in Cambridge* (New York, 1917); James B. Scouller, *History of the Presbytery of Argyle of the United Presbyterian Church* (Newville, PA, 1880), pp. 88–93; Rev. James Harper, *History of the Associate Reformed Synod of New York and United Presbyterian Synod of New York* (Philadelphia, PA, 1877), pp. 26–30 and 46–63; Patricia V. Bonome, *Under the Cape of Heaven* (New York, 1986), pp. 133–35; James Price, "Origin and Distinctive Characteristics of the United Presbyterian Church of North America," paper read before the Presbyterian Historical Society, November 19, 1900, pp. 87, 88, 91, 94, 97, 98, 100, 103; James MacNaughton, Jr., *The Argyle Patent and Its Early Settlers* (Hopkinsville, KY, 1999), p. 416; *The United Presbyterian Churches of the Cambridge Valley 1769–1969* (Cambridge, NY, 1969), pp. 23, 43, 62, 63; *National Anti-Slavery Standard*, vol. 17, no. 4, June 14, 1856, p. 2; JGN-AL6, p. 322; Gilbert Hobbs Barnett, *The Anti-Slavery Impulse, 1838–1844* (New York, 1964), pp. 94–95; Victor B. Howard, "The Anti-Slavery Movement in the Presbyterian Church," (PhD dissertation, Ohio State University, 1961), pp. 8, 47, 40n, 42n, 179, 204; Robert Hastings Nichols, *Presbyterianism in New York State* (Philadelphia, 1963), pp. 122–25; David Steele, "History of the Reformed Presbyterian Church of North America," paper read before the Presbyterian Historical Society, March 16, 1896, p. 42; Ira Berlin, *Freedom: A Documentary History of Emancipation*, ser. 1, vol. 1 (New York, 1987), p. 161; Gordon Leidner, "Measuring the Presidents," *Columbiad*, vol. 2, no. 1 (Spring 1998); *Washington County Post*, March 28, 1862; Andrew E. Murray, *Presbyterians and the Negro—A History* (Philadelphia, PA, 1966), pp. 127, 128; Fred A. Shannon, *The Organization and Administration of the Union Army* (Cleveland, OH, 1928), p. 606; C. Duncan Rice, *The Scots Abolitionists* (Baton Rouge, LA, 1991), p. 120; *Washington County Post*, vol. 74, no. 29, May 10, 1861, p. 2; ibid., vol. 74, November 22, 1861, p. 2; ibid., vol. 75, no. 19, May 8, 1863, p. 2; ibid., vol. 75, no. 606, Nov. 7, 1862, p. 2; Seth Eyland, *Evaluation of a Life* (New York, 1884), pp. 150–51; Henry James Ford, *The Scotch-Irish in America* (Hamden, CT, 1966), pp. 253–56; Kevin Phillips, *The Cousins' War* (New York, 1999), pp. xiii, xxi, 177–82; Dave Thornton, "The Civil War Editor: Rufus King Crocker" (unpublished typescript, n.d.), p. 45; WVR-L, to his parents dated July 29 and March 28, 1862 (copies in author's possession); Samuel Eliot Morison, *The Oxford History of the American People* (New York, 1965), p. 518; W. Stanford Reid, *The Scottish Tradition in Canada* (Toronto, 1976), p. 120; *Washington County Post*, vol. 74, no. 548, September 20, 1861, p. 2; Eugene R. Fingerhut, "Assimilation of Immigrants on the Frontier of New York 1764–1776" (PhD dissertation, Columbia University, 1962), pp. 44–46; Albert Barnes, *The Church and Slavery* (reprint, New York, 1969), pp. 197–98; Rev. A. M. Stewart, *Camp, March and Battlefield* (Philadelphia, PA, 1865), p. 1; Randall

M. Miller, *Religion and the American Civil War* (New York, 1988), pp. 118, 122; Robert E. Thompson, *A History of the Presbyterian Churches in the United States* (New York, 1845), p. 10; George P. Hutchinson, *The History behind the Reformed Presbyterian Church, Evangelical Synod* (Cherry Hill, NJ) pp. 30, 39, 44–45; E. C. Aft, *Elgin, An American History* (Elgin, IL, 1984), pp. 32–34; Islay V. H. Gill, *History of Washington County, N.Y.* (Washington County Historical Society, 1956), pp. 49, 50; Jennie M. Patten, *History of the Somanauk United Presbyterian Church* (Chicago, IL, 1928), pp. 57–59, 244, 253–54; *Cornsilk Quarterly*, vol. 4, no. 2 (Summer 1985), p. 41; Corp. John C. Gourlie (Company D., 123rd N.Y.) letter to his sister dated August 26, 1864 (copy in author's possession); Kenneth A. Perry, ed., "We Are in a Fight Today," *The Civil War Diaries of Horace P Mathews and King S. Hammond* (123rd N.Y.) (Bowie, MD, 2000), pp. xix, 39, 125; *Presbytery Reporter*, vol. 5, no. 6, February 1860, p. 166; Benedict Maryniak, "Union Miliary Chaplains," *Faith in the Fight*, ed. John W. Brinsfield (Mechanicsburg, PA, 2003), p. 7; James Mac Naughton, Jr., *The Mac Naughtons of Argyle* (Glens Falls, NY, 1994), pp. 312–15; Margaret Leech, *Reveille in Washington* (New York, 1991), p. 109; Philip S. Paladun, *"A People's Contest,"* (New York, 1988), pp. 14–15, 10; *Presbytery Reporter*, vol. 5, no. 6, February 1860, p. 166; Allen E. Guelzo, *Lincoln's Emancipation Proclamation* (New York, 2004), p. 151; James Webb, *Born Fighting* (New York, 2004), p. 81; CS-AL, p. 576.

7. James R. Arnold, *The Armies of U. S. Grant* (London, 1995), pp. 158–59; Allan Nevins, ed., *A Diary of Battle* (New York, 1962), p. 318; *Report of the Provost Marshall General, Executive Documents of the House of Representatives*, 39th Congress, 1st session, 1865–66 (Washington, DC, 1866), p. 39; JMM-BC, p. 720; Gabor Borritt, *Why the Confederacy Lost* (New York, 1992), p. 127; Reid Mitchell, *Civil War Soldiers* (New York, 1988), pp. 64, 158; JTG-MS., p. 27; EJH-US, p. 111; Robert Hunt Rhodes, *All for the Union* (New York, 1985), pp. viii, 135, 230; HSC-CWA, p. 443.

8. Ross family records and correspondence; Gabor Borritt, *Why the Confederacy Lost* (New York, 1992), p. 121; Harvey Reid Papers, Box 2, Scrapbook No. 1, Folder 3, University Archives and Area Research Center, University of Wisconsin—Parkside, Kenosha, WI; Charles W. Wills, *Army Life of an Illinois Soldier* (Carbondale, IL, 1996), p. 235; LGB-H36, p. 624; Mark H. Dunkelman, *Brothers One and All* (Baton Rouge, LA, 2004), p. 205.

9. JMM-OF, pp. 52–61; Clement Eaton, *A History of the Southern Confederacy* (New York, 1954), p. 45; Reid Mitchell, *Civil War Soldiers* (New York, 1988), p. 154; JTG-MS, pp. 41, 178; Russell F. Weighley, *History of the United States Army* (New York, 1967), p. 255; David W. Blight, *Union and Emancipation* (Kent, Ohio, 1997), pp. 110, 111, 114–15, 128; *Washington County People's Journal*, vol. 10, no. 33, August 13, 1863; ibid., vol. 10, no. 31, July 30, 1863; PSP-PAL, p. 212; William H. Ross, (93rd N.Y.), letters to his brother Daniel, dated November 5, 1861, and February 6, 1862 (copies in author's possession); JEN-AL, p. 466; William C. Davis, *Lincoln's Men* (New York, 1999), p. 58; JTG-MS, pp. 41, 42, 59; Reid Mitchell, *Civil War Soldiers* (New York, 1988), p. 15; EJH-US, p. 100; Randal C. Jimmerson, *The Private Civil War* (Baton

Rouge, LA, 1988), p. 227; Allen G. Guelzo, *Lincoln's Emancipation Proclamation* (New York, 2004), p. 79; Eric Foner, *Reconstruction* (New York, 1988), pp. 11–18; JTG-MS, pp. 123–29.

Chapter 2. Stones River

1. *Elgin Daily Courier*, April 5, 1962; LGB-H36, pp. 18, 20; Newton Bateman and Paul Selby, eds., *Historical Encyclopedia of Illinois and History of Kane County* (Chicago, 1904), p. 689; T. M. Eddy, *The Patriotism of Illinois*, vol. 1 (Chicago, IL, 1866), pp. 113–14; David R. Wade, "The Hard-Charging 36th Illinois," *America's Civil War*, July 1999, p. 8; Ken Bauman, *Arming the Suckers* (Dayton OH, 1989) p. 113.

2. LGB-H36, pp. 310–13, 326 332, 338, 339, 340, 387, 388; Col. F. T. Sherman (88th Ill.), letter to Illinois governor Richard Yates, dated January 13, 1863, Illinois State Historical Society; RM-S, pp. 102, 103; Lt. Col. Joseph B. Mitchell, *Decisive Battles of the Civil War* (New York, 1955), p. 111; William F. E. Shanks, *Personal Recollections of Distinguished Generals* (New York, 1866), pp. 137–38; OR, ser. 1, vol. 20, part 1—Reports, pp. 347, 348, 352, 355, 356, 358, 360; PC-TS, pp. 4, 8, 9; William Sumner Dodge, *History of the Old Second Division* (Chicago, 1864), pp. 384–88, 446–47; EJH-US, p. 113; James L. McDonough, *Stones River* (Knoxville, TN, 1980), pp. 78. 98, 119; PHS-M, p. 209; WML-EG, pp. 202, 204, 208, 209, 211, 212; William F. Fox, *Regimental Losses in the Civil War* (Albany NY, 1889), pp. 10, 363; RO-SI, pp. 84–85, 87, 89, 90, 105; JB-CaC, pp. 24, 32; JMM-BC, pp. 516–20; RHS-HD, p. 149; James A. Connolly, *Three Years in the Army of the Cumberland* (Bloomington, IN, 1987), pp. 134n, 151–53; Robert Cheeks, "Little Phil's Fighting Retreat," *America's Civil War*, January 1997, pp. 35–40; Jo Ann B. Wilkinson, *400 Days to Perryville* (Perryville, KY, 1970), pp. 48–51; Thomas B. Buell, *The Warrior Generals* (New York, 1997), p. 194; Kenneth P. Williams, *Lincoln Finds a General*, vol. 4 (New York, 1956), pp. 130, 263; ibid., vol. 5, p. 142; Francis T. Miller, *The Photographic History of the Civil War*, vol. 4 (New York, 1959), pp. 264–65; JES-RN, pp. 244, 324–25; Peter Cozzens, *The Darkest Days of the War* (Chapel Hill, NC, 1997), p. 312; Brayton Harris, *Blue and Gray in Black and White* (London, 1999), pp. 290–91; Kenneth W. Noe, *Perryville* (Lexington, KY, 2001), pp. 276–87, 342–44, 379–80; EJH-BB, pp. 118–20; Horace Cecil Fisher, *A Staff Officer's Story* (Boston, 1960), p. 66; RED-CW, p. 189; WVR-L, to his parents, brother, and sister dated July 22, July 26, July 27, July 29, August 31, and September 2, October 2, and October 24, 1862 (copies in author's possession); William J. K. Beaudot, *The 24th Wisconsin Infantry in the Civil War* (Mechanicsburg, PA, 2003), p. 130; LJD-DG, pp. 201, 202; Joseph Hergesheimer, *Sheridan* (New York, 1931), pp. 23, 27; Wallace P. Benson (36th Ill.), *A Soldier's Diary* (Algonquin, IL, 1919), p. 29; *Report of the Adjutant General, State of Kansas*, vol. 1 (Topeka, KS, 1886), p. 214; Shelby Foote, *The Civil War Red River to Appomattox* (New York, 1974) p. 136.

3. Captain A. Kilbrook, (24th Wis.), letter, dated January 15, 1863, to the parents of a private in his company killed in action (copy in author's possession); Amandus Selsby (24th Wis.), letter, to his parents, dated February 8, 1863 (copy in author's possession); LGB-H36, pp. 339, 341, 345–47, 388–89; RM-S, pp. 104–06; Henry A. Castle "Sheridan with the Army of the Cumberland," *MOLLUS, District of Columbia Commandery*, vol. 2, 1897–1903, p. 168; *In Memoriam John Lendrum Mitchell* (Milwaukee, WI, 1906), pp. 26–27; Francis F. McKinney *Education in Violence* (Detroit, MI, 1961), pp. 184, 187; DE-L, to his father and mother, dated January 8, 1863 (copy in author's possession); Thomas B. Buell, *The Warrior Generals* (New York, 1997), p. 200; RM-S, pp. 100, 105, 106, 108; James McDonough, *Stones River* (New York, 1997), pp. 81, 83, 85, 101, 107, 110, 111, 112; PHS-M, pp. 209, 220–22; WML-EG, pp. 215, 221; RO-SI, p. 92; T. M. Eddy, *The Patriotism of Illinois* (Chicago, 1866), pp. 235, 236, 360; WVR-L, to his parents, dated January 2, 1863; Charles Lewis Francis (88th Ill.) *Narrative of a Private Soldier* (Brooklyn, NY, 1879), pp. 113–16; Pvt. Freeman S. Dunkler (36th Ill.) letter to his parents, dated January 2, 1863 (copy in author's possession); *Detroit Sunday Tribune*, November 3, 1895, p. 14; David R. Wade, "The Hard-Charging 36th Illinois," *America's Civil War*, July 1999, p. 8; Kenneth T. Williams, *Lincoln Finds a General*, vol. 4 (New York, 1959, pp. 266–72; JES-RN, p. 50; Alfred Pirtle, "Stone River Sketches," *MOLLUS, Ohio Commandery*, December 1904, pp. 6–8; WML-EG, p. 217; C. Knight Aldrich, ed., *Quest for a Star* (Knoxville, TN, 1999), pp. 22–23; Horace Cecil Fisher, *A Staff Officer's Story* (Boston, 1960), pp. 66–67; 1st Lt. E. M. de Bruin (Sill's aide), letter to Mrs. Douglas, Sill's sister, dated February 11, 1863 (Archives of the Ross County Historical Society, Chillicothe, OH); EJH-BB, pp. 197–213; Thomas B. Buell, *The Warrior Generals* (New York, 1997), p. 266; Arthur M. Manigault, *A Carolinian Goes to War* (Chapel Hill, NC, 1983), pp. 56, 57; OR, ser. 1, vol. 20, part 1—Reports (no. 50, General Sheridan), pp. 348–51; *Tennessee Historical Quarterly*, vol. 41, no. 3 (Fall 1982), pp. 281–83; Chuck Lawlin, *Civil War Sourcebook* (New York, 1991), p. 123; LJD-DG, pp. 205–08, 210, 211; Robert C. Cheeks, "Little Phil's Fighting Retreat," *America's Civil War*, January 1997, pp. 35–40; James Nourse, diary entry dated December 31, 1862 (microfilm, Special Collections, Duke University); Peter Cozzens, *No Better Place to Die* (Chicago, IL, 1990), p. 122; Arza Bartholomew, Jr., (21st Michigan), letter to his wife, dated January 5, 1863; Pvt. R. H. Watson (36th Ill), letter to his sister, dated April 11, 1863 (copy in author's possession); *Confederate Veteran*, vol. 16 (1906), p. 451; Col. Sherman (88th Ill.), letter to Gov. Richard Yates, January 13, 1863.

4. LGB-H36, p. 389, 393–96; Henry A. Castle "Sheridan with the Army of the Cumberland," *MOLLUS, District of Columbia Commandery*, vol. 2, 1897–1903, pp. 168–69; Pvt. R. H. Watson (Company D., 36th Ill.) letter to his sister (date illegible) (copy in author's possession); OR, ser. 1, vol. 20, part 1—Reports, pp. 209, 348, 351, 352, 353; John G. Parkhurst, "Recollections of Stones River," MOLLUS, Michigan Commandery (Detroit, MI, 1890), pp. 8–9; Francis F. McKinney *Education in Violence* (Detroit, MI, 1961), p. 188; Thomas B. Buell, *The Warrior Generals* (New York, 1997), pp. 200–01; James Barnet, ed. *Martyrs and Heroes of Illinois* (Chicago, IL, 1865), pp. 158–59; James L. McDonough,

Stones River (Knoxville, TN, 1980), pp. 115, 116, 118, 120, 121, 122, 123, 129; PHS-M, pp. 222–35; WML-EG, pp. 222, 224, 227, 233, 237, 238; AHG-HP, p. 322; OR—Supplement—Records of Events, vol. 10, p. 632; DE-L, to his parents; Kenneth T. Williams, *Lincoln Finds a General*, vol. 4 (New York, 1959), pp. 267, 268, 276; *Troy Daily Times*, January 10, 1863; Peter G. Tsouras, *Military Quotations of the Civil War* (New York, 1998), p. 240; WML-EG., pp. 220, 222, 227; Nathaniel C. Hughes, Jr., *The Pride of the Confederate Artillery* (Baton Rouge, LA, 1997) p. 85; Horace Cecil Fisher, *A Staff Officer's Story* (Boston, 1960), pp. 60–67; Eric J. W. Henborg, *Little Phil* (Dulles, VA, 2002), p. 9; William J. K. Beaudot, *The 24th Wisconsin Infantry in the Civil War* (Mechanicsburg, PA, 2003), pp. 148–72; Lt. Col. G. C. Kniffen, "The Battle of Stones River," *Battles and Leaders of the Civil War*, vol. 3, ed. Thomas Yoseloff (New York, 1956), pp. 618–19; Pvt. John Sackett (36th Ill.), letter to his father, dated January 17, 1863 (copy in author's possession).

5. LGB-H36, pp. 390, 392; Henry A. Castle "Sheridan with the Army of the Cumberland," *MOLLUS, District of Columbia Commandery*, vol. 2, 1897–1903, pp. 168–70; WML-EG, p. 235; RO-SI, p. 97; Pvt. Oscay Pecoy (36th Ill.), diary entry dated January 1, 1863 (copy in author's possession); WKK-AL, p. 229; Pvt. John Ely (88th Ill.), diary (copy in author's possession); C. Knight Aldrich, ed., *Quest for a Star* (KnoxvilleTN, 1999), p. 24; JES-RN, p. 53; S. Austin Thayer (Headquarters, 14th Army Corps) letter to William Green, dated January 7, 1863.

6. CS-AL, p. 342; JMM-BC, pp. 669–70; RM-S, pp. 117, 128, 129; WML-EG, pp. 242, 249; Lt. R. V. Marshall (22nd Ind.), *A Historical Sketch of the Twenty-second Regiment Indiana Volunteers* (Madison, IN, 1877), p. 26; JB-CaC, p. 95; RHS-HD, p. 152; Pvt. C. A. Halsey (36th Ill.), letter to his friend Benjamin, dated February 18, 1863 (Stones River National Battlefield Park); JES-RN, pp. 43, 59; LGB-H36, pp. 382, 384–85, 393, 402, 406; EJH-BB, p. 234; LJD-DG, p. 227; Pvt. George Cummins (36th Ill.), letter to his friend Maggie, dated April 1, 1864 (copy in author's possession); *Cincinnati Commercial*, January 31, 1863.

Chapter 3. Chancellorsville

1. FAL-TF, p. 78; Robert S. Robertson, *Diary of the War* (Fort Wayne, IN, 1965), p. 60; Jennings Cropper Wise, *The Long Arm of Lee* (New York, 1959), p. 574; EL-GH, p. 141; military records of the Ross brothers, National Archives; JB-CaC, p. 200; JMM-BC, p. 849; JES-RN, pp. 172–73; *Washington County Post*, vol. 75, no. 593 (September 19, 1862), p. 2; ibid., no. 18, May 1, 1863, p. 2; *Troy Daily Times*, September 1, 1862; Peter G. Tsouras, *Military Quotations from the Civil War* (New York, 1998), pp. 24, 206; Stephen W. Sears, *On Campaign With the Army of the Potomac* (New York, 2001), pp. 185, 197; Olivia Coolidge, *The Statesmanship of Abraham Lincoln* (New York, 1976), p. 137; Margaret Leech, *Reveille in Washington* (New York, 1941), p. 284; David E. Johnson, *A Funny Thing Happened on the Way to the White House* (New York, 1983), p. 52; JMM-BC,

p. 585; John K. Hensel, "The Good Steward: Major General George Gordon Meade," (PhD dissertation, Temple University, 2000), pp. 80–82.

2. Brigadier General A. S. Williams, Special Order No. 43, dated March 17, 1863, National Archives Record Group 393, Records of U.S. Army Continental Commands, Inventory, vol. 2, entry 5472, p. 407; Muster Rolls, Twelfth Army Corps, National Archives Record Group 393, Records of U.S. Army Continental Command; David Donald, ed., *Why the North Won the Civil War* (Baton Rouge, LA, 1960), p. 33; LVLN-GC, p. 280.

3. OR, ser. III, vol. 1—Correspondence, p. 23 (John Bigelow, Jr.); JGC-NH, pp. 146–47; R4US, undated pamphlet (copy in author's possession); FAL-TF, pp. 34, 65, 77; Rossiter Johnson, *Campfire and Battlefield* (New York, 1894), p. 518; *Cincinnati Enquirer*, vol. 26, no. 63, May 12, 1863, p. 1; Stewart Sifakis, *Who Was Who in the Civil War* (New York, 1986), pp. 558–59; David G. Martin, *The Chancellorsville Campaign* (Conshohocken, PA, 1991), p. 34; OR, ser. III, vol. 4—Union Correspondence, p. 62; *Washington County People's Journal*, vol. 10, no. 27, July 2, 1863; *Annual Report, Association of West Point Graduates for 1897* (West Point, NY, 1897), obituary of Clermont L. Best, p. 79; Pvt. William Hutton (123rd N.Y.) letter to his father, dated July 16, 1863 (William Hutton papers, Minnesota Historical Society); Nathan Appleton, *History of the Fifth Massachusetts Battery* (Boston, 1902), p. 64; JMM-A, p. 135; PVS-SL, p. 117; Stephen W. Sears, *Gettysburg* (New York, 2003), p. 38; Jenkin Lloyd Jones, *An Artilleryman's Diary* (Madison, WI, 1914), pp. 29, 102; LT-GG, pp. 143–44; Ezra T. Warner, *Generals in Blue* (Baton Rouge, LA, 1964), pp. 451–53; Andrew N. Morris, "Forgotten Decisiveness," (PhD dissertation, University of Kansas, 1966), p. 183; Fairfax Downey, *Sound of Guns* (New York, 1955), pp. 121, 124.

4. FAL-TF, p. 77; LJD-CG, p. 13; Francis A. Lord., *Civil War Collectors Encyclopedia* (New York, 1965), p. 24; Ashley Halsey, ed., *A Yankee Private's Civil War* (Chicago, 1961), pp. 37–38; Augustus Buell, *The Cannoneer* (Washington, DC, 1890), pp. 22–23; OR ser. III, vol. 4—Union Correspondence, pp. 62, 65, 66; Robert Russell Booth, *Memorial of Lt. F. B. Crosby, USA* (New York, 1864), pp. 19–28; *America's Civil War*, March 1997, p. 80; Fairfax Downey, *Sound of Guns* (New York, 1955), p. 138.

5. Grady McWhinney, *Attack and Die* (University, AL, 1982), p. 123; Thomas Dean, *Cannons* (Gettysburg, PA, 1985), pp. 17–18; CS-AL, pp. 360–61; DHK-H93, pp. 268–70, 395, 579; Command and General Staff School, *Chancellorsville Source Book* (Fort Leavenworth, KS, 1937), p. 29; Jerry Finch (Company D, 123rd N.Y.) letter to his mother, dated April 25, 1863 (copy in author's possession); KJB-S, pp. 32–33; ERB-IN27, pp. 300–01; Pvt. John Cutter, (123rd N.Y.) Letter to his mother, dated April 17, 1863 (Minnesota Historical Society); Pvt. William E. Rich (Company H, 123rd N.Y.), letter to William Law, dated April 7, 1863 (copy in author's possession); Ernest J. Stackpole, *Chancellorsville* (Harrisburg, PA, 1958), p. 21; William K. WKK-AL, pp. 247–48; Nathan Appleton, *History of the Fifth Massachusetts Battery* (Boston, 1902), p. 64; KJB-S, p. 33; DHK-H93, pp. 268–71; James P. Brady, *Hurrah for the Artillery* (Gettysburg, PA, 1992), p. 209.

6. Charles Royster, *The Destructive War* (New York, 1991), pp. 199–200; Command and General Staff School, *Chancellorsville Source Book* (Ft. Leavenworth,

KS, 1937), p. 291; David G. Martin, *The Chancellorsville Campaign*, (Conshohacken, PA, 1991), p. 90; OR, ser. I, vol. 25, part 1—Reports, no. 23 (Henry J. Hunt), p. 248; ibid., report no. 279 (Capt. Fitzhugh), p. 721; Alfred H. Guernsley, *Harper's Pictorial History of the Civil War* (New York, 1866), p. 486; OR Supplement—Record of Events vol. 46, p. 542; Ray F. Nichols, *The Stakes of Power* (New York, 1961), p. 129; *Washington County Post*, vol. 75, no. 18 (May 1, 1863), p. 2; ERB-IN27, pp. 300–01; Aurelia Austin, *Georgia Boys with "Stonewall" Jackson* (Athens, GA, 1967), pp. 60–61; William C. Davis, *Lincoln's Men* (New York, 1999), p. 144; Capt. Norman F. Weer (Company E, 123rd N.Y.), letter to his parents, dated April 1, 1863 (copy in author's possession); Ned Bradford, compiler, *Battles and Leaders of the Civil War* (New York, 1956), p. 324; Olivia Coolidge, *The Statesmanship of Abraham Lincoln* (New York, 1976), pp. 137–38; Doris K. Goodwin, *Team of Rivals* (New York, 2005), pp. 513–16; Pvt. Henry Mosier (Company H, 123rd N.Y.), letter to Uncle Asa, dated April 24, 1863.

    7. Ernest B. Furgurson, *Chancellorsville* (New York, 1992), p. 45; WW-L, pp. 387–89.

    8. HSC-BG1, p. 261; Robert C. Cheeks, "So Perfect a Slaughter," *America's Civil War*, May 1990, p. 37; Samuel P. Bates, *The Battle of Chancellorsville* (Meadville, PA, 1882), pp. 119, 121; HCM-R123, p. 30; JB-CoC, pp. 325–28, 343; Jedediah Hotchkiss, *The Battlefields of Virginia* (New York, 1867), p. 65; H. John Cooper, *Chancellorsville, 1863* (London, 1972), p. 34; William R. Hillyer, "Chancellorsville, May 2 and 3, 1863," *MOLLUS, District of Columbia Commandery*, 1904, p. 15; Theodore A. Dodge, *The Campaign of Chancellorsville* (Boston, MA, 1881), pp. 132–33; C.F. Morse, letter to Mr. Adams, dated May 3, 1911 (LC Manuscript Collections); *New York Times*, vol. 12, no. 3265 (May 7, 1863), p. 1; JGC-NH, p. 169; OR, ser. I, vol. 25, part 1—Reports, report no. 156 (Capt. Osborn), p. 484; ibid., report no. 23 (Gen. Hunt), p. 249; Augustus Choate Hamlin, *The Battle of Chancellorsville* (Bangor, ME, 1896), pp. 107, 110, 111; Edmund R. Brown (Company C, 27th Ind.), *The Twenty-Seventh Indiana Volunteer Infantry* (Gaithersburg, MD, 1899), p. 323; *Annual Report, Association of West Point Graduates*, 1897 (West Point, NY, 1897) p. 81; Kenneth T. Williams, *Lincoln Finds a General*, vol. 5 (New York, 1959), p. 184; Bessie Mell Lane, ed., *Dear Bet* (Clemson SC, 1979), p. 84; John J. H. Love papers (LC Manuscript Division), pp. 26–27; John C. Waugh, *The Class of 1846* (New York, 1994), p. 429; LT-GG, p. 149; LVLN-GC, pp. 280–81, 290–91; PVS-SL, p. 270; JES-RN, p. 182; Pvt. John Law Marshall (Company G, 123rd N.Y.), letter to his parents, dated May 14, 1863; PC-NA, pp. 250–52, 257; Thomas Yoseloff, *Battles and Leaders of the Civil War*, vol. 3 (New York, 1956), pp. 179–81.

    9. KJB-S, p. 53; JGC-NH, p. 173; OR, Supplement—Record of Events, vol. 46, p. 545; AMC-L, to his father, dated May 8, 1863 (Minnesota Historical Society); Capt. H. O. Wiley (Company K, 123rd N.Y.), letter to the *Granville Register*, dated April 8, 1863 (copy in author's possession); PVS-SL, p. 236.

    10. Maj. Gen. J. F. C. Fuller, *Grant and Lee* (Bloomington, IN, 1957), p. 190; JB-CoC, p. 342.

    11. OR, ser. 1, vol. 25, Part 1—Reports, report no. 267, p. 699 (Col. Ross); ibid., report no. 270 (Col. McDougall), p. 705; Samuel P. Bates, *The Battle of Chancellorsville* (Meadville, PA, 1882), p. 120; RC-D, p. 78, (typescript

copy in Bancroft Public Library, Salem, NY); H. John Cooper, *Chancellorsville, 1863* (London, 1972), p. 39; LT-GG, p. 147; HCM-R123, p. 30; Albert Castel, *Articles of War* (Mechanicsburg PA, 2001), p. 71; Michael C. Hardy, *The Thirty-Seventh North Carolina Troops* (Jefferson, NC, 2003), pp. 133–36; Stephen W. Sears, *Chancellorsville* (New York, 1996), p. 318.

12. Pvt. J. L. Marshall (Company G, 123rd N.Y.), undated letter (NYHS), pp. 13, 14; David E. Johnson, *A Funny Thing Happened on the Way to the White House* (New York, 1983), pp. 246–47.

13. KJB-S, p. 55; *Cincinnati Commercial*, vol. 23, no. 269 (May 16, 1863), p. 1; Gregory Coco, *The Civil War Infantryman* (Gettysburg, PA, 1996), p. 101.

14. MQ-CM, p. 196; JGC-NH, pp. 176–77; LVLN-GC, p. 303.

15. James I. Robertson, Jr., *The Stonewall Brigade* (Baton Rouge, LA, 1963), pp. 185–87; Col. Samuel E. Pittman, "The Operations of General Alpheus S. Williams in the Chancellorsville Campaign." *Michigan MOLLUS* (Detroit, 1888), p. 15; Heros Von Borcke, *Memoirs of the Confederate War for Independence*, vol. 2 (New York, 1938), p. 235; *Cincinnati Daily Enquirer*, vol. 26, no. 163 (May 12, 1863), p. 1; Samuel P. Bates, *The Battle of Chancellorsville* (Meadville, PA, 1882), pp. 120, 124–25, 127–28; OR, ser. I, vol. 25, part 1—Reports, report no. 157 (George B. Winslow), p. 488; Capt. John S. Crary, Co. H. 123rd New York, letter to the *Salem Press* dated May 19, 1863; WW-L, pp. 378–79; John G. Paxton, ed., *The Civil War Letters of General Frank (Bull) Paxton* (Hillsboro, TN, 1978), p. 99.

16. Julius Higley (123rd N.Y.) letter to his sister, dated May 18, 1863 (copy in author's possession); John L. Marshall (123rd N.Y.), undated letter, p. 15 (copy in author's possession); Edward E. Marvin, *Fifth Regiment Connecticut Volunteers* (Hartford, CT, 1889), p. 27; RC-D., pp. 81–82; Jennings Cropper Wise, *The Long Arm of Lee* (New York, 1959), p. 497; Pvt. S. Atwood (123rd N.Y.), letter to the *Salem Press*, dated May 26, 1863 (copy in author's possession); AMC-D, entry dated May 4, 1863; AMC-L, to his father dated May 8, 1863 (copy in author's possession); *Washington County Post*, vol. 75, no. 21 (May 22, 1863), p. 2; John L. Marshall (Company G, 123rd N.Y.), letter to his father, dated May 14, 1863; Marshall, diary entry, p. 15 (NYHS Manuscript Department); Marshall, undated letter to Rev. H. Brown (NYHS Manuscript Department); John G. Paxton, ed., *The Civil War Letters of General Frank (Bull) Paxton* (Hillsboro, TN, 1978), p. 99; Charles W. Turner, ed., *Letters from the Stonewall Brigade* (Natural Bridge Station, VA, 1992), p. 79; memoir of George A. Woodruff, 1st Lt. 1st U.S. Artillery, p. 83 (U.S. Military Academy Library); HCM-R123, p. 31; John Law Marshall (Company G, 123rd N.Y.), letter to his parents, dated May 14, 1863; PC-CC, pp. 92–94; James MacNaughton, Jr., *MacNaughtons of Argyle* (Glens Falls, NY, 1994), pp. 298–99; Stephen W. Sears, *Chancellorsville* (New York, 1996), p. 330.

17. HCM-R123, p. 31.

18. New York Monuments Commission, *Slocum and His Men* (Albany, 1904), pp. 165–66; JB-CoC, p. 352; Heros Von Borcke, *Memoirs of the Confederate War for Independence*, vol. 2, (New York, 1938), p. 238; HSC-BG1, p. 26; Col J. E. Gough, *Fredericksburg and Chancellorsville* (London, 1913), p. 240; Col. Samuel E. Pittman, "The Operations of General Alpheus S. Williams in the Chancel-

lorsville Campaign," *MOLLUS, Michigan Commandery*, (Detroit, 1888), p. 15; Spencer G. Welch, *A Confederate Surgeon's Letters to his Wife* (New York, 1911), p. 51; Edmund R. Brown (Company C, 27th Ind.), *The Twenty-Seventh Indiana Volunteer Infantry* (Gaithersburg, MD, 1899), p. 344; WW-L, pp. 377–79; Ned Bradford, compiler, *Battles and Leaders of the Civil War* (New York, 1956), p. 331; Stephen W. Sears, *Chancellorsville* (New York, 1996), p. 332.

    19. Col. Samuel E. Pittman, "The Operations of General Alpheus S. Williams in the Chancellorsville Campaign." *Michigan MOLLUS* (Detroit, 1888), pp. 16–17; George S. Bernard, *War Talks of Confederate Veterans* (Petersburg, VA, 1892), pp. 56–57; RC-D, pp. 79, 82; Nathaniel Steven Rowell, (123rd N.Y.), Civil War diary, p. 12 (copy in author's possession); James I. Robertson, Jr., *The Stonewall Brigade* (Baton Rouge, LA, 1963), pp. 186–88; WCM-L, to his wife, dated May 10, 1863 (copy in author's possession).

    20. OR, ser. 1, vol. 25, part 1—Reports, report no. 157 (George B. Winslow), pp. 487–88; JB-CoC, pp. 358–59; *New York Times*, vol. 12, no. 3265, p. 1 (May 7, 1863); MQ-CM, p. 199; LVLN-GC, pp. 306–07.

    21. Col. Samuel E. Pittman, "The Operations of General Alpheus S. Williams in the Chancellorsville Campaign." *Michigan MOLLUS* (Detroit, 1888), pp. 16–17; Nathaniel Steven Rowell, diary, p. 12 (copy in author's possession); CJ-WC, p. 81; Capt. John S. Crary, (123rd N.Y.), letter to the *Salem Press*, May 19, 1863; AMC-D, entry dated May 4, 1863; *Washington County Post*, vol. 75, no. 21 (May 22, 1863), p. 2; Ned Bradford, compiler, *Battles and Leaders of the Civil War* (New York, 1956), p. 333.

    22. JB-CoC, p. 358; D. Augustus Dickert, *History of Kershaw's Brigade* (Newberry, SC, 1899), p. 216; OR, ser. 1, vol. 25, part 1—Reports, report no. 270 (Archibald L. McDougall), p. 705; Jedediah Hotchkiss, *The Battlefields of Virginia* (New York, 1867), p. 71; C. F. Morse, letter to John Bigelow, dated January 13, 1912, p. 5 (LC Manuscript Collections); David G. Martin, *The Chancellorsville Campaign* (Conshohocken, PA, 1991), pp. 153–54; RC-D, pp. 82–83; Capt. John S. Crary (Company H, 123rd N.Y.), letter to the *Salem Press*, dated May 19, 1863 (copy in author's possession); HCM-R123, pp. 31, 219; Pvt. James F. Wallace (Company D, 123rd N.Y.), letter to Amanda, dated May 7, 1863 (copy in author's possession); Sgt. Henry Sartwell (Company D, 123rd N.Y.), Military Service Record (NA Record Group 94); Sergeant L. R. Coy (123rd N.Y.), "Volunteer Life in the Army as seen in the War of the Rebellion," speech given in York, Nebraska, February 25, 1892 (copy in author's possession); HCM-R123, p. 31; Pvt. John Marshall (123rd N.Y.), letter to his parents, dated May 14, 1863 (copy in author's possession); LVLN-GC, p. 308–09; Col. A. S. McDougall (123rd N.Y.), letter to M. Fairchild, Esq., dated June 7, 1863; Stephen W. Sears, *Chancellorsville* (New York, 1996), p. 321; James Crane (3rd Wis. staff member of Gen. Thomas Ruger), letter to friend, n.d. (copy in author's possession).

    23. Charles E. Slocum, *The Life and Services of Major General H. W. Slocum* (Toledo, OH, 1913), pp. 90–91; HSC-BG1, p. 262; OR ser. I, vol. 25, part 1—Reports, report no. 258 (Henry W. Slocum), p. 670; ibid., report no. 23 (Henry J. Hunt), p. 249; Theodore A. Dodge, *The Campaign of Chancellorsville* (Boston, MA, 1881), p. 139; RC-D, pp. 80, 82–83; Lt. R. S. Robertson (93rd N.Y.),

letter to his parents, dated May 14, 1863; W. H. Armstrong, letter to Dear Sir, dated June 3, 1863 (copy in author's possession); Lt. Col. James C. Rogers (123rd N.Y.), letter to the *Sandy Hill Herald*, May 7, 1863 (copy in author's possession); Stephen W. Sears, *Chancellorsville* (New York, 1996), pp. 333–34.

24. HSC-BG 2, pp. 20–22; Sergeant L. R. Coy (123rd N.Y.), "Volunteer Life in the Army as Seen in the War of the Rebellion," paper read February 25, 1892, to Robert Anderson Post no. 32, GAR (copy in author's possession); Stephen W. Sears, *Chancellorsville* (New York, 1996), p. 344.

25. RL-ND, p. 456; Stephen W. Sears, *Chancellorsville* (New York, 1996), pp. 335–36.

26. Dr. Jay Luvaas and Col. Harold W Nelson, *Battles of Chancellorsville and Gettysburg* (Carlisle, PA, 1988), p. 255; Charles E. Slocum, *The Life and Services of Major General H. W. Slocum* (Toledo, OH, 1913), p. 165; MQ-CM, p. 199.

27. D. Augustus Dickert, *History of Kershaw's Brigade* (Newberry, SC, 1899), p. 216; OR, ser. 1, vol. 25, part 1—Reports, report no. 65 (Winfield S. Hancock), p. 314; Theodore A. Dodge, *The Campaign of Chancellorsville* (Boston, MA, 1881), pp. 139–40; JB-CoC, p. 362.

28. Dr. Jay Luvaas and Col. Harold W Nelson, *Battles of Chancellorsville and Gettysburg* (Carlisle, PA, 1988), p. 273; LVLN-GC, p. 312; Fairfax Downey, *Sound of Guns* (New York, 1955), p. 150.

29. JB-CoC, pp. 362, 368–69.

30. KJB-S, pp. 61–62; JB-CoC, p. 372; HSC-BG2, p. 262; PC-NA, p. 263.

31. JB-CoC, pp. 362, 368.

32. KJB-S, p. 68; Gary W. Gallagher, *Stephen Dodd Ramseur* (Chapel Hill, NC, 1985), p. 62; Gary W. Gallagher, *Extracts of Letters of Major General Bryan Grimes* (Wilmington, NC, 1986), pp. 34–35; Pvt. John A. Larmon, (123rd N.Y.), letter to his uncle Thomas, dated May 18, 1863 and published in *The Washington County Peoples' Journal*; Sgt. Major Charles H. Church (3rd Regiment, Michigan Volunteers) *Civil War Letters* (Rose City, MI, 1987), p. 34.

33. OR, ser. I, vol. 25, part 1—Reports, report no. 259 (Clermont L. Best), pp. 675–76.

34. OR, ser. I, vol. 25, part 1—Reports, report no. 279 (Robert H. Fitzhugh), p. 724; ibid., report no. 281 (Edward D. Muhlenberg), p. 726; *Annual Report, Association of West Point Graduates, 1897*, p. 83; Robert Russell Booth, *Memorial of Lt. F. B. Crosby, USA* (New York, 1864), pp. 19–28; Rice C. Bull (123rd N.Y.), letter to his brother, dated September 8, 1863.

35. HCM-R123, pp. 32–33; WWB-L, to his cousin Abbie, May 15, 1863 (New York State Archives SC 12780); MQ-CM, p. 202; KJB-S, p. 86; AMC-L, to his father, dated May 8, 1863; *Washington County Post*, vol. 75, no. 21 (May 22, 1863), p. 2; RC-D, p. 88.

Chapter 4. After Chancellorsville

1. Dr. Daniel C. Brinton, "From Chancellorsville to Gettysburg, A Doctor's Diary," *Pennsylvania Magazine of History and Biography*, vol. 89, no. 3, July 1965, pp. 301–02; Col. Charles Morse, "The Twelfth Corps at Gettysburg," MOLLUS

Massachusetts, vol. 14 (1918), pp. 7–8; James P. Brady, *Hurrah for the Artillery*, (Gettysburg, PA, 1992), p. 223; New York Monuments Commission, *In Memoriam Henry Warner Slocum* (Albany, NY, 1902), p. 196; DHK-H93, p. 399; Charles C. Fennell, Jr., "The Attack and Defense of Culp's Hill" (PhD dissertation, West Virginia University, 1992), p. 64; David Shultz, "A Combined and Concentrated Fire," *North and South*, vol. 2, no. 3 (March 1999), p. 48; Captain Robert G. Carter, *Four Brothers in Blue* (Norman, OK, 1999), pp. 252, 254.

   2. EL-GH, pp. 150, 152; OR, ser. 1, vol. 25., part 1—Reports, report no. 23 (Henry J. Hunt) p. 252; JB-CoC, pp. 39, 45; David G. Martin, *The Chancellorsville Campaign* (Conshohocken, PA, 1991), p. 34; LT-GG, pp. 187, 188; David Shultz, "A Combined and Concentrated Fire," *North and South*, vol. 2, no. 3 (March 1999), p. 45; L. Van Loan Naisawald, "Did Union Artillery Make the Difference," CWTI, July 1963, p. 310, 316; Edward J. Stackpole, *Chancellorsville* (Harrisburg, PA, 1958), pp. 26–27; Stephen W. Sears, *Gettysburg* (New York, 2003), p. 313; John K. Hensel, "The Good Steward: Major General George Gordon Meade," vol. 1, part 1 (PhD dissertation, Temple University, 1980), 200, pp. 118–19.

   3. MQ-CM, pp. 178, 204–05; *Washington Country People's Journal*, vol. 10, no. 20 (May 14, 1863); ERB-IN27, p. 350; Roger Pickenpaugh, *Rescue by Rail* (Lincoln, NE, 1998), p. 74; Albert Castel, *Articles of War* (Mechanicsburg, PA, 2001), pp. 69, 71, 74; WW-L, p. 396; LT-GG, pp. 146–48; Lt. R. S. Robertson (93rd N.Y.), letter to his parents, dated May 14, 1863 (copy in author's possession).

   4. Edward J. Stackpole, *Chancellorsville* (Harrisburg, PA, 1958), p. 298; Stewart Sifakis, *Who Was Who in the Civil War* (New York, 1988), pp. 598, 599; *Correspondence of John Sedgwick*, vol. 2 (New York, 1903), p. 109; Louis M. Starr, *Bohemian Brigade* (Madison, WI, 1987) p. 200; David G.Martin, *The Chancellorsville Campaign* (Conshohocken, PA, 1991), p. 26; W. S. Nye, *Here Come the Rebels* (Baton Rouge, LA, 1965), p. 27; LT-GG, p. 3; JES-RN, p. 218; Francis A. Walker, *General Hancock* (New York, 1894), pp. 92–93; 1st Lt. Haviland Gifford (93rd N.Y.), letter to his father, dated October 23, 1864 (Gilder Lehman Collection, GLC 456008, Pierpont Morgan Library); WW-L, p. 384; Brian Melton "Where is Slocum?" *Civil War Historian*, vol. 2, no. 4 (September/October 2006), pp. 47–50; Col. Charles F. Morse (2nd Mass.), letter published in HSC-CWA, pg. 198.

   5. Geoffrey C. Ward, *The Civil War* (New York, 1991), p. 210; *Cincinnati Daily Enquirer* vol. 26, no. 168 (May 18, 1863), p. 3; Noah Brooks, *Abraham Lincoln* (New York, 1885), pp. 358–59; WKK-AL, p. 249.

   6. Lt. Clermont L. Best, telegram to Brig. Gen. Henry J. Hunt dated May 9, 1864 (LC Manuscript Division) William Clark, *History of Hampton Battery F* (Pittsburgh, 1909), p. 53; Joseph Todd (Hampton's Independent Pennsylvania, Battery F), diary, p. 7 (U.S. Army Military History Institute Carlisle Barracks PA); CS-AL, p. 364; Jennings Cropper Wise, *The Long Arm of Lee* (New York, 1959), p. 574; Willard Glazier, *Battles for the Union* (Chicago, 1875), p. 246; JB-CoC, pp. 359, 368; Col. J. E. Gough, *Fredericksburg and Chancellorsville* (London, 1913), p. 244; Edward J. Stackpole, *Chancellorsville* (Harrisburg PA, 1958), p. 294; JGC-NH, p. 161; JB-CoC, p. 346; David Shultz, "A Combined and Concentrated Fire,"

North and South, vol. 2, no. 3 (March 1999), p. 49; RED-CW, p. 284; Stephen W. Sears, *Gettysburg* (New York, 2003), p. 344.

7. Francis A. Lord, *They Fought for the Union* (New York, 1960), p. 81; LT-GG, p. 187; PVS-SL, p. 129.

8. James R. Cotner, "Horsepower Moves the Guns," *America's Civil War*, March 1996, p. 37; *North and South*, vol. 2, no. 2 (January 1999), p. 58; PVS-SL, pp. 117, 124.

9. Muster Rolls, Twelfth Army Corps (National Archives Record Group 393, Records of the U.S. Army Continental Command); JSC-L, to his wife, Hattie, dated June 2, 1863 (New York State Library MS 13820); James R. Arnold, *The Armies of U. S. Grant* (London, 1995), p. 83; Francis B. Heitman, *Historical Regiments of the Untied States Army*, vol. 1 (Washington, DC, 1903), p. 850; PVS-SL, pp. 127, 130, 339; John D. Billings, *Hardtack and Coffee* (Boston, 1887), pp. 184–87; Jenkin Lloyd Jones, *An Artilleryman's Diary* (Madison, WI, 1914), pp. 102, 143, 154; Fairfax Downey, *Sound of Guns* (New York, 1955), p. 121; Frank Wilkeson, *Turned Inside Out* (Lincoln, NE, 1997), pp. 22–23.

10. Steven B. Ash, "White Virginians under Federal Occupation," *The Virginia Magazine*, vol. 98, no. 2 (April 1990), pp. 179–81; Ernest B. Furgurson, *Chancellorsville* (New York, 1992), p. 58; John Warwick Daniel Papers, Box 23 (Manuscript Collection, Alderman Library, University of Virginia); W. S. Nye, *Here Come the Rebels* (Baton Rouge, LA, 1965), pp. 4, 14, 15; JMM-BC, pp. 645–47.

11. Stephen W. Sears, *Gettysburg* (New York, 2003), pg. 101; Noah Andre Trudeau, *Gettysburg* (New York, 2002), pg. 6; Maj. Gen. Sir Frederic Maurice, *An Aide-de-camp of Lee* (Boston, 1927), pp. 186–89; Irving Werstein, *The Adventure of the Civil War Told with Pictures* (New York, 1964), p. 91; John Warwick Daniel Papers, Box 23 (Manuscript Collection, Alderman Library, University of Virginia); Willard Glazier, *Battles for the Union* (Chicago, 1875), p. 246; Jennings Cropper Wise, *The Long Arm of Lee* (New York, 1959), pp. 249, 598–99; CJ-WC, p. 249; Charles C. Fennell, Jr., "The Attack and Defense of Culp's Hill" (PhD dissertation, West Virginia University, 1992), pp. 73, 78–79, 83; Jeffrey Rogers Hummel, *Emancipating Slaves, Enslaving Free Men* (Peru, IL, 1996), p. 208; W. S. Nye, *Here Come the Rebels* (Baton Rouge, LA, 1965), pp. 5, 9; JMM-BC, p. 650; Richard Wheeler, *Lee's Terrible Swift Sword* (New York, 1992), p. 406; Lynda Crist, ed., *The Papers of Jefferson Davis*, vol. 9 (Baton Rouge, LA, 1997), p. 244; CS-AL, pg. 365.

12. F4US, undated pamphlet (copy in author's possession); OR, ser. I, vol. 28, part 2, pp. 20, 30–31; John W. Schildt, *Roads to Gettysburg* (Parsons, WV, 1968), p. 160; Jennings Cropper Wise, *The Long Arm of Lee* (New York, 1959), p. 599; CS-AL, p. 409; JGC-NH, p. 179; OR, Supplement—Record of Events, vol. 46, p. 565; Charles W. Snell, "Harpers Ferry Becomes a Fortress," Harpers Ferry National Monument, 1959, pp. 52–53; JES-RN, p. 226; ERB-IN27, pp. 359, 362; RL-ND, p. 477; Brayton Harris, *Blue and Gray in Black and White* (London, 1999), p. 277; Wilbur S. Nye, *Here Come the Rebels* (Baton Rouge, LA, 1965), p. 225; Corp. John Gourlie (123rd N.Y.) letter to his sister Marie, dated June 23, 1863 (copy in author's possession); WCM-D, entries dated June 18, June 19, June 24, June 29 (copies in author's possession); Lt. R. S. Robertson

(93rd N.Y.), letter to his parents, dated July 3, 1863 (copy in author's possession); LT-GG, p. 150.

13. Richard Wheeler, *Witness to Gettysburg* (New York, 1987), p. 93; Joseph Todd (Hampton's Independent Pennsylvania, Battery F), diary, pp. 470–71; *Cincinnati Daily Enquirer*, vol. 26, no. 205 (June 30, 1863), p. 2; George E. Tumas, *Victory Rode the Rails* (Indianapolis, IN, 1953), p. 276; Ernest B. Furgurson, *Chancellorsville* (New York, 1992), pp. 346–47; Alfred A. Nofi, *The Gettysburg Campaign* (New York, 1986), p. 53; Stephen W. Sears, *Gettysburg* (New York, 2003), pp. 120, 300; JGN-AL7, p. 226; Richard Moe, *The Last Full Measure* (New York, 1993), p. 253; Merlin E. Sumner, ed., *The Diary of Cyrus B. Comstock* (Dayton, OH, 1987), p. vi.

14. MQ-CM, pp. 221–23; William Swinton *Campaigns of the Army of the Potomac* (New York, 1871), pp. 320–24; John W. Schildt, *Roads to Gettysburg* (Parsons, WV, 1968), p. 336; Richard Wheeler, *Witness to Gettysburg* (New York, 1987), p. 95; John D. McKenzie, *Uncertain Glory* (New York, 1997), p. 144; "Eye Glass" (123rd N.Y.), letter to *The Washington County People's Journal*, dated June 23, 1863 (copy in author's possession); LT-GG, pp. 1, 2, 3; RL-ND, p. 492; JES-RN, p. 231; ERB-IN27, pp. 360–61; James W. Bellah, *Soldiers' Battle* (New York, 1962), p. 99; WKK-AL, pp. 257–58; Lynda Crist, ed., *The Papers of Jefferson Davis*, vol. 9 (Baton Rouge, LA, 1997), p. 386.

15. Pvt. Levi Eaton (123rd N.Y.), letter to his wife, dated July 6, 1863 (copy in author's possession); WWB-L, to his uncle, dated July 5, 1863 (copy in author's possession); ERB-IN27, p. 361–62; Stephen W. Sears, *Gettysburg* (New York, 2003), pp. 19, 105–06.

Chapter 5. Gettysburg

1. MQ-CM, p. 225; Alpheus Williams letter to his daughter dated July 6, 1863 (copy in author's possession); RC-D, entry dated July 1, 1863 (copy in author's possession); JGC-NH, p. 183; AMC-D, entry dated June 30, 1863 (copy in author's possession); Mark M. Boatner, *The Civil War Dictionary* (New York, 1959), p. 926; JMM-BC, p. 652; RC-D, p. 120 (copy in author's possession); Stephen W. Sears, *Gettysburg* (New York, 2003), p. 52.

2. Sgt. L. R. Coy (123rd N.Y.), letter to his wife, dated July 2, 1863 (copy in author's possession); George A. Thayer, "Gettysburg, As We Men On The Right Saw It," *Ohio MOLLUS* vol. 2 (1886–1888), pp. 30–33; James P. Brady, *Hurrah for the Artillery* (Gettysburg, PA, 1992), p. 226; Gen. A. S. Williams, letter to his daughter, dated July 6, 1863 (copy in author's possession); RC-D, pp. 121–22 (copy in author's possession).

3. Anthony J. Milano, "A Call of Leadership," *Gettysburg Magazine*, no. 6 (January 1992), p. 71; LT-GG, p. 146; HCM-R123, p. 47, Stephen W. Sears, *Gettysburg* (New York, 2003), p. 191.

4. HCM-R123, p. 47; RC-D, entry dated July 2, 1863, p. 122 (copy in author's possession); JGC-NH, p. 185; Charles C. Fennell, Jr., "The Attack and

Defense of Culp's Hill" (PhD dissertation, West Virginia University, 1992), p. 115.

5. "Gettysburg," Department of Tactics, Intelligence & Military Science (Fort Huachuca AZ, 1986), p. 47; OR, ser. 1, vol. 27, part 1—Reports, report no. 314 (Edward D. Muhlenberg), p. 870; OR, ser. I, vol. 27, part 2—Reports, report no. 505, pp. 505, 543–44; New York Monuments Commission, *Slocum and His Men* (Albany, 1904), p. 178; Percy G. Hamlin, *"Old Bald Head"* (Strasburg, VA, 1940), pp. 150–51; EL-GH, pp. 160–61; Lt. E. R. Geary (Knap's Battery F), letter to his mother, dated July 17, 1863.

6. Cecil Battine, *The Crisis of the Confederacy* (London, 1905), p. 250; RC-D, entry dated July 1, 1863, p. 121 (copy in author's possession); Jennings Cropper Wise, *The Long Arm of Lee* (New York, 1959), p. 628.

7. Sgt. L. R. Coy, (123rd N.Y.), letter to his wife Sarah, dated March 12, 1863 (copy in author's possession); RC-D, entry dated July 2, 1863, pp. 123–24.

8. EL-GH, pp. 150, 160, 161, 169; Stephen W. Sears, *Gettysburg* (New York, 2003), p. 355; LT-GG, p. 189.

9. RL-ND, p. 523.

10. Cecil Battine, *The Crisis of the Confederacy* (London, 1905), p. 253; James W. Bellah, *Soldiers' Battle* (New York, 1962), p. 137; John M. Gibson, *Those 163 Days* (New York, 1961), p. 17; Stephen W. Sears, *Gettysburg* (New York, 2003), p. 356.

11. New York Monuments Commission, *Slocum and His Men* (Albany, 1904), pp. 180–81; Charles C. Coffin, *Four Years of Fighting* (New York, 1970), p. 289; Percy G. Hamlin, *"Old Bald Head"* (Strasburg, VA, 1940), p. 202; James W. Bellah, *Soldiers' Battle* (New York, 1962), p. 146; HSC-BG2, p. 622; RC-D, entry dated July 2, 1863 (copy in author's possession), p. 124; Joseph E. Persico, *My Enemy, My Brother* (New York, 1977), p. 182.

12. OR, ser. 1, vol. 27, part 1—Reports, report no. 274 (Archibald L. McDougall), pp. 783–84; ibid., report no. 275 (Warren W. Packer), p. 789; Sgt. L. R. Coy, (123rd N.Y.), letter to his wife, dated July 6, 1863 (copy in author's possession); Lt. George Robinson (Company H, 123rd N.Y.), letter to his wife, dated July 5, 1863 (copy in author's possession); RC-D, pp. 124–25 (copy in author's possession); soldier in the (123rd N.Y.), unsigned letter dated March 12, 1865, published in the *Washington County People's Journal*, vol. 12, no. 13 (March 30, 1865) (copy in author's possession); HCM-R123, pp. 35, 53.

13. OR, ser. 1, vol. 27, part 1—Reports, report no. 293 (John W. Geary), p. 830; Charles C. Coffin, *Four Years of Fighting* (New York, 1970), pp. 289–90.

14. OR, ser. 1, vol. 27, part 1—Reports, report no. 314 (Edward D. Muhlenberg), p. 870; Harry W. Pfanz, *Gettysburg—Culp's Hill and Cemetery Hill* (Chapel Hill, NC, 1993), p. 288; Charles C. Fennell, Jr., "The Attack and Defense of Culp's Hill" (PhD dissertation, West Virginia University, 1992), pp. 165,166; LT-GG, pp. 152, 153; David Shultz, "A Combined and Concentrated Fire," *North and South*, vol. 2, no. 3 (March 1999), p. 52.

15. Muster Rolls, Twelfth Army Corps (NA Record Group 393, Records of the U.S. Army Continental Command); New York Monuments Commission,

Notes to Chapter 5

Slocum and His Men (Albany, 1904), p. 181; David Shultz, "A Combined and Concentrated Fire," *North and South*, vol. 2, no. 3 (March 1999), p. 52.

16. OR, ser. 1, vol. 27, part 1—Reports, report no. 282 (H.H. Lockwood), p. 804; ibid., report no. 285 (John H. Ketcham), p. 810.

17. John Purifoy, "The Artillery at Gettysburg," *Confederate Veteran*, vol. 32 (1924), p. 425; Harry W. Pfanz, *Gettysburg—Culp's Hill and Cemetery Hill* (Chapel Hill, NC, 1993), p. 285.

18. Augustus Buell, *The Cannoneer* (Washington, DC, 1890), pp. 22–23; John Purifoy, "The Artillery at Gettysburg," *Confederate Veteran*, vol. 32 (1924), p. 285.

19. OR, ser. 1, vol. 27, part 1—Reports, report no. 272 (Alpheus S. Williams), p. 777; JGC-NH, p. 192.

20. OR, ser. 1, vol. 27, part 1—Reports, report no. 273 (Thomas H. Ruger), p. 780; Abner Doubleday, *Chancellorsville and Gettysburg Campaigns of the Civil War*, vol. 6 (New York, 1887), pp. 186–87; MQ-CM, p. 230; EL-GH, p. 170; Philo B. Buckingham (aide to General Williams), letter to his wife, dated July 7, 1863 (American Antiquarian Society, Worcester, MA); Harry W. Pfanz, *Gettysburg—Culp's Hill and Cemetery Hill* (Chapel Hill, NC, 1993), p. 287; JGC-NH, pp. 192–93; Stephen W. Sears, *Gettysburg* (New York, 2003), pp. 361, 364; Noah A. Trudeau, *Gettysburg* (New York, 2002), pp. 428–31.

21. EL-GH, pp. 170, 171; James W. Bellah, *Soldiers' Battle* (New York, 1962), pp. 131, 148; OR, ser. 1, vol. 27, part 1, Reports, report no. 314 (Edward D. Muhlenberg), p. 870; ibid., report no. 285 (John H. Ketcham), p. 810; ibid., report no. 290 (Nirom M. Crane), p. 820; Edward E. Marvin, *Fifth Regiment Connecticut Volunteers* (Hartford, CT, 1889), p. 275; Rev. Edward O. Bartlett "*The Dutchess County Regiment*" (Danbury, CT), pp. 32–34; LT-GG, pp. 187, 188.

22. Sgt. L. R. Coy (123rd N.Y.), letter to his wife, dated July 6, 1863 (copy in author's possession); Harry W. Pfanz, *Gettysburg—Culp's Hill and Cemetery Hill* (Chapel Hill, NC, 1993), p. 291; James W. Bellah, *Soldier's Battle* (New York, 1962), p. 148; Charles C. Fennell, Jr., "The Attack and Defense of Culp's Hill" (PhD dissertation, West Virginia University, 1992), p. 167; JGC-NH, pp. 193–19; Wiley Sword, *Mountains Touched With Fire* (New York, 1995), p. 134; William Alan Blair, *A Politician Goes to War* (University Park, PA, 1995), p. 240; Stephen W. Sears, *Gettysburg* (New York, 2003), p. 38; Lt. George I. Robinson (123rd N.Y.), letter to his wife, dated July 5, 1863 (copy in author's possession).

23. OR, ser. 1, vol. 27, part 2—Reports, report no. 509 (W. G. Lewis), p. 574; ibid., report no. 293 (John W. Geary), p. 828; ibid., report no. 272 (Alpheus S. Williams) p. 775; John O. Casler, *Four Years in The Stonewall Brigade* (Gerard, KS, 1906), p. 174; Col. Charles F. Morse, "The Twelfth Corps at Gettysburg," *Massachusetts MOLLUS* vol. 14, (1918), p. 32–33; HSC-BG2, p. 622; Percy G. Hamlin, "*Old Bald Head*" (Strasburg, VA, 1940), pp. 154–55; Jack McLaughlin, *Gettysburg: The Long Encampment* (New York, 1963), pp. 122–12; Harry W. Pfanz, *Gettysburg—Culp's Hill and Cemetery Hill* (Chapel Hill, NC, 1993), pp. 287–88; Charles C. Fennell, Jr., "The Attack and Defense of Culp's Hill" (PhD dissertation, West Virginia University, 1992), p. 173; RC-D, p. 126 (copy in author's possession); *Gettysburg Magazine* no. 5 (July 1991), p. 120; HCM-R123, p. 50.

24. Cecil Battine, *The Crisis of the Confederacy* (London, 1905), p. 251; George Augustine Thayer, "The Heroic Period of the Union," *MOLLUS, Ohio Commandery* (Cincinnati, OH, 1886), p. 20.

25. OR, ser. 1, vol. 27, part 1—Reports, report no. 293 (John W. Geary), pp. 828–29; David Nichols (Battery E, Pennsylvania Light Artillery), letter to his father, dated July 9, 1863 (U.S. Army Military History Institute, Carlisle Barracks, PA); David Nichols, diary entry dated July 3, 1863 (copy in author's possession); HSC-BG2, p. 622; OR, ser. 1, vol. 27, part 2—Reports, report no. 72 (J. A. Walker), p. 519; Harry W. Pfanz, *Gettysburg—Culp's Hill and Cemetery Hill* (Chapel Hill, NC, 1993), p. 285; Joseph E. Persico, *My Enemy, My Brother* (New York, 1977), p. 183.

26. John W. Storrs, *Twentieth Connecticut* (Ansonia, CT, 1886), pp. 93–94; New York Monuments Commission, *Slocum and His Men* (Albany, 1904), p. 183; MQ-CM, p. 230; Muster Rolls, Twelfth Army Corps (NA Record Group 393, U.S. Army Continental Command); Samuel Toombs, *Reminiscences of the War* (Orange, NJ, 1878), pp. 80–81.

27. Joseph E. Persico, *My Enemy, My Brother* (New York, 1977), p. 183; Sgt. Fayette Hale (Co. K 123rd N.Y.) letter to the *Granville Register*, dated August 8, 1863 (copy in author's possession).

28. HCM-R123, pp. 49–50; Comte de Paris, *The Battle of Gettysburg* (Philadelphia, 1886) pp. 199–200; OR, ser. 1, vol. 27, part 1—Reports, report no. 276 (William B. Wooster), p. 794; ibid., report no. 273 (Thomas H. Ruger), p. 781; New York Monuments Commission, *Slocum and His Men* (Albany, 1904), p. 184; Sgt. L. R. Coy, (123rd N.Y.), letter to his wife, dated July 5, 1863 (copy in authors' possession); EL-GH, p. 171; *Chicago Evening Journal*, vol. 23, no. 142 (July 6, 1863), p. 1; RC-D, pp. 126–27; AMC-D, entry dated July 3, 1863 (copy in author's possession); LT-GG, p. 149; Jeffrey D. Wert, *Gettysburg* (New York, 2001), p. 92; Lt. George I. Robinson (123rd N.Y.), letter to his wife, dated July 5, 1863 (copy in author's possession).

29. James I. Robertson, *The 4th Virginia* (Lynchburg, VA, 1982), pp. 27, 28; OR ser. 1, vol. 27, part 1—Reports, report N. 314 (Edward D. Muhlenberg), p. 871; ibid., report no. 274 (Archibald L. McDougall), p. 785; L. Van Loan Naisawald, "Did Union Artillery Make the Difference," CWTI, vol. 2, no. 4 (July 1963), p. 35; Pvt. John Gourlee (123rd N.Y.), letter to his sister Jennie, dated July 6, 1863 (U.S. Army Military History Institute, Civil War Miscellaneous Collection); ERB-IN27, p. 391.

30. Glenn Tucker, *High Tide at Gettysburg* (Saybrook, CT, 1994), p. 323; Edwin B. Coddington, *Gettysburg Campaign* (Dayton, OH, 1979), p. 471; Randolph H. McKim, *A Soldier's Recollections* (New York, 1910), p. 187; David Shultz, "A Combined and Concentrated Fire," *North and South*, vol. 2, no. 3 (March 1999), pp. 39 and 54; Jeffrey B.Wert, *Gettysburg* (New York, 2001), pp. 54–55, 93.

31. John Gourlee (123rd N.Y.), letter to his sister Jennie, dated July 6, 1863 (U.S. Army Military History Institute, Civil War Miscellaneous Collection); John J. H. Love (12th Corps surgeon), "History of the Twelfth Corps" (undated typescript manuscript), p. 38 (LC Manuscript Collection); W. G. Bean, *The Liberty Hall Volunteers* (Charlottesville, VA, 1964), p. 150.

32. OR ser. I, vol. 27, part 1—Reports, report no. 293 (John W. Geary), p. 831; Ken Bandy and Florence Freeland, eds., *The Gettysburg Papers* (Dayton, OH, 1986), p. 871; James W. Bellah, *Soldier's Battle* (New York, 1962), p. 151; J. Watts De Pryster, *Gettysburg and After* (Gaithersburg, MD, 1987), p. 21; RC-D, entry dated July 4, 1863, p. 130 (copy in author's possession); ERB-IN27, p. 394; AMC-L, to his brother, dated July 5, 1863 (copy in author's possession); Geo. Robinson (123rd N.Y.) letter no. 40 to his wife, dated July 5, 1863 (copy in author's possession); James W. Bellah, *Soldiers' Battle* (New York, 1962), pp. 133–34; Richard Wheeler, *History of the Battle of Gettysburg* (New York, 2001), pp. 263–65; Noah Andre Trudeau, *Gettysburg* (New York, 2002), pp. 123, 535; Glenn Tucker, *High Tide at Gettysburg* (Saybrook, CT, 1994), pp. 382–385.

33. Tidball, "Artillery Service," papers of Henry Jackson Hunt (LC Manuscript Division, ms. No. 26864), p. 690; Charles C. Coffin, *Four Years of Fighting* (New York, 1970), p. 290; Chaplain Edward D. Neill, ed., *Glimpses of the Nation's Struggle*, 2nd ser. (St. Paul, MN, 1890), pp. 46–47; J. G. Hamilton, ed., *The Papers of Randolph Abbott Shotwell*, vol. 1 (Raleigh, NC, 1929), p. 33; Noah Andre Trudeau, *Gettysburg* (New York, 2002), p. 524; Stephen W. Sears, *Gettysburg* (New York, 2003), p. 185.

34. William E. Birkhimer, *Historical Sketch of the Artillery, U.S. Army* (New York, 1968), pp. 214–15; Tidball, "Artillery Service," papers of Henry Jackson Hunt (LC Manuscript Division, ms. no. 26864), pp. 466, 687–90; Douglas Southall Freeman, *Lee's Lieutenant's* (New York, 1942), p. 645; EL-GH, pp. 150–51; Charles E. Slocum, *Services of Maj. Ge. H. W. Slocum* (Toledo, OH, 1913), p. 111; David Shultz "A Combined and Concentrated Fire," *North and South*, vol. 2, no. 3 (March 1999), p. 40; JMM-BC, p. 664; JES-RN, pp. 291–92; Aurelia Austin, *Georgia Boys with "Stonewall" Jackson* (Athens, GA, 1967), pp. 66–67; Rod Gragg, *Covered With Glory* (New York, 2000), p. 209; LT-GG, p. 149; Stephen W. Sears, *Gettysburg* (New York, 2003), pp. 38, 471, 472, 498, 499, 507.

35. *National Tribune*, vol. 11, no. 37, whole no. 557 (April 14, 1892), p. 4; Francis A. Lord, *They Fought for the Union* (New York, 1960), p. 17; CS-AL, pp. 579–80. Muster Rolls, Twelfth Army Corps (NA Record Group 393, Records of the U.S. Army Continental Command); F4US; and OR, Supplement, ser. 1, vol. 51, part 1, p. 647.

Chapter 6. Chickamauga

1. Richard M. Ketchum, ed., *The American Heritage Picture History of the Civil War* (New York, 1960), p. 57; Michael Anderson Hughes, "The Struggle for Chattanooga" (PhD dissertation, University of Arkansas, 1991), pp. 99–102; RL-ND, pp. 558, 561, 565; Brigade Order Book, 14th Corps, 3rd Division, 1st Brigade (NA Record Group 94); Lt. Henry Drake (24th Wis.), letters to his brother John, dated April 22, May 22, May 24, July 12, 1863 (copies in author's possession); Pvt. George A. Cooley, (24th Wis.) diary entries dated July 1, July 4, August 9, August 15, 1863 (Wisconsin Historical Society Archives; JMM-

BC, pp. 669–72; John B. Turchin, *Chickamauga* (Chicago, 1888), pp. 88–89, 96, 99–101, 111, 112, 114, 116; PC-TS, pp. 40, 377, 379, 382, 384, 385–91, 466–68; *Elgin Weekly Gazette* (June 10, 1863); Frederick D. Williams, *Civil War Letters of James A. Garfield* (East Lansing, MI, 1964) p. 296; Lt. Alfred Pirtle, *Leaves from My Journal*, pp. 54–78 (copy in author's possession); PHS-M, pp. 280–84; AHG-HP, p. 531; Mark M. Boatner, *The Civil War Dictionary* (New York, 1959), p. 498; JB-CaC, pp. 5, 24; LGB-H36, pp. 413–14, 422, 433, 434, 438–40, 441, 444–45, 448, 454, 456–57, 469; JES-RN, pp. 295–96; *History Today*, July 2000, p. 24; PC-TS, pp. 117, 225; JES-RN, p. 296; Ruth C. Carter, *For Honor, Glory and Union* (Lexington, KY, 1999), pp. 166, 186, 192, 199; Kenneth W. Noe, *Perryville* (Lexington, KY, 2001), pp. 230–31; Joseph Hergesheimer, *Sheridan* (New York, 1931), pp. 61, 79; LJD-CG, p. 231; WVR-L, to his parents, dated January 28, May 17, May 25, June 5, 1863 (copies in author's possession); DE-D, entry dated August 9, 1863 (copies in author's possessioin); David R. Wade "The Hard-Charging 36th Illinois," *America's Civil War* (July 1999), pp. 88, 90; Sgt. R. H. Watson (36th Ill.) letter to his sister, dated April 11, 1863 (copy in author's possession); Col. F. T. Sherman (88th Ill.), diary entry dated April 16, 1863 (copy in author's possession); Chauncy Peck (21st Mich.) letter to his brother, dated August 16, 1863 (copy in author's possession); Pvt. George Cummins (Company C., 36th Ill.), letters to his friend Maggie, dated February 17, April 16, August 30, 1863; ibid., to Mr. M. L. Todd, dated August 25, 1863 (copy in author's possession); JMM-BC, pp. 669–70.

2. *National Tribune*, vol. 24, no. 49, Whole no. 1310 (October 4, 1906), p. 1; Francis F. McKinney *Education in Violence* (Detroit, MI, 1961), pp. 252–55; JMM-BC, p. 675; PC-TS, pp. 7, 140, 168, 288, 310, 311, 358, 359, 382–90, 427, 468, 501–02, 511, 521; John B. Turchin, *Chickamauga* (Chicago, 1988), p. 234; Gates P. Thruston, "Chickamauga," *Southern Bivouac*, vol. 62 (1886–1887), pp. 411, 414, 415; James R. Arnold, *Chickamauga, 1863* (London, 1997), p. 68; John D. McKenzie, *Uncertain Glory* (New York, 1997), p. 205; RM-S, p. 135; LGB-H36, pp. 461–75, 495; John Ely (88th Ill.) diary entries dated September 20 and October 19, 1863 (copies in author's possession); Clarence C. Buell and Robert V. Johnson, eds., *Battle and Leaders of the Civil War*, vol. 3 (New York, 1888), pp. 663, 666, 670; William M. Owen, *In Camp and Battle with the Washington Artillery* (Boston, 1885), pp. 286–87; JB-CaC, pp. 76, 126; AHG-HP, p. 546; Steven E. Woodworth, *Six Armies in Tennessee* (Lincoln, NE, 1998), pp. 114–18; Henry P. Mann (15th Ill. Cavalry) diary entry dated September 20, 1863 (University of Missouri-Rolla, Historical Manuscript Collection); Clyde C. Walton, ed., *Private Smith's Journal* (88th Ill.) (Chicago, 1953), p. 96; Pvt. George A. Cooley (24th Wis.) diary entry dated September 20, 1863 (copy in author's possession); T. M. Eddy, *The Patriotism of Illinois* (Chicago, 1866), p. 72; Charles A. Dana, *Recollections of the Civil War* (New York, 1963), p. 115; Ruth C. Carter, *For Honor, Glory and Union* (Lexington, KY, 1999), pp. 27, 28, 158, 200, 201; Frederick D. Williams, *Civil War Letters of James A. Garfield*, vol. 5 (East Lansing MI, 1964), pp. 258–259; JES-RN., pp. 296, 333, 336, 339, 340; Maurice Marcoot, *Five Years in the Sunny South* (University Microfilms International, Ann Arbor, MI, 1990), p. 37; *The Papers of Philip Sheridan*, Microfilm reel no. 72 (LC Manuscript Division);

RED-CW, p. 326; Alfred Pirtle (aide to General Lytle), letter to his father, dated September 23, 1863 (FCHS, Lytle Collection), p. 427; PC-BL, p. 427; JB-CaC, pp. 36, 118–21, 125–27, 135; Horace Cecil Fisher, *A Staff Officer's Story* (Boston, 1960), p. 89; C. Knight Aldrich, ed., *Quest for a Star* (Knoxville, TN, 1999), pp. 50–52; EJH-BB, p. 234; Cyrus K. Remington, *A Record of Battery I, First N.Y. Light Artillery* (Buffalo, NY, 1891), pp. 34, 55; Alfred Pirtle, letter to his sister, dated September 19, 1863 (FCHS, Lytle Collection); Alfred Pirtle, "Lytle's Last Sacrifice," unpaged typescript (Louisville, KY, 1920), (FCHS Lytle Collection); James L. McDonough, *Chattanooga, A Death Grip on the Confederacy* (Knoxville, TN, 1984), pp. 41–42; Lily Lytle, letter to dear uncle, dated October 5, 1863 (Letter no. 60, Box 31, Lytle papers, Cincinnati Historical Society); David J. Endres "Rectifying the Fatal Contrast," *Ohio Valley History* vol. 2, no. 2 (Fall 2002), pp. 27, 30; LJD-CG, p. 336; Ezra T. Warner, *Generals in Blue* (Baton Rouge, LA, 1964), p. 181; *Personal Recollections of John M. Palmer* (Cincinnati, 1901), pp. 186–87; PC-BL, pp. 310–15, 376–89, 442–50, 466–68; Arthur M. Manigault, *A Carolinian Goes to War* (Columbia, SC, 1983), pp. 97–98; Richard A. Baumgartner, Chickamauga (Huntington, WV, 1997), pp. 172–73.

3. LGB-H36, pp. 456–79, 482, 800–08; OR, ser. 1, vol. 31, part 2—Reports, report no. 122 (Col. Silas Miller), pp. 583–84; Pvt. W. W. Gifford (Company D, 36th Ill.), unpaged diary (Chickamauga and Chattanooga National Military Park); Richard M. Ketchum, ed., *The American Heritage Picture History of the Civil War* (New York, 1960), p. 420; JMM-BC, p. 674; Henry A. Castle, "Sheridan with the Army of the Cumberland," *MOLLUS, District of Columbia Commandery 1897–1903*, vol. 2, pp. 177–78; PC-TS, pp. 226–28; Francis F. McKinney, *Education in Violence* (Detroit, MI, 1961), p. 259; Michael Anderson Hughes, "The Struggle for Chattanooga," (PhD dissertation, University of Arkansas, 1991), pp. 118–19; PHS-M, pp. 284–87; JB-CaC, pp. 172, 197; OR—Supplement—Record of Events, vol. 10, p. 633; B. F. Scribner, *How Soldiers Were Made* (New Albany, IN, 1887), p. 159; JMM-BC, p. 674; JES-RN, pp. 19, 325; Alfred Pirtle (aide to General Lytle), letter to his father, dated September 23, 1863 (FCHS, Lytle Collection); Pvt. John Ely (88th Ill.), diary entry, dated October 19, 1863 (copy in author's possession); Pvt. W. W. Gifford (36th Ill.) undated letter to his wife (copy in author's possession); Steven E. Woodworth, *This Grand Spectacle* (Abilene, TX, 1999), p. 39; Augustus Buell, *The Cannoneer* (Washington, DC, 1890), pp. 669–71; Theodore W. Blackburn, *Letters from the Front* (Dayton, OH, 1981), p. 155; Pvt. George Cummins (36th Ill.), letter to Maggie, dated April 1, 1864 (copy in author's possession); Robert G. Athearm, *Soldier in the West: The Civil War Letters of Alfred Lacey Hough* (Philadelphia, 1957), pp. 150–51.

Chapter 7. Missionary Ridge

1. William F. E. Shanks *Personal Recollections of Distinguished Generals* (New York, 1866), pp. 268, 271; Clyde C. Walton, ed., *Private Smith's Journal* (88th Ill.) (Chicago, 1953), p. 104; Pvt. George A. Cooley (24th Wis.), diary entry dated

September 30, 1863 (copy in author's possession); Stewart Sifakis, *Who Was Who in the Civil War* (New York, 1988), p. 259; LGB-H36, pp. 488–89, 500–03, 540; Lester L. Swift, "The Preacher Regiment at Chickamauga and Missionary Ridge," *Lincoln Herald* (1970) p. 57; Richard M. Ketchum, ed. *The American Heritage Picture History of the Civil War* (New York, 1960) p. 420; WML-EG, pp. 372–73; Col. Francis T. Sherman (88th Ill.) letter to his father, dated October 25, 1863 (Chicago Historical Society); JB-CaC, pp. 143, 176; T. M. Eddy, *The Patriotism of Illinois*, vol. 1 (Chicago, IL, 1866), p. 314; WVR-L, to his parents, dated November 3, 1863 (University of Wisconsin Special Collections); Steven E. Woodworth, *Six Armies in Tennessee* (Lincoln, NE, 1988), pp. 137–38, 144; JES-RN, pp. 367–68; Maurice Marcoot, *Five Years in the Sunny South* (University Microfilm International, Ann Arbor, MI, 1990), p. 39; CS-AL, p. 432; PVS-SL, p. 75; William B. Haberton, *Homeward Bound* (Mechanicsburg, PA, 2001), p. 50; C. Knight Aldrich, ed., *Quest for a Star* (Knoxville, TN, 1999), p. 69; CWTI (September/October 1992), pp. 22, 24; Michael A. Hughes, "The Struggle for Chattanooga" (PhD dissertation, University of Arkansas, 1991), pp. 163–70; Lt. R. S. Robertson (93rd N.Y.), letter to his parents, dated September 13, 1863 (copy in author's possession); Doris K. Goodwin, *Team of Rivals* (New York, 2005), pp. 558–59; JES-RN, pp. 352–53; Earl Schenck Miers, *The American Civil War* (New York, 1961), p. 224; Lt. George Robinson (123rd N.Y.), diary entry dated November 25, 1863.

2. Earl Schenck Miers, *The American Civil War* (New York, 1961), pp. 236–37; *The National Tribune*, vol. 20, no. 15, whole no. 1014 (January 17, 1901), p. 2; William F. Smith, *From Chattanooga to Petersburg* (Boston, 1893), pp. 9–12; W. C. McClean (123rd N.Y.) letter to his brother, dated October 3, 1863 (McClean Family Papers, File no. SC 20811, Manuscript and Special Collections, NYSL); WML-EG, p. 368; Thomas B. Buell, *The Warrior Generals* (New York, 1997), p. 280; HCM-R123, pp. 69–75; RC-D, entry dated October 5, 1863 (copy in author's possession); Carroll Bateman, *The Baltimore and Ohio* (undated pamphlet), p. 17; Lt. George Robinson (123rd N.Y.) letters to his wife, dated September 9, September 20, October 12, 1863; ibid., diary entries dated September 26, October 12, 16, 31, 1863 (copy in author's possession); ERB-IN27, p. 447; Roger Pickenpaugh, *Rescue by Rail* (Lincoln, NE, 1998), pp. 53–54, 69, 70, 73, 74, 77, 82, 92, 95, 97, 98, 106–07, 148; CJ-WC, p. 82; JB-CaC, pp. 57–58; James P. Brady, *Hurrah for the Artillery* (Gettysburg, PA, 1992), pp. 290–93; Patrick Abbazia, *The Chickamauga Campaign* (New York, 1988), p. 141; Lynda L. Crist, ed., *The Papers of Jefferson Davis*, vol. 9 (Baton Rouge, LA, 1997), p. 416; CWTI (September/October 1992), pp. 24, 58; Thomas J. Morgan "Reminiscences of Service with Colored Troops," *Personal Narratives of Events in the War of the Rebellion*, vol. 5 (Rhode Island Soldiers and Sailors Historical Society, Wilmington, NC, 1993), pp. 81–84; WW-L, pp. 422, 424–25; LJD-CG, pp. 345–47; Kenneth A. Perry, ed., "We Are in a Fight Today," *The Civil War Diaries of Horace P. Mathews and King S. Hammond* (123rd N.Y.) (Bowie, MD, 2000), p. 15; "E. S. R." (123rd N.Y.), letter to his parents, published in the *Whitehall Chronicle*, January 15, 1864 (copy in author's possession); JES-RN, p. 352; Bruce Catton, *Never Call Retreat* (New York, 1967), p. 244; R4US; Frederick H. Dyer, *A Compendium of the War of the Rebellion*, vol. 3 (New York, 1959), p. 1704; Noah A Trudeau, *Like Men of War* (Edison, NJ, 1988), pp. 336–37.

3. RC-D, pp. 160–61; RC-L, to his wife, dated November 19, 1863 (copy in author's possession); JGC-NH, pp. 202–03; MQ-CM, pp. 268,269, 272; New York State Monuments Commission, *In Memoriam Henry Warner Slocum* (Albany, NY, 1904), p. 47; OR, ser. I, vol. 31, part 1—Reports, pp. 768, 777; HCM-R123, pp. 66, 70, 73; Russell F. Weigley, *Quartermaster General of the Union Army* (New York, 1959), p. 290; AHG-HP, p. 560; Wilbur D. Jones, Jr., *Grants in the Cornfield* (Shippensburg, PA, 1997), p. 34; C. Knight Aldrich, ed., *Quest for a Star* (Knoxville, TN, 1999), p. 69; Charles W. Wills, *Army Life of an Illinois Soldier* (Carbondale, IL, 1996), p. 231; Cyrus K. Remington, *A Record of Battery I, First N.Y. Light Artillery* (Buffalo, NY, 1891), pp. 39, 42; LJD-CG, p. 385; Lt. George I. Robinson (123rd N.Y.), letter to his wife, dated October 12, 1863 (copy in author's possession); ibid., diary entries dated October 21, 30, November 1, 7, 1863 (copy in author's possession); James A. Connolly, *Three Years in the Army of the Cumberland* (Bloomington, IN, 1987), p. 134; Rice C. Bull (123rd New York), diary entry, p. 96 (copy in author's possession).

4. Lt. Richard H. Watson, (36th Ill.) letter to his sister Jennie, dated November 21, 1863 (AMHS, Civil War Miscellaneous Collection); Thomas B. Buell, *The Warrior Generals* (New York, 1997), p. 290; RM-S, p. 138; PC-SH, pp. 107, 261; WML-EG, pp. 370. 372; WVR-L, to his parents, dated November 5, 1863 (University of Wisconsin Manuscript Collections); JES-RN, pp. 356–57, 362–63; Maurice Marcoot, *Five Years in the Sunny South* (University Microfilms International, Ann Arbor, MI, 1990), p. 40; Roger Pickenpaugh, *Rescue by Rail* (Lincoln, NE, 1998), pp. 153–54; Thomas B. Buell, *The Warrior Generals* (New York, 1997), pp. 193, 269, 351; LGB-H36, pp. 509, 514, 519, 571, 578; JB-CaC, pp. 70–71, 139, 182–83, 186; JMM-DS, pp. 163–64; Carol K. Bleser, *Intimate Strategies of the Civil War* (New York, 2001), p. 129; Joseph O. Jackson, ed., "Some of the Boys . . ." (Carbondale, IL, 1960), pp. 126–27; Michael Anderson Hughes, "The Struggle for Chattanooga," (PhD dissertation, University of Arkansas, 1991), pp. 179, 189–91; LJD-CG, pp. 387, 426; Joseph Hergesheimer, *Sheridan* (New York, 1931), pp. 130–31; GP-LW, pp. 321, 322; Richard Henry Avens, *Peaceful Warrior* (New York, 1991), p. 31; KJB-S, pp. 97, 99; HCM-R123, p. 73; Kenneth A. Perry, *The Fitch Gazeteer,* vol. 3 (Bowie, MD, 1999) p. 350; JYS-PG10, p. 19; Lt. George Robinson (123rd N.Y.), dairy entried dated October 30, November 15, 1863 (copy in author's possession).

5. LGB-H36, pp. 519, 520, 524, 525, 526, 527, 528, 617–18; OR ser. I, vol. 31, part 2—Reports, report no. 28 (Col. Francis T. Sherman), pp. 194–95; ibid., report no. 29 (Porter C. Olson), pp. 196–98; Peter B. Kellenberger (36th Ill.) letter to his friend, dated December 19, 1863 (LC Manuscript Division); James Barnet, ed., *Martyrs and Heroes of Illinois* (Chicago, 1865), pp. 159–62; John Ely (88th Ill.) diary entry dated November 23, November 24, 1863 (copy in author's possession); CWTI, "The Battles for Chattanooga," vol. 10, no. 5 (August 1971), p. 30; PC-SH, pp. 257–79; W. H. Newlin, *A History of the Seventy-Third Regiment of Illinois Infantry Volunteers* (Springfield, IL, 1890), pp. 264–66; PHS-M, pp. 304, 306, 308–10; JB-CaC, pp. 222, 223; SPH-WT, pp. 174–74; Steven E. Woodworth, *Six Armies in Tennessee* (Lincoln, NE, 1988), pp. 150–80, 196; Private correspondence from Fort Edward Historical Association

to author, dated October 13, 1983; Watson, op. cit., pp. 119–22; James A. Connolly, *Three Years in the Army of the Cumberland* (Bloomington, IN, 1987), pp. 151–52; unpublished after-action reports by Col. R. L. Gibson, December 13, 1863; Chickamauga-Chattanooga NBP, Office of the Historian; ERB-IN27, pp. 291, 292; eds. of Time Life Books, *Voices of the Civil War-Chattanooga* (Alexandria, VA, 1998), p. 127; Maurice Marcoot, *Five Years in the Sunny South* (University Microfilms International, Ann Arbor, MI, 1990), p. 41; Lt. Edward K. Ward (4th Tenn.), letter to his sister, dated December 8, 1863 (Gilder Lehrman collection, Pierpont Morgan Library, GLC 2232 no. 27); John B. Lindsley, *Military Annals of Tennessee* (Spartan, SC, 1974), p. 188; JB-CaC, pp. 223, 225, 228; C. Knight Aldrich, ed., *Quest for a Star* (Knoxville, TN, 1999), pp. 69, 88, 89, 190n; Joseph Hergesheimer, *Sheridan* (New York, 1931), pp. 137, 138; Society of the 74th Illinois Volunteer Infantry, *Campaigns of the 74th Illinois Volunteer Infantry* (Rockford, IL, 1903), pp. 24–25, 125–28; Steven E. Woodworth, *Six Armies in Tennessee* (Lincoln, NE, 1988), pp. 40, 88–89; Lenette S. Taylor, "The Supply for Tomorrow Must Not Fail," (Kent, OH, 2004), p. 169; Judith Lee Hallock, *Braxton Bragg and Confederate Defeat* (Tuscaloosa, AL, 1991), p. 138; Stephen Chicione, *John Basil Turchin and the Fight to Free the Slaves* (Westport, CT, 2003), p. 168; Michael V. Sheridan, "Charging with Sheridan up Missionary Ridge" in PC-BL, pp. 454, 463; PC-TS, p. 379; RED-CW, p. 344; HSC-CWA, pp. 648–49.

6. OR ser. I, vol. 30, part 2—Reports, report no. 28 (Col. Francis T. Sherman) p. 195; William F. G. Shanks, *Personal Recollections of Distinguished Generals* (New York, 1866), pp. 150, 153; T. J. Stiles, ed., *In Their Own Words* (New York, 1995), p. 198; RM-S, pp. 143, 145; John Ely (88th Ill.) diary entry dated November 25, 1863 (Chickamauga and Chattanooga NMP Library); PC-SH, pp. 270, 286, 287, 306; W.H. Newlin, *A History of the Seventy-third Regiment of Illinois Infantry Volunteers* (Springfield, IL, 1890), pp. 265, 266; LGB-H36., pp. 527, 528, 530; PHS-M, pp. 311, 312, 322, 324; RO-SI p. 133; AHG-HP, p. 562; T. M. Eddy, *The Patriotism of Illinois*, vol. 1 (Chicago, IL, 1866), p. 416; JB-CaC, pp. 226–27; David R. Wade, "The Hard-Charging 36th Illinois," *America's Civil War* (July 1999), p. 90; Steven E. Woodward, *Six Armies in Tennessee* (Lincoln, NE, 1998), p. 200; eds. of Time Life Books, *Voices of the Civil War-Chattanooga* (Alexandria, VA, 1998), p. 132; Maurice Marcoot, *Five Years in the Sunny South* (University Microfilms International, Ann Arbor, MI, 1990), p. 42; Michael Anderson Hughes, "The Struggle for Chattanooga" (PhD dissertation, University of Arkansas, 1991), pp. 155, 159; *MOLLUS-Wisconsin Commandery*, vol. 2, 1896, p. 204; C. Knight Aldrich, ed., *Quest for a Star* (Knoxville, TN, 1999), p. 86; Glenn V. Longacre, ed., *To Battle for God and the Right* (Chicago, 2003), p. 136n; Judith Lee Hallock, *Braxton Bragg and Confederate Defeat* (Tuscaloosa, AL, 1991), pp. 127, 130, 135–37, 139; PC-BL, p. 465; OR Supplement, ser. I, vol. 31, part 1—Reports (Col. Gibson, Louisiana Brigade) pp. 113–17; Maj. Francis Campbell (13th and 20th Louisiana Regiments) pp. 120–21; Alexander K. McClure, *The Annals of the Civil War* (New York, 1994), pp. 186–87; Wilbur F. Hinman, *The Story of the Sherman Brigade* (Alliance, OH, 1897), p. 456; Leverett M. Kelley, Congressional Medal of Honor Citation, dated April 4, 1900.

7. LGB-H36, pp. 529–30, 533–36; *Elgin Daily Courier*, November 27, 1963; Victor Hicken, *Illinois in the Civil War* (Urbana, IL, 1966), pp. 234, 236; OR ser. I, vol. 30, part 2—Reports, report no. 29 (Lt. Col. Porter C. Olson), p. 197; *New York Times*, November 29, 1863; Pvt. John Ely, (88th Ill.), diary entries dated November 24, November 25, November 26, 1863 (copies in author's possession); PC-SH, pp. 278, 287, 308; Wiley Sword, *Mountains Touched With Fire* (New York, 1995), p. 303; James Lee McDonough, *Chattanooga* (Nashville, TN, 1984), p. 215; RM-S, p. 145; William F. Smith, *From Chattanooga to Petersburg* (Boston, 1893); Henry Fuller (88th Ill.), letter to his father, dated November 25, 1863, *Henry Fuller Papers* (SC 531, Illinois State Historical Society); JB-CaC, pp. 232–33; James A. Connolly, *Three Years in the Army of the Cumberland* (Bloomington, IN, 1987), p. 158; Steven E. Woodworth, *Six Armies in Tennessee* (Lincoln, NE, 1988), pp. 200, 202–03; Charles A. Dana, *Recollections of the Civil War* (New York, 1963), pp. 141–42; Larry M. Strayer, *Echoes of Battle* (Huntington, WV, 1991), p. 18; Jim R. Cabannis, *Civil War Journal and Letters of Washington Ives*, (4th Fla, C.S.A.) (Jackson MS, 1987), p. 53; Thomas J. Ford (24th Wis.) *With the Rank and File* (Milwaukee, WI, 1898), p. 29; Brooks D. Simpson, *Ulysses S. Grant* (New York, 2000) pp. 240, 242, 247; C. Knight Aldrich, ed., *Quest for a Star* (Knoxville, TN, 1999), pp. 87, 88; PC-BL, pp. 459, 460, 462, 463, 465; DE-L, to his parents, dated November 26, 1863; Pvt. George Cummins (36th Ill.), letter to Maggie, dated April 14, 1864 (copy in author's possession); JES-RN, p. 393; CS-AL, p. 448–49.

8. 36th Illinois Regimental Order Book (unpaged), (NA); William C. Buchanan (36th Ill.), diary entries dated March 31, April 4, 1864 (copy in author's possession); LGB-H36, pp. 291, 546, 549–53, 558, 559, 564, 566–74; DE-L, to his brother, dated April 3, 1864, noted that "at most every station they come to, some of [the soldiers] would get on the cars." (Day Elmore was a private in Lank's Company E) (copy in author's possession); Melancton J. Ross pension and medical records (NA, RG94); *Illinois Adjutant General's Report* vol. 3, rev., pp. 35–36; *Aurora (Illinois) Daily Beacon*, vol. 5, no. 50 (December 10, 1863), p. 1; ibid., vol. 17, no. 862, page 1 (February 25, 1864); ibid., vol. 6, no. 12, p. 1 (March 24, 1864); George A. Cummins (Company F, 36th Ill.), letter dated April 14, 1864 (Illinois State Historical Library); Newton Bateman and Paul Selby, eds., *History of Kendall County, Illinois* vol. 2 (Chicago, 1904), p. 776; James R. Arnold, *The Armies of U. S. Grant* (London, 1995), p. 144; OR ser. I, vol. 37, part 2—Reports, report no. 27 (Sheridan) pp. 102–03; John—(123rd N.Y.), letter dated February 27, 1864 (copy in author's possession); WVR-L, to his parents, dated January 9, 1864 (University of Wisconsin Manuscript Collection); Pvt. George A. Cooley (24th Wis.), diary entry dated November 28, 1863 (copy in author's possession); John D. McKenzie, *Uncertain Glory, Lee's Generalship Re-examined* (New York, 1999) pp. 349–58; Daniel R. Ross and Melancton J. Ross, military service records (NA, Record Group 94); F4US; HCM-R123, pp. 79–85; Col. Francis T. Sherman (88th Ill.), letter to his family, dated December 21, 1863 (Chicago Historical Society); OR—Supplement vol. 10, part 2, Record of Events, p. 634; PHS-M, pp. 325, 328; RO-SI, p. 141; unsigned letter written by a soldier in the 123rd N.Y.,

published in *The Washington County People's Journal*, vol. 11, no. 10 (March 10, 1864); T. M. Eddy, *The Patriotism of Illinois*, vol. 1 (Chicago, IL, 1866), pp. 133, 134; David R. Wade, "The Hard-Charging 36th Illinois," *America's Civil War*, July 1999, p. 90; Thomas B. Buell, *The Warrior Generals* (New York, 1997), p. 280; Bruce Catton, *This Hallowed Ground* (New York, 1956), pp. 319–20; CS-AL, pp. 423, 437, 438; OR—Supplement, Record of Events, vol. 46, part 2, pp. 547–48; Joseph Hergesheimer, *Sheridan* (New York, 1931), p. 338; *Washington County Post*, vol. 75, no. 52 (December 25, 1863), p. 2; Maurice Marcoot, *Five Years in the Sunny South* (University Microfilms International, Ann Arbor, MI, 1990), p. 44; *The Papers of Philip Sheridan* Reel no. 83, p. 228 (LC Manuscript Collection); Lt. George Robinson (123rd N.Y.), letter to his wife, dated April 24, 1864 (copy in author's possession); Rachael Sherman Thorndyke, *The Sherman Letters* (New York, 1969), p. 226; William Hutton (123rd N.Y.) letter to (illegible) dated January (?), 1864 (copy in author's possession); *The Daily Chronicle* (Washington, DC), January 1864; C. Knight Aldrich, ed., *Quest for a Star* (Knoxville, TN, 1999), pp. 88, 97–99; Thomas J. Morgan, ed., *Personal Narratives*, 3rd ser., no. 13 (Soldiers' and Sailors' Historical Society Of Rhode Island, Providence RI, 1885), pp. 11, 15, 18–20, 22; *Kendall County Record*, May 7, May 12, 1864; Henry J. Aten, *History of the 85th Regt Ill. Volunteer Regiment* (Hiawatha, KS, 1901) p. 139; *Salem Press* vol. 15, no. 1 (May 3, 1864); Pvt. John L. Marshall (Company G, 123rd N.Y.) letter to his parents, dated January 20, 1864, and to his cousin, dated January 22, 1864 (copies in author's possession); Mark M. Boatner, *The Civil War Dictionary* (New York, 1959), p. 765; WW-L, pp. 443, 445; Glenn V. Longacre, *To Battle for God and Right* (Chicago, 2003), pp. 138–43, 153; LJD-CG, p. 379; DE-L, to his parents, dated December 6, 1863 (copy in author's possession); Pvt. George Cummins (36th Ill.), letter to Maggie, dated April 1, 1864 (copy in author's possession); JYS-PG10, pp. 250, 255; Brian Melton, "Where Is Slocum?" *Civil War Historian*, vol. 2, no. 4 (September/October 2006), pp. 50, 51; Herman Hattaway, *How the North Won* (Urbana, IL, 1983), p. 422; Pvt. Artemus Harrington (Company G, 123rd N.Y.) letter to his parents, dated February 22, 1863 (copy in author's possession); JYS-PG10, p. 354; Fred A. Shannon, *The Organization and Administration of the Union Army 1861–1865* (Gloucester, MA, 1965) p. 69; Lt. Robinson (123rd N.Y.) diary entry December 18, 1863 (copy in author's possession); ibid., letter to his wife, dated April 24, 1864 (copy in author's possession); WCM-L, to his father, dated January 1, 1864 (copy in author's possession); Lieutenant Robinson (123rd N.Y.) letters to his wife, dated March 30, April 24, 1864 (copies in author's possession); Wilbur F. Hinman, *The Story of the Sherman Brigade* (Alliance OH, 1897), p. 458. James A. Padgett, "With Sherman Through Georgia and the Carolinas," Part 1, *Georgia Historical Quarterly*, vol. 32, p. 289; Battery F 4th U.S. undated pamphlet (copy in author's possession).

Chapter 9. Battle of the Wilderness

1. JGN-AL8, p. 355; Maj. Gen. Grenville M. Dodge *The Battle of Atlanta* (New York, 1965), p. 154; Noah Andre Trudeau, *Bloody Roads South* (Boston, 1988),

p. 9; Ernest B. Furguson, *Chancellorsville* (New York, 1992), p. 47 DHK-H93, pp. 65, 66; Gerald F. Linderman, *Embattled Courage* (New York, 1987), p. 36; Herman Hattaway, *How the North Won* (Urbana, IL, 1983), p. 524; Richard H. McMurry, *The Road Past Kennesaw: The Atlanta Campaign of 1864* (Washington, DC, 1972), p. 3; Maj. Gen. J. F. C. Fuller, *Grant and Lee* (Bloomington, IN, 1957), pp. 209–10; Richard Wheeler, *Sherman's March* (New York, 1978), p. 15; *Washington County Post*, March 28, 1862; James R. Arnold, *Grant Wins the War* (New York, 1997), p. 315; David E. Long, *The Jewel of Liberty* (Mechanicsburg, PA, 1994), p. 197; William H. Ross, military service record (NA, RG 94).

2. William Sumner Dodge, *History of the Old Second Division* (Chicago, 1864), p. 156; Captain B. H. Liddell Hart, "Sherman," *Civil War Chronicles*, p. 20; Stephen E. Ambrose, "Fort Donelson: Disastrous Blow to the South," CWTI, vol. 5, no. 3 (1966), p. 8; Robert Leckie, *From Sea to Shining Sea* (New York, 1993), p. 566; Don Lowry, *No Turning Back* (New York, 1992), p. 20; Captain Louis C. Duncan, *The Medical Department of the United States Army in the Civil War* (Gaithersburg, MD, 1987), p. 353; Shelby Foote, *The Civil War: A Narrative* vol. 3 (New York, 1974), pp. 128, 129, 136; Russell F. Weighley, *The American Way of War* (Bloomington, IN, 1977), pp. 142–43; HP-CG, p. 373; Regimental Order Book, *Ninety-third New York*, Company C (NA, Record Group 94); Lt. Col. Thomas Wilson, "Feeding a Great Army," CWTI, vol. 4, no. 10 (February 1966), p. 32; Adam Badeau, *Military History of Ulysses S. Grant*, vol. 2 (New York, 1881), pp. 107–08; FAL-TF, p. 118; WWB-L, to Maggie Jane Getty, dated April 21, 1864 (New York State Archives, SC12780), p. 241; Second Army Corps, vol. 56 (NA, RG393, pt 2, Gen. Order no. 8); Robert S. Robertson, *Diary of the War* (Fort Wayne IN, 1965) pp. 154–55, 158; *Harper's Weekly*, vol. 8, no. 370 (January 30, 1864), p. 67, and no. 375 (March 5, 1864), p. 147; John Crisfield, *History of Washington County, N.Y., 1738–1878* (Interlaken, NY, 1991) p. 176; Henry N. Blake, *Three Years in the Army of the Potomac* (Boston, 1865), pp. 267, 268; FAL-TF, p. 118; JSC-D, 1864, entries on pp. 11, 14, 20, 26, 39–41 (typescript copy in author's possession); Emil & Ruth Rosenblatt, eds., *Hard Marching Every Day* (Lawrence, KS, 1992), pp. 204, 206; Francis A. Walker, *History of the Second Army Corps* (New York, 1886), p. 408; Gordon C. Rhea, *The Battle of the Wilderness* (Baton Rouge, LA, 1994), p. 202; Guard Book, Consolidated Morning Reports and Regimental Order Book, pp. 4, 7; Ninety-third New York, RG 94 (NA); Gamaliel Bradford, *Union Portraits* (Freeport, NY, 1968), p. 83; Gabor S. Borrit, *Lincoln's Generals* (New York, 1994), p. 165; Gerald F. Linderman, *Embattled Courage* (New York, 1987), pp. 263–64; Stephen B. Oates, *A Woman of Valor-Clara Barton in the Civil War* (New York, 1994), p. 215; Charles A. Dana, *Recollections of the Civil War* (New York, 1963), p. 59; six letters, written by the Ross brothers to one another, are in the author's possession (the original letter written by William to his mother, is in the National Archives as part of her dependent's pension application); General C. M. Wilcox "Lee and Grant in the Wilderness," *Annals of the War* vol. 1, no. 46, January 12, 1878, p. 147; Arthur C. Cole, *The Era of the Civil War* (Urbana, IL, 1987), pp. 234–35, 260–63; Stephen W. Sears, *To the Gates of Richmond* (New York, 1972), pp. 347–48, 355; the Civil War records of these four brothers are in the National Archives, the New York State Division of Military and Naval Records, and the Office of the Secretary of the State of

Illinois; David S. Sparks, ed., *Inside Lincoln's Army* (New York, 1964), pp. 360–61; Larry M. Strayer, *Echos of Battle* (Huntington, WV, 1991), p. 18; Henry N. Blake, *Three Years in the Army of the Potomac* (Boston, 1865), pp. 273–74; JSC-D, p. 42 (copy in author's possession); Emil & Ruth Rosenblatt, eds., *Hard Marching Every Day* (Lawrence, KS, 1992), pp. 208, 209; Francis A. Walker, *History of the Second Army Corps* (New York, 1886), p. 405; Robert S. Robertson, *Diary of the War* (Fort Wayne, IN, 1965), p. 143; George T. Fleming, *Life and Letters of General Alexander Hays* (Pittsburgh, 1919), p. 552; James D. Horan, *Matthew Brady* (New York, 1955), p. 55; Ezra J. Warner, *Generals in Blue* (Baton Rouge, LA, 1977), pp. 170, 223–24; William B. Jordan, *Red Diamond Regiment* (Shippensburg, PA, 1996) p. 109; *Southern Historical Society Papers*, vol. 23 (Chapel Hill, NC, 1895), p. 248; Gilbert Hays, *Under the Red Patch* (Pittsburgh, 1908), p. 278; JSC-D, entries on January 4, February 2, February 9, February 12, 1862 (copies in author's possession); Rossiter Johnson, *Campfire and Battlefield* (Boston, 1894), pp. 353, 354; DHK-H93, pp. 370, 371, 373, 375; Ken Bandy, *The Gettysburg Papers*, vol. 2 (Clayton, OH, 1978) p. 1026; Alexander Gardner, *Gardner's Photographic Sketch Book* (New York, 1959), opposite plate 55; Otto Eisenchime, *The Civil War* (New York, 1956), p. 354; Warren W. Hassler, Jr., *Commanders of the Army of the Potomac* (Baton Rouge, LA, 1962), p. 161; HCM-R123, p. 65; Gary W. Gallagher, ed., *The Wilderness Campaign* (Chapel Hill, NC, 1997), pp. 68–70, 75; Merlin E. Sumner, ed., *The Diary of Cyrus B. Comstock* (New York, 1987), p. 260; AHG-HP, p. 624; *Glens Falls Republican*, January 5, 1864; *Washington County Post*, January 8, 1864; Jurgen Herbst, *The Once and Future School* (New York, 1996), p. 70; JMM-BC, p. 488; DHK-H93, pp. 30, 32–34, 36–38, 393; Lt. Chester Swain (93rd N.Y.), letter to his sister, dated January 3, 1863 (copy in author's possession); James R. Arnold, *The Armies of U. S. Grant* (London, 1995), p. 24; WWB-L, to Cousin Em, dated November 9, 1863 (copy in author's possession); Ernest B. Furguson, *Not War But Murder* (New York, 2000), pp. 7, 17; Brooks D. Simpson, *Ulysses S. Grant* (New York, 2000), pp. 262, 264, 286; DHK-H93, pp. 37–38; Rod Gragg, *Covered With Glory* (New York, 2000), p. 181; U.S. Census of 1860, Little Rock Township, Kane County, Illinois; CS-AL, pp. 297, 464; Charles W. Wills, *Army Life of an Illinois Soldier* (Carbondale, IL, 1996), p. 22; Loume R. Speer, *Portals to Hell* (Mechanicsburg, PA, 1997), p. 82; Margaret Leech, *Reveille in Washington* (New York, 1941), pp. 166, 212–13, 217, 339, 384, 385; William R. Plum, *Civil War in the United States* vol. 2 (Chicago, 1882), pp. 128–30; *Personal Memoirs of John H. Brinton* (New York, 1914), p. 61; Pvt. Robert Knox Sneden, *Eye of the Storm* (New York, 2000), p. 101; JES-RN, pp. 77, 94; John C. Waugh, *Reelecting Lincoln* (New York, 1997), pp. 121, 127–28, 130; Ethan S. Rafuse, *George Gordon Meade and the War in the East* (Abilene, TX, 2003), p. 14; Lt. R. S. Robertson (93rd N.Y.) letters to his parents, dated July 28, September 1, November 4, November 19, December 30, 1863 (copies in author's possession); Doris K. Goodwin, *Team of Rivals* (New York, 2005), pp. 451–52; 1st Lt. Haviland Gifford (93rd N.Y.) letter to his father, written in early October 1863 (copy in author's possession); Kevin C. Murphy, ed., *The Civil War Letters of Joseph C. Taylor of the 37th Massachusetts Volunteer Infantry* (Lewiston, NY, 1988), p. 164n; DHK-H93, pp. 362–63, 368, 369; Frederick Phisterer, *New*

York in the War of the Rebellion (Albany, N.Y., 1912), p. 4493; Penrose E. Mark, *Red: White: and Blue Badge* (Harrisburg, PA, 1911), pp. 260–61; John K. Hensel, "The Good Steward: Major General George Gordon Meade" (PhD dissertation, Temple University, 1980), vol. 2, part 2, pp. 646, 652, 657–59; Captain Robert G. Carter, *Four Brothers in Blue* (Norman, OK, 1999), pp. 66–67; *Report of the Provost Marshall General Executive Documents of the House of Representatives, 39th Congress 1st Session 1865–1866* (Washington, DC, 1866), p. 161; Pvt. John Haley (17th Me.), diary entry, p. 146 (copy in author's possession).

    3. George T. Fleming, *Life and Letters of General Alexander Hays* (Pittsburgh, 1919), p. 552; Gabor S. Borritt, ed., *Lincoln's Generals* (New York, 1994), p. 165; Second Army Corps, vol. 56, RG 393, pt. 2, entries 166 and 167; JSC-D, entry dated March 10, 1864 (copy in author's possession); William B. Jordan, *Red Diamond Regiment* (Shippensburg, PA, 1996), p. 124; Glenn Tucker, *Hancock the Superb* (Indianapolis, IN, 1954), p. 173; Gary W. Gallagher, ed., *The Wilderness Campaign* (Chapel Hill, NC, 1997), p. 93; James R. Arnold, *The Armies of U. S. Grant* (London, 1995), p. 169; Brayton Harris, *Blue and Gray in Black and White* (Washington, DC, 1999), p. 260; JES-RN, p. 94; WWB-L, to cousin Libbie, dated July 14, 1863 (copy in author's possession); Francis A. Walker, *General Hancock* (New York, 1898), p. 157; *Morning Chronicle* Washington, DC March 11, March 15, 1864; Richard Wheeler, *On Fields of Fury* (New York, 1991), p. 46; Pvt. John Haley (17th Me.), diary (Dyer Library, Saco, ME), p. 232; John C. Waugh, *Reelecting Lincoln* (New York, 1997), p. 127; Bruce Catton, *Never Call Retreat* (London, England, 2001), p. 300; A. M. Gambone, *Hancock at Gettysburg...and Beyond* (Baltimore, MD, 1997), p. 183; Frank Wilkeson, *Turned Inside Out* (Lincoln, NE, 1997), p. 37; OR ser. 3, vol. 3—Correspondence, pp. 748–749; OR—Supplement, ser. 1, vol. 27, part 1—Reports, p. 74; William F. Fox, *Regimental Losses in the Civil War* (Albany, NY, 1889), p. 69.

    4. DHK-H93, pp. 57–60, 546; Gilbert Hays, *Under the Red Patch* (Pittsburgh, 1908), pp. 225–26; Ruth L. Silliker, ed., *The Rebel Yell and the Yankee Hurrah* (Camden, ME, 1985), pp. 139, 141–44; Alexander Gardner, *Gardner's Photographic Sketch Book* (New York, 1959), opposite Plates 55 & 60; William B. Greene (Company G, 2nd U.S. Sharpshooters 1864–65), diary entry April 23, 1864 (Collection of Wiley Sword); JYS-PG10, p. 362; JSC-D, entry dated May 5, 1864 (typescript copy in author's possession); Oliver W. Davis, *The Life of David Bell Birney* (Philadelphia, 1867) pp. 212, 215; George R. Agassiz, *With Grant and Meade from the Wilderness to Appomattox* (Lincoln, NE, 1994), pp. 144, 266; George T. Fleming, *Life and Letters of General Alexander Hays* (Pittsburgh, 1919), pp. 565–66; RED-CW, p. 393; Frederick Phisterer, *New York in the War of the Rebellion*, vol. 1, (Albany, NY, 1912), p. 62; WWB-L, to his uncle, dated May 11, 1864 (New York State Archives, SC 12780); JSC-D, entries dated March 30, April 15, April 16, April 17, April 19, April 22, April 29, 1864 (copies in author's possession); WWB-L, letter to his friend Maggie, dated April 21, 1864 (copy in author's possession); Second Army Corps, vol. 56, General Order no. 8 and Guard Reports (NA, RGE 393); DHK-H93, p. 585; Robert S. Robertson, *Diary of the War* (Fort Wayne, IN, 1965), pp. 154–55; William F. Fox, *Regimental Losses in the Civil War* (Albany, NY, 1884); Percy G. Hamlin, *"Old Bald Head,"*

(Strasburg, VA, 1940), p. 167; Power J. Tracy, "From the Wilderness to Appomattox: Life in Lee's Army of Northern Virginia" (PhD dissertation, University of South Carolina, 1993), pp. 7–9; Robert S. Robertson, *Diary of the War* (Fort Wayne, IN, 1965), p. 158; JSC-D, entries dated April 22, April 26, 1864 (copies in author's possession); Francis A. Walker, *History of the Second Army Corps* (New York, 1886), p. 405; *Chicago Evening Journal* vol. 25, no. 82 (April 29, 1864), p. 1; L. A. Rose (military telegraph operator, Second Army Corps), diary entry dated May 5, 1864 (LC MSS); Frederick Phisterer, *New York in the War of the Rebellion*, vol. 4 (Albany, New York, 1912), p. 3042; WWB-L, to Maggie Jane Getty, dated April 21, 1864 (N.Y. State Archives, SC 12780), p. 241; WWB-L, to Cousin Libbie, dated May 1, 1864; Richard Wheeler, *On Fields of Fury* (New York, 1991), pp. 47, 75; JYS-PG10, pp. 175–76; JYS-PG11, pp. 362–63; Gilbert Hays, *Under the Red Patch* (Pittsburgh, 1908), pp. 225–26; 93rd N.Y. Bound Records, Consolidated Morning Reports (NA, RG 94); William S. McFeely, *Grant* (New York, 1981), p. 165; JGN-CW, pp. 90–91; Warren W. Hassler, Jr., *Commanders of the Army of the Potomac* (Baton Rouge, LA, 1962), p. 206; Philip N. Racine, ed., "Unspoiled Heart," *The Journal of Charles Mattocks of the 17th Maine* (Knoxville, TN, 1994), p. 129; Clarence Edward Macartney, *Grant and His Generals* (New York, 1953), p. 34–35, 40; William B. Jordan, *Red Diamond Regiment* (Shippensburg, PA, 1996), pp. 124, 125, 128; Power J. Tracy, "From the Wilderness to Appomattox: Life in Lee's Army of Northern Virginia" (PhD dissertation, University of South Carolina, 1993), p. 13; OR, ser. I, vol. 38, part 1, pp. 221–29; Medical and Surgical History of the War of the Rebellion, 1st part, Medical Volume, p. 148; Douglas Southall Freeman, *R. E. Lee* vol. 3 (New York, 1935), p. 268; Nancy Scott Anderson, *The Generals* (New York, 1988), p. 363; RL-ND, pp. 581–82; Gaillard Hunt, *Israel Elihu and Cadwallader Washburn* (New York, 1925), pp. 209, 369; Lt. McHenry Howard, "Notes and Recollections on Opening the Wilderness Campaign," *Massachusetts MOLLUS*, vol. 4 (Boston, 1965), p. 95; JSC-D, May 3, 1864, p. 46 (copy in author's possession); Marcus B. Toney, *The Privations of a Private* (Nashville, TN, 1905), p. 74; Herman Hattaway, *How the North Won* (Urbana, IL, 1983) p. 525; William B. Jordan, *Red Diamond Regiment* (Shippensburg, PA, 1996), p. 124; Emmet Crozier, *Yankee Reporters 1861–65* (New York, 1956), pp. 377, 381; Louis M. Starr, *Bohemian Brigade* (New York, 1954), p. 296; Earl Schenck Miers, *The Last Campaign* (New York, 1988), p. 31; Sylvannus Cadwallader, manuscript "Four Years with Grant" (1896) (Illinois State Historical Library, Springfield, IL), pp. 365, 373; Henry N. Blake, *Three Years in the Army of the Potomac* (Boston, 1865), p. 279; JYS-PG11, p. 396; FAL-TF, pp. 261–62; R. Plum, *The Military Telegraph During the Civil War* (Chicago, 1882) p. 130; HP-CG, p. 149; Gerald F. Linderman, *Embattled Courage* (New York, 1987), p. 123; *Chicago Evening Journal*, vol. 25, no. 82 (April 29, 1864); JGN-AL8, pp. 91, 355; L. A. Rose, diary (LC Manuscript Division); Theodore Lyman, jounal entry dated May 3, 1864 (Massachusetts Historical Society); Charles A. Page, *Letters of a War Correspondent* (Boston, 1899), p. 47; Marcus B. Toney, *The Privations of a Private* (Nashville, TN, 1905), p. 72; William B. Jordan, *Red Diamond Regiment* (Shippensburg, PA, 1996), p. 122; John R. Young, *Around the World with General Grant*, vol. 2 (New York, 1879), p. 299; William S. McFeely, *Grant* (New York,

1981), p. 165; JSC-D, entries dated May 2, May 4, 1864 (copies in author's possession); AHG-HP, p. 624; *Washington County Post*, March 28, 1862; Mark M. Boatner, *The Civil War Dictionary* (New York, 1959), p. 65; Gary W. Gallagher, ed., *The Wilderness Campaign* (Chapel Hill, NC, 1997), pp. 95, 172; Francis A. Walker, *History of the Second Army Corps* (New York, 1886), p. 157; Brooks D. Simpson, *Ulysses S. Grant* (New York, 2000), p. 285; Lloyd Lewis, *Captain Sam Grant* (Boston, 1950), pp. 396, 406; Rachael Sherman Thorndyke, *The Sherman Letters* (New York, 1969), p. 225; *Morning Chronicle* March 18, March 24, April 30, 1864; Carol K. Bleser, *Intimate Strategies of the Civil War* (New York, 2001), p. 131; CS-AL, p. 459; John D. Billings, *Hardtack and Coffee* (Boston, 1887), p. 180; JYS-PG10, pp. 370, 434; J. G. Hamilton, ed., *The Papers of Randolph Abbot Shotwell*, vol. 2 (Raleigh, NC, 1929), p. 464; JTG-MS, p. 187; William B. Jordan, *Red Diamond Regiment* (Shippensburg, PA, 1996), p. 129; Pvt. J. Reynolds (105th Pa.) letter to his mother, April 23, 1864; Pvt. John W. Haley (17th Me.) undated diary entries, pp. 133, 145 (Saco, ME Public Library); John C. Waugh, *Reelecting Lincoln* (New York, 1997), p. 122, 156; Mark Grumsley, *And Keep Moving On* (Lincoln, NE, 2002), pp. 13–14; George Bowen (12th N.J.) diary entry dated May 1, 1864 (copy in author's possession); John Minor Botts, *The Political Life of the Author Vindicated* (New York, 1866), p. xiii; Frederick Phisterer, *New York in the War of the Rebellion* (Albany, NY, 1912), pp. 62, 305; JYS-PG10, pp. 275–76, 337, 550, 555–56; *Albany Argus* and the *Messenger*, undated issues containing letters authored by soldiers in the 93rd and dated April 23 and April 21, 1864, respectively (in author's possession); Warren Wilkinson, *Mother May You Never See the Sights I Have Seen* (New York, 1990), p. 62; Ezra J. Warner, *Generals in Blue* (Baton Rouge, LA, 1977), p. 370.

 5. Robert V. Johnson and Clarence C. Buell, eds., *Battle and Leaders of the Civil War*, vol. 4 (New York, 1888), pp. 152–53; William S. McFeely, *Grant* (New York, 1981), p. 167; Maj. Gen. J. F. C. Fuller, *Grant and Lee* (Bloomington, IN, 1957), pp. 214–15; Sylvannus Cadwallader, manuscript "Four Years with Grant" (1896) (Illinois State Historical Library, Springfield, IL), p. 372; Clement Eaton, ed., *Confederate Military History*, vol. 3 (New York, 1962), p. 432; Captain Louis C. Duncan, *The Medical Department of the United States Army in the Civil War* (Gaithersburg, MD, 1987), pp. 321–22; George R. Agassiz, *With Grant and Meade from the Wilderness to Appomattox* (Lincoln, NE, 1994), pp. 87, 156; JSC-D, entries dated February 21, May 4, 1864 (copy in author's possession); John Laird Wilson, *Pictorial History of the Great Civil War* (New York, 1881), p. 276; J. Willard Brown, *The Signal Corps, U.S.A.* (Boston, 1896), p. 382; Charles C. Coffin, *Four Years of Fighting* (New York, 1970), p. 315; Nancy Scott Anderson, *The Generals* (New York, 1988), p. 364; Kenneth P. Williams, *Lincoln Finds a General*, vol. 1 (Bloomington, IN, 1949), p. 12; Gene Smith, *Lee and Grant* (New York, 1984), p. 190; Noah Andre Trudeau *Bloody Roads South* (Boston, 1988), p. 42; Adam Badeau, *Ulysses S. Grant*, vol. 2 (New York, 1881) pp. 104–05; JGN-AL8, p. 360; T. Harry Williams, *McClellan, Sherman and Grant* (New Brunswick NJ, 1962), p. 81; HP-CG, p. xv; Clifford Dowdey, *Lee's Last Campaign* (Boston, 1960), pp. 68, 84; Warren W. Hassler, Jr., *Commanders of the Army of the Potomac* (Baton Rouge, LA, 1962), pp. 195, 199; Maj. Gen. Ulysses S. Grant III, *Ulysses S. Grant*

(New York, 1969), p. 217; Louis M. Starr, *Bohemian Brigade* (New York, 1954), p. 297; Andrew D. Long, *Stonewall's "Foot Cavalrymen"* (Austin, TX, 1965), p. 18; H. John Cooper, *Chancellorsville, 1863* (London, 1972), p. 35; AHG-HP, p. 626; Lloyd Lewis, *Captain Sam Grant* (Boston, 1950), p. 365; JB-CaC, p. 186; PVS-SL, p. 257; Margaret Leech, *Reveille in Washington* (New York, 1941), p. 386; Pvt. John Haley (17th Me.), diary entry, p. 233; William B. Jordan, *Red Diamond Regiment* (Shippensburg, PA, 1996), p. 132; Brooks D. Simpson, *Ulysses S. Grant* (New York, 2000), p. 292.

  6. Thomas B. Buell, *The Warrior Generals* (New York, 1997), p. 306; JGN-AL8, pp. 358, 360; DHK-H93, pp. 62, 230; Gen. L. A. Grant "Vermont Brigade at the Wilderness," *The National Tribune*, vol. 16, no. 16, Whole no. 807 (January 28, 1897), p. 2; Edward S. Steere, *The Wilderness Campaign* (Harrisburg, PA, 1960), pp. 203, 211; Noah Andre Trudeau *Bloody Roads South* (Boston, 1988), pp. 62–63; HSC-BG2, p. 373; Henry N. Blake, *Three Years in the Army of the Potomac* (Boston, 1865), p. 279; JSC-D, entry dated May 5, 1864 (copy in author's possession); Merlin E. Sumner, ed., *The Diary of Cyrus B. Comstock* (New York, 1987), p. 264; JYS-PG10, p. 399, Bruce Catton, *Never Call Retreat* (London, England, 2001), p. 354; Morris Schaff, *The Battle of the Wilderness* (Boston, 1910), pp. 128, 129, 132, 133; Gregory A. Coco, *The Civil War Infantryman* (Gettysburg, PA, 1996), p. 134.

  7. Nelson V. Hutchinson, *History of the Seventh Massachusetts Volunteer Infantry* (Taunton, MA, 1890), p. 176; Walter S. Goss, "A History of the 7th Regt of Mass. Volunteers," (Rare Book and Manuscript Division, New York Public Library), pp. 181–84; JSC-D, entry dated May 5, 1864 (copy in author's possession); Lt. Col. W. W. Swan "Battle of the Wilderness," *MOLLUS-Massachusetts Commandery*, vol. 4 (Boston, 1905), pp. 138, 139, and Addenda; Alfred S. Roe, *The Tenth Regiment Massachusetts Volunteer Infantry* (Springfield, MA, 1909), p. 257; Brig. Gen. Hazard Stevens, *The Wilderness Campaign* (Boston, 1905), p. 190; Ezra J. Warner, *Generals in Blue* (Baton Rouge, LA, 1977), p. 170; John D. McKenzie, *Uncertain Glory* (New York, 1997), p. 147; David M. Jordan, *Winfield Scott Hancock* (Bloomington, IN, 1988), p. 115; Edward S. Steere, *The Wilderness Campaign* (Harrisburg, PA, 1960), p. 40, 137, 139, 188, 200; Penrose G. Mark, *Red, White, and Blue Badge* (Harrisburg, PA, 1911), p. 253; J. H. Stine, *History of the Army of the Potomac* (Washington, DC, 1893), p. 602; OR ser. I, vol. 36, part 1—Reports, report no. 154 (Gen. Getty), pp. 676–77; ibid., report no. 72 (Lt. Col. Neeper), pp. 482–83; Maj. W. G. Mitchell, daily memorandum, pp. 350–51; George T. Fleming, *Life and Letters of General Alexander Hays* (Pittsburgh, 1919), pp. 596–98; WWB-L, personal correspondence, dated May 7, 1864 (New York State Archives, SC12780); DHK-H93, pp. 60–65, 535–36, 547, 548, 553, 554, 567, 581, 583–84, 586; *Annals of the War* (Philadelphia, 1879), pp. 493–95; Capt. C. A. Stevens, *Sharpshooters* (Dayton, 1984), p. 401; John Robertson, ed., *Michigan in the War* (Lansing MI, 1882), p. 245; D. G. Grotty, *Four Years Campaigning in the Army of the Potomac* (Grand Rapids, MI, 1874), p. 126; Elisha Hunt Rhodes, *All For the Union* (Lincoln, RI, 1985), p. 144; Joseph Keith Newell, "Ours," *Annals of the 10th Regiment* (Springfield, MA, 1875), pp. 257–59; Col. John S. Crocker, *Memoirs*, dated May 1864, Regiments—93rd NYSV (Manuscript collection,

NYHS); Brig. Gen. Charles P. Mattocks, "In Six Prisons," *War Papers, MOLLUS, Maine Commandery* vol. 1 (Portland, ME, 1898) p. 162; OR ser. 1, vol. 38, part 1Reports, report no. 15 (Hancock), pp. 318–20; Lt. Col. Wm. Y. Ripley (First U.S. Sharpshooters), *Vermont Rifleman in the War for the Union* (Rutland, VT, 1883), pp. 144–46; Robert C. Johnson and Clarence C. Buell, eds., *Battles and Leaders of the Civil War*, vol. 4 (New York, 1888), pp. 154–57; Capt. Charles H. Brewster (10th Mass.), letter to his mother, dated May 11, 1864 (copy in author's possession); William E. S. Whitman, *Maine in the War for the Union* (Lewiston, ME, 1865) p. 453; William Kent, "A Wilderness Memory," CWTI, vol. 28, no. 1 (1989), pp. 35–36; Captain George Verrill, "The Seventeenth Maine at Gettysburg and in the Wilderness" *War Papers, MOLLUS Maine Commandery*, vol. 1 (Portland, ME, 1898), pp. 273–75; JSC-D, May 5, 1864, p. 47; Regimental Order Book 93rd NY RG 94, National Archives, entry dated March 26, 1864; Philip N. Racine, ed., *"Unspoiled Heart," The Journal of Charles Mattocks of the 17th Maine* (Knoxville, TN, 1994), pp. 135–36; David M. Jordan, *Winfield Scott Hancock* (Bloomington, IN, 1988), p. 115; Robert G. Scott *Into the Wilderness With the Army of the Potomac*; George R. Agassiz, *With Grant and Meade from the Wilderness to Appomattox* (Lincoln, NE, 1994), p. 92; Francis A. Walker, *General Hancock* (New York, 1895), p. 164; Lt. Col. W. W. Swan "Battle of the Wilderness," *MOLLUS-Massachusetts Commandery*, vol. 4 (Boston, 1905), pp. 140, 141; Don Lowry, *No Turning Back* (New York, 1992), p. 179; Rev. D. X. Junkin, *Life of Winfield Scott Hancock* (New York, 1880), p. 134; Edward S. Steere, *The Wilderness Campaign* (Harrisburg, PA, 1960), p. 192; Jacob Seibert (93rd Penn.), letter to his father, dated May 14, 1864 (Harrisburg Civil War Roundtable Collection); Thomas B. Buell, *The Warrior Generals* (New York, 1997), p. 301; G. G. Benedict, *Vermont in the Civil War*, vol. 1 (Burlington, VT, 1886), pp. 423–24; Ruth L. Silliker, ed., *The Rebel Yell and the Yankee Hurrah* (Camden, ME, 1985), p. 195; Mark Grumsley, *And Keep Moving On* (Lincoln, NE, 2002), p. 39; Pvt. John Haley (17th Me.), diary (Dyer Library, Saco, ME), pp. 237–38; Perry D. Jamieson, *Winfield Scott Hancock Gettysburg Hero* (Abilene TX, 2003), pp. 90–93, 95; *Portland (Maine) Daily Press*, May 9, 1864; Mason W. Tyler, *Recollections of the Civil War* (New York, 1912), pp. 142–45; Maj. Gen. Henry Heth, unpublished after-action report, May 4–December 7, 1864 (Fredericksburg and Spotsylvania NMP), pp. 1–4; DHK-H93, pp. 63, 64; LT-GG, p. 65; Bruce Catton, *Never Call Retreat* (London, England, 2001), pp. 354–56; Morris Schaff, *The Battle of the Wilderness* (Boston, 1910), pp. 140–41, 150, 164, 169, 172–75, 185.

8. Rev. A. M. Stewart, *Camp, March and Battlefield* (Philadelphia, 1865), p. 377; *New York Monuments Commission, Final Report of the Battlefield of Gettysburg*, vol. 2 (Albany, NY, 1900), p. 712; Augustus Woodbury, *The Second Rhode Island Regiment* (Providence, RI, 1875), p. 235; Stewart Sifakis, *Who Was Who in the Civil War* (New York, 1988), p. 306; Warren W. Hassler, "Harry Heth, Lee's Hard-Luck General," CWTI , vol. 5, no. 4 (July 1966), p. 13; HSC-BG2, p. 373; James I. Robertson, *General A. P. Hill* (New York, 1987), pp. 255–59; Oliver W. Davis, *Life of General D. B. Birney* (Philadelphia, 1867), p. 215; *New York Times*, vol. 13, no. 3938 (May 8, 1864), p. 1; Gilbert A. Hays Papers, John M. Yahres (63rd Penn.), letter to Gilbert A. Hays, dated March 24, 1917

(Historical Society of Western Pennsylvania); JSC-D, entry May 5, 1864 (copy in author's possession); George T. Fleming, *Life and Letters of General Alexander Hays* (Pittsburgh, 1919), pp. 599–602; Francis A. Walker, *General Hancock* (New York, 1898), p. 288; Philip N. Racine, ed., *"Unspoiled Heart," The Journal of Charles Mattocks of the 17th Maine* (Knoxville, TN, 1994), pp. 135–36; Lt. Col. Chas. B. Merrill, *Report, Northern Monthly*, vol. 1; no. 8 (October 1864), p. 555; Lt. Col. Wm. Y. Ripley (First U.S. Sharpshooters), *Vermont Rifleman in the War for the Union*, (Rutland, VT, 1883), p. 145; Wiley Sword, *Sharpshooter* (Lincoln, RI, 1988), pp. 46, 50; Charles Harvey Brewster, *When This Cruel War Is Over*, ed. David W. Blight (Amherst, MA, 1992), p. 292; William Kent, "A Wilderness Memory," CWTI, vol. 28, no. 1 (March 1989), pp. 37–38; FAL-TF, p. 62; Mahon and Danysh, *Army Lineage Series: Infantry*, pp. 18–19; OR ser. 1, vol. 36, part 1—Reports, report no. 71 (Maj. McConihe, 93rd N.Y.), p. 467; FAL-TF, pp. 29, 61; William F. Fox, *Regimental Losses in the Civil War* (Albany, NY, 1889), p. 419; John W. Forney, *Life and Military Career of Winfield Scott Hancock* (Philadelphia, PA, 1880), p. 228; Nelson V. Hutchinson, *History of the Seventh Massachusetts Volunteer Infantry* (Taunton, MA, 1890), pp. 174–76; OR, ser. 1, vol. 48, part 2—Correspondence, p. 411; Gaillard Hunt, *Israel, Elihu and Cadwallader Washburn* (New York, 1925), p. 209; OR, ser. 1, vol. 48, part 1—Reports, p. 122; George T. Fleming, *Life and Letters of General Alexander Hays* (Pittsburgh, 1919), p. 552; John S. Crocker (93rd N.Y.), memoir, (NYHS); EJH-US, pp. 73, 74; KJB-S, p. 56; Edward S. Steere, *The Wilderness Campaign* (Harrisburg, PA, 1960), p. 242; CWTI, May 1962, p. 17; Don Congdon, ed., *Combat: The Civil War* (New York, 1967), pp. 477–78; WWB-L, to his uncle, dated May 9, June 29, 1864 (New York State Archives, SC12780); H. H. Cunningham, *Doctors in Grey* (Baton Rouge, LA, 1958), p. 118; John Michael Priest, *Civil War*, vol. 10, no. 6, issue 38 (November–December 1992), p. 53; William Swinton, *Campaigns of the Army of the Potomac* (New York, 1871), pp. 425–26; General C. M. Wilcox "Lee and Grant in the Wilderness," *Annals of the War*, vol. 1, no. 46 (January 12, 1878); Mason W. Tyler, *Recollections of the Civil War* (New York, 1912), p. 146; CS-AL, p. 508; Emmet Crozier, *Yankee Reporters 1861–65* (New York, 1956), pp. 382–90; Louis M. Starr, *Bohemian Brigade* (New York, 1954), p. 299; Don Congdon, ed., *Combat: The Civil War* (New York, 1967), pp. 477–78; Penrose E. Mark, *Red: White: and Blue Badge* (Harrisburg, PA, 1911), p. 352; H. H. Cunningham, *Doctors in Blue* (Baton Rouge, LA, 1958), p. 115; Helen Todd, *A Man Named Grant* (Boston, 1940), p. 211; Gaillard Hunt, *Israel Elihu and Cadwallader Washburn* (New York, 1925), p. 209; Don Lowry, *No Turning Back* (New York, 1992), p. 20; *Glens Falls Republican*, May 17, 1864; *Glens Falls Messenger*, vol. 9, no. 25 (June 17, 1864); *Washington Post*, May 20, May 27, 1864 (letter of S. M. Peters, [93rd N.Y.], dated May 19, 1864); Colonel Parsons, "The 10th (Mass.) Regiment—Salient Points in A History," MOLLUS, *Massachusetts Commandery*, April 3, 1901, p. 7; Lt. William L. Bramhall (Company E, 93rd N.Y.) letter dated May 10, 1864; *New York Tribune*, May 20, 1864; David Craft, *History of the 141st Regiment, Pennsylvania Volunteers* (Towanda, PA, 1885), pp. 175–77; Rod Gragg, *Covered With Glory* (New York, 2000), pp. 181, 205; Capt. J. K. Newell, *"Ours," Annals of the 10th Regt. Mass. Volunteers* (Springfield, MA, 1875), pp. 257–59;

JMM-CC, p. 74; Elisha Hunt Rhodes, *All For the Union* (Lincoln, RI, 1985), p. 146; Edward P. Bridgman (37th Mass.), *Early Recollections and Army Experiences*, pp. 68, 69; James B. Pond Papers (Clements Library, University of Michigan); Ruth L. Silliker, ed., *The Rebel Yell and the Yankee Hurrah* (Camden, ME, 1985), p. 144; Peter B. Dalton, *With Our Faces to the Foe* (Union, ME, 1998), p. 300; William E. S. Whitman, *Maine in the War for the Union* (Lewiston, ME, 1865), p. 453; Lieutenant Hunt, letter dated May 8, 1864 (copy in author's possession); Robert Hunt Rhodes, *All For the Union* (New York, 1985), pp. 144–46; David M. Jordan, *Winfield Scott Hancock* (Bloomington, IN, 1988), p. 135; DHK-H93: memoir of Lt. C. T. Barnes (93rd N.Y.), p. 278; ibid., memoir of Col. Pulford (5th Mich.), p. 93; ibid., memoir of Lt. George Blackman, p. 302; ibid., memoir of Col. Crocker, pp. 63–65; ibid., memoir of Sgt. A. J. Gibbs, pp. 61–62; OR—ser. I, vol. 51, part 1—Supplement, Reports (Lt. Col. Charles Merrill, 17th Me.); Corp. Frank Rood (93rd N.Y.) letter to his parents, dated May 6, 1864 (copy in author's possession); LT-GG, pp. 53–54.

9. Edward S. Steere, *The Wilderness Campaign* (Harrisburg, PA, 1960), pp. 231, 234; William Roscoe Thayer, *The Life and Letters of John Hay* (New York, 1929), p. 211; DHK-H93, pp. 67, 547, 548; WWB-L, to his uncle, dated May 9, 1864 (copy in author's possession); General C. M. Wilcox "Lee and Grant in the Wilderness," *Annals of the War*, vol. 1, no. 46 (January 12, 1878), p. 493; *Confederate Military History*, vol. 4 (Atlanta, 1899), p. 234; T. P. Williams, *The Mississippi Brigade of Brig. Gen. Joseph R. Davis* (Dayton, OH, 1999), pp. 133, 135.

10. David Wallace Adams, "Illinois Soldiers and the Emancipation proclamation," *Journal of the Illinois State Historical Society*, vol. 67, no. 4 (September 1974), p. 100; HSC-BG2, p. 193; Russell F. Weighley, *Way of War* (Bloomington, IN, 1973), p. 143; OR ser. 1, vol. 46, part 1—Reports, report no. 70 (Brig. Gen. Byron R. Pierce), pp. 785–87; WWB-L, to his uncle, dated May 9, 1864 (copy in author's possession); Captain Louis C. Duncan, *The Medical Department of the United States Army in the Civil War* (Gaithersburg, MD, 1987), pp. 320–22, 324, 328, 331, 332, 333; Webb B. Garrison, *A Treasury of Civil War Tales* (Nashville, TN, 1988), p. 195; William L. Stone, ed., *Washington County New York: Its History* (New York, 1901), p. 339; George W. Pearsall (55th N.C.), (George W. Pearsall Collection, North Carolina Archives); Lt. Chester Swain (93rd N.Y.), letter to George, dated May 16, 1864 (copy in author's possession); *Civil War Letters of Sgt. Major Charles H. Church* (17th Me.) (Rose City, MI, 1987), p. 34; T. P. Williams, *The Mississippi Brigade of Brig. Gen. Joseph R. Davis* (Dayton, OH, 1999), p. 139; DHK-H93, pp. 69–70, 286–88.

11. Sgt. L. R. Coy (123rd N.Y.), diary entry dated May 15, 1865 (copy in author's possession); KJB-S, p. 244; John S. Crocker (93rd N.Y.), service and medical record (NA, R. G. 94); DHK-H93, pp. 498–99, 630; WWB-L, to his uncle, dated May 9, 1864; Russell F. Weighley, *Way of War* (Bloomington, IN, 1973), pp. 118, 125–26; *Salem Press*, May 17, 1864; Quartermaster General's Office, *Names of Officers and Soldiers Found on the Battlefields of the Wilderness and Spotsylvania Court House, VA*, General Orders no. 58 (no. II) (Washington, DC, 1865); William L. Stone, ed., *Washington County, New York: Its History* (New York, 1901), p. 339; Frederick H. Dyer, *Compendium of the Civil War*, vol. 3

(New York, 1959), p. 1442; *Salem Press*, July 11, 1865; *Washington County Post*, June 17, 1864; Dave Thornton, "The Civil War Editor: Rufus King Crocker" (unpublished typescript, n.d.), p. 58; Margaret Leech, *Reveille in Washington* (New York, 1941), p. 398; T. P. Williams, *The Mississippi Brigade of Brig. Gen. Joseph R. Davis* (Dayton OH, 1999), p. 135; Lt. R. S. Robertson, letter to his parents dated May 14, 1864 (copy in author's possession); OR ser. I, vol. 38, part 1, pp. 121–22; Frederick Phisterer, *New York in the War of the Rebellion* (Albany, NY, 1912), p. 299; J. Mark Bollinger (National Park Service ranger, Andersonville National Historic Site) private correspondence with author dated November 22, 1988; DHK-H93, pp. 288, 547; Walter Clark, ed., *Histories of the Several Regiments and Battalions from North Carolina* vol. 3 (Wendell NC, 1901), p. 305; ibid., vol. 2, p. 446; Pvt. Alexander Frank (48th N.C.) letter to his father dated May 19, 1863, Alexander Frank Papers, Duke University Perkins Library.

Chapter 10. The Battle of Kolb's Farm

1. Hamlin A. Cole, *Mine Eyes Have Seen the Glory* (Cranbury, NJ, 1975), p. 157; W. H. Chamberlin, "The Skirmish Line in the Atlanta Campaign," *MOLLUS, Ohio Commandery*, vol. 3, pp. 182–83; WTS-M, vol. 2, p. 395; RL-ND, p. 340; John Macdonald, *Great Battles of the Civil War* (New York, 1992), p. 156; William M. Kelly, "A History of the Thirtieth Alabama Volunteers" (MA thesis, University of Alabama, 1927), pp. 151, 155; Noah Andre Trudeau, *Like Men of War* (New York, 1998), p. 335n; Peter G. Tsouras, *Military Quotations from the Civil War* (New York, 1998), p. 244; Lt. Alonzo T. Mason (Company A, 123rd N.Y.), letter to his wife, dated August 2, 1864 (NYHS), p. 4; David Evans, *Sherman's Horsemen* (Indianapolis, IN, 1996), pp. xii and xxiii; W. T. Sherman, letter to Secretary of War, dated May 8, 1861 (copy in author's possession); *Harpers New Monthly Magazine*, vol. 30, no. 179 (April 1, 1865), p. 645; J.D. Cox, *Military Reminiscences of the Civil War*, vol. 2 (New York, 1900), p. 24; Sam R. Watkins, "*Co. Ayteh*" (New York, 1962), pp. 125–26; Larry M. Strayer, *Echoes of Battle: The Atlanta Campaign* (Huntington, WV, 1991), pp. 130, 132, 133–34.

2. The descriptions of these two encounters with the Rebels on May 1, by KJB-S, pp. 44–48; HCM-R123, pp. 25–28, substantially agree with the report of Col. Archibald L McDougall, as published in OR, ser. I, vol. 25, part I, pp. 704–05. However, both describe the skirmish line as a picket line. If the purpose of the movement was to make a feint toward Fredericksburg, and thus distract the enemy's attention from the major troop movement, it would have been imperative to skirmish rather than picket; HCM-R123, p. 214; Kenneth A. Perry, ed., "We Are in a Fight Today," *The Civil War Diaries of Horace P. Mathews and King S. Hammond* (123rd N.Y.) (Bowie, MD, 2000), p. xix; Ned Bradford, *Battles and Leaders of the Civil War* (New York, 1956), p. 591; JES-RN, p. 18; Pvt. Albert E. Higley (22nd N.Y.) letter to his father, dated September 27, 1862 (copy in author's possession).

3. *Louisville Daily Journal*, vol. 34, no. 221 (July 6, 1864), p. 1; Union Soldiers and Sailors Monuments Association, *The Union Regiments of Kentucky*

(Louisville, 1897), p. 418; B. F. Scribner, *How Soldiers Were Made* (New Albany, IN, 1887), pp. 250–51, 275; George F. Crain, *Soldiering with Sherman* (DeKalb, IL, 2000), p. 104; *Morning Chronicle*, April 19, 1864.

 4. Among the eighty-two accounts identified by the author are fifteen reports published in OR; stories in twenty-seven newspapers and magazines; eight regimental histories, and thirty-two letters and other personal narratives on Sherman's Atlanta campaign.

 5. OR. ser. I, vol. 7, pp. 32; Edward O. Bartlett, *The Duchess County Regiment* (Danbury, CT, 1907), pp. 93–95; B. F. Scribner, *How Soldiers Were Made* (New Albany, IN, 1887), p. 250; *Cincinnati Daily Gazette*, June 20, 1864; HCM-R123, p. 88; ERB-IN27, p. 469, 507–09; Albert Castel, *Articles of War* (Mechanicsburg, PA, 2001), pp. 71–74; gunner in Battery M (name illegible), letter dated June 25, 1864 (copy in author's possession; *People's Journal*, June 30, 1864; Orlando Brown, Jr. (14th Ky.), letter to his father, dated May 5, 1862 (copy in author's possession); Alan Nevins, *The War for the Union* (New York, 1971), p. 367; Lt. Col. Robert E. Ellis, "From Atlanta to the Sea," *The Military Engineer*, vol. 50, no. 344 (November 1959), p. 440; Charles Royster, *Destructive War* (New York, 1991), p. 300; WW-L, p. 466; Pvt. Noah Rich (123rd N.Y.), letters to his parents, dated June 21, June 26, 1864 (copies in author's possession); Sgt. Rufus Mead "With through Georgia to the Sea and the Carolinas," *Georgia Historical Quarterly*, vol. 32 (1948), p. 296.

 6. The service records of the seventeen men who were captured—one officer and sixteen enlisted men—indicate that thirteen went to Andersonville, where one died "from improper treatment" less than two months after imprisonment. Thirteen received invalid pensions for diseases contracted in prison, including scurvy, dropsy, heart conditions, rheumatism, lung diseases, and typhoid fever. Two of these men were described as walking skeletons when they were released from prison. Three escaped, including Lt. Walter F. Martin, who was imprisoned in the Charleston, S.C., city jail. One was wounded, captured, and died in a Confederate hospital in Atlanta. Six were paroled. Company H, Daniels company, suffered the most casualties—five captured, one killed in action, one mortally wounded, two wounded and captured who died in Confederate hospitals, and one wounded, who recovered in a Union hospital—a total of ten casualties; HCM-R123, pp. 88, 101–05, 112; Pvt A. B. Cone (Company G, 123rd N.Y.), memoir, "Inside Views of Sherman's Campaign," pp. 15–17; Sarah Blackwell Temple, *The First One Hundred Years* (1935), pp. 278–79; *Letters from Confederate Soldiers*, vol. 2 (Georgia Department Of Archives and History, Atlanta, 1940), p. 41; Ezra T. Warner, *Generals in Blue* (Baton Rouge, LA, 1964), pp. 271–72; Richard A. Baumgartner, *Kennesaw Mountain*, June 1864 (Huntington, WV, 1988), pp. 79–85; Frank J. Welcher, *Coburn's Brigade* (Carmel, IN, 1999), p. 214; KJB-S, pp. 128–35; HCM-R123, pp. 90, 101–05; AMC-D, entry dated June 22, 1864 (copy in author's possession); RC-D, pp. 72–74, 244–49; RC-L, to his wife, dated June 24, 1864 (copy in author's possession); Eldon B. Richardson, *Kolb's Farm: Rehearsal for Atlanta's Doom*, pp. 5–11; Sergeant L. R. Coy (Company K. 123rd N.Y.), diary entry dated June 22, 1864 (copy in author's possession); OR, ser. I, vol. 38, part II—Reports, pp. 32–49; Edwin E. Marvin, *Fifth Regiment Connecticut*

Volunteers (Hartford, CT, 1889), p. 316; MQ-CM, pp. 327–29; "A June Evening Before Atlanta," *National Tribune* (Washington, DC) (October 26, 1905), p. 3; *Detroit Advertiser and Tribune*, vol. 36, no. 3 (July 19, 1864), p. 8; *Washington County People's Journal* vol. 11, no. 28 (July 14, 1864); Col. George W. Gallup (14th Ky.), letters to his wife, dated June 22, June 23, June 30, 1864 (Kennesaw Mountain Historical Association); OR, ser. 1, vol. 38, part 3—Reports (Confederate), p. 814; B. F. Scribner, *How Soldiers Were Made* (New Albany, IN, 1887), p. 256; Wilbur D. Jones, *Grants in the Cornfield* (Shippensburg, PA, 1997), p. 42; Noah G. Hill (Company K, 123rd N.Y.), letters to his parents, June 21, June 26, 1864 (copies in author's possession); Kenneth A. Perry, ed., "We Are in a Fight Today," *The Civil War Diaries of Horace P. Mathews and King S. Hammond* (123rd N.Y.) (Bowie, MD, 2000), p. 125; John B. Lindsley, *Military Annals of Tennessee* 1st ser. (Spartanburg, SC, 1974), p. 480; Albert Castel, *Articles of War* (Mechanicsburg, PA, 2001), p. 715; Albert Castel, *Decision in the West* (Lawrence, KS, 1992), pp. 290–95; David Evans, *Sherman's Horsemen* (Indianapolis, IN, 1996), p. xxxiii; David P. Conygham, *Sherman's March Through the South* (New York, 1865), pp. 128, 130, 131; *Washington County People's Journal*, June 30, 1864; Pvt. Harlan P. Martin (Company E., 123rd N.Y.), letter to his mother, dated June 28, 1864 (copy in author's possession); Surgeon John A. Lair, letter to his parents, dated September 14, 1864 (copy in author's possession); WCM-D, entry dated June 22 (1864), (copy in author's possession); WCM-L, to his mother, dated June 23, 1864 (copy in author's possession); *Civil War Times Illustrated*, April 1964, p. 33.

  7. Nathaniel C. Hughes, Jr., *General William J. Hardee* (Baton Rouge, LA, 1965), p. 207; OR, ser. 1, vol. 38, part 2, Reports, report no. 175 (Hooker), pp. 14–15; John M. Schofield (LC Civil War Manuscript Collection no. 65), pp. 96–97; Jacob D. Cox, *Atlanta* (New York, 1882), pp. 113–14; *Macon Daily Telegraph* June 27, 1864; WW-L, pp. 422, 437–39, 464, 467–68; AMC-D, entry June 22, 1864 (copy in author's possession).

  8. Jacob D. Cox, *Military Reminiscences of the Civil War*, vol. 2 (New York, 1900), pp. 302–03; JGC-NH, pp. 212, 213; Albert Castel, *Decision in the West* (Lawrence, KS, 1992), p. 299.

  9. Stephen E. Ambrose, *Upton and the Army* (Baton Rouge, LA, 1964), pp. 63–65, 79–80.

  10. *Cincinnati Daily Gazette*, vol. 75, no. 310 (June 25, 1864), p. 1.

  11. Burke Davis, *Sherman's March* (New York, 1980), pp. 289–95; FAL-TF, p. 325.

Chapter 11. From Prisoner to Guard

  1. Dennis P. Kelly, park historian, Kennesaw Mountain National Battlefield Park, private correspondence with the author, dated August 9, 1983; A. M. Colton (42nd Georgia Regiment), letter to his wife, dated June 23, 1864 (copy in author's possession); William M. Armstrong, "Cahaba to Charleston: The

Prison Odyssey of Lt. Edmund E. Ryan," *Civil War History*, vol. 8, no. 2, p. 221; Dr. Daniel R. Ross, typescript memoir dictated to his son (undated) (copy in author's possession); RC-D, entry dated June 22, 1864 (copy in author's possession); pension records (NA Record Group 94); Richard Wheeler, *Sherman's March* (New York, 1978), p. 28; Lonnie R. Speer, *Portals to Hell* (Mechanicsburg, PA, 1997), pp. 261, 269.

    2. Richard B. Harwell, ed., *The Union Reader* (New York, 1958), pp. 286–91; JGN-AL7, p. 467; Ovid L. Futch, *History of Andersonville Prison* (Gainesville FL, 1908), pp. 81, 99–100; Francis T. Miller, ed., *The Photographic History of the Civil War* (New York, 1912), p. 84; Victor Hicken, *Illinois in the Civil War* (Urbana, IL, 1966), p. 352; John L. Ransom, *Andersonville Diary* (Auburn, NY, 1881), pp. 92, 117; H. M. David, *Fourteen Months in Southern Prisons* (Milwaukee, WI, 1865), pp. 153–55; Daniel R. Ross, typescript memoir (undated); RC-D, entry dated June 22, 1864 (copy in author's possession); Robert E. Denny, *The Civil War Years* (New York, 1992), p. 474; Pvt. Robert K. Sneden, *Eye of the Storm* (New York, 2000), p. 230.

    3. Told to author by Charles Ross, a grandson of Dr. Daniel Ross, and by his daughter, Ethel Padgett; Ovid L. Futch, *History of Andersonville Prison* (Gainesville, FL, 1908), pp. 32–33; H. M. David, *Fourteen Months in Southern Prisons* (Milwaukee, WI, 1865), p. 158.

    4. H. H. Cunningham, *Doctors in Gray* (Baton Rouge, LA, 1958), p. 207; Donna Padgett, personal correspondence with author dated April 20, 1989, describing Dr. Ross's aversion to onions because of his prison experience.

    5. Ovid L. Futch, *History of Andersonville Prison* (Gainesville, FL, 1908), pp. 82, 113; William Marvel, *Andersonville* (Chapel Hill, NC, 1994), pp. 148–49.

    6. OR, ser. II, vol. 8—Correspondence, p. 593; ibid., ser. II, vol. 7, pp. 583–84; Ovid L. Futch, *History of Andersonville Prison* (Gainesville, FL, 1908), pp. 84–85.

    7. Peter A. Brannon, "The Cahawba Military Prison, 1863–1865," *Alabama Review*, vol. 3, no. 1 (January 1950), pp. 163; William Marvel, *Andersonville* (Chapel Hill, NC, 1994), pp. 176–80; John Cannan, *The Atlanta Campaign* (Conshohocken, PA, 1991), p. 83.

    8. Ovid L. Futch, *History of Andersonville Prison* (Gainesville, FL, 1908), p. 227; Raymond F. Baker, *Andersonville* (Washington, DC, 1972), p. 7; OR, ser. II, vol. 8, p. 593; *Salem Press*, vol. 15, no. 36 (January 3, 1865); Pvt. Robert K. Sneden, *Eye of the Storm* (New York, 2000), pp. 249, 255, 258; Lonnie R. Speer, *Portals to Hell* (Mechanicsburg, PA, 1997), pp. 262, 277–78; Lynda L. Crist, ed., *The Papers of Jefferson Davis*, vol. 11 (Baton Rouge, LA, 2003), p. 16; Henry Hitchcock, *Marching with Sherman* (New Haven, CT, 1927), pp. 135, 150; William Marvel, *Andersonville* (Chapel Hill, NC, 1994), pp. 109, 204, 225.

    9. Dr. Daniel R. Ross (123rd N.Y.), typescript memoir; pension records (NA Record Group 94); H. M. David, *Fourteen Months in Southern Prisons* (Milwaukee, WI, 1865), pp. 328, 329, 330, 332, 333, 334; Lessel Long, *Twelve Months in Andersonville* (Huntington, IN, 1886) pp. 86–87, 104, 109; Captain Willard W. Glazier, *The Capture, the Prison Pen and the Escape* (Hartford, CT, 1868), pp. 331–32; Asa B. Isham, *Prisoners of War and Military Prisons* (Cincinnati,

OH, 1890), p. 362; John McElroy, *This Was Andersonville* (New York, 1957), pp. 167–92, 204–07, 216; Ovid L. Futch, *History of Andersonville Prison* (Gainesville, FL, 1908), p. 96; Francis T. Miller, ed., *The Photographic History of the Civil War* (New York, 1912), p. 84; RED-CW, pp. 466, 484, 486–90; Jim Miles, *To the Sea* (Nashville, TN, 1989), p. 112; Frederick Phisterer, *New York in the War of the Rebellion* (Albany, NY, 1912), p. 309; AHG-HP, p. 670; RED-CW, pp. 466, 484, 486, 488–89; *Chicago Tribune*, June 24, 1864; Pvt. Robert K. Sneden, *Eye of the Storm* (New York, 2000), pp. 264, 268, 270, 271; Michael P. Johnson, ed., *Abraham Lincoln, Slavery and the Civil War* (New York, 2001), p. 324n; George S. Bradley, *The Star Corps* (Milwaukee, WI, 1865), p. 203; Reid Mitchell, *Civil War Soldiers* (New York, 1988), p. 189; Rossiter Johnson, *Campfire and Battlefield* (New York, 1894), p. 415; William Marvel, *Andersonville* (Chapel Hill, NC, 1994), p. 234; W. A. Croffut, *Fifty Years in Camp and Field* (New York, 1909), pp. 457, 458, 461.

10. P. Dempsey Memoirs (New York State Archives, file no. 17698); Pvt. Robert K. Sneden, *Eye of the Storm* (New York, 2000), p. 272.

11. John McElroy, *This Was Andersonville* (New York, 1957), pp. 218–21, 226–30, 236, 238–39, 245; P. Dempsey Memoirs (New York State Archives, file no. 17698); (NA record groups 94 and 249—Records of the Commissary General of Prisoners); RED-CW, p. 504; KJB-S, p. 193; HCM-R123, pp. 141–42; Henry Hitchcock, *Marching with Sherman* (New Haven, CT, 1927), p. 150; William Marvel, *Andersonville* (Chapel Hill NC, 1994), pp. 225–28.

12. John McElroy, *This Was Andersonville* (New York, 1957), pp. 218–21, 226–30, 236, 238–39, 245; P. Dempsey Memoirs (New York State Archives, file no. 17698).

13. OR, ser. II vol. 6, p. 1124; William O. Bryant, *Cahaba Prison* (Tuscaloosa, AL, 1990) p. 17; Lonnie R. Speer, *Portals to Hell* (Mechanicsburg, PA, 1997), pp. 255–56.

14. Jesse Hawes, *Cahaba* (New York, 1888), p. 21.

15. James L. Conrad, "Held Captive at Cahaba," CWTI, vol. 21, no. 7, pp. 14–15; OR ser. II, Vol 7, pp. 998–1001; Peter A. Brannon, "The Cahawba Military Prison, 1863–1865," *Alabama Review*, vol. 3, no. 1 (January 1950), pp. 172–73; Alex W. Cawthon, letter to Dr. Thomas M. Owen, dated October 21, 1910 (Alabama Department of Archives and History); *Alabama Review*, vol. 15, no. 4, October 1962, p. 280; William O. Bryant, *Cahaba Prison* (Tuscaloosa, AL, 1990), pp. 24, 32, 52, 74, 75, 83; Alston Fitts, *Selma* (n.d.), p. 48; Lonnie R. Speer, *Portals to Hell* (Mechanicsburg, PA, 1997), pp. 257–58.

16. William B. Hesseltine, *Civil War Prisons* (Columbus OH, 1930), pp. 154–57, 168–73; Peter A. Brannon, "The Cahawba Military Prison, 1863–1865," *Alabama Review*, vol. 3, no. 1 (January 1950), pp. 168–71; Dr. Daniel Ross (123rd N.Y.), memoir (typescript copy in author's possession); William O. Bryant, *Cahaba Prison* (Tuscaloosa, AL, 1990), pp. 100, 101, 108; William Marvel, *Andersonville* (Chapel Hill, NC, 1994), p. 234.

17. Dr. Daniel Ross (123rd N.Y.), memoir (typescript copy in author's possession); Joseph G. Vale, *Minty and the Cavalry* (Harrisburg, PA, 1886) pp. 433, 442; William Forse Scott, *4th Iowa Veteran Volunteers* (New York, 1893), pp.

456–57; Robert Selph Henry, *"First with the Most" Forrest* (New York, 1991), pp. 431–32; Gen. James H. Wilson, correspondence to James E. Kelly, dated February 9, 1910 (LC Manuscript); James Larson, *Sergeant Larson of the 4th U. S. Cavalry* (San Antonio, 1935); James H. Wilson, *Under the Old Flag*, vol. 2 (New York, 1912), pp. 229–31; Chas. O. Brown, Narrative of Personal Experiences in the Battle of Selma (typescript unpaged, Illinois State Historical Society); James Pickett Jones, *Yankee Blitzkrieg* (Athens, GA, 1976), pp. 89, 91; Lewis M. Hosea, "The Campaign of Selma," *Sketches of War History, Ohio MOLLUS*, vol. 1 (Cincinnati, OH, 1888), pp. 99–100; E. N. Gilpin, "The Last Campaign: A Cavalryman's Journal," *Journal of the U.S. Cavalry Association*, vol. 18 (Leavenworth, KS, 1938), pp. 639–40; OR ser. I, vol. 49, part 1—Reports, p. 480; Major Elbridge Colby, "Wilson's Campaign of 1865," *The Journal of American Military History Foundation*, vol. 2, no. 4 (1938), pp. 210–14; Jerry Keenan, "Wilson's Selma Raid," CWTI (January 1963), pp. 38, 40, 41; Edward G. Longacre, *From Union Stars to Top Hat* (Harrisburg, PA, 1972), pp. 207–08; Capt. W. E. Doyle, "the Wilson Raid," *National Tribune*, vol. 10, no. 23, Whole no. 491 (January 8, 1891), p. 1; Edward Smith, "Wilson's Famous Road," *National Tribune*, vol. 10, no. 23, Whole no. 491 (June 2, 1910); John W. Rowell, *Yankee Artillerymen* (Knoxville, TN, 1975), pp. 248, 254; Capt. J. Harvey Mathes, *General Forrest* (New York, 1902), pp. 345–47; Adelia Brownell "Civil War Service in Selma, Alabama," *Cincinnati Historical Society Bulletin* vol. 24 (1966), p. 324; Edward G. Longacre, *Mounted Raids of the Civil War* (Lincoln, NE, 1975), p. 317; Joseph G. Vale, *Minty and the Cavalry* (Harrisburg, PA, 1886), pp. 431–33, 437; EL-GC, pp. 206–09; Noah Trudeau, *Out of the Storm* (New York, 1994), pp. 160, 164, 165; OR, ser. I, vol, 49, part 1, Reports, report no. 33 (Winslow), p. 480; ibid., report (Wilson) pp. 360–61; T. F. Dornblasser, *Saber Strokes of the Pennsylvania Dragoons* (Philadelphia, PA, 1884), pp. 210, 215; Brian S. Wills, *The Confederacy's Greatest Cavalryman* (Lawrence, KS, 1992), p. 310; Charles O. Brown (3rd Ohio Cavalry), memoir (n.d.), pp. 3–5 (Illinois State Historical Library); William Forse Scott, *The Story of a Cavalry Regiment* (New York, 1893), pp. 450–51; Jerry Keenan, *Wilson's Cavalry Corps* (Jefferson, NC, 1998), pp. 169–72; *North and South*, vol. 2 (January 1999), p. 83; extracts from records of Sgt. Thomas W. Giles, (4th U.S. Cavalry), typescript entry dated April 2, 1865, (Selma Public Library); Alston Fitts, *Selma* (n.d.), p. 53; Gen. James H. Wilson, diary entry dated April 2, 1865 (Historical Society of Delaware); JES-RN, p. 153; PC-BL, p. 151; Glenn W. Sunderland, *Lightning at Hoover's Gap* (New York, 1969), pp. 203, 205–07; Earl Schenck Miers, *The General Who Marched to Hell* (New York, 1951), p. 211.

    18. James Pickett Jones, *Yankee Blitzkrieg* (Athens GA, 1976), p. 89, 9; *National Tribune*, vol. 13, no. 26, whole no. 660, new ser., p. 1; EL-GC, p. 209.

    19. Samuel Eliot Morison, *The Oxford History of The American People* (New York, 1965), p. 698; Lewis M. Hosea, "The Campaign of Selma," *Sketches of War History, Ohio MOLLUS*, vol. 1 (Cincinnati, OH, 1888), p. 101; Dr. Daniel Ross (123rd N.Y.), memoir (typescript copy in author's possession); Lauren H. Ripley (4th Mich. Cavalry), "Personal Reminiscences of the Flight and Capture of Jeff Davis," p. 4 (February 17, 1894, Michigan Historical Collections, Bentley Historical Library, University of Michigan); John W. Rowell, *Yankee Artillerymen*

414   Notes to Chapter 11

(Knoxville, TN, 1975), p. 256; JMM-BC, p. 825; James Nourse (Chicago Board of Trade Battery), diary entry dated April 2, 1865 (Duke University Special Collections Library); Keenan, *Wilson's Cavalry Corps* (Jefferson, NC, 1998) H. M. David, *Fourteen Months in Southern Prisons* (Milwaukee, WI, 1865) William Marvel, *Andersonville* (Chapel Hill, NC, 1994) H. M. David, *Fourteen Months in Southern Prisons* (Milwaukee, WI, 1865) Ovid L. Futch, *History of Andersonville Prison* (Gainesville, FL, 1908) typescript unpaged, pp. 173–76; extracts from records of Sgt. Thomas W. Giles (4th U.S. Cavalry), typescript entry dated April 2, 1865 (Selma Public Library), entry dated April 4, 1865.

20. OR, *Medical and Surgical History of the War of the Rebellion* part 1—Appendix, p. 328; OR, ser. 1, vol. 49, part 1—Reports, pp. 362, 381, 407, 474; ibid., part 2—Correspondence; William B. Hesseltine, *Civil War Prisons* (Columbus, OH, 1930), p. 237; Dr. Daniel Ross, memoir (undated) (typescript copy in author's possession); Major Elbridge Colby, "Wilson's Campaign of 1865," *The Journal of American Military History Foundation*, vol. 2, no. 4 (1938), pp. 216–20; Henry P. Beers, *Guide to the Archives of the Government of the Confederate States of America* (Washington DC, 1968), p. 250; E. N. Gilpin, "The Last Campaign: A Cavalryman's Journal," *Journal of the U.S. Cavalry Association*, vol. 18 (Leavenworth, KS, 1938), p. 653; *National Tribune* January 15, 1891, p. 2; EL-GC, pp. 220–21; Frederick H. Dyer, *Compendium of the Civil War*, vol. 3 (New York, 1959), p. 1442; James Nourse (Chicago Board of Trade Battery), diary entry dated May 3, 1865 (Duke University Special Collections Library); Ovid L. Futch, *History of Andersonville Prison* (Gainesville, FL, 1908), p. 117; *Selma Union*, vol. 1, April 8, 1865 (Pierpont Morgan Library, Gilbert Lehrman Collection, GLC 1187); F. H. Bailey (4th Mich.) letter to his parents, dated May 15, 1865 (Bentley Historical Library, University of Michigan); Joseph O. Jackson, ed., *Some of The Boys* (Carbondale, IL, 1960), p. 248; William Marvel, *Andersonville* (Chapel Hill, NC, 1994), pp. 238, 240, 241, 245.

21. Dr. Daniel Ross, memoir (undated) (typescript copy in author's possession), his recollections as related to the author by his children; Daniel R. Ross, affidavit dated October 21, 1868, in connection with his application for commutation of rations while a prisoner of war (NA RG 94 Records of The Adjutant General's Office, 1780s–1917); RG 92 Entry 1450, Daily Reports of Vessels: Fort Monroe, Virginia, Vessel file, Star of the South (Office of the Quartermaster General); OR, ser. I, vol. 49, part 1, Reports, pp. 537–38; Joseph G. Vale, *Minty and the Cavalry* (Harrisburg, PA, 1886), pp. 464–65; E. N. Gilpin (3rd Iowa Cavalry), memoir dated April 23, 1905 (LC Manuscript Division); RED-CW, p. 569–70; E.N. Gilpin, "The Last Campaign: A Cavalryman's Journal," *Journal of the U.S. Cavalry Association*, vol. 18 (Leavenworth, KS, 1938), p. 674; *A Memorial of the Great Rebellion: A History of the Fourteenth Regiment New Hampshire Volunteers* (Boston, 1882), pp. 342–43; *New York Tribune*, May 22, 1865; *Atlantic Monthly*, vol. 16, no. 95 (September 1865), p. 346; Henry Potter (4th Mich.), letter, dated May 19, 1865 (Michigan Historical Collections Bentley Historical Library, University of Michigan); Alf J. Mapp, Jr., *Frock Coats and Epaulets* (New York, 1963), p. 121; J. G. Dickinson, *War Papers MOLLUS, Michigan Commandery*, vol. 1 (Detroit, 1913), p. 13; William A Schmitt, *The Last Days of the Lost Cause* (Clarksdale, MS, 1949) pp. 28–29; *The Register of the Kentucky Historical Society*, vol. 64, no. 4 (October 1966), pp. 274–76; OR,

ser. I, vol. 43, part 2—Correspondence, pp. 559–61; Evening News Company, *Historic Bridgeton, 1686–1936* (1936), p. 232; EL-GC, p. 220; Hathaway Recollections (1865), (University of North Carolina, microfilm reel no. M2954, Vol. 8); EL-GC, p. 223; *Official Records of the Union and Confederate Navies*, ser. 1, vol. 2, pp. 145–47; Burke Davis, *The Long Surrender* (New York, 1985), pp. 155–56; 215, 221, 223; OR, ser. 1, vol. 49, part 2—Correspondence, pp. 847, 868; *Washington County People's Journal*, vol. 12, no. 22, June 1, 1865; *Sandy Hill Herald* (quoting the *Philadelphia Enquirer*), vol. 17, no. 12 (May 30, 1865), p. 2; James Nourse (Chicago Board of Trade Battery), diary entry dated May 13, 1865 (Duke University Special Collections Library); Maj. Gen. J. H. Wilson, telegram to E. M. Stanton, dated May 15, 1865 (LC Manuscript Division); William B. Halberton, *Homeward Bound* (Mechanicsburg, PA, 2001), p. 101; William C. Davis, *An Honorable Defeat* (New York, 2001), p. 351; Navy Department, *Civil War Naval Chronology* (Washington, DC, 1971), p. V-99; *Daily Chronicle*, vol. 3, no. 174 (May 25, 1865), p. 1; Lynda Crist, ed., *The Papers of Jefferson Davis*, vol. 9 (Baton Rouge, LA, 1997), pp. 563, 583–84; OR, ser. 1, vol. 49, part 2—Correspondence, pp. 745, 760; ibid., ser. I, vol. 47, part 1—Reports, p. 36.

22. Pension records (NA Record Group 94); Record Group 249, Records of the Commissary General of Prisons; JMM-BC, pp. 799–800; Shelby Foote, *The Civil War: A Narrative Red River to Appomattox* (New York: 1974), pp. 1012, 1013.

Chapter 12. Capture of Atlanta

1. John Cannan, *The Atlanta Campaign* (Conshohocken, PA, 1991) p. 163; A. A. Hoehling, *Last Train From Atlanta* (New York, 1958), pp. 450, 455–56, 516; WCM-D, entries dated September 4, September 12, September 29, October 7, October 16, October 29, November 12, 1864 (copies in author's possession); *Salem Press*, vol. 15, no. 12 (July 19, 1864); AMC-D, entries dated September 2, September 29, 1864; OR—Supplement vol. 46, part 2—Record of Events, p. 567; JMM-BC, p. 774; SPH-WT, p. 241; Pvt. John Cutter (123rd N.Y.), letters to his father, dated September 4, September 7, September 22, October 11, October 24, 1864 (copies in author's possession); William Alan Blair, ed., *A Politician Goes To War* (University Park, PA, 1995), pp. 203, 207, 211; Frank L. Byrne, ed., *Civil War Letters of Harvey Reid* (Madison, WI, 1965), pp. 196, 198; *Washington County Post*, vol. 76, no. 30 (July 15, 1864), p. 2; ibid., vol. 76, no. 35 (August 26, 1864), p. 1; *Sandy Hill Herald*, vol. 16, no. 26 (September 6, 1864), p. 2; New York State Census of 1865; Col. James L. Selfridge, Brigade Report, dated December 26, 1864 (Office of the Washington County Historian, Fort Edwards, NY); Robert E. Denny, *The Civil War Years* (New York, 1992), pp. 456–65; Thomas B. Buell, *Warrior Generals* (New York, 1997), p. 375; WCM-L, to his father, dated September 3, September 29, 1864 (copies in author's possession); WCM-D, entry dated September 2, September 13, 1864 (copies in author's possession); Albert Castel, *Articles of War* (Mechanicsburg, PA, 2001), p. 75; David E. Long, *The Jewel of Liberty* (New York, 1997), p. 212; Albert Castel,

Decision in the West (Lawrence, KS, 1992), pp. 527–28, 532–33, 543, 548, 552, 553; Richard Wheeler, *Sherman's March* (New York, 1978), p. 50; Brooks D. Simpson, *Ulysses S. Grant* (New York, 2000), p. 377; KJB-S, p. 167; RED-CW, pp. 444, 449, 453, 460, 477; Margaret Leech, *Reveille in Washington* (New York, 1941), pp. 430–32; Pvt. Levi Eaton (123rd N.Y.), letter to his parents, dated September 4, 1864 (copy in author's possession); Bruce Chadwick, *The Two American Presidents* (Secaucas, NJ, 1999), p. 388; John C. Waugh, *Reelecting Lincoln* (New York, 1997), pp. 231–32, 296–98; LJD-DG, pp. 417–18, 428; Brian C. Melton, " 'Stay and Fight It Out': Henry W. Slocum and American's Civil War," (PhD dissertation, Texas Christian University, 2003), pp. 149, 151; Lynda L. Crist, ed., *The Papers of Jefferson Davis*, vol. 2 (Baton Rouge, LA, 2003), pp. 8, 14, 20; Capt. David P. Conygham, *Sherman's March Through Georgia* (New York, 1865), pp. 216, 254; Robert G. Athearn, *Soldier in the West: The Civil War Letters of Alfred Lacey Hough* (Philadelphia, 1957), p. 216n; MQ-CM, p. 343; WTS-M, vol. 2, p. 151; Pvt. Levi Eaton (123rd N.Y.) letter to his wife, dated September 4, 1864 (copy in author's possession); Military Engineer No. 344, Nov.–Dec. 1959, p. 440; James A. Padgett, "With Sherman Through Georgia and the Carolinas," vol. 32, pp. 303, 305, 309, 311, 315, 321; Larry M. Strayer, *Echoes of Battle: The Atlanta Campaign* (Huntington, WV, 1991), pp. 318, 319, 320; Earl Schenck Miers, *The General Who Marched to Hell* (New York, 1951), pp. 159, 160.

2. HCM-R123, pp. 132, 133; WDM-D, entry dated November 2, 1864 (copy in author's possession); S. A. Armstrong (32nd Wis.), letter to "Friend Rosa Stone," dated October 31, 1864 (copy in author's possession); letter to his mother dated October 14, 1864 (copy in author's possession); Lt. Col. Robert R. Ellis, *Military Engineer* vol. 52, no. 345 (January 1960), p. 4; AMC-D, entry dated November 2, 1864 (copy in author's possession); AMC-L, to his brother, dated October 24, 1864 (copy in author's possession); RED-CW, p. 475; Frank J. Welcher, *Coburn's Brigade* (Carmel IN, 1999), pp. 270, 271, 275; Captain Cutler (Company H, 123rd N.Y.) letter to William Law, dated October 28, 1864 (copy in author's possession); Thomas B. Buell, *The Warrior Generals* (New York, 1997), p. 384; letter to the *Whitehall Chronicle* dated October 24, 1864 signed by "Volunteer," (123rd N.Y.) (copy in author's possession); Richard M. McMurry, *Atlanta, 1864* (Lincoln, NE, 2000), pp. 177, 180; HP-CG, p. 203; JGN-AL9, p. 477; WTS-M, vol. 2, pp. 641, 643, 646; Anne J. Bailey, *The Chessboard of War* (Lincoln, NE, 2000), pp. 16, 50, 51; Kenneth A. Perry, ed., "We Are in a Fight Today," *The Civil War Diaries of Horace P. Mathews and King S. Hammond* (123rd N.Y.) (Bowie, MD, 2000), p. 25; CS-AL, pp. 618, 619, Albert Castel, *Decision in the West* (Lawrence, KS, 1992), p. 553; William Alan Blair, ed., *A Politician Goes To War* (University Park, PA, 1995), p. 210n; Private Harrington (Company G, 123rd N.Y.) letter to his parents, dated November 7, 1864 (copy in author's possession); Rev. George S. Bradley, *The Star Corps* (Milwaukee, WI, 1865), p. 179; MQ-CM, p. 348; WCM-L, to his father, dated October 20, November 6, 1864 (copies in author's possession); WCM-D, entries dated October 17, October 21, October 22, October 23, October 24, November 17, 1864 (copies in author's possession); William A. Blair, *A Politician Goes to War* (University Park, PA, 1995), p. 160(n).

3. John D. Ross military service record (NA); WCM-D, entry dated November 12, 1864 (copy in author's possession); RC-D, entry dated November 12, 1864 (copy in author's possession); A. A. Hoehling, *Last Train From Atlanta* (New York, 1958), pp. 521, 538–39; JGC-NH, p. 218; MC-CM, p. 356; WCM-D, entries dated September 12, September 17, 1864 (copy in author's possession); Capt. David P. Conygham, *Sherman's March Through Georgia* (New York, 1865), pp. 187, 242; Herman Hattaway, *How the North Won* (Urbana, IL, 1983), p. 663; OR, ser. 1, vol. 32, part 1—Reports, pp. 26, 27; JTG-MS, pp. xii, 15, 16, 17, 20, 33, 197–98; AHG-HP, p. 685; AMC-L, to his father and brother, dated November 13, November 27, 1864 (copies in author's possession); Victor Davis Hanson, *The Soul of Battle* (New York, 1999), pp. 138, 139, 141, 147, 151, 158, 161, 212, 224; Peter G. Tsouras, *Military Quotations from the Civil War* (New York, 1998), p. 61; Richard M. McMurry, *Atlanta, 1864* (Lincoln, NE, 2000), pp. 50, 190; Richard Wheeler, *Sherman's March* (New York, 1978), p. 17; Ned Bradford, *Battles and Leaders of the Civil War* (New York, 1956), p. 592; General Williams' letter on Sherman's *Memoirs* (unpaged typescript, n.d.) (copy in author's possession); Capt. D. W. Whittle, (72nd Ill.) diary entry dated November 22, 1864 (copy in author's possession); Russel F. Weigley, *The American Way of War* (Bloomington, IN, 1973), pp. 145, 148; Henry Hitchcock, *Marching with Sherman* (New Haven, CT, 1927), p. 58; CS-AL, pp. 620, 627; KJB-S, p. 171; JMM-BC, p. 809; Jim Miles, *To The Sea* (Nashville, TN, 1989), pp. 20, 33.

4. OR, ser. 1, vol. 44—Reports, Correspondence, etc., pp. 207, 221, 226, 228; Captain Louis C. Duncan, *The Medical Department of the United States Army in the Civil War* (Gaithersburg, MD, 1987), pp. 222, 354, 356, 357, 358, 360, 362, 363, 364; John D. Billings, *Hardtack and Coffee* (Boston, MA, 1887), p. 365; Rossiter Johnson, *Campfire and Battlefield* (New York, 1894), pp. 420, 421, 422; Alexander A. Lawrence, *A Present for Mr. Lincoln* (Macon, GA, 1961), p. 196; John D. Ross military service record (NA); Mark Coburn, *Terrible Innocence* (New York, 1993), p. 158; A. A. Hoehling, *Last Train From Atlanta* (New York, 1958), p. 530; Peter G. Tsouras, *Military Quotations from the Civil War* (New York, 1998), p. 138; JTG-MS, p. 101; W.T. Sherman, *Memoirs of General William T. Sherman*, vol. 2 (New York, 1875), pp. 642, 655; Col. James L. Selfridge, 1st Brigade, 1st Division, 20th A. C. Special Order 74, November 10, 1864.

Chapter 13. March to the Sea and Beyond

1. Jim Miles, *To the Sea* (Nashville, TN, 1989), pp. 30, 33; Robert V. Johnson and Clarence C. Buell, eds., *Battles and Leaders of the Civil War*, vol. 4 (New York, 1888), p. 672; A. A. Hoehling, *Last Train From Atlanta* (New York, 1958), pp. 520–21, 523; MQ-CM, p. 355; WCM-D, entries dated October 15, November 14, November 15, 1864 (copies in author's possession); John E. Barrett, *Sherman's March Through the Carolinas* (Chapel Hill, NC, 1956), p. 32; JGC-NH, pp. 151–52; Richard T. Van Wyck, *A War to Petrify the Heart* (Hensonville, NY, 1997), p. 265; HP-CG, pp. 332–33; Frank L. Byrne, ed., *Civil War Letters of*

418   Notes to Chapter 13

Harvey Reid (Madison, WI, 1965), pp. 200–01; *Sandy Hill Herald*, vol. 16, no. 44 (January 10, 1865), p. 2; RED-CW, p. 487; Peter G. Tsouras, *Military Quotations from the Civil War* (New York, 1998), p. 31; HCM-R123, p. 134; CS-AL, p. 249; WW-L, p. 19; PVS-SL, pp. 237, 239; W. T. Sherman, *Memoirs of General William T. Sherman*, vol. 2 (New York, 1875), p. 633; Capt. David P. Conygham, *Sherman's March Through Georgia* (New York, 1865), pp. 237–38.

  2. Peter Batty and Peter Parish, *The Divided Union* (Topsfield, MA), p. 184; KJB-B-S, pp. 178–79; Frank L. Byrne, ed., *Civil War Letters of Harvey Reid* (Madison, WI, 1965), p. 204; HCM-R123, pp. 134, 138; JTG-MS, pp. 104, 105; WW-L, pp. 96, 100; PVS-SL, pp. 241, 249, 269; Charles W. Wills, *Army Life of an Illinois Soldier* (Carbondale, IL, 1996), p. 372; Anne J. Bailey, *The Chessboard of War* (Lincoln, NE, 2000, p. 57; Henry Hitchcock, *Marching with Sherman* (New Haven, CT, 1927), p. 91; Theodore W. Blackburn, *Letters from the Front* (Dayton, Ohio, 1981), p. 172.

  3. Clarence C. Buell and Robert V. Johnson, eds., *Battle and Leaders of the Civil War*, vol. 4 (New York, 1888), p. 672; SPH-WT, p. 256; JMM-BC, p. 431.

  4. Jim Miles, *To the Sea* (Nashville, TN, 1989), pp. 168–69; SPH-WT, pp. 271 and 301; Col. Selfridge, Brigade Report, dated December 26, 1864; Don Congdon, ed., *Civil War* (New York, 1967), pp. 454–55; HCM-R123, p. 135; JB-CaC, p. 198; JTG-MS, pp. 102–03; WW-L, p. 21.

  5. Col. S. M. Bowman and Lt. Col. R. B. Irwin, *Sherman and His Campaigns* (New York, 1865), pp. 283–84; Hathaway Recollections (1865), (University of North Carolina, microfilm reel no. M2954, vol. 8), p. 654; Ashley Halsey, *A Yankee Private's Civil War* (Chicago, 1983), p. 143; Jim Miles, *To the Sea* (Nashville, TN, 1989), pp. 43, 56, 57, 112–14; HCM-R123, pp. 134, 140, 145–47; John Cannan, *The Atlanta Campaign* (Conshohocken, PA, 1991), pp. 147–48; KJB-S, pp. 174–75, 190–91, 194, 195; WCM-D, entries dated November 2, November 26, November 29, December 3, 1864 (copies in author's possession); Rossiter Johnson, *Campfire and Battlefield* (New York, 1894), p. 421; JGC-NH, p. 224; *Generals' Reports of Service*, vol. 9 (A. S. Williams) Adjutant Generals Office (NA), pp. 34–37; Robert V. Johnson and Clarence C. Buell, eds., *Battle and Leaders of the Civil War*, vol. 4 (New York, 1888), p. 675; AHG-HP, p. 688; SPH-WT, pp. 256, 258; Frank L. Byrne, ed., *Civil War Letters of Harvey Reid* (Madison, WI, 1965), p. 206; RED-CW, pp. 492, 494–95, 497; Burke Davis, *Sherman's March* (New York, 1988), pp. 60, 62, 69, 82–83, 88, 96; Anne J. Bailey, *The Chessboard of War* (Lincoln, NE, 2000), pp. 114, 123; Capt. David P. Conygham, *Sherman's March Through Georgia* (New York, 1865), p. 275; WW-L, p. 85; RED-CW, p. 497; William R. Plum, *Civil War in the United States* vol. 2 (Chicago, 1882), pp. 248–50; Capt. D. W. Whittle (72nd Ill.), diary entries dated November 13, November 22, December 6, 1864 (copies in author's possession); Brian C. Melton, "'Stay and Fight It Out': Henry W. Slocum and American's Civil War," (PhD dissertation, Texas Christian University, 2003), p. 167; JMM-BC, p. 810; Henry Hitchcock, *Marching with Sherman* (New Haven CT, 1927), p. 156; William Marvel, *Andersonville* (Chapel Hill, NC, 1994), pp. 222–23; RC-D, entries dated November 20, November 29, November 30, December 3, 1864 (copies in author's possession).

6. RC-D, entries dated December 9, December 10, December 11, December 12, December 15, December 16, December 21 (1864) (copies in author's possession); RC-:L, to his wife, dated December 24, 1864; OR, ser. 1, vol. 44, Reports, Correspondence, etc., pp. 309, 44, 45, 46, 208–09, 218, 221–22, 224–26, 229; Charles C. Jones, Jr., *The Siege of Savannah* (Albany, NY, 1874), pp. 75, 78–86, 115, 117; WCM-D, entries dated December 9, December 10, December 11, December 12, December 16, December 18, 1864 (NYHS); WCM-L, to his parents, dated December 17, 1864, February 1, February 7, 1865 (NYHS); Brig. Gen. Alpheus Williams, diary entry dated December 9, 1864 (Burton Historical Collection, Detroit Public Library); HCM-R123, pp. 145–46; Jim Miles, *To the Sea* (Nashville, TN, 1989), pp. 43, 56–57, 124, 129, 199–200; Col. S. M. Bowman and Lt. Col. R. B. Irwin, *Sherman and His Campaigns* (New York, 1865), pp. 283–84, 289–90, 295, 338; Charles E. Slocum, *Services of Major General H. W. Slocum* (Toledo, OH, 1913), pp. 238, 242; Ashley Halsey, *A Yankee Private's Civil War* (Chicago, 1983), pp. 137, 143; *Executive Documents, House of Representatives*, 1st Session 39th Congress, 1865, Report of the Secretary of War (Washington, DC, 1866), p. 639; Herman Hattaway, *How the North Won* (Urbana, IL, 1983), p. 654; George S. Bradley, *The Star Corps* (Milwaukee, WI, 1865), pp. 213–15; Henry Hitchcock, undated letter to his wife (LC Manuscript Collection); Capt. David P. Conygham, *Sherman's March Through Georgia* (New York, 1865), p. 289; WTS-M, vol. 2, pp. 195, 212; General A. S. Williams, journal entries dated December 9, December 10, December 12, December 15, December 17, 18, December 19, December 20, December 21, 1864 (copies in author's possession); *Civil War Chronicles*, vol. 2, no. 3 (Winter 1893), p. 11; A. S. Williams, Report of Service, vol. 9, Adjutant General's Office, pp. 32–40 (NA, RG 94); Louise B. Hill, *Joseph E. Brown and the Confederacy* (Westport, CT, 1939), pp. 189–90; Charles C. Coffin, *Four Years of Fighting* (Boston, 1866), p. 430–31; Pvt. John Cutter (123rd N.Y.), letter to his father, dated December 18, 1864 (copy in author's possession); KJB-S, pp. 195–96; JMM-BC, pp. 816, 838; James A. Connolly, *Three Years in the Army of the Cumberland* (Bloomington, IN, 1987), p. 363; Col. Selfridge, Brigade Report, dated December 26, 1864, RED-CW, pp. 500, 506; Frank J. Welcher, *Coburn's Brigade* (Carmel, IN, 1999), p. 301, HCM-R123, pp. 145–46; Burke Davis, *Sherman's March* (New York, 1988), pp. 91, 96–99, 111, 128; William Alan Blair, ed., *A Politician Goes To War* (University Park, PA, 1995), pp. xxii, 217; Anne J. Bailey, *The Chessboard of War* (Lincoln, NE, 2000, p. 129; Brian C. Melton, "'Stay and Fight It Out': Henry W. Slocum and American's Civil War," (PhD dissertation, Texas Christian University, 2003), p. 172; Capt. David P. Conygham, *Sherman's March Through Georgia* (New York, 1865), pp. 291–93; KJB-S, pp. 195–99, WCM-D, entries dated December 9, December 12, December 14, December 15, December 18, December 23, 1864 (copies in author's possession).

7. WCM-D, entries dated December 21, December 22, December 24, December 25, December 30, December 31, 1864, and January 1, January 2, 1865 (copies in author's possession); RC-L, to his wife, dated December 24, 1864, January 1, 1865 (copies in author's possession); HCM-R123, pp. 149–50; KJB-S, pp. 198–99; Jim Miles, *To the Sea* (Nashville, TN, 1989), p. 251; Gen.

A. S. Williams, letter to Pitt, dated April 21, 1865 (Burton Historical Collection, Detroit Public Library); John W. Stepp, *Mirror of War* (Englewood, NJ, 1961), p. 312; SPH-WT, p. 264; James A. Connolly, *Three Years in the Army of the Cumberland* (Bloomington, IN, 1987), pp. 361, 370; *Sandy Hill Herald*, vol. 17, no. 1 (March 14, 1865), p. 2; John E. Barrett, *Sherman's March Through the Carolinas* (Chapel Hill, NC, 1956), p. 27; *New York Herald*, December 25, 1864; Burke Davis, *Sherman's March* (New York, 1988), p. 122; Albert Castel, *Decision in the West* (Lawrence, KS, 1992), pp. 76–77; Anne J. Bailey, *The Chessboard of War* (Lincoln, NE, 2000), p. 170; WTS-M, p. 746; Brian C. Melton, "'Stay and Fight It Out': Henry W. Slocum and American's Civil War," (PhD dissertation, Texas Christian University, 2003), p. 173; Maj. George W. Nichols, T*he Story of the Great March* (Williamstown, MA, 1972), pp. 98–99; Robert K. Sneden, *Eye of the Storm* (New York, 2000), pp. 274–75, 277n, 278; Burke Davis, *Sherman's March* (New York, 1988), p. 129.

8. General Geary, letters to his wife, dated December 27, 1864, and January 1, 1865, from Savannah (copies in author's possession), p. 19; KJB-S, p. 196; WCM-D, entries dated January 2, January 5, January 7, January 9, January 12, January 15, 1865 letter to his father dated January 9, 1865 (copies in author's possession); John E. Barrett, *Sherman's March Through the Carolinas* (Chapel Hill, NC, 1956), p. 41; HCM-R123, p. 151; JTG-MS, pp. 82–83; JMM-BC, pp. 820, 826; Maj. George W. Nichols, T*he Story of the Great March* (Williamstown, MA, 1972), p. 179; WCM-L, to his mother, dated January 3, 1865 (copy in author's possession).

9. KJB-S, pp. 201–35; HCM-R123, pp. 153–73; Jim Miles, *To the Sea* (Nashville, TN, 1989), pp. 216–21, 239, 251–63; Peter Batty and Peter Parish, *The Divided Union* (Topsfield, MA, 1987), p. 189; Gen. A. S. Williams, diary entries dated February 8, March 2, March 3, 1865 (copies in author's possession); Gen. A. S. Williams, letter to Pitt, April 21, 1865 (copy in author's possession); WCM-D, entries dated January 16, January 17, January 18, January 19, January 26, January 31, March 2, March 4, March 7, March 11, March 12, March 13, March 14, March 15, March 23, March 30, May 3, 1865 (copies in author's possession); T. Harry Williams, *McClellan, Sherman and Grant* (New York, 1951), p. 74; Herman Hattaway, *How the North Won* (Urbana, IL, 1983), p. 657, 669–70; Robert V. Johnson and Clarence C. Buell, eds., *Battle and Leaders of the Civil War*, vol. 4 (New York, 1888), pp. 683–84, 687, 754, 755; Robert Hale Strong, *A Yankee Private's Civil War* (Chicago, 1961), p. 102; Richard T. Van Wyck, *A War to Petrify the Heart* (Hensonville, NY, 1997), p. 301; Pvt. John Cutter (123rd N.Y.), letter to his father, dated February 2, 1865 (copy in author's possession); Herman Hattaway, *How the North Won* (Urbana, IL, 1983), p. 666; JMM-BC pp. 669, 841; *Washington County People's Journal*, vol. 12, no. 11 (March 16, 1865); ibid., vol. 12, no. 13 (March 30, 1865); Jeffrey Rogers Hummel, *Emancipating Slaves, Enslaving Free Men* (Chicago, IL, 1996), pp. 278–79; Sgt. Lorenzo R. Coy (123rd N.Y.), diary entry dated April 1865 (copy in author's possession); SPH-WT, pp. 273, 277; JMM-BC, p. 826; RHS-HD, p. 183; James A. Connolly, *Three Years in the Army of the Cumberland* (Bloomington, IN, 1987), pp. 380, 386; John S. Bowman, *The Civil War Day by Day* (Greenwich, CT, 1989), p. 203; Colonel James L. Selfridge, Brigade Report, March 24, 1865; JES-RN, p. 159; Frank

J. Welcher, *Coburn's Brigade* (Carmel, IN, 1999), pp. 356–57; *North and South*, vol. 2, no. 2 (January 1999), p. 53; JTG-MS, pp. 79, 87, 106, 113–14, 140, 162; Albert Castel, *Decision in the West* (Lawrence, KS, 1992), p. 71; PVS-SL, p. 76; John M. Gibson, *Those 163 Days* (New York, 1961), p. 204; John E. Barrett, *Sherman's March Through the Carolinas*, (Chapel Hill, NC, 1956), p. 158; CS-AL, p. 660; Maj. George W. Nichols, *The Story of the Great March* (Williamstown, MA, 1972), pp. 235, 252, 257, 268, 271, 275–76; W. T. Sherman, *Memoirs of General William T. Sherman*, vol. 2 (New York, 1875), pp. 772, 780; HSC-CWA, p. 792: RED-CW, pp. 544–47, 550; Margaret Leech, *Reveille in Washington* (New York, 1941), p. 446; Pvt. John L. Marshall (Company G, 123rd N.Y.), letter to his parents, dated April 8, 1865 (copy in author's possession); RED-CW, p. 518; Anne J. Bailey, *The Chessboard of War* (Lincoln, NE, 2000), pp. 17, 131; Brian C. Melton, "'Stay and Fight It Out': Henry W. Slocum and American's Civil War" (PhD dissertation, Texas Christian University, 2003), pp. 172–73; Burke Davis, *Sherman's March* (New York, 1988), pp. 225–26, 241, 247; Charles Royster, *Destructive War* (New York, 1991), p. 346; Walter Millis, *Arms and Men* (New Brunswick, NJ, 1984), pp. 119–20; Pvt. Levi Eaton (123rd N.Y.), letter to his wife, dated January 15, 1865 (copy in author's possession); Noah A. Trudeau, *Like Men of War* (Edison, NJ, 1998), pp. 356–57; CS-AL, p. 661; RC-L, to his wife, dated January 16, 1865 (copy in author's possession); RC-D, entries dated January 1 through January 28, 1865 (copy in author's possession).

10. KJB-S, pp. 237–38; HCM-R123, pp. 173–74; Jim Miles, *To the Sea* (Nashville, TN, 1989), p. 173; Gen A. S. Williams, letter to Pitt, dated April 21, 1865 (Burton Historical Collection, Detroit Public Library); Robert V. Johnson and Clarence C. Buell, eds., *Battle and Leaders of the Civil War*, vol. 4 (New York, 1888), pp. 679, 754; Col. S. M. Bowman and Lt. Col. R. B. Irwin, *Sherman and His Campaigns* (New York, 1865), pp. 369–70; James A. Padgett, *With Sherman through Georgia and the Carolinas* (n.d.), pp. 74–77; AHG-HP, p. 721; *Washington County Post*, vol. 77, no. 13 (March 13, 1865), p. 2; WCM-D, entries dated March 23, April 4, April 8, 1865 (copies in author's possession); WTS-M, p. 788; John E. Barrett, *Sherman's March Through the Carolinas* (Chapel Hill, NC, 1956), pp. 191, 198; JTG-MS, pp. 23, 25, 26;CS-AL, pp. 679–80; HSC-CWA, p. 753; Maj. George W. Nichols, *The Story of the Great March* (Williamstown, MA, 1972), pp. 285–88; Pvt. John Marshall (123rd N.Y.), letter to his parents, dated April 8, 1865 (copy in author's possession); Burke Davis, *Sherman's March* (New York, 1988), p. 246–47; MQ-CM, p. 380; Harvey Reid, HQ aide, 2nd Brig., 3rd Div., 20th Corps) written in Goldsboro, NC, March 28, 1865 (copy in author's possession).

11. KJB-S, pp. 238–41; HCM-R123, pp. 174–76; Jim Miles, *To the Sea* (Nashville, TN, 1989), p. 263; Sergeant Lorenzo R. Coy (123rd N.Y.), diary entry dated April 10, 1865 (copy in author's possession); General Williams, diary entry dated April 10 and 12, 1865 (copy in author's possession); RC-D, entry dated April 10, 1865 (copy in author's possession); JGC-NH, p. 218; *Washington County People's Journal*, vol. 12, no. 18 (May 4, 1865); WCM-D, entry dated April 10, 1865 (copy in author's possession); John E. Barrett, *Sherman's March Through the Carolinas* (Chapel Hill, NC, 1956), pp. 158, 203, 204; Olivia Coolidge, *The Statesmanship of Abraham Lincoln* (New York, 1976), pp. 13, 16, 28, 30, 182–84: MQ-CM, p. 381.

Chapter 14. Victory and the Grand Review

1. HCM-R123, pp. 176–85; KJB-S, pp. 240–43, 247; Jim Miles, *To the Sea* (Nashville, TN, 1989), pp. 264–67; Sgt. Lorenzo R. Coy (123rd N.Y.), diary entries dated April 12, April 17, April 22, April 28, April 29, April 30, May 11, 1865 (copies in author's possession); WCM-D, entries dated April 12, April 14, April 28, April 30, May 2, May 10, 1865 (copies in author's possession); RL-ND, pp. 651, 653; Capt. David P. Conygham, *Sherman's March Through Georgia* (New York, 1865), pp. 384, 403; Katharine M. Jones, *When Sherman Came* (Indianapolis, IN, 1964), pp. 287, 288; Robert Hale Strong, *A Yankee Private's Civil War* (Chicago, 1961), pp. 196–97, 203; W. C. McMurray, *History of the 20th Tennessee Infantry Regiment* (Nashville, TN, 1904) pp. 354–56, 358; RED-CW, pp. 563, 568; Webb Garrison, *Civil War Tales*, (Nashville, TN, 1988), pp. 236–37; JTG-MS, pp. 51, 157; Pvt. John Cutter, (123rd N.Y.), letters to his father, dated April 20, May 22, 1865 (copies in author's possession); John E. Barrett, *Sherman's March Through the Carolinas* (Chapel Hill, NC, 1956), pp. 236, 255, 269–70; *Washington County Post*, vol. 77, no. 19 (May 12, 1865), p. 2; Frank J. Welcher, *Coburn's Brigade* (Carmel, IN, 1999), pp. 365, 367–68, 371, 374–75; John E. Barrett, *Sherman's March Through the Carolinas*, (Chapel Hill, NC, 1956), pp. 235, 248–49, 254; Pvt. John Cutter (123rd N.Y.), letter to his father, dated April 20, 1865 (copy in author's possession); AMC-D, entries dated April 18, May 11, 1865; William C. Davis, *Lincoln's Men* (New York, 1999), p. 241; Burke Davis, *Sherman's March* (New York, 1988), p. 288; Henry Hitchcock, *Marching with Sherman* (New Haven, CT, 1927), p. 307; JMM-BC, p. 853.

2. KJB-S, pp. 244–45; HCM-R123, pp. 185–87; Brig. Gen. Alpheus Williams, diary entry dated May 15, 1865; WCM-D, entry dated May 15, 1865 (copy in author's possession); Pvt. John Cutter (123rd N.Y.), letter to his sister, dated May 22, 1865 (copy in author's possession); Frank J. Welcher, *Coburn's Brigade* (Carmel, IN, 1999), pp. 377, 380; AMC-D, entry dated May 15, 1865 (copy in author's possession).

3. HCM-R123, pp. 189–90; KJB-S, pp. 246–48; WCM-D, entries dated May 25, June 8, June 10, June 11, 1865; RC-D, entry dated May 26, 1865 (copy in author's possession); Shelby Foote, *The Civil War, A Narrative* (New York, 1974), p. 1017; Sgt. L. R. Coy (123rd N.Y.), diary entries dated May 15, May 19, May 23, 1865 (copy in author's possession); WCM-D, entries dated June 10, June 11, 1865 (copies in author's possession); Charles Royster, *The Destructive War* (New York, 1981), pp. 405–15; Theodore F. Upson, *With Sherman to the Sea* (Bloomington, IN, 1958), pp. 176–77; Margaret Leech, *Reveille in Washington* (New York, 1941), pp. 416–17, 510, 512–13; Morgan E. Dowling, *Southern Prisons* (Detroit, 1870), p. 491; Stanley Kimmel, *Mr. Lincoln's Washington* (New York, 1957), pp. 214–15; William B. Jordan, Jr., *Red Diamond Regiment* (Shippensburg, PA, 1996), pp. 246–47; FAL-TF, p. 325; Robert Hale Strong, *A Yankee Private's Civil War* (Chicago, 1961), pp. 210–11; AMC-D, entries dated May 24, June 11, 1865 (copies in author's possession); Reid Mitchell, *The Vacant Chair* (New York, 1993), p. 208; *Washington County Post*, vol. 77, no. 24 (June 16, 1865), p. 2; Victor Davis Hanson, *The Soul of Battle* (New York, 1999), pp. 123, 126; Frank

J. Welcher, *Coburn's Brigade* (Carmel, IN, 1999), pp. 380–81; Peter G. Tsouras, *Military Quotations from the Civil War* (New York, 1998); Brooks D. Simpson, *Ulysses S. Grant* (New York, 2000), p. 449; Burke Davis, *Sherman's March* (New York, 1988), pp. 285, 288–96; WCM-L, to his mother dated June 1, 1865 (copy in author's possession); Noah Brooks, *Washington in Lincoln's Time* (New York, 1958), pp. 270–83; William B. Holberton, *Homeward Bound* (Mechanicsburg, PA, 2001), pp. 25, 27; Albert Castel, *Decision in the West* (Lawrence, KS, 1992), p. 77; Mills Lane, ed., *"War is Hell"* (Savannah, GA, 1974), p. 2; *Daily Chronicle*, vol. 3, no. 174 (May 25, 1865), p. 1; James P. Jones, *"Black Jack" John A. Logan and Southern Illinois in the Civil War Era* (Tallahassee, FL, 1967), p. 262; AMC-D, entries dated May 19, May 20, May 22, May 23, May 24, 1865 (copies in author's possession); Charles Royster, *A Revolutionary People at War* (New York, 1979), pp. 405–17; Capt. George W. Pepper, *Sherman's Georgia Campaign* (Zanesville, OH, 1866), p. 479; Kenneth A. Perry, ed., "We Are in a Fight Today," *The Civil War Diaries of Horace P. Mathews and King S. Hammond* (123rd N.Y.) (Bowie MD, 2000), p. 34; Capt. George I. Robinson (123rd N.Y.), letter to his wife, dated May 19, 1865 (copies in author's possession); Jennifer C. Bohrnstedt, ed., *Soldiering with Sherman* (DeKalb, IL, 2000), p. 164; LT-GG, p. 143; Stanley Kimmel, *Mr. Lincoln's Washington* (New York, 1957), pp. 210–16; Andrew Ward, *The Slave's War* (New York, 2008), p. 253.

4. Service, Medical, and Pension records of Daniel, Melancton, and John Ross (NA Record Group 94); 1865 New York State Census, Salem Township; Jim Miles, *To the Sea* (Nashville, TN, 1989), p. 267; WCM-D, entries dated May 24, May 29, June 10, June 11, 1865 (copies in author's possession); Sgt. L. R. Coy (123rd N.Y.) diary entry dated June 10, 1865 (copy in author's possession).

5. Ross family records; 1865 New York State Census of Washington County; Ezra T. Warner, *Generals in Blue* (Baton Rouge, LA, 1964), pp. 451–53, 560; DHK-H93, pp. 499, 500, 505.

Epilogue

1. Col. Francis Sherman (88th Ill.), letter to his father, February 1863 (copy in author's possession); Charles Royster, *A Revolutionary People at War* (New York, 1979), pp. 8, 16–20, 48–49, 64, 102, 367; JTG-MS, pp. 48, 49; Bell Wiley, *The Life of Billy Yank* (Indianapolis, IN, 1952), p. 40; Allan R. Millett, *For the Common Defense* (New York, 1984), pp. 55, 57, 63; Benjamin Quarles, *Lincoln and the Negro* (New York, 1962), pp. 129, 221–23; Gabor Borritt, *Why the Confederacy Lost* (New York, 1992), pp. 115–16; *Washington County People's Journal*, vol. 10, no. 29 (July 16, 1863); RHS-HD, p. 172; JMM-SE, p. 124; LaWanda Cox, *Lincoln and Black Freedom* (Columbia, SC, 1994), p. 4; Wilbur D. Jones, *Grants in the Cornfield* (Shippensburg, PA, 1997), p. 33; Richard M. Ketchum, ed., *American Heritage Picture History of the Civil War* (New York, 1960), pp. 252, 418; JMM-CC, pp. 92, 116, 119, 126; WKK-AL, p. 233; JMM-DS, p. 201; Joseph Allen Frank, *With Ballot and Bayonet* (Athens, GA, 1998), pp. 69–70; Joyce Appleby, *Inheriting the*

Revolution (Cambridge, MA, 2000), p. 248; WVR-L, to his parents, dated June 9, 1863, July 27, 1862 (copies in author's possession); Jenkins Lloyd Jones, *An Artilleryman's Diary* (Madison, WI, 1914), p. 47; Kevin Phillips, *The Cousin's War* (New York, 1999), pp. xiii, xxi, 92, 177–82; EJH-US, pp. xi, 194, 197; Roger Butterfield, *The American Past* (New York, n.d.), p. 172; Randal C. Jimmerson, *The Private Civil War* (Baton Rouge, LA, 1988), p. 34–41; GP-LW, p. 339; Michael S. Green, *Freedom, Union, and Power* (New York, 2004), p. 23; Allen G. Guelzo, *Lincoln's Emancipation Proclamation* (New York, 2004), pp. 160, 161, 195, 232; John C. Waugh, *Reelecting Lincoln* (New York, 1997), p. 85; *Whitehall Chronicle*, May 8, 1863; Arthur M. Schlesinger, Jr., *The Crisis of the Old Order* (New York, 2002), p. ix; J. F. Cleveland, comp., *The Tribune Almanac* (New York, 1865), p. 48; Bertram Wyatt-Brown, *Lewis Tappan and the Evangelical War Against Slavery* (Baton Rouge, LA, 1997), p. 337; Samuel Eliot Morison, *Oxford History of the American People* (New York, 1965), p. 509; Christian J. Heidorf, *Shoulder Arms* (Glens Falls, NY, 1998), pp. 72–73, 85; Marie Rulkotter, "Civil War Veterans in Politics," (PhD dissertation, University of Wisconsin, 1938), pp. 2, 4, 27n, 28; *Abraham Lincoln, Great Speeches* (Mineola, NY, 1991), p. 97.

   2. JTG-MS, p. 202; David Long, *The Jewel of Liberty* (New York, 1997), p. 257; O. O. Winther, *The Soldier Vote in the Election of 1864* (Albany, NY, 1944), p. 445; Josiah H. Benton *Voting in the Field* (Boston, 1915), p. 312; "Soldier Voting in 1864: The David McKelvy Diary" *Pennsylvania Magazine of History and Biography*, vol. 115, no. 3 (July 1991), p. 383; JYS-PG12, pp. 212–15. Jeffrey H. Jones, *Marching to Save a Union* (West Conshohocken, PA, 2007), p. 255; Michael Burlingame, *Inside Lincoln's White House* (Carbondale, IL, 1997), p. 240; OR, series 1, vol. 44, part 1, p. 228.

   3. JMM-CC, pp. 117–30; JTG-MS, p. 50; Gabor Borritt, *Why the Confederacy Lost* (New York, 1992), pp. 122, 141–51; *The Washington County People's Journal*, vol. 11, no. 21 (May 26, 1864); ibid., vol. 10, no. 4 (October 29, 1863); ibid., vol. 11, no. 36 (September 8, 1864); CS-AL, pp. 157, 273; David E. Long, *The Jewel of Liberty* (Mechanicsburg, PA, 1994), p. 251; Christian J. Heidorf, *Shoulder Arms* (Glens Falls, NY, 1998), pp. 73, 86; Jeffrey Rogers Hummel, *Emancipating Slaves, Enslaving Free Men* (Chicago, 1996), p. 207; AHG-HP, pp. 669–70; *Washington County Post*, March 13, 1863, September 30,1854, and October 17, 1864; JMM-BC, pp. 716, 804, 839–40; James I. Robertson, *The Concise Illustrated History of the Civil War* (Harrisburg, PA, 1979), pp. 32–34; Gordon Leidner, "Measuring the Presidents" *Columbiad*, vol. 2, no. 1 (Spring 1998), pp. 62–63; RHS-HD, p. 121, 179; David Wallace Adams "Illinois Soldiers and the Emancipation proclamation," *Journal of the Illinois State Historical Society*, vol. 67, no. 4 (September 1974), pp. 408–17; WVR-L, to his parents, dated March 21, 1862, and May 30, 1863 (copies in author's possession); Alma Lutz, *Susan B. Anthony* (Boston, 1960), p. 58; LaWanda Cox, *Lincoln and Black Freedom* (Columbia, SC, 1994), p. 13; Dr. Daniel R. Ross (123rd N.Y.), typescript memoir (in author's possession); AMC-L to his sister, dated December 5, 1864 (copy in author's possession); Ruth L. Silliker, ed., *The Rebel Yell and Yankee Hurrah* (Camden, ME, 1985), pp. 218, 219, 268; Gary W. Gallagher, ed., *The Wilderness Campaign* (Chapel Hill, NC, 1997), pp. 79–88; Tommy Bogger, *Readings in Black*

and White (Portsmouth, VA, n.d.), p. 21; *America's Civil War* (September 1998), p. 62; David Long, *The Jewel of Liberty* (New York, 1997), pp. 215–16, 256; LGB-H36, pp. 675, 687–88; Thomas J. Morgan, "Reminiscences of Service with Colored Troops in the Army of the Cumberland," *Personal Narratives*, Rhode Island Soldiers and Sailors' Society, 3rd ser., no. 13 (Providence, RI, 1885), pp. 35, 41, 44, 46, 47, 48; *Troy Daily Times*, July 28, 1862, August 27, 1862, and January 2, 1863; Linda J. Altman, *Slavery and Abolition in American History* (Berkeley Heights, NJ, 1999) p. 101; Orville C. Robinson (123rd N.Y.), letter to E. H. Snyder, dated September 1, 1863 (copy in author's possession); James R. Arnold, *Grant Wins the War* (New York, 1997), pp. 70–71; Capt. Culver (Company H, 123rd N.Y.), letter to William Law, dated October 28, 1864 (copy in author's possession); correspondence by "Eyeglass" (Lt. Alonzo T. Mason [123rd N.Y.] Collection, NYHS Library); Henry Martin, *The Hairstons* (New York, 1999), p. 151; William C. Davis, *Lincoln's Men* (New York, 1999), pp. 92–105, 152, 211, 213, 218, 220, 223, 252; Joseph Allen Frank, *With Ballot and Bayonet* (Athens, GA, 1998), pp. 67, 69, 70, 127; David Donald, ed., *Why the North Won the Civil War* (Baton Rouge, LA, 1969), p. 86; Peter G. Tsouras, *Military Quotations from the Civil War* (New York, 1988), pp. 151, 227; DE-L, to his parents, dated November 8, 1864 (copy in author's possession); Wendell H. Stephenson, *The Political Career of General James H. Lane*, vol. 3 (Topeka, KS, 1930), pp. 129, 131; 1st Lt. Haviland Gifford (93rd N.Y.), letter to his father, dated November 5, 1863 (Pierpont Morgan Library, Gilbert Lehrman Collection, GLC 4560.09); William C. Davis, *Lincoln's Men* (New York, 1999), pp. 107, 205, 222–23, 229, 231, 246; *Glens Falls Messenger*, June 8, 1863; Col. Oliver Edwards (37th Mass.), letter to his mother, dated January 13, 1863 (Gilbert Lehrman Collection GLC 2163 no. 6); letter from "H.O.W." (a soldier in the 123rd) to his hometown newspaper, dated August 13, 1863; EJH-LV, pp. 30–33, 96, 97, 111; WKK-AL, pp. 251, 269, 272, 273; Pvt. John Cutter (123rd N.Y.), letter to his father, dated December 18, 1864 (copy in author's possession); Bruce Chadwick, *The Two American Presidents* (Secaucas, NJ, 1999), p. 390; *Daily Chronicle* (Washington, DC), March 22, 1864; Charles Sterling Underhill, *"Your Soldier Boy Samuel"* (Buffalo, NY, 1929), p. 67; JTG-MS, pp. 48, 59; KJB-S, p. 196; Catherine Clinton and Nina Silbers, eds., *Divided Houses* (New York, 1992), p. 69; JMM-DS, p. 197; James I. Robertson, Jr., *Soldiers Blue and Gray* (Columbia, SC, 1988), pp. 31, 35; Michael Vorenberg, "The Deformed Child: Slavery and the Election of 1864," *Civil War History*, vol. 47, no. 3 (September 2001), p. 255; *Gazeteer of the County of Washington, NY*, 1849, p. 14; T. Harry Williams, "Voters in Blue: The Citizen Soldiers of the Civil War," *Mississippi Valley Historical Review*, vol. 3, no. 2 (September 1944), pp. 199–200; C. Knight Aldrich, *Quest for a Star* (Knoxville, TN, 1999), pp. 32, 69; Herbert A. Donovan, *The Barnburners* (Philadelphia, PA, 1974), p. 106; Gerald Sorin, *The New York Abolitionists* (Westport, CT, 1971), p. 127; Hugh Davis, "The New York Evangelist, New School Presbyterians and Slavery, 1837–1857," *American Presbyterians*, vol. 68 (1990), p. 15; Stephen W. Sears, *On Campaign with the Army of the Potomac* (New York, 2001), p. 185; H. Jack Long, *The Wit and Wisdom of Abraham Lincoln* (Cleveland, OH, 1942), pp. 214, 221; George S. Bradley, *The Star Corps* (Milwaukee, WI, 1865), p. 179; CS-AL, pp.

157, 556, 579, 612, 644; *People's Journal*, January 8, 1863, May 26, 1864, June 2, 1864; ibid., July 14, July 16, November 10, and November 21, 1864; Rossiter Johnson, *Campfire and Battlefield* (New York, 1894), p. 415; E. R. Mann, *The Bench and Bar of Saratoga County* (Ballston Spa, NY, 1876), p. 294; Olivia Coolidge, *The Statesmanship of Abraham Lincoln* (New York, 1976), pp. 116, 132, 133, 150; James M. McPherson, *What They Fought For* (Baton Rouge, LA, 1994), pp. 42, 43, 62, 69; David E. Johnson, *A Funny Thing Happened on the Way to the White House* (New York, 1983), p. 52; Joseph O. Jackson, "*Some of the Boys...*" (Carbondale, IL 1960), p. 210; Pvt. John Marshall (Company E, 123rd N.Y.), letter to his parents, dated April 8, 1865 (copy in author's possession); Margaret Leech, *Reveille in Washington* (New York, 1941), p. 438; WVR-L, to his parents, dated July 29, 1862, August 2, 1863 (copies in author's possession); HCM-R123, p. 131; Jane H. Kobelski, *Readings in Black and White* (Portsmouth, VA, n.d.), p. 21; David W. Blight, *Union and Emancipation* (Kent, OH, 1997), pp. 114, 115, 119; John R. Brumgardt, "Overwhelmingly for Old Abe," *Lincoln Herald* vol. 78 (Winter 1975), p. 155; *Aurora Beacon*, February 25, 1864; *Washington County People's Journal*, February 9, 1865; *Washington County Chronicle*, January 13, 1865; JES-RN, p. 12; Randal C. Jimmerson, *The Private Civil War* (Baton Rouge, LA, 1988), pp. 39, 45–48, 96, 181, 183; GP-LW, pp. 196, 265, 296–99; John C. Waugh, *Reelecting Lincoln* (New York, 1997), p. 312; John Hay, *Lincoln and the Civil War* (Westport, CT, 1939), p. 242; Pvt. John Gourlie (123rd N.Y.), letter to his brother, dated November 3, 1864 (copy in author's possession); *Lincoln Herald*, vol. 54, no. 3, p. 23; James A. Padgett, ed., "With Sherman through Georgia and the Carolinas: Letters of a Federal Soldier," part 2, *Georgia Historical Quarterly*, vol. 33, no. 1 (March 1949), pp. 52–55; Kevin C. Murphy, ed., *The Civil War Letters of Joseph K. Taylor of the Thirty-seventh Mass. Volunteer Infantry* (Lewiston, NY, 1998), p. 153; Samuel P. Timmons (1st Ohio), letter to "Kind Father," dated February 17, 1863 (copy in author's possession); *Troy Daily Times*, August 16, 1862; "Soldier Voting in 1864: The David McKelvy Diary," *Pennsylvania Magazine of History and Biography*, vol. 115, no. 3 (July 1991), pp. 372, 375, 378, 383; *Sandy Hill Herald*, letter signed by "W. B. P. Co. D. 93rd NY," dated August 14, 1863 (probably William B. Peck) (copy in author's possession); JYS-PG12, p. 213; James M. Greiner, *Subdued by the Sword: A Line Officer in the 121st New York Volunteers,* (Albany, NY, 2003), p. 83; PSP-PAL, p. 26; *Atlantic Monthly*, vol. 14, issue 84 (October 1864), p. 518; OR ser. III, vol. 5—Correspondence, pp. 660–63; Noah A. Trudeau, *Like Men of War* (Edison, NJ, 2002), pp. 59, 349, 466; David E. Long, *The Jewel of Liberty* (New York, 1997), p. 177; HSC-CWA, p. 51.

Glossary

abatis: An obstacle or barricade of felled trees with bent or sharpened branches directed toward an enemy.

ball: Start of battle.

bluebelly: Slang for Union soldier.

broadside: A sheet of paper printed on one or both sides, for distribution or posting.

bummer: Forager.

butternuts: Slang for Confederates, derived from their homespun jackets dyed with butternuts.

canister: A metal cylinder packed with shot that scattered when fired from a cannon.

casemates: An armored compartment for artillery.

casualties: Statistic referring to those who were killed, wounded, or captured/missing.

coffee coolers: Stragglers.

contraband: "Stolen" runaway slaves who were considered property rather than people without any identity of their own.

copperheads: Peace Democrats, so called because of their poisonous views.

countermarch: March in reverse direction, over ground just covered.

Covenanting Presbyterian Church: A branch of the Presbyterian Church that adheres to the belief that slavery is a sin in God's eyes, and that the Bible is the supreme law of the land. Covenanting refers to a decree that when man's law—including the king's—conflicted with God's, they would obey His law.

deadline: An escape prevention no-man's zone inside the prison wall.

develop: Identify the enemy's location.

double-quick: A very fast marching pace.

dress: Straighten.

drop trail: Horses were hitched to the tongue, known as the trail, at the rear of the gun wagon so they could pull the gun into position; when so positioned, horses would be unhitched and the tongue—or trail—dropped to the ground.

effective: Soldier who was fully equipped and ready for battle.

epaulments: Earthworks.

feeler: A skirmisher who keeps in advance and on the flanks of the main column to scope out the land and the enemy.

fresh fish: Epithet used to describe new arrivals in Confederate prison.

galloper: Courier on horseback.

grape: A cluster of small projectiles fired together from a cannon to produce a hail of shot.

graybacks: Slang for Confederate soldier; also slang for lice.

guide left, right or center: Keep in alignment with the man to the left, right, or center when marching.

invest: To surround (a place) with military forces or works in order to prevent approach or escape; to besiege.

ironclads: Hardtack.

Glossary

Kansas-Nebraska Act: The 1854 act that created the territories of Kansas and Nebraska, and allowed settlers to decide whether or not slavery would be permitted.

limber: The two-wheeled vehicle used to tow a field gun or caisson, pulled by a team of horses; also a verb meaning to attach a gun or caisson to the limber in preparation for moving to a new position.

Lincolnite: A supporter of Abraham Lincoln; also a member of an Illinois regiment in the Civil War.

mess: The group of soldiers who share meal preparation and eat together.

minié ball: A cone-shaped bullet with a hollow base that would expand when fired.

Napoleon: A smoothbore brass cannon that was effective at close range, used to fire shot and canister.

New School Presbyterian: A group that split from other Presbyterians over slavery and other issues.

parole: The conditional release of a prisoner of war, under which the parolee agrees he will not take up arms against the enemy until exchanged for a prisoner from the other army.

Parrott gun: A longer-range gun than the Napoleon with a rifled barrel that fired ten- or twenty-pound shot.

picket line: Perimeter patrol.

pioneers: Foot soldiers whose job was to build or improve roads and dig entrenchments ahead of the army.

prebounty men: Soldiers who enlisted before large bounties were offered to attract recruits.

Presbyterian Covenanters: Followers of the Covenanting Presbyterian church.

rations: One ration was a day's worth of meals for one man.

red legs: Artillerymen.

redoubt: A temporary or permanent fort system, usually earthworks.

rifle-musket: A musket in which the interior of the barrel has been rifled, or grooved in a spiral pattern to prevent the bullet from tumbling or wobbling.

Secosh: Misspelling of "secesh," a slang term for secessionist, a supporter of the South's right to secede from the Union.

skillygalee: Hardtack.

stand of colors: The regimental flag carried into battle by a flag bearer to guide the soldiers and keep them oriented to their regiment.

sutler: Civilian merchants who were common fixtures at military encampments and some prisons.

tattoo: A signal played on a drum, bugle, or trumpet to alert soldiers to go to quarters.

terrible execution: Extremely effective rifle or artillery fire.

three-year men: Soldiers who enlisted for a three-year period after already having served a shorter enlistment period.

thrown out: Positioning skirmishers on a line in advance of the battle line.

USCT: U.S. Colored Troops.

veteranize: Enlist as a Veteran Volunteer; only Union soldiers who first enlisted for three years by early 1862 were eligible to veteranize by enlisting for another three-year stint starting in December 1863.

Bibliographic Essays

The most time-consuming research involved in writing this book, by far, was locating the almost 2,000 personal narratives written by more than 300 soldiers in the three regiments and brigades in which the Ross brothers fought. In my thirty-year search, I consulted Civil War letter collections in countless libraries and historical societies, both public and private, as well as the National Archives military reference section, Library of Congress Manuscript Collection, and the Army Military History Institute.

I have drawn from all of these for background and cite the personal narratives that best describe the soldiers' motivation to fight, and the campaigns, marches, and battles in which they participated. All social historians I have read agree that these personal accounts contain as accurate and complete a record as exists of how soldiers felt about the war and why they fought it. The letters of the Veteran Volunteers illustrate clearly they had the strongest moral commitment. There were several very literate soldiers in each of the three regiments in which the Ross brothers fought, and their extensive letter collections were especially important sources.

Countless scholarly works helped put the personal narratives in context. They have been invaluable in their interpretations of the reasons for, and results of, the battles and campaigns in which the Ross brothers and their comrades fought as well as their contributions to the outcomes.

In all cases, I drew heavily on *Official Records for the War of the Rebellion*, plus other Civil War records in the National Archives, including brigade and regimental order books, and military and pension records of individual soldiers. To access invaluable information contained in rare, out-of-print books, I relied on the help of interlibrary loan services throughout the country.

Why, How, and When They Fought

I used twenty-four principal sources to trace the impact of the Ross family's church on their lives in New York. The best source on the Washington

County Reformed Presbyterians is James B. Scouller's *History of the Presbytery of Argyle (New York) of the United Presbyterian Church* (Newville, PA, 1880). Of the eleven personal letters written by seven soldiers regarding their religious convictions, the five written by three soldiers in the 36th Ill. best indicate their moral stance against slavery.

More books have been written about Abraham Lincoln than about any other president. I consulted twenty-eight to determine his private as well as public views on slavery, the impact he had on his soldiers, his Emancipation Proclamation, and the growing support for it. The most helpful were Carl Sandburg's *Abraham Lincoln* (New York, 1966), James M. McPherson's *For Cause and Comrades* (New York, 1997), *Battle Cry of Freedom* (New York, 1988), Joseph T. Glatthaar's *The March to the Sea and Beyond* (New York, 1985), and Doris K. Goodwin's *Team of Rivals* (New York, 2005).

Chancellorsville

Pvt. Dan Ross's military service record, National Archives RG94, documents his record as an artilleryman in Battery F, 4th U.S. Seventy-seven letters, diaries, and other personal narratives by thirty-three officers and soldiers who fought with him at Chancellorsville, as well as eleven contemporary newspaper accounts, describe the action of his artillery brigade in support of General Williams's division, to which it was assigned, as well as those of the 123rd N.Y. and the loss of confidence in Hooker's generalship among men and officers after Chancellorsville. Twenty-eight regimental and other unit histories also were helpful, particularly Henry C. Morhous's Reminiscences of the 123rd Regiment NYSV (Greenwich, New York, 1879) and Rice C. Bull, Soldiering [123rd N.Y.] (Novato, CA 1977), as were twenty-two contemporary newspaper and journal reports.

The best sources consulted to determine how green cannoneers were trained include L. Van Loan Naisawold's *Grape and Canister* (New York, 1960), Jenkin L. Jones's *An Artilleryman's Diary* (Madison, WI, 1914), August Buell's *The Cannoneer* (Washington, DC, 1890), and Fairfax Downey's *Sound of Guns* (NewYork, 1955).

For understanding why and how the battle was fought and its contribution to the total war effort, I drew heavily on Edward J. Stackpole's *Chancellorsville* (Harrisburg, PA, 1958), Stephen W. Sears's *Chancellorsville* (New York, 1996), Ernest F. Furgurson's *Chancellorsville* (New York, 1992), John Bigelow, Jr.'s *Campaign of Chancellorsville* (New Haven, CT, 1910), and Milo F. Quaife's *From the Cannon's Mouth* (Detroit, 1959).

Bibliographic Essays 433

After Chancellorsville

I examined general officers' accounts of General Hooker's conduct of the Battle of Chancellorsville, why he lost it, and the impact of the loss on civilian and military morale in both the North and the South. Seventy-seven personal narratives and eleven contemporary newspaper accounts fill in details of the action experienced by Dan Ross's Battery F, the 123rd N.Y., and the rest of General Williams's division and the battle's aftermath.

The two previously cited regimental histories of the 123rd N.Y. were also very helpful. For a description of how they were reequipped and trained for their next encounter with the enemy and their march to Gettysburg for that encounter, these histories provided many details.

Gettysburg

Pvt. Dan Ross illustrates with clarity how inexperienced cannoneers were recruited and trained in early 1863 to fill the hopelessly inadequate ranks of the Army of the Potomac artillery. The effectiveness of their on-the-job training is revealed in the comparison of their initial performance at Chancellorsville, their first battle, in comparison to how much more effective they were at Gettysburg three months later. I have found no comparable comparisons in Civil War literature regarding the recruitment, training, and operations of the artillery.

Edward E. Longacre's *A Biography of General Henry Jackson Hunt* (New York, 1977) is by far the best treatment of Hunt's role in both Chancellorsville and Gettysburg.

Stones River, Chickamauga, and Missionary Ridge

Lank's 36th Ill. is a classic example of a Veteran Volunteer regiment. The men not only enlisted at the outset of the war, but reenlisted under extremely adverse circumstances and fought to the very end of the war. The men's dual commitment to fight to the war's end so as to restore the Union and establish equal rights for all men, including slaves, is clearly revealed in the 128 letters, diary entries, memoirs, and journals written by fifty-two officers and soldiers, half of them in Lank's regiment and brigade. Fifteen contemporary newspaper and journal accounts and thirty-four regimental and other unit histories—most of them in Lank's and other brigades in General Sherman's division—also document how they became more and more inured to hardship and melded into an increasingly powerful fighting machine.

One of the most complete regimental histories I have read, *History of the Thirty-sixth Regiment Illinois Volunteers*, by L. G. Bennett and William M. Haigh (reprint, Marengo, IL, 1999), was compiled by its members. Both authors served in Lank's Company E, Haigh as chaplain. This history is rich with details about all four battles Lank fought in, as well as the time between them. For information on their early battle experience, I relied on Kenneth W. Noe's *Perryville* (Lexington, KY, 2001).

How the 36th Ill. fought at Stones River is best described in twenty-eight letters and diary entries and three contemporary newspaper accounts. For the overall battle scene and Stones River's contribution to the total war effort, I drew heavily from two books by Peter Cozzens—*No Better Place to Die* (Chicago, 1960) and James L. McDonough's *Stones River* (Knoxville, TN, 1980).

To examine the Lincolnites' role in the massive undertaking of establishing a supply base at Murfreesboro, I also consulted forty letters and other personal narratives, plus two contemporary newspaper accounts. To examine the Battle of Chickamauga and its significance to the war, I drew heavily on B. Turchin's *Chickamauga* (Chicago, 1888), John Bowers's *Chattanooga and Chickamauga* (New York, 1994), and Cozzens's *This Terrible Sound* (Chicago, 1992).

Personal narratives offer a previously unpublished explanation of why Sheridan's soldiers stormed Missionary Ridge, contrary to Grant's orders. They also provide colorful descriptions of the 1,200-mile train ride Hooker's 20th Corps (including Dan's Battery F) and the 123rd N.Y. took from Virginia to Tennessee, which are more complete than heretofore published.

Detailed regimental and brigade after-action reports of the four principal bloody battles in which Lank fought before he was blinded appear in the *Official Records*. The significance of these battles to the war in the West and Lincoln's concern about them and their generals—Buell, Rosecrans, Sherman, Thomas, Sheridan, and Grant—is best addressed in James M. McPherson's *Battle Cry of Freedom* (New York, 1988), and Peter Cozzens' three books—*The Terrible Sound* (Chicago, 1992), *The Darkest Days of the War* (Chapel Hill, NC, 1997), and *The Shipwreck of Their Hopes* (Urbana, IL, 1994). Other valuable sources include John L. McDonough's *Stones River* (Knoxville, TN, 1980) and *Chattanooga* (Nashville, TN, 1984), John Bowers's *Chickamauga and Chattanooga* (New York, 1994), and Kenneth W. Noe's *Perryville* (Lexington, KY, 2001).

Battle of the Wilderness

No country crossroads in North America ever heard such volleys of musketry as did the intersection of Brock and Orange Plank roads in central Virginia on May 5, 1864. The Battle of the Wilderness was perhaps the most confused, disorganized, and least documented conflict of the Civil War by both armies.

The "fog of war" over this battle can only be lifted by examining the rich personal narratives—letters, diaries, memoirs, journals, and regimental histories of the participants—plus newspaper accounts by on-the-scene correspondents. Of the five brief after-action reports by regimental commanders in Hays's brigade in the *Official Records*, four were written more than three months later, after a dozen other battles had been fought. However, Hays's Brigade Order Book and other records in the National Archives, never before cited, were most helpful. Reconstructing the battle through on-the-scene accounts by participants and observers, supported by the other records in the National Archives, shed significant new light on how Hays's brigade, and particularly the 93rd N.Y., prevented what could have been a fatal Confederate breakthrough of the Union line.

This is believed to be the first in-depth attempt to lift the fog. One hundred nineteen personal narratives written by forty-eight officers and soldiers, Union and Confederate; twenty-one regimental histories; and twenty-four newspaper and magazine articles in fourteen publications were pieced together. Many of the firsthand accounts were published in David H. King's *History of the Ninety-Third New York* (Milwaukee, WI, 1895). Colonel Crocker's unpublished diary also was invaluable. Together they shed a whole new light on how this battle was fought, as well as on the 93rd New Yorkers' decision to veteranize during the winter and spring prior to this battle.

To set this opening battle in the context of the overall campaign, I relied most heavily on the seminal work of Edward Steere's *The Wilderness Campaign* (Harrisburg, NY, 1960). Morris Schaff's *The Battle of the Wilderness* (Boston, 1910), and Noah Trudean's more recent *Bloody Roads South* (Boston, 1988) were also extremely helpful.

Kolb's Farm

In the dozens of volumes written about Sherman's march on Atlanta, no more than several paragraphs in each have been devoted to the all-day skirmishing activity that preceded the Battle of Kolb's Farm, June 22,

1864. The one exception is Richard A. Baumgartner's *Kennesaw Mountain, June 1864* (Huntington, WV, 1988). Yet in the *Officials Records* it was described in fifteen after-action reports, fourteen of which were written by Union officers and one by a Confederate. As a result, it is an extremely well documented, classic example of how Sherman relied on seasoned skirmishers to aggressively feel his enemy's strength and guide his flanking movements so as to avoid head-on, bloody battles and thereby forcing General Johnston to continuously retreat. Fortunately, the 123rd New Yorkers were highly literate soldiers. Details of how skirmishers maneuvered and protected themselves, as well as one another, are clearly revealed in thirty-two letters, diaries, memoirs, and journals written by twenty-one officers and soldiers. That includes twelve in the 123rd. One lieutenant, five sergeants, and one private wrote diaries, and five others wrote letters. Two regimental histories of the 123rd include descriptions of their skirmishing. Twenty-seven contemporary newspaper and journal accounts and eight additional regimental and other unit histories also describe the battle. Taken together with the fourteen after-action reports by their officers, a detailed picture emerges of the toll it took in killed, wounded, and captured soldiers on both sides.

The two regimental histories are Sergeant Henry C. Morhous's *Reminiscences of the 123rd Regiment N.Y.S.V.* (Greenwich, NY, 1879) and K. Jack Bauer's *Soldiering: The Civil War Diary of Rice C. Bull* (Novato, CA, 1977).

Albert Castel's *Decision in the West* (Lawrence, KS, 1992) provides the best account of the relevance of the Battle of Kolb's Farm to the conduct of Sherman's march on Atlanta.

Prisoner to Guard

The three best works that portray the gruesome conditions of Southern Civil War prisons, especially Andersonville, during the ten months that Pvt. Dan Ross was incarcerated, especially in Andersonville, are: William B. Hesseltine's *Civil War Prisons* (Columbus, OH, 1930), William Marvel's *Andersonville: The Last Depot* (Chapel Hill, NC, 1994), and Ovid L. Futch's *History of Andersonville Prison* (Gainesville, FL, 1968).

Twelve books and memoirs, including Dan's, of those incarcerated at about the same time as Dan offered further details about what inmates in Confederate prisons experienced. To determine the lifelong impact of the appalling prison life on these men, I used the military, medical, and pension records from the National Archives of nine who were captured with Dan to determine the prison-related diseases on which their pensions were based.

I used Dan's memoir and thirty-two participant accounts by twenty-six officers and horse soldiers, plus seven regimental and other unit histories, to recount the raid on Selma, one of the most successful cavalry raids in the war, and its results. Altogether, these sources provide a more complete record than I have found of that battle. In his memoir, Dan described what he witnessed of the battle from his unique vantage point on the roof of a four-story building.

The description of Dan's release, subsequent attempt to rejoin his regiment, and his assignment as a guard to take the Confederate President Jefferson Davis to prison at Fortress Monroe are contained in his memoir. I supplement it with six reports by officers and soldiers who also guarded Davis, nine contemporary newspaper and journal accounts, and Lynda L. Crist's *The Papers of Jefferson Davis*, vol. 11 (Baton Rouge, LA, 2003). Altogether, these sixteen sources provide a more complete description than any other account of his trip to prison.

Capture of Atlanta

Sherman's men were acutely aware of the significance of capturing Atlanta and were hell-bent to do so. When they did, they wrote extensively about it. To best illustrate their views as well as the reaction of their folks back home, I cited forty-eight of their letters and diary entries, and reviewed articles in four of their local newspapers.

Preparations for converting Atlanta into a springboard for Sherman's further march to Savannah and beyond are also extensively chronicled. I relied mainly on Albert Castel's *Decison in the West* (Lawrence, KS, 1992), John Cannan's *The Atlanta Campaign* (Conshohocken, PA, 1991), and Larry T. Daniel's *Days of Glory* (Baton Rouge, LA, 2004). The two regimental histories of the 123rd filled in many details.

March to the Sea and Beyond

John's military, medical, and pension records, plus other records in the National Archives document the unqualified family commitment of their blood and treasure to the war effort. Local newspaper accounts describe the storm and drought; other public and family records recount the financial reverses the family suffered, and the loss of the family farm is recorded in their county courthouse.

The battle-hardened 123rd N.Y. soldiers' commitment to the dual purpose of the war and to Lincoln's leadership—and that of other regiments in their division—is revealed in 219 letters, as well as diaries, memoirs, and journals written by twenty-two officers and soldiers. Fourteen of them served in the 123rd N.Y. They also clearly illustrate the high morale in Sherman's army and the supreme confidence they had in Sherman and the officers under him.

Eleven contemporary newspaper reports reveal the same moral commitment as do the two regimental histories of the 123rd N.Y. Twenty-one other regimental and unit histories in Sherman's army were used to complete the analysis.

Six other publications by men who served in Sherman's army, four of them on his staff, were particularly insightful into both Sherman's management and the campaign's impact on both Union and Southern morale. They are Capt. George W. Pepper's *Sherman's Georgia Campaign* (Zanesville, OH, 1866), Theodore Upson's *With Sherman to the Sea* (Bloomington, IN, 1958), George W. Nichols's *The Story of the Great March* (Williamstown, MA, 1972), Henry Hitchcock's *Marching with Sherman* (New Haven, CT, 1927), James A. Connolly's *Three Years in the Army of the Cumberland* (Bloomington, IN, 1987) and Capt. David P. Conygham, *Sherman's March Through Georgia* (New York, 1865). *From the Cannon's Mouth* is a collection of letters and diary entries written by General Alpheus Williams, under whom the 123rd had served almost from its inception.

Joseph Glatthaar's *The March to the Sea and Beyond* (New York, 1985) is as complete an analysis of the men in Sherman's army as has yet been published. Sherman's personal views of the caliber of his men and how he selected them is clearly revealed in his *Memoirs of General W. T. Sherman*, vol. 2 (New York, 1990).

Victory and the Grand Review

The victory celebration by Sherman's army at Goldsboro, North Carolina, when they heard of Lee's surrender at Appomattox—and of General Johnston's surrender to Sherman shortly thereafter—was recorded in twenty-six letters and diary entries by men and officers in the 123rd N.Y. Their reactions to Lincoln's assassination before the surrender negotiations began at Goldsboro are included in many of these personal narratives along with vivid accounts of their march from Goldsboro to Washington, DC, for the Grand Review.

John G. Barretts's *Sherman's March Through the Carolinas* (Chapel Hill, NC, 1956) provided the best overall view of how the surrender proceedings were conducted.

The description of the Grand Review of Sherman's army before President Johnson and Generals Grant and Sherman is more complete than any other I have read. Contemporary sources, including five newspaper accounts, vividly describe how soldiers prepared for and participated in the review and how crowds reacted, as well as what else the men did as sightseers in the nation's capital while awaiting their discharge from the army. This overwhelming vote for Lincoln cast by his soldiers in the 123rd N.Y. was recorded in his diary by the officer who tabulated it.

Epilogue: A Legacy of Sacrifice

An analysis of soldiers' votes in the 1864 presidential election was assembled from a number of sources, including votes conducted in five prisons. The growth in emancipation sentiment and allegiance to "Father Abraham" is revealed in thirty-five letters and memoirs written by twenty-three soldiers and officers—seventeen of whom were in the three regiments in which the Ross brothers served. Twenty-seven editorials and news reports published in their hometown newspapers and nine regimental and other unit histories support the thesis that support grew for emancipation as the war progressed.

Wider and wider acceptance of the commitment to the twin goals of the war by both soldiers and citizens is clearly revealed in James M. McPherson's *What They Fought For* (Baton Rouge, LA 1994), Earl J. Hess' *The Union Soldier in Battle* (Lawrence, KS, 1997), and Joseph Allen Frank's *With Ballot and Bayonet* (Athens, GA, 1998), as well as McPherson's *For Cause and Comrades* and Glatthaar's *The March to the Sea and Beyond*, both previously cited. McPherson's *Battle Cry of Freedom* superbly traces the growing support for emancipation as the war ground on to a final conclusion.

Index

10th Illinois, 20, 59
  Will's enlistment, 20, 60
  duty at Cairo, Ill., 59–60

123rd N.Y. regiment, 25–27, 159–64, *200*
  Chancellorsville, 73–91, 100, 341
  Dan's enlistment, 25, 63
  Gettysburg, 108–15, 120–21
  Grand Review, 262, 342–48
  John's enlistment, 287
  Johnston's surrender, 336, 339
  Kolb's Farm, 242–61, 263
  Lincoln's assassination, 336–37
  march through Carolinas, 323–32
  march to the Sea, 297, 301–13
  march to Washington, 339–42
  occupation of Atlanta, 288–300
  occupation of Savannah, 318–21, 323
  recruitment, 11, 18–19, 23, 33
  siege of Savannah, 313–18
  total wartime casualties, 33
  train transport to Tennessee, 157–59
  winter of 1863–64, 186–88

36th Illinois, 21, 30–33, 40, 44–46, 54, 57, 128, 130, 151, 154, *176*, 181, 183
  Chickamauga, 136–48
  Lank's 1st enlistment, 21
  Lank's 2nd enlistment, 182
  Missionary Ridge, 170–79
  Perryville, 42
  Recruitment, 39
  Stones River, 45
  Total wartime casualties, 33, 44

7th NY (Black Horse), 21–22, 24, 61
  Dan's enlistment, 21, 60

93rd New York, 21, 32, 199, *200*,205, 207, 208, 210, 233, 237–38, 363
  Battle of Wilderness, 221–32
  headquarters and guard duty, 201–07
  recruitment, 11, 21, 23–24
  total wartime casualties, 33
  Will's 1st enlistment, 20
  Will's 2nd enlistment, 22, 32
  winter camp life 1863–64, 203–14

Abolition, 2–3, 10, 34–35, 351, 354–55, 365
  civilians' growing support for, 15–18
  political support for, 13–15
  religious support for, 8, 10–14, 17
Andersonville Prison, 266–68, 270–71, 280, 287, 308
Anthony, Susan B., 17
Anti-slavery societies, 13, 17, 19
Army supply lines, 54, 102, 170, 249, 259
  Grant's "Cracker Line," 163, 308
  Meade's spring 1864 supply line, 212, 216–17, 222
  Rosecrans's Chattanooga campaign, 127, 128, 130–31

442 Index

Army supply lines *(continued)*
  Savannah, 313, 318, 321
  Port of Wilmington, 322, 325, 328
  Atlanta and march to the sea, 195, 288, 295, 304–05
Artillery, *118*, 125
  Horses, care and training, 98–99
  Battery F, 4th U.S., 66–68, 73, 76, 77, 89, 90, 108, 110, 112, 114, 121, 126, 156, 187, 201, 216, 245
  Napoleon 12-pounders, 69–70, 113
  recruitment and training, 65–70, 98, 113
  skills needed, 98
  uniforms, 66

Barnburners, 15
Barnes, Capt. Dennis E., 71, 197, 207, 209, 213, 225, 233
Barnes, Lt. C. T., 197, 233, 235
Beecher, Rev. Henry Ward, 17, 140
Best, Capt. Clermont L., 67, 73, 76–78, 81–83, 85–86, 88–90, 94, 98, 100
Birney, Brig. Gen./Maj. Gen. David B., 14, 78, 205, 207, 209–10, 216, 223–24, 230, 238, 274
Black soldiers
  casualties, 359, 360, 399
  duties, 160, 187
  fighting skills, 358, 359, 360,
  numbers, 360
  reaction to Emancipation Proclamation, 192
  reverence for Lincoln, 333
  treatment as prisoners, 270
  white soldiers' attitude toward, 158, 160, 183–84, 279, 354, 356–61
Blackshear Prison, 270, 271
Bragg, Lt. Gen. Braxton, 42–46, 55–57, 64, 128–32, 134, 137, 148, 150, 154–56, 160, 163–65, 168–73, 175, 177–78, 180, 189, 191, 194, 243, 267, 291
Braman, Lt./Capt. W. W. (93rd NY), 202, 208, 209

Brown, Georgia Governor Joseph E., 296, 307
Brown, John, 16, 132, 215, 302, 332
Bull, Sgt. Rice C. (123rd NY), 26–27, 363
Burnside, Maj. Gen. Ambrose, 64, 132, 182, 199, 277, 355

Chancellorsville, Battle of
  battlefield conditions, 72–73
  Confederate casualties, 82, 88
  dates, 59
  map, *80*
  morale, 63, 65, 97, 100, 106
  outcome, 90–91, 93–106
  regimental casualties, 82, 88, 90–91
  role of 123rd NY, 77–78, 81–83, 85–87, 90–91
  role of Battery F, 77–78, 85, 87–91
  significance of battle, 94, 95–97, 100–01
  supplies, 59, 62, 64, 73, 100
  Union casualties, 88, 90–91
  weather conditions, 63, 65, 72, 78
Chaplains, role of, 11, 28, 155, 163, 168
  Barber, L., 227
  Bartlett, Edward, 257
  Gordon, Henry, 11, 22, 25, 28, 64
  Forsyth, James G., 11, 28
  Haigh, William M., 41, 184
  Stewart, A. M., 11
  White, Myron, 295, 333
Charleston Prison, 292
Chase, Salmon P., Assistant Secretary of War, 2
Chicago Evening Journal, 153
Chicago Tribune, 248
Chickamauga, Battle of
  Confederate casualties, 150
  dates, 127
  Lytle's brigade, role of, 133–51
  map, *135*, *139*
  outcome, 148, 150–51
  regimental casualties, 149, 151
  role of 36th Ill., 133–51

Union casualties, 145, 150–51
use of artillery, 137, 138, 140, 142, 146
Cincinnati Daily Commercial, 89, 97
Cincinnati Daily Enquirer, 97
Cincinnati Daily Gazette, 241, 261, 356
Comparison to Revolutionary War soldiers, 12, 352
Confederate prisons
 Andersonville, 28, 144, 151, 237, 263–72, 280–81, 284, 286–88, 292, 308, 340, 367, 368
 Blackshear, 270, 271
 Cahaba (Selma, Castle Morgan), 267, 270, 272–74
 Charleston, 267–68, 271–72, 286, 292,
 Florence, 267, 270–72, 286
 Macon, 264, 266
 Millen (Camp Lawton), 267–71, 273, 309
 Thomasville, 270, 280, 320
Confederate views
 slavery, 1, 2, 15, 37, 39, 67, 190, 270
 black soldiers, 270, 279, 330, 357–61; *see also* USCT
Cook, Sgt. Albert (123rd NY), 91, 294
Cooper Union Speech by Lincoln, 16
Copperheads, 91, 101, 158, 193, 288, 294, 357, 363
Courage, moral, 33, 36, 172, 177, 230, 351, 352
Courage, physical, 33, 42, 45, 54, 55, 67, 68, 89, 105, 133, 142, 161, 165, 179, 226, 253, 359
Covenanting Presbyterians, 7–11, 13–14, 17, 19–21
Coy, Lt. L. R. (123rd NY), 27
Crocker, Col. John S., 23–25, 64, 203–05, *204*, 207–11, 213–14, 219–220, 224, 226–28, 230–31, 236, 340, 349, 357
Crosby, 1st Lt. Franklin B., 67, 77, 90
Cruikshank, Lt. Robert (123rd NY), 26–27, 59, 183, 292, 294, 298, 322

Cummins, Pvt. George A. (36th Ill.), 127, 130
Cutter, Pvt. John (123rd NY), 72, 363

Dana, Charles A., Assistant Secretary of War, 134, 145, 151, 181
Davis, President Jefferson, 57, 102, 105, 189–91, 211, 243, 265, 274, 280, 282, 306–07, 333, 336, 339, 342, 347, 368
 relationship with Gen. Robert E. Lee, 102, 190–91, 211, 274
Douglass, Frederick, 13, 17
Dred Scott decision, 16

Elections
 1860, 2, 4, 16, 18, 26, 353, 364
 1864 soldier vote, 269–70, *293*, 352, 361–64
 1864 popular vote, 19, 364
Elmore, Pvt. Day (36th Ill.), 30, 55, 128, 180, 183, 363
Emancipation (*see also* anti-slavery), 10, 13–14, 19, 23, 28, 34–35
 soldiers' support for emancipation, 3, 4, 34–35, 209, 355–57, 359–61, 364–65
Emancipation Proclamation, 3, 4, 14, 19, 25, 55, 65, 192, 193, 355, 356, 357, 358
 civilians' reaction to, 14, 193
 Covenanter church support of, 6, 14
 final, 55
 growing support of, 35, 356–57, 361–62
 newspapers' response to, 19
 officers' and soldiers' reactions, 65
 preliminary, 355
 slaves' reactions, 192, 357, 358
Enlistment bounties and bonuses, 27–31, 63–64, 287, 352

Fitzhugh, Capt. Robert H., 73
Florence Prison, 267, 270–72, 286
Floyd, Lt. John G., 74, 76, 87–90

444 Index

Forrest, Gen. Nathan B., 276–78, 295
Free Soil Party, 15, 16
Fugitive Slave Act, 10, 15–16, 37, 354

Garfield, Col. James, A., 137
Geary, Brig. Gen. John W., 87, 108, 113–15, 117–19, 122, 260, 317, 319, 321, 323
Getty, Brig. Gen. George W., 221–24, 226–27, 230
Gettysburg, Battle of
   12th Corps casualties, 121
   artillery casualties, 121
   battlefield conditions, 110, 112–13
   Confederate casualties, 121–23
   dates, 107
   map, *116*
   morale, 106
   preparations for, 107–09
   role of 123rd NY, 111–12, 114–15, 120–21
   significance of battle, 110
   Union casualties, 121–23
   use of artillery, 110, 114, 117, 119–21
   weather conditions, 117
Glens Falls Messenger, 208
Gifford, Lt. Haviland (93rd NY), 96, 201
Gibbs, Sgt. A. J. (93rd NY), 229
Gordon, Rev. Henry, 11, 22, 25, 28, 64
Gourlie, Corp. John C. (123rd NY), 28, 292–93
Grand Review, *343,* 344–50
Granger, Maj. Gen. Gordon, 145, 147–48, 154, 170–71, 174, 180–81
Grant, Col./Brig. Gen./Maj. Gen./Lt. Gen. Ulysses S., 200–01, 205–06, 212, 216, 218
   Cracker Line, 163, 308
   Missionary Ridge, Battle of, 153, 161–66, 168–70, 173, 175, 179, 189
   as commander of Northern armies, 198, 204, 205

   relationship with Congressman Washburn, 204, 215
   relationship with Lincoln, 212
   relationship with Meade, 209, 212, 218
   relationship with soldiers, 206–07, 210
   Wilderness, Battle of, 199–200, 206, 209, 212–13, 215–17, 220, 222–23, 230, 232, 234, 236
Gray, Capt. Norman, 61, 63
Gray, Capt./Maj. Henry C. (123rd NY), 77, 82, 91, 336
Greusel, Col. Nicholas, 46–48, 51, 55, 57

Haigh, William H., 41, 184,
Halleck, Maj. Gen. Henry "Old Gramps," 71, 97, 104, 212, 284, 294, 297, 298, 354
Halsey, Pvt. C. A. (36th Ill.), 56
Hancock, Maj. Gen. Winfield Scott, 32, 205–07, 209, 213–17, 219–27, 230, 234–36, 238, 274, 281, 282, 341
Hardee, Lt. Gen. Wm. J. (CSA), 50, 52, 212, 260, 313, 316, 323, 329
Harper's Ferry, 16
Hay, John, 22, 153, 206
Hays, Brig. Gen. Alexander, 205, 207–10, 214, 220, 224, 226–30, 236, 237, 274
Hemenway, Lt. Lucius, 178, 186
Heth, Brig. Gen. Henry (CSA), 79, 198, 224
Hill, Maj. Gen. A.P. (CSA), 76, 220
Hobbs, Capt. A. M., 39, 54, 144, 184
Hood, Lt. Gen. John Bell (CSA), 242, 249, 250, 252, 293, 295, 318, 324, 336, 339, 359
Hooker, Maj. Gen. Joseph, 64, 65, 71, 72, 93, 94, 333, 336
   role at Chancellorsville, 64, 67, 73–75, 78, 84, 88, 91, 95, 96, 97, 106
   role at Kolb's Farm, 245–47, 255, 258–61, 274

Index

Howard, Maj. Gen. Oliver Otis, 75, 77, 97, 307, 333, 344
Hunt, Brig. Gen. Henry J., 65, 88–94, 98–99, 105, 109–10, 112–14, 121, 126

Irrepressible conflict, 2, 38

Jackson, Lt. Gen. Thomas J. "Stonewall" (CSA), 67, 75–77, 79, 91, 122
Johnston, Lt. Gen. Joseph E. (CSA), 131, 199, 200, 242–43, 247–49, 265, 280–82, 286, 297, 328, 333, 336–37, 339
Jonesville Academy, 18, 22

Kane County, Illinois, 19, 20, 39, 184
Kansas Nebraska Act, 2, 10, 15–16, 24, 37
Knipe, Brig. Gen. Joseph F., 95, 102, 160, 163, 251, 254–55, 257–59
Kolb's Farm, Battle of, 28, 241–43, 258
   battlefield conditions, 251
   Confederate casualties, 259
   Dan's capture, 28, 257
   dates, 249
   map, *250, 252*
   morale, 249
   outcome, 259
   regimental casualties, 259
   role of regiment, 259–60
   significance of battle, 242, 248
   skirmishing, 242–44, 246–48, 251, 253–58
   supplies, 249
   Union casualties, 259
   weather conditions, 249

Laiboldt, Col. Bernard, 53, 136, 138, 141–42, 148
Lee, Lt. Gen. Robert E. (CSA), 64, 73–75, 79, 100–05, 107–08, 111, 114, 120–24, 154, 190–92, 194–95, 198–202, 211–13, 215–18, 220–21, 232, 234–37, 245, 274, 290–91, 318, 321, 323, 327, 333, 335, 337, 341, 360
Liberty Party, 14, 15, 208
Lincoln, Abraham
   1864 soldier vote for, 269–70, 361–64
   assassination, 280, 284, 336–37, 340, 342, 344–48
   battlefield visits, 63, 70–72
   calls for volunteers, 3, 6, 11, 20–22, 24–26, 29, 32, 35, 39, 67, 102, 203, 241, 287, 357
   Declaration of Independence, 3
   devotion of soldiers to, 63, 71–72, 352–53
   election in 1860, 2, 4, 16, 18, 353
   election in 1864, 4, 19, 288–95, 317, 327
   Emancipation Proclamation, 3, 4, 6, 14, 19, 25, 55, 65, 192, 193, 355–58
   growing support for, 361
   growing support by Veteran Volunteers, 362
   Kansas-Nebraska Act, 2
   religious influences on, 7, 11, 14
   views on generals 43–44, 56, 96–97, 103–05, 150, 153, 156, 158, 181, 187, 198, 206, 212
   views on slavery, 15–16, 22, 27, 34, 37, 315, 353, 355, 365–66, 368
   views on preserving the Union, 16, 22–23, 34, 97, 365, 368
Lincoln-Douglass debates, 17
Longstreet Lt. Gen. James (CSA), 74, 102, 111, 115, 124, 132, 134, 137, 141, 145, 148, 154, 182, 189–90, 194–95
Lyman, Lt. Theodore, 210, 211, 230
Lytle, Brig. Gen. William, 128–34, 136–43

Macon Prison, 264, 266
Manigault, Brig. Gen. Arthur M., 141, 142, 326
Marshall, Pvt. John L. (123rd NY), 186, 330

Martin, Lt. Walter E. (123rd NY), 292
McClellan, Maj. Gen. George B., 24, 62–64, 199, 269–70, 288–90, 292–95, 353–55, 357, 362–64
McConihe, Maj./Lt. Col. Samuel, 230, 239, 349
McCook, Maj. Gen. Alexander M., 44, 47
    Chickamauga, 129, 130, 132–35, 137–38, 142, 144–48, 154
    Stones River, 44–46, 48, 50–52
McDougall, Col. Archibald L., 66, 182, 244, 246
    Chancellorsville, Battle of, 75, 83, 86, 91
    Gettysburg, Battle of, 102, 120
    recruiting activities, 18, 25
    religion, 25
    Republican background, 25
McKean, NY Cong. James B., 18
McLean, Sgt. Clark (123rd NY), 246, 288, 319, 320, 330
Martin, Lt. Walter E., 292
Meade, Maj. Gen. George Gordon, 105
    as head of Army of the Potomac, 104–05
    Chancellorsville, Battle of, 97
    Gettysburg, Battle of, 106–07, 109–11, 113, 115, 117, 122–26
    relationship with Grant, 209, 212, 218
    respect of officers, 105, 106
    sending troops to Rosecrans, 154
    Wilderness, Battle of, 203–07, 209–12, 219–24, 230, 232, 234
Millen Prison (Camp Lawton), 267–71, 273, 309
Miller, Capt./Maj./Lt. Col./Col. Silas T., 51, 55, 127–29, 143–44, 146–47, 149, 151, 153, 165–66, 178–79, 181–85
Minty, Col. Robert H. G., 278
Missionary Ridge, Battle of, 169–79
    battlefield conditions, 171–76

    dates, 168
    map, *167*
    morale, 171–74
    outcome, 177–79
    role of regiment, 166, 169, 177–79
    significance of battle, 189–91
    supplies, 163
    weather conditions, 171
Missouri Compromise, 1, 37
Morgan, New York Governor Edward, 18, 24, 25
Morhous, Sgt. Henry C. (123rd NY), 253
Mower, Maj. Gen. Joseph A., 332–33
Mud march, 64–65
Muhlenberg, Lt. Edward D., 90, 99, 104, 111

New York Times, 76, 85, 101, 174, 331, 348
New York Tribune, 2, 96, 284
Newspapers
    Cincinnati Daily Chronicle, 97
    Cincinnati Daily Commercial, 89, 97
    Cincinnati Daily Gazette, 261
    Chicago Evening Journal, 153
    Chicago Tribune, 248
    New York Times, 76, 85, 101, 174, 331, 348
    New York Tribune, 2
    Troy Daily Times, 19, 26, 27; *see also* Washington County newspapers
Norton, Lt. Col. Franklin, 244

Old White Church (Salem, NY), 8, 9, 26, 27
Olson, Lt./Capt./Maj./Col. Porter C., 51, 53, 55, 57, 127, 144, 151, 165, 171, 180–81

Patrick, Brig. Gen. Marsena, 103
Pecoy, Pvt. Oscar (36th Ill.), 55
Perryville, Battle of, 40, 42, 57
Phillips, Wendell, 17
Porter, Horace, 163, 291, 333

Index

Quakers, 12, 13, 17, 158

Reeder, Pvt. Walter V. (36th Ill.), 21, 39, 41, 42, 128, 183, 352, 354, 359
Reformed Presbyterian Churches in Washington County, 11, 17, 20, 26
Republican Party, 2, 14–16, 18, 194, 353, 364
Robertson, Lt. R. S. (93rd NY), 96, 104, 201, 238
Robinson, Lt./Capt. George I. (123rd NY), 156, 160
Rogers, Lt. Col./Col. James C., 18–19, 25, 246, 348
Rosecrans, Maj. Gen. William S., 43, 44, 47, 54, 56, 127, 129, 131–32, 136, 141, 145, 150, 161
Ross, Anna Marie, 6, 18, 22, 349, 365, 367
Ross, Charles Wesley, 5–7, 9, 16, 28, 287, 365, 367
Ross, Charlotte Burch, 6, 349, 366
Ross, Col. Samuel, 82, 95
Ross, Daniel Reid "Dan," 18, 20, 22, 60, 61, 66, 157–58, 182, 201, 244, 333, *366*
   Andersonville, 257, 264–67
   artillery training, 66–70
   Battle of Selma, 274–78
   capture, 28, 257
   Chancellorsville, 75–89
   change in rank, 66
   correspondence with family, 22–24, 60–63
   enlistments, 6, 22, 25–27, 63–64
   Gettysburg, 114–22
   guard duty in Tennessee, 160–86, 302
   guarding Jefferson Davis, 282–86, 342
   infantry training, 64
   Kolb's Farm, 249–60
   other duties, 24, 279–80, 281–82
   pension, 367
   post-war life, 365–68
   return to 123rd NY, 187
   reunions with family, 64, 74, 201, 348–49
   skirmishing, 33, 242–43, 253
   Selma imprisonment, 272–74
   West Virginia, 286, 366–68
Ross, John Doty, 20, 27, 28, 287–88, *302*, 319, 333, 342
   capture of Atlanta, 296
   Chancellorsville and Wilderness battlefields, 341
   enlistment, 6, 28, 287
   Grand Review, 342, 347–48
   injury, 311–12
   march to Savannah, 299–316
   march through Carolinas, 323–31, 333–35
   post-war life, 365
   reunion with Dan, 348–49
   training, 288, 296–97
Ross, Margaret Reid, 5–9, 12, 17, 287, 365
Ross, Melancton "Lank," 6, 18, 22, 39, *40*, 41, 44, 55, 133, 151, 154, 160, 163, 199
   Chickamauga, 134–47
   enlistments, 6, 21, 27, 31, 39–40, 183–84, 203
   furlough, 184
   hospitalizations, 185–86, 188, 349
   injury, 28, 185, 274
   Missionary Ridge, 168–78
   move to Illinois, 19–20
   Perryville, 42
   post-war life, 24, 367
   Stones River, 44–54
Ross, William Henry "Will," 5, 9, 18, 20, 22, 28, 33, 35, 59–60, 122, 197–99, *198*, *200*, 214, 229, 238, 341, 351201,
   Battle of the Wilderness, 207, 216–32
   changes in rank, 64, 197
   commissary sergeant duties, 197

448 Index

Ross, William Henry "Will" *(continued)*
  correspondence with family, 5, 22–24, 27, 32, 60–63
  death, 28
  enlistments, 6, 20, 22–24, 27, 31, 59, 197, 202
  furlough, 202
  headquarters and provost guard duty, 62–63, 71, 89, 105, 117, 201, 205, 207
  move to Illinois, 19–20, 22
  recruiting for the 93rd NY, 23–24, 60–61
  reunions with family members, 64, 74, 201, 202
  training, 59, 209
Ross correspondence & memoirs, 5, 22–24, 27, 32, 60–63, 277, 368
Ross family, 11–12
  anti-slavery and pro-Union sentiments, 3–4, 6–7, 10–12, 19, 22
  attachment to community, 36, 365
  commitment to education, 18, 22
  commitment to family, 60–61, 367
  country of origin, 7
  farm life and practices, 5, 20, 22, 24, 28, 60–61
  historical background, 6–12
  religious convictions, 6, 10, 12
Ruger, Brig. Gen. Thomas, 79, 84, 86, 109–10, 112, 114–15, 122
Rugg, Lt. Sylvannus T., 99, 112, 124, 163

Salem Press, 25, 363
Savannah, Georgia, 268, 295, 312–14, *314*, 316, 318–21
Schofield, Maj. Gen John M., 259, 330–31, 333, 336
Scott, Maj. Gen. Winfield "Old Fuss & Feathers," 204
Scots, 8, 9, 12, 14, 20
Selfridge, Col./Brig. Gen. James L., 312, 326
Selma
  Battle of Selma, 274–78
  black troops organized in, 279, 359

Cahaba Prison (Castle Morgan), 267, 272–74
  prison hospital, 273–74, 279
  role in Confederacy, 191, 278
Sheridan, Maj. Gen. Philip H., 40, 42, 44–45, 67, 183, 274, 290
  Chickamauga, Battle of, 127–34, 136–49, 151
  Missionary Ridge, Battle of, 153, 155, 164–66, 168–75, 179–81, 189
  Stones River, Battle of, 45–48, 50–57
Sherman, Col./Brig. Gen. Francis T., 127, 130, 162, 164, 167–69, 171, 174–75, 179–81
Sherman, Maj. George D., 144, 151, 169, 171
Sherman, Maj. Gen. William T., 1–3, 30, 40, 161, 164, 187–88, 212, 236, 266, 268, 280, 351
  Atlanta, 189, 199–200, 241–49, 266–67, 288–300
  Grand Review, 339–48
  Kolb's Farm, Battle of, 241–49, 258–62
  March to the sea and beyond, 271, 301–03, *303*, 306–13, *310*, 315–28, 331–38
  Missionary Ridge, Battle of, 170, 173
Sherman's army, 32–35, 185, 352, 361
  treatment of runaway slaves, 321–22, 326, 346
Sherman, Sen. John, 212, 355
Sill, Brig. Gen. Joshua W., 45–48, 50–51, 56
Skirmishing, 33, 226, 241, 243–48
  dangers of, 241, 244, 247
  importance of, 33
  Sherman's reliance on, 241–42
  skills required, 242, 244
Slocum, Maj. Gen. Henry Warner, 67–68, *68*, 302
  12th Corps at Chancellorsville, 78, 82, 84–88, 91, 93–95

12th Corps at Gettysburg, 103, 105, 107–08, 110–15, 117, 119, 124
12th Corps in Tennessee, 156, 159–60, 163
20th Corps at Atlanta, 286, 289, 291, 293, 302
anti-slavery views, 67
Army of Georgia, 302, 304, 307–08, 311–12, 316–17, 319, 325, 327–28, 330–31, 341–42, 347–48
  march to the sea route, *303*
  postwar career, 349
  relationship with Hooker, 75, 84, 95–97, 156, 161, 187
  relationship with Meade, 105, 110
  transfer to Vicksburg, 187
  troops reviewed by Lincoln, 71–72
Smith, Gerrit, 17
Stanton, Edwin M., Secretary of War, 71, 153
Stevenson, Brig. Gen. Carter L. (CSA), 246, 256, 259, 336
Stones River, Battle of, 44–57
  battlefield conditions, 45–47
  Confederate casualties, 56
  dates, 45
  location, 45
  map, *49*
  morale, 45
  outcome, 56
  regimental casualties, 54
  road conditions, 44
  role of regiment, 45, 48, 50, 52–53, 55
  significance of battle, 56–57
  supplies, 43
  Union casualties, 54–55, 56
  weather conditions, 45, 47, 48
Stuart, Maj. Gen. J. E. B. (CSA), 79, 81, 84, 88
Surrender at Goldsboro, N.C., 329–31

Terry, Gen. Alfred H., 322, 330, 336
Thomas, Maj. Gen. George. H., 40, 44, 52, 55, 131, 134, 137–38, 145–46, 148–50, 153, 155, 161, 163–66, 168–70, 172–73, 179, 181, 183, 188, 258, 259, 295, 302, 318, 321, 358–60
Thomasville Prison, 270, 280, 320
Train troop movement to Tennessee, 157–59
Troy Daily Times, 19, 26, 27
Tubman, Harriet, 13

Ulster Scots, 7–8
Uncle Tom's Cabin, 16
Underground railroad, 16, 17, 19, 356, 367
US Colored Troops (USCT), 160, 183, 279, 321, 326, 359

Veteran Volunteers
  band of brothers, 33
  bounties and other incentives, 202–03, 182–84
  commitment to ending slavery and saving the Union, 30, 36, 182–84, 260, 330, 338, 351, 353–55, 357–59, 361–63, 365, 368
  comparison to Revolutionary War soldiers, 183, 351–52, 354,
  creation of Veteran Volunteer program, 29–30
  devotion to company officers, 33
  devotion to Hancock, 208, 222
  devotion to Lincoln, 353–54, 361, 363–64
  devotion to regimental officers, 32–33
  devotion to Sheridan, 45, 57, 179
  devotion to Sherman, 288–89, 322
  devotion to Thomas, 161, 179
  duties, 33, 172–73, 183, 221, 224–30, 312
  family traditions, 352
  fighting skills and discipline, 33,
  honoring the Declaration of Independence, 352
  numbers of, 20, 30, 32–33, 182–83, 202, 208, 297, 361
  other reasons for reenlisting, 30–32, 33, 36, 275, 297

Veteran Volunteers *(continued)*
  recruiting, 164, 202, 206
  religious views, 36, 356

Ward, Gen. William T., 332
Washburn, Cong. Elihu B., 204, 213, 215, 358
Washington County, New York, 13, 15–18, 21–23, 26–28, 76, 202, 289, 342
  religious history, 8–10
  support for Lincoln, 4, 16, 362
Washington County newspapers, 363
  Salem Press, 25, 363
  Washington County Chronicle, 365
  Washington County Peoples' Journal, 16, 19, 25, 100, 356, 361, 365
  Washington County Post, 19, 24, 25, 287, 362
  Whitehall Chronicle, *19*, 354
Watson, Pvt. R. H. (36th Ill.), 53, 127
Wheeler, Brig. Gen. Joseph (CSA), 50, 296, 308, 326, 335

Wide Awakes, 18, 25
Wilderness, Battle of
  battlefield conditions, 224, 226
  dates, 197
  location, 223
  map, *225*
  morale, 212, 215–16
  preparations for, 209–13, 215
  regimental casualties, 233
  road conditions, 215, 223
  role of regiment, 226–30, 233
  significance of battle, 234
  supplies, 207, 211–12, 216–17
  Union casualties, 235, *239*
  weather conditions, 214–15
Williams, Brig. Gen. Alpheus Starkey, 72, *73*, 78–79, 84–88, 91, 95, 103–15, 122–25, 159–63, 187, 245–46, 251–59, 289–90, 294, 307, 311, 316–26, 329–35, 340, 346–49
Wilson, Maj. Gen. James H., 254, 274–83
Wirz, Capt. Henry, 264–66, 280–81